A *Backwoods Home* Anthology:

The Fifth Year

Published by
Backwoods Home Magazine
P. O. Box 712
Gold Beach, OR 97444
www.backwoodshome.com

A Backwoods Home Anthology

Copyright 1997 by Backwoods Home Magazine

ISSN No. : 0-9655203-1-5

All rights reserved

Editor: *Dave Duffy*

Senior Editor: *John Silveira*

Art Director: *Don Childers*

Contributors:

Dynah Geissal, Don Fallick, Sherry Wietelman, Kristen Rogers, Richard Blunt, J. Darlene Campbell, Jim Slater, Larry Elliott, Ron Brackin, M.C. Wright, Melinda C. Long, Ted Sponem, Charlotte Jones, Gene Willis, Jennifer Stein Barker, John and Linda Janetos, Lucy Shober, Sally Denney, Michael Simmons, Charles Sanders, Martin P. Waterman, Bonnie Gelle, Audrey Stallsmith, H. Scott Kaufmann, Robert L. Williams, Monta Hulsing, Jeff Heikenfeld, Vernon Hopkins, Pat Ward, Cleoral Lovell, Vern Modeland, Whitney M. Bollier, Charles Bryant O'Dooley, Steven F. Minner, Chris and Mike Braet, Dory Hulburt, Marjorie Burris, Dorothy Ainsworth, Mary Pipes, Eric and Birney Dibble, Randy Atkins, Judith Blucher, Ralph LaPlant, Tok Thompson, Christopher Maxwell, Atty. Sandra R. Bullington, CPA, Edie L. Norling, Greg & Bonnie Chaney, J.D. Hooker, Edwin A. Towne, Jr., Ray Lagoe, Skip Thomsen & Cat Freshwater, Jayn Steidl Thibodeau, Knight C. Duerig, Barbara Sorensen Fallick, David Jensen, Phil Wilcox, Serena Somers, Joe Radabaugh, Anita Evangelista, William Shepherd, Shari Prange, Bill Palmroth, Jill Fox.

A Backwoods Home Anthology

Introduction

Welcome to The Fifth Year, another anthology of *Backwoods Home Magazine* articles. This one covers Issues 25 through 30, which were published in 1994. No matter the year, the articles, of course, are timeless because they are of a "how-to" nature. If you'd like to see the other volumes, namely, The Best of the First Two Years, The Third Year, and The Fourth Year, just give us a call at 1-800-835-2418. An order form is at the end of this book.

In these uncertain times, the anthologies will comprise a comforting companion to people seeking self sufficiency and assurance that they can take care of themselves and their family in any emergency, or just because they want to.

I'm proud to have been associated with the writers whose articles comprise this volume.

— Dave Duffy

*This anthology is dedicated
to the memory of Lucy Shober,
and to the other writers
who made its contents possible*

Profiles of Writers

Darlene Campbell	22
Ralph LaPlant	26
Dynah Geissal	26
Don Fallick	30
Rev. Dr. J.D. Hooker	33
Richard Blunt	35
Kristen Rogers	38
Marjorie Burris	42
Robert L. Williams	42
Mick Sagrillo	46
Skip Thomsen	48
Linda Robie	49
Larry Elliott	55
Jennifer Stein Barker	63
Charles A. Sanders	67
Margaret C. Wright	70
Tim Green	79
Jan Cook	79
Phil Wilcox	87
Dave Jensen	92
Sally Denney	102
Martin P. Waterman	109
Audrey Stallsmith	109
Ted Sponem	111
Don Childers	137
Mary Pipes	144
Ilene Duffy	151
Chris Braet	160
Lucy Shober	174
John Janetos	180
Dory Hulburt	183
Jeff Heikenfeld	218
Annie Duffy	261
Dave Duffy	276
Carole Perlick	299
Edie Norling	307
John Silveira	319
Dorothy Ainsworth	326

Contents

Issue Number 25

- *Whether it's small town or big time, the environment or health care, the government is not the answer (commentary)* — **14**
- *Planning is an essential key to achieving the country life* — **15**
- *Some tips on moving to your country home* — **18**
- *Supplement your income by teaching others your skills* — **23**
- *Make a patchwork baby bunting from scraps* — **25**
- *Make better pizza at home than you can buy* — **27**
- *How we bought our country home* — **31**
- *The solar-powered silent partner* — **34**
- *Home-schooling — Is it right for your kids?* — **37**
- *Some homeschooling ideas* — **39**
- *Child-led learning* — **41**
- *Native of the forest: a guide to growing ginseng* — **43**
- *The timberwolf woodbox* — **49**
- *A tale about tenure in the neighborhood* — **50**
- *Winter ch-ch-ch-ch-chores* — **51**
- *The bow and arrow: low tech tool for food, entertainment* — **52**
- *Cooking with dried fruit* — **54**
- *Planning a move from the city to the country* — **56**
- *Just for kids — You in the big night sky* — **64**
- *Living the country life* — **66**
- *Explore the world with shortwave* — **68**

Issue Number 26

- *Forget conspiracies (commentary)* — **72**
- *Driving back country roads — different skills needed at every turn* — **73**
- *The miracle of a country birth* — **78**
- *Make delicious wine at home* — **80**
- *Grapes—with 3000 varieties, you can grow them just about anywhere in North America* — **83**
- *Garden huckleberries—these hardy, firm berries are easy to grow, as tasty as blueberries* — **86**
- *Short season gardening* — **87**

- *Kiwi fruit—healthy, delicious, exotic, pest-and disease-resistant, low-maintenance... — 89*
- *The 10 most useful herbs — 93*
- *Tips for cold-climate herb growing — 95*
- *Some herb garden recipes — 96*
- *My favorite soup recipes — 98*
- *Try an isolated gain passive solar house — 101*
- *Simplified concrete and masonry work — 103*
- *Just for kids—Killing some time — 105*
- *Raising sheep — 107*
- *Free supplies for your homestead — 110*
- *Improving poor garden soil — 112*
- *Dueling duck — 113*
- *Edible landscapes are Jim Gibbons' livelihood — 114*
- *Muzzleloaders—art, science, and a piece of history — 116*
- *Deer discourology — 118*
- *Synopsis of sourdough — 119*

Issue Number 27

- *Self reliance—the key to happiness (commentary) — 24*
- *How to care for and feed the family pond — 125*
- *Good-bye old friend — 129*
- *Raising water buffalo—are they better than cattle? — 130*
- *Moon over Bogus Brook — 131*
- *Here are 5 simple things that make our life easier — 132*
- *Determined woman builds distinctive vertical log studio — 133*
- *Choosing and using a wood cookstove — 142*
- *Mick Sagrillo—Wizard of Wind — 145*
- *Three great bread recipes — 148*
- *Quick and easy veggie food — 152*
- *Learn the basics of wall framing — 154*
- *Health care begins at home — 157*
- *Build a fieldstone chimney — 159*
- *Start a home-based food business — 161*
- *Making your own sourdough yeast — 163*
- *Make a lifeline before you need it — 164*

- *Build an earth-sheltered log cabin* — **165**
- *Handguns are useful tools for the homesteader* — **167**
- *Trading your city house for a country homestead —will it be a taxing move?* — **170**
- *How to build a low-cost log lifter* — **173**

Issue Number 28

- *The beast is at the door again (commentary)* — **176**
- *For a truly independent energy system, your choices are solar, wind, and water* — **177**
- *The great cow caper* — **181**
- *Lucky duck* — **183**
- *Raising fish in the farm pond* — **184**
- *How ya gonna keep 'em down on the farm—after they've seen the mall?* — **190**
- *Independent energy runs Backwoods Home Magazine* — **193**
- *Looking behind the Declaration of Independence* — **195**
- *Chinese cooking* — **201**
- *Just for kids—sun-kabobs and solar sizzle* — **207**
- *Designing for solar heating* — **209**
- *The gosling that lived* — **214**
- *Micro-hydropower—a working example* — **215**
- *Here's a low-cost, low-tech refrigerator that really works* — **219**
- *The care of lead acid batteries* — **220**
- *Sun oven cookery* — **221**
- *Build a 12-volt power plant from the junkyard* — **223**
- *Firewood: how and what to buy* — **225**

Issue Number 29

- *Bad laws, good solutions (commentary)* — **228**
- *Here are some home-based businesses that are worth trying* — **229**
- *Use your own sawmill to cut lumber prices* — **233**
- *Raising goats as a business is a profitable and fun venture* — **235**
- *You have to learn to shovel crap before you learn to be the boss* — **238**
- *Grow an independent living with a cut flower business* — **245**
- *Here are three ways to build a stanchion* — **248**
- *From Martha and Abigail to Dolley and Louisa, America's earliest First Ladies were fascinating* — **250**

- *Making sourdough bread* — 258
- *Old-fashioned desserts* — 262
- *Odd-jobbin' can be a country goldmine* — 264
- *Help your children to read by teaching them the phonic basics* — 270
- *PV as a country business?—if you're a jack-of-all-trades* — 273
- *Here's how to start a part-time, one-person mail order business* — 274
- *Try an ex-military truck for rugged, reliable service* — 277
- *Install a remote telephone line* — 282

Issue Number 30

- *Note from the publisher—Liquid apple pie and Fred Johnston* — 286
- *Politics, self reliance... (commentary)* — 287
- *American food—it's as varied as the melting pot* — 288
- *Collecting old phonograph records is fun and educational* — 295
- *Try traditional early American fried squirrel* — 298
- *Barbecue a whole goat (and more) in an imu* — 300
- *Your throw-away fish can be keepers if you know how to prepare them right* — 302
- *David and the D-4...a story about growing up* — 305
- *Building an expensive log house—the cheap way* — 308
- *Making and using a solar cooker* — 314
- *Poor man's shrimp cocktail on perch, and...* — 318
- *Sourdough with substance* — 320
- *How to keep those excess eggs* — 322
- *Some thoughts about my wood cookstove* — 324
- *Preventing and surviving stove and chimney fires* — 325
- *Venison recipes* — 327
- *Converting your gas car to electric is no shocker* — 329
- *Just for kids—some pioneer recipes* — 324
- *Pemmican—the all purpose food* — 337
- *Former first ladies—beautiful, brilliant, crazy* — 338
- *Turkeys—fun and profitable and not as dumb as you think* — 347
- *Learning in the pickle patch* — 349

Index of articles in previous issues and anthologies — 351

FREE VITA-MIX

January/February 1994
No. 25
$3.50 U.S.
$4.50 Canada

Backwoods Home magazine

... a practical journal of self reliance!

MOVING TO THE COUNTRY

BLUNT'S PIZZA

GROWING GINSENG

SOLAR WATER PUMP

PLAN YOUR OWN HOUSE

DON CHILDERS

My View

Whether it's small town or big time, the environment or health care, the government is not the answer.

Ever notice how government involvement, whether at the local level or at the national level, tends to short circuit sensible citizen action and replace it with silly government action?

Here's a good one: You're now a criminal in the town of Ojai, California if you fail to sort your recyclables from your trash.

Never mind that Ojai citizens are already among the best recyclers on the planet. John Silveira, the senior editor of BHM who is a member of that conservative/libertarian group of meanies who don't trust environmentalist political activists as far as they can throw them, recycles just about everything that comes into his house. In fact he hardly ever throws anything away. You can imagine how the liberals in Ojai recycle if that's how a conservative/libertarian does it.

But that wasn't good enough for the Ojai City Council. They wanted a law so they could punish non-recycling suspects. In fact, since between 10 and 20 percent of Ojai residents don't subscribe to the city's trash service, the law also makes it illegal for them not to subscribe to the service. City councilors said that part of the law was necessary so the city could easily compare the public utility subscriber list with the trash collector's list to make sure all residents were being monitored for proper disposal of recyclables.

And there you have it, ladies and gentlemen: the main reason why people like me distrust most political do-gooders who make it into the halls of power. They aren't interested in solving problems nearly as much as they are interested in tossing their weight around.

Ojai do-gooders have just passed a law to solve a problem that doesn't exist. And they're going to make Ojai residents criminals if they don't use the city's trash service.

It is a consistent complaint heard in conservative circles that political do-gooders, such as environmental activists, social engineers, health reformers, and the rest of the reformers who want to transform America into their version of Paradise, are far more interested in wielding power over people than they are in doing good for people.

To us distrustful conservatives, Ojai is an example of where the do-gooders want to take us—into the prison camp of forced reform, whether it's reform for the environment's sake or for the sake of any number of causes on their agenda. Never mind seeking consensus, seeking voluntary action—or even admitting that voluntary action governed by people's sense of self interest is even a possibility. They want to shove it down everyone's throats because they think they know what's good for everyone.

And no, I'm not one of those insensitive conservatives who doesn't give a damn about the environment. Don't get environmental awareness mixed up with power-hungry activism. I too recycle everything in my house, and the BHM office has recycling bins all over the place. I'm just against power-grabbing morons passing oppressive laws in the name of a good cause. The laws do much more to oppress others than they do to solve an environmental problem.

The Ojai City Council's approach to solving a non-existent problem is similar to the approach politicians and political activists at all levels of government often take to solve problems that either don't exist or that can be better solved by voluntary action.

The current national debate over health care is the most important example on the national level.

The premise has been set forth that the American health care system does not work well enough. That's a matter of debate. It sure doesn't work well enough for some people, but it works pretty good when compared to other factors, such as the high level of technical accomplishment in the American system and the really lousy health care systems of most other nations.

But here's the real problem: Now that the federal government has taken it upon itself to "solve" the nation's health care problem, the solutions that are being proposed have nothing to do with allowing voluntary systems—in this case the free market forces this nation is based upon—come into play, even though there is plenty of evidence to suggest that voluntary systems, that is, people operating in their own best self interest, would work.

The government's solutions revolve around a government-mandated national health care plan that will effectively transfer 14 percent of the Gross Domestic Product—or an amount equal to 14 percent of the goods and services produced in the United States—to the federal government so a bunch of politicians can administer it.

I can't imagine a worse solution. Has anybody seen what the federal politicians have done with the nation's other big health care plans—Medicare and Medicaid? What makes us think they are going to do any better with a new, bigger one?

Why aren't free market solutions being considered? How about allowing whoever wants to become a doctor become a doctor, so long as they can prove their competency? There are plenty of people out there who could handle medical school. Let the free market—consumers demanding quality, low-cost medicine—determine how many doctors there should be.

How about allowing people to save for their own medical care in the form of a tax-free IRA-type savings account, or at least allowing them to pay their medical insurance premiums with before-tax dollars.

Considering only solutions that turn the nation's health care system over to a bunch of politicians and bureaucrats doesn't make any sense. The government runs nothing right that I can see. Why would it run a health care system any different? All we'll end up doing is transferring 14 percent of our individual freedom to a bunch of politicians who are no different than the power-hungry imbeciles of the Ojai City Council.

Government solutions that haven't worked in the past should not be recycled. They should be thrown out with the trash. ∆

COUNTRY LIVING

A Backwoods Home Anthology

Planning is an essential key to achieving the country life

By Dynah Geissal

In 1971 we moved from a large metropolitan area to a town in Montana. My main interest was to achieve a better life for myself and my children. We were choosing to keep our lives in our own hands. No boss to answer to, but also no paycheck. The food that we have for each year is the result of how hard we worked, how good our decisions were and the unpredictability of nature.

Why do we do it? When farm life is especially difficult and when the money coming in just isn't sufficient, a little part of me envies the person with the nine to five. Then I look back over the events that led me to this life and it seems inevitable since early childhood. There were many choices along the way, but it seems that they all led in one direction.

You may have decided to move to the country but are unsure how to go about it. My experience may give you some tips, ideas, and guidelines that will be helpful.

Plan and study

Plan your move at least a year ahead of time, if at all possible. During that year, research, research, research! Study everything you can that may be helpful to your upcoming life in the country. Relevant books include those on homesteading, raising livestock, gardening and so forth. If you have never gardened, give it a try. You will gain valuable information that will be helpful later on.

If you have money, save it. Don't start stocking up on things you think will be useful. Better to have the extra money and then buy what you need when you actually need it. Your transition will go much more smoothly with the extra financial resources rather than with objects that may prove to have doubtful value.

Check it out first

Find out about areas that interest you as possible places to live and then visit them. If the region is noted for its severe winters, a summer visit is not adequate, and vice versa. When I moved to Montana, for example, I didn't have a clue as to how cold the weather could be or how long the cold could last. The free-standing gas heater in the living room of our five-room apartment appeared adequate to

The Fifth Year

15

me. The snow began on Halloween and did not let up until the end of March. The wind roared through the leaky windows. The pipes froze and frost covered the walls in the four unheated rooms.

My five-year-old and 18-month-old were piled in blankets and sleeping bags at night and got along just fine. The new baby wore a knit hat and mittens to bed and only her little face showed from under the mound of blankets that covered her; she was never sick or cold. However, my older son didn't fare as well. One morning, he started to cry as he put on his winter boots to walk the few blocks to school. Upon examination, I found that the insides were coated in ice. At that point we knew we couldn't go on this way.

We arranged to trade a tricycle for an old wood heater that we had seen in the neighborhood. Getting the monstrous thing into our upstairs apartment was an adventure in itself, but we were in high spirits as we anticipated the warmth that would soon be ours. We went to the hardware store, purchased a bow saw for $15 and cut firewood with that all winter. I don't recommend it, but it can be done.

A temporary move

When you have chosen a locale that you like, visit various towns. Some small places are small-minded also and resent outsiders. You may never feel at home in a place like that. Another town just down the road may be full of friendly folks. Stop into a cafe, shop in a grocery store. See how you're treated. It doesn't take long to get a feel for a place.

Ask the locals about possible places to rent or to buy. Are they eager to help, or do they act as if you have the plague? Check out the school system, if you have children. Are people generally pleased with what they have? Do they seem committed to the

Dynah Geissal with Mocha, the queen of her goat herd.

schools? To their community in general?

If you're moving from an urban area and are generally unfamiliar with rural life, I strongly suggest trying life in a town of your choice before actually moving out into the country. You will acquire many building blocks for success by establishing a network of friends. They will become a valuable support system later on, and you will learn much of what you need to know from such people. You'll begin to get a feel for the area and to learn various characteristics about the outlying regions that you could never discern as an outsider.

Making a living

After choosing a place that feels right to you, how do you intend to make a living? What skills do you have, and are they needed in a small town? If not, are you willing to take a drop in wages to live in your chosen place? A resourceful person can usually find some way to make a living, but is that what you want to do?

Don't count on making a living off the land for a good many years. Take a hard, honest look at yourself. Are you a self starter? A highly self-motivated person? Or do you need a set job where you know what needs doing, you do it and you go home? Be truthful now! A certain kind of person can make the most of a situation and make a buck doing it. But don't kid yourself. If that person isn't you, set up your work situation ahead of time. Still, it's good to have some goals in mind, even if they change later on.

In the beginning we supported ourselves by baby-sitting and by bicycle repair out of our home. Baby-sitting was a natural with three children in the family. We learned bicycle repair from books and through trial and error. Two years later when we made our move to the country, these jobs went with us. Had we tried to develop them in the country, success would have been much more difficult to achieve. During the time in town, however, we developed a clientele and a market.

The point here is that money can be made using skills you either already have or can fairly easily develop. It's important to be alert to possible sources of income at all times. People with "real" jobs don't have the time to do everything for themselves and that's where you can cash in. The possibilities are endless.

A handy list

Here's a list of just some of the things my husband and I have done for money:
- auto mechanics
- bicycle repair
- baby sitting
- leather work
- welding
- pole furniture construction
- table making, plain but well-crafted
- wood stove construction
- by-the-day farm labor
- chimney sweeping
- fence building
- rototilling
- firewood cutting
- sale of kitchen-crafted goodies
- willow chair making
- children's toys—from wooden sailboats to gym sets
- barn building
- construction of livestock equipment such as hay feeders and stock racks
- house painting
- handy work such as window replacement, pump repair, plumbing, roofing, remodeling work, hauling, and weatherizing.

After you've moved to your chosen area and started to develop some useful skills, you'll want to look for that country place. What sort of place do you envision? Will you learn to grow most of your own food? Will you provide your own fuel? Will you work out of your own home? Of course, all these things are subject to change and will evolve on their own as you discover your talents and hone your skills. These things and many more got us by in the past. It took about seven years after we found our farm to make a real go of it, monetarily speaking.

Keep dreams flexible

I had been living in town for a year, and thought I knew exactly where I wanted to move. It was incredibly beautiful, sparsely populated, and had an excellent school system. We had spent quite a bit of time camping in the area during the summer and truly loved the place. But when it came time to find a place to live it proved to be impossible. We drove every road, advertised, talked endlessly to people everywhere, and found nothing. We spent an entire summer and came up empty handed.

Hoping to find something vacant during the winter, we tried again and only then realized how naive we were. The three feet of snow in our town grew to six in the country area of our choice. Only the main roads were plowed and the wind screamed through the passes at twice the velocity it moved through town. The only vacancy we found was a summer cottage totally unequipped for winter. "Growing season" was a term that didn't concern me then, but it turned out to be only 60 days as compared to the already none-too-generous 90 days in town.

Spring arrived and my need to find a place became more urgent. With one child in school, it seemed important to move as soon as the term ended to allow plenty of time for acclimation before the fall term began.

How I found my place

One day, a person came up to me in the park and asked if I were "looking to move to the country." I said, "Yes," and listened to his story. He said he rented a place in the country. When he had moved there it had been vacant for many years and he had done extensive renovation. However, his oil stove had leaked and fire had trashed the living room and covered the entire rest of the house with oily, black soot. He didn't have the heart to start again but also didn't want to leave the elderly landlord with such a mess. I agreed to look at the place.

Well, Montana in spring is not a pretty sight, and it doesn't get better until around June. Before that, most everything is about as bleak as you can imagine. When I first came to the house in early May I said, "No, I can't live there." But when school ended and I still hadn't found a place, I went back and looked again. This time there were leaves on the trees and the pastures were green. The cattails and reeds and sedges were lush along the creek. I decided that, yes, I could live there after all. And so I made a two-year commitment, not wanting to move the children too often but also having my heart set on a place in the woods. I didn't want to be a farmer.

One thing led to another. Someone gave me a chicken, and later, two goats. Somebody in town could no longer keep their ducks and geese. Another person grew tired of their rabbits. A friend asked me to raise some calves for her. And I became a farmer.

I grew to love this half section of land as if it were my own. I learned the ways of the coyotes and the bald eagles, of the red fox and the arctic fox, of the great blue heron and the great horned owl. I discovered the whistling swans with their sounds so high in the sky they seem everywhere and nowhere. I've seen black bears and badgers and 30 deer just outside my window. I've seen buzzards and osprey and kingfishers and thousands of Canadian geese. I've seen the creek dark with ducks and mergansers and alive with bitterns, stilts, godwits, curlews, and snipes. And my soul is in the land. It's been 20 years now. The kids are long gone — grown, with lives of their own. And I'm still a farmer.

So take things as they come and be open to what may befall you. It could prove to be absolutely right. ∆

Some tips on moving to your country home

By Don Fallick

Moving to the country can be an exciting experience. I should know. I've done it four times! The first time was probably the easiest. My wife and I were young, unencumbered by children, and didn't know enough to be scared. I'd like to think I've learned a few things along the way.

Travel light

The first lesson to be learned, and to be re-learned over and over, is to refrain from hauling the remains of your urban lifestyle with you to clutter up your new home. Unless your "junk pile" is necessary for earning your living, you will be glad, eventually, that you left it behind.

If you make your living as a carpenter, for instance, you'll need to take your tools with you, but try to refrain from moving your scrap lumber pile. Last time I moved, I left $200 worth of new 2x6 lumber, which I had bought for half-price. As soon as I got to my new home, I needed 2x6s, and had to pay three times as much for them. This sort of thing almost always happens in a move. It was very aggravating, but a quick bout with a calculator proved that it would have cost me more to move the lumber than it cost me to replace it. This is obvious, when you think about it. Lumber haulers use the most cost effective way to get their goods from one place to another. Private moving trucks and trailers just can't compete.

Moving new tools

Even moving tools can get you in trouble. Name brand tools cost about the same in all regions of the country. If you buy new tools and move them, you probably won't save or lose money on the purchase price, but you will lose the cost of moving them. Worst of all, you won't be able to take them back to the dealer where you purchased them if they prove defective.

On my second move to the country, I had already learned the principle of selling all my junk and investing in durable goods. I decided to invest my yard sale profits in a new chainsaw; a tool I did not have, knew I would need, and could buy from a national company. I bought the best (most expensive) one Sears sold, took it home and fired it up to make sure it worked, and moved it 1000 miles.

Chainsaw troubles

Alas, when I reached my new home in the woods of the Pacific Northwest, and actually started using the saw to lay in a supply of firewood, I discovered it was a lemon. It literally spent more time in Sears' shop than it did in mine. Before I moved, I made sure there was a Sears store in Spokane, the nearest city to my new home. I didn't realize it was 50 miles away, or what that would mean if I was out in the woods when the darn thing busted. After only a couple of such incidents, I tried to get the Sears store to take back the saw, or at least exchange it. It turned out the saw I bought was a discontinued model, and my local Sears store wouldn't take it back, since they hadn't sold it to me. They did honor the saw's warrantee, and fixed it for free every time I brought it in for the first year, but I was stuck with the saw. Had I kept my yard sale money and bought a saw locally, I'm sure I would have avoided a big, expensive hassle.

The modern homesteader

The homesteaders of the last century nearly made a religion out of traveling light. A common pioneer's boast was

that he could carry all of his tools on his back. To a certain extent, this was true, since the pioneers generally made their own tool handles on the spot.

Generally, a pioneer carried a boring auger, an axehead, a knife, a chisel, a sawblade for a bow saw, and a plow coulter. The modern homesteader may choose from a much lengthier list of tools. (See "things to take" at the end of this article.)

Non-electric appliances

If you are considering moving to a homestead where electricity is not available, and you've never lived without it, there are some things you should know. First of all, living without electricity need not be a hardship. There's very little that can't be done somehow, without electricity. The bad news is that many things that are quick and easy with electricity require time and forethought to do without it.

Light is a good example. Kerosene or gasoline lights can be as bright as electric, but it they require the proper lamps, wicks, chimneys, and in some cases, mantles. All but the lamps are consumables, that is, you have to expect to replace or replenish them frequently. You may not be able to find the exact right chimneys, wicks, or mantles right away in your new home, so it's a good idea to take spares. You'll need some fuel, too. It's dangerous to move lamps full of flammable liquids, so you'll need a fuel can, and a bulb siphon. You ought to know how to operate this equipment, of course.

Burned nose

I'll never forget my first encounter with a kerosene lamp. I was visiting in the area I later moved to, and my hosts lit the kerosene lamp in my bedroom and left me to go to bed myself. When I was ready, I tried to figure out how to put out the fire. I tried turning the wick down, but it just smoked. Then I tried to blow out the flame, and burned my nose! I thought I could blow it out, if only I could remove the chimney, but it was too hot to touch, and I burned my fingers. Finally, I gave up and sought out my hosts, who nearly died laughing, but did show me how to place my hand at an angle to reflect my breath down the lamp chimney and blow out the flame.

Some activities can be mechanized, even without electricity. Treadle sewing machines are a good example. The old fashioned sewing heads may still be in good enough shape to sew with, but most can't backstitch, and none can zig-zag.

Fortunately, newer machines with external motors can be easily adapted to run by treadle power. This usually involves nothing more than removing the motor and enlarging the hole in the treadle unit top so the newer sewing head will fit. I learned to sew on such a machine, and it worked just fine.

Treadle sewing machines are now considered antiques, which means the price is outrageous and the treadle unit may be beyond repair. If you can find a reasonably priced treadle machine that works, or even the treadle unit, do buy it and move it. You may not be able to find one near your new home.

The same goes for wringer washing machines. Since Maytag stopped making them about 10 years ago, they have become "collectibles," which means the quality and availability goes down and the price goes up. Maytag still does make parts for their wringer washers, so that's the best brand to buy, if you get a choice. Before our divorce Jj and I owned four, one good Maytag and one good Speed Queen, plus a "parts machine" for each. We moved all of them, and never begrudged the space they took.

Since my remarriage, we have traded the Maytags for a modern washer and gas dryer. They don't work any better than the old machines, but they're much faster, and they are automatic. With 11 people in the family, this has become important.

Wood heat

Living without electricity takes knowledge and equipment that most modern urbanites simply don't have. So does living with wood heat. Besides wood, wood-butchering skills, and tools (see *Backwoods Home Magazine* The Best of the First Two Years and The Third Year), you'll need a stove to burn it in. My family has gone for years without a "heat stove." Our five bedroom house in northeastern Washington State still is heated only by the cook stove downstairs in the kitchen, and the sun. (See "Semi-Underground House" in BHM Issue # 9.)

Most people use two stoves, though, one for heating and one for cooking. The range is often fueled by propane, rather than wood. Wood ranges require large amounts of small pieces of wood. This requires lots of work from the wood-butcher. Regulating a wood range is an art, not a science, and can't be learned in a day. But their biggest drawback is that they are hot in the summertime. Even folks who love to cook on wood stoves frequently use a propane stove in the summertime, or build a summer kitchen in a shady spot outside the house.

Propane is a by-product of petroleum production, and burns clean. Of course, if you can pick up dry deadwood in the forest for free, a propane stove might be considered a luxury of a sort. Unless you have a stove that you just treasure, I wouldn't recommend moving one. They're heavy and bulky to move or store, and readily available used, in most parts of the country. And you can get a reasonably priced, small gas range new from your propane dealer.

Wood stoves are even heavier and bulkier, but new ones are extremely expensive, and old ones may not be available in your new location. Many areas regulate or even prohibit the sale of older type wood stoves. Check your local regulations before you move, if you're thinking of moving a wood stove.

Propane appliances

Propane can take the place of electricity for making bright, clean-burning gas lights, and for running propane powered refrigerators and freezers. If you own a propane refrigerator, by all means, take it with you. New ones are frightfully expensive, and used ones are generally unavailable.

Gas lights are as much an improvement over kerosene as gas stoves are over wood stoves. Using them is nearly as simple as using electric lights, and the light they produce is white. New gas lights are still manufactured by the Humphrey Light Company, who have been making them for about a century. They're as safe as any modern gas appliance, but the disadvantage is that they are expensive, and not portable. It takes five to light our 35-foot long "great room," and they cost $50 each, not counting the copper supply tubes and the mounting kits, which are not cheap. If you're planning on installing gas lights, and you have access to such hardware cheap, it's worth buying it and moving it.

Storage

If you tried to move all the things it would be good to have, you'd probably need two moving vans. This is definitely not "traveling light." The idea is not to go out and buy stuff to move, but rather to avoid leaving behind something that's really hard to replace and necessary in your new lifestyle. Nevertheless, if you are not moving into a big, old farmhouse, you will likely end up with a lot of stuff to store when you arrive.

The first time I moved to the country, I moved a motor home onto a 17-acre parcel of land that the previous owner had used as a cattle ranch. Some of the cattle were still there. While we were waiting for him to come get them, we stored our household furnishings under a tarp, inside an old corral. True to the contrary nature of cattle, the cows broke into the corral when we weren't home and spent hours trampling and messing on our curtains, dishes, and furniture. The owner was apologetic, but never did make good our loss.

The second time we moved to the country we were wiser. We located a self-storage facility in the closest city and stored our excess stuff there, under lock and key. It was better than being destroyed by cattle, but still, it was expensive ($40/month and up) and inconvenient. Every time we needed something from storage, we had to drive 40 miles to the storage facility. Then, like as not, what we wanted was on the bottom, at the back.

After packing and unpacking our rented storage room about a dozen times, I decided to drop everything else I was doing and build a storage building near the house. It took me and a neighbor a couple of mornings to frame up a shed out of green poles. As the wood dried, the notched and tied joints we made have gotten tighter, instead of splitting out, as nailed joints would do. We nailed on "siding" recycled from metal gas station roofing, and roofed the shed with 1/2" plywood and roll roofing. The whole shed cost only $50 to build, was roomier than our rented storage space, and a lot more convenient. One more argument in favor of doing things yourself!

3 moves equal 1 fire

How you actually make the move depends on many factors. I have moved with a moving company, a rented truck, a pickup truck and trailer, even a small car and trailer. If your road is good enough, and your bank balance large enough to take the strain, a moving company is the easiest way to go. You can take everything you think you'll need, and the company will fix or replace anything that breaks. And things will break. A friend of mine in the Air Force says, "Three moves are as good as a fire," when it comes to destroying furniture.

Rented moving trucks

Few of the people in my circle of friends can afford this kind of luxury, and most live in places where moving vans can't go. The rest of us have to do the job ourselves. I have rented moving trucks and "cube vans" from all the major, national "one way" companies. There's little difference between them, except for price.

Don't be ashamed to bargain. These firms want your business! Call a month ahead and give them a chance to beat each other's prices. If Ryder quotes a price that's lower than U-Haul, call U-Haul back and tell them. Then call Ryder back and ask them to beat U-Haul's latest offer. Keep it up until they tell you it's their best offer, then choose the one that's best for you. The last time I moved, I saved nearly $100 over the quoted price of the truck, plus I got an extra day and 50 extra miles free. Not a bad return for an hour's worth of telephone calls! Also, it's a good idea to pack a broom where you can get at it easily after you've unloaded the truck. Most rental dealers charge a $20 cleaning fee if the truck is returned dirty.

A big advantage of rentals is that the truck owner is responsible for any mechanical breakdowns, flat tires, etc. When I moved to Washington State from Wisconsin, our rented truck had a bad front-end alignment. I struggled with it all the way to South Dakota, then called Ryder. Turned out there was a shop that could fix it, right in town. Ryder checked with the shop, found out it would take all day to fix, and gave us an extra day free truck rental, plus a night's free lodging and two free meals for the whole family. We were only about 50 miles from DeSmet, home of Laura Ingalls Wilder, so we all got in the car and took the whole day to go sight-seeing, free!

Adventures in moving

Not all breakdowns are as fun to remember. I once helped my friend Vernon Lamps move from Wisconsin to El Paso, Texas, a distance of 2000 miles. Vernon had an old pickup, converted to a flat-bed, a large, old station wagon, and two home-made trailers to pull. Everything was packed as high and tight as we could get it, with excess baggage and furniture tied on top of the wagon, and outside of the truck and trailers. We really did look like something out of The Grapes of Wrath.

The rig was heavy, and difficult to handle, but everything mostly went OK until we reached the vicinity of Enid, Oklahoma. That's where we broke down.

Vernon had built the motor himself, and didn't want my help fixing it, so I spent my time staring out the window. I noticed an extraordinarily large number of trucks traveling along the road, lots of old cars full of men, and a manufacturing complex so big that we could see it more than 20 miles away. Enid is a small town, but for 50 miles in all directions we had 4 lanes of divided highway. I couldn't figure it out.

Obviously, the huge factory had something to do with all this traffic, so I got out my binoculars and started scanning. I got the shock of my life! There were guided missile launchers concealed in the trees a few hundred yards away, camouflaged tanks, and soldiers with guns pointed right at us! Then I remembered where I had heard of Enid, Oklahoma. It's the site of the Pantex plant, where most U.S. nuclear bombs and warheads are made. Most of those trucks were really armored vehicles in disguise, and the cars full of "farmers" were most likely full of G-men, with automatic weapons on the floor. And there we were, looking very suspicious. About the time I got my heart rate under control, Vernon got the carburetor fixed, and we got out of there fast.

Not all of my moves have been so exciting, but breakdowns are a fact of life in pulling heavy weights long distances, over strenuous terrain. A nationally recognized auto club card, such as AAA or Montgomery Wards, can be a God-send. I personally prefer AAA, because I like their free trip-planning service. Good, up-to-date maps are essential, unless you know the route well and have driven it recently. AAA membership is the cheapest and best "insurance" I know of, for making your move a smooth one.

Paper or plastic?

I am generally a disbeliever in using credit cards, but moving is an exception. Moving trucks drink large amounts of fuel, and long moves may necessitate overnight stays in out-of-the-way motels or campsites. When you arrive, you may have unforeseen expenses, plus planned-for expenses such as food, utility fees, etc. Many of the places where you'll stop will not accept out-of-town checks.

This means you'll either have to carry a large amount of cash, or some kind of "plastic money." 24-hour, automatic teller machines outside your state may not recognize your ATM card, but everybody takes Visa and MasterCard.

If you can't get credit, or just dislike it as intensely as I do, there's still a way out. Ask your bank about a Visa or MC debit card. You deposit a certain amount of cash, and each time you use the card, your account is debited the appropriate amount. You can't withdraw any more than the amount you originally deposited, but the card looks (and works) exactly like a Visa or MC credit card. You can even stick it in an ATM and withdraw cash, if you need to, in virtually any town in America. It's lots better than carrying hundreds of dollars in money.

Just make sure that each driver has enough plastic or paper money to last the trip. On my last move, we got separated, and hadn't agreed on any meeting places along the way. We each had to make it with what we had on hand, and I came pretty close to running out of gas before I found an ATM that would take my card. Barbara had the Visa. If I ever have to move again, we're going to have a CB radio for each rig.

Things to move (if you have them)

Tools:
- Chainsaw, bow saw, ax, hatchet, splitting maul, wedges, logging chain, hard-hats & other safety gear.
- Garden cart, tiller, hoes, rakes, spades, hoses, sprinklers.
- Mattock, shovels, pick, wheelbarrow.
- Carpentry tools, mechanic's tools. electrician's tools, mason's tools.
- Generator. Bring electric tools if you have room, even if you won't have electricity right away. Good used tools don't bring much at yard sales and can be expensive to replace.
- Sewing machine/serger. If you have a treadle sewing machine, bring it!
- Kitchen tools, especially canners and food-processing tools. Don't bother moving canning jars.
- Spinning wheel, loom, other crafts tools you use.
- Animal husbandry tools/tack.
- Tools of your trade.
- All the rope you have.

- Come-alongs, and extra cable.
- Hunting/fishing/ trapping gear.

Furnishings:
- Sleeping bags, blankets, quilts, bedding, and towels.
- Beds with good mattresses. If pressed for space, just bring the mattresses. Good, cheap mattresses are hard to find. Used bed frames and box springs are easy.
- Folding chairs (don't take much space).
- Table (knocked down).
- Dressers, at least 2 drawers for each family member. Expect to pay $5-10/drawer and up for good, used dressers.

Books:
- References, including back issues of *BHM*.

Appliances:
- Wringer washing machine, or new washer/dryer in good condition.
- Gas range if you have room (can be converted to propane). No one likes a wood stove in the summertime.
- Gas refrigerator.
- Gas lights. Bring copper supply tube if in good condition.
- Lamps. Without electricity, bring all the kerosene lamps you can get. Camping lantern.
- TV, VCR, stereo, video games, computers: aren't you moving away from all this stuff? Leave it behind if you can.

Clothes:
- As appropriate for extremes of climate you are moving to, in sizes as will be required in season.
- Boots and leather gloves.
- Rubber boots (called "irrigators" or "Wellingtons").
- Wide-brim hats for everyone. For sun shade and to keep off ticks.

Supplies:
- Matches, flashlight batteries, candles.
- Well-stocked first-aid kit.
- Betadyne (keeps mosquitoes off).
- Benadryl (neutralizes bee & wasp stings).
- Waterless hand cleaner. Removes pitch, safe for kid's hair & clothes. Use before washing with soap.
- Soap, dish detergent, laundry detergent. You'll want 'em right away.
- Flour, dried beans, cornmeal, cooking oil, and oatmeal.
- You'll tire of it fast, but you won't starve.

Vehicles:
- Pick-up truck, preferably four-wheel drive or with limited-slip (Positrac) differential and "off road" tires.
- High gas mileage "second rig" for long commutes or shopping trips. Subarus and Toyotas are popular because they're available in four-wheel drive, and have adequate ground clearance. No car with less than 6" ground clearance is a bargain in the country. ∆

A BHM Writer's Profile

Darlene Campbell

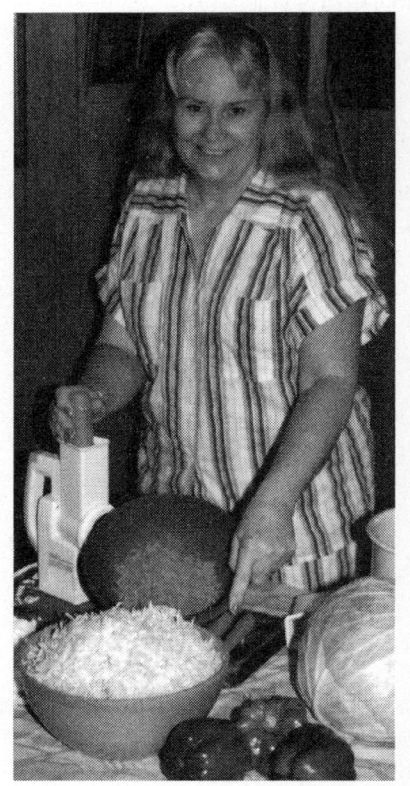

Country living is probably the biggest influence in Darlene Campbell's life. She recalls helping to raise calves and rabbits with her father, and as a youngster she wanted to become a veterinarian. She began writing in elementary school, where she had a serial published in the school newspaper. An early marriage and two tours in Japan put veterinary medicine out of the picture, but her desire to write continued.

Her homesteading career began in the desert foothills of Arizona, where she lived with her husband and children without utilities. A generator, gas lights, and gas refrigerators provided the comforts of life. Water was hauled in a tanker and gravity-fed to the house. She raised goats, pigs, rabbits, calves, chickens, turkeys, horses, and Samoyed dogs.

In 1979, she moved with her family to eastern Oklahoma, where she grew a garden large enough to can 300 quarts of vegetables a season, raised rabbits, and learned to tan hides. She helped her husband develop their farm into a certified tree farm by clearing brush and thinning overgrown stands of pine and cedar.

She devoted more time to her writing and got a job with the local newspaper as the features editor. She was associate editor for *Country Christian Magazine*. She has written many articles and has sold two books to a publisher. Today Darlene writes about raising animals and cooking, and she publishes a newsletter, *The Christian Homesteader*, from her home. She has eight children, fourteen grandchildren, and two great-grandchildren.

MAKING A LIVING

A Backwoods Home Anthology

Supplement your income by teaching others your skills

By Sherry Wietelman

People have been passing skills to the next generation since the beginning of civilization. In ancient times, skilled craftsmen trained young apprentices who became skilled craftsmen and trained other young apprentices. Apprenticeship was the accepted method of teaching others a skill for thousands of years.

Now, more than ever, there is a need for teaching others how-to skills. As office workers lose their positions because of downsizing in large corporations, they find that they have no skills to support themselves and their families. Adults needing training or retraining have created opportunities for skilled craftspeople and artisans to develop and teach adult education classes. Those people who have skills can share their expertise with others and get paid for it at the same time.

When many of us inventory our skills, we sell ourselves short by thinking we don't know anything that anyone else would want to learn. Many people are surprised at what other people will pay to learn. Cabinetmaking, fence-building, sewing, jelly-making, converting to wind or solar power, home maintenance, organic gardening, starting a compost heap, furniture construction or refinishing, and simple auto maintenance are just a few of the many possibilities for adult classes. And college degrees aren't a necessary teaching credential, because it's your experience and basic know-how that people want.

Whether your motivation is financing an independent lifestyle or passing down skills from one generation to the next, teaching others what you know can be satisfying and fulfilling. But before you decide to teach a class, there are five steps you need to learn in order to make your classes the best they can be.

Choosing a subject

The first step to take toward teaching an adult class is to analyze what you can and want to teach. The best teachers are those who enjoy what they're doing and want to share their knowledge and skills with others. You must also analyze your possible audience and think about locations where you can hold your class. Community centers, churches and continuing education programs at community colleges are all possibilities. You will need an appropriate and safe place to teach your class.

Planning a curriculum

Once you've decided on what to teach, you'll need to decide how much to teach, or the scope of the class. You can't possibly teach your students everything you know, so you have to decide just how much information is necessary for them to become competent at the tasks they are learning. If you're teaching students how to change the oil in their cars, they don't need to know how the engine works or the history of cars in America. They need to know where the oil plug is, how to take it off and put it back on safely, and how to put more oil in. Giving your students too much information will frustrate and confuse them. But remember—the safety of your students is your responsibility. You will need to teach them any safety rules first.

When you've decided what your audience needs to know, you'll need to break it down into small chunks. Just as you learned to walk before running, your students will need to learn certain information before other information. Arranging the small chunks of information and simple

The Fifth Year

tasks in the proper order is called sequencing. Sequencing the information will help students connect the chunks of information more easily and quickly.

Preparing lessons

Once you have decided what to teach, how much of it to teach and the order to teach it in, you will be ready to prepare for your first class. You must answer questions such as, "What will I do the first class meeting?" Preparing a written outline will ensure that you cover everything you need to cover the first class meeting. Your students will also need to know whether you will provide the tools, equipment and/or supplies that they need or whether they should bring their own. Handouts for your students, such as a class syllabus or agenda, written objectives for students to meet during the class, and procedure sheets for students to refer to while practicing skills, are other items you will need to think about and possibly prepare.

Don't overlook the Consumer Information Catalog as a source of free or low-priced materials for your class. Universities engaged in research and county extensions are other sources of low-cost information. They often produce fact sheets which are generally inexpensive and provide the most current information available. Oklahoma State University and the Oklahoma County Extension Service in Stillwater, Oklahoma, publish an extensive collection of fact sheets on agricultural, environmental, and home economics topics.

You can also check in the government documents area at large public and university libraries for information published by the federal government. Other good sources are trade and professional organizations, which publish current literature on the occupation or interest they represent. Whatever your source of information, make sure the information you give your students is the most current available.

Facilitating learning

If you've done your homework up to this point, you should now be prepared to instruct your students. When you are giving students background information, it is helpful if you try to relate it to something they already know. Explaining why the information is important will also help them better understand and retain the information. However, for the hands-on skills, you will need to demonstrate correct procedures and allow each student plenty of time to practice afterwards. As an example, say you are teaching a bicycle maintenance class. When instructing students about fixing a flat tire, you'll need to demonstrate the procedure, then allow each student to fix a flat. Circulate while they are working and correct any mistakes you see by reteaching the part they didn't get.

Evaluating results

As a teacher, you will want to continually evaluate your students. There are two types of evaluation. The first type, formative evaluation, occurs when you are circulating and watching the students fix their flat tires. You are evaluating how well they understood your demonstration of the procedure. The second type, summative evaluation, occurs at the end of a block of instruction. It can be a written exam or a hands-on performance check that looks at both procedure and product.

The product in the flat tire example would be the repaired tire. The criteria you would use to evaluate the tire might be that it must hold 30 pounds of air for a minimum of three hours. Summative evaluation gives you a picture of how much information and skills your students have learned, and more importantly, how well you have taught them. Keep in mind that adult students aren't necessarily interested

Flow chart

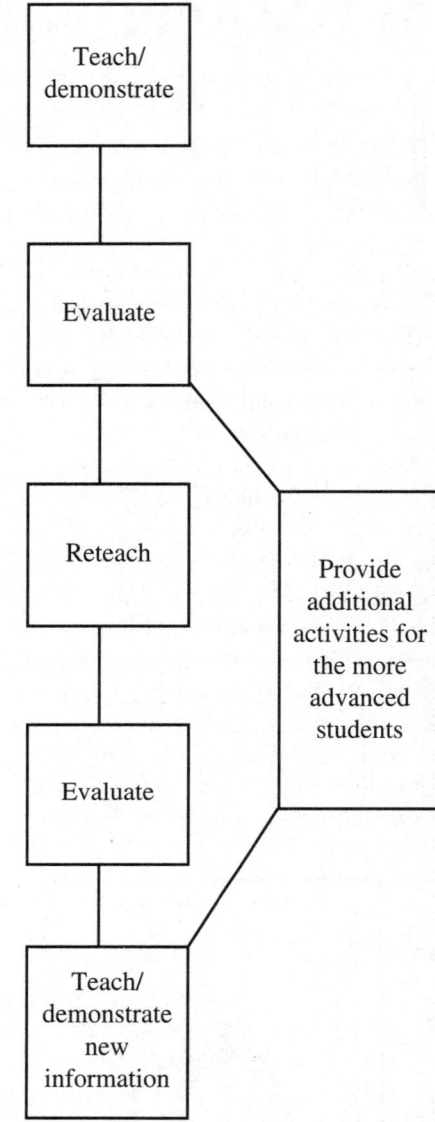

in receiving a grade, but they are interested in succeeding.

Teaching others what you know can be fulfilling and rewarding. Nothing feels quite as good as seeing one of your students succeed in learning a new skill. Whether you've organized a class for profit or taught your grandchildren how to churn butter, you've made a positive impact on another person. And, if you've done it right, you've made new friends for the rest of your life. ∆

Make a patchwork baby bunting from scraps

By Kristen Rogers

Everybody who knits or crochets eventually winds up with bags and bags of little balls of different colored yarns that are too small to do anything worthwhile with, but too big to throw away. I had several such collections, and when little Becca was born, I decided that the time had come to design a practical, inexpensive, heavy bunting for her to wear outside in the spring or to sleep in during the cold, winter nights when the wood stove burns low.

What I came up with is the bunting shown in the photos. It works up quickly and easily, has no fancy stitching and is very washable, since I made Becca's in acrylic yarns. You could embellish it by embroidering flowers and so forth in each square, but I liked the idea of the plain blocks, making a patchwork quilt sort of an idea. It fits little ones from 3 months to a year, and you can leave the bottom seam open and lengthen the body for older babies.

Materials:

Knitting worsted: 8 oz. white, small amounts (approx. 1 oz. of each) 7 different colors to make 35 patches; 18" zipper; 7 knitting bobbins; 3 holders; ½" button; Size 6 knitting needles (or size needed to obtain gauge; Size G crochet hook.

Gauge: 4 st=1"; 5 rows = 1"

Instructions:

Using white yarn, cast on 114 st. K 6 rows.

Begin pattern as follows:

Row 1:

Using white, K2, change to 1st color, K14, change to white, K2, change to 2nd color, K14, change to white, K2, change to 3rd color, K14, change to white, K2, change to 4th color, K14, change to white, K2, change to 5th color, K14, change to white K2, change to 6th color, K14, change to white, K2, change to 7th color, K14, change to white, K2.

Row 2:

Using white, K2, change to 7th color, P14, change to white, K2, change to 6th color, P14, change to white, K2, change to 5th color, P14, change to white K2, change to 4th color, P14, change to white, K2, change to 3rd color, P14, change to white, K2, change to 2nd color, P14, change to white, K2, change to 1st color, P14, change to white, K2.

Continue this pattern for 16 rows—a total of 18 rows per square. With white, K 4 rows. Begin following pattern again for another 18 rows, varying color placement. Repeat pattern 3 more times for a total of 5 full-block rows of different color patchwork squares. Increase 1 st on the last row. Attach white.

Yoke:

Row 1: K1, P1, using white.

Row 2: P1, K1. These two rows form the ribbing pattern. Work in ribbing for 27 st and place on holder to form the upper front. Bind off 4 st for underarm. Rib next 53 st and place on holder for back. Bind off 4 st for other underarm. Complete the row in ribbing pattern.

Upper left front:

Work 27 st in ribbing, dec 1 st at armhole edge on next round and every other row until 25 st remain. Work even until length from 1st row of ribbing measures 3 ½. Rib across 14 st, place remaining 11 st on holder. Continue working 14 st on needle in ribbing pattern, dec 1 st at neck edge every row until 9 st remain. Work even until length from 1st ribbing row is 5". Bind off.

Upper right front:

Place 27 st from holder onto needle. Keeping to ribbing pattern, dec 1 st at armhole next row and every other row until 25 st remain. Work even until length from 1st ribbing row is 3½", ending at the neck edge. Work across 1st 11 st, place on holder. Work

A Backwoods Home Anthology

remaining 14 st. Complete as with the other side.

Back:
Place 53 st on needle and knit in the ribbing pattern. Dec 1 st at each end of next row and every other row until 9 st remain. Continue working in ribbing pattern until length from 1st ribbing row is 4½". Bind off 9 st at beginning of next 2 rows. Place remaining 31 st on holder. Sew shoulder seams.

Collar:
Place 11 st from right front holder onto needle. Place 31 st from back holder and 11 st from left front holder onto needle. Working in Kl, Pl ribbing patters, work until the collar measures 1". Bind off.

Sleeves:
Beginning at the lower cuff, cast on 26 st. Work in Kl, Pl ribbing for 1½". Inc 10 st evenly across the last row 36 st total. Work in garter st (all knit stitches), inc 1 st at each end every 8th row until there are 42 st. Work until the piece measures 6½" from beginning, or until desired length. Bind off 2 st at beginning of next 2 rows, dec 1 st at each end of 3rd row and at the end of every 4th row after that until 28 st remain. Dec 1 st each end of every other row until 18 st remain. Work 1 row even. Cast off. Repeat for second sleeve. Sew sleeves to armhole edges. Sew side seams. Sew button to right edge of collar. Using a crochet hook, attach yarn to the top left edge of collar, ch 7, attach to lower left edge of collar to form button loop. Tie off and weave yarn end into collar. Sew zipper in place and sew remaining front seam to bottom of bunting. Bottom seam can be left open for older babies or sewn closed for little ones. Δ

A BHM Writer's Profile

Ralph LaPlant's writing follows his work and interests. He concentrates on prehospital emergency medical care and outdoor camping and survival skills. In photography, his area of concentration is nature. He has travelled to Glacier Park for moose, Wyoming for landscapes, the Boundary Waters Canoe Area Wilderness of Minnesota for its beauty, and twice to Churchill, Manitoba to photograph polar bears. He has lived in a two-room log cabin in a remote area of Minnesota without electricity, using a generator when necessary, and pumping water by hand.

A BHM Writer's Profile

Dynah Geissal

Dynah Geissal and husband Bob have been subsistence farmers for 21 years and figure they are 90% food self-sufficient.

They bought 40 acres of bare land in the mountains of western Montana and lived in a tipi at 4600 feet while constructing shelters and pens for the livestock, as well as building the house in which they now live. The Geissals also provide their own water from their hand-dug well and their own electricity from solar panels.

Dynah has been a mainstay writer for *Backwoods Home Magazine* for years, sharing her and her husband's extensive self reliance knowledge in clear, concise, and engaging articles.

Dynah Geissal's log cabin

RECIPES

A Backwoods Home Anthology

Make better pizza at home than you can buy

By Richard Blunt

If the first thing that comes to mind when you think "pizza" is a somewhat round, tasteless, orangy-red pulpy mass that's been delivered to your house by a pimply-faced high school kid who swears he's not late (all the while your 14-year-old daughter is standing behind the door swooning), then I hope this month's column will excite your curiosity and provide you with the information and incentive to have some fun and try making pizza, right there in your very own kitchen. Unfortunately, the neighborhood pizzerias have established the criteria for what we think of as good pizza. But that stuff is not good pizza and pizza does not have to be a second-rate food. Some of the world's best known and respected chefs have devoted serious attention to it. Professionals like James Beard and Julia Child have used their talents to create some wonderful pizza delights, and you can start creating your own, knowing you're in good company.

There are just two parts to any pizza: the crust and the topping. Both require some attention to detail during preparation to ensure a first-class finished product. Some special equipment is also desirable to get the best results. However, I could walk into almost any kitchen in America, right now, and make a good pizza with just the equipment I found there.

The equipment

Let's examine the equipment first. The very best pizza is baked in a wood-fired brick oven on a pizza stone. The pizza stone produces a light, crispy, evenly baked crust. Getting a wood-fired brick oven may be beyond the means of the average pizza gourmet, but the stone baking surface is easy to obtain and will provide good results in the average kitchen oven. Specialty shops sell pizza stones in round and rectangular shapes, in various thicknesses, and they last practically forever.

For my own use, I use 5 1/2-inch square by 1/2-inch thick **quarry tiles**. They are cheap, available in all building supply stores, and will cover a standard-sized rack in most domestic ovens, without modification. To place these tiles in my oven, I move one of the racks to the lowest position in the oven and place the tiles on it, covering as much of the rack as possible. I do this so that most of the heat in the upper part of the oven is coming through the stone rather than around it on convection currents.

If you do not wish to use a pizza pan, but cook directly on top of the stone, transferring the pizza to and from the oven will require a **pizza paddle**. These can also be purchased in specialty shops. For myself, I use a pizza pan for the first few minutes of cooking, just enough to let the crust get firm, then I slide the pan out from under the pizza and continue cooking the pizza directly on the stone.

If you don't wish to buy a pizza paddle, you can make your own using a few basic tools, some 3/8-inch plywood, and a little imagination.

Pizza pans come in a variety of sizes. The most common sizes are 12, 14, and 16-inch diameters and are made of aluminum or black enameled steel. I think you get best results using enameled steel.

Another piece of equipment is a **food thermometer**. To accurately measure the temperature of liquids being combined with the yeast, you should use a food thermometer. You'll find I use a food thermometer in quite a few of my recipes. It's going to be worthwhile for you to get one.

Before we get into the recipes, here are a few preparation tips that will help you make a first-class pizza every time.

The first concerns the flour. It's best to use **high-gluten bread flour** when making pizza dough. Gluten is the protein that provides strength and elasticity to the dough. Both of these qualities are important when combining flour with yeast. Though unbleached all-purpose flour can be substituted for bread flour, it has less gluten and you'll have some loss of quality. If you mix whole wheat flour with white flour, on a 50-50 basis, you can produce an interesting crust, both in flavor and in texture. Also, substituting yellow corn meal for 1/4 of the bread flour will give you a crust with a light crispy texture.

The Fifth Year

When measuring flour for use with the dough, use the **"scoop and level"** method. Scoop the flour from it's container with the correct size measuring cup, then level the flour to the top of the cup with the straight edge of a knife or spatula. Spooning the flour into the measuring cup means lots of air and less flour, and tamping the flour down into the measuring cup means more flour and a heavier crust. To avoid this, just scoop it out with your measuring cup, use a knife to level it in the cup, and you'll get the same amount of flour every time. This is how I measured all the flour when testing the recipes for this column.

Kneading is a very important procedure when making any baked product to which you've added yeast. It activates the gluten in the flour and evenly distributes the yeast cells throughout the dough. This is necessary if you expect the dough to rise properly and bake to a light and even texture. Depending on the type of flour used, sufficient kneading will take from 10 to 20 minutes. Kneading the flour also burns calories and will allow you to eat an extra slice of the pizza, if it really turns out good, without feeling any guilt. You'll know you've kneaded the dough enough when it no longer feels sticky and it's developed an elastic texture. A good test to determine when the kneading is complete is to make an indentation in the dough with your finger. If it springs right back, you're done. If the dent stays, knead it some more.

Cake yeast and **dry granulated yeast** both work well. I use the dry granulated variety. For one thing, it's easier to store. In dried yeast, the yeast cells are dormant and durable. In cake yeast, they're already active and easily destroyed during storage.

A vast assortment of cheeses will give your pizza added interest. In addition to the traditional whole-milk mozzarella, I've used other soft cheeses like provolone, swiss, cheddar, soft jack, camembert, fontina, and brie. Hard cheeses like aged jack, parmesan, and asiago can also be used, independently or in combination with a selection of soft cheeses, to produce the taste delight of your choice.

Due to space limitations, all the recipes in this article are made with tomatoes. This is not meant to imply that using tomatoes is the only way to make good pizza. There's a slew of recipes that depend on other vegetables, meats, and sauces that result in a first-class pizza. I have also included one of my all-purpose tomato sauce recipes in this article. This sauce can be used on pasta as well as pizza. But, when short of time, I've even used the bottled pizza sauce you find in your local market. Really. I make up for the loss in quality with added toppings.

The first recipe is my version of the traditional pizza dough.

Classic pizza dough

> 2 3/4 cups flour
> 1 tsp salt
> 1/2 cup warm water (100 to 110 degrees F.)
> 1 pkg (1/4 oz.) yeast (dry granulated)
> 1/4 tsp granulated sugar
> 1/2 cup cool water (room temperature)
> 2 Tbsp olive oil
> 1/4 to 1/2 cup flour (for kneading)
> additional olive oil (to oil bowl)

1. Combine the flour and salt in a suitable size mixing bowl, mix and set aside.

2. Combine the warm water, yeast, and sugar. Mix this and set it aside to proof. Proofing lets you know that the yeast is still active. It's when a layer of foam appears on top of the mixture within five minutes. If this doesn't happen, the yeast you've used is not active and you'll have to discard what you have and start again.

3. After the yeast has proofed, combine it with the cool water, oil, and flour-salt mixture. Stir this with a heavy spoon until it forms into a ball. Dust the counter with a little flour and place the dough on the floured area. Now, knead the dough for about 10 to 20 minutes while adding flour to the counter to prevent the dough from sticking. Not all flours are the same, so it may be necessary to add a little more or a little less flour than the recipe calls for to get the desired result. Of course, since you can't take flour out, remember any mistake you make on the too-much side for next time.

4. Transfer the dough to a well-oiled bowl, one large enough to allow the dough to double in volume. Cover it with a clean cloth and let it rise until it's doubled in size. This will take from one to two hours, depending on the room's temperature.

5. After the dough has risen to twice it's original size, punch it down and transfer it to a lightly-floured board. Now, knead for one minute to remove any air bubbles. Cut this into two equal-size balls, cover them and let them rest for five minutes.

6. You are now ready to form two 12 to 14-inch round pizza shells or two 12 by 15-inch shells on rectangular cookie sheets. Forming a pizza shell can be a little tricky, but with a little practice you can become good at it. The tossing and spinning method used by the pros has never interested me, and my kitchen ceiling is better for it, too. What I have always used is the old-fashioned rolling pin

method. I suggest that you do the same until you get a little experience or a little more daring.

After the dough has rested for five minutes, lightly flour the counter and begin rolling the dough to the desired size and thickness. When not using a pizza pan, and after the shell has reached its proper size, gently roll the shell onto

> 2 1/2 cups bread flour
> 1/2 tsp salt
> 2 Tbsp grated parmesan cheese
> 1/4 tsp garlic powder
> 1/4 tsp dried basil leaf
> 1/8 tsp dried thyme leaf
> 1/8 tsp dried oregano leaf
> 1/8 tsp dried red pepper flakes (optional)
> 1 pkg dry granulated yeast
> 1/2 cup warm water (between 100 and 110° F.)
> 1/2 cup buttermilk (room temperature, not cold)
> 2 Tbsp peanut oil
> 1/4 cup bread flour (for kneading)
> additional peanut oil (to oil the bowl)

the rolling pin, and transfer it to a pizza paddle that has been dusted with corn meal.) Finish shaping the shell by working the dough with your fingers and pressing with your hands. When using a pan, follow the same procedure but lightly oil the pan before sprinkling on the corn meal. The thickness at this time should be about 1/8 inch. Cover the shell with a cloth and set it aside for 15 minutes.

Add the topping of your choice (more on the topping later) and transfer the pizza to the quarry-tile or stone surface in a preheated 425-degree oven. Bake it for about 10 minutes or until the undercrust and the edges are evenly browned and the cheese topping is melted and bubbling.

This next recipe is a variation on the classic dough recipe. I've added ingredients to the dough to give it a flavor that will balance the dough against the toppings which I'm going to recommend.

> 1/2 cup onion, finely diced
> 3 Tbsp olive oil
> 3 1/2 cups fresh, ripe plum tomatoes, peeled, seeded, and chopped
> 2 cloves fresh garlic, finely diced
> 1/2 tsp dried thyme
> 4 twists of freshly ground black pepper from a pepper mill (If you've read my previous columns, you know why I use freshly ground

Garlic and herb pizza dough

Measure, combine, and mix the flour, salt, parmesan cheese, garlic powder, dried herbs, and red pepper flakes. Proceed as in the previous recipe, substituting the buttermilk for the cool water and the peanut oil for the olive oil. Please do not let my selection of herbs limit you. There's a vast world of flavors available for your use; to vary this recipe use your imagination.

The sauce

Here's a recipe for an all purpose tomato sauce. I use it for both pizza and pasta. The recipe produces about two cups of sauce, enough for two pizzas.

> 1 each prepared pizza shell
> 2 Tbsp olive oil
> 1 to 1 1/2 cups pizza sauce or chopped fresh tomato
> 1 cup whole-milk mozzarella cheese, shredded
> 1/4 cup provolone cheese, shredded

All-purpose tomato sauce

1. Saute the onions in the olive oil until tender.
2. Add the tomatoes and simmer over a low heat for 10 minutes, stirring frequently to prevent sticking.
3. Add the garlic and thyme. Continue to cook over a low heat for about 20 minutes more. Let the sauce thicken some if it's to be used on pizza (if the sauce is too thin it will make the crust soggy), but don't let it get too thick if it's to be used on pasta. If the sauce becomes dry, that is, too much like tomato paste, add a little red wine or tomato juice before using it on the pizza.
4. Remove the sauce from the heat, stir in salt and pepper to taste, and allow it to cool.

Toppings

You are now ready to make a first-class pizza. Here are a few topping ideas. The first is a version of the tomato and cheese pizza, using three popular cheeses.

Tomato and cheese pizza

> 2 or 3 sweet Italian sausages
> 3/4 cup fresh mushrooms, thinly sliced
> 2 Tbsp fresh oregano leaves

The Fifth Year

> 1/2 cup chopped clams, fresh cooked or canned
> 1/4 cup Bermuda onion, minced
> 2 cloves fresh garlic, minced
> 1 tsp dried savory leaves

1. Brush off any excess flour from the prepared shell and lightly brush the shell with olive oil.
2. Sprinkle on half of the parmesan cheese, then evenly spread the chopped tomato or pizza sauce.
3. Evenly spread the mozzarella and provolone cheeses.
4. Finish off with the rest of the parmesan cheese and the leaf oregano.
5. Bake as directed earlier.

With a selection of various cheeses, tomatoes, and seasonings as a base, you can develop a wide variety of interesting, tasty pizzas. Here are a few combinations that I have enjoyed over the years. For each of these combinations, follow the assembly procedure outlined in the previous recipe, up to the addition of the tomato or tomato

> 1/2 cup fresh broccoli, diced to 1/2" chunks
> 1/4 cup fresh fennel bulb, diced to 1/4"
> 1 fresh sweet red pepper, thinly sliced
> 1 tsp dried rosemary leaves
> 2 tsp olive oil

sauce. If hard grating cheese, like parmesan, is not one of your cheese selections, omit that step.

Italian sausage topping

Bake the sausages in a 350 degree oven until just cooked through. Allow them to cool then peel off the skin and chop the sausage into chunks. After spreading the tomato sauce, evenly spread the sausage and mushrooms. Finish with your selection of cheeses and the oregano. Bake as usual.

Clam topping

After adding the tomatoes or tomato sauce to the pizza, sprinkle on the clams and the onion. Now add your selection of cheeses and finish with the garlic and savory leaves. Bake as usual.

Broccoli topping

Saute the broccoli, fennel, and pepper in the olive oil until just tender. Add the rosemary leaves and immediately remove from the heat and set aside to cool. With this topping, assemble the pizza completely, then spread the vegetable and herb mixture on top of the cheeses. The subtle anise flavor of the fennel bulb opens the door to using a wide variety of cheeses. I urge you to try cheeses like camembert, soft jack, fontina, and brie. You'll discover a vast world of flavor delights in the humble pizza.

Well, that's it. I hope that I have excited your interest enough for you to give homemade pizzas a try. But, as I pointed out earlier, pizzas can be made without tomatoes and they can even be made without cheeses. You can use cream sauces, fruits and vegetables, various meats, and you can even use aromatic spices. There are many nontraditional toppings and someday we'll talk about them when I come back to pizzas in future columns. ∆

A BHM Writer's Profile

Don Fallick

Don Fallick has been writing for Backwoods Home Magazine since issue number eight, but he's been reading BHM since the first year. He built his own home on his first homestead in western Colorado in 1976. Since then, Fallick has lived in Wisconsin, Washington State, and Utah. His homesteading activities have included owner-built construction, homeschooling, independent energy, horse-power, harvesting wild foods and game, homebased business, cooking, and "raising everything but his standard of living."

Fallick and his bride Barbara have 10 children betwen them. All have been homeschooled. When he is not writing for BHM, he works as a surveyor and substitute school teacher. At one time or another, he has also been a carpenter, nurse aide, factory worker, locksmith, editor, and commercial pilot. He has a wide range of interests, and says that he tries to do "everything that interests him." Current projects include a lengthy "how to" book, three books of guitar music, and two children's stories.

COUNTRY LIVING

A Backwoods Home Anthology

How we bought our country home

By J. Darlene Campbell

I must confess that our move to the country was not at all planned. It happened so quickly and so unexpectedly that even now I suspect we were merely following our destiny. I was divorced with five children and had always longed for a country place. Then I met and married John, who shared this dream of living on a few acres and having livestock and a small garden. Even with both of us working, we didn't dare think of buying our dream place, since supporting a ready-made family meant having no money left at the end of the month to put away for our future.

Both of us are bargain hunters. We scan the ads looking for bargains of all sorts, so it was not unusual that when I spotted an ad in a Sunday, 1969, newspaper selling bare desert land, I made a comment about it to John. By this time we had been married over four years and had a sixth child. But still dreaming about a future in the country, John said it sounded good, so we decided to take a drive out to look at it. It was situated some 25 miles from our home in north Phoenix, Arizona.

We arrived with all six children in tow and turned them loose as we walked over bare land with the real estate sales person. We fell in love with the quiet, the natural beauty, and the wide open spaces where children can run to their hearts' content. We selected five acres to call ours, signed a contract and then went home wondering how we would pay for it.

We discussed the possibility of selling our home and called a real estate broker to give us some idea of how much we could get for it. When we said how much we needed in order to pay off the mortgage and still have something left over, the broker almost laughed. She said our home would never sell for that sum. Let me say here that land values were just on the brink of escalating.

We put aside our thoughts of selling our home and moving to the country, but we decided to hold onto the land for future use; perhaps we would go there on weekends and work at putting up fences and such. I was raising purebred puppies which I sold for pet and show and, with three litters ready to sell, we made the down payment on the land.

A few weeks later a lady knocked on our door and asked if we wanted to sell our home. She was a real estate sales person looking for a house in that particular school district for a client. We were surprised but told her that if the price was right we would sell. To our amazement, the appraisal came back and our house was sold!

Now we had 30 days to get out! We knew we wanted to move onto our land, but there was no house, no electricity, no sewer, and no water. In fact, it was going to be quite an experience for the next three years without electricity.

Making do

John immediately located a house that needed to be moved because a freeway was going in. He bought it and paid to have it moved to our country place. He got a reduction on the moving costs by providing some of the labor himself. Then he ordered a custom-made tank trailer for hauling water behind our pickup. Little did we know we would be doing this for the next eight years. He also bought a gasoline operated generator to power a used wringer washing machine.

Other things we quickly bought were propane gas lights, gas refrigerators, and a gas space heater. One of the most exciting days of our lives was the day they moved the old house onto the property. It looked like some wrecked battleship sitting alone in the desert. Not very pretty, but we loved it.

By this time we had depleted the cash derived from selling the house, but we were still bargain hunting. I came home from work one day to find a note on the dresser. "I've gone to move our garage," it said. "What garage?" I wondered. Later I learned that John had called around until he located a garage to be torn down and moved. The materials were available free to anyone who would do the work. He rebuilt it on our property, and that became our barn.

Our first livestock purchase was at an auction. We bought five crossbred calves. They immediately took sick

The Fifth Year

with shipping fever. We learned to use veterinary skills to save them, but later lost the heifer to pneumonia. And of course there were chickens and turkeys and rabbits.

We bathed children in a washtub by heating water on the cook stove, and we learned numerous other techniques for living on the land. The day the boys brought home four five-foot-long rattlers, all stoned to death, I knew they were learning to survive.

John built us a new home on that first five acres. Our family grew by two more children and we lived there to see the power lines come in, bringing with them the city folks, a very different breed. We sold our little place without the aid of a realtor. It was no longer bare land. It had a new three-bedroom home, barn, shop, kennel, corrals, and chicken coop, all hand-constructed by John, and it was completely fenced.

Then we moved to southeast Oklahoma and purchased 18 acres of woodland. It is bordered on two sides by the Ouachita National Forest and abounds with wildlife, wild fruits and nuts. It was in sad need of repair, and John set to work restoring the woods and constructing buildings. Secluded and close to nature, we hope to live out our lives here.

The power of willpower

There are thousands of people just like us who are dreaming of a place in the country where they not only can live self-sufficiently, but debt-free. Since most of these people start out in debt, buying a few acres may seem impossible on their income. Yet it can be done with perseverance, determination, and willpower. Yes, willpower.

The largest obstacle to getting out of debt or saving enough money for the down payment on a country place is lack of willpower and the lack of desire to do without simple pleasures (or perhaps extravagant pleasures) in order to make the move. Having raised eight children, we faced the same problems as other families. There were always expenses, expected and unexpected, such as medical expenditures, school clothes, automobile insurance, automobile repairs, taxes, and holidays where everyone is expected to give, give, give.

An ace in the hole

Early in our marriage, I had invested in what I call my ace in the hole, the raising of purebred puppies which I sold at premium prices for show and pet. Even with both my husband and me working, it took the sale of these puppies to meet some of the financial obligations. I strongly advise everyone to have an ace in the hole. Not necessarily the same one that worked for us, but some means of paying expenses that your earnings will not cover. If you have a talent such as auto repair, gunsmithing, typing, or child care, use it as your ace to squirrel away savings or meet other obligations that otherwise drain your savings.

Plastic peril

Too many Americans rely on that plastic credit card for buying needful items or paying expenses. The plastic card is the quickest way to find yourself so deep in debt that a country place will never become reality. However, if you have already fallen into this trap, use your willpower to immediately curtail using the card; put it away in a safe place. Notice I did not say cut it up, because it is true that sometimes you must rely on one to be secure. I am talking about using the card only for emergencies like being admitted into a hospital, or paying insurance premiums on the jalopy, or buying auto license plates. Never use it for clothes, even school clothes, or eating out, or purchasing extras such as televisions, camcorders, or other things you can do without.

Now that you aren't using the card, draw up a budget plan. Make a list of all your income, excluding your ace in the hole. Then list all your set expenses such as payments on credit cards, utilities, house payments, loans, doctor bills, food expenditures—anything that you know you must pay each month. Total both lists and subtract your monthly expenses from your monthly income. Anything left? If so, set a portion of it aside in a savings account and use the rest for such necessities as clothes and auto repairs.

Now consider your ace in the hole. You can use the income provided by your talent in one of two ways: put all of it into the savings account and draw from that account only when extra expenses pop up that your monthly income will not cover; or use it immediately to pay those things including taxes, auto insurance and school expenses.

By the time you have gotten this far, you are probably wondering how you will buy clothes if you don't use your credit cards. If you can sew, begin now to make most of your clothing. Its really quite easy, though time consuming. Repair worn clothing or update the style by adding a few fashion touches here and there.

When I was raising my children, I saved all outgrown clothing for the next child in line. I realize today that children going to school in the city will not wear hand-me-downs, but if they want to move to the country perhaps they will be willing to make a few exceptions. You can also shop wisely at sales, yard sales included, to dress your children well. Never throw away a worn-out garment before removing buttons, snaps or zippers for recycling in your sewing box. The garment can then be cut down to make something else such as strips for making hooked rugs, squares for quilts or pot holders. Even if you don't use the items now, you will need them some day. I moved two boxes of quilt scraps to the country and used them all, some for quilts, some for carseat throws. I soon found they also made wonderful doll clothes for Barbies I found at yard sales, which helped at Christmas time.

If you work outside the home it is important to dress well. But do you really need a new wardrobe every season? I think not. Some cities have resale shops where better quality clothing is sold on consignment. Don't be embarrassed to shop there. If the city is some distance from your place of employment, no one will ever know the difference. And bear in mind that one day you will be working on your own farm, feeding and watering stock and planting a garden, and all those expensive clothes will just hang in the closet.

Make this an adventure and you will soon find that you have money left over for buying things you will later need in the country. I found my first pressure canner at a yard sale while we were still living in town, and it still works perfectly after all these years of hard use. Just recently I found an electrical breaker box for a workshop that I picked up for $5. John said it saved him roughly $80 to $100.

Now, here's another ace in the hole. If you are paying on a home, consider the market value. When you are ready to sell your home and move to the farm, the equity you have built up will help make the down payment. If you are renting, consider buying a small place and fixing it up. The improvements you make on a house in town will increase its resale value. When you sell, you will see that you actually were saving a little money each month in the way of mortgage payments.

Own your own life

Once you have begun to save a little and have learned to do without credit cards, you will be paying cash for everything. Sound impossible? It's really not. Everything you own will belong to you outright, and any money left at the end of the month is another step toward your move to the country.

If you still aren't coming out ahead at the end of each month, try negotiating with creditors to lower your payments and make them more manageable. However, lowered payments mean a longer pay-off time, so the date you set to buy a country place may have to be postponed a little.

There is no better life than being free of debt, raising your own meat and vegetables, and training your children to appreciate the land. It's well worth the investment in time and effort. ∆

A BHM Writer's Profile

Rev. Dr. J.D. Hooker

The family of J.D. Hooker lives back off a gravel road, in rural Dekalb County, Indiana. Now they are raising donkeys and wolf/German shepherd hybrids—a unique and highly competent type of working dog. He and his wife of 25 years have four daughters, a granddaughter, and two grandsons.

"For us," says Hooker, "the backwoods type lifestyle is the perfect way to live and raise a family. He admits that they do have decades of experience in living independently, but says, "It's only because so many years have passed while we've been busy enjoying our way of life!"

The solar-powered silent partner

*By Jim Slater
(with Larry Elliott)*

When my wife Jessie and I moved to our new place on the High Desert of Central Oregon, we knew that a steady, reliable supply of water would be our prime consideration. With 160 acres of dry, parched desert, our first major project would have to be a water well.

We had looked long and hard at the lay of the land before we bought it to make sure that a well could be drilled and pumped without bankrupting us.

To our west is an area where deep wells and dry holes are common. We could not afford to end up with either of these. Typically a well in this area ends up at 700 to 800 feet and leaves the land owner with a bill of over $15,000 even if it's only a dry hole. To the north and south of us steep buttes are dotted with small springs that run cold and clear year round, even during our recent seven-year drought. We were hoping that this high water table could be found somewhere on our place.

Even if we could find water, the next obstacle that would need to be overcome would be that the nearest power line was two miles away and, at $6 per foot to get it here, this option would be out of the question. Any energy we would use to pump water would either have to be portable (gas, diesel, etc.) and easily purchased or we would have to produce it ourselves. An AC submersible pump and generator was considered first, then a windmill or perhaps a gasoline powered jack pump. At this stage we had not even heard of a solar pump.

Looking for water

Two sites were chosen on our property as likely to have water. A well driller recommended by a friend was called in to look things over. At the first site he was shown, which happened to be located next to our cistern installed up the hill from the house, he looked at the dark red rock formation and said "Don't look like you will do any good here. I've drilled in this type before and never had any luck." He asked to see something else. At this point our options had just dropped by 50%. I then told him we had picked another area because it was located near a hillside spring and close to the junction of two large gullies that drained hundreds of acres, the only drawback being that it was very remote and near the top of a steep hill. "Well let's see it," he said. Our spirits where lifted when he took a look at some hard grey rock and told us that if he could set up his rig on this remote spot, there would be a good chance of finding water. Since one of my wife's many talents happened to be dowsing, it seemed like a good idea to let her try her hand in verifying the driller's observation. After a few quick passes, Jessie said, "Drill here." As it turned out, they were both right. The well came in at 185 feet and better than 5 gallons per minute. Not only did this solve our water problem, but it also proved we were right to question the conventional "wisdom" of the locals who said it couldn't be done.

Next problem

Now that our first problem was out of the way, we had to face the problem of how to get the water out of the ground and then deliver it many hundreds of feet down to our house and cistern, as well as pasture. Since the well pump would now be situated 950 feet up a steep and fairly inaccessible hill, we didn't feel like having to supply any pump that would need fuel. Packing a gas can uphill on skis or snowshoes just did not appeal to us. We gave some thought to using a windmill, but the well is protected from the wind. A new source of energy would have to be found.

About this time a friend of ours loaned us a solar products catalog. Little did we know that so many products existed for folks like us who live beyond the grid. After reading the section on water pumping and looking at solar panels and trackers, it all

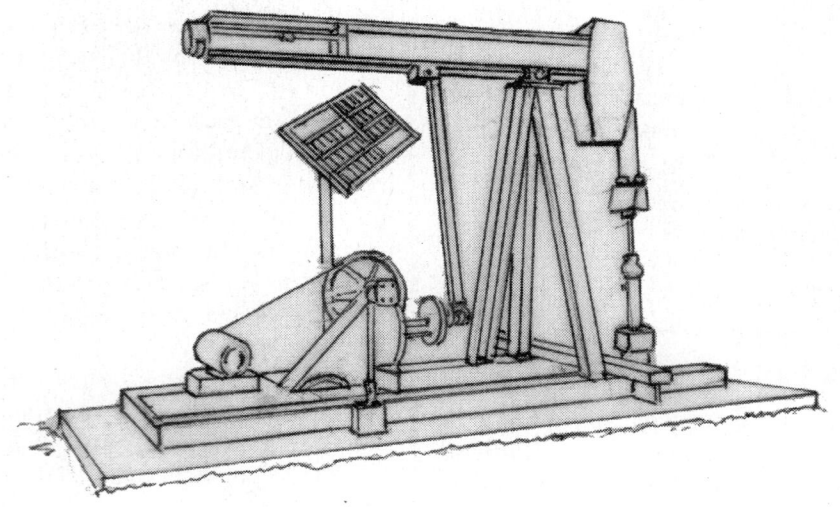

began to sound good. Since all advertising should be taken with a grain of salt, we decided to talk to others who may have already had experience with solar pumping. A rancher friend of ours said that he knew people further east of us who were using a solar pump with good results. A rancher will be the first to tell you if something does or doesn't work. We heard only positive comments, which was what I wanted to hear.

The solution found

A local solar distributor and installer was next contacted. We told him that we wanted to get a solar pump but needed to make sure we got the right one. We had decided on a DC submersible with a passive tracker. He asked if we had considered a jack pump. We replied that we had, but the cost was too high for our budget. He said, "I just happen to have a used jack with a motor and controller I'd like to sell." After spending the rest of the day checking out the jack and doing a lot of arithmetic, we called him back and said, "Let's do it."

The main reason for choosing the jack pump over the submersible, besides the cost, was that should something go wrong with the motor, repairs would be quite easy and relatively inexpensive. In a jack pump the motor is above ground, not in the well. A simple belt and pulley connect the motor to a gear box. A gas motor could be attached if need be, or perhaps a bicycle pulley, although not very practical. Also, by attaching a larger motor and more panels, the output of the pump could be increased in the future if needed.

After a few weeks, we had all the equipment necessary to complete the pump installation. The well driller was called back to help set the pipe and well cylinder, and all went along with only some minor problems. The first time water began flowing out the discharge pipe we knew we had a winner and that at least our first two problems had been overcome.

How it works

For all of you who may not be familiar with the components that make up a complete solar pumping system and have only a little knowledge of how it works, a brief description is in order.

In our system, six used Arco (now Seimens) M-51 photovoltaic panels are wired in series to produce the voltage necessary to drive the motor. These panels are mounted on a Zomeworks passive tracker (requires no electric motors or external power source) which orients the panels toward the sun as it travels across the sky.

The electric power produced by the panels flows to a controller which, in our system, is a 600-watt Australian Energy Concepts Maximizer. This power is then fed to a 1/3 hp permanent magnet motor that drives a 60:1 ratio gear box through a belt and

A BHM Writer's Profile

Richard Blunt

Richard Blunt is the Backwoods Home Magazine Food Editor. His articles in BHM are more than just collections of recipes. They are instructions for how to create a dish, then vary it to suit your tastes. He explains how each step and ingredient affect the final product. His column is written to appeal to all readers, from beginners who want to learn how to cook well to experienced chefs who want to experiment and broaden their horizons.

Blunt is well qualified for the task. His career in the food industry spans more than three decades. What began as a desperation job as a teenage pot washer in Cambridge, Massachusetts, developed into a 30-year learning experience that has found him presiding over the kitchens of exclusive restaurants in the Greater Boston area. Since then, he has worked as a senior manager for three large food management companies. He lives in Connecticut with his wife and three children.

pulley arrangement that also serves to further increase the ratio between motor and gear box rpm. This wide gear ratio serves to keep the pumping action slow and very powerful due to the high torque generated.

The rotary motion of the gear box is then converted to reciprocating up and down motion using an eccentric, in a manner somewhat similar to the method used to drive steam locomotive wheels. This up and down motion is transmitted to a cable and walking beam (very similar to oil field pumps that look like giant prehistoric birds bobbing their heads up and down) that pulls a 7/16" steel rod up and down inside the well pipe. This rod then drives a piston and cylinder located at the bottom of the well in an up and down motion that lifts water to the surface. The water is truly "jacked" to the surface with each stroke. Our well cylinder travels about 18" with each stroke and with a 1 7/8" piston delivers over 1.5 gallons per minute in full sun.

At some point, we shall increase this production by using a larger cylinder and motor, and by adding two extra solar panels. The tracker we purchased had room for a total of eight panels, so we will have room for them without any modifications. This is something to keep in mind if you may be looking to do as we have done.

The entire pump assembly is housed in a small A-frame shed that serves to keep ice, rain and snow, as well as critters, off the pump. Since we have cattle roaming about our area, a barbed wire fence was built around the pump and the solar tracker to prevent damage. Even if you don't have cattle, deer can do a lot of damage if they decide to use your tracker as a scratching post.

After we were assured we would have a steady supply of pure water, the hardest phase of the entire project had to to tackled. We had to dig a trench and lay pipe the entire distance (over 1000 feet) to our house and cistern. Instead of simply digging trenches and laying pipe, we decided to carefully design the entire system to give us maximum water to several different sites and do it without having our bitter cold winters freeze pipes and leave us without water.

Our water project became a real test of our commitment to living off the grid and on an isolated ranch. Our pipeline had to be laid in a ditch that dropped down a steep slope for over 950 feet and had to be dug through a lot of rock. 250 feet of this ditch had to be dug and backfilled by hand. After all the backbreaking digging was done, 1 1/4" PVC pipe was laid down the entire length. Care was taken to ensure that all sections would be self draining each night.

The pipe terminates at an underground 1800 gallon cistern. The cistern is located about 300 feet from the house with a drop of about 50 feet. A separate pipe comes out the top of the cistern to act as an overflow. This overflow is piped past the house to the barnyard where it fills a stock pond and stock tank. We use a system of valves to direct this water. A 5-foot piece of 12-inch water main fits around both valves and stands vertically above them. The top is plugged with foamboard and covered with a piece of plywood. This valve box is insulated from freezing by filling large plastic garbage sacks with fiberglass insulation. Using duct tape to hold it together, I rolled up a two and one half foot section of unfaced insulation to about a 12-inch diameter coil and placed it in the garbage sack. This insulates from ground level to the top of the valves.

Since our system is gravity fed, our water pressure at the house is about 22 P.S.I. This is somewhat lower than standard city water pressure, but serves us very well and is more than enough to allow use of a tankless water heater. We have kept all of our pipe sizes a little larger than required to lower the friction and give better water delivery.

We had one of the coldest winters on record this year, and no part of the water system froze. The jackpump output was enough to keep us and our livestock well supplied with water even though we hardly saw the sun for the two months of December and January. We are very happy with our water system. Last summer we were blessed with a beautiful vegetable garden. Carrots, potatoes, bush beans, corn, strawberries, pumpkins, onions, cukes and more all grown with water pumped by the sun and on land that, until then, was dry and brown and stripped of moisture. The horses now drink cold, clear water on the hottest days of summer and splash in their own pond to cool themselves.

We did a lot of planning and hard work to accomplish these things, but has all been worth it.

The Maximizer, or LCB, used in this system is without a doubt the most important component of all. This controller can be best described as an electronic gearshift. It converts amps to volts or vice versa. In our system, six photovoltaic panels, each producing 2.3 amps at about 17.3 volts, are wired in series (positive to negative, etc.) to give a total of 2.3 amps (remember, in series circuits only the voltage adds) at about 104 volts. In very bright sun this voltage and current can be even higher.

Since our motor requires around 90 volts to operate at full speed, the Maximizer converts (using switching technology found in computers) the excess voltage to current to supply the three amps needed by the motor. This allows the pump to operate at maximum efficiency even in low sun conditions. On overcast days or when a cloud passes overhead the voltage of the panels stays around 96 volts, but the amps decrease. In this condition the motor would normally stop. The Maximizer now "shifts gears" and supplies additional amps at a lower voltage and keeps the pump running. The only time our pump stops is in total darkness or in groundfog. ∆

HOME EDUCATION

A Backwoods Home Anthology

Home-schooling — Is it right for your kids?

By Ron Brackin

By way of introduction, I confess that I am not one of you. I am a suburbanite who loves to visit wholesome Lancaster farms and rustic ranches in Jackson Hole but must return to the land of fast food, deadlines, and traffic jams just as surely as the buzzards return to Hinkley.

Nevertheless, I have an enormous admiration for families who renounce their urban citizenship, load up the family Conestoga, and head off to carve out a home in the wilderness.

You are, by definition, an independent sort and therefore perfect candidates for home schooling (provided, of course, that you have children).

A home school can be designed to conform to virtually any lifestyle. It is almost infinitely malleable. But in that flexibility lies its chief difficulty. In short, there are so many curricula, teaching philosophies, and variations that the inquirer may be easily overwhelmed.

To prevent this, and since you are back-to-basics folk, we will turn momentarily from the clutter of ideas, resources, and techniques and begin at the beginning.

Ask the right questions

Why would you consider teaching your children at home? (Check all that apply.)
__ They'll get a better education.
__ They'll learn our family's values.
__ We don't want to miss our children's childhood.
__ Home schooling will protect them from drugs and violence.
__ We believe it's biblical.
__ All our friends home school.
__ There isn't a school within 100 miles.

Home schooling requires a pretty significant commitment on the part of the entire family. And, like anything else, it can be discouraging from time to time. When the tough times come, you will inevitably ask yourself, "Why are we doing this, anyway?" And that's when you will need good reasons to keep going.

So spend a good amount of time, discussion, and prayer on this first question. It's your foundation. And anyone who has hewn his own cabin knows the importance of a solid foundation when the storms hit. Generally speaking, every reason you have for home schooling is like a foundation stone. The more you have, the stronger your foundation.

So let's examine a few of these reasons.

A better education

Will your children get a better education if you teach them at home?

You don't have to do much research here. The bottom line is: you will get out of it what you put into it. It will help if you begin to look at education holistically, as they say. In other words, you look for every opportunity in the daily act of living to apply and reinforce what you are teaching.

As examples of what you can do, point out the principles of physics, anatomy, and physiology involved in splitting logs. Make use of weights and measures in the kitchen and workshop. Apply foreign language study to correspondence with overseas penpals or vacations. Develop new outlets for creative writing assignments, like journals, family newsletters, and correspondence with famous personalities. Take the lead from groups like Junior Achievers, Future Farmers, and 4H Clubs. The real issue you must address in your analysis, though, is whether you are prepared to make this kind of intense commitment.

Family values

Just what are your family's values? One of the first things to do is sit down and write them out. Discuss them. Prioritize them. You probably did something similar before moving to the backwoods or your mountain or island or wherever you've sunk your roots. You determined the relative importance of career, convenience, construction, maintenance, planned development, proximity to schools and supplies, medical facilities, emergency services, etc. Now do the same thing concerning the value of religion, work ethic, virtue, education, health, entertainment, and comfort. Identify, in descending order, what is most important to you.

Then, once you've laid out what you believe in and what's important to you, ask yourself whether your children will have those values reinforced in public or private school. If not, here's another stone for your foundation.

Sharing your children's childhood

While some parents dread holidays and summer vacation because their children are under foot, others wish the holidays would never end. They're not content to capture childhood moments on Kodak; they want to savor them day by day and treasure them in their hearts. They actually enjoy having the little rascals around and being the ones to teach them how to read, write, and do sums, revealing creation to them one flower at a time, and opening the windows of history to let in the light of man's dealings with his God and his fellow men. Decide how much you desire that kind of

The Fifth Year

involvement and how much time you will actually have to devote to it.

No drugs or violence

Protection from drugs and violence is an issue still hotly debated in and out of the home.

Some say children will never be able to cope in the "real world" if they are protected from it by being taught at home. They need to relate with their peers, they say. Socialize. Obviously, no one wants his son or daughter exposed to drugs or violence, but the belief here is that drugs and violence are a part of life, and children need to learn to deal with it.

Others maintain that the children are not being sheltered at home, they are being equipped.

Rather than being "thrown to the lions" when they are ill-prepared to deal with such things as peer pressure and fear, they are given the time and space to grow strong in their character and convictions. Military enlistees, for example, are sent to boot camp to be toughened up and taught discipline and proficiency with their weapons. They are trained in a protected environment before being sent to the front.

It's biblically correct

Whether or not home schooling is biblical is another widely discussed issue within the Judeo-Christian community. Both the Torah and the Bible place responsibility for the education of children on the shoulders of their parents. While there are those who believe this means only religious training, others make no such distinction between secular and sacred and believe God is relevant to and involved in every area of their lives. You must carefully evaluate your own position on this matter.

Everybody's doing it

Having the support of others who home school is invaluable. However, teaching your children at home simply because others are doing it will not sustain you through the seasons of pressure and doubt. You will need to know that it's right for you, not for your next-door neighbor (assuming, of course, that you have a next-door neighbor other than beavers and pine trees).

No choice

And home schooling just because it's your only option can be just as frustrating. While you may be less tempted to quit (what else can you do?), having no way out could also make you cranky and a bit difficult to live with.

A family affair

One more thing before we move on. You may have noticed the conspicuous absence of the pronoun "I" in our checklist. Trust me, if home schooling begins as "mother's little project" or "that thing mom does"—if the family is not in agreement and committed to its success—you would do well to say "thanks, anyway," and go out and plant a truck garden. While single moms and single dads have successfully taught their children at home, and continue to do so, it's definitely tougher alone. And it's worse still when there are folks around who might help but are not interested.

Dads don't have to teach the 3 R's in order to be actively involved. They should at least be school principals. And when things get rolling, you'll find that the teaching goes on in the kitchen, basement, barn, field, woods—everywhere and every time parents and children are together. You should now be able to answer the first question and be ready to tackle the second. This one will take a bit more time, but that's okay. There's no hurry—there only seems to be.

Finding the right resources

If, after going through this checklist, you decide that homeschooling is the right choice for you and your children, you must then begin researching how to go about it. Several homeschool associations and suppliers advertise regularly in *Backwoods Home Magazine*. You should contact several of them and choose those who seem to have the same interests and values you have.

The best ones will also be able to give you information about local support groups. The laws vary considerably throughout the country, so be sure you research what the legal requirements are concerning home education in your state and local area.

Home schooling is not right for everyone. But then again neither is homesteading. And who'd have ever thought you'd be living in the woods like the three bears, on a mountain like Heidi's goat, or in the desert like John the Baptist? Certainly not I!

(Ron Brackin writes for Home Study International, (1-800-782-4769) and teaches the Writing Christian Workshop, a full-day seminar designed to prepare home school parents to motivate and train their children to write. He is an author and journalist and lives with his wife, Annie, and their four children in Plano, Texas.) Δ

A BHM Writer's Profile

Kristen Rogers

Kristen Rogers lives in her backwoods home where she cooks, gardens, writes, and generally domesticates. When she's not cooking, Rogers can usually be found at the local farmer's market or selling her wares at the "Gourmet Gardener" outlet.

Rogers has written several articles for Backwoods Home Magazine on a variety of topics, including her struggles with Child Protective Services. She also writes a gourmet gardening column for a local newspaper.

HOME EDUCATION

Some homeschooling ideas

By Don Fallick

It was a typical three ring circus around our house when Dave called to ask me to write this article. Two of the kids, and some of their friends, were up on the garage roof putting on new shingles. Our 12-year-old daughter was changing the tire on the car, with the help of her 14-year-old sister. The rest of the kids were decorating the house for a birthday party, or were in the kitchen baking a cake. Barbara and the birthday girls were driving around picking up party guests. I kept pretty busy running up and down the ladder giving instructions when needed and advice when asked. Once in awhile I got to hammer a nail.

Curriculum

While we worked, we talked. Neal, the seven-year-old, learned the names of the different kinds of workers who build a house—masons, carpenters, sheet rockers, painters, glaziers, and roofers—and what each one does. Tali, the 12-year-old, learned the importance of safety in jacking up a car: "I don't know how you feel about your legs, but I wouldn't trust that jack enough to put my legs under the car!" Amy, the 14-year-old, tried roofing and learned that faster isn't necessarily better. Fourteen-year-old Soren learned the importance of precision and accuracy, while 13-year-old Camilla learned that if you try to "whip" volunteers, you'll end up baking the cake yourself. Seven-year-old Halley and 11-year-old Thora learned that good workers can choose their jobs and don't have to put up with unpleasant employers, if they're willing to work hard.

All got practice in following written and spoken directions, measuring, calculating, and seeing a job through to completion—valuable lessons taught, but not always learned, in classrooms. Informal discussions included science fiction, computers, and biology. "Did you know that tomatoes are considered berries, but strawberries are not?" Soren asked. This sparked a lively contest to think of other biological anomalies, with the younger children joining right in.

Homeschooling is contagious

During the course of the afternoon the two birthday kids returned with their guests, held their party, and played games in the yard. After the party, most of the guests wanted to come up on the garage roof to help shingle. They seemed to have more fun hammering nails than they had playing party games, to the surprise of no one in our family. Children love to mimic adults, especially when they can do the things adults do "for real." And there's nothing more real than work, whether it's feeding critters, gardening, or fixing the roof.

The homework "trap"

Most of the homeschoolers I know try to take "teaching moments" like these and use them to educate their kids. But some of them then fall into the same trap that classroom teachers do—they make "homework assignments" which have little of the immediacy or naturalness of the genuine learning environment. For example, there's a temptation, after a Saturday work project such as ours, to assign each child to write a composition about "What I Learned Last Saturday." This is totally artificial, and signals the children that they are being "taught" something. Instead, we encourage the kids to write letters to grandparents, distant friends, or pen pals, or even to keep a diary or journal. We never ask to see the letters or journal entries. Nevertheless, we do see most of them, because the kids bring them to us for help with spelling, punctuation, grammar, and composition.

Motivation

We do not insist that corrections be made. If they want to send letters spelled "their way," that's their business. We do share with them letters from the grandparents to us,

The Fifth Year

commenting on the "unusual" spelling, or even asking for a translation! Often the "offender" is unable to translate his or her own letter. This is usually sufficient motivation for the child to start seeking help with spelling, etc. The only thing "artificial" we do is to ask grandparents to write only to children who write to them, except for special occasions such as birthdays and holidays. The thrill of getting "real letters" in the mail is great motivation for a child who sees "big kids" and adults receiving such mail all the time. Especially when that child lives in the backwoods and has little personal contact with others.

Part-time homeschool

"Natural learning," as practiced in the Fallick family, need not be reserved for home schooled kids. It works equally well for children who spend part or most of their day in public school, too. In fact, our children have been in and out of public schools, to the frequent consternation of school officials. Being teachers ourselves, Barbara and I are not scared of them. We use the schools to supplement our home-based instruction. When we are able to keep one parent in the home full-time, we homeschool those children who want to homeschool. When we have both had to work outside the home, we've sent the kids to public school and confined our homeschooling to weekends. Sometimes, some of our kids have gone to school part-time.

I confess that my own preference is to be able to stay home with the kids. Not everyone is crazy enough to want to stay home with nine children, and this option may not be right for you. But I firmly believe almost any parents can homeschool their children at least part-time. If we can do it, with me working full-time, writing part-time, and janitoring part-time, and Barbara student-teaching in the mornings, taking classes in the afternoons, working part-time, and running a family of eleven, you can too!

Fitting it in

Yes, our schedule is pretty hectic, but homeschooling actually helps. For example, several of the older kids take turns helping me at my janitoring job. My boss doesn't mind, as long as the work gets done, and done right. The first two or three times, each child just follows me around and watches what I do. We keep up a running dialog, so the child learns why each job is done the particular way it is.

Gradually, the child begins to do things suited to his or her ability, until he or she can do one part of the job alone. Then I set the child to doing that part of the job while I do another part, thus halving my time. I now have enough children trained that I can count on having two or three with me on any given evening. What used to take four or five hours now takes one and one-half at most, and we all get home in time for supper.

I pay each kid about half of what I get for the job that kid has done. There aren't many 12-year-olds in our area who can earn $3.50 per hour! Of course, I'm making $3.50 per hour on the labor they do, too. Far from feeling cheated, the kids all feel proud that they can contribute so much to the family's support and still have money left over "to burn."

The real world

Mopping floors and vacuuming offices may not seem "educational." But we talk while we work, and what we talk about is educational. After all, kids—especially teenagers—don't want to talk to their parents about intimate stuff. But they are anxious to find out what you know, as long as they think they are the ones directing the conversation.

The whole point is that children enjoy learning about the real world, especially when they can see the connection between what they are learning and their actual environment. And they love to show off what they know. Praise their knowledge sincerely, and you'll never need to give them a test! In fact, a positive attitude is your most important asset as a homeschooler. If you view learning as fun, and if you obviously enjoy sharing what you know with them, your kids will share your passion. Even if they can't see the connection between studying history, say, and being a good citizen, they'll still learn to love history if you have a good time telling them your favorite stories of the past, even if it's just "war stories."

Most children are very literal minded. They haven't yet developed the ability to see relationships that are obvious to adults. Small wonder they act so childish. But kids see their parents working, or at least going off to work, every day. Naturally, they want to work, too.

Appropriate "lessons"

The trick, especially with small children, is to find some real work that they are capable of doing. When we are weeding, we give the small kids the job of pulling the small weeds. Sure, I could hoe down a square yard of tiny weeds in the time it takes my seven-year-old to pull one. But that's not the point. The weeds will be back every year, but my son will never be seven again.

There's a story about an old farmer who let his boys care for the family calves. They didn't always do the job right, and the grown cattle were neither as big nor as healthy as they should have been. The farmer's neighbor called him lazy, and said if he'd raised the calves himself, they'd have brought much more at the market. The old farmer responded, "That's just the point! You thought I was araisin' calves, but I was araisin' sons!" ∆

HOME EDUCATION

A Backwoods Home Anthology

Child-led learning

By M. C. Wright

Everyday, all day, is school for our family. If we go for a walk we examine trees, birds, bugs, rocks, and dirt. Everything is up for grabs. We can spend hours examining the way an airport works. Going to the grocery store is a study in the science of food production, gardening, math, and artistic display. The list goes on and on. One venture to the health food store was to be a study of herbs and tonic, a planned field trip by mom and son to buy a few herbs for personal use.

Research

In preparation for the visit we read about the plants, learned where they grow and what each part of the plant is used for. We cut out pictures of herb plants and put them in a notebook we keep, along with a short written description of each herb and its medical purpose. We also drew plans for a small herb garden we want to plant. Homeschoolers have to be flexible, seeming to often wander off onto other trails of learning, and this was one of those times. The herbal plants' needs led us to studying soil nutrients. Plants need water, but "where does all that water come from?" "Let's find out!" "Wow, look how many herbs we can grow in our box!" "How many herb leaves does it take to make a pound?" "Oh no! How many pounds of dirt are in the planter box?" "How are we going to know if our dirt is good for plants?" On and on we went—but back to the trip to the health food store.

We set off with the list of herbs we needed to make a blend of herbal oils used for colds and flu. Benjamin and I spent a few minutes looking at the dried bulk herbs, and decided to buy a few ounces of comfrey. We weighed the crunched leaves on a big scale and kept measuring till we had four ounces. Putting the leaves in a bag and marking the bag with weight and cost took some figuring (math, writing, and spelling involved). Deciding on the oils we needed for our concoction was a matter of reading labels, and then figuring out how many bottles of each we needed for our recipe. We figured the cost of our purchase on the calculator, and after getting all of our herbal treasures together, we headed to the front of the store. We stopped by the goodie counter for some white chocolate sticks (used for bribery) and then were ready to check out. By this time I felt really pleased. We had learned about herbs and measurements, had figured weights and money, and had had a good time. I hadn't once had to say, "Don't touch!" and, for us, that's a big success.

Something new

As I wrote the check, the building trembled and, while I pondered whether it was an earthquake or my imagination, I heard a roar like a train coming through the building. At that point, I was ready to grab Benjamin and toss him under the counter to save his life. Luckily, he is a very observant 10-year-old and, not being shy, he yelled, "Mom, look! It's a tank!" Sure enough, a huge green army tank was coming down the main street in town. Benjamin ran around looking for the door but, in his excitement to get outside with that clanking, noisy monster, he couldn't find the door. Thank goodness it wasn't a fire! He would have perished for sure.

As any ever alert homeschooling mom would be, I'm always ready to assist my child with whatever he is interested in, right? Forget the herbs, purse, checkbook and the shocked cashier. Get that child outside!! Well, our luck was in. There were two, count them, two huge, green, roaring, infernal machines going down the street. Which meant we had more time to decide the best way to handle this situation. After a full body tackle and a football carry, I managed to get the hyper-ventilated bundle of energy outside the store. While he was standing there yelling, "Mom get the car, follow those tanks!" I realized I had left all my valuables on the counter in the store. No way would that child go back in the building. He could still see smoke coming out of the tanks' exhausts and was determined to follow them, whether on foot or by car.

After a mad dash to retrieve my belongings from the nice, but shocked, cashier, I hurried back out to protect the child I had abandoned on the sidewalk. Benjamin, being small and fast, beat me to the car still yelling, "Mom, follow those tanks !" "Ok , buckle up! Which way did they go?" (Remember, child-led learning.) Fortunately, it was a Saturday morning, so traffic was light and, despite observing the posted speed limit, we caught up with the objects of our pursuit within three blocks. Now I could see why it was so easy to catch them. Ten miles an hour tops was the speed at which our convoy (the two tanks and us) progressed through the business district and into a residential area.

All that time my child was taking in those humongous contraptions with all the admiration of a true devotee. Now, personally, I see nothing that fantastic about a couple of tanks. But I'm a good sport, so we kept following as they ground along at a snail's pace. After about twenty minutes, I began

The Fifth Year

A BHM Writer's Profile

Marjorie Burris

Since 1970, when Marjorie Burris and her husband bought their 40-acre homestead in the central Arizona mountains, necessity has forced them to learn self-sufficiency. They use native plants for medicine, cure their own meat, and maintain and repair all their equipment.

Burris grew up in southern Illinois, but has lived most of her adult life in the west. She is a registered nurse, specializing in operating room nursing. Her greatest pleasure has been watching her three boys grow up in the backwoods. Now they bring their own children to the homestead to pass along backwoods values and skills.

Burris began writing after she retired from nursing. Her articles and stories have appeared in *Backwoods Home Magazine* and other publications.

---

thinking about the grocery shopping still to do and the laundry to be picked up. I knew Benjamin had memorized every detail of "his tanks," and I was convinced that I wouldn't be a bad mother and ruin him for life if I insisted we go about our business and leave the tanks to fulfill their mission without us.

Contact

"No way! Just a little longer and they will stop," he said with childish faith. And sure enough, they did finally turn into a gas station and—believe it or not—pull up to the pumps. The man in the first tank opened the top cover to his machine and climbed down. He proceeded to fill up the gas tank. Benjamin, who is not shy and is well enough adjusted socially that he feels comfortable talking with adults, decided it would be in his best interest to have a detailed conversation with the gentlemen. I, being a level-headed individual and not accustomed to chasing tanks through the middle of town, was a little bit apprehensive about parking so obviously and staring at the men and their machines. I don't fit the profile of a terrorist (I hope), so I had to make a quick decision as to how far this encounter would go. Deciding not to stifle Benjamin's enthusiasm, I drove the car within a reasonable and safe distance.

Benjamin got the four men's permission to look at the machines and then proceeded to have a long talk with them. He learned how much the tanks weigh, how fast they travel, how much gas they hold, and how long the gas lasts. He learned about the guns on the top and the size of their bullets. The men demonstrated how they see to drive, which thrilled my homeschooled kid. He asked questions about how they got "picked" to drive the tanks, and was told a little bit about joining the National Guard. You can guess what Benjamin wants to be when he grows up! Last week it was a "shark-chaser," this week it's a tank driver.

A learning experience

When the men finally headed back to their shops, we went on our way. A note will be dispatched to the local National Guard Unit to thank the men for their time and kindness. After going to the grocery and laundry, we stopped by the library and came home with several books about the Army, tanks, and famous battles. Probably for the next few days we will learn more about tanks and all the things and people associated with them than we would ever have learned if we had not gone to the health food store. But that's okay, home schoolers have to be flexible. I have to remember to call the cashier and tell her I'll be in next week to pick up the bag of herbs that I left on the counter. ∆

A BHM Writer's Profile

Robert L. Williams

Robert L. Williams is the author of 27 published books, more than 3,000 stories and articles, and 10 television scripts, in addition to his regular contributions to *Backwoods Home Magazine*.

Born in Hayesville, North Carolina in 1932, Williams has been a U.S. Army tank mechanic, professional baseball player, and educator. He devoted 30 years to teaching English and literature— first in high school, then on the college and university campus.

In 1989 Williams saw his pre-Civil War house demolished by a tornado. He and his wife Elizabeth and their son Robert III used a chain saw to build their new house from trees uprooted by the storm. The first story published about their house appeared in *Backwoods Home Magazine*, issue No. 16. Their story is the subject of a book called <u>Starting Over</u>, available from BHM.

Native of the forest: a guide to growing ginseng

By Melinda C. Long

Ginseng is a perennial herb that is native to backwoods of the eastern half of the United States. Its root is valuable, especially some wild varieties that bring an unbelievable $38 to $52 an ounce. Prices have been rising steadily over the years.

Wild ginseng has nearly disappeared, and what is left is hard to find. Since the days of mountain men and beaver trappers, ginseng has been dug on a regular basis and sold to the Far East. Now some states have laws that establish hunting seasons for ginseng just like they do for deer and squirrel.

Wild ginseng can still be found, but the days of finding a patch worth a small fortune are gone. Today almost all ginseng is cultivated.

Domestic ginseng brings only a fraction of what wild ginseng is worth—$18 to $68 per pound—but it will grow faster. In four years you can have a domestic root ready for market, while wild ginseng takes ten.

It takes a few years before you can harvest a crop of ginseng, but you don't have to worry about a drop in demand. Chinese have used ginseng as an aphrodisiac and cure-all for at least a thousand years, and its popularity shows no sign of decline. If anything, it's rising, and as most people involved with ginseng will tell, not enough people are taking advantage of the opportunities. You will always find a market for ginseng.

It is an inconspicuous plant. Ginseng blends well into woodland foliage and isn't easy to spot until mid-August or September when its berries turn scarlet red and its leaves turn yellow. Then, right from the center of the plant stands a well-formed cluster of berries. The plant will be one to two feet tall and have three or four branches on a main stem. Each branch has five leaves that meet at a central point at the end of the branch where the leaves spread out evenly, like the fingers on your hand. Domestic plants may grow double stems, but their leaves and berries are the same wild plants.

Getting started

Seeds take eighteen months to germinate, so you'll want to buy stratified seed when you're ready to plant. Stratified seed is seed that has been kept in moist sand for a year and is ready to use when you are. It's best to start out small with ginseng. Never order more than you can afford to lose. Ginseng can be difficult to get started, and seed is expensive. Seed costs between $100 to $150 a pound and it takes about one hundred pounds to sow an acre. But smaller quantities are available. An ounce costs about $15 and will sow approximately forty square feet.

You can also start by planting young roots. They will give you a one- or two-year head start. Roots sell for about eighteen dollars per hundred for one-year roots, and two-year-old roots cost between $25 to $30 per hundred.

You can plant seeds or roots in the spring or fall. Make your inquiries early. By late spring or fall, mail-order seed and roots may be sold out or high-priced. Try to deal with a reputable source.

Dealers not only sell mature roots, they also sell their seed and young roots to growers. Dealers have a natural tendency to make growing ginseng sound like the easiest "get-rich-quick" scheme in the world, and they may encourage you to buy more seed than you need.

If your roots or seed arrive before you are ready to plant, don't let them dry out. Store roots in the refrigerator or in damp humus soil. Keep the seed in moist sand, also in the refrigerator. Wash sand away through a screen when you are ready to plant, or sow the sand along with the seed.

Planting ginseng

There are two methods of cultivating ginseng. You can plant in the woods, placing ginseng in its natural habitat, or you can use artificial shade. The main thing to remember about ginseng is that it's a shade-loving plant.

Artificial shade is made by building sheds over plant beds that have a lath roof or have straw scattered over chicken wire that has been stretched across the top. Posts are set before the beds are made. Lath roofs are built in sections and laid in frames on the roof so they can be removed in winter and won't bend or buckle under the weight of the snow. If your area is not too windy, straw will stay in place with tobacco sticks or boards laid on top. You can extend the roof overhang to reduce the need for sides on your

This ginseng plant is ten years old. Growing ginseng in pots makes it easy to monitor growth.

shed. Some growers think lath sides are necessary and others don't. The main thing is to keep the plants well shaded.

You should lay out the beds so they will get the most natural shade. By running your shed north to south, and your beds in short rows east and west, the sunshine won't bear down on any one area of plants too long during the day.

You can plant ginseng in any good garden soil, but a rich humus soil is preferred. Work the beds up eight or nine inches deep and mix in a combination of leaf mold, rotted wood, shredded leaves and old manure. Drainage is very important and so is ventilation, not only for air circulation around the plants but also for ventilation in the soil around the roots so they won't rot. If there is any doubt about drainage adequacy, you should put in a drain tile under each bed. Raise the beds a few inches above your paths. Have sloping sides on the beds or hold the sides in place with edge boards.

You can plant seeds or roots, or to get a head start plant a combination of both. For roots, rows are eight inches apart. Set the tiny roots three inches deep eight inches apart in the row. Seeds are planted one inch deep, two inches apart in rows six inches apart.

You'll want to encourage your domestic ginseng to grow quicker, and using organic fertilizer is best. You don't want to use chicken manure or bloodmeal. They contain nitrogen that burns the roots on contact. Strong fertilizer may also cause the plant to grow too fast, creating lots of green foliage at the expense of the root.

Organic fertilizer has the best balance. Rock phosphate is inexpensive. Bone meal is good but it costs more. Potash is very good, and composts of shredded leaves, grass clippings and a bit of manure that has broken down over several months are also helpful.

You can fertilize woodland ginseng but one of the reasons for planting in the woods is to duplicate as close as possible the "wild" root that brings prices so much higher. A main trait of wild ginseng is its slow growth. No chemical difference has been detected between wild and domestic ginseng, but buyers can tell the difference.

The crown, an area between the top of the root and the stem, is much longer than on a domestic plant. Also, the crown has rings that indicate its age the same way rings on a tree will tell its age. Wild roots are usually thinner and somewhat gnarled.

Planting ginseng in the wild

Planting in the woods has advantages. Shade is convenient and the soil is already mixed. Find the best location for your patch. Ginseng is somewhat particular about where it grows, yet not any more so than other woodland plants like mayapple or maidenhair fern. Still, finding an excellent location could be the secret of success in growing ginseng in the woods. You have to keep a balance of factors in mind when making a decision, and you must choose a

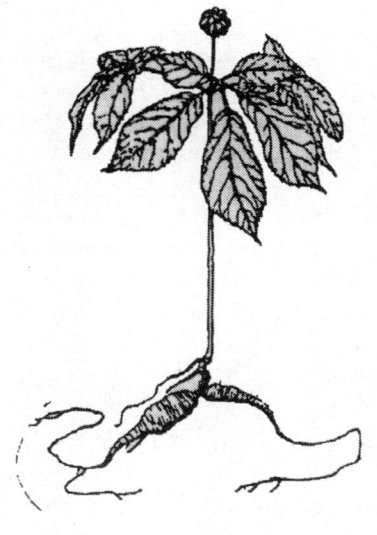

Wild ginseng plant

place that won't be disturbed for years.

Keep in mind that ginseng likes well-drained soil, but don't forget that it also likes a certain amount of moisture. Ginseng seedlings are not strong like corn seedlings are. If the ground is too dry, ginseng can't push through. Then the seedling will break off and die. Locate your garden on a gentle slope with an eastern or northern exposure. Plant up and down instead of horizontally on the slope.

In the woods, you'll have plenty of shade to choose from and ginseng likes cool deep shadows. It likes to grow near hardwoods such as oak, hickory, poplar, ash, beech, etc. It isn't partial to any one particular type of hardwood but prefers, instead, to grow near a mix of hardwoods.

It's good to plant near medium sized trees for two reasons. Their branches are lower and give a better shade cover than older trees that have lost their low branches and have their shade starting much higher on the trunk. Also, older trees make good timber. You'll need to keep future logging possibilities in mind when thinking of your location. You hope your wild ginseng patch will be undisturbed for at least ten years.

Anywhere you find mayapple, bloodroot, golden seal (yellowroot), or luscious ferns of any kind growing in the woods you know that particular spot has the right loamy soil conditions that ginseng loves. Now all you need for your woodland preparations are your seed or roots for planting, a pair of gloves, a rake, maybe pruning shears to cut away underbrush, and a small hoe or hand-held garden cultivator.

Select a spot that is not too close to tree trunks. You need the trees' shade but you don't want their roots sapping all the food and water away from your plants. Cut away any underbrush in the area and rake aside the leaf litter. Scatter the seeds by hand, then turn the seeds under no deeper than an inch with the small hoe or cultivator, or even by hand if the soil is soft enough. Return the loose soil and leaf litter. But don't pile the covering on too thick. Mice love to eat ginseng and a pile of leaves is an invitation for winter homes.

The reason why this method of cultivation is simpler than the artificial shade is because you are disturbing the soil as little as possible. This reduces the risk of disease, especially blights that lie dormant in the soil. You may not be able to keep as close a watch on a wild patch (although for some backwoods readers a wild patch may be as close as the backyard), but it can thrive with less attention in its natural environment.

Wild ginseng still needs maintenance though, especially in the first year. You can barely see the new seedlings when they first appear. They look like small bean sprouts and have only two small leaves, but you want to resist the temptation of pulling the weeds up around them. Even though the weeds may be choking their air circulation, you don't want to disturb the soil and activate disease.

Instead, "mow" the weeds down with a weed-eater or break the weed tops off by hand.

In the first year, you do have to spray fungicide on the wild plants regularly every week to give them a good, solid start. Later on, the method of minimal weed control will reduce the amount of spraying that needs to be done. After the first year, the plants will only need spraying occasionally or when the weather is exceptionally hot and wet.

Pests and disease

It has been said that everything in the woods likes ginseng, and judging from the number of pests ginseng attracts, it must be true. Deer like the leaves and mice can be a particular problem. They can easily wipe out a newly planted bed of roots in no time.

My parents plant their young roots in wire guards to ward off mice. The wire guards are similar to the type used around tulip bulbs to protect them from mice.

You can stop some of the mouse damage by emptying a small box of D-Con into a pint jar and laying the jar on its side in the garden. Camouflage it with a piece of bark or leaves. If moles are a problem, leave poison peanuts in their trail. Other pests of ginseng include mites, snails, birds, and even muskrats.

Using fungicide is part of the regular maintenance of ginseng, especially in domestic gardens where the soil has been thoroughly worked through. Commercial sprays work fine. Zineb is a chemical you can start with. Cultivated plants should be sprayed every week and after every rain.

The worst disease to plague ginseng is the blight called "alternaria." Alternaria is a fungus that is dreaded mainly for its destruction to the seeds. When ginseng is struck, the leaves look as if they were scalded, like boiling water had been poured on the plant. The leaves wilt and hang limp. If the weather is wet, alternaria can spread fast with an entire garden going down in a day or two. Fortunately, the disease does not harm the roots. By the time it strikes, usually in hot weather around the middle of July, the bud has already formed on the root for next year's growth. Alternaria will kill plant tops and destroy seeds, but the root will produce a healthy plant again next spring.

Alternaria can be exacerbated by inadequate drainage, plant spacing that is too close, and even fertilizer. Ginseng is accustomed to slow growth. Fertilizer can weaken a plant by encouraging it to grow too fast and disturbing its normal growth cycles. Prevent this disease if you can. Sometimes seeds are lost to birds and rodents but nothing wipes out a whole generation of seed like alternaria.

Seeds

Berries turn red and ripen at different times, depending on your location. In the south they are ready in August and in the north, September. The berries won't wait until frost to fall to the ground. They will fall not long after they're ripe. You can pick berries every day as they ripen or you can wait until the whole pod is ready. There are two or three seeds in each berry.

After the berries are picked, separate the seeds by storing them in moist sand. In four to six weeks, the berry pulp will dissolve. Now you are ready to plant your seeds or stratify them for future use. If you have too much seed to store in the refrigerator, use a screened box that can be buried in the ground. Place seed between layers of moist sand in the screen box and bury it eight inches in a cool shady place.

Roots

The ideal time to dig roots is when the plant has turned yellow in the fall, and the stem is no longer green. A root dug at this stage will lose less weight after drying than a root that is dug in the summer.

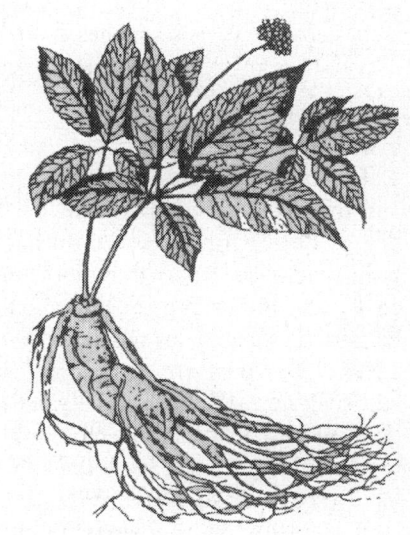

Typical shape of domestic ginseng plant

It's hard to predict the shape a ginseng root will take. It has a tendency to branch. The most unusual shapes are valuable. Roots that resemble the human form are considered potent by Oriental buyers. You want to lift the root out whole without scraping the outer skin.

When you are ready to dig, it's best to use tools that will loosen the soil rather than turn it. A long thin steel spike or wooden stick works well to loosen the soil, then you can finish digging the root out with your hands.

A Swiss army knife is helpful when you are digging in the woods. Sometimes you have to saw through tree roots. Many times ginseng will grow under tree roots or between rocks and boulders.

A full-grown root generally measures one inch wide and four inches long, and weighs about one ounce when it's green. It takes approximately seventy-five roots to make a pound. Fresh roots lose two-thirds of their weight when completely dry.

A great deal of the market value depends on how the roots are dried, so it's very important that the drying process be carried out carefully and thoroughly. The first thing a buyer inspects is the dryness of a root. Buyers want a root that is completely dry and fairly crisp.

Remove dirt from the roots by spraying them over a screen rack with a water hose. Don't let roots sit in water too long. They will waterlog and the inside of the root will never dry as pure white as it would have been otherwise. Roots draw moisture easily and the drying process should be started as quickly as possible.

Even after they are dried they can still soak up moisture, so you want to do your best to dry them thoroughly the first time around. Sometimes they have to be dried all over again.

Depending on the weather and humidity, it takes between two to four weeks to dry roots and you don't want the drying period to move too fast or too slow. Too fast, and the outer shell dries before the inside; too slow, and the inside of the root is discolored.

It's best to let roots dry naturally. Sunlight tends to burn, so dry roots indoors. They need good ventilation. Places like the attic in your house or among the eaves in a shed or garage will work. Spread the roots in a single layer on screen racks.

Markets

Before sending your roots to market, they should be so dry that they break before bending. Most ginseng is exported to Oriental countries, and if there is a possibility they will take on moisture during shipping it will cause a dealer to lower your price.

You can find dealers who buy through mail-order by checking the classified ads under the heading "Plants, Roots & Herbs" in outdoor and farming magazines. Always contact dealers by mail first and ask for a price list. The market fluctuates a lot and you can expect prices to go up or down every year.

When you ship to a buyer, pack roots in a box as full as possible with crumpled newspaper. Roots get damaged if they shake around too much.

With a lot of money involved in growing ginseng, some people prefer to deal with buyers in person. Most metropolitan areas of large cities have Oriental sections, and you can always find a buyer there. A grower in my area of southern Indiana prefers to deal face-to-face, and since he is an over-the-road truck driver, he took his first crop for sale to Chinatown in Los Angeles. He had no trouble at all making a sale.

He had been there before and noticed how they packaged their roots for retail. The roots were cleaned with the hair-like root strands cut away, and the packages lay in neat rows in styrofoam trays covered with Saran Wrap, just like the cuts of meat at the supermarket. He cleaned his roots the same way by cutting the stringy roots off and throwing them away. The Oriental buyers were not pleased. They showed him a package that contained nothing but the hair-like roots and it had a price of twenty dollars on it. So although a root will look neater without all the tiny, stringy roots, don't remove them. Even they are worth some money.

How much profit you ultimately wind up with will depend on how much you plant. A quarter of an acre will produce seventy-five pounds of dried roots. A wild patch of this size would be worth at least $18,000. A

> ### A BHM Writer's Profile
>
> **Mick Sagrillo**
>
>
>
> Mick Sagrillo has written wind power articles for *Backwoods Home Magazine*, and he has regular wind power columns in several other independent energy publications. He founded Lake Michigan Wind and Sun, Ltd., which manufactures, repairs, and sells wind generator components and systems across the U.S. and in 29 foreign countries.
>
> An avid alternative energy enthusiast, Sagrillo is a founder and director of half a dozen major wind energy, renewable resource, or environmental organizations. When he's not teaching wind energy workshops around the country, Sagrillo lives with his wife, Lynn, on their small homestead in northeast Wisconsin.

quarter acre of domestic-grown brings a profit starting around $3,700.

One acre will produce five hundred pounds of dried root, and that translates into a small fortune no matter how you look at it. But starting out, it's a good idea to begin slowly and become familiar with ginseng.

An experienced grower from Wisconsin, Robert Romang, says you need to develop a keen sense of timing when it comes to ginseng. Knowing the right amount of time to dry a root properly or find a wild plant in the fall before its leaves and berries drop takes a little practice. But it's worth the time.

Marathon County, Wisconsin, produces millions of dollars of domestic ginseng, and Wisconsin is the world's third largest exporter of ginseng, after China and Korea.

Laws

In 1978, the Federal Government declared wild ginseng an endangered species. Now most states in the eastern half of the U.S. have created regulations on gathering it, establishing a hunting season that starts in August and coincides with the ripening seeds.

Summer digging is forbidden and plants have to be a certain size before they can be considered legal to harvest. It is illegal to dig small wild plants that have three or less main leaf stems. Plants this size have little root value but produce a lot of seed. The fear that wild ginseng may become extinct spills over into regulations concerning domestic-grown.

A commercial license is required in most states to buy, trade or sell ginseng. Check with authorities to find the specifics of the ginseng laws in your area.

Ginseng can grow in almost all areas of the United States, except south Florida. A soil pH of 5½ to 6 is best. Ginseng likes soil that is slightly acid. Growing ginseng is an activity that can become a small business, a sideline income or a hobby. It requires patience, diligence and dedication. But in the end, no other herb pays off better than ginseng.

For further information:

- **American Ginseng Gardens,** Box 440, Flag Pond, TN 37657, (615) 743-3700. A reputable dealer that sells seed and young roots to growers. The management is happy to supply information in getting started and managing a new crop. They also have a 2-hour video tape available that shows how to hunt and grow ginseng. Cost: $19.95 + $5 postage and handling.

- **Ginseng and other Medicinal Plants** by A.R. Harding. c. 1972 revised ed. Illustrates and describes how to grow ginseng, goldenseal and other valuable roots and herbs. Order from Fur-Fish-Game, 2878 E. Main St., Columbus, OH 43209. Cost $6.00 + $1.50 postage and handling.

- *The Business of Herbs*, Northwind Farm, Route 2, Box 246, Shevlin, MN 56676. Publication that brings research news, market trends and other information to people interested in making money with all kinds of herbs, including ginseng.

Uses of ginseng

Ancient people believed the spirit of God dwelled in ginseng. There was no other explanation for its tremendous rejuvenating power. In A.D. 200 a Chinese emperor declared ginseng a panacea, a remedy for all ills and diseases. Claims such as these, that ginseng is an elixir of life, led to scientific research in Russia, Sweden, Korea, China, Japan, Germany, the United States and Argentina. Scientific findings are consistent with those of ancient herbalists.

Ginseng contains vitamins B1, B2 (riboflavin), B12, biotin and pantothenic acid which enhance the endocrine glands and stimulate the nervous system. It also has significant amounts of iron, copper, manganese, potassium, calcium, sulfer, magnesium, phosphorus, silicon, and sodium, enzymes, carbohydrates and germanium, an ingredient that is instrumental in the formation of red blood cells.

Ginseng root also contains panacene, which is a tranquilizer and pain reliever. At the same time, panaxin is present, which acts as a stimulant. This seems paradoxical, but ginseng's medicinal qualities don't cancel each other out. They yield when the situation calls for it or activate depending on the need of the body.

In 1958, Russians coined the term "adaptogen" when their tests revealed that ginseng affects the whole body, and that it activates automatically to help correct any illness, no matter what it might be. An experiment done with mice showed that ginseng had no noticeable effect on a healthy mouse, but as soon as an ailment appeared ginseng went to work to put the body back on "course."

Ginseng also reduces stress and fatigue. By restoring a chemical in the brain called norepinephrine, the mind is replenished and brought back into focus. When the body is over-worked and overstimulated, norepinephrine is depleted.

Research and clinical use have shown that ginseng can also help to normalize blood sugar levels in diabetics, boost the immune system, reduce cholesterol, enhance cancer-fighting drugs, improve pulmonary functions, improve vision and hearing, strengthen the nervous system and increase sexual energy.

Ginseng improves blood sugar levels and blood circulation to the brain, and both of these conditions affect mental performance. Elderly people are especially prone to poor circulation. Tests done in Argentina found ginseng increased blood flow to the cerebral and carotid arteries, which are main arteries of the brain. Memory and concentration improved in ninety percent of the elderly patients tested.

Scientists believe ginseng does the trick through its positive effect on the hypothalamus and pituitary glands because they play a major role in how the brain functions.

Experimentation is the key in choosing the best variety of ginseng to use. We react differently to different medicines, so choosing the best one becomes a matter of personal choice.

Health food stores usually carry a variety of ginseng products. Capsules, powders, extracts and instant teas are the most common forms. The ginseng root itself is not as convenient but is preferred by many people who use ginseng regularly.

The American Medical Association suggests taking two or three grams a day for maxium results. One capsule equals about one gram. All herbs are mild, so it will take about a month for you to feel the cumulative effect of this dosage. If you want to feel the effects of ginseng sooner, say in five days, you can take six to nine capsules a day. But if you feel hyper, irritable or nervous, you may be taking too much. Ginseng is generally completely safe but there are situations when it should not be used. It can make conditions worse when you have a cold, flu, fever or bronchical problem. Consult a competent practitioner of herbal medicine during these times. "Congestive" symptoms such as constipation or obesity don't respond well to ginseng. And people with high blood pressure should be careful in using high doses. Huge amounts of ginseng are considered most stimulating, and women who use large amounts may find menstrual cycles altered. Yet, on the other hand, a cup of ginseng tea every day will help restore estrogen levels in women whose ovaries have been removed. Because ginseng increases the levels of sexual hormones, young children shouldn't take ginseng regularly. But it won't hurt them to take it occasionally when they are recovering from an illness and their energy is down.

Ginseng won't change your life overnight, but scientific research shows it does increase vitality. And it is versatile, able to correct most imbalances in the body. Check this powerful herb out for yourself, then decide how it works best for you.

Sources for further information where you can find ginseng and learn more about herbal medicine:

- **California School of Herbal Studies,** PO. Box # 39, Forestville, CA 95436 707- 887- 7457. Catalog costs one dollar. No correspondence course available, but they are helpful in referring other sources of information on herbal studies.
- **Rosemary Gladstar,** P.O. Box # 420, E. Barre, Vermont 05649. Correspondence course. Send SASE for information.

These companies sell a variety of mental-enhancement and life extension drugs and products that are not sold in the U.S. Write and ask for their catalog:

- **InHome Health Services,** P.O. # 3112, CH-2800 Delemont, witzerland
- **Interlab,** BCM Box # 5890, London WCIN 3XX, England. ∆

A BHM Writer's Profile

Skip Thomsen

Skip Thomsen is the author of three books and many magazine articles, most of them dealing with independent power of some sort. Thomsen wrote The Modern Homestead Manual and his deisel generator book, More Power To You, to share his experience of more than 15 years homesteading 108 acres in Oregon "from the ground up." Both books are available through Backwoods Home Magazine.

Thomsen says he has wanted to move to the country and homestead since he was a child growing up in the San Francisco Bay area. He has lived in a tiny cabin on a few acres, as well as his owner-designed and built home on his huge Oregon spread. Now he is searching for the "perfect" place on Hawaii's Big Island, and a new partner to share it with.

Besides his frequent articles for BHM, Thomsen is currently working on a book of photo essays about photovoltaic (solar electric) systems that work. It will be specifically oriented toward Hawaii and any other place where people do not believe that solar is a viable alternative to grid power.

BUILDING

The timberwolf woodbox

By Ted Sponem

Here's an easy-to-make woodbox that doesn't cost much. It can be made from a single 4' x 8' sheet of plywood and 25 feet of 1" x 2" stock to reinforce the corners and bottom.

Cut the plywood according to the drawing. Use a compass or a coffee can to draw the radius for the bottom cut-outs. Keep in mind that one side of the plywood will be the wrong side for outside surfaces.

Attach the corner 1 x 2s to the side pieces. The front and back overlap the sides. The corners of the bottom will have to be notched to clear the corner 1 x 2s.

I usually install the bottom of the box six inches up from the floor, but it can be put on the bottom. With the bottom raised, it's easier to reach that last piece of firewood. Also, it gives you a place to sweep the dust.

The kindling shelf, if installed, can be located from six to ten inches from the top. Use a 1 x 2 for the front edge. The lid and front edge need some edges beveled for a good fit. Use small "T" hinges and a cabinet door handle for the lid. Stain or paint to suit yourself.

Black metal "wall angles," used for suspended ceilings, can be added to the corners for reinforcing and a decorative "ironbound" look. Toss the scraps into the woodbox to start your firewood supply. ∆

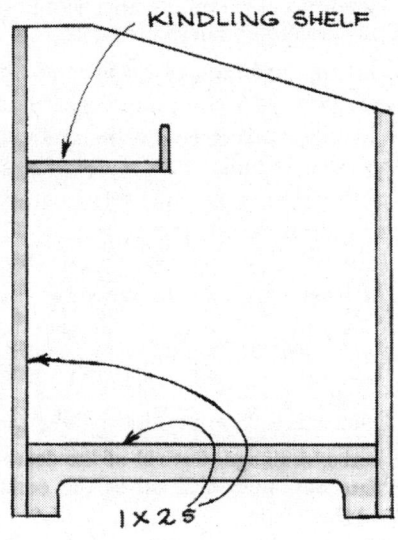

A BHM Business Profile

Linda Robie

Linda Robie is Backwoods Home Magazine's office manager. She had previously worked for 10 years as an Assistant Registrar in a co-ed high school in southern California and 8 years as a mental health worker in Oregon. With a keen eye for detail, she maintains BHM's subscriber database and is responsible for the remarkably few complaints the magazine gets from its subscribers.

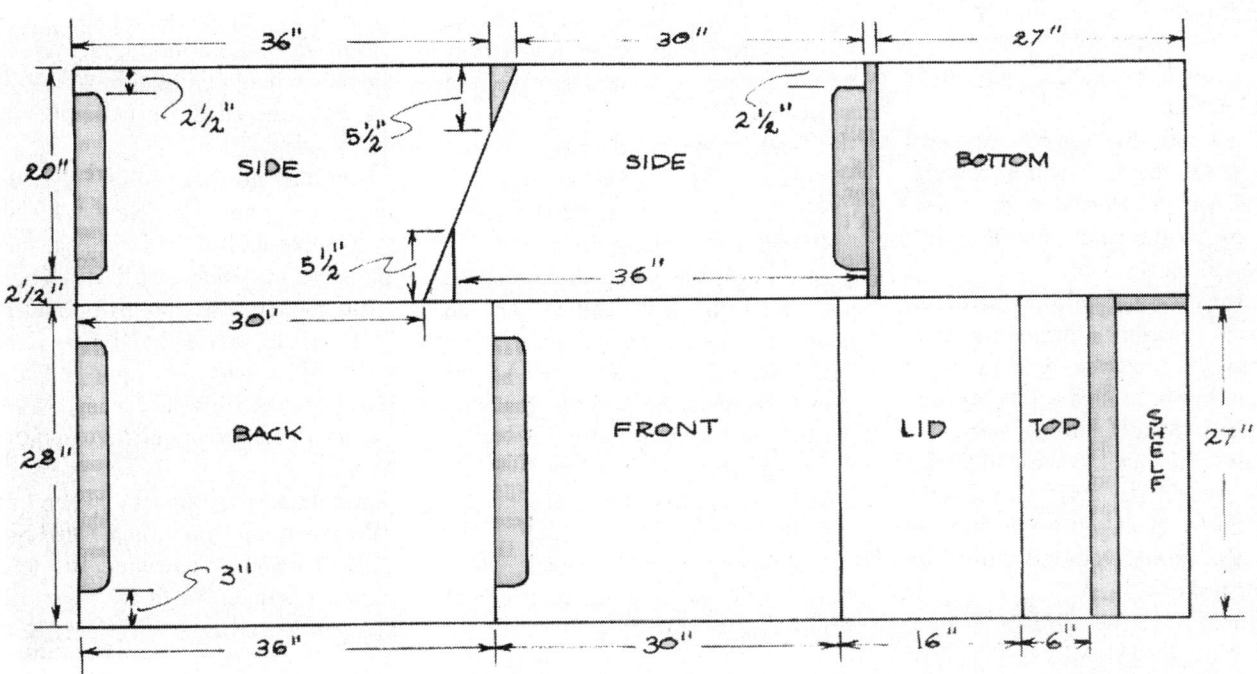

The Fifth Year

A tale about tenure in the neighborhood

By Charlotte Jones

Back in the early '70s, the man bought an acre of land outside of town. Okay, it was up north of town, about a mile from where the old city dump was, back in the '40s.

There were no trees. Few neighbors, and those lived down the road a piece. No paved streets. Just a lot of weeds. Certainly no place your New Jersey relatives would want to visit.

The land was in a low tax district. Translated, that means an undesirable area. Undesirable to some. It would be home to him and his family.

He built a little house. It was never big enough, even when he built it. But it'd do.

He put in a septic tank, although his mother-in-law called it a cesspool. A "witch" with a divining rod located where he could get a working well. Sure enough. The rig finally struck water, but the family had to ration it. They had to choose between cleaning, showering, or flushing in any given hour.

He called it workable. His family called it pitiful.

So the family lived in the too-small house while the kids were growing. They closed the front door if anyone drove by so the road dust wouldn't settle on the coffee table.

But they could relax and drink lemonade on a hot afternoon instead of aerating a fancy lawn. They could hang clothes on a clothesline, as God intended. Since there were no sidewalks, they had no snow to shovel in the winter. His wife could walk down the road at midnight and the worst that could happen would be meeting a skunk.

The man had a pet bird for several years. Not the gilded cage type of bird, but a pretty little meadowlark that perched on the clothesline wire every morning and sang to him. He and that bird shared many confidences.

The man planted trees on his land over the years. The deer ate all the leaves and the trees died. That was okay. He'd rather have deer than trees anyway.

Their few neighbors lived the same way his family lived. It was country. And the nights were very, very quiet.

Their fire protection was volunteer neighbors. Their police protection was the overworked sheriff, who arrived in less than three minutes the one time they needed help.

There was no neighborhood association. There wasn't any need for one.

There were no covenant restrictions. No one complained about their lifestyle. They just lived and let live. It was more than satisfactory, thank you.

Then one day the acre next to his went up for sale. He wanted that land. He often took evening strolls around his one acre parcel and he felt terribly proud. He would be almost royalty if he owned two acres.

He called the real estate agent whose phone number was on the sign and asked about the cost of the land. "$10,000," the realtor said.

He thought there must be a mistake and he had his wife call back in an hour. But no, that was the right figure. $10,000. $10,000? That was more than twice what he paid for his acre. An identical acre at more than twice the price! There was no way he could afford $10,000 for a piece of land just to walk around on.

A couple of weeks later there was a "sold" notice attached to the real estate sign.

A month later another acre down the road had a "for sale" sign on it. When he called about that acre, he was quoted an asking price of $12,000. For one identical acre.

Soon a "sold" banner was draped across that sign, too.

Then there were rumors—housing complex, development, growth, a park, city utilities, higher taxes.

Soon the rumors were gone, and change became a reality.

There were surveyors, backhoes, concrete trucks, and electric hammers popping.

Out of the bare prairie around his acre grew two-story houses, ranch style houses, tri-level houses, colonial houses, and mine-shaft style houses. Up went fences. In came refrigerators, twenty-foot trees, carpeting, and sod.

Into those houses moved couples, families, singles. On the new sod toddlers played. In the street children threw balls. In the backyards dogs barked.

Then there were petitions: Pave the road. Put in street lights, sidewalks, curbs, drainage. Get rid of the deer. Save the whales.

Mists of insecticides and liquid fertilizers clouded the neighborhood and little yellow warning flags waved in yards as proudly as daffodils.

"Officials" held public meetings in the new school gymnasium.

And door-to-door salespersons proliferated.

Now that all those folks are settled in, the next thing they want is for him to live like they do. He can't see why. He doesn't ask that they live like him.

But there are grumblings about his clothesline, his dirt driveway, his "natural" lawn, his unpainted mail box, his weeds, his old car.

Doesn't tenure count for anything? Naaaaa.

But there's an acre of ground for sale down south of town across the field from an abandoned shopping center. It's quiet out there... especially at night. ∆

COUNTRY LIVING

Winter ch-ch-ch-ch-chores

By Dynah Geissal

The winter goes on and on. We haven't had a "real" winter for eight years. Eight years of drought, and the drought hasn't ended. The snow we get just stays and piles up so it looks like a lot. Because of the cold the snow holds little moisture. The seemingly endless 20-below nights, coupled with the ferocity of the east wind, blow the warmth out of this old house. Baby rabbits must spend the night in the house and the baby chick pen in the brooder house is swaddled in blankets. Water dishes and buckets freeze almost as soon as they're set out. It seems that we spend most of the day thawing and refilling them.

When we used to have real winters, we could count on being snowed in for stretches of a couple of weeks at a time. Sometimes it was not only our quarter mile driveway that was impassable, but the one mile of dirt road out to the pavement as well. We would leave the truck and haul the battery the 1¼ miles to the house if the blizzard came while we were away from the house. It didn't matter much. We're well stocked and could last all winter, if necessary.

We've gotten spoiled though in the last few years. In the fall we put off bringing the horses down from the hills above the house. We had planned to bring them down in October, but the weather was so nice. Then we thought, November. They're so happy up there. They hate having to stay in the barnyard all winter. They crib, they harass the goats, they get ornery, and they get hay bellies from eating out of sheer boredom.

So December came and they stayed in the hills. When snow came we drove the truck up to feed and water. It wasn't much of an extra chore, and they were so happy. Even when the winds came along with 30-below nights, they were snug in the low areas among the trees. Plenty of horses around here have bare pasture and seem to be okay. I worried a little but they stayed fat, healthy, and happy.

Then came another snow storm that dumped new snow on the old, and wind drifted it over the driveway. When we drove out, it would refill the tracks by the time we got back 15 minutes later. It got to be too much. Going the ¾ mile to the horses was turning into a major daily struggle.

"It's no big deal," I said. "It's only ¾ of a mile. I'll ski up, pulling the toboggan with their hay and water." After all, I think nothing of skiing six or eight miles with a backpack full of food and clothes to spend a winter night in the backcountry.

Crossing the first field took a bit longer than I expected, but what the heck. Even if it took an hour, it would be worth it not to have to drive out. As I started up the first hill, I had a revelation: Skis were not the best choice for this job. I should have worn snowshoes. The weight of the toboggan, carrying enough hay and water for two 1400-pound horses, required more force to pull than I, on skis, could muster. I had to sidestep up the hill. That worked all right but was slow and took a lot of energy. Step, step, tug. Wrap the rope around my wrist and do it again and again.

By the third hill I was starting to doubt my sanity. These are long, steep hills. I have a lot of endurance, but my skiing skills are not the best. With one hand pulling the toboggan, I could use only one pole. This was harder than I expected. As I contemplated the last stretch up to the ridge, the horses suddenly materialized on top. That sight gave me the necessary strength to make the final push.

I spent a few minutes visiting but the wind was coming up again, so I started for home. I looked down the way I had come. Mighty steep, but if I made it up I could make it down, I thought. I pushed off and started down. Suddenly the thought occurred, "I only have one pole. Uh oh. Well, too late now. I'm going awfully fast though." Then the next thought. "The empty toboggan is probably going faster than I am and is going to run into me."

I held my arm out to the side just as the toboggan raced by. But the rope was wrapped around my wrist and, with a jerk and a whoosh, I was yanked even faster down the hill. Wow! I'm a conservative skier, not used to speed like this.

With one hill to go, I abandoned the toboggan to do a little skiing in a more normal fashion before going home. As I reached the top of one of my favorite hills, I noticed a bald eagle that I had seen earlier perched there, surveying the hills below. It didn't hear me. I watched from less than 20 feet away until I got cold and said, "I see you." It turned its massive head toward me and lumbered off airborne down the valley.

Tomorrow I believe I'll wear the snowshoes. ∆

The Fifth Year

A Backwoods Home Anthology

SELF-SUFFICIENCY

The bow and arrow: low tech tool for food, entertainment

By Gene Willis

For thousands of years the bow and arrow have been used to hunt for food and to defend people, property and even countries.

In modern times archery is still used to hunt and has also become a sport which can be an inexpensive form of family entertainment.

Once the bow and arrows are purchased they can be reused many times if cared for and used properly. There is a wide variety of tackle that can be used with the bow, but all that a beginner will need is a quiver, arm guard, and perhaps a shooting glove (more about these later).

Several types available

There are several types of bows available and each has its own particular advantages and disadvantages.

The **long bow** is a straight wooden stave six feet or more in length with a string attached to both ends. This type of bow was used in Europe for centuries in both hunting and military applications.

If you remember Kevin Costner's Robin Hood film, you will have seen the long bow used. The long bow is simple, very sturdy, and requires little maintenance. It also imparts a fair amount of kinetic energy to the arrows fired from it.

Its disadvantages are that the length makes it a bit unwieldy, slow to shoot because of its long draw, and changes in the weather can affect the performance. Hot, humid weather causes it to be slightly weaker and cold weather increases the stiffness.

Another type is the **recurve bow**. The recurve is shorter than the long bow and is usually made of laminated fiberglass and wood.

Recurve bows have the advantage of being impervious to weather, being shorter and easier to handle, and being faster shooting. However, care must be taken with the recurve not to damage the arms of the bow. This will result in a misalignment of the bow which would throw the arrows off course.

The **compound bow** is a modern innovation. It is short and powerful

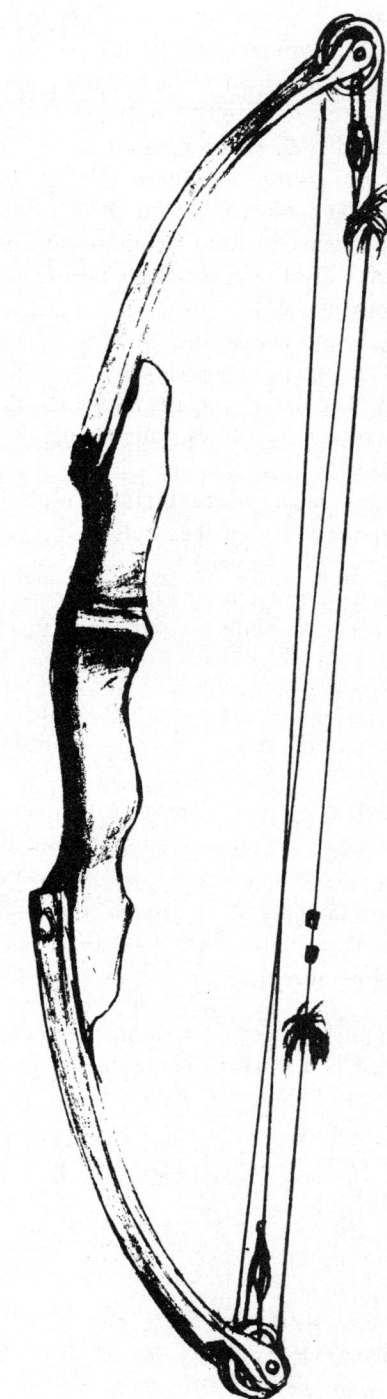
Compound bow

Traditional long bow on the left and modern recurve bow on the right

52   *The Fifth Year*

and uses a series of pulleys to increase the mechanical advantage of the system.

Many models can be adjusted to change the draw weight (the amount of force required to pull the string back) higher or lower. A disadvantage of the compound bow is that its moving parts can break or wear. Also, tools must be used for these adjustments. Ever lose, misplace, or forget a tool you need?

For sport shooting or hunting the compound is a good choice.

The **crossbow** imparts a high kinetic energy to the arrows, called bolts, that it fires.

One nice characteristic of the crossbow is that it is held and fired like a rifle. Anyone with rifle experience can learn to shoot it fairly quickly. In addition, since you don't have to hold the bowstring back yourself, your aim can be much steadier and much heavier draw weights can be used.

If you decide on a crossbow, buy a better quality one. Some of the cheaper ones that I've used in times past have the tendency to fire just by bumping the bow—not very nice!

Accessories

The first accessory that you will need is a quiver. There are several types of these to choose from. The best known is the back or sling quiver, which is worn by being strapped over the back at an angle. If you plan on carrying larger numbers of arrows, then the sling quiver is for you. Some of these hold 50 arrows.

A small quiver is the belt quiver, which (surprise!) is worn on your belt at waist height. The belt quiver only holds about a dozen arrows but is a little more convenient to use. There are also some bows which have an arrow rack that allows five to six arrows to be carried very accessibly.

Pin sights can also be purchased for some bows. These sights give the archer a reference point for sighting in on the target. While not necessary, a pin sight can be very handy.

Another interesting accessory is a small rod and reel which screws right into the front of any bow made for it. This device is used with a long, prong-tipped arrow for fishing. One really critical archery accessory you must get is an arm guard. The arm guard does just that: guards your arm against being grazed, usually quite painfully, by the bow string upon releasing the arrow.

A shooting glove should also be considered if you plan to shoot

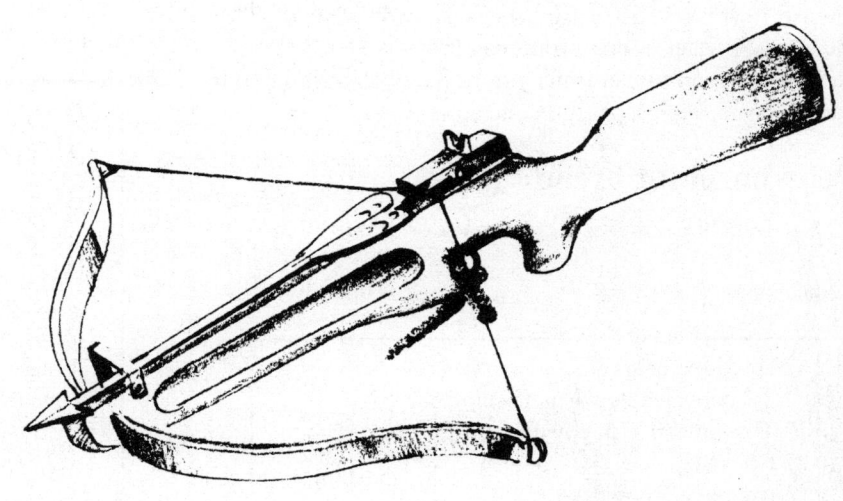

Crossbow

frequently or for a long duration. When you first start practicing archery, your fingertips will probably be sore. This soreness is caused by the continual friction from drawing and releasing the bow string.

There is a gadget out now called a bow string release which grips the string instead of holding the string with your fingers.

What's it good for?

Now you may be thinking, "This is all very interesting, but what real use is a bow and arrow today?" Well first of all, archery is just plain fun. It's a form of exercise and recreation that the entire family can enjoy together. The bow and arrow can also be an inexpensive, quiet and effective tool in becoming more self-sufficient.

Most states have special hunting seasons for bowhunters, and bowhunters are often allowed extra deer tags. In some states bowhunters are allowed to take antlerless deer and to hunt in zones where rifle hunting is not permitted. Decent archery skills can help you become better prepared for an uncertain future.

The ammunition is reusable and the whole system is low maintenance. It is also much more difficult for a "loaded bow" to accidentally discharge.

Shooting a bow does have some drawbacks. (No pun intended of course!) Using a bow accurately requires some practice and a familiarity with your particular bow's characteristics. And obviously, a bow does not have as great a range as a firearm, nor can it be fired as rapidly. But in spite of these few disadvantages, the bow is a durable, useful, and fun tool. Δ

Cooking with dried fruit

By Jennifer Stein Barker

It's winter and, if you've been learning from the articles in *BHM*, your pantry is stocked with the produce you grew last summer. The fruit you've dried makes great snacks. It also makes a good garnish for Indian curries or Armenian lentil soup. You can chop it and add it to hot cereal for a sweet-tart start in the morning, or cook it with fresh apples for hot fruit compote (see Winter Breakfasts, *BHM* No.19, p.49).

Dried fruit shines in baked goods. Fruit cakes, muffins, quickbreads, tarts, almost any baked good can be adapted to use dried fruit instead of fresh. The flavor will be more intense if you use dried fruit, because even after soaking there is less water in dried fruit than in fresh. Here are some recipes designed to use fruits you're likely to have in your pantry: pears, apples, peaches, and apricots.

Pear-hazelnut bread

This sweet bread makes a great snack or dessert.

Makes one 5" x 9" loaf.

> 1 cup dried pears
> 1 2/3 cups whole wheat pastry flour
> 3 Tbsp. buttermilk powder
> 1 tsp. soda
> 1 tsp. baking powder
> 3/4 cup water (from soaking)
> 3 Tbsp. oil
> 1/4 cup honey
> 1 egg, beaten
> 3/4 cup chopped hazelnuts

Put the dried pears in a small bowl and pour just enough boiling water over to cover them. Let them soak while you prepare the other ingredients. Prepare a 5" x 9" loaf pan by oiling it and lining with baking paper. Preheat the oven to 400 degrees.

Sift together the flour, buttermilk powder, soda, and baking powder. In a medium bowl, whisk together the water (pour the soaking water off the pears, and add enough hot tap water to make 3/4 cup), oil, honey, and egg. Chop the hazelnuts and slice the pears, and have them ready on the side. Add the dry mixture to the wet all at once, and whisk together to combine thoroughly. Fold in the nuts and pears, and scrape the mixture into the prepared pan.

Bake at 400 degrees for 15 minutes, then turn oven down to 375 degrees and continue baking for another 45 minutes, or until the top is golden and firm, and the bread tests done. Cool on a wire rack.

Apricot vlaii

Vlaii is a Dutch treat that can be enjoyed for breakfast, as a coffee cake, or as a not-too-sweet dessert. Peaches can be substituted for the apricots, though it might be best to slice them.

Makes one 10" circular vlaii.

Dough:

> 2/3 cup warm water
> 1 Tbsp. yeast
> 1 tsp. honey
> 1/4 cup oil
> 3 Tbsp. honey
> 1/4 tsp. salt
> 1 1/4 cups whole wheat bread flour
> 1/2 cup whole wheat pastry flour
> Filling:
> 3 cups (about 1 lb.) dried apricots
> 1/3 cup honey
> 1 1/2 cups water

For dough: in a medium bowl, dissolve the yeast and 1 tsp. honey in the warm water and let sit in a warm place for ten minutes, or until the yeast foams up. Stir in the oil, salt, and three tablespoons honey. Stir in the bread flour and beat until the dough is stretchy. Stir in the pastry flour.

Turn the dough out onto a lightly floured board, and knead eight to ten minutes until smooth and elastic, adding just enough flour to prevent dough from sticking. Place the dough in an oiled bowl, turn over so the oiled surface is on top, and cover. Let rise until doubled, one hour or more.

Meanwhile, combine apricots, 1/3 cup honey, and water in a medium saucepan. Bring to a boil, then reduce heat and simmer uncovered, stirring occasionally, until apricots are tender, 10 to 15 minutes. Remove apricots to a dish and set them aside, leaving syrup in the pan. Boil syrup, uncovered, over medium heat until reduced to about 1/3 cup. Watch closely and stir frequently. Set aside.

Oil a 10-inch tart pan or springform pan with removable rim. Punch down the dough and form it gently into a disc.

Transfer the dough to the pan, and pat it out over the bottom and three-fourths of the way up the sides of the pan. Arrange the apricots (overlapping slightly) over the dough. Spoon the syrup evenly over the fruit. Gently press the dough edge down to where it is level with the fruit.

Preheat the oven to 375 degrees (let the vlaii rise ten minutes while the oven is heating). Place a large cookie sheet on the top rack to shield the vlaii from too direct heat. Place a small pan of hot water on the bottom of the oven. Bake the vlaii on the middle rack until the crust is well-browned, about 40 minutes.

Loosen the rim of the pan from the crust, and remove. Serve warm; or cool, cover, and serve later.

Apple-oat crumb cake

This is a sweet, dark cake with a topping full of goodies.

Makes one 9" x 9" cake.

Cake:

```
2/3 cup dried apples
1 cup rolled oats
1 2/3 cups whole wheat pastry flour
1 1/2 tsp. soda
1 tsp. cinnamon
1/4 tsp. nutmeg
1/4 cup oil
2/3 cup honey
1 Tbsp. molasses
1 cup water (use soaking water)
2 eggs, beaten
```

Topping:

```
1 Tbsp. oil
3 Tbsp. honey
1/2 tsp. cinnamon
1 tsp. vanilla
3/4 cup rolled oats
1/2 cup coconut
1/2 cup chopped nuts
```

Place the dried apples in a small bowl, and pour just enough boiling water over to cover them. Prepare a 9"x 9" cake pan by oiling it and lining it with baker's paper. Preheat the oven to 350 degrees.

Make the topping by heating together, in a medium saucepan, the oil, honey, cinnamon, and vanilla. Stir to blend well, then add the oats, coconut, and nuts. Stir to coat all ingredients. Set aside.

Returning to the cake, put the oats in a large bowl. Sift together the flour, soda, cinnamon, and nutmeg, add to the oats, and stir to blend well. In a medium bowl, whisk together the oil, honey, and molasses. Add one cup of hot water (use soaking water, and fill to 1 cup with hot tap water), and whisk in. Add the beaten eggs and whisk to blend well. Chop the soaked apples and have them ready to add.

Add the liquid mixture to the dry. Stir just until all ingredients are thoroughly moistened, and stir in the chopped apples. Pour into the prepared pan. Crumble the topping mixture over the batter in the pan. A lot of it will sink in, but don't worry—there's plenty! Bake 35-40 minutes. Check after 20 minutes, and if the top is browning too quickly, put a foil cover over it loosely (or an empty cookie sheet on the shelf above it). Serve warm or at room temperature. Δ

A BHM Writer's Profile

Larry Elliott

Larry Elliott is an inventor/tinkerer/business owner living on 40 acres of central Oregon's high desert. For more than 20 years, he has been active in designing, using, and selling equipment for securing energy independence, and he designed and installed the photoelectric system that provides electricity for Backwoods Home Magazine's remote Oregon office. He has been writing for BHM since 1993.

Elliott has incorporated solar electric, wind generators, and energy conservation into his present homestead, as well as his previous farm in western Pennsylvania in the 1970s. He owns and operates Solar Tech, an independent energy firm that has installed many rural independent energy systems.

Planning a move from the city to the country

By John and Linda Janetos

I was born in Chicago almost 40 years ago, and I was ready to leave as soon as I found out where I was. I've never been much of a city person. The hustle and bustle don't do a thing for me. I joined the Boy Scouts at age 11. That was one of the things that influenced me most to get out of the city. After getting out of the army in the early '70s, I vowed never to return to Chicago.

False starts

My first stop was Arizona for a year. Too darn hot for me. My first real homestead was a log cabin outside of Brattleboro, Vermont. My second was in the Rocky Mountains of Colorado. Then I moved to the wilderness of Alaska for my third homestead. These places were all rented cabins. It's hard to come up with a rent check every month when you're in the woods. I never raised animals for food; I used to hunt to eat. Talk about motivation!

Whenever I needed money, I would have to go to an urban area to work for awhile. I've had several businesses over the years to support the homesteads, but sometimes it wasn't enough. My problem was that I never had enough money to set myself up for self-sufficiency because I could never get ahead financially. I needed a plan.

I decided to move back to Chicago to earn enough money to buy a nice homestead and set up a business so I wouldn't have to worry about money again. Moving beyond the sidewalks doesn't have to mean being dirt poor. You can be comfortable if you take your time and think. I'm going to relate some of the things that my wife and I have done to become independent. Perhaps some of our experience will help you.

We're not going to talk about country jobs or mistakes other people have made. There are several great articles in *BHM* that cover these and other subjects. Skip Thomsen did a good article in Issue No. 15 about why people fail to make a country lifestyle work. This is recommended reading for anyone considering such a move.

This article is intended to help you get out of the city to the country. I'm going to give you some basic guidelines, and I'm assuming that you're not rich. This article is intended for people with limited funds. I'm also assuming that you really, really want to do this, because you need the desire. No article can give you that. You have to want to do it. It's not as hard as it seems, as long as you're prepared.

So, let's get down to business. For the purpose of this article, we will be discussing homesteading. That means to live as self-sufficiently and independently as possible by raising your own food, creating your own income, producing your own power, etc.

First things first

The first thing that I recommend you do is read about other people who are doing what you want to do. The best way is to subscribe to publications that are geared toward a back-to-the-land lifestyle, like the one you're reading now. *Countryside and Small Stock Journal* is another good one. Read the letters from readers that write to the magazines. Read the articles. These people talk about their experiences, good and not so good. You'll have both. I suggest reading for a year before you make a decision either way. It may seem like a long time, but it's not. Never be in a hurry to make a decision that will affect your life and your well-being. A wrong one could cost you dearly, so be sure you know what you want.

The plan

Next, you need to develop a plan. If you're single, it will be easier to move but harder to run a homestead. I believe that you have more options if you're single, and you don't have the pressure of mouths to feed while you're making the transition to a country life. Of course if done properly, there shouldn't be any pressure. That's why you're moving to the country, remember.

It takes at least two people to run a decent-sized homestead. There is always some kind of work that needs doing. You can do it by yourself, but it will be harder and more time consuming. You're going to want to have plenty of time for fishing.

Unless you're a confirmed hermit, find a mate to share your homestead with you. Find someone before you start, someone who shares your dreams and needs. This is where being single has an edge: you can try to find someone who has homesteading or related experience. This person will become your most important ally, or your worst enemy, so choose wisely. Check out the classifieds in this magazine and *Countryside* for people seeking mates. Obviously, if you live in a big city, there will be a smaller percentage of people with homestead skills in the classifieds. Read them. You never know what kind of person you'll come across. I met my wife through a classified ad in the *Chicago Sun-Times* newspaper. She has worked on a hog farm and also as a veterinary assistant; she has skills that are useful on the homestead.

If you're married, that's a different story. The whole family is going to have to want to homestead, and you'll have to learn together. Either that, or dump the old man and find someone who does want to do it!

Once you decide to give homesteading a try, start to keep a journal. Write down your needs and your goals and steps that you will take to reach them. Write down all of your ideas, listing pros and cons. This will eventually become your plan for the future.

Get your feet wet

You can talk and think about homesteading all you want, but you'll never get a real feel for it unless you do it. Once you buy a place, it's too late to decide that you don't like the lifestyle. I suggest spending some time on a homestead or a farm.

Every large city has farmland within a couple hours distance. Spend your vacation working on a farm. See if you would like it. If you don't know any farmers, the best place to meet them is at county fairs. Keep your eye on the newspaper for fair dates and locations. There will be thousands of farmers there. Most that I've run into were glad to talk to me about raising different kinds of animals. Talk to a couple and offer to work on their farm for a week or two for free. Tell them about your plans and ask for suggestions.

I don't think many farmers would turn down a couple of weeks worth of free labor. I know I wouldn't. Tell them you want to learn about as many different aspects of farm life as you can. Ask questions, but don't talk too much. Pay attention and listen. If you find that the work and lifestyle suit you, then you are ready for the next step. Keep in mind that two weeks on a farm is different than a commitment to a lifestyle. Look ahead. Are you going to want to do this five years down the road? Ten years? Twenty years?

Decisions, decisions

Now that you have decided to give homesteading a try, exactly what is it that you want to do? And, where do you want to do it? Do you want to raise animals? Or crops? Or a combination? The type of lifestyle you decide on will probably have an impact on your choice of location. A ski lodge wouldn't do well in the Arizona desert. Nor would a mountain climbing school in Kansas. What do you do for a living? What skills do you have? Will you be earning your living solely from your homestead? If you run into financial trouble, will you be able to find a job within a reasonable distance?

It will be easier if you are going to stay in an area with which you are already familiar. Lots of people from Chicago go to Wisconsin and Michigan for vacation. They wind up buying property in these places because they are familiar with the area. Sometimes, you can get great deals in areas that you're not familiar with. But wherever the location, decide what type of homestead and enterprise you would like and start gathering information about it.

My wife, Linda, and I decided that we wanted to operate a catfish farm. Several factors affected our decision. I was formally trained as a chef, though there wasn't much call for culinary artistry in previous places I had chosen to live. But at least I had learned that people always have to eat, whether times are good or bad. Fish is becoming more popular with consumers, and people are increasingly concerned about the quality of fish being harvested from natural waters, as well as about shortages caused by over harvesting. My wife and I happen to like to fish, an important consideration.

A catfish farm has to be in the right geographic location for maximum production. You can't successfully raise catfish in Idaho because catfish grow best in warm water, and it's not that warm up there. Trout, on the other hand, would thrive in the colder temperature. Raising livestock in extremely cold climates, such as Zone 3, would be more expensive because of the need to heat shelter, if animals were housed indoors, and/or increased feed to maintain the animals' body heat, if they remained outdoors. The cold causes stress also, for both people and animals. So, decide what type of business operation and climate you would like for yourself, and let's move on to the next step.

Budget

As you have probably guessed, this idea of yours is going to cost some money, the amount depending on what you want to do. You can buy a working homestead or build your own. Whatever you do, you will have to decide how much money you want to spend as well as how much you have available to spend. City dwellers usually make more money than country people. Some of the reasons are higher cost of living, labor unions, and competition for good labor. I assume that you have a job. If not, get one! You're going to need money to do this right.

Linda and I decided that we wanted to spend a maximum of $30,000 for a minimum of 40 acres. A house on the property would be nice, but I was prepared to build one. We were looking for a derelict homestead that already had utilities—electricity, well, septic, phone. We figured we would tear down the house and build a new one around the existing utilities. Depending on the area we chose to move to, we figured on saving from $5,000 to $20,000 just by not having to bring in the utilities.

We planned on digging our own ponds for the catfish farm. That would cost another $25,000 to $50,000, depending on the size operation that we wanted. We contacted the Illinois Department of Fish and Game to acquire information on aquaculture (fish farming). They sent us "tons" of literature, for no charge, and they offered to help us every step of the way in starting our operation. There are agencies out there to help you also, so find them and use them.

Our original budget was $100,000 to buy property, build a house, dig the ponds, and purchase necessary equipment for the fish farm. Set yourself a budget, but keep it flexible. You may have to change it. We did. Once you have come up with a rough one, it's time for the next step.

Choosing a location

We developed several guidelines in choosing a location for ourselves. Weather was a factor. It had to be warm enough most of the year to maximize catfish production. Terrain was also a factor. It's harder to dig a pond on the side of a mountain than it is on level or rolling land. Also, the soil characteristics would dictate whether water could be held in a pond or would soak into the ground. Price was probably the most important factor for us. We wanted to buy in an area where we could get the most for our money. We would rather have a shack on 100 acres than a mansion on one acre. Taxes were also a consideration, as were the strictness of building codes. As you can see, we looked for the same things that we would look for if we were moving anywhere—quality and proximity of schools and shopping, political and social climate, economic growth and future possibilities.

My wife and I called a national real estate company that specializes in farm and country property and had them send us their nationwide listing catalog. The company was United National Real Estate, and they have an 800 number. You can get it by calling 1-800-555-1212. Ask for their catalog. They have listings in most of the 50 states. You can compare property prices in different areas. You can call realtors to find out about taxes and other local data.

After you have found an area that you might be interested in, go there.

Call the realtor that lists the property you want to see. Sometimes, real estate agents will pick up the tab for your motel and meals if you make a trip to see a property they list. Ask them if they will do that; it doesn't hurt to ask. Horace Yancey of Yancey Real Estate in Oxford, Arkansas built a brand new guest house next to his real estate office for prospective buyers to spend the night in after looking at his offerings. Other agents may do this too. You never know unless you ask. All they can say is no; they can't take away your birthday for asking.

Look at a lot of places, and take your time. You're looking for the place where you'll be spending the rest of your life, so don't let anyone rush you into making a decision. An old realtors' trick is to tell you that they have someone interested in the property, so they can force you into a commitment. Don't ever sign anything at this point. If they do sell a property, don't worry, there will be plenty more. I know. I've looked at hundreds. The point is that it's your money. Don't spend it on anything that you're not 100% sure of. And never buy a property without looking at it in person! After looking at our real estate guide, my wife and I decided to look further at southern Missouri and northern Arkansas. The property was reasonably priced, the taxes were low, and the climate suited our fish farming requirements.

Shopping for property

Once you have decided on a general area, start to gather information about it before you visit. Contact local chambers of commerce and other organizations and have them send you literature. If you are a member of a club or an organization such as the Elks, Kiwanis, or VFW, see if there is a local chapter in your area of interest. Call them up and tell them your plans. They will be more than happy to help you.

Once you have information on an area, call several realtors and arrange to go look at properties. Be sure to have a good idea what you're looking for. Ask the realtors to arrange several properties for you to see in one trip. Remember, give yourself plenty of time to look. Don't rush. I like to use several realtors because I pit them against each other to give me the best deal. They all want that commission, and I like to see how hard they are willing to work for it.

Sometimes agents will accompany you to the properties, sometimes they won't. If they don't stand to make a good commission on a piece of land, they will generally send you by yourself. That is fine, since you won't feel as pressured that way.

Whether you're buying a house or just a piece of property, I suggest looking at the place while it's raining. That way you can see if there is a possible flooding situation or if the house has problems with leaks or seepage.

As with buying anything, be careful! People will be less than honest with you in order to sell you something. A person selling a house because of termites will probably not tell you. If he did, then he couldn't sell you the house. Inspect not only the house, but the property as well. It should take you at least two hours to inspect a property that you are interested in.

Start with the land. Does it have any low spots? Any swampy areas that would breed mosquitoes? Any wetlands that are protected by law? How about timber and pasture? Suitable soil for growing? Abundant water supply? How about poisonous snakes and critters? (But if you don't like bugs and critters, then you probably won't like the country.)

How about the neighbors? Go over and talk to them. Will their lifestyle conflict with yours? If you want to be certified organic and the neighbors use chemicals that leach onto your property, you would have trouble. Or if they have 15 dogs that bark all night or might come after your chickens, you would have trouble. Find these things out before you buy a place; it will be too late once you have signed the papers. How about the property lines? Are they clearly marked to avoid confusion? How's the fencing? What's the general condition of the property? Has it been cared for or neglected? You can usually get a better deal on neglected property.

Make notes about what you observe while you are on the property, while things are fresh in your mind, and estimate costs for repairs, replacements, etc. That way, you won't forget things, and you can review all of your notes once you have finished looking. Take pictures of the properties, and compare different ones. Write down the pros and cons for each one. Be honest and objective. You want the best deal for your money. Any reputable agent will understand that, so if one doesn't, find a new agent.

We looked for seven years, at hundreds of properties—from primitive to ultra-sophisticated—in at least 20 states, before we found the right property last year. It was kind of a fluke that we found it, but nevertheless we did. Our friends and family used to laugh at us because every weekend we were going on a quest for the perfect place.

Finally, we were looking through a three-month-old real estate catalog called Ozark Mountain Living and there it was—a little tiny ad that said "Catfish Farm For Sale." It said there were seven ponds on a little under 20 acres. We called the realtor and found out that there was a 14-year-old house on the property. It was less property than we wanted, but we went to look at it anyway.

The seven ponds turned out to be four fish ponds, two small stock ponds, and one dry hole in the ground. The ponds were good-sized, having a total of about five surface acres. The stock ponds were in a fenced pasture. There were eight fruit trees, tons of blackberries, and numerous oak, hickory, cedar, and walnut trees, not to mention everything else that grows in the Arkansas Ozarks. There were deer, bobcat, wild turkey, coyote, mink, and a host of other animals and birds on the property. There were even a couple of acres of marsh that now have become our wildlife refuge.

The house was 1000 square feet, wood framed with brick veneer in front. Enclosing the carport would add a third bedroom and increase the square footage to 1200. There was a 500-foot deep well, septic system, electricity, phone, propane furnace, water heater, and cook stove. The house and property had been rented out by the owner for the last seven years. It was really neglected, but the layout was nice. The house sat on a hill and faced south for passive solar efficiency. It was surrounded by huge trees that shaded the house in the summer. I couldn't have laid the house out better myself.

The taxes were $167 a year. This year they went down to $155. How many places have you lived where the taxes went down? We looked at the place several times and talked to the neighbors and the locals. The farm was one mile from a town of 350 people and about 12 miles from a town of 6,000 people. The stores are in the larger town.

We bought the place for $26,000. It was smaller than we wanted property-wise, but it had everything that we were looking for. The catfish farm was already established, and the house was already livable. The pastures, nut trees, fruit trees, and blackberries were a bonus that will increase the income we can make from the property. It took a while to find our place, but it was worth it.

House inspection

It is very important that you take your time when inspecting a prospective house. People have been known to improve the cosmetic appearance of a house to conceal flaws and problems. During inspection, you should have the following items: a flashlight, a camera with flash, a notebook and pen, a clean one-gallon bottle with tight-fitting lid, and a ladder.

Don't worry about imposing on the homeowners. They want to sell the house. Ask a lot of questions, and look—really look—at everything, inside and out. Remember, once you buy a house, it's yours. You can't give it back to the seller, so it's important to know what you're buying. It's okay to buy a house that needs work, but you don't want any major surprises. We had to rip the floor out of our farmhouse because the previous renters had four dogs that had peed all over the floor, and it had soaked into the wood. Surprise!

Figure the amount of work that needs to be done to the house and include that in the price that you are paying. If you can't do the work yourself, you will have to pay someone to do it for you. Add that to the cost too. If you buy a house for $30,000, and it needs $10,000 worth of work, then you'll be paying $40,000, not including interest if you must finance the house. So be observant and take your time.

Checklist

The following is our checklist of things to look for when inspecting a prospective house.

1. Look at the outside of the house for its condition and possible repair needs. Check soffitt, fascia, gutters, siding, exposed foundation, window and door seals, porch, and railings. Check wood for insect damage. Check for external water damage.

2. Find out if the property is in a flood plain. If it is, don't buy it. Check around the house for low spots that could indicate possible flooding problems in the future.

3. Take your ladder and climb up on the roof. How does it look? Any patchwork? Walk on the roof. Does it feel strong or does it give under your weight? Is the chimney okay? Check for rotting wood and insect damage. Are the shingles in good shape? What about the television antenna?

4. How's the view? Does your neighbor have a ragged old barn or 14 acres of junk that you have to look at every day? If he was going to get rid of the stuff, he would have done it by now. Stay away from those places if they offend your sensibilities.

5. Bring your ladder in the house and climb up in the crawl space under the roof. Any signs of water damage or leaks? Insect damage? What's the condition of the trusses? Is there adequate insulation for the climate? Any pines exposed? Take your flashlight up there with you. Don't count on a homeowner to supply you with any equipment.

6. Work your way down from the crawl space to the main floor. Is the house expandable, if need be? Do the floors squeak? What is the condition of carpets and floors? Any signs of settling (cracks over doorways, for example)? Is the woodwork in good shape? Are the windows tight? Do all electrical outlets work? Make sure! Is the ceiling water damaged? Is the paint peeling? Is it lead based? Are there adequate closets and storage space? Do doors close right? What's the condition of the electrical system? Does it have fuses or circuit breakers? Is the house wired for 220? Does it have washer and dryer hookups? Central air conditioning? Is there a furnace? Have the owners turn the furnace on, even in summer, so you can make sure it works. You won't want any surprises when you really need it later on. While you're at it, have them turn on the air conditioning. Are there easy exits in case of fire?

7. Check the bathroom. Does the toilet flush okay? Turn on the shower. Is there adequate water pressure? Do the sink and tub drain all right? Is there plenty of hot water? Is there water damage around the tub or shower? How about the floor? Is the lighting okay? Is there enough storage for bathroom stuff? Is there a window? Check the hot water heater. How old is it? Any signs of leaks on the floor around it? How old is the septic system? Will it meet your household needs?

8. Check the kitchen. Turn on hot and cold water in the sink. Does it drain okay? Taste the water!! Does it taste all right? Believe it or not, I know a fellow who bought a house without testing the well water, and then he did nothing but complain about the taste. Not too smart, huh? Fill your clean gallon bottle with tap water and have it tested by a certified laboratory. This will be one of the most important things that you do. Be certain of the water quality. How's the cabinet and counter space? Do any appliances come with the place? What is their condition? Take plenty of notes and pictures. If you look at several places, these will help you remember what you looked at. Is the water from a city or a well? Is gas natural or propane? Is there fuel oil? What about electricity and telephone service?

9. Check the basement or crawl space if there is one. Any sign of flooding or seepage? Does it smell musty? Is there any insect damage? Are there cracks in foundation walls? What is the condition of floor joists above? Ductwork? Pipes? Water pressure tank? Any leaks in anything?

10. Ask the owner whether you may call again if you have other questions regarding the property.

Never make a commitment after looking at a house once. After you have looked at several properties, sit down and have a meeting with all family members involved. Review your notes and photographs. Discuss pros and cons of each property, and get input from everybody. After you have narrowed your choices, go look at the first choice again. Linda and I went back three different times before we made our decision to buy the place.

Remember to meet the neighbors before you buy a place. Go into the town you will be patronizing and do some shopping. Talk to people. Eat in the restaurants. This will be your new home. Will you fit in? Do you like the people, and do they like you? Tell people about your plans to move into the area. How do they react? Do they seem helpful or standoffish?

Many country people distrust city folks. And many city folks think that country people are just hicks. But think about it. To run a successful working homestead you need skills in business, bookkeeping, advertising, agriculture or livestock, mechanics and engineering, some veterinary medicine, carpentry, and Lord knows what else. Doesn't sound like a hick to me. It sounds like a person who has a pretty good handle on life. How many city folks have this many skills? Not many.

A lot of city folks have know-it-all attitudes, when they don't know squat. Don't move to the country with a city attitude. It won't work. If you want to be a decent, helpful neighbor, you'll be able to make friends wherever you settle down. Country living means slowing down to a lower gear in life, just like downshifting to a lower gear in your car. The pace is slower, and people aren't in so much of a hurry. Can you adapt to that lifestyle? It will take awhile, at least a year, so give yourself time.

These are questions that you have to answer before you buy a place. Don't be in a hurry to make the wrong move. Relax. If you talk your decision over with others, they may bring up points you have overlooked. Talk to friends and family. I didn't get much support from my family. They think I'm nuts. They considered my move to Alaska as the point when I "went over the edge." It's too bad, really. I have a lot of experiences and dreams to share with them, but they can't understand because they've been trapped in the city their whole lives. All of them, that is, except my mom. She grew up on a farm in the old country, and she can't understand why I would want to work as hard as she had to. She and her sister had to hitch themselves to the plow and pull it. I told her it's not like that anymore, but she remains unconvinced.

Once you decide to buy the place, there are still several things that have to be done. Have you found out about mineral rights or water rights? Make sure they come with the property. Are any back taxes due? You can find out from the county tax collector. Is the title free and clear? The real estate agent should arrange for a title search and tax check, but you are ultimately responsible for these, so be sure that you find out.

Once you have given the realtor or owner a down payment or earnest money, it will be very hard to get it back from them, should you decide to back out of the sale. Protect yourself with the contract. You can put anything in it as long as it is agreeable to both parties. This is called a rider. Find out what things stay with the house after you buy it—carpeting, appliances, ceiling fans, etc.—and include them in the rider. Make the laboratory report for the drinking water a condition of sale, and put that

in the rider. You don't want to buy a place if it has bad water. Also, be sure to make a final inspection after the previous tenants move out to ensure that well, septic, and other things all still work. We added that to our rider. Make sure you write down everything in the contract that you want as conditions of sale. They will have to be approved by the seller.

You can take the contract to a lawyer if you want, though I don't have much use for lawyers. There is no legal requirement that you have one. Just read the whole contract and make sure you understand everything. If you don't, ask questions. If you're not satisfied with the answers, don't sign anything until you are. Remember, once you sign your name, you've made a legal obligation as an adult. Be sure of what you're buying, and you'll never be sorry.

Obviously, the best way to buy a property is with cash. That way, you don't have to pay someone for the use of their money. But paying cash is not essential. A majority of homeowners finance their homes with various lending institutions. I don't really trust banks myself, although we are financing our farm with one right now. The area where we lived in Chicago has average home prices of $100,000. The average person gets a 30-year note for about $1,000 a month. I may not be a space shuttle technician, but it only took me about 30 seconds to figure out that at the end of that 30-year note, those people will have paid $360,000 for a $100,000 house. $260,000 in interest? That sounds like loan sharking to me. Don't they put the mob in jail for doing that? I guess we can tell who runs the country!

Owner financing is when the seller of the property assumes the role of a bank. You give them a pre-arranged down payment, and make monthly payments for a set number of years. You still pay interest, but you don't go through a credit check like you would with a bank. The down payment is generally smaller than that required by a bank and there is less time spent on paperwork. You can close almost immediately. With owner financing, you can tailor a contract to suit your needs, if it is agreeable to both parties.

You have less flexibility with a contract from a lending institution. The foreclosure process is different. Most owner-financed contracts say that on the day you get two payments behind on your contract, after notice by registered letter, the property reverts back to the initial owner. No courts, no lawyers, no nothing. You lose your down payment and any payments that you have made up to that point. You also lose any improvements that you have made to the property (barn, garage, etc.). You just pack up your stuff and move out. It seems pretty cold, but it's not much different than a bank contract. Only a bank will usually give you three months before they start foreclosure action. They also keep your deposit, payments to date, and improvements. The only difference is that they give you an extra month before they take your home.

Some people will also swap for land. Do you have anything worth money? An extra car, a boat or motorcycle? Any skills you could trade? I know a guy who traded a 19-foot cruiser (boat) for five acres in Wisconsin. He built his dream home there. Be creative! Think! There are ways to finance your place if you want it badly enough. If you do have to finance with a bank, try to get the shortest time possible on the note. The longer the loan, the more interest you have to pay.

When we bought our place, we put $5,000 down and financed the rest through the savings and loan that held the deed to the house. We planned to continue living in Chicago until we paid the place off. The savings and loan gave us a $21,000 loan even though I didn't have a job! I was working construction and was on seasonal layoff. Linda had a job, and that helped get us the loan.

Making the deal

There is no rule that says you must pay the asking price for a property. Real estate agents try to get the most for a property because they work on commission. Make sure that the owner actually gets your offer. When shopping for your house, keep your eyes and ears open for clues that might save you some money. People sell property for different reasons. When we were looking at our farm, I asked the agent how much the place sold for new, 14 years ago. He said about $48,000. I was surprised. It was listed in the real estate guide for $35,000. When I first called the realtor about the place, he said the price had been reduced to $32,000. When we went to his office before

A country moment

Backwoods Home Magazine's solar-powered office in southern Oregon

going to see the place for the first time, the price had been lowered to $29,500. They had lowered the price by $5,500 and we hadn't even opened our mouths yet!

Turns out, the place was originally bought by a fellow who retired from General Motors in Michigan. He had rented it out for the last seven years. He had gotten three months behind on his payments, and the bank was starting foreclosure, so he was in a hurry to sell. I found out that he owed $26,000 to the bank. I offered to pay that amount to keep him from being foreclosed, but the realtor said he wouldn't go for it. I told him to give the owner my offer, anyway.

The realtor wasn't too thrilled because he had a commission coming, and there wouldn't be anything extra for him. The owner had already decided to give the house up to the bank if he couldn't sell it. I stuck to my guns. It was my money and if I couldn't get the deal that I wanted, I was walking. The owner was willing to have me pay off his note and keep his credit rating halfway decent. The problem was with the real estate agent. He had put time and money into selling the property and said he

had $2,500 coming. I offered him $1,000 cash for his fee, and he jumped on it.

We took a five-year note for $21,000 principal at a fixed ten percent interest rate. Our payments are $443.00 a month for five years, and the total interest we were scheduled to pay would come to about $6,000, for a total pay back of $27,000. During the first three months after we got the place, I put a large part of my paycheck toward the principal on the house, since I was back to work by then. We paid $6,000 on the principal in those three months, in addition to our regular payments. That really knocked the interest down, but it takes two incomes to do that. We lived on Linda's income while we put mine toward the house. We've had the place for 15 months now and have made over 40 payments on it. We only owe about $7,000 more on the place. We won't move there until after we get the loan paid off, since we don't want to be saddled with a house payment. If I have to work to cover a house payment, that's less time that I can spend fishing! Anyway, the point is, give yourself a limit and stick with it. If someone doesn't give you the deal you want, find someone else. Spend only what you can afford, and only you know what that is.

Since we will now only wind up paying about $30,000 for our place, after interest, we have been able to lower our budget from $100,000 to $50,000. Who can gripe about that much savings? Since we didn't have to build a house, bring in utilities, or dig ponds, we saved a bunch of money. We need to build a barn and shop and other small buildings. We also need a tractor and some equipment. I figure that will cost $20,000. With the money we saved, I've designed a complete alternative energy power plant for the homestead, which will total about $10,000. It will be a hybrid system which uses photovoltaic modules, a hydroelectric system operated by the runoff from our ponds, and a diesel generator. We were thinking about wind, but after monitoring the wind speed in the area for a year, we decided that it didn't blow hard enough.

Getting the funds

Unless you have a rich relative that just left you a couple of million in their will, you will have to work, just like we do. I used to own a business, but found that I could make more money, per hours worked, by working for someone else. I went into construction and got a union job. One of the advantages of living in the city is that the wages are higher than in the country. Use this to your advantage. Work all the overtime that you can while you're young, and don't fritter away your money. I bring home $1,000 a week, but I have to work 70 hours a week for it. I don't mind; it won't be much longer now. We live on Linda's check and put mine into the house. We also have cut our expenses considerably, although the cost of living is much higher in cities. A decent one-bedroom apartment in Chicago costs about $500-600.

Stop spending your money on anything but your goals and your essential living costs. Stop eating out and cook at home. It's cheaper. We eat out once a week to reward ourselves for being tightwads, but we have a $20 limit for dinner for both of us. You have to set goals and a budget and stick to them.

The following are things that we have given up and the savings we have realized as a result.

Sunday paper: $5 / mo.
Meals out 4 times/week: $240 / mo.
Junk food and snacks: $40 / mo.
Credit cards (interest): $3-400/ yr.
Groceries from
   non- discount stores: $80 / mo.
Smoking (both of us): $175 / mo.
Visits to gin mills: $50 / mo.
Professional haircuts
   (Linda cuts mine): $100 / yr.

The biggest savings came from selling Linda's car and keeping my mini pickup. It costs a lot to keep a car in Chicago. License fees alone are over $120 a year, not to mention the cost of mandatory insurance. Cars are nice, but if you can get by with public transportation for awhile, you can save a lot of money. We need one car because we make so many trips to our farm. But by selling the second one, we've saved over $2,000 a year. We just ride our bicycles or walk. We've learned to adjust.

All the things I've listed above save us about $10,000 per year. What we are most pleased about is how we figured a way to get free rent. Since our goal was to rent as cheaply as we could, in order to pay on the farm, we were renting a dumpy little basement apartment for $350 a month, and I didn't even want to pay that much. I wanted a free place to live, and then I got a brainstorm! I placed an ad in the local paper offering to help take care of an elderly person or couple in exchange for free room and board. We received several replies, and moved in with a nice 78-year-old woman who is in pretty good health. We make a couple of meals a day for her and do household chores (laundry, shopping, cleaning, mopping, lawn care and minor repairs). She has a washer and dryer, so we save an extra $20.00 a month by not going to the laundromat. Altogether, we've saved about $6,000 a year by moving in with her. Add that to the above figure, and we're saving $16,000 per year. That's more than the per capita income in many states!

My advice to you is to just use your head, relax, and be creative! Be clear about your goals, flexible and patient in working toward them. You too can make your homesteading dreams come true! Δ

A BHM Writer's Profile

Jennifer Stein Barker

Jennifer Stein Barker grew up in Vermont, where healthy cooking has always been popular. As an adult living in the Cascade Mountains of Washington, she owned and cooked at Garrison Springs lodge, a backcountry ski lodge. As her reputation for good food grew, she began writing for Backwoods Home Magazine in 1989.

When she met her husband Lance and moved to Oregon, Barker began working on a cookbook (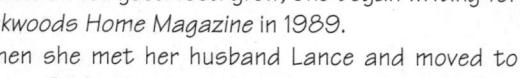The Morning Hill Cookbook now available through Backwoods Home) and teaching whole foods cooking courses at the Blue Mountain Community College extension in John Day.

The Barkers live on 40 acres in the Pine woods of Bear Valley, with three cats and a three-acre garden. She was last seen digging beets, turnips, and kohlrabi out from under the snow.

Just for kids — You in the big night sky

By Lucy Shober

There is a Native American tribe called the Anishinabe. These people, who live close to the great lakes, tell the story of a brave and determined fisher (this is a little animal in the weasel family). The fisher lived in a time when the earth was cold and snow always covered the ground. He knew that behind the clouds, in the sky, there was a land where it was always warm, so he set about chewing a hole in the sky to let that warmth flow onto the earth. The fisher worked hard, and pretty soon that good balmy air began to flow through his hole and warm up the world below.

Just as things began to turn green under the melting snow though, the people who lived in the sky realized that the fisher was taking some of their heat and began shooting him with arrows. When an arrow struck him he fell through the sky, but since he had died while trying to help his friends on earth, his body was carried magically back up into the heavens so that his loved ones could see him forever. And that is how Native Americans say the big dipper came to be.

You probably know that most people think of the big dipper as part of the constellation of the Great Bear, Ursa Major. Constellations are groups of stars which we can look at in different ways so that they become pictures. It's hard to believe that ancient people could have really seen some of those images in the stars! Their imaginations must have had to work pretty hard to come up with the flying ponies, emperors and dragons with which they decorated the night sky.

Some of the constellations are a little overwhelming to try and figure out, but a good library book on stars will help you out. After you identify a few of the easier ones, why not try and make up some of your own? There are crawfish and ducks, clown faces and pizza supremes up there just waiting for you to discover them! Winter is a great time to spread your blanket and gaze upward, because the atmosphere which covers the earth tends to be clearer. Make up your own stories to go with your star shapes, and then chart the stars in your constellations and draw pictures around them just like the Greek people of yesteryear did.

Each star is identified by its own set of letters and numbers, but did you know that you could have a star named after yourself or someone that you love? The International Star Registry will record a star in your name into its vault in Switzerland. For information, you can write to them at 1821 Willow Road, Northfield, IL, 60093, or call (708) 441-8520.

If you want to, you can put yourself into the night sky while sitting at the kitchen table! Follow the directions below to make a dreamy world of your own, and then use your library book to answer the questions in the stellar quiz.

You will need a shoe box, an old photo of yourself, scissors, paste, a sharp pointed object (like an ice pick), moss or grass, pebbles and twigs, a scrap of cloth, your imagination, a flashlight or lamp, and the help of an adult friend!

Have you ever seen those little peep shows that people make with a shoe box? Your project will be like those, only with a cosmic twist.

First, cut out the star map on this page and paste it to the lid of your shoe box. (By the way, do you recognize any of the constellations?) Now with adult help, punch a hole into each star on the paper, punching all the way through the box lid. Then, make a little door at one end of the box itself (see picture).

Next, take the photo of yourself (a full-body photo looks best), cut away everything except your body, and fold it into a sitting position. Decorate the inside of the box with the twigs and moss, etc. Then paste the cloth scrap onto the box floor. Maybe you could try and make the box look like your own backyard! Now paste yourself (the photo, that is) onto the cloth so that it looks like you have settled onto your favorite blanket. Put the top onto the box and hold it up to a lamp or shine a flashlight over the top while looking through the door.

There you are—sharing the big night sky with two bears and a dragon! It's easy to put yourself in lights. Just lie back and let your imagination take you for a ride!

Stellar quiz

1. It takes the same amount of time to _____ as it does for the light of the sun (our planet's own star) to reach the earth.

A. Take a hot bath and wash your hair (35 min., 46 sec.).

B. Clean up your room (2 hrs., 59 min., 13 sec.).

C. Bake a batch of chocolate chip cookies (8 min., 20 sec.).

2. The zodiac is a _____.

A. Group of stars in the shape of a grizzly bear.

B. Group of twelve star pictures in the sky.

C. Scientific name for our galaxy.

3. Our galaxy is named _____ and it is shaped like a _____.

A. Zagnut, basketball.

B. Milky Way, frizbee.

C. Zenith, badmitten birdie. ∆

Answer: C,B,B.

Draco (the dragon), Ursa Major (Big Bear), and Ursa Minor (Little Bear).

Living the country life

By Sally Denney

Moving to the country can be a dream come true, or it can be a nightmare. The wide open spaces can fill you with fulfillment or send you spiraling into despair if you haven't fully researched the house, the property and the community you plan to call home.

When we moved to the country we were met by friendly-seeming country folks who were taking bets on how long we would stay. The house we moved into was in desperate need of repairs. The roof leaked, the foundation was falling in, and the wiring was last updated in the early 1950s. We knew all of that and bought it anyway. We had completely remodeled our house in town and had gained quite a bit of hands-on experience. We were eager to start a new project, and what better place to do it than in the country?

So we packed up our furniture, family, and dreams, and dug into the task of fixing the old homestead up to a better condition than her original one. We were so busy with remodeling that we didn't come up for air for two years. When we finally peeked out the pristine new windows of our mansion on the hill, we discovered that several community feuds were being waged around us.

Neighbor problems

Our homestead is located at the dead end of a long, gravel, country road. The entrance to our lane is near a house whose inhabitant hadn't yet accepted lawnmowers and who didn't own sheep. His lawn was usually long enough to bale for hay and he had no intention of changing his way of life. This drove his neighbor to the north crazy, because he was a mowing fanatic who trimmed his lawn three to four times a week. Somehow, they decided that we were the ones to settle their dispute and were constantly running to us to report on the other's latest escapades. We dubbed them the Hatfields and the McCoys and listened intently, but didn't agree with either one. Had we learned about the neighborhood feud before we moved here (that's the first thing we should have done), we might have given the property a second look. But now that we're here, we try to make the best of a difficult situation.

We learned, after moving, how friendly the neighbors were by asking for someone to plow a small space for our garden. They said their equipment was too big to plow a garden space (never mind that we owned 23 acres and didn't care how big a plot they plowed). They just preferred saying no to helping us. In the long run, that has proven to be good because we learned how to be self-sufficient. Now they occasionally ask us for favors, and we try to accommodate them—unless our equipment is too small.

School problems

The second thing we should have done was read old newspaper articles about the community, because we landed on the edge of two small towns with a joint public school system. When the towns consolidated to bring better education to their children, they never abandoned their competitive desires to better their own communities. They continued arguing over the location of the high school they had built twenty years before, and now they needed to either add on or build a new one, but didn't have enough tax base to do so.

No matter whether families homeschool or not, they have to pay property taxes, and due to the ongoing school dispute, the tax rate has risen every year since we've been here. Meanwhile, the two communities are still fighting about whose town is best and least dependent on the bigger cities nearby. We should have attended a few school board meetings before moving so we could be more informed about school politics because, like it or not, our dollars would be involved. The only good thing about this situation is that the school board is elected, not appointed, or we would probably be paying even higher property taxes than we are.

Another area that deserved some investigation before moving was the local public library. Had we visited the one in our small town, we would have seen how inadequate it is. The library received the minimum budget to work with, and the librarians tended not to look for improvements because they felt they were already overworked during the twenty hours a week that they were open. As the town's weekly school reporter, I once wanted to advertise that the library hosted a children's story hour so that more children would attend, but the librarian said she didn't want the publicity. Too many children would show up, and they didn't have the staff to handle it. They wouldn't foster volunteer programs because they said it was easier to do the work themselves, and then they complained that they were overworked. I now pay a fee to use the larger library in a nearby city.

Church

We did visit the local church when we first moved and found the people very helpful there. I truly believe that our church attendance was the only reason we were eventually accepted into the community. So before you commit to moving, you might want to visit local churches a few times to learn more about your prospective neighbors and to let them know you.

Best source of information

If the property is like ours and located in a very small township, it is also a good idea to talk with the local tax assessor before buying. This person is usually a fountain of information on everything from soil conditions to well depths to the legal obligations of property line fences. He or she may also be the person to contact should your sheep, cows, pigs, or chickens ever be troubled by stray dogs. We have learned that if the tax assessor doesn't have the answer, he knows someone else who does.

Find out all you can about the local fire department as well. Is it volunteer? What is its response time? How many miles is it from your home? My sister, who lives nearby, had a small fire in her home, but by the time the volunteer fire department arrived on a below-zero evening, my husband had already put out the fire with an extinguisher. It was a good thing he had, because after the department arrived they realized that the pump truck had not been refilled after responding to the previous fire. I strongly recommend investigating such critical concerns before you buy. Your findings will determine the price of your home insurance, something else it is nice to know about in advance.

Learn about local celebrations, festivals and events. I once inspired my children to complete their chores quickly so that we could attend the town's annual festival, but when we arrived we found that the entire event consisted of a soft drink stand on the town square. Ten years later, my children still laugh about the big buildup I gave them, and the look on my face when we arrived.

But we love it

In spite of our learning experiences, we have come to find our community to be a delightful place. The scenery is spectacular, the peace and quiet are worth the lack of hoopla at the festivals, and the people have finally grown quite friendly towards us. I enjoy their company far more than I ever did my neighbors in town. When a country neighbor has traveled a long way to see me, it is because they really wanted to and not because they just had a whim to step out the back door and holler across the fence.

We have also discovered that if you settle in one spot long enough, the problems start solving themselves. Our neighbor that never mowed his lawn moved away. The library has been appropriated more funds. The festival has improved yearly. The towns finally compromised on the schools and are building a new middle school, leaving the high school where it was. And the fire department—well, we haven't had to call them. I'd better check into that! Δ

A BHM Writer's Profile

Charles A. Sanders

The rugged, wooded hills of southern Indiana are home to Charles A. Sanders, his wife Patti, and their three children. Sanders built their heavily-insulated, south-facing, wood heated house in 1979. They have 39 acres of timber and pasture, where they grow timber, a few cattle, and hay. They can, freeze, and dry hundreds of quarts of vegetables from their large garden each summer. The Sanders raise their own beef, and augment it with small game and deer from the surrounding woodlands. Their orchard keeps them in apples and pears. They keep bees for pollination and honey.

Sander's interest in the land carries over into his occupation. He has been a conservation officer for 19 years, and serves as a district firearms instructor. Sanders spends his vacation time as a member of Indiana's Inter-Agency Wildland Fire Crew, and he has fought wildfires in Oregon, Idaho, Montana, Minnesota, and Kentucky, as well as his own state. Writing is an especially strong interest. Besides writing for *Backwoods Home Magazine*, Sanders is writing a common-sense, down to earth, present-day homesteader's guide. His other interests include trapping, reading, radio, and winemaking.

A Backwoods Home Anthology

AMERICANA-SOCIETY

Explore the world with shortwave

By Michael Simmons

Do you ever wonder if there is more to the evening news than the usual "drivel" shown us night after night, week after week on the boob tube? Do you ever wonder just how biased, slanted, or edited the news stories are, carefully controlled by unseen hands? Would you like to know how other nations and peoples view world situations? Does hearing news the American networks never report sound appealing? If so, then shortwave radio can be the best way to explore a world of news and programming which is less tainted by commercial (or political) interests.

News and entertainment

Shortwave radio is the primary source for news and entertainment in most of the world except for the United States, where TV and FM radio predominate. In many nations (virtually all the third world countries), the TV broadcast stations are controlled and/or owned by the government and in some cases are only operated for part of the day. Since that means the news is what the leaders want it to be, the people naturally want to hear more of what is going on from outside their country. They can only do so by shortwave.

Since there are millions of people who are working outside of their own countries (Americans alone who are working abroad number 2.5 million), shortwave broadcasters produce plenty of quality news and entertainment broadcasts almost around the clock for these folks.

The British Broadcasting Corporation (BBC) and the Voice of America (VOA) are the favorite shortwave news sources for most everyone around the world. Their news contents are very complete, containing far more items than you'll ever hear on CNN news.

Remember, in some other countries, the media are often tightly controlled by their governments, so people are often dubious of their contents. They value the news broadcasts of the BBC and VOA because of the total lack of propaganda or political bias, and the BBC and VOA news directors guard that reputation most carefully.

Germany, Switzerland, Russia, the Netherlands, Australia and even the Vatican, operate very powerful shortwave transmitters for excellent worldwide coverage. They broadcast news about their internal affairs, and offer popular programs about various topics such as technological and medical developments in their countries.

Do you like to learn about new types of folk music? Shortwave is a great way to discover, right in your home, diverse music styles performed throughout the world.

Ever wonder what soap operas are like in other countries? The BBC broadcasts soaps on occasion to their countrymen working abroad, and some can be quite humorous.

With Russia struggling toward democracy, its All Union Radio can be very interesting these days. Although it is still very much the voice of the government, experienced listeners can derive much satisfaction by listening and interpreting what is really going on over there.

During world crises, shortwave will provide tantalizing nuggets of up-to-the-minute news on what's happening, perhaps right from where it is happening. During Operation Desert Storm, thousands of Americans bought shortwave radios, creating a backlog clear to Japan. They could listen directly to the statements and opinions of dozens of countries throughout the world, rather than to the patchy reporting brought by the domestic news services.

During the Tieneman Square massacre in Peking, one shortwave (SW) listener caught a brief broadcast from Radio Beijing late one evening on 9690 kiloHertz (kHz) that sounded extremely odd. In rough English, the amateurish-sounding announcer talked about thousands of deaths at the hands of soldiers and even began denouncing the government. He further stated that nothing further could be said because of the circumstances. A female voice suddenly came on, and nothing further about the massacre was mentioned. NBC News carried an item on this event during the next day's evening news, but what a thrill to catch it "first hand."

Clandestine stations operating illegally under the noses of an oppressive government can provide fascinating listening, especially during times of civil unrest or war. These are usually the voices for revolutionary political groups and are in the native language. However, a few broadcasts such as the anti-Castro broadcasts originating in Florida are in English.

Want to listen to some really bizarre alternative programming? Pirate stations can offer truly "off-the-wall" programming that will range from hilarious to obscene. Stateside, pirate stations are usually low-powered, illegal operations broadcasting around 7415 to 7420 kHz, mostly on weekend and holiday evenings, especially during the evening hours. As they are not obeying Federal Communication Commission rules at all, anything goes. With names like Radio Freddie's Nightmare, KRUD, and Radio Free Euphoria, you can imagine what you can expect. Just make sure the young 'uns are in another room.

Many shortwave programs have considerable educational content which can be a boon to homeschoolers. You may catch art news from Radio France, science news from Radio Canada, bawdy comedies from Radio Sweden, recipes from RBI, Germany, all there for your listening enjoyment.

Shortwave bands

To begin with, shortwave frequencies are between the AM broadcast frequencies and the low VHF communications channels. If you could twist the tuning knob on your AM receiver past 1620 kiloHertz (kHz), the usual upper limit for broadcast radios, on up to 3000 kHz, you would be on the bottom edge of the SW band. It extends to 30,000 kHz or 30 Megahertz (MHz). Different kinds of stations operate on the shortwave frequencies in different groups of frequencies called bands. The most useful SW broadcast bands for listeners in North America are the 49, 40, 31, 25, and 19 meter bands (there are others, but these are the most listened to). Please refer to the chart at the end of this article to determine the range of frequencies within each band.

The usefulness (or "receivability") of these bands changes with the time of day and year. During the day, the 19 meter band is active, followed by the 25 meter band later on. During the early evening hours, say 6 o'clock EST, the 31 meter band will start to come alive with European stations beginning their North American broadcasts. These broadcasts usually stay on until 11 p.m. EST or later, until the band changes transmission characteristics—that is, dies. Late night listening can be continued on the lowest frequencies, the 41 meter band.

Summertime static and other factors make the 41 and 40 meter bands less useful from April to September, but during the cold winter months, these and the 31 meter band really come alive. The 19 and 25 meter bands, and to some extent the 31 meter band, are more useful during the summer.

Our sun's storm and solar flare activity can also have a lot to do with shortwave reception. Every 11 years, the sunspot activity is at a high, which makes shortwave signals stronger on the 19 and 25 meter bands, but limits 40 and 41 meters. During sunspot minimums, the 19 and 25 meter bands suffer, while the 40 and 41 meter bands boom. The 31 meter band, which is in between the two, seems to suffer only during years of very low sunspot activity. All bands can be "wiped out" temporarily by solar storms, which can happen very suddenly, anytime. If you ever tune around on your shortwave and find it dead, don't panic. It may only be a solar storm in progress, which will pass within a few hours or days.

Buying equipment

As to what kind and brand of shortwave receiver you should get, that can get as involved as what type of car or home is best for you. New receivers can range from $29.95 to well over $2000 for communications-grade equipment. Performance generally increases with price, although anything over $200 is for serious listening only. If you are wanting only to get your feet wet to see if you like it, then your initial expense should be around $100. Sets costing $50 or less may suffer enough performance-wise to turn you off against shortwave needlessly.

A shortwave receiver is judged by its ability to hear weak stations (or sensitivity), its ability to pull apart close-together stations (or selectivity), and the quality of its frequency readout, which includes accuracy and readability.

During the evening hours, the big shortwave stations such the BBC and Radio Switzerland will be beaming toward the North American continent, producing whopping signals. It will not take extra-good sensitivity to pull them in satisfactorily.

In fact, these stations can come in so strongly that really good receivers must reduce their sensitivity to avoid distortion of the signal. Good sensitivity needed to dig out the weak stations such as those in third world countries is sought after by serious SW listeners, but isn't necessary for the beginning or casual listener.

The second characteristic of the SW receiver is probably the most important: selectivity, or the ability to slice away unwanted stations crowding in on your intended frequency. The SW bands are limited in size, frequency-wise, so the broadcast stations must squeeze in, big and small, right next to each other. Occasionally they are on top of each of other, but no receiver can do anything about that. A cheaply constructed receiver with poor selectivity may have two stations coming in at the same time, which can be very aggravating. The better receivers will have ceramic and/or crystal filters to "slice away" unwanted stations.

The high-powered European SW stations will usually come through fine by sheer brute force. They are so powerful that no other stations can be heard through them. If you are only interested in listening to them, you'll do well most of the time. But let's say you find a very interesting program coming from a medium powered station with a bigger one nearby. Then you may have problems pulling them apart. This is where the better receivers will allow you to hear the weaker station, not the stronger.

The frequency readout is important too, so you can find your favorite stations consistently night after night. The better receivers now have digital readouts which will put you precisely on frequency immediately. The nice ones also have frequency memories so you can bring up your favorite stations instantly once they've been programmed. The less expensive receivers use the old fashioned mechanical tuning with the knob and slide dial. These don't have the accuracy of the digital units, of course, but with a little experience you can tune in your favorites quite well.

If you only want to buy the non-digital types, you should get the units which only tune the broadcast portions of the SW bands to make it easier to tune. Receivers which have all the frequencies between 3000 and 30000 kiloHertz can have crowded dials, making it more difficult to tell which frequency you are tuned to.

Reception and noise

Once you have bought your receiver, consider putting a wire antenna outside your house or apartment. The aerial, clipped to the whip antenna provided with the unit or onto the antenna jack on the rear (always there on good units), will dramatically increase the signal strengths. Radio Shack sells an antenna kit for under ten dollars.

You should purchase a copy of Popular Communications magazine, which usually carries a listing of the English broadcasts, times, and frequencies. This will eliminate frustration caused by hunting around the dial. Note: the times and frequencies are always changing for various reasons, so don't be surprised if you have to tune around the listed frequency to find the intended station. It happens all the time.

A chart of frequencies is shown to give you an idea where the major stations might be found, but the frequencies may change by the time you read this. If a station does change its frequency, it usually moves by only 5 or 10 kiloHertz.

Read the owner's manual included with your receiver for tips which can enhance your listening enjoyment.

If you have a problem with electrical noise, move the set around to a quiet spot away from computers, fluorescent lights, and TV sets. These are like miniature noise transmitters which can "bleed" into your set. An outside antenna located away from noise sources will help greatly. Plugging the set into different wall outlets can help tremendously, too.

Shortwave stations know that there are many listeners out there who are not familiar with their programming and will give out plenty of information about their programs. The big ones may even offer program guides free if you write them at the addresses given you. If you do write to them, include a report of what you heard from them, plus the time and frequency you heard them, and you may get a beautiful card or certificate confirming your reception report. These are known as QSL cards or reports, and can be great fun to collect.

As you gain experience, you may want to hunt around for exotic stations such as those pirates; then you will really be hooked, like many thousands of other Americans.

Popular stations:

Voice Of America: 6130, 7405, 9775, 11695
Radio Canada: 9750
All Union Radio, Russia: 7220
BBC, England: 6175, 7330, 9915, 11750
WWCR, Tennessee: 7435
KTBN, Utah: 7510
Radio Beijing, China: 11715
Radio Madrid, Spain: 9530
Radio Netherlands: 6163
Radio RSA, S. Africa: 7270
Swiss Radio, Int'l.: 9885
Radio Sofia, Bulgaria: 9700
Government time stations:
WWV, United States—5000, 10000, 15000 (all hours)
CHU, Canada—3330, 7335, 14670

These frequencies may vary somewhat over the months, but not by much. If you can't find a particular station using the above frequencies, tune on either side a bit and it should be there. For a very complete tuning guide, consult the most recent issue of Popular Communications magazine, sold at many grocery stores. ∆

A BHM Writer's Profile

M. C. Wright

Born and educated in a small town in southern Mississippi, Margaret Clark (M.C.) Wright still has the accent to prove it. She was raised by her grandmother and a loving nanny while her mom worked outside the home. Wright married her high school sweetheart; they have been together 35 years. She is mother to four children and "Mamaw" to seven grandchildren.

Wright and her family have travelled extensively, following the electrical construction trade. They landed in Idaho 20 years ago and are still there. Wright is now working at a local women's shelter as an advocate for victims of domestic violence.

Wright cooks from scratch, sews, quilts, gardens, and takes care of the animals. Her favorite attire is a denim skirt, sweatshirt, and Birkenstocks with socks, which she describes as a real fashion statement. She began writing after taking some journalism classes—a hobby turned serious. She says, "I love the idea of other people being interested in my lifestyle, and hope I can inspire them to follow their dreams."

March/April 1994
No. 26
$3.50 U.S.
$4.50 Canada

FREE $500 KIT

Backwoods Home magazine

...a practical journal of self reliance!

SPECIAL GARDENING ISSUE

- 10 USEFUL HERBS
- HOME FOUNDATIONS
- BIRTH OF A KID GOAT
- GROWING HUCKLEBERRIES

My View

Forget conspiracies...

Political conspiracy theories have two things in common: the conspiracy is enormous in size, and the conspirators are largely invisible so nobody gets a chance to take action against them. Such is the case with one of the most popular conspiracy theories many patriotic Americans currently cling to—the New World Order conspiracy.

With this country's inexorable march into a welfare-type system similar to the ones that exist in Western Europe and Canada, many people in the U.S. believe a grand international conspiracy is at the bottom of it. I find this tremendously tragic, because those who cling to conspiracy theories as explanations for their woes, not only do nothing to combat the alleged conspiracy but they unwittingly aid the restructuring of America into the welfare state they so fear.

The most popular conspiracy theory of our time involves a host of nefarious organizations and people: the Trilateral Commission, the Council on Foreign Relations, the Bilderbergers, David Rockefeller, even on occasion your typical historical scapegoats—Jews and the Papacy—all hooked up in one grand conspiracy to slam dunk America into a Global Government under the control of the New World Order that will make virtual slaves of us all.

The conspiracy is so big that none of the myriad of publications and organizations that have sprung up to warn people of it ever offer any solutions on how to stop it. It is always stuff we can't quite touch—U.N. troops in secret training camps on American soil or hundreds of newly-built concentration camps waiting to imprison Americans who oppose the imminent visitation of the New World Order.

Proponents of the New World Order conspiracy promote it much like you'd promote a religion: total belief is necessary or you are a suspect conspirator too. When Bo Gritz, the 1992 Populist Party Presidential candidate and himself a believer in the New World Order conspiracy, publicly stated he doubted the existence of concentration camps in America, another noted conspiracy theorist immediately branded Gritz a CIA-plant and thus a defacto member of the New World Order conspiracy.

That makes it a clean sweep for the New World Order in the last Presidential election. According to the conspiracy theorists, all the major candidates—Clinton, Bush, and Perot—were sponsored by the New World Order. Now Gritz the heretic is one of them too. Slam dunk it is for the New World Order. Now I guess this article makes me a conspirator as well. Tsk, tsk. Shame on me.

But of course Bo Gritz and my election to the ranks of the New World Order conspirators suits the conspiracy theorists just fine. Because that is the nature of these conspiracies—everyone and everything is involved. Even NAFTA, the recently-enacted free trade agreement, is alleged to be a part of the New World Order master plan. It is that broad.

These conspiracies are so big that they can't be stopped because they have too many powerful people and the intrigue is too perfect and all encompassing. We are all doomed.

...and do something productive!

And that is what makes me so damned mad about these alleged grand conspiracies like the New World Order. Adherents to them use them as an excuse to do nothing. America is perched on the chasm of socialism and we have a bunch of phony patriots running around yelling, "The sky is falling." What they need is a good kick in the behind and a knock on the head with someone asking them, "Hello, is anybody home."

This country doesn't need a grand conspiracy trying to take it over. Socialism is winning by default. Conspiracy theorists are so preoccupied with invisible monsters that they don't see the fox who presently occupies the White House, nor the weasels in Congress who are passing laws that will make the existence of a New World Order academic. Clinton is no puppet of the New World Order; he is a clever politician who just happens to think socialism and big government work. Neither do congressmen belong to some secret global order; they are politicians doing what politicians have always done—vying for more power, for their share of the nation's wealth.

Even if there were a grand conspiracy, burying your head in the sand won't combat it. What we can combat is what we can see and touch, and we can see and touch Clinton, the U.S. Congress, our declining public education system, a decaying value structure in America, and lots more. If you don't like socialism, join political forces with others and fight it; don't hide in the woods with your Mini 14.

"They got Randy Weaver," you say. That's right, they did. So what did you do about it. Buy more ammo and hide in your bunker? Did you write a letter to a congressman or newspaper to express your outrage, join a political action group to put your views into action? Or did you bury your head in a conspiracy newsletter and grumble?

Many believers in a New World Order conspiracy like to cite the writings of our founding fathers, our Constitution, and our great patriots when they cry about how terrible things are. But our founding fathers never believed that grand conspiracies had any teeth worth running from. Otherwise we'd still be owned by England.

Our founding fathers believed that every individual can control his or her own future, that every individual can make a significant contribution to safeguarding the freedoms of all of us. And they were right. It wasn't by accident that this nation, based on individual liberty and individual responsibility for keeping that liberty safe, was born. It was brought about by clear thinking people who did not cower before real or imagined conspiracies.

American institutions and values are being severely tested these days, but the fight against socialism is very winnable if enough people stand up, speak out, and take some kind of action. So far you conspiracy adherents are putting up one Chicken Little fight. ∆

COUNTRY LIVING

Driving back country roads — different skills needed at every turn

By Don Fallick

When I first moved to the backwoods in 1985, nobody could tell me anything about driving. I could drift corners with the best of them, had played at road racing, had a clean driving record, and hadn't had an accident for 15 years. I had driven Colorado mountain roads, rural routes and city streets, had survived half a dozen Wisconsin winters, and I learned to drive on the freeways of Los Angeles. But I knew nothing about real back country driving.

Speed kills—TIRES!

The first, costly, lesson I learned was that driving on gravel requires slower speeds than driving on pavement. Speeds that are merely scary on asphalt can eat up your tires in a hurry on gravel—if they don't kill you. Driving on freshly laid gravel is very much like driving on ball bearings, with this one difference: ball bearings don't have sharp corners. After replacing four new tires in three months, I made a conscious decision to slow down. Even though I was capable of high-speed driving on our "county road," I found I simply couldn't afford it. Only after I slowed down did I learn the real advantages of slower driving.
- Tires last much longer.
- Gas mileage increases dramatically.
- You have time to enjoy the scenery along the way.
- You arrive at your destination relaxed.

But the most important difference is in the attitude of the driver. When you intend to go slowly, you allow time for the trip and don't feel the sense of urgent haste that pushes city drivers to "compete" with each other. You've got time to be neighborly, to stop and help another traveler in distress if you should happen to meet one, or even just to say "Hi!"

Keeping to the middle

One of the first things most city folks notice about back country driving is the absence of other cars on the road. In the last eight years, I can recall every time I've encountered as many as six cars in a 25-mile round trip to town. Most country drivers follow an old adage that advises you to "keep it in the middle of the road." This makes good sense when the shoulders range from soft to non existent and opposing traffic is something to write home about. Still, it's not a bad idea to keep to the right when cresting a hill, at least in the daytime. At night, you can see the oncoming car's headlights in plenty of time to get out of his way.

Often, the middle of the road will have ruts that can be unpleasant to drive in. I try to "drive down" the ruts by driving on the high spots whenever I can. With a county government that grades the road twice a year "whether it needs it or not," it's up to those of us who use the road to take the best care of it that we can.

Watch for sleepers . . .

Taking care of the road includes taking care not to bother the residents. In the city, cars seem to have the right of way, regardless of what the law says. Country folks take a different view. Kids and animals are used to playing, or even sleeping, in the middle of the

road. This is not unreasonable when traffic is a once-a-day occurrence. If you drive by and bury your neighbors in dust, they won't like it, or you, much. It's polite to slow way down when passing livestock, houses, people, and even when meeting oncoming vehicles. Some old timers even stop to let oncoming cars go by. Anyone displaying that much courtesy deserves to be treated with respect.

Depending on your location, you may expect to meet slow-moving tractors and farm machinery, or fast-moving logging trucks, etc. at appropriate times of the year. In open country you can see them a long way off, and your only challenge may be containing your temper until they can get out of your way. In the mountains, where turnouts may be miles apart, such vehicles often use CB radio to warn other traffic. Your neighbors will be able to tell you what channel to monitor. It might seem an unnecessary expense, but it could keep you from becoming a hood ornament on a logging truck.

...cattle and horses...

Cars and tractors are not the only thing you'll find in the middle of a country road. Besides the proverbial dog sleeping there, back country drivers frequently encounter livestock, wildlife, and horses. Each of these must be dealt with differently, but the key to success is to see and recognize the danger early and slow down immediately.

Escaped cattle along, or in, a road are an obvious menace. They have no instinctive fear of cars, and may be very slow to get off the road. Sounding the horn may encourage them to leave, but if not, the best course is to proceed past them very, very slowly. Cattle do respect creatures that are bigger than they are and will step aside to allow you to pass once they recognize your superior size. Unfortunately, cattle are not known for good eyesight, so you may have to get really close before they can see you clearly.

If you can tell where the cows got out, and there are other cattle still where they belong, it's polite to fix the fence or gate, at least temporarily. And always notify the owner, if you can find him. Cattle are expensive, and the owner will thank you for telling him his cows are out. If you can't identify or find the owner, the sheriff will probably know whose cows they are and how to reach him. Eastern Washington State is not known as a big cattle area, yet the most common item in the sheriff's log in Lincoln County is a report of escaped cattle.

Horses are a different story. Backwoods horses who rarely see a car are generally terrified of passing vehicles, and usually bolt across the road just in front of you as you pass. One pitch-black night I passed a black horse in the dark, and it ran directly in front of me. The car was demolished, the horse died, and my family and I had to strip in the middle of the road and shake the broken glass out of our clothes. Spoiled my whole day. Even horses with riders may be spooked by passing cars. So always pass horses very slowly, and never honk at a horse!

...sheep...

If you live in sheep country, you know that from a distance, sheep look like nothing more than large, white rocks by the side of the road. They aren't likely to bolt into the road like horses, but they may very well wander into it before you get there. Horn honking doesn't seem to have much effect on sheep, for some reason, but moving very, very slowly through a small flock of sheep does seem to work. Your best bet with a large flock is just to wait. In a large flock, the sheep won't let each other move out of your way. Eventually the flock will cross the road, and you can resume your journey. Just pretend you're at a railroad crossing.

The biggest danger from sheep is that you may encounter a flock unexpectedly, just over the crest of a hill or around a curve, at highway speed. An 80 lb. sheep hitting your windshield at 50 mph can easily kill you. If you live in a sheep herding area, you'll likely be aware of the danger, but sometimes sheep herders drive their flocks as far as 100 miles to summer or winter pasture, so it's a good idea to take a second look at any large, white rocks you see.

...and wildlife

From early evening to late morning is the best time to spot deer on the road, though they may be found crossing at any time of the day. Deer will usually get out of your way if they possibly can, especially if they hear you coming. Unfortunately, like horses, they will sometimes bolt in front of you when spooked. Deer repellers, available in sporting goods stores, produce an ultrasonic whistle which scares the deer away. They work. They also repel some other animals. I do not know their effect on horses, but since they are powered by the airstream flowing across your bumper, slowing way down for horses may avoid problems. Ask before you buy.

Although deer present the greatest wildlife danger to motorists, they are not the only danger. Besides the unpleasantness of hitting a skunk, porcupines and badgers can ruin your tires, and even small, innocuous creatures like rabbits can wreck a car moving at high speed. I once saw a Pontiac with the whole front end stove in to the firewall. When I asked the owner what he hit, he answered, "Would you believe, the biggest damn jack rabbit I've ever seen?"

Prepare for snow driving

CB radio can be used to summon help in the event you break down or get stuck, but if you are really remote, you will probably have to cope with your own emergencies. Most folks living in snow country expect to get stuck in the snow at least once each winter. This can be a disaster or an inconvenience, depending on how you're equipped.

Probably the most comforting thing you can have in the car with you in a blizzard is another person. But as an absolute minimum for winter driving, you need:

Snow tires: "All-season radials" will not do. They are ordinary road tires, made of rubber that can stand low and high temperatures. They may have tread patterns similar to snow tires, but real snow tires will work much better. If ice might be a problem, get studded snow tires, siped tires, or walnut shell retreads.

Metal studs tear up bare roads, are legal in only a few states, and then only during a certain season, which varies with the state. Studs wear down quickly when driving on bare roads, so it's best to put them on just before it snows, and get them off as soon as the last snow melts. This can be expensive unless you have them mounted on an extra set of wheels so you can change them yourself.

Siped (rhymes with "typed") tires are ordinary, new snow tires which have had extra grooves cut across the tread to increase traction on icy or wet pavement. It works very well, but does shorten the life of the tire. Don't try to save the $7-$10 per tire siping fee by doing it yourself. Without a siping machine you are sure to ruin the tire. Ask your tire dealer about siping.

Walnutshell retreads are used tires retreaded with rubber containing ground-up walnut shells. Really. They are very "sticky" on icy or wet pavement, and lots cheaper than studs or siped tires, but they wear out really fast. Plan on buying a set every winter.

If deep snow or muddy roads are likely to be a problem, ask for "mud lugs"—tires with extremely deep tread patterns. Buy your snow chains after you choose your tread patterns. Tires of the same "size" with different treads can vary greatly in actual dimensions.

Serious chains: Practice putting them on before it snows. It will be harder in the snow. Drive no faster than 30 mph with chains on, and get them off as soon as you're out of the snow. Cheap chains are only good for paved roads and a couple of inches of snow at the most. Their guarantee will do you no good if they break 40 miles from civilization. "Cable chains" are only useful for icy pavements, where they do work well. For serious snow, get serious chains with the biggest, thickest links your car will take, preferably with lugs welded to the cross-chains. They cost a lot, but they work. Treat 'em right and they'll last for years.

A heater that works and an exhaust system that won't gas you with carbon monoxide (CO). CO is a colorless, odorless gas that first gives you a headache, then puts you to sleep, then kills you. There are CO detectors available, but they're expensive and unreliable. The best defense is to have your exhaust system checked in the fall.

In addition, carry with you in the vehicle:

A shovel: Better yet, two shovels a wide one for digging out of snow drifts, and a narrow one for clearing snow out from under a car that's been "high centered."

A flashlight: For putting chains on at night. Spare batteries, too, or better yet, a spare flashlight.

A large pair of pliers, for putting on cold chains. I like pump pliers such as Channel-Loks. You also need some soft wire for tying back loose chain ends, and extra rubber "chain tighteners." A hunk of cardboard for lying down on in the snow, and a towel and an extra pair of gloves, for drying and warming your hands afterward, can be real handy.

A bag of cheap kitty litter: It's cheaper than traction sand, works far better, and doesn't freeze solid in your trunk.

A tow chain or tow rope, and a come-along.

An axe or bow saw in wooded country.

If all else fails, the following will help you keep warm overnight: **a mylar "space" blanket, a fat candle or "canned heat" and matches, some hard candy to eat, and a metal cup or pot** (or even some aluminum foil) to melt snow in for drinking.

Desert driving

In the desert you're more likely to break down than to get stuck. You'll need an extra fan belt and the tools to replace it. I've heard that a pair of pantyhose will work, but I've never known anyone who actually succeeded. Some electrician's tape, for fixing hoses, may get you where you're going. If you do get stuck in the sand, traction mats may help. Pieces of old carpet don't usually work well. Always carry water in the desert, for you and for your vehicle. Under no circumstances should you ever drink water from the radiator. Even if it's had no antifreeze in it for years, it can still kill you.

Know where your car's cooling system thermostat is and how to remove it. Sudden overheating, when there's no other, obvious cause, may be caused by a stuck thermostat. If you can't unstick it, or don't know how, removing the thermostat entirely will cure the problem temporarily. In hot weather the thermostat is not usually necessary anyway.

If you do get stuck or break down in very hot weather, don't try to go for help in the daytime. Stay in the shade and wait for night to travel on foot. It may get quite cool at night in the desert, even in the summer, so keep a jacket with you, just in case. A "space blanket" with the shiny side in can keep you warm at night, or with the shiny side out it can protect you from the sun, especially if you've brought a couple of tent poles, rope, and tent pegs.

Mountain driving

Besides the obvious dangers of overheating on steep climbs or losing brake effectiveness on long downgrades, mountain country can present other challenges to the backwoods driver.

Fallen trees can block roads. It's a good idea to keep a chainsaw with you in the mountains, or at least a good, big bow saw. I have had the experience of driving down a "one way" hill, only to find my way blocked by a downed tree. Fortunately, I was only about a quarter mile from home, so I was able to walk home and get the chainsaw. Even so, a quarter of a mile seems a lot longer, carrying a saw and gas.

Mountains can affect the way you handle snow and ice. When I first moved to Washington, my neighbors showed me how to get out of the canyon in snowy weather. Many mountain or canyon roads have a particular "trick" to driving them during bad weather. You may find that you can make it up a particular hill if you can pass a certain spot at the bottom at a particular speed. You may have to back up and "take a run at it," or you may need to drive on the wrong side of the road in certain places, to avoid ruts, mud, icy spots, etc.

Only a neighbor can tell you exactly how to navigate your particular hazards, but some general principles apply:

1. Downhill is more dangerous than uphill. To keep your speed down, pump the brakes hard, in a rapid rhythm. This will slow you down without overheating the brakes and making them fade.

2. Shift into low gear, low drive range, and/or four-wheel drive (as applicable) before starting downhill. It's easier to keep your speed down than it is to get it down. And if your speed does pick up, you may not have time to downshift.

3. Be prepared to stop by running into a snowdrift, bushes, or even by scraping against the side of a bluff. It's much better to deliberately wreck the car, under control, than to run off a steep, twisty mountain road out of control. Do not deliberately run into a tree, or into a ditch. Hitting a tree can kill you, and driving into a ditch can flip the car over. Always wear seat belts, just in case. Two friends of mine went off a crooked mountain road and tumbled 1500 feet. The one wearing a seat belt suffered a broken jaw and minor injuries. The other one died.

Mountain cars

Front-wheel drive cars climb hills much better than rear drive, but rear drive is much better for going down. You can gear down, and the slower-turning rear wheels will tend to pull the car straight in a skid. With front-wheel drive, either braking or downshifting may make the front wheels skid. The only way to improve your steering traction with front drive is to accelerate. But on a steep, slippery downhill road, you can quickly reach the point where improvement in steering from acceleration is negated by the hazards of increased speed.

If you drive two vehicles regularly, make them both either front drive or rear drive. Your first reaction in a front-wheel skid in a rear-drive car should be to back off the gas pedal, but in a front-drive car you should step on the gas. The wrong "instinctive" reaction in an emergency could easily kill you, so it's better to develop the same instinct for use in all your vehicles.

You may be able to slow down by using the parking brake. It activates only the rear brakes, so it won't make the front wheels skid. But the rear brakes are only about half as powerful as the front brakes, and will burn out faster. If allowed to lock, they will burn out immediately. If you have a lever-type brake, hold the button in while applying the brake, to prevent brake lock-up. If the parking brake is applied by a foot pedal, hold the release knob out while applying the brakes. Use parking brakes sparingly, and check for excessive wear frequently.

Another way to increase steering efficiency is to use high traction tires on the front wheels. This can help steering on a rear drive car, too. For years, before I had either front drive or four-wheel drive, I used studded snow tires or walnut shell retreads on all four wheels every winter. When you live at the bottom of a steep, mile-long grade, good steering traction is essential.

Four-wheel drive cars and trucks are by far the best for going up or down hill. They also cost at least $2000 more than a comparable front or rear-drive rig. Maintenance costs more with four-wheel drive, and tires must be purchased four at a time, to avoid getting "drive-line wrap" (this makes it hard to shift out of four-wheel drive and can eventually damage the drive train). If you do get drive-line wrap, try backing up a short distance before shifting into two-wheel drive. Gas mileage will be less with four-wheel drive.

A good compromise between the utility and the expense of four-wheel drive is two-wheel drive with a limited-slip (positive traction) differential. On any car, the right and left drive wheels must be able to turn at different rates, so the car can corner without dragging a wheel. Unfortunately, if one wheel is on a no-traction surface, it will spin, while the other drive wheel does nothing. A limited-slip differential prevents wheel-spinning on slick surfaces, increasing traction on marginal surfaces tremendously. The effective increase is almost as much as four-wheel drive and costs much less. In many cases, a limited-slip differential can be retrofitted to your current vehicle. They do cost significantly more than a normal differential, need more repairs, cost more to maintain, and decrease gas mileage.

Consider a winch

There are some circumstances where positive traction will not help. If both your drive wheels are off the road, on ice, or high-centered, they'll both spin. You either need four-wheel drive or a winch. If most of your "dangerous" driving takes place in wooded areas, the winch may be the better idea. A reasonable winch should cost less than four-wheel drive, and can be moved to your next car. It uses gas and wears down only when actually in use.

Be sure to tell the dealer what you want it for. Some cheap winches can only pull straight ahead. You want one that can pull at a fairly wide angle. It need not be able to lift the entire weight of the car. Usually, just getting the drive wheels back on solid ground will do. Make sure that mounting and appropriate cables are included, or find out what they'll cost. If you're not sure there will always be a tree to anchor your winch to, four-wheel drive may still be the way to go. Best bet if you can afford it: four-wheel drive and a winch.

London fog

Whatever kind of rig you've got, driving it in the backwoods is not going to be like "civilized" driving. Navigation can be a problem where road signs are non-existent, and even landmarks may be few and far between. As you become intimate with the roads near your home, you'll find yourself navigating by the shape and texture of the road itself. The wheat fields above the canyon I call home are sometimes subject to nighttime fogs as thick as London's. Friends from the city are terrified to drive in them.

I was too, the first time. In fog so thick you couldn't see the headlights of an oncoming car 50 feet away, I wondered what would keep someone from climbing up my rear bumper, assuming someone else was crazy enough to be out in such weather. I need not have worried. There were others out in the fog, but they were all going as slowly as I was. I drove, and my passenger walked with her hand on the hood of the car. When we came to the turns, I just followed her hand. We made it home, and that's the bottom line. It took awhile, but in the backwoods it ain't when you get there that matters, it's whether. ∆

The miracle of a country birth

By Sally Denney

We are greenhorns, beginners in large animal husbandry, although we have owned several pets: dogs, cats, rabbits, guinea pigs, hamsters, and chickens. We have until now been city bound, so we've always had our large animals spayed or neutered.

But now we've moved to the country, and the upcoming birth of our new goat kids will be our first family experience of the miracle of birth outside of the clinical setting of a hospital. We are anxious, to say the least.

As our two does (nannies) head closer to their estimated due dates, we are vigilantly checking on them. Being novices, we are alert for any sign of an impending birth. We have our iodine and baby food jar ready (they are needed for dipping kid navels to prevent infection), old towels and hair dryer (needed for drying our prospective kids—we have been warned to dry a Nubian's ears thoroughly or the tips will freeze in the low spring temperatures), white thread, and sterile scissors, all packed into a hand basket, waiting by the back door ready for a quick trip to the barn.

The basket reminds us that we will soon be seeing what we've been awaiting since last October. Its supplies remind us that veterinarians we are not and our apprehension sends me once again to my goat books and my husband once again to check on the expecting mothers.

Time drags and, while we wait, we drive our goat owning friends and neighbors crazy with questions.

"What do you think?" I'll call them and ask every time one of the does makes a grunt or a different move.

"The goat books say..." has been one of my standard lead sentences. I've said it so often to the lady I bought and bred our goats from that she suggested maybe I should read the books to the goats and then they will know what they are supposed to be doing.

The goats think we're strange. We go to their stalls and stand around looking at them as if they are our prize watermelons. The goats are generally excited about our presence. They normally fight for their fair share of petting. But now they are growing bored with us. They fall asleep and we continue to wait.

The youngest of the two nannies is having a discharge. Is this a sign? A neighbor, who has been in the goat business for a number of years, stopped over and told us, after a quick inspection, not to expect any babies for at least four days. "Their udders aren't full enough...they'll be tight and hot before they go." To my consternation, she says this in front of the goats and now I'm sure they will take the four days' leeway as a reprieve.

Materials to have on hand for a large animal birth:
White thread or iodized navel clamps
Scissors
Iodine
Small jar (baby food jar is ideal) for iodine
Old towels
Hair dryer
Bucket for carrying supplies

The oldest nanny looks at me as the neighbor leaves and I'm sure she's grinning with an I-could-have-told-you-that expression.

A week later the discharge is thicker and coming faster. We are eagerly anticipating the big event. But is this discharge something or nothing?

Every two hours I check on the young doe. She seems normal, except that every time the cat tries to enter her pen, she nips at the cat, chasing her away. This isn't normal for her . . . the young nanny is very friendly to everyone, including our black cocker spaniel.

Noon. Nothing has happened.

At 3:30 p.m. I mosey on down to the barn just to see if there is any change. One of the does is breathing heavy and grunting. A tiny black hoof breaks from the vaginal opening. Is it

a front or a back leg? I pray for a front.

I pray for a speedy delivery and that everything is normal for the goat and for me, as I'm home alone. The children are on the school bus heading home and my husband is at work.

I run to the house for my basket. I telephone my husband, but he isn't in. I hope he is on his way home.

I return to the barn. The nanny is pushing but hasn't lain down. The books and the lady I bought her from said she would lie down when the time is close.

They were wrong.

The hoof reappears and a few minutes later another hoof appears. A nose a second later and then the kid hits the ground. I jump into the stall with towels. Together the doe and I clean this new life.

The young doe licks my hair in a thank you. I dry the new kid with a hair dryer.

Five or ten minutes later the mother starts contracting again. My husband arrives shortly before this happens. He says he sees a nose. I'm still drying the first kid and I don't look immediately. The nanny bellows. I take a look. The second kid is coming breech.

Will he suffocate before he's born?

As the mother contracts, I gently pull. A minute later a new buck enters the world coughing and spitting. I use the aspirator on him and begin drying his thick fur with towels and the hair dryer.

We have two new goats, a buck and a doe. One at a time, I pick them up and dip their navels. When they are down, they begin looking for their first meal.

They stand on wobbly legs. Our first miracle down on the farm. Δ

A BHM Computer Wizard's Profile

Tim Green

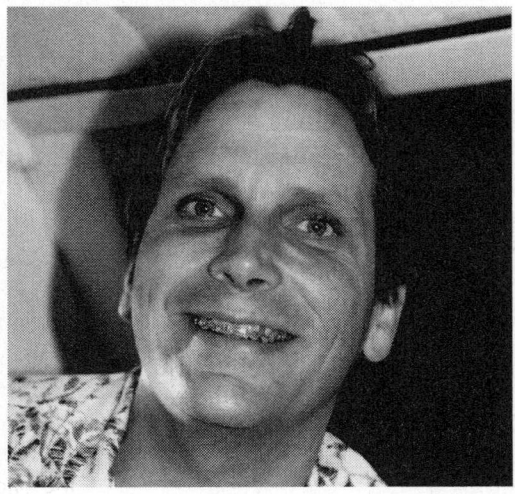

Tim Green is more than just *Backwoods Home Magazine*'s computer wizard. Without his faith, encouragement, and financial assistance BHM might never have been started. Years ago when Dave Duffy, *BHM*'s founder and publisher, was an aspiring carpenter, he remodeled a large garage for Green, turning it into a rental apartment. Little did Duffy know that he would be living there two years later while starting a magazine. The first issues of *BHM* were put together on the floor of Tim Green's garage.

Later, Green designed and set up the computer network that allows our staff to create pages, layouts, subscriber lists, etc. He can frequently solve our computer problems by phone. Green is a partner in the magazine and he and Duffy are personal friends. Tim Green lives in Ventura, California, with his wife. His business e-mail address is tge@pacbell.net.

A BHM Writer's Profile

Jan Cook

Jan Cook has been with *Backwoods Home Magazine* since the beginning, as a writer, an editor, and as the principal typist for entire issues. She has at various times been *BHM*'s crafts editor. In her "other life" she has been a technical writer for the Department of Defense for 15 years.

Jan calls herself a creative seamstress but her latest passion is machine embroidery, and she embellishes anything she finds on the floor—which has taught her husband and son to pick up after themselves.

She is currently helping to organize a group of those who are interested in machine embroidery; those interested can reach her at JaninSoCal@aol.com.

Jan says she's a cut-to-the-chase kind of person with little tolerance for things that are supposed to work but don't. She believes in life's simpler things, like poems should rhyme and people should be as good as their word.

Make delicious wine at home

By Charles Sanders

The art and practice of wine making is an ancient and time-honored one. My guess is that some early man let his grapes or juice sit a little too long, and a strange, yet not unpleasant, taste accompanied ingestion of the fermented foodstuff. After gorging himself on the mysterious concoction, he probably ended up collapsing on the floor of the cave, and began seeing pink mastodons walking across the ceiling. Perhaps he decided that he could repeat the experience by deliberately allowing the grapes to ferment. The rest is history.

From the days of early man, allowing natural fermentation of fruit and juice to occur in crude vessels, to the high-tech, computer-controlled stainless steel wineries of today, the basic process of winemaking has remained unchanged. Very simply put, wine is made when yeast converts fruit sugar to alcohol. Winemaking involves influencing and controlling the fermentation process to obtain wine of a desired flavor with the desired degree of sweetness and alcohol content.

The home winemaker can make a multitude of tasty and well made wines. As with the other foods produced on the homestead, you will know exactly what ingredients are in the finished product. You do not need to use potentially harmful chemicals, clarifying agents, etc., and can still end up with superb wines, suitable for serving to even the most finicky friends. Of course, not every wine will please every taste, but that, again, is one of the pleasures of making your own wine. You can experiment with ingredients, sugar content, yeast types, and fermentation methods. It is a good use of fruit produced on the home place. In many cases, even home-produced honey can be used to sweeten your wines. And, in fact, even bad wine can be permitted to complete the fermentation process by exposing it to air, resulting in some good and very useable vinegar.

If you record information about your ingredients and procedures, you will know how to repeat your successes and discard the failures. In addition, good wine recipes are often passed on to offspring, much as a grandfather passes down a treasured shotgun. Essentially, home winemaking is just another part of being as self-sufficient as possible. By possessing the knowledge and ability to make your own fine wines at home, you can save a good deal of money, depending upon your level of wine consumption.

The U.S. Bureau of Alcohol, Tobacco, and Firearms permits the head of a household to make up to 100 gallons of wine or beer for each adult in the household, with a 200 gallon limit. Such production is limited to beverages produced for consumption in the home. I'd suggest that you locate the ATF office serving your area in a directory listing federal government agencies and contact them for further information. Note, too, that the regulations apply to the making of wine and beer only, and not whiskeys, brandies, or other distilled spirits.

The actual process of making wine is not overly complicated. However, it does take a bit of time in the kitchen and some space where you can allow the fermenting juice to do its thing. Simple setups such as the one illustrated are very serviceable and dependable. In fact, I use one or more of the jug-and-tube arrangements nearly every time I make wine. For larger batches, 5 or 6 gallon glass jugs are available from winemaker suppliers or some industrial outlets. The caps of these large jugs can be fitted with a commercially available air lock or can easily, and at no cost, be rigged up to work just like the milk jug and tube, as illustrated.

For the more ambitious winemaker who anticipates many evenings of wine guzzling around the winter woodstove, I'd recommend purchasing a used whiskey barrel or two to

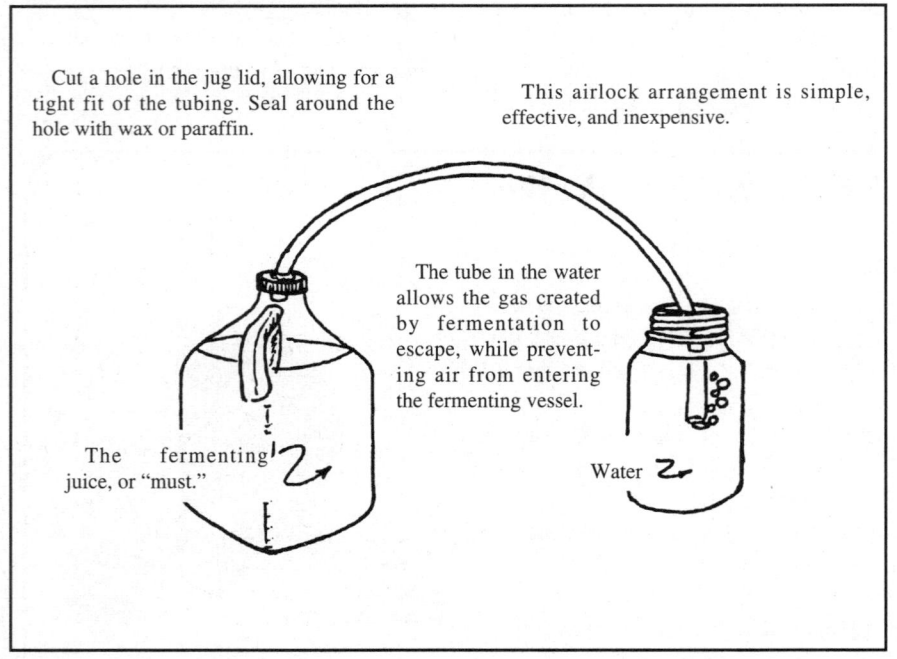

Cut a hole in the jug lid, allowing for a tight fit of the tubing. Seal around the hole with wax or paraffin.

This airlock arrangement is simple, effective, and inexpensive.

The tube in the water allows the gas created by fermentation to escape, while preventing air from entering the fermenting vessel.

The fermenting juice, or "must."

Water

Materials: one or more plastic milk jugs, one quart jar, approximately 2 to 2½ feet of plastic tubing for each vessel, and a punch for making the hole in the lid.

use as fermenting vessels. But remember that it takes a pretty good wine appetite to down 50 gallons of homemade wine. Additionally, especially for the beginner, a one or two gallon mistake is easier to get rid of than a 50 gallon one.

So, follow the general directions given here and enjoy some mighty tasty wine that you'll be delighted to serve to your friends. Once you get the hang of it, don't be afraid to experiment with ingredients or to adjust the sugar content to better suit your taste. You will make a few mistakes, but even some of those will be quite drinkable! After a while, though, you will end up with a favorite wine of your own making and will likely have a hard time answering requests for samples of bottles of the delightful drink.

The accompanying illustration shows how easily a home fermentation setup can be made for little or no cost at all. As you can see, an ordinary plastic milk jug is simply recycled to become the fermentation vessel. The cap of the jug is punched to accommodate a length of plastic tubing, which in turn runs into a jar of water. This arrangement forms the air lock and provides an escape for the gases forming within the fermentation jug, yet allows no air to get into the vessel to spoil the wine. The tubing which I used was just the size to allow me to use a fired .357 magnum pistol case to neatly punch the hole in the plastic jug lid. The tubing fit tightly into the hole, but I sealed it with a bit of melted candle wax just to make sure there were no leaks. You can easily make several of these jugs and tubes and run them all into the same vessel of water.

The recipes below are the same ones that we use at home to make many fine wines. Try them yourself, and adjust the ingredients, if necessary, to make the wine acceptable to your taste. This first recipe includes the essential method to be used with the other, following, recipes. On subsequent recipes, additional instructions are included as necessary. Remember, though, that the basic process is included in this first recipe.

Grape wine #1

Either black, green, or white grapes may be used for this recipe, and the resulting wine will please just about anyone.

| 4 lb. grapes |
| 3½ lb. sugar |
| 1 oz. dry yeast (or one envelope dry yeast) |
| 1 gal. water |

Pick the grapes from the stalks and crush them by hand. Pour the boiling water over them and leave to soak for 48 hours. Strain and put the juice through a jelly bag or similar material to remove as much of the fine pulp as possible. Put the juice in a large pan and heat slightly. Add the sugar to the warm juice (the sugar will dissolve better in the heated juice than if it were cold). When the sugar is dissolved, sprinkle the yeast on top and stir in. Put the soon-to-be wine into the fermenting vessel, attach the air lock, and ferment for fourteen days, or until bubbles are no longer emitting from the plastic tube.

After fermentation is complete, siphon the new wine into a clean container, being careful not to shake the container and disturb the sediment in the bottom. The purpose of siphoning new wine is to separate the liquid from the sediment (also called the lees), which settles to the bottom. So be careful when siphoning not to let the wine go back through the tube and stir up the lees. The process of siphoning off the wine to allow the sediment to settle out is called "racking." Usually only one time is necessary to produce a good clear wine.

However, the wine may be racked two or three times to produce even greater clarity. For a second or third racking, place the container in a cool place for several months, and again siphon off the wine. It should now be ready for bottling and/or drinking. If this wine is stored in gallon plastic jugs or in corked glass bottles, it will continue to age and improve in quality.

Raspberry wine
(My personal favorite)

| 4½ lb. raspberries |
| 3½ lb. sugar |
| 1 oz. yeast |
| 1 gal. water |

Crush the raspberries, pour the boiling water over them and leave to soak for 48 hours. Strain the juice and pulp through a jelly bag. Heat the strained juice to near boiling and simmer for two minutes. Pour the hot liquid over the sugar and stir until all the sugar is dissolved. Allow the brew to cool, and then sprinkle the yeast on top and stir in. Funnel into the fermenting vessel and attach an air lock. Ferment for fourteen days, or until fermentation ceases. Bottle as with Grape #1. Enjoyed on a cold winter evening, this wine is pure ambrosia!

Cherry wine

| 6 lb. black cherries |
| 4 lb. sugar |
| 1 oz. yeast |
| 1 gal. water |

Crush the cherries and pour the boiling water over them. Leave to soak for 48 hours. Strain through a piece of muslin and then through a jelly bag. Heat the juice to near boiling and simmer for a couple of minutes. Pour the hot juice over the sugar and stir until all the sugar is dissolved. As soon as the sweetened juice is cool, sprinkle the yeast on top and stir in. Put into the fermenting vessel, attach an air lock and ferment for fourteen days. Bottle as with Grape #1.

Blackberry wine

| 5 lb. blackberries |
| 4 lb. sugar |
| 1 oz. yeast |
| 1 gal. water |

Crush the berries, pour the boiling water over them. While the pulp is still hot, strain through a piece of muslin and then put through a jelly bag. Heat the strained juice to near boiling and simmer for a couple of minutes. Pour the hot juice over the sugar and stir until all the sugar is dissolved. As soon as the brew is cooled, add the yeast and stir it in. Put into the fermenting vessel and attach an air lock. Let the wine work for two weeks, or until fermentation ceases. Bottle as with Grape #1.

Honey-berry wine

| 1 cup honey |
| 1 cup crushed strawberries |
| 4 lb. sugar |
| 1 oz. yeast |
| 1 gal. water |

Put the honey and fruit into a large vessel. Boil half the sugar in a quart of water for a couple of minutes. Cool and add to the honey and fruit. Put in a gallon of boiled and cooled water. Add the yeast. Boil the remaining sugar in a quart of water. Cool and add. Put the brew into the fermenting vessel and work until all fermentation stops. Bottle. This is a good one!

Up-north whisky

This is not a real whisky, that is, a distilled liquor. The wheat added to the wine gives it a "whisky-like" appearance and taste. It is another very good wine.

| 2 lb. wheat |
| 2 lb. raisins |
| 4 large oranges |
| 4 lb. sugar |
| 1 oz. yeast |
| 1 gal. water |

Heat the water to boiling and pour over the sugar. Stir until dissolved and add the wheat and chopped-up raisins. Cut up the oranges and squeeze, adding the freshly squeezed juice to the rest of the brew. Allow it all to cool, and then add the yeast and stir in. Pour into fermenting vessel and allow to work until all fermentation stops, usually in two to three weeks. Strain and bottle.

Strawberry wine

| 4 lb. strawberries |
| 2½ lb. sugar |
| 1 oz. yeast |
| 1 gal. water |

Boil the water and pour it over the crushed fruit. Let stand for a few hours, stirring occasionally. Strain well through a jelly bag. Heat the mixture to near boiling and simmer for two minutes. Pour over the sugar and stir until all is dissolved. Allow the whole mess to cool, sprinkle the yeast on top and stir in. Put it to working in the fermenting vessel, and once all fermentation has ceased, bottle.

Welch wine

This is an easily prepared wine using frozen grape juice concentrate. Tasty! You can also try the recipe using white grapes. It makes a delightful white wine.

| 7 12-oz. cans frozen grape juice concentrate |
| 7 or 8 lbs. sugar |
| 1 oz. yeast |
| 5 gal. water |

Mix the juice concentrate into the warm water. Make sure that all the juice dissolves. Add the sugar to the mixture, stirring until all is dissolved. As soon as everything is cooled to approximately room temperature or slightly above, add the yeast and stir in. Pour into your fermentation vessels and attach air locks. Let the wine work until all signs of fermentation stop. Siphon off and bottle.

"Blue fox" grape wine
(Using wild Fox Grapes)

| 8 lb. wild grapes |
| 5 lb. sugar |
| 1 oz. yeast |
| 2 gal. water |

Strip the grapes from the stalks and crush them in a large crock or pan. Pour the boiling water over the fruit and let soak for 48 hours. Strain the juice through muslin, and then through a jelly bag. Heat the juice to near boiling and add the sugar, stirring until all is dissolved. Once the mixture is cooled, add the yeast and stir in. Funnel into the fermenting vessel and attach the air lock. Let it work for fourteen days, or until fermentation ceases. Siphon off and bottle.

Country peach wine

| 5 lb. fresh ripe peaches |
| 4 lb. sugar |
| 1 oz. yeast |
| 1 gal. water |

Cut up the peaches and remove the stones. Heat the water to boiling and pour over the fruit. Let stand for a few hours. As soon as the mixture cools well, crush the fruit well by hand. Let the mixture stand for 48 hours. Crush the fruit well again, then strain through fine muslin. Heat the juice to boiling and simmer for 10 to 12 minutes. Next, pour the hot juice over the sugar and stir until well blended. Allow the whole solution to cool, then add the yeast by sprinkling it into the juice and stirring. Put the liquid into the fermenting vessels and allow it to work for about fourteen days, or until it stops. Siphon off and bottle. This one is a real taste of summer on a cold winter day!

As with most other facets of self-reliant living, try to use what you have or can make or scrounge. Experiment with your own types of fruit and proportions of ingredients. ∆

Grapes — with 3000 varieties, you can grow them just about anywhere in North America

By Martin P. Waterman

It is unfortunate that a fruit as desirable, productive, and useful as the grape is not more widely grown. Most would-be grape growers do not consider planting this fruit because of the perception that grapes are difficult to grow. Fortunately, nothing could be further from the truth. Growing grapes is not as difficult as many believe.

There are more varieties of grapes (3000 plus) than any kind of fruit. This does not include several native species that have been and are being used to successfully breed grapes that can survive in practically every region of the world.

North America is blessed with many native varieties. While these native varieties provided ample food for the Indians and settlers, their best use has been as an aid in breeding with high quality grapes originating in Europe, Asia and the Middle East. The best of both worlds is being bred into grapes ideally suited for our North American climate. This is often necessary since grapes originating from outside this continent tend to be finicky and prone to diseases, pests, stress from temperature extremes, and other maladies while the North American grapes are naturally well-adapted to our climate.

Due to breeding and improved methods of culture, the day when every gardener in the United States can grow grapes has arrived. Whether you garden under the frigid temperatures of the great plains or in humid subtropical south Florida or high in the Rocky Mountains, you should be able to find a variety that can take the worst that Mother Nature can dish out.

Grapes can be used for wine, fresh eating, raisins, jellies, jams and preserves. They can also be added to many meals and desserts. Craft people have an affinity with the vine since the canes can be used to make baskets or Christmas wreaths.

Valiant is one of the hardiest and most dependable grapes for the garden. Developed in South Dakota, this grape is rumored to be able to survive temperatures of -50° F! In blind taste tests, the juice and jam from this grape rival those of Concord, the standard grape of the processing industry. The author averages 17-22 pounds of fruit per vine.

With so many uses, some planning is advisable when you ponder the growing of grapes. This will put you in a better position to be able to choose the right variety for your own particular needs.

There are three pieces of advice I give anyone who wants to grow grapes. First, do not pay much attention to the uses that are traditionally associated with a variety. I have grown hundreds of varieties of grapes and one of my first mistakes was to allow other people and their perceptions to influence my grape growing. For instance, I grow many wine grapes. For the most part, many of them will never see the inside of a wine bottle. However, the same characteristics that make wine grapes excellent for making wine, such as high sugar and intense fruity flavors also make them far tastier than most table grapes. Wine grapes are rarely sold for eating because they usually have straggly clusters and small berries. For wine grapes, a higher concentration of skin to pulp is desirable, since the skin contains most of the flavor and color. Another reason that you may never get to taste wine grapes is that they command a much higher price than for table grapes. Conversely, many dessert or eating grapes make wines that most people would feel excel over the over-oaked and much touted French and California vintages. Home made wines are some of the best wines I have tasted, many of them coming from non-traditional grape varieties (the thought of which would make a wine connoisseur cringe).

The other piece of advice is try as many varieties as you can and then keep the varieties that do best in your area. Grapes are easy to propagate from dormant cuttings and a single mature vine can provide enough cuttings for over 100 new vines.

Don't grow commercial varieties. In the majority of cases, they are usually only grown for characteristics that make them tough enough to endure handling and storage. They also tend to be very neutral flavored in order to please a wide group of tastes. Grapes can mimic almost any fruit flavor. Riesling has hints of apple while Cabernet Sauvingnon is often compared to black currants. Each grape has its own individual flavor and personality. When I give some of my more flavorful or muscat grape varieties to people to taste, they usually say that they had no idea a grape could be so packed with flavor.

Commercial grapes also tend to have small berries. Commercial growers do not like large berries and clusters. For the home gardener, however, large clusters and berries are welcomed. Some varieties (when cluster thinned) can produce breathtaking five-pound clusters a foot and a half in length. It pays to shop around and find the grape varieties that are most likely to serve your needs.

Grape culture

Since all grape varieties and their hybrids are descended from wild stock, their needs are not elaborate. Once you understand a few basic principles about grape growing, you can become a competent backyard viticulturist.

There are some basic rules to growing grapes that relate to planting, site selection, pruning, training and disease control.

Grapes can be planted in the spring or the fall. If planted in the spring, you can use bare-rooted material as long as the vine is dormant and the roots are not allowed to dry out.

Grapes can be successfully planted in the autumn if they are potted. Vines should be planted at least eight feet apart because a vine after the sixth or seventh year can become very large. Many of the newer vines, once established, become quite vigorous. When planting your vine, remember it has to be carefully removed from the pot and placed in a hole which has been prepared for it using a good loose soil mix and some moisture. Unless the vine is severely root bound, care should be taken not to disturb the roots unless the vine is dormant. If the hole is dry, it will act as a wick and remove moisture from the vine, so be sure to moisten the sides and bottom of the hole. The hole should be large enough so that the new vine will have at least one and a half to two feet of loose soil in all directions in order for the roots to expand.

In the autumn, even though the vine will become dormant and shed its leaves, its roots will continue to take up nutrients until the very cold weather arrives. In the spring, the roots will become active again before the buds push. Even though the vine may appear barren and dormant above ground, the roots will be busy growing and gathering nutrients. By spring, the vine will be on its way to becoming established. This is important because the grower has a vine that is better prepared to survive summer droughts than a vine planted in the spring. In addition, by planting a vine in the fall, fruiting can often be advanced by a full year. Furthermore, a vine that is healthier is in a better position to fight off the pressure of pests and diseases.

With site selection, there are three very important rules to follow. Choose a location to maximize the sun's light and establish good air and water drainage. Any area that will reflect heat is of extra value. Try growing a vine against a wall, a fence or near a patio, and you will be able to speed ripening and decrease the negative effects of winter.

Air drainage serves two purposes. The first is frost protection. Frost flows like a river seeking lower altitudes. Therefore, do not plant grapes at the bottom of a hill or valley unless there is a large body of water nearby capable of retaining heat. The other type of air drainage is a good steady breeze. Grapes that are grown where there is good air circulation are less likely to succumb to mildews.

Water drainage is also important. By planting your grapes on a hill for good frost drainage, you may also be able to have good water drainage. Grapes will not tolerate growing in wet, poorly drained areas.

All grapes need to be pruned. In the wild, grapes rarely fruit. Most of the vine's energy goes towards vegetative growth instead of fruit production. By pruning as much as 80% of the old growth away, you are forcing nutrients and growth into fewer buds and the result is annual fruit production. Grapes have always been known as great producers. Some varieties in California will produce over 25 tons per acre. In some markets, wine can be purchased cheaper than milk or orange juice.

Since grapes have the natural habit of being climbers, they commonly will climb a tree trying to reach sunlight and thus can easily grow over 100 feet in height. Of course, this result is not desired. When you prune a grape vine, you may have to cut off as much as two thirds to three quarters of the fruitful buds. There are hundreds of pruning methods available and you can find a good argument for the usage of almost all of them. However, there is one constant rule to follow. For most vines that are over three years old, you should prune the vines so that 30 buds remain plus 10 extra buds for each additional pound of wood. The first year, the vine should be pruned to form one or two trunks. Vines with two trunks or multiple trunks are becoming popular. In New York State, growers have found that a vine trained to two or more trunks will always have one trunk survive in those exceptionally cold winters that can happen every few decades or so.

The shaping that you use will depend on the purpose you have in mind for your vines. All vines need some type of support. Increasingly, this support comes in the form of some type of training. Grapes can be trained to cover arbors, walls, chain link fences, archways and, of course, trellises. A short trellis in the backyard makes a useful backyard divider, and in the summer when it is covered with foliage and fruit, it also acts as a convenient privacy hedge. If you plan to grow several vines on a trellis, most books on pruning will show a number of different methods for training grapes in a vineyard.

The basic way to grow grapes organically is to choose a good site and then choose several varieties of disease resistant vines and hope for the best. Fortunately, many of the new grapes have a great deal of disease resistance.

The major problems with grapes come from mildews but these can be controlled with sulphur sprays. Many of the newer varieties are superior at resisting mildews. Some kinds of grapes at the supermarket have so much sulphur spray residue left on them that I suppose that you could use them to make gunpowder. In the autumn, when most of the rains come, a favorable environment is created for the development of mildews. If you choose early ripening grapes such as the ones recommended in this article, you may be able to grow no spray grapes unless you are in a very humid area. However, mildews late in the season seem to benefit a vine. I have talked to several grape growers and breeders who have told me that when you spray a vine late in the season, the vine has a tendency to put out new succulent growth. This depletes the vine of nutrients and this new growth is killed during the winter. By not spraying the mildews, you help to defoliate the vines, to slow down their growth and to mature good dark wood and thus help them to survive the winter.

A good strategy is to grow a variety of different grapes. This way, statistically, most will not be affected by weather, insects or diseases in the same season.

Sources

The best way to locate and purchase grape varieties is to write various nurseries and request their catalogs. These names can usually be found in any gardening magazine. Seedless grapes tend to be the most popular choices. If you want to grow wine varieties, visit wineries in your area. Most wineries will give or sell you cuttings and will be able to tell you which grapes are best suited for growing in your area.

There has often been difficulty finding grape vines that can take cold temperature extremes. The two best sources for hardy grape material are the new hybrids being developed by Cornell University in Geneva, New York and the varieties bred by private breeders such as Elmer Swenson. Elmer Swenson, a retired dairy farmer, has been breeding grapes in Wisconsin for over 50 years and his varieties provide much of the basis for the wine industry in Minnesota.

Most nursery catalogs will tell you the zones suitable for their grapes. If you desire a hardiness zone map, the new giant USDA Plant Hardiness Zone Map (S/N 001-000-04550-4) is available for $6.50 from the Superintendent of Documents, Government Printing Office, Washington, D.C., 20402. You can call the order desk at (202) 783-3238. While you are at it, you may want to ask for a catalog of their publications.

Another useful guide is <u>Growing Grapes in Minnesota</u>, which is a 62 page booklet on growing grapes in cold climates. It is available for $5.50 plus $1.50 postage & handling from the Minnesota Grape Growers Association, P. O. Box 10605, White Bear Lake, Minnesota, 55110. This book will answer any question you are likely to encounter, from building a trellis to variety selection. If you are serious about growing grapes, you will probably want to join this excellent organization that is at the forefront of hardy grape growing. Minnesota growers are in U.S.D.A. zones 2B to 4B.

Lake Sylvia Vineyard Nursery (Rt. 1 Box 149, South Haven, Minnesota, 55382) will send you their catalog free if you send an S.A.S.E. They feature hardy varieties with most of them developed by grape breeders such as Elmer Swenson and Dave MacGregor.

Lake Sylvia Vineyards Nursery has also released two of Elmer Swenson's hardy seedless selections: E.S. 3-20-36 and E.S. 3-22-18 which are hardy to about -35F and -30F respectively. E.S. 3-20-36 is very early with small red seedless berries that are almost candy-like in flavor. E.S. 3-22-18 is a blue grape with larger berries and a larger bunch. The future looks good for hardy seedless grapes. The University of Minnesota is currently evaluating some excellent selections that I believe will revolutionize grape growing in the north, at least for the small grower and hobbyist.

Another source is theNew York State Fruit Testing Cooperative Association (NYSFTA), P.O. Box 462, Geneva, New York, 14456-0462. The $10.00 annual membership fee entitles each member to the annual catalog, newsletters, and the privilege of purchasing plant material and notification of the annual meeting. NYSFTA distributes grape varieties developed by Cornell University and other breeders and has a wide variety of fruits.

Some of the early seedless varieties available at Geneva can survive in the southern part of the state. Notable seedless varieties are Einset, Reliance, and Interlaken.

Another resource worth considering is the North American Fruit Explorers, Route 1, Box 94, Chapin, Illinois, 62628. This organization is a conglomeration of fruit hobbyists who trade ideas, discoveries, and plant materials. The centerpiece of the organization is their quarterly journal *Pomona*, which is entirely written by members. The coordinator of Fruit Test Groups and Consultants is Lon Rombough (13113 Ehlen Rd., Aurora, Oregon, 97002). He is a specialist at locating hard to find grapes and has one of the largest and most unique private collections in the nation.

(Martin P. Waterman is a frequent contributor to this magazine. His grape breeding program is internationally recognized. He plants several thousand seedlings from his crosses each year, striving to develop hardier seedless and wine grape varieties for the north.) Δ

Garden huckleberries — these hardy, firm berries are easy to grow, as tasty as blueberries

By Bonnie Gelle

You know how your neighbor has been telling you plant Wonder Worker Carrots. You'll love them. And Aunt Em says, "You've never seen such great squash as Indiana Jones Early Yellow." So you shrug and think, "Yeah, sure! For me, they'd sprout, curl up, and blow away."

One summer, my mother was raving about growing great huckleberries when she was young. My curiosity aroused, I checked with our County Extension Agent who said, "They don't grow well this far north."

Trying something new

I overcame my distrust of well-intentioned advice and the discouragement of an expert and ordered Garden Huckleberry seeds from Stokes Seeds in 1987. I planted a 15-foot row. Now I'm hooked.

This itty-bitty seed has almost 100% germination and needs no TLC in my northern Minnesota garden. It grows into a healthy three-foot wonder which yields the easiest fruit to harvest and makes wonderful blue fruit treats.

Stokes Seeds of Buffalo, NY, is one of the few companies offering seeds of Solanum melanocerasum, or Garden Huckleberry. I've ordered my vegetable seeds from them for the past 10 years because all their seed packets offer the most helpful planting and harvesting advice. The huckleberry packet even contains a recipe for pies.

That packet also includes the advice to start huckleberries indoors, transplanting outside after danger of frost. I've done that but find that my blue fruit plants can be direct seeded successfully. I'm for anything that eliminates extra time and effort.

Care and maintenance

I direct-sow these tiny seeds sparsely into a row that increases in length yearly. I've been amazed at the germination.

When the seedlings are three inches tall, I thin them to a spacing of three inches. When they are six inches tall, I thin again to leave a foot between the healthy youngsters.

Since I have my row of huckleberries spaced 30 inches from my other vegetable plantings, I can cultivate them the same time I take the Allis Chalmers "G" and the cultivator through the beans, carrots, and sweet corn. Eventually the vigorous growth of these bushes shades out weeds, so all I need to do is cultivate weekly until they get too tall for that. They even seem to do well where the garden is shaded part of the day.

The plants resemble short trees by late July. Clusters of tiny white blossoms dot the bushes, and berries begin to form. Within a month, the berries swell and turn from olive green through stages of purple until they are a glossy blue-black. The berries are very firm and usually ½ to ¾ inches in diameter.

Harvesting

Harvesting begins as soon as the berries are usable, which is usually early- to mid-September. Some sources say that huckleberries are better after a light frost. There's no such thing in my neck of the woods, so I don't take chances. I get 'em while the gettin's good.

Huckleberries are seedier than blueberries but just as tasty. What I don't use as they mature, I throw into pint-size freezer bags for use during the winter. Huckleberries are greatest in the all-American blue fruit pie. I also like to use them in muffins, syrup, and jelly.

Let me invite you to try huckleberries. You'll get hooked too!

Here are some ways I use this blue fruit:

Huckleberry muffins

Preheat oven to 350°.
Wash & drain 1½ cups fresh or frozen huckleberries.
Pour ½ cup orange juice over ½ cup rolled oats. Stir. Let stand while you prepare the dry ingredients.

---
2 cups flour
½ cup sugar
1½ tsp. baking powder
½ tsp. salt
½ tsp. soda
½ tsp. cinnamon

To the oatmeal and juice, add:

---
1 slightly beaten egg
½ cup oil

Stir in the dry ingredients. Add the huckleberries.
Fill muffin cups 2/3 full of batter. Bake at 350 degrees about 25 minutes or until the tops look light brown.

Blue fruit pie (huckleberry version)

Prepare your favorite two-crust pastry recipe. Line pie plate with bottom crust. Fill with mixture of:

> 3 cups fresh or frozen, drained huckleberries
> 1 cup sugar
> 4 Tbsp. flour
> 1 tsp. cinnamon
> Dash of salt

Dot with margarine. Cover with top crust. Bake pie at 350 degrees for approximately 1 hour.

Huckleberry cake

Sauce: Cook 2 cups huckleberries in ½ cup water in small saucepan. Boil 1 minute. Stir in 1 cup sugar and 1 Tbsp. cornstarch. Continue cooking, stirring constantly, until the sauce thickens and looks clear. Set aside to cool.

Cake batter: Use any yellow cake mix. Prepare according to package directions, except diminish the water by ¼ cup. Pour into greased and floured 9 x 13 pan.

Add 1 Tbsp. of lemon juice to cooled sauce and swirl sauce over the cake batter (the sauce will sink to the bottom of the pan while the cake bakes).

Bake for the time recommended on the package. Let cool. Cut into pieces and flip over for serving. Good with ice cream or whipped cream, or sprinkle powdered sugar on each slice as you serve it. Δ

A BHM Writer's Profile

Phil Wilcox

Phil Wilcox, a mostly retired East Coast transplant, lives on his semi-remote 20 acres about 100 miles north of San Francisco, California. He designs, sells, and installs remote solar home power systems. His own cabin is solar powered with propane for cooking and refrigeration, and he heats his home with wood.

Phil also has a deep love for hot springs and travels North America in search of them. He photographs and writes about them for Aqua Thermal Access, publisher of guide books on the subject. As time permits he also writes for other publications and tries to find time for working in his vegetable garden, fishing, camping, swimming, four-wheeling, hiking and otherwise enjoying Mother Nature. He would like to find a young lady to join him in these adventures. He may be reached at: P.O. Box 1460, Lower Lake, CA 95457

Short season gardening

By Dynah Geissal

I've read just about every gardening book in my public library, but most of them are virtually useless for someone in my situation. A few have a brief section on short season gardening, but the advice is quite limited. If you are trying to learn to garden in an area with fewer than ninety frost free-days, this article is for you.

Montana is not noted for its lengthy growing season, but combined with the problems of altitude and latitude, I also live in a frost pocket. My garden regularly loses at least a week on each end of the season, compared to gardens only five miles away. As an example, light frosts are common all over the area the first week of July, but at my house thirty degrees is the rule.

Around here June 1st is the traditional time for setting out tomato plants, but even then it's a gamble. Having lost mine the year before, I prudently waited until June 15th. When everyone lost their plants June 5th, I gloried in my foresight only to lose mine on the 16th. For two years in a row we've had killing frosts on August 25th.

None of these horror stories are unusual for Montana, except for the fact that we had five years of exceptional weather that spoiled us. Those were drought years that carried with them ideal gardening weather. We only get about twelve inches of moisture a year (mostly it is snow), but our water table is only five feet down so watering was never a problem.

During those years we got enough tomatoes for canning, where ordinarily tomatoes are ripened inside after the season with only a few ripening on the vine. We got plenty of full size ears of corn for freezing, and green beans and winter squash were abundant. One year we even got peppers, which is almost unheard of.

The moral is that we forgot to rely on the vegetables that get us through most years: cole crops, root crops and greens. Face it, tomatoes and peppers are more fun than turnips and cabbage. I learned my lesson this year, as did many other people. We had babied tomato plants in my green room for the entire spring and neglected my cole crops. I had raised three hundred basil plants, but only ten turnips.

The tomato and pepper plants sat stunted until the end of July. In August they began to flower, and the frost hit on the 25th. Fifty-degree days coupled with forty-degree nights were not conducive to growth for these warmth loving plants.

My advice is to find out what grows well in your area and then consider anything else a bonus. An emphasis on cole crops, root crops, and greens is probably your best bet. Take into consideration which of the following apply to you; late or early frosts; cold nights; cool days and cold nights; or all of the above.

It's extremely important to obtain seeds that are suitable for your climate. It is even better if the seeds are locally grown. Those seeds will be adapted to your area specifically. If cold soil is a problem, local seed companies will have produced seed that can do quite well in that situation. Normal tomato seeds, for example, wouldn't have much of a chance in fifty-degree soil. The same is true of corn. I buy all my seeds from Garden City Seeds in Victor, Montana. The people there are very conscientious and helpful, and the seeds are very good and getting better.

While we're on the subject of seeds, consider getting open pollinated ones whenever possible. These are seeds that have reproduced naturally. They produce plants true to form each year. Hybrid seeds, by contrast, are crossbred. Such seeds cannot be saved because their offspring are not predictable. You can help maintain plant diversity by growing and saving open-pollinated seeds.

Some people may be interested in heirloom seeds. These seeds have been handed down, and growing them is another way to help preserve natural diversity. They are the building blocks for so-called improved varieties and need to be preserved for future generations.

Some plants will have to be started much earlier than seed catalogs advise. For example, I start peppers and basil at the end of January, tomatoes at the end of February and cole crops at the end of March. You'll have to weigh the problems caused by such early planting against the benefits. As an example, in an old house that is heated with wood, as mine is, the rooms can be quite cold during this time. In order to get good germination, I put my seed trays on top of my brooder box. The bottom heat gets them going really well. Later growth may be really retarded, though.

Another problem is that by the time the plants can be set out in June they will be huge. That means they will take up a tremendous amount of space inside. It also means that the plants are much more susceptible to transplant shock. These plants are not bred to have such an extended lifetime, so some of them, such as broccoli, may bolt before producing a real crop. I've found that living with the above challenge is necessary for me to get a decent harvest most years.

If your frost free season is ninety days, don't expect to have success with a tomato that the catalog or packet says takes ninety days to maturity. A seventy day requirement is the maximum. That's because cold soil and cold nights retard growth and production. Likewise don't choose a corn that is supposed to take more than seventy-five days. Corn doesn't need as much warmth as tomatoes but still will be slowed by cool temperatures.

A rich soil is more important for short season gardens than it is for others. For one thing, your plants will need readily available nutrients for fast growth, and a friable soil warms much earlier than a packed soil. In addition, your plants will have an easier time growing in a fluffy soil as compared to one that is compacted.

If you use deep bedding in your barn or chicken house, you can put it right into your garden, either in the fall or 2-4 weeks before planting in the spring. It is almost impossible to use manure that is too hot when you garden in a cold climate, as long as you dig it in before planting. The manure will help to warm the soil, and by the time the plants are up, it is unlikely that the manure will burn them. Don't use this method with potatoes, however, as fresh manure can cause scab.

If you don't use deep bedding for your animals, compost your manure with other organic materials to get more bulk and a greater range of nutrients.

Raised beds warm up faster than a flat garden. Be sure not to mulch until the soil is thoroughly warm or you'll insulate the soil from the warmth of the sun. Be sure your garden has plenty of sunlight. Your plants will need all the coaxing they can get. At the end of the season a killing frost is frequently followed by a week or two of warm weather. Learn to predict a frost. A low pressure system will likely hold in warmth, but a high pressure system can produce clear, cold nights for my part of the country. A Pacific weather system will likely bring moisture, but not frost late in the summer. An Arctic weather system, however, is likely to bring dry cold. Find out what's true in your area.

Try to get through that first frost. Leaving a sprinkler on will help as well as covering your plants with plastic, cloth or straw. To preserve your plants through a killing frost down to around twenty-eight degrees, you'll need to use covering and sprinkling together all night. I've saved even the basil for up to four days with this method before the weather warmed up.

A well watered garden will hold heat better than a dry garden, and plants that are not drought stressed are better able to stand up to frost. On the other hand, wet ground warms up more slowly than dry ground.

There are two types of plants that will help you in your admittedly difficult job of short season gardening. One is perennials. Instead of using precious time on flower beds that need planting every year, rely on ones that come back year after year. Also plant asparagus, strawberries, raspberries, horseradish, rhubarb, sunchokes and perennial herbs. (Be sure the herbs are indeed perennial in your climate. Rosemary, for example, is a perennial but cannot withstand Montana winters.)

Native plants will also help you in your quest for a successful short season garden. They are mostly maintenance free and are a good way to enjoy seeing what the lands looked like before people entered the picture. A meadow of native grasses is beautiful and never needs mowing or watering. A wildflower garden likewise will take care of itself and will compete well with weeds if the ground is tilled the first year after the first weeds come up. Natural plants are intriguing, and once you get involved with them you'll want to learn more and more.

I hope I've given you some ideas that will help you in your gardening prospects. Short season gardening is challenging to say the least, but it can be very rewarding, sometimes frustrating, and always a learning experience. Good luck! ∆

FARM/GARDEN

A Backwoods Home Anthology

Kiwi fruit — healthy, delicious, exotic, pest- and disease-resistant, low-maintenance...

By Martin P. Waterman

If one could custom design a new fruit for the North American climate, ideally one would want a fruit that could be grown in almost every area and survive with relatively little maintenance. With all the concern there is over pesticide use, it should be very disease and pest resistant and, ultimately, this new fantasy fruit should produce bountiful harvests that are healthy, delicious and exotic.

Apparently, and unbelievably so, the kiwi (*Actinidia*) seems to satisfy these and other important requirements and this is probably responsible for its meteoric rise in popularity: first as supermarket fruit and then as a popular offering at nurseries and garden centers.

Still, despite its new found fame, there is much to learn about the many different varieties of kiwi that are available. The reason for this is that kiwis are not native to our country and many of the available varieties and hybrids have only been introduced in the last few years.

A number of different texts are becoming available but unfortunately these texts concentrate on the grocery store varieties and rarely mention any of the many other types of kiwis which are commonly offered by nurseries and garden centers.

Because of this, it has been a learning experience for many kiwi growers, to say the least, as they have tried to figure out the proper cultural needs of this unusual plant.

It has been postulated that there may be as many as 50 varieties of Actinidia, depending on whom you believe. There seems to be no argument concerning the fact that there are at least three dozen distinct varieties.

And now that more and more fruit hybridizers are experimenting with kiwis, we are certain to see many more specially adapted varieties for commercial and home use. The kiwi breeders are creating more self-fertile varieties. They are working to improve fruit quality and size, in addition to improving vines so that they are more productive, hardier, and better able to hold their fruit.

The genetic diversity contained in the many species of kiwi has blessed growers with a large range of areas where it can be successfully grown. However, this diversity has also created the need for special requirements for many of the species. This includes (among other things) making certain that the *A. kolomiktas* that can exist in the coldest areas of the United States receive shade from the sun, as well as seeing that the *A. deliciosa* in warm areas such as southern California receive enough cold. This is hard for some people to comprehend as most believe the kiwi is a tropical fruit that belongs with such things as bananas, mangoes, and papayas.

A. deliciosa, *or fuzzy kiwi*

Kiwi history

Actinidia have a fascinating history. Actinidia are vines that are native to Asia and are found distributed from India to the island of Sakhalin near Japan. In the wild, they tend to be climbers, often growing to over 100 feet, particularly when they can find a tree nearby. In China, all parts of the vine are put to good use. The leaves are rich in starch, protein and vitamin

The Fifth Year

C, which has made them an ideal food for pigs. The roots are used to make insecticide and the stalks are used to make glue. This glue is used for construction materials which include wax and other papers which are used for traditional calligraphy and paintings. The plant is also used for herbal cures such as improving blood circulation and lactation, reducing fevers and as a treatment for sprains, contusions and boils.

From its wilderness roots in the wild, kiwi fruit made the journey to New Zealand and then to the United States in the 1930's. The varieties from New Zealand that were brought to the U.S. were A. deliciosa a name that recently replaced the previous A. chinensis probably to help give the fruit a more appealing scientific name. The common name, Chinese gooseberry, was also changed along the way to help assist in the marketing and promotion, so that the "kiwi" would no longer be confused with the tart gooseberries that most people think of when the name is mentioned.

As perfect as some claim the kiwi is, it is important to know that it is not without some shortcomings. For instance, late spring and early fall frosts can be damaging to the vines. Cats are attracted to the vines, which contain a substance similar to catnip. Site selection can sometimes solve the frost problems, and a plastic tree guard or similar protection will help to fend off the felines. High winds can also be damaging because they can remove much of the crop from the vines.

It is also important to know that every variety has a different winter chilling requirement. A certain amount of chilling, a given number of hours at below 45° (7° C), is needed in order for the vines to bear a crop. Growers in Florida found out about chilling the hard way when they tried unsuccessfully to grow some of the commercial varieties grown in California.

Cultivation requirements

Requirements do vary between different kiwi types, but there are many necessities that are required by all Actinidia. Because of their growth habits, some kind of support or trellis system must be used. These can span from a simple grape style trellis, to very elaborate designs that feature the female vines on one overhead level and the male vines (for pollination) on a higher level.

In commercial terms, it is not uncommon for a grower to need to spend $20,000 to $30,000 per acre to establish kiwis, a good portion of this money being spent for the trellis system. However, for the backwoods grower, a fence could be the ideal support, especially when dealing with some of the less vigorous vines such as the kolomitkas.

It is common for some home growers to plant kiwis near a tree so that the vine will have something to climb. The drawback of this type of system is that, like the vine, you too may have to become a climber in order to get to the fruit.

Fortunately, many nurseries provide trellis designs and other culture information so that different styles can be considered. For growing around the homestead, the kiwi lends itself well to use as a landscape plant because it can be trained to climb archways, arbors or up the side of a building.

Kiwis also need to be pruned in order to remain healthy and to provide fruit on a regular basis. Pruning serves a number of functions, including balancing fruitfulness and vegetative growth, allowing the right amounts of air and sun penetration, and directing the vine to grow in the required direction.

Soil pH should be maintained between 5.0 and 6.5, and the soil should be able to provide adequate nutrients, because kiwis are heavy feeders. The soil will also need to be well drained, or you run the risk of your vines succumbing to crown rot.

One requirement of all kiwis, particularly in their first year, is a regular supply of water. Watering is also crucial to insure good fruit set. In California, kiwi plantings are among the heaviest water users of any crop, due to their expansive leaf area and large root systems. The serious backwoods grower may want to consider an underground irrigation system in dry areas.

A nurseryman's dream

Actinidia easily roots from softwood cuttings. This has helped to increase the number of kiwi being grown and make it one of the easier plants to propagate for nurserymen and growers. One nurseryman takes cuttings in the spring from his stock plants and then is able to take cuttings at least twice from the first set of cuttings before autumn arrives. Because of the high demand, many kiwis are sold without properly developed root systems. This often makes them prone to injury and even death in their first year.

Another troublesome element which has given the kiwi a bad name in some circles is that most of them require a male pollinator. Therefore, many customers may have ended up with just one kiwi which, in most instances, will never fruit. Many of the newer kiwi varieties, however, are self-fruitful and this will help alleviate the problem. Kiwi fruit can also be started from seeds, and some of the seed saver groups are now beginning to have inventories of many of the rare varieties, in addition to the popular ones. There is variability in the kiwi seedling, and most will differ in some manner from the parents. However, many new improved selections are discovered this way.

Varieties

Probably the greatest determining factor for kiwi survival is choosing the correct variety for your site. The following are the most common and important varieties that are being offered by nurseries and garden centers:

A. arguta is hardy from -10° to -30° (-23° C to -34° C) depending on whether the vine is young or one of the several clones that are damaged at -10° (-23° C). There is a great variation in habit of *A. arguta* and many growers are reporting different results.

A. arguta also goes under the name of "Hardy Kiwi." It is one of the most vigorous of the kiwis, so that considerable pruning is necessary to keep it under control.

Argutas have smooth leaves, stems and fruit. The fruit is smaller than the regular supermarket fuzzy kiwi and will only keep for two months under refrigeration.

Argutas also need a pollinator, except for the Issai. Many varieties are proving to be popular. Ananasnaja came from Belgium and features some of the largest fruits of the argutas. Ananasnaja translates from Russian to mean "pineapple-like." The Issai is becoming more and more popular due to the fact that it is self-fertile. Coming from Japan, the Issai features compactness and the ability to produce fruit, often the year after planting.

All these good features are not without a down side. The Issai is probably the least hardy of the argutas. Another variety developed by Professor Elwyn Meader is named, simply the Meader kiwi. This kiwi was selected by him because of its productivity and its sweet, medium sized fruit. Also worth mentioning is a variety simply known as 74-79 which some think is the best of a numbered series from the experiment station at Chico, California. In areas where 74-79 does well, it produces large, sweet fruit. One of the biggest complaints that I have heard concerning the argutas is that they can take over five years to begin to fruit. However, I also understand the results are well worth the wait.

A. deliciosa is really the king of kiwis. It is the kiwi first made popular in New Zealand and is now being grown commercially in many countries, from Chile to Israel. These are the largest fruited kiwis and are also known as fuzzy kiwi.

A. deliciosa can need at least 220 frost free days, and they are only hardy to about 0° (-18° C), depending on the particular variety. Many varieties should have their trunks wrapped so that the bark at the base of the plant does not freeze and separate from the trunk, thereby girdling the vine. There are many varieties of A. deliciosa and tales abound about the new material that is being developed and tested, particularly in New Zealand, that is said to offer some substantial improvements over existing varieties.

The most popular variety of those introduced from New Zealand is the Hayward kiwi. It is adapted to both commercial and backyard use and is noted for its large, attractive fruit. Blake is another self-fertile variety, but the fruit is smaller than the Hayward about the size of a small egg. Vincent is a low chill kiwi for warmer areas of California and Florida. Apparently, Vincent may only require as little as 150 hours of below 45° (7C°) temperatures to produce its heavy crops. Another variety worth mentioning is called Saanichton 12 from Canada. This variety, which has been grown on Vancouver Island for over 30 years, is large and sweet and does not suffer too much winter damage. It has also proven itself to be a good variety for the home grower.

A. kolomitka is the hardiest of the edible species. The kolomitkas have given hope to northern growers because of their ability to survive temperatures of -50° (-65° C). With hardiness like that, it is no wonder that one nursery has named them "Arctic Kiwi." The fruit of *A. kolomitka* is smooth skinned rather than fuzzy and can be eaten like a grape when fresh, or a raisin when dried. The green fruit is grape shaped and many people consider them the best tasting of the kiwis, even surpassing the larger A. deliciosa. The flavor has been described as having hints of strawberry and pineapple. The vine is compact and seldom reaches more than 15 to 20 feet.

A. kolomitka vines need a pollinator, so a male vine must be purchased which should pollinate up to a dozen female plants. Kolomitkas only need 130 frost-free days for fruit to mature.

There are some features unique to the kolomitkas. They need shade, even into U.S.D.A. Zone 4 and cooler climates. The reason for this is that they are native to Manchuria and Soviet Asia and are used to a shaded forest environment. Without shading, the leaves of the vines tend to get scorched by the sun. Some innovative solutions to this problem have been developed. Some people grow grapes on an overhead trellis system such as a Geneva Double Curtain and then let the kiwis grow along lower trellis lines.

Another unique feature is the variegated leaves. These appear on both the male and female vines, but the male vines are usually more spectacular. The male kolomitka has gone in and out of fashion in the nursery industry, especially in England, as an ornamental vine because of its beautiful variegated leaves with bands of green, pink, and white.

A. kolomitka is very high in Vitamin C and is a rich source of minerals and fiber, with a natural sugar content that can go as high as 30 percent.

A. kolomitka fruit can be easily dislodged by the wind, particularly when it is ripe. However, with its yields reported as high as 75 pounds for a mature vine, this may not be an insurmountable problem.

Fruit breeders are already working with the kolomitka to lend its hardiness to other kiwis as well as improving existing kolomitkas.

Of the many varieties available there have been some that have shown some superiority. These include

Krupnopladnaya (meaning "large fruit" in Russian), Arnold Arboretum (a fine quality, sweet, early ripening variety) and Pautske. Many find the taste of these varieties far superior to that of the supermarket kiwis, which are not always ripe and have often been stored for extended periods of time.

Some of my favorite kolomitka varieties that I am growing are Pozdanya (late ripening, large with less fruit drop), Sentyabraskaya (love the name and the vigorous growth) and Krupnopladnaya.

A. polygama is hardy to -30° (-34° C) or colder. The fruit tends to be orange in color, and the round shaped leaves are often large and variegated. Some of the varieties are self-fertile and do not need a male vine in order to set fruit.

Once you are officially a kiwi grower, your thoughts will probably stray to thinking about what to do with all the fruit. There have been many figures tossed about concerning the miraculous ability of these vines to produce. Varieties such as Abbott, Monty, and Vincent have shown that even here in America they can bear over 250 pounds per vine in their eighth and ninth year.

Realistically, a few varieties properly cared for should provide the grower with an ample supply of fruit. If you lack spousal support for growing kiwi (male or female), it is good to know that the kiwi is versatile in the kitchen and good tasting. Uses vary, from meat tenderizer to being a star performer in ice creams, sorbets, yogurt and desserts—just the beginning for imaginative cooks.

About the only thing the kiwi grower is likely to tire of is the constant harping of backyard "experts" who'll tell you that "you can't grow them here." Just smile politely and nod your head; they'll find out soon enough. Just remember, if you live just about anywhere below timberline and south of the Arctic Circle, chances are that there's a kiwi variety for you.

For more information

Actinidia Enthusiasts Journal (P. O. Box 1064, Tonasket, Washington, 98855) is an annual newsletter featuring the latest information on kiwi, including sources of material and new methods of culture. It is an excellent reference source for kiwi growers. Past issues are also available.

The Oregon Exotics Rare Fruit Nursery (1065 Messinger Road, Grants Pass, Oregon, 97527) is an unbelievable resource for the backwoods grower. They have hundreds of rare and exclusive fruit, nut, and vegetable varieties from around the world, many of which have never been grown to any extent in North America. If you want to be on the cutting edge of growing and try exotic material, this is the place. Catalog is $2.

- Edible Landscaping
  P. O. Box 77
  Afton, Virginia
  22920
  (Catalog is $1)

- Northwoods Nursery
  28696 S. Cramer
  Molalla, Oregon
  97038
  (Catalog is free)

- Corn Hill Nursery
  R.R. 5, Petitcodiac
  New Brunswick, E0A 2H0
  Canada
  (Catalog $2)

(Martin Waterman is a kiwi breeder and grower and writes for several horticultural magazines and journals in North America from the comfort of his backwoods home.) ∆

A BHM Writer's Profile

Dave Jensen

Dave Jenson lives with his family in a log cabin on his parent's farm in southern Washington. He is a stay-at-home dad. His wife, Misoon, is a translator. They heat their cabin and hot water with wood from logging slash.

Dave divides his time between babysitting his two children, Jennifer, 6, and Sam, 4, and caring for his growing flock of old trucks. They are mostly Dodges, but he also has a '64 Toyota FJ40 and a '56 International S120.

FARM/GARDEN

The 10 most useful herbs

By Audrey Stallsmith

With the current bewildering variety of herb plants and seeds available, it is sometimes difficult to tell which ones are primarily for show, and which ones you will actually be able to use. Angelica, for example, is pretty, but it is also BIG. And, unless you can develop a passion for candying stems or flavoring liqueurs, there is not much you can do with it. So, if your space is limited and you prefer your plants to work for their keep, here are ten that are guaranteed to satisfy: caraway, chives, parsley, sage, catnip, chamomile, lemon balm, rosemary, dill, and mint.

If you are a salad lover, be sure to include the first three. When I'm tossing together lettuce, tomatoes, and cucumbers in late summer, I always chop up a few leaves of each of these to add spice. Caraway (*carum carvi*) was the first plant after the spring bulbs to bloom in my garden last year. Its delicate white flowers are something like Queen Anne's Lace, and they can be used in bouquets. Don't use too many of them this way though, because you're going to want most to go to seed. The seeds can be easily stripped off the plant after they turn dry and brown, and are an important ingredient in numerous recipes especially rye bread. Caraway, along with dill and fennel, was one of the seeds carried to prayer meetings in colonial times to help curb the appetite. Chewing caraway seeds will also help dispel a bellyache. Since caraway is a biennial, you'll probably have to wait until the second year for flowers and seeds, but you'll get plenty of feathery leaves with a licorice-like taste the first summer.

Probably the most widely used herb, with the possible exception of parsley, is chives (*allium schoenoprasum*). Its spiky leaves will add an onion-like flavor to any dish without all that peeling and weeping. Once established, you'll have chives forever, and its round pink flowerheads are an extra bonus. Those flowers can be used for tinting and flavoring white vinegar to be used as salad dressing. There is also a garlic chive available (*allium tuberosum*).

Parsley (*petroselinum*) also needs little introduction. Its value as a seasoning and garnish is well known. Parsley is sometimes slow to germinate. It reportedly has to go to the devil and back seven times before sprouting! Warmth and plenty of moisture should speed the process. Soaking the seedbed with boiling water might help if you're in a hurry. As with most herbs, the newest leaves are the best-tasting. The curly type (*petroselinum crispum*) is the most popular, but there are plainer-leafed varieties that reputedly taste just as good.

Sage (*salvia officinalis*) is a must for use in stuffings for meat and poultry. Salvia means well, and sage was originally one of the most touted medicinal herbs. "He who would live for aye [forever] must eat sage in May." It has come to symbolize good health and long life. Since it is antiseptic, you might try using it as a mouthwash. Sage tea is also said to darken gray or brunette hair when used as a rinse. Plants tend to become woody after several years, and should then be replaced. Do not confuse culinary sage with the flower garden salvias or with clary sage, which is more com-

monly used in perfumery than in cooking.

Gardeners who are also lovers of felines should put in a good supply of catnip (*nepeta cataria*). Keep it well away from any other plants you value, though, because your cats will roll in it, play with it, chew on it, and just generally rhapsodize over it! It will also make a soothing tea for your colds, fevers, and digestive ailments, if you can find any after your cats are done with it! Dry some to make stuffed toys for them. And don't just limit yourself to one variety. Your options include camphor, lance-leaved, and lemon types, as well as Chinese, Greek, Himalayan, Persian and Russian species.

Chamomile (*anthemis noblis*, *chamaemelum nobile*, or *chamomilla recutita*) symbolizes humility and best wishes. This meek little daisy-like herb is a natural sedative. Steep some of the dried flowers to make a bedtime

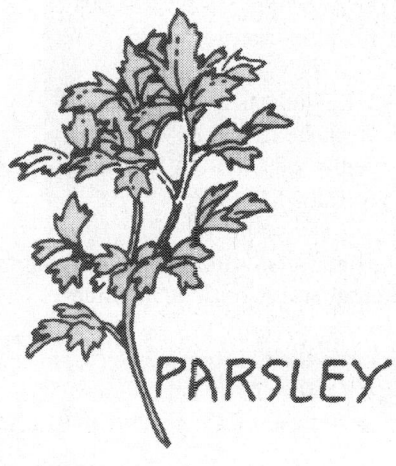

tea or a rinse for blonde hair. Anthemis noblis will also make a sweet-smelling lawn if clipped and not allowed to bloom.

Worth growing for its fresh scent alone, lemon balm (*melissa officinalis*) can also be used to garnish and add flavor to summer drinks and fruit salads. Balm tea is said to be beneficial in treatment of fevers, colds,

and nausea. Try rubbing fresh leaves on insect bites.

Rosemary, that's for remembrance, Shakespeare's Ophelia said. Besides smelling heavenly, this herb (*rosmarinus officinalis*) is extensively used in cooking and cosmetics. Often described as stimulating and enlivening, it is said to encourage hair growth. Whether or not this is true, a rinse of rosemary will make your locks glossy. It is best used on normal or oily hair, since it does tend to have a slight drying effect. Rosemary has a reputation for being hard to grow from seed. In fact, some say that only about one in seven rosemary seeds will sprout. That is why, when I was starting plants indoors last spring, I recklessly planted an entire package of rosemary and ended up with over seventy-five seedlings! I gave them no special treatment, sowing in ordinary potting soil and, when they germinated, putting them under fluorescent lights in a cool basement. In hot Mediterranean-type climates, rosemary is perennial and evergreen, but in Pennsylvania, I have to replant every year. (You can take cuttings from one year's plants and keep them indoors until the next spring. Just don't over-water.)

Dill (*anethum graveolens*) is as popular with vegetable gardeners as with herb fanciers. The seeds are a must for pickles, and can even be used in fruitcakes. The leaves are often added to potato salads. Dill tea is said to relieve indigestion and strengthen fingernails. Some also assert that it has a soothing effect on babies and suggest tucking a small sachet of it in the crib.

The clean, sharp scent of the mints (*menthas*) will help you feel cooler on a muggy summer day. You can make jellies or teas from peppermint (*mentha piperita officinalis*) or spearmint (*mentha spicata*), or simply use them as a garnish for lemonades and punches. Keep in mind that they are invasive, and may take over your garden if the roots are not contained. You can plant them in a sunken bottomless bucket or build little underground walls of slate or stone to separate them from their neighbors. There are mints available for every taste, including anise, apple, basil, Egyptian, ginger, grapefruit, Korean, lemon, lime, Moroccan, mountain, orange, pineapple, silver, and several variegated types.

An herbal infusion, or tea, can be made from any of these herbs by pouring a cup of boiling water over ¼-ounce of the dried, or ½-ounce of the fresh, herb and letting the brew stand (covered) for ten minutes before straining out the herb.

Most of the top-ten herbs are also easy-care plants. Caraway, rosemary, and dill need full sun. Most of the others will tolerate partial shade, and the mints prefer a shady, moist location. Chives, sage, catnip, lemon balm, and the mints are perennials. Chamomile can be either annual or perennial, depending on which species you plant. Caraway, dill, and parsley will self-sow. Only rosemary and the annual type of chamomile should need yearly replacing.

Be warned that herb gardening is addictive, and that you may find yourself, like me, growing more and more

of the less practical plants just for the smell of it!

Both of the following have a good selection of herb seeds:

- Park Seed Company
Cokesbury Road
Greenwood, SC 29647-0001
(catalog free)

- J. L. Hudson, Seedsman
P. O. Box 1058
Redwood City, CA 94064
(catalog $1)

For 25-cent sample seed packets and herb plants at reasonable prices:

- Le Jardin Du Gourmet
P. O. Box 75
St. Johnsbury Center, VT 05863 ∆

Tips for cold-climate herb growing

By Jennifer Stein Barker

There are plenty of books and magazines on the subject of herb-gardening, but if you live in a cold climate such as the Inland Northwest, all the publications seem to assume you don't garden. My favorite gardening magazines have blank spots on the map where all the mountains are between the Cascades and the Rockies. They don't recognize the existence of anything colder than USDA zone 5 or 6 (I live in zone 4a). Extension agents have been known to respond to questions about problems in our area without even looking at the plants: "It's winter kill," "You can't grow anything there."

You can grow a garden, herbs included, in a climate where summer nights rarely stay above 50°, and the frost-free season averages 16 days. It takes perseverence, care for your plants, and a willingness to experiment. Some plants, like oregano, will sprawl all over the herb garden even in the severest of climates. Mints also seem to be able to take just about anything. Other plants, like thymes and sages, may survive with a little coddling and proper management, and tender ones like basil haven't a chance of surviving on their own, but can be managed as seasonal plants and grown outdoors under cover for that big pesto harvest.

The best way to find winter-hardy plants is to experiment. If one cultivar of an herb doesn't survive, try another cultivar. Mother of thyme, a creeping ground-cover with round, easy-to-pick leaves, is as hardy as the day is long. Lovage and tarragon spring up faithfully each year. I've lost purchased anise hyssop twice to early frosts, while seed-grown hyssops self sow each year to spring up all over the garden. Chamomile, garlic, and chives seem to stand up to anything the weather can throw at them. Winter-hardy herbs are not limited to culinary varieties. Medicinals and fragrance herbs like beebalm, horehound, and lavender can be hardy too.

For those herbs which are borderline winter-hardy here, like english thyme and dwarf sage, I've developed a management technique which will ensure their survival during winters when the same plant, unmanaged, dies next to it. In summer, as you cut the herb for cooking or drying, make the cut near the bottom of the stem, so that you take most of an individual stem each time. This ensures that the plant stays compact and produces new growth at the bottom. Always cut the longest stems back first, so that the plant doesn't become "leggy" and strung out. Never cut more than 1/3 of the total foliage off the plant. With the coming of cold weather in the fall, plant growth will slow down, and then you should stop cutting the plant completely. After the ground has frozen, lay a thick layer of mulch around the stem, and lightly over the top of the plant, to minimize temperature swings during winter thaws. Remove this mulch as early in the spring as the snow melts off it, or when severe weather (single digit and below at night) eases.

Some tender herbs, like basil, haven't a hope of surviving past the first frost without help. After much experimentation, we found that African Basil maintains the best flavor of any windowsill-grown basil, and it can withstand cooler outside temperatures than most. Cuttings from our indoor plant placed in a glass of water in a sunny place will root within a few weeks. They are then planted in small pots and "hardened off" outside to strong sunshine and cooler temperatures. This is done gradually, an hour at a time at first, up to a full day after a few weeks.

When the basil plants are ready, and the temperature has warmed to the point where the nights are usually frost-free (some places there are no guarantees, even in July), we plant them out into a raised bed where the soil is rich and the drainage is good. Over the top of the bed are placed heavy wire hoops, and over the hoops is draped a polyester row-cover. This is a spun-bonded polyester fabric that comes in various widths and is available at garden centers, usually used for starting tender seedlings in the spring. It is weighted down with small rocks around the edges to keep it from blowing off. In our cold climate, we use it to moderate the temperature all season long on all sorts of crops, from herbs to lettuce to potatoes. The basil thrives under it, and will grow in a month into plants a foot in diameter.

Your local nursery should acquire their plants with the local climate in mind (if they don't, perhaps you should be the local nursery), but mail-order sources may provide a wider selection from which to choose. One source here in the Northwest with a catalog which gives straight information about cold hardiness is:

Goodwin Creek Gardens
Box 83
Williams, OR 97544
(503) 846-7357
(catalog, $1)

Herb growing can be a great joy, and one that is not limited to warm climates and rich soils. In harsher places, the key words are: experiment, be creative, and enjoy your successes, whatever they may be. Δ

Some herb garden recipes

By Jennifer Stein Barker

The use of herbs can turn everyday foods into something very special. They enrich and enliven foods, and complement flavors in subtle and delicious ways.

One of the secrets of cooking with herbs is to use the freshest herbs you can find. If it's not the season to go and pick herbs straight out of the garden, you can get good flavor out of most dried herbs, but they must be the freshest you can obtain. You should be aware that many herbs in the grocery store may have been picked years before you see them on the shelves. If you can't pick and dry your own, the best place to buy them is from the bulk container of a whole-foods grocery or health-food store. Not only are they likely to be fresher, they are most certainly cheaper to buy in bulk.

It is also more economical to buy in bulk because you need not buy any more of an herb or spice than you will use in a year. Fresh crops of herbs are processed and appear in the bulk bins in late fall or early winter each year. That is the best time to buy your year's supply.

How you store herbs is very important. Light and heat will destroy their flavor. Look for a cool, dark cupboard, and store herbs in colored glass jars or opaque containers to keep light from them. If you use a lot of a certain herb, like basil for instance, the freezer is a good place to store most of it while you only keep out what you will use in a month or so.

Start right now by checking your existing herbs. Open the jars and take a little of each into your hand. Crumble the leaves and smell them. Do they smell fresh and aromatic? If they smell more like straw, start by replacing them, and then try the following recipes to open up a whole new world of herbal cooking.

Marinated vegies with feta and Greek olives

Serve this as a side dish with your best Greek dinner, or a main dish with lots of crusty Sesame Ring bread to sop up the marinade. This goes great with Rosemary potatoes. Serves 4 as a side dish, or 2 as a main dish.

Marinade:

```
1/3 cup olive oil
1/4 cup red wine vinegar
1 Tbsp. fresh lemon juice
freshly-ground black pepper
1 clove garlic, minced
herbs to taste:
thyme, basil, oregano, dill, rosemary (choose 2 or
    3, fresh if possible)
1/4 lb. feta cheese
1/2 jar black Greek olives
```

Vegies:

```
1 green pepper
1 ripe tomato
1 stalk broccoli
1 carrot
1/2 red onion
1/2 cucumber, peeled
```

Prepare marinade: In a 2- or 3-quart bowl that has a tight-fitting lid, mix marinade ingredients with a small whisk. Start with 1/4 cup of fresh herbs, or 4 teaspoons of dried herbs. Taste, and add more if you like.

Prepare vegies: cut the broccoli into bite-sized pieces. Steam them over boiling water until just barely tender, and add them warm to the marinade. Dice and add the green pepper, tomato, red onion, and cucumber.

Refrigerate the salad at least 4 hours before serving. Stir it about once an hour, and return it to the refrigerator. Just before serving, arrange the salad on a bed of washed leaf lettuce, and decorate it with chunks of the feta cheese, and the Greek olives. The olives can be pitted with a cherry pitter if desired.

Rosemary potatoes

Serve as a side dish with Greek food, or as a main dish accompanied by a Greek salad and a hearty Sesame Ring. I prefer Yukon Gold potatoes in this, but any waxy yellow potato will do. Serves 3-6.

```
2 lb. yellow potatoes, diced 1/2"
1 Tbsp. olive oil
2 cloves garlic, minced
1 onion, halved and sliced thin
2½ tsp. rosemary
¼ tsp. thyme
1½ Tbsp. lemon juice
1 Tbsp. tamari
```

Scrub and dice the potatoes, leaving the skins on. In a steamer basket over a pan of boiling water, steam the potatoes until they are tender. Save the steaming water for stock.

Meanwhile, heat the olive oil in a deep heavy skillet, preferably cast iron. Add the onion and garlic and braise and reglaze. Crush the rosemary and thyme lightly in a mortar and pestle, and when the onions have acquired a golden glaze, add the herbs, lemon juice, and tamari. Turn the heat down to low, and allow the juice to reduce a little and the flavors to blend as the mixture bubbles gently.

When the onion-herb mixture has reduced to a thick sauce, and the potatoes are tender, toss the two together until the potatoes are well coated. Serve immediately.

Minestrone

This is a chunky, beany minestrone with a traditional flavor. Serves 4:

> ½ cup dry chickpeas
> ½ cup dry red beans
> ½ cup dried baby limas
> 1 Tbsp. olive oil
> 1 medium onion, diced
> 2 garlic cloves, minced
> 1 cup sliced celery
> 3 cups stock or water
> ½ tsp. fennel seed
> 1/8 tsp. celery seed
> ¼ tsp. chervil
> 2 red potatoes, diced
> 2 carrots, chunked
> 2 Tbsp. tamari
> 1/8 tsp. Tabasco
> ¼ cup dry red wine
> 2/3 cup pasta shells
> 1 cup fresh or frozen green beans, cut 1"

Wash and soak the beans overnight in separate containers. In the morning, discard the soaking water and cook the beans in separate pans with plenty of water, just until they are barely tender. Drain them and save the cooking water to use as the stock. Set aside (if you want to skip this step, just open 15 oz. cans of three different beans and drain the stock from them. Set beans and stock aside).

In a 6 quart stockpot or Dutch oven, heat the olive oil over medium-high heat and add the onion. Braise and reglaze, using a little wine or water for the braising liquid, until the onion is golden and transparent. Add the garlic and celery and a little water, and braise until the celery is tender. Add the stock or water, using the bean cooking liquid.

In a mortar, crush the fennel seed and celery seed together. Add them to the soup. Add the chervil, crushing it between your fingers. Add the potatoes, carrots, tamari, tabasco, red wine, and the beans. Bring to a boil, reduce the heat, and simmer for 5 minutes. Add the pasta shells and the green beans (and more stock or water if necessary), and cook until the pasta is tender, about 10-12 minutes more after the pot reaches the boil.

Noodles with pine nuts and squash

Serves 4:

> 1 lb. whole wheat noodles
> 6 dried tomato halves
> 1 onion, chopped
> 1 clove garlic, minced
> 2 Tbsp. olive oil
> ¼ cup pine nuts
> 4 oz. fresh mushrooms
> 1 lb. summer squash (zucchini,
>   crookneck, or pattypan)
> ¼ cup chopped fresh herbs,
>   or 4 tsp. dried herbs
>   (marjoram, thyme, basil)
> 1 Tbsp. lemon juice
> 1 Tbsp. tomato paste
> grated cheese (opt.)

Cover the dried tomato halves with boiling water, and soak for 15 minutes, or till soft. Save the water. Slice the tomatoes finely. Bring 8 quarts of water to a full boil in a large kettle.

Heat the olive oil in a large heavy skillet over medium-high heat. Add the onion and garlic and saute until they begin to turn golden. Add the saved tomato soaking water, and continue cooking until the water evaporates and the juices turn brown on the bottom of the pan. Add more water an ounce at a time, and cook off until the onions are golden ("braise and reglaze"). Add another ounce of water, and the pine nuts and mushrooms. As the water evaporates, add more an ounce at a time only as necessary to prevent burning, until the mushrooms and nuts begin to brown. Then add the squash, the sliced soaked tomatoes, and the herbs, lemon juice, and tomato paste. Turn the heat to low, cover the pan, and allow to simmer gently, stirring frequently, while you cook the pasta. Add more water to the sauce if necessary to keep from sticking.

Cook the pasta as you normally do, then toss with the sauce. Serve with grated cheese if desired. ∆

My favorite soup recipes

By Richard Blunt

"If you can boil water, you can make good soup." This was a proclamation Chef Sully made one morning just as he was putting his two stock pots on the stove.

Sully was the morning chef and I was the breakfast cook and salad man at a well known restaurant in Cambridge, Massachusetts. When he made these pronouncements, it usually meant he was about to teach me something.

During the previous two weeks, he had been teaching me how to prepare fresh soup stocks. Before each lesson he made a statement, like the one above, and I think I've remembered every one of them down through the years. The content of each aphorism always related directly to what he was going to teach. Already being familiar with this, it seemed to me that knowing how to boil water was all that was necessary to make good soup.

But the first thing that became clear to me was how little I knew about boiling water. There are four levels of boil: simmer, gentle boil, boil, and hard boil. Each has a specific purpose in soup and stock preparation. What I thought was simmer turned out to be halfway between a gentle boil and a boil.

Over the years I have discovered that many amateur cooks have developed the same misunderstanding I had, and it often leads to poor results in the kitchen. To get the best idea of what constitutes the various levels of boil, try this experiment: Place a small pot (3 or 4 quarts) half filled with water on a stove burner set at medium heat. Watch closely as the water heats up. Small bubbles will start forming on the bottom of the pot. They will start rising, but will not reach the surface. There is also a sluggish movement of the water. This, my friends, is a simmer.

As the water gets hotter, the bubbles will rise from the bottom of the pot a little faster. When the bubbles just start breaking the surface, you have a gentle or light boil. As the water gains more heat, the bubbles become larger and rise actively to the surface and then you have established a boil.

In its final stage, the hard boil produces turbulence all over the surface of the pot. As far as I can determine, a hard boil is useless in the preparation of good soups and stocks.

How do we use the other three levels of boil? Good question. Understanding the meaning of the terms simmer, light boil, and boil has great importance when preparing soups.

Simmering is used when cooking soups and stocks for a long period of time. The extended cooking extracts flavors from the ingredients to flavor the stock. The low agitation prevents fat and other undesirable products from emulsifying and making the stock cloudy.

The gentle boil serves the same function as the simmer, and will do it a little faster. But only use the gentle boil when you plan to stay near the pot and keep your eye on things. A gentle boil can turn into a full boil and ruin a soup very quickly.

The boil is used to reduce the quantity of liquid in a soup or stock and concentrate flavors. Before you try to reduce or concentrate a stock, however, it is important to strain it and remove all the fat.

Now, with the stages of boiling under our belts, let's get to two soups I'll help you to prepare in this issue. Both are examples of how much fun soup is to make, and both offer the cook the opportunity to use his or her imagination.

Sully taught me that a good soup must be fresh and taste of the things from which it is made. He told me to pay attention to how the soups are put together and to try to understand how I should have a special taste, aroma, and consistency in mind when planning a soup. A classic example of this is the vegetable soup recipe I'm about to introduce. If you follow my directions, I think you'll see how your interest and imagination in soup making can be put to the test with this recipe.

Traditionally this soup is made with a plain water base. As a change, I've included beef stock in the liquid. It's a different taste I want to achieve, and I feel that my beef stock contributes to the flavor of the soup without overpowering the other ingredients. For the beans in this recipe, you can select from a wide variety. I've chosen dried white beans and fava beans for use here (fava beans are also known as bread beans). White beans are mild, and fava beans have a noticeable flavor without being too strong. If you prefer a milder soup, use all white beans or use fresh beans of any of several other varieties, in the same quantities listed in the recipe.

I've included in this recipe a flavoring mixture that I add to the soup just before I serve it. It adds a real distinction to this soup. The French call it *pistou* and it's very similar to the pesto Italians use on pasta. Pistou, however, is used in soups.

The pistou recipe, which follows the soup recipe, can also be changed to suit your taste. Decrease the amount of basil and season to your personal taste. The traditional recipe calls for Parmesan cheese as an ingredient and for passing grated Parmesan, to be sprinkled on the soup separately, after the soup has been served. Other cheeses like

Emmenthal, Swiss, Romano, or Asiago can be used in place of the grated Parmesan to contribute subtle flavor changes just before sampling the first spoonful. I also use curry powder as a seasoning, though traditional recipes call for a pinch of saffron.

Here is my recipe. Give it a try.

Vegetable bean soup with pistou

> ¾ cup dry white beans
> ¼ cup dry fava beans
> 4 cups water
> 2 Tbsp light olive oil
> ½ cup white onions (diced medium)
> 2 fresh garlic cloves (minced)
> ¼ tsp curry powder
> 1 cup fresh tomatoes (peeled, seeded, diced) OR canned tomatoes (diced)
> ¾ cup fresh carrots (peeled and diced medium)
> ¾ cup fresh green beans (cut in ½" sections)
> 1½ cups fresh zucchini squash (diced medium)
> 1 fresh sweet pepper (red or green, diced medium)
> 1½ cups fresh boiling potatoes (peeled and diced medium)
> ½ cup vermicelli noodles
> salt and fresh black pepper, to taste
> ½ cup freshly grated cheese (Parmesan, Romano, Asiago, Swiss, Gruyere)

Preparation

1. Combine the white and fava beans with the four cups of water, set on the stove and bring to a light boil. Allow the beans to boil for two minutes, remove from the heat and let the beans soak for one hour. Return the beans to the heat, bring them to a simmer, and cook them until they're tender. This will take between 1 and 1½ hours. Drain the beans and save the bean stock.

2. In a 4 or 5 quart sauce pan, heat the oil over a medium heat. Add the onions and garlic and saute them for about 2 minutes, then add the curry powder and continue sauteing until the onions are tender. Don't brown them.

3. Add the tomatoes and cook for another 2 minutes.

4. Add enough water to the bean stock to make 8 cups of stock and add this along with the beef stock to the sauteed onions and garlic mixture. Add the carrots and potatoes.

Simmer this, partially covered, until the vegetables are tender.

5. While the soup is simmering, prepare the pistou, according to the recipe that follows, and set it aside at room temperature.

6. When the carrots and potatoes become tender, add the green beans, zucchini, sweet peppers, and noodles. Continue to simmer uncovered until all the vegetables become tender. Add the beans and let the mixture cook until the beans are heated. If the soup is too thick, add a little boiling water to thin it.

Pistou

This is the flavoring that gives this soup its distinctive character.

> 3 large cloves fresh garlic
> 1/3 cup fresh basil leaf OR 2 Tbsp dried basil
> 3 Tbsp fresh thyme leaf or 2 tsp dried thyme
> 4 Tbsp grated Parmesan cheese
> 2 Tbsp tomato paste
> 4 Tbsp olive or peanut oil
> ¼ tsp salt

Preparation

1. With a mortar and pestle, a wooden spoon and a bowl, or a blender, mash the basil, thyme, and garlic into paste.
2. Stir in the tomato paste, Parmesan cheese, and salt.
3. Now, beat in the olive oil, one Tbsp at a time.

Serving

1. Thin the pistou with a little soup.
2. Ladle the soup into a tureen and slowly combine the pistou mixture with the soup while stirring with a spoon. Sample frequently, until you get a taste you like.
3. Serve the soup at once, complementing it with your favorite bread. Pass the grated cheese.

Next is a soup for which I've been creating variations for years. Onion soup is the first soup I ever made as a professional. It is a classic soup and is enjoyed in many versions all over the world. Enjoyed for breakfast by French farmers and served for a late evening or early morning meal for French show girls. Few foods in the world can claim this kind of versatility.

I am sure that you will have fun preparing it and experience a great deal of pride and satisfaction serving it to your friends and family.

Here is one of my favorite versions of this wonderful soup.

French onion soup (Gratinee)

> 4 Tbsp butter or margarine
> 1 tsp peanut oil
> 2½ lbs. (approximately 7 cups) onions (peeled and thinly sliced)
> ½ Tbsp sugar
> 2 cloves fresh garlic (finely minced)
> 2 Tbsp white flour
> 1 cup white vermouth (or other dry white wine)
> 6 cups chicken stock
> 4 cups beef stock
> 1 bay leaf
> salt to taste
> fresh ground black pepper
> 8-10 slices French bread (½" thick)
> 6 Tbsp butter or margarine (melted)
> 12-16 slices Emmenthal or other Swiss cheese sliced 1/8" thick (or 1½ to 2 cups shredded)

Preparation

1. Peel the onions, then cut them in half and thinly slice them, cutting across the grain.

2. In a 4 quart sauce pan heat the oil and margarine/butter over low heat. Stir in the onions and cook, partially covered, over low heat for abut 10 minutes or until the onions are translucent and tender.

3. Stir occasionally to prevent sticking.

4. Now, remove the cover, add the sugar and stir to blend. The sugar serves two purposes. One is to help the onions brown and the other is to increase their sweetness. If you are making this soup in the spring, with a fresh batch of onions from the garden, this is the time of year when onions are at their sweetest, so omit the sugar.

5. Leaving the cover off of pot, turn up the burner to a medium heat. Now add the garlic and continue to saute the onions until they are golden brown. Stir them frequently to prevent them from burning. Reduce the heat if any signs of burning show. The browning process takes about 20 minutes.

6. Sprinkle the flour in with the browned onions while stirring constantly. Continue to cook for another two minutes. This additional cooking of the flour prevents it from leaving a raw taste and powdery texture in the soup.

7. Remove the pot from the heat and allow it to cool for a couple of minutes. Return the pot to a medium heat and add the wine. Bring this to a boil, and cook it until the wine is reduced by half. (This, incidentally, boils off all the alcohol.)

8. Reduce the heat and add the beef and chicken stocks along with the bay leaf. Allow the soup to simmer very slowly, uncovered, for 1½ hours. Add salt and fresh ground black pepper during the last 15 minutes of cooking.

Croutons for topping

While the soup is simmering, preheat your oven to 325°. Lightly coat both sides of the French bread slices with melted butter or margarine. Place the bread on a cookie sheet and put it in the oven to brown. When the up side of the bread has browned, turn it over and brown the other side. When completely browned, remove from the oven and set aside.

To serve

I have included two ways to serve. One requires more work, but it's worth it.

1. Place a crouton into each serving bowl and ladle in soup. Pass grated Parmesan cheese separately.

2. This method of service adds a real touch of distinction and character to the soup. It is also what adds the name Gratinee to the soup. Gratinee refers to the fact that you are now adding cheese to it.

3. Heat the oven to 370°. Ladle the soup into an oven-proof soup tureen or individual oven-proof soup bowls. When using the individual bowls, place one crouton into each bowl. With the tureen or an oven casserole, use as many croutons as it takes to cover the entire surface of the soup. Now cover with a layer of sliced or shredded cheese. Place into the oven and bake for 10 to 15 minutes, or until cheese melts and starts to brown. It will be easier to get the individual bowls into and out of the oven by placing them on a cookie sheet.

As an alternate way of serving, make a one dish meal with this soup and serve it with freshly baked French bread, a good salad and a robust red wine.

Soup and bread are great table companions. In a future article, I will share with you a couple of bread recipes that go well with both of these soups, or with any soup recipe. ∆

Try an isolated gain passive solar house

By H. Scott Kaufmann

How would you like to cut your annual heating bill in half? This can be made possible with the use of passive solar energy systems.

Every three days, the sun showers the earth with more energy than all of the fossil fuels on earth. Yet less than 5% of America's houses use any type of solar energy system. This may be because the solar energy systems of the past were expensive and required builders to totally redesign the house around the solar energy system. With the passive energy design, the house itself becomes the energy system, and as a result a traditional looking house is still possible. Also, the passive design can be built for only about 5% more than the normal construction costs, compared to up to 25% more for the active system (solar collection dishes or panels mounted on a roof).

Active solar systems

The active solar energy system uses solar collection panels, storage tanks, an energy transfer mechanism, and an energy distribution system. This type of system always employs some kind of working fluid which collects, transfers, stores, and distributes the collected solar energy (see Fig. 1). To handle this working fluid, extensive plumbing must be installed in the house. Also, large storage tanks are used to hold the heated fluid until it is needed. Because of the plumbing and storage tanks involved, the house is designed around the energy system. People don't want to live in energy systems, they want to live in houses. And because of the plumbing, tanks, and the structural modifications that must be made to the house, the initial expenditure for an active system can be very costly. With the advent of passive solar homes, these concerns are alleviated.

Passive solar systems

The passive solar energy system reduces energy consumption by paying close attention to site orientation, and the use of large amounts of south facing windows to allow low angle winter sunshine into the structure. These are the collection devices. And the house itself, along with proper insulation, is the storage device. There is no fluid involved, only air, in the passive solar design. And there is no

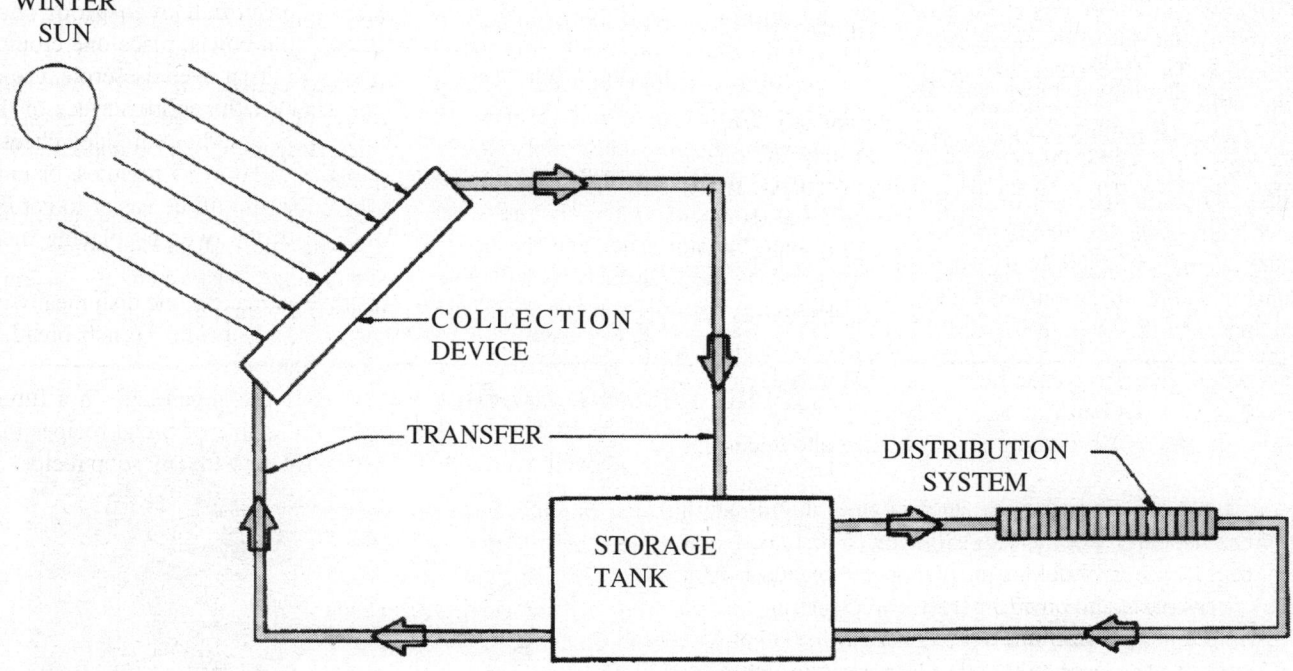

Figure 1. Active solar system

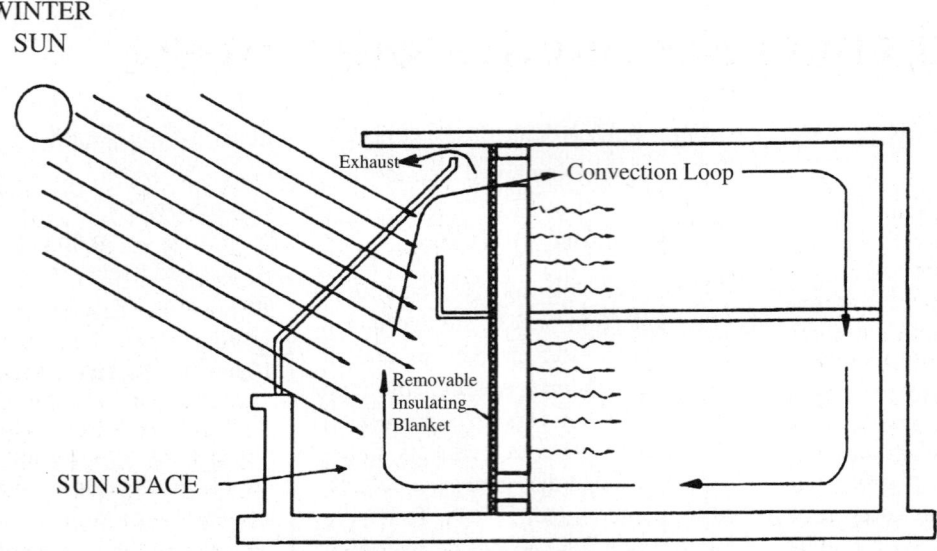

Figure 2. Isolated gain system using a sun space

mechanical means of collecting, storing, or distributing the energy.

Isolated gain system

There are many variations to the passive solar design. But one of the most effective and attractive is the isolated gain system (see Fig. 2). The isolated gain system consists of a greenhouse, sun porch, or other south facing room attached to the main part of the house. This space acts as both the solar collector and storage area, and serves a useful function of transferring excess heat to the main part of the house. The sun space is often combined with some sort of thermal mass (material that conducts heat), such as plants and soil, or masonry within the sun space. In this way the system can provide heat in two ways according to the temperature outside.

For daytime operation, solar radiation passes through the windows into the sun space and heats up the thermal mass within. Heat is then transferred throughout the rest of the house by means of vents, ducts, windows, or doors. As the space is being heated during the day, the warm air is allowed to escape to the main part of the house and cool air enters. This then forms a natural convection loop that evenly distributes the warm air.

At night the sun space cools slowly as heat is released by the thermal mass within the sun space. If the wall between the sun space and the house is used as thermal mass, it will give off heat to both the sun space and the house. For this reason an insulated shutter can be placed on the sun space side of the thermal wall to reduce heat entering the space.

Because the passive solar system uses traditional building methods and materials, this type of system can be built for only 5 to 10 percent over the normal cost of new home construction. Also, an isolated gain system is a good solution for retro-fitting an existing house by adding on the sun space. Besides cutting fuel bills by 40% or more, there is the added advantage of interesting living space added to your home.

So with all this free, renewable energy available to heat our homes, consider using a passive energy system to heat your home. Δ

A BHM Writer's Profile

Sally Denney

Sally Denney lives on a 23-acre farm in Warsaw, Indiana. She has been married to her husband, Randy, for 25 years. They have four children, Mrs. Matthew (Shelley) Boruff, Tonya, Nicholas, and Timothy. They have one grandson, Skyler James Boruff.

Her hobbies are crafting, gardening, quilting, and painting. Besides Backwoods Home Magazine, she has written for Quilt World, Grit, Good Old Days, Rural Heritage, and various other magazines. She is currently working on a book titled The Art of Display for Crafters.

She is a part-time employee of The Papers, Inc. in the editorial department.

Simplified concrete and masonry work

By Robert L. Williams

If you are willing to sweat a great deal, endure aching muscles, and expend time and energy, you can do much of your concrete and masonry work around the house or farm. Your early work will not be extremely pretty or professional, but the money you save and the pride you take in your work can offset minor problems.

The keys to do-it-yourself masonry (and, indeed, hundreds of other jobs around the homestead) are inseparable from several very important economic factors. First, can you afford the time to do the work yourself? Ask this one basic question: Can I earn what I would have to pay a professional during the time it would take me to do the job? If so, you may want to hire the masonry people.

Depending upon your part of the country and whether you hire union or non-union workers, professionals or part-time masons, and whether you will be allowed to help with the work, the job can vary by several hundred dollars. A mason, for instance, might charge you $2 for every cement block he lays. If a wall has 300 blocks in it, you will pay $600, in addition to the cost of the blocks, the mortar, and other ingredients of the job.

If you can spare the time, however, you can do virtually any of the simple masonry jobs needed. Start, if you are building a foundation wall, by digging the footings and setting up the batter boards. These are simply stakes and cords stretched along the footing excavations to guide your construction work in order to have perfectly square corners and true walls all around.

Set the stakes at the corner at least four feet from the corner itself, and where the cords cross, the angle should create a perfectly square corner. One quick way to determine whether the corner is square is to measure from the point where the cords cross out one line 9 feet and 12 feet down the other line. Mark the spot and then measure diagonally from mark to mark. The distance should be 15 feet.

If you are working on a very small structure or very large one, you can use the same basic formula of multiples of 3, 4, and 5 (3x3=9; 3x4=12; 3x5=15). You can use 3, 4, and 5, or 30, 40, and 50 . . . as long as 3, 4, and 5 are multiplied by 3.

Measure the length of the footing carefully to see that it is divisible in length by 16. This is the length of a typical cement block and its mortar joint. For instance, if your wall is to be 40 feet long, this equals 480 inches (40x12). Divide 480 by 16 (the length of the block plus joint) and you get 30. Thus you know that you will not be left with an odd length to try to fill at the end of a course of blocks.

If, for sheer example, you want a wall 43 feet long. You will have 516 inches which, divided by 16, is 32.25. You will be forced to deal with one-fourth of a block in each course. Avoid this.

Footers or footings should be deep enough to be below the frost or freeze line. When footings are dug, you are ready to mix concrete. You will need a container such as a mortar box if you plan to mix a large amount of concrete. For smaller amounts a wheelbarrow will work. You will also need a hoe and the basic concrete ingredients: Portland cement, sand, gravel, and water.

We have used the 1-3-5 formula for years and have found it to work perfectly for concrete footings, floors, and other basic uses. This formula says that you will use one measure of Portland cement, three measures of sand, and five of gravel (the sand and gravel are often called fine aggregate and coarse aggregate). You can also use the 1-2-3 formula.

To mix a whole bag of Portland cement, start by pouring five gallons of water into the mortar box or pan. Then add the Portland cement and mix it thoroughly (don't just wet it!) with the water. Then add the sand a small amount at a time until it, too, is mixed thoroughly. Finally, add the gravel a shovelful at a time until it is well mixed. Add more water if the mixture is too dry. It should be a thick-soup consistency.

Shovel the concrete mixture into the footing trench. To assure a level footing, you can space stakes along the trench and drive them down until the top (or other mark) of the stake is perfectly level with all other stakes and with the desired depth of the concrete. Shovel in concrete until, when smoothed, the concrete reaches the top mark of each stake. You can remove the stakes when the desired level is reached.

When you mix mortar, use essentially the same methods. The formula is 1:3 (one measure of masonry cement to three measures of sand, plus enough water to form a mixture of a plastic consistency. You want it thin enough to work easily and thick enough to hold its shape—sort of like thin pudding.

Start with two gallons of water (for a large batch of mortar) and ten shovels of sand. Mix the sand and water well and then add the masonry cement (Type II). Gradually add the rest of the sand and cement mix and water as needed.

To lay blocks, first set up a guide line by driving two stakes at least two feet past the end of the footing and aligned with the outside edge of the footing and the batter board cords which denote the exact location of the outside of the foundation wall. The guide line should be stretched tightly and should be eight inches high. A cement block is 7.5 inches high, and you will need a half-inch of mortar under it to bring it to a height of eight inches.

Lay a mortar bed over the top of the footing. Make it thick enough to support the weight of the block; you do not want the block resting on the footing surface but within the mortar bed.

The first block should be a corner block: that is, one with a square end rather than the traditional "ears" of the regular course or stretcher blocks. Set the block in the mortar bed so that the end of the block is aligned exactly with the batter board cord and the outside edge is aligned with the guide line.

Push the block down firmly into the mortar bed until the top of the block is aligned with the guide line. The outside edge of the block should be as close as possible, at all points, to the guide line without touching it. Never let the blocks touch the guide line.

To lay the next block, stand it on end and use the trowel to cut into the mortar and scoop a load onto the blade. "Butter" the ears of the block by holding the trowel with your fingers around the handle and the thumb across and parallel to the metal part of the trowel handle.

Lower the trowel with the point at five o'clock and let the point barely graze the outside edge of the block side as close to the corner as possible. With a swift motion, rake the trowel along the outside edge of the block end until you have applied a thick bead of mortar inside the grooves at the end of the block. Do not try to butter the other end of the block.

Lift the block by grasping the thick sides of the core partition in the middle of the block. With two hands holding the block, gently position it near the first block, and as you lower the second block into the mortar bed, push the block gently but firmly against the first one so that the mortar is compressed between the two blocks.

Now, with a guide line set up along the other side of the corner, lay a block that butts into the side of the first block. Butter the end of the block as you did before. You now have the first two blocks of the corner.

The third block is laid so that it stretches across the first two blocks. In other words, half the new block will rest on each of the first two blocks to establish a bond among all three blocks. Before you lay the block (which will be another corner block so that the outside end will align smoothly with the other blocks) lay a mortar bed over the first two blocks so that the third block will not actually touch either of the first two blocks but will rest instead on the mortar bed so that another bond is formed.

Next, lay blocks at the ends of the two blocks resting in the mortar bed. You now have four blocks in the first row or course of blocks. Then lay, as you did before, two second course blocks that will butt into the first block in the second course.

In this fashion, keep laying block until the corner is waist high. You can even build the corner as high as you plan to take the wall, as long as you are reasonably certain that the corner is true in all respects.

Then go to another corner and repeat the process until all four corners are started. At this point, begin to complete the first course of the first wall. Keep the blocks aligned with the guide line. Notice that the guide line should be even with the top of the blocks at all points in the course.

Keep your mortar joints as close to the same thickness as you possibly can. This includes the mortar bed joints as well as the joints between blocks.

You should keep checking every block by using a level from end to end and from side to side. If one side is too high, use the butt of the trowel handle to tap the high point down until it is level with the rest of the wall. Use the level vertically against the side of the wall to see that the wall isn't leaning in or out at all. Correct even the tiniest problems while they are still easy to remedy.

Remember to double-check the length of the wall to see that you will be able to fit a whole block or a half-block into the final space in each course. As you work, note the bonding of the blocks. Keep the bonding such that each block should span half of the two blocks below it.

As you lay each block, use the edge of the trowel to cut away all mortar that is squeezed out between blocks. Fling this mortar back into the mortar pan.

If you need a mortar board to make your work easier, build one by locating a square or rectangle of plywood about 12 to 15 inches in each direction. Locate scrap lengths of 2-x-4s and stand these far enough apart so that you can lay the square of plywood over the 2-x-4s and then nail the plywood to the 2-x-4s. Load this surface with mortar and carry it to your work station.

If you wish to add brick veneer to the foundation wall, leave enough room on the footing for the width of a brick. When you lay the bricks, do the work exactly as you did the blocks. Just think of the bricks as miniature blocks. Concentrate on bonding, mortar joints, mortar beds, vertical and horizontal trueness, and neat and consistent work at all times.

In at least alternate courses you will need to break a block down the center in order to have the courses work out exactly. You can buy special blocks that can be broken easily and exactly. If you don't have these, you can break a regular stretcher block by tapping the outside surface just beside the partition for the core. Tap until the tinny sound suddenly deepens. Then turn the block over and tap the surface of the opposite side until the same deep tone is heard. The block will then break, with a little practice on your part, in a fairly straight line.

The half block will then fit into the final space left in the course of blocks. You may need to use a hammer or masonry hammer to chip gently at the irregular edges that protrude from the block. You will also break a few blocks at the wrong places, but this is all part of learning basic masonry.

The methods described here will not in any sense of the word make you a professional mason. But with practice and a degree of experimentation you can learn to do a very creditable job of laying bricks and blocks, and you can save yourself a great deal of money and emerge from the work with sore and aching joints and muscles but with a sense of pride that you are one major step closer to complete self-reliant living. ∆

Just for kids—Killing some time
(create an afternoon time warp)

By Lucy Shober

There is a book that describes a time warp as being a kind of bubble, a place in time that doesn't really fit into what we know of as history. How often have you wished that you could spend one or two days in a big bubble like that? Maybe the time that you accidentally spelled your name in permanent ink on the bathroom wall. Wouldn't it have been nice to just go to sleep in a big vacant bubble until the flack from that blew over? What about those sickly tense minutes spent at the doctor's office staring at a tray of sterile needles, wondering which one was for you? How about the dentist? The principal's office? Sunday evenings at nine o'clock with three hours of homework that you've been putting off?...

Enough!! Stop! It's probably making you knee-weak just thinking of some of life's little episodes, so let's escape! How about taking some of that precious stuff (time) to move a hundred years forward or a million years back in history? Take an afternoon to forget today. With a little imagination, it's easy, and you don't even need a note from your parents! Follow these steps to remove yourself to the Jurassic age, then whiz on up to the year 2094. It's a breeze! Just remember to come back in time to finish conjugating those verbs before English class tomorrow.

First of all you must wash all of today out of your mind. Fill up a sink with warm sudsy water, take a deep breath, and sink your face and hands. Blow all of the air out of your lungs, and with each bubble you make, pretend that something that's been bugging you is being carried away. Lift up your head for another breath, plunge again and let those warm time bubbles escape with every last worry in your brain. When this is finished, dry off with a towel, and you're ready for an afternoon in the twilight zone!

Prehistoric fish fossil prints

To escape to the Jurassic period you will need to have gathered these materials before your head dunk:

- some old absorbent rags.
- a box of salt.
- a fresh dead fish (mullet is pretty cheap, most places)
- some tempera paint.
- four or five sheets of newsprint or construction paper.

With these materials, you can make what looks like a real fish fossil. First take the fish and rub it all over with salt. Do its head and tail on both sides too. This will remove all the slimy film that protects the live fish from bacteria while it swims through the water. Now wipe the salt off with the rags. Pick a color (or colors) of tempera and spread a thin layer over the whole fish body on one side. Don't use too much! Now wipe the excess off with a rag and place the newsprint

or construction paper over the fish's body and press down firmly.

It might take two or three tries, but with practice you can come up with some really beautiful fossil-like prints. If you get a really nice one, you could even frame it, they're that pretty!

Make a time capsule

After you've cleaned up that mess, let's head for the future! You will have fun scouting around the house for items to go into your time capsule.

A time capsule is like a present for someone *not* in the present: a gift for a friend in the future. In your gift box (or capsule) you will show your friend little tid-bits of what your life and world was like in the year 1994. You won't be here anymore, of course, in the year 2094, so the person who opens your time capsule will be kind of like the ultimate one-way pen-pal. An old oatmeal box works best for this project. You must paint it, or wrap it in aluminum foil, or even glue beads and other decorations onto it. Anything to make it look special to some child of the future. Label it too, with the words "Time capsule, to be opened in the year 1994," and your name and the date.

Inside your box, you should put the filled out information sheet from this page, and the following signs of these times.

1. A folded-up first page of your local newspaper.
2. A favorite article from *Backwoods Home Magazine*, perhaps one that gives some "how to" information (raising chickens or maybe some great recipe).
3. A plastic bag with a few strands of your hair in it.
4. A copy of the alphabet and numbers from one to one hundred (just in case things change drastically!).
5. A picture of you and one of your family.
6. (This is the fun part!) Anything that you think is wonderful about the times in which we live. Maybe a couple of sticks of bubble gum, or your favorite candy bar. If you're from the south you might throw in a bottle of tabasco sauce! Perhaps your favorite fish lure, or a tape of yourself or your favorite band singing. Put some seeds from the garden in too, and even some joke items like a plastic ice cube with a fly in it. Put explanations in to let them know what you were like back in the good old days of 1994. They will love the nostalgia, and you will have a great time providing it.

When your capsule is full, put the top onto the box and either glue it or tape it firmly. You must put your capsule in a safe place, maybe in the bottom of a box in the attic. If you're really into it, check around with your adult friends to see who might have some extra space in a safety deposit box at the bank.

Now just forget about it. If you can stand not to open it, you sure will make the day of some lucky child who happens upon your 1994 time capsule in the year 2094. What a trip to the future! ∆

Time capsule information sheet

My name_____

My hobbies_____

My pets_____

About me and my family:

What we like to eat:_____

This is what we do all day long:_____

Father_____

Mother_____

Siblings (brothers and sisters)_____

Here is a picture of my house and yard. I drew it myself.

Raising sheep

By Monta Hulsing

Sheep have always been one of man's liberators. In one animal you have a source of meat, milk, leather, and fiber. Having an animal that provided such a variety of needs allowed primitive man to move into areas of the world that were previously uninhabitable. As mankind progressed from a hunter-gatherer society to a more agrarian lifestyle, the sheep readily adapted to domestication. Sheep can be raised successfully in areas that are unsuitable for anything except growing grass. They can tolerate hot, semi-desert environments as well as the harsh winters near the arctic circle. This remarkable animal has been a part of human civilization and has made life easier for mankind for millennia. Many nomadic tribes even built their homes out of wool in areas of the world where other building materials were scarce or nonexistent.

Meat and milk products

Meat was probably the first use humans had for sheep. The sheep converts forage into meat more efficiently than any other ruminant. A shepherd can raise five sheep per acre just letting them graze freely, and one who practices rotational grazing can triple that number. Lambing in the spring, you can produce a crop of nice lean, meaty lambs for your freezer, or to sell, on grass alone. On a small scale it is always possible to sell freezer lambs direct to the customer and make several times more than market prices would bring you, and at quite a savings for the customer, also. In fact, I know of people who have gone into the retail specialty market and have a small rural shop that specializes in lamb grown on their farm, and lamb cookery. If one had the wherewithal to obtain or grow organically produced feed, it would be possible to go into the organically raised meat business, and that is a product where the demand is always greater than the supply.

Author Monta Hulsing with Zeus, a champion Lincoln ram.

One of the major reasons I raise sheep is the quality of life that you can achieve producing your own meat. One trip to a feedlot operation to spy out the methods used, and I almost became a vegetarian. The single most cost effective thing a beef producer can do is use the hormone based growth implants. Another item of concern is the antibiotics and other medicines that are routinely fed to feedlot animals. We're told by the drug companies that all these chemicals are out of the meat of the animal if a certain number of days pass before slaughter, yet I wonder how many unscrupulous producers simply process these animals regardless.

I no longer buy meat at the grocery because I do not want to risk feeding my family and friends the residues from these treatments. People who raise their own meat, be it beef, poultry, pork, rabbit, fish, or lamb, knows what they are getting (and not getting) when they put meat on the table.

Yogurt, which was originally made with ewe's milk, was enjoyed by the many nomadic tribes around the world for thousands of years before it became so popular with the health minded modern world. The Vikings and other early European peoples used sheep milk for their cheeses as well as yogurt. Today the sheep dairy business is small and specialized, but thriving and gaining in popularity and acceptance.

Sheepskins and wool

Sheepskins were the superior pelts for garments, since they have fleece rather than hair. Most animal hairs are hollow fibers, and while they can be very warm, especially on the animal, they are actually quite fragile compared to sheepskin. A single wool fiber can be bent twenty thousand times before breaking—compared to about two thousand for the next most durable natural fiber, silk, and a mere 75 times for most synthetics. We have all seen rabbit fur coats in department stores. One of the first things I noticed about these rabbit skin coats is the tendency to shed. The few deerskins I have seen tanned with the hair on them, have been decorating someone's wall, or used in some other relatively limited way. Not so sheepskins. There are numerous companies and individuals that make many varied articles with sheepskins, everything from baby booties to steering wheel covers. It can even be tanned in such a way as to make it machine washable.

Early man discovered another use for sheep hides. Sheepskins were washed and soaked in lime to remove the fat and the fiber, stretched and scraped thin, and then rubbed with pumice and chalk. This produced a smooth white writing surface known as parchment. Parchment was much more durable than most primitive papers; some parchment scrolls have been found that date back to 1500 BC. Vellum, which is made from lambskins, is a higher grade of parchment, and historically has been used for university diplomas, maps, and legal documents.

Mankind almost certainly used sheep for food long before discovering the value of wool. But when he learned the advantages of clothing his body with wool garments, he discovered a sheep's true worth. It is not synthetically produced, and therefore does not contribute to the world's abundance of environmentally destructive chemical wastes. Wool is the easiest of natural fibers to work with. Historically in this country, children began doing the family's wool processing at about age five. Even if you have no carding, spinning and weaving skills, you can felt your wool and end up with a very good fabric for many uses, including garments. Felting was probably one of the earliest of wool processing methods. Felting compacts the wool, making it warmer, sturdier, and more water resistant, without being heavy in weight. It makes very good outerwear, and the nomads on the plains of central and western Asia used felt for yurts, their tentlike homes. Even today, in our modern technological world, yurts still decorate the landscape from Turkey to eastern Mongolia.

Other products

There are two other important items that come from sheep. Lanolin, a byproduct of wool processing, has been used for creams and lotions that soothe the skin and protect it, as well as a base for medicinal creams. Just going out to the barn and handling some sheep is a good remedy for chapped or dry hands in the winter. The tallow from sheep has been made into soap for centuries. Sheep tallow soap, better known as saddle soap, is extremely gentle, and can really be used for any cleaning need. Sheep tallow was also added to beeswax to make candles.

Lincoln longwools

I started out raising sheep about ten years ago, and since I was a weaver and had a friend that wanted to learn to spin, I chose a "wool" breed. That livestock experience was rather short lived, but when I wanted to resume raising sheep about five years ago, once again I chose a "wool" breed. This time it was Lincoln Longwools.

Lincolns are an old breed of sheep, dating back to the mid-18th century in Lincolnshire, England, where selective breeding was practiced to improve the flocks of primitive sheep. In books and records from the era, it comes to us that Lincolns were most likely the parents of all the English longwool breeds. A breeders' society for those who raised Lincoln sheep was started in 1796, and in this country the American National Lincoln Sheep Breeders' Association was founded over 100 years ago, in 1891.

The NLSBA now maintains a white sheep registry and a natural colored sheep registry to accommodate the different breeders of Lincolns in this country. Lincolns are considered a rare breed. Lincolns make up less than one percent of the 11 million sheep in this country. In 1992 there were 136 breeders listed in the membership directory.

As I am writing this, I can look out my front window and see my sheep. Stretched out before me in the fields are sheep of many hues and colors. I have white Lincolns, black Lincolns, and a collection of the various "blues" which run the range of nearly-white silvers, through the grays and pewters to the charcoals. Their fleeces shine with the luster that is part of a Lincoln's heritage. Recently shorn, they are masses of tight curls that in time will become deeply crimped locks, which over the course of a year could reach lengths of 10 inches or even more. It is not uncommon to have 20 pounds of wool come off of a Lincoln. I have crossbred sheep whose fleece weight will triple the amount of fleece I will get from their non-Lincoln mothers.

Lincoln fleece is an amazing fiber. It is a very strong fiber, used historically for rugs and the heels and toes of socks. The white and silver colors take dye fabulously, giving intense colors and shades. Along with the natural variation of color in Lincolns, they seem to acquire very interesting natural sun bleachings. I have had fleeces turn up with brown and even red highlights, which is a boon to the handspinner and weaver.

Lincoln Longwools are considered to be a coarse wool breed. People who know something about wool often dismiss Lincoln wool as being too coarse for anything except rugs and carpets. As a Lincoln breeder I have found their wool to be very versatile. Its length makes it extremely easy to spin, and the hogget—first shearing off of the lambs—is soft enough to make beautiful sweaters. The wool from yearlings and older sheep, when spun by hand, is much softer than many commercial yarns used to make outerwear. Any garment made with Lincoln wool will be very durable. Needless to say, the rugs I weave will probably outlast me.

The Lincoln is a large sheep, well muscled and sturdy. Even though they are thought of as a wool sheep, they yield excellent carcasses, having a wide loin and large rear legs. A Lincoln ram typically weighs in at 250 lbs. or more and ewes can reach 200 lbs. They are a hornless breed of sheep that exhibit vigor and stamina, and have an aura of self assurance in their stance.

In Lincolnshire, the land consists of low rolling plains type grasslands, where the sheep live their lives entirely outdoors. They lamb in late winter on the sometimes snowy hillsides. On this continent, they live with ease in areas as varied as New England, the Midwest, the Pacific Northwest, and the high plateaus of Mexico, taking snow, rain, and heat in stride.

It is said that Lincolns grow slowly, but I have found that to mean that they do not reach full growth until after the second year. A result of this is that Lincolns are unusually long lived sheep. It isn't uncommon to find a 12-year-old ewe still productive in lambs and fleece. The ewes are excellent mothers, attentive, with good milk supplies. Lincolns in England produce, on average, a 150% lambing rate. Here in this country higher ratios are noted. This year I only had one ewe that didn't give me twins, a yearling I was saving out for showing, that was inadvertently bred last year. Other breeders I know have ewes that routinely give them triplets and I know of at least one breeder that gets quads from some of their ewes. The lambs are hardy, able to take harsh weather right from the beginning. They reach market weights at an age comparable with other breeds.

In commercial operations, Lincoln rams can really excel. Their value in a crossbred program can be seen in the vigorous growth and increased wool production of the lambs. The lambs inherit many of the Lincoln's traits of disease and parasite resistance. Heat tolerance and feed conversion are another benefit of crossing Lincoln rams with ewes of other breeds.

Lincolns are calm and gentle sheep. I can walk right up to any of my breeding rams and take ahold of them. With a little encouragement the sheep will follow me from pasture to pasture as we rotate their grazing land. I take sheep to our local elementary school for a sheep and wool demonstration and they tolerate the children's affection very well.

All these things are things you can find out by reading literature about Lincolns or talking to Lincoln breeders. We all love to talk about our wonderful "exotic" sheep. I would like to also add that some of the simple pleasures of sheep raising come from seeing lambs bounding across the field, wearing handcrafted garments, trying that new recipe for lamb chops, and that feeling of contentment that comes from "doing your own thing...."

(Monta Hulsing sells NLSBA registered white and colored Lincoln sheep and hand woven rugs from Hulsing's Black Sheep Farm, Rt 1, Box 478, Williams IN 47470.) ∆

A BHM Writer's Profile

Martin P. Waterman

Martin P. Waterman, a frequent contributor to Backwoods Home Magazine, writes on the science of gardening and horticulture. He also writes on technology issues including computers, communications, and genetics, and how these sciences influence our lives.

Waterman is a rural based writer living in British Columbia, Canada. He spends much of his time writing, gardening, breeding hardy fruit for the north, or on Internet, where he can be reached at:

martin_waterman@bc.sympatico.ca

A BHM Writer's Profile

Audrey Stallsmith

Audrey Stallsmith, 35, is a free lance writer whose first book, The Body They May Kill, was put out by Thomas Nelson Publishers in 1995. She currently has a contract with Waterbrook Press for a series of mystery novels with herbal themes. The first of these, Rosemary for Remembrance, is scheduled for release in April of 1998.

Single, Audrey lives with her parents on a small dairy farm in western Pennsylvania. Her intersts include herbs and heirloom flowers, oil painting, cryptic crosswords, old lace, beads, and Border Collies. Her favorite authors are C.S. Lewis, G.K. Chesterton, and Dorothy Sayers.

A Backwoods Home Anthology

SELF-SUFFICIENCY/MONEY

Free supplies for your homestead

By Jeff Heikenfeld

A couple years ago my wife and I moved from our rented townhouse to a farm in the country. Since we were buying a house in need of everything, a barn and several other outbuildings, I knew we would need a lot of material. I have always read the local bargain sheet and free advertising newspapers. I noticed every once in a while an ad would appear asking for something, like a bed for free, as well as ads offering things for free. The free ads are a good source to use except for the fact that most times the items are gone by the time you make the call.

In the past, I had run ads asking for specific items I wished to purchase. I recently purchased a rototiller this way. The tiller was a two-year-old Troybilt. A friend shared the expense with me, and we each paid $200 for a tiller that would have gone for $1000 at today's prices.

The beauty of this type of ad is that it puts you in direct touch with the person who has the item without them having to tell the whole world that they have it. To solicit materials for my homestead, I thought I would run a free ad saying what I wanted. "Ask and ye shall receive." Since I wasn't paying for the ad, I had nothing to lose. After a couple of tries, I came up with two ad versions that I thought were pretty good. If you want to do this, you may write a better one. My ads were as follows:

> Wanted: Brick, lumber, paint, nails for reconditioning old barn and farmhouse, can use anything. Phone 737-1541, ask for Heik.
>
> Free: Have truck, will haul away lumber, plywood, bricks, nails, storm windows, tarpaper, etc. Needed to renovate old farm buildings and house, call 737-1541, ask for Heik.

The phone calls started when the paper came out. I was working as a car salesperson, so I put both my home and work number in the paper. Since I only got paid if I sold a car, I wasn't cheating my employer. (Advice: Don't get fired for a load of stuff. Use your work number only if it doesn't cause problems.) If I was with a customer, I would take the name and number of the caller and return the call as soon as I could. Remember, nobody else knows this person has a garage full of stuff to get rid of, but it doesn't take too long before they tell someone, so be prompt.

My first call was from a man moving off his farm after forty years. He gave me a pickup load of old buckets, doors, tools, wire, nails, wash tubs, rope, etc. He was chuckling to himself the whole time he was loading the stuff. "Oh, you'll need this," he would say. Almost everything was usable stuff that he had failed to sell at his yard sale, so this was good for him and for me.

The second call was from a man who remodeled old houses to resell. He gave me three loads of used brick, 15 new oak cabinet doors, a working dishwasher, a stainless steel sink, two windows with casements, and assorted windows and screens and scrap lumber. I went over several times when he called me. He wouldn't say much, just his last name and, "There's (whatever it was) sitting out for you." I always went the same day he called since the neighborhood was known for having materials disappear.

The only thing you need is a way to carry the stuff. A pickup is best, but a trailer could do the same job. Obviously, you also need the energy to do the work, but if you bought a homestead you'd better have it anyway! The car dealership had a truck I could use. I was always careful not to take a nice truck so I wouldn't scratch up a good paint job, and so my benefactor would not think I had more money than he did. One time while picking up three bundles of new cedar shake shingles, I was told how nice my truck was. When I told the man it wasn't mine, he became a whole lot happier. So if you have a new truck, borrow an older one. Even if you think you're only going once, you might get another call or referral from the person if you conduct yourself properly.

Enlist the help of friends and family. They are additional free advertisers for you. My dad found me an entire kitchen, full of cabinets, and my mother-in-law found storm windows and screens from a whole house. They are now earmarked for the second story of the barn.

Friends may give you a lot of things if you talk about the farm with them. I have been given lumber, firewood, coal, stained glass lamps, fence posts, etc.

There is no way to tell you everything else I have been given, so I'll just list a few examples:

- 8 pickup loads of red pine lumber and roof tin from an old shed
- 2 pickup loads of concrete block
- 1 pickup load of shingles

- 1 coal boiler, scrap lumber, and 10 new 2x4s
- 2 40-pound boxes of nails, plus a roll of black plastic for gardening

People are glad to see you. The fella with the nails said, "I wish I had seen your ad sooner. I already put two 40-pound boxes in the trash!" The man with the eight loads of lumber said, "I was taking this to the dump until my dad saw your ad." He saved, and I saved.

There are a few guidelines I use. Suit yourself, but no doubt you'll find out what works and what doesn't quickly enough. My guidelines:

- Use free ads.
- Take everything. You can pass on what you don't need to others, friends, Salvation Army, etc.
- Be specific in what you ask for.
- Be grateful.
- Keep your word.
- Don't look too prosperous.
- Get good directions, and call before you go.
- Unload excess stock periodically, swapping or giving it away. You can't keep it all.
- Keep your eyes and ears open. I got 25 roof trusses this way.
- Keep a basic tool kit with you. You might need to take something apart.
- Keep a list of what you still need, so you can alter your ad.

You can get whatever you want free, if you can afford to wait for it. If you need it immediately, buy it. All this collecting can really amass a pile of supplies quickly. Your wife will probably label you a junkman, and your friends may kid you a lot, but you'll save big dollars. ∆

*When I was a boy,
Fishing,
We would gut the trout
Alive,
Bread them,
Then throw them in a sizzling skillet,
Right there on the bank,
And eat them immediately.
One day,
One slipped from my hand
Just after I had gutted it
And it slipped from my hand
And fell back into the water.
I watched it
Swim away
Until it reached the bottom
And the safety of its comrades,
Its entrails
Still on the rocks beside me.*

John Earl Silveira
Ojai, CA

A BHM Writer's Profile

Ted Sponem

Born in 1951, raised on a Wisconsin dairy farm, Ted Sponem is a freelance carpenter and soldier of misfortune. He builds mandolins and mountain dulcimers along with a variety of children's toys (adults like them too.)

Ted is interested in wind and solar power in its various forms, as well as aviation, old time music, backwoods living, and reading. He has been known to take part in occasional fur trade era rendevous. He hates politics...if con is opposit of pro, is congress opposite of progress?

Improving poor garden soil

Here in the Siskiyou mountains of southern Oregon, where *BHM*'s office is located, the land is very poor for gardening. The soil is primarily gray clay that turns to brick when the sun hits it, and it has plenty of rocks.

When we started planning our garden here at the office, we went to a few long term residents at neighboring Fall Creek Ranch to find out how they manage such productive gardens here. For those in similar situations, this is what they told us.

From Vernon Hopkins:

Having had the pleasure of growing lush vegetable gardens in deep, rich topsoils at my former home, it was a challenge to improve this garden area when I came here more than 30 years ago. There was an inch or two of topsoil over a heavy clay base. Deep growing vegetables grew twisted and misshapen as they were forced to penetrate the heavy soil.

The nearby feeder for the replacement heifers furnished an abundance of manure mixed with hay. With the front bucket on the tractor, this fresh manure (mixed with the soil around the feeder) was heaped to the depth of more than one foot over the entire garden area. This was spaded into the clay base, leveled and planted.

Earthworms, attracted by the large supply of their favorite foods, moved in, multiplied and soon turned this covering of manure into inches of rich top soil. By adding a few inches of manure each year for worm food, there is no reason to deep till, as worms are nature's plowmen.

Once the right soil is provided for plants (manure and organic matter homogenized by earthworms) you can sit back and watch it grow, or as some enthusiastic gardeners would say, "drop in the seeds and jump back."

A raised border separating the garden area from the lawn was made by heaping a foot wide by one- foot- high mound of manure mixed with hay. Under this border, potatoes were planted. In mid-summer, by lifting the edge of the border, we could harvest the larger of the new crop for a mess of new potatoes and peas.

From Pat Ward:

Planting a garden in the Southern Oregon Cascades can be done with minimal effort. Having a multitude of cow byproducts is the secret. You cover a plot with a thick layer of mixed cow manure and old hay, till it, then throw in some seeds, water, and jump back.

Maybe not quite that easy, but basically that's it. Cow manure is best because it has less weed seeds in it, due to the cow's digestive tract. Dairies are a good source if you don't have your own cows. It's not necessary to till the ground after the first time. You just build your own soil with continuous applications of cow manure, and you will have a beautiful loamy garden. In fact my Dad's soil got so loamy and soft that he couldn't grow corn. It would fall over because the soil was so rich the roots didn't have to go deep to get their nourishment. You can use other ingredients to build and fertilize your garden. Chicken manure is very good but should be mixed with the dirt as it is very hot and can burn little seedlings. Horse manure is good except for the weed seeds. It can be heated to kill the seeds. You can also build up your soil by burying your kitchen garbage in your garden. It's very good for the soil. I hate to see good garbage go to the garbage man when it does so much good in the garden. It does take longer to decompose though.

Garden plots: you can design your garden in many ways. Raised gardens are very popular, attractive, and kind of expensive. You need railroad ties, planks, rocks or other material that is strong enough to make a frame about 8 to 12 inches high. Wood frames are usually square cornered shapes. With rocks your imagination can run wild. It's a lot of work but the end results are usually worth it. Fill your frames with manure in the fall. You can also just start building up a spot in the yard.

Another help is to get your seeds and seedlings from a local supplier who understands the needs of your climate. The best source I have found for this region is Nichols Garden Nursery, 1190 N. Pacific Highway, Albany, OR 97321-4598. Δ

A country moment

Swallows court each other in northern California. (Frank Tickle photo)

COUNTRY LIVING

Dueling duck

By Cleoral Lovell

The day we brought him home our two dogs were not sure what he was. Neither was he. Donald Duck pressed his advantage and convinced both quadrupeds that two legs were superior. He lowered his bill to the ground, waved his extended neck like an eel, and rushed Mac. Our terrier backed away, completely perplexed by his new playmate's tactics. Ace the pup decided he'd be braver. He raced forward, yapping hysterically at this queer creature. For his trouble he got a healthy nip on his ear that sent him into retreat.

Donald had been given to us by one of my husband's friends because he had become a nuisance. (The duck, not the friend.) There was only one boy at their house and Donald was his pet. The drake would tolerate pants legs and sneakers, but just let a pair of nylons and heels cross his line of vision! The lady of the house was tired of being pursued by a web footed quacker, so we inherited Donald.

I had hoped, by being especially nice to him and serving him extra helpings of corn and special tid-bits, to win favor in his beady eyes. Not this belligerent duck! His paranoid ego demands that at least one adult, preferably female, and every cat and dog in the neighborhood be terrorized before he can be even faintly happy. He is as above accepting bribes as a Supreme Court justice, and he enjoys literally biting the hand that feeds him.

Occasionally he will lull me into a false sense of security by a temporary truce. Sometimes it's because he is too busy soaking up sunshine or splashing under the downspout. Sometimes he is too busy making life miserable for the world of worms and insects to bother to charge me. This is the exception, not the rule.

Sometimes I protect myself by fending him off with an empty clothes basket or the lawn broom. He delights in these games where he pits only his bill and speed against the weapon of my choice. I have become quicker of foot than at any time since I was on the girl's track team in grade school!

Until he came to live with us, the most water Donald had ever seen at one time was a pailful. The first time we introduced him to our pond proved more entertaining than a Jerry Lewis movie. His antics resembled the routine of a prima donna in an aquacade. When he tired of gliding, diving, and whirling clockwise and counterclockwise, he flapped his wings until all of him was out of the water except his feet. Then he settled back down with a contented gurgle that was a cross between the bubbling of a baby and the burp of an overstuffed gourmet.

On our first trip down to the pond with Donald, we thought we would just leave him there to enjoy his initiation to his natural habitat. But upbringing crowded out instinct. Before we were halfway to the house, a distance of 300 feet, Donald overtook us, waddled past indignantly and led the procession. He was angry and weaving from side to side like a tipsy drum major.

Since he has agreed to co-existence with our four children, our pets (provided they keep their distance), and with me (provided I'm armed), he has proved to be a valuable addition to our household. He has taken on the role of watchdog. (Or should I say watchduck?) We have thought of posting a sign: "Beware of the duck!" to protect visitors' ankles. Usually a "nice doggy" or a friendly pat on the head will send our dogs into a tail-wagging ecstasy, but no one has found the proper password for Donald.

Just when I feel that Donald and I have reached an amicable understanding, he wounds not only my pride but my anatomy afresh. Nursing my latest red bruise about a week ago, I announced (yes, in his presence!) that he would look good stuffed and roasted.

Our daughter voiced the opinion of the other five members of the family: "Donald? For dinner? Not that duck! He's got too much personality to end up on a platter!"

Maybe I'll be more inclined to agree after my black and blue marks fade. ∆

The Fifth Year

Edible landscapes are Jim Gibbons' livelihood

By Vern Modeland

It's not a new idea. But it is gaining new fans. And it's an idea that has plenty of work-from-home income potential. What you need is a green thumb, and the enthusiasm of Jim Gibbons.

Gibbons lives on a tree-filled lot in the north part of Los Angeles. By most backwoodsers' standards, that's not a first choice location for homesteading. And the lot measures what some homesteaders would allow is a skimpy 60-by-100 feet. Its one other feature that's immediately noticeable to anyone who happens by is that all available space surrounding the Gibbons house on that 600 square-foot lot is bursting with growing, healthy, edible things.

No artificially-nurtured carpet of rich green grass and none of the Southern California-conventional palm trees or flowering ornamentals for Gibbons. He grows fruit trees—175 of them—and enough other practical plants to keep his family of four supplied with all the fruits, vegetables and herbs they want the year around. There's even surplus, to offer up as refreshing, and sometimes surprising, samples for the growing number of folks who drop in at the Gibbons place in Grenada Hills, California, just to see what he's up to.

Backyard jungle

"My backyard is a jungle of fruit trees. Lots of varieties. Small and close together."

Gibbons keeps his mini-orchard close-cropped. He prunes the trees 8-10 feet in height, for easier harvesting and to encourage growth. Under and around the fruit trees, vegetables and herbs thrive. Popular strains grow side by side with the new varieties that he constantly experiments with. His latest fancies include egg fruit, white sapote, and lucma.

Gibbons, as you might have guessed by now, is an advocate of edible landscaping. And he's making a living from helping cityfolks turn unused or under-used little spots into fertile plots on which to grow food to supplement or replace the neighborhood supermarket's fare of commercially grown and treated green-stuff.

Edible landscapes have global history. In the Philippines and Micronesia, people rely on kitchen gardens for a significant portion of their fresh produce. In Europe's newly-democratic states, folks are struggling to re-learn old ways and develop independent gardens following the collapse of state-run food supply systems.

"Instead of relying on [commercial] agriculture to produce all our food, we can become growers of much of our own produce," Gibbons has written.

"Fruit can be produced for just pennies a pound at home, whether there's a full front and back yard or just some containers on a patio."

Landscape feeds tenants

Gibbons cites the example of one Los Angeles client who has sought his help. She owns an apartment building, he explains. It's located in an area where incomes are limited.

Gibbons was contracted to remove all the existing landscaping around the apartment building, enrich the soil, then replant the space with vegetables, herbs and fruit trees.

"The tenants now help themselves to the harvest. I keep it planted. They keep it going."

Even the children, seven to fifteen years of age, have become involved, he says with pride about that project.

"People are continually surprised to find out how much they can grow in a little space. And in the cities, there's land that is good for no other use that can be producing food. Utility and city-owned corridors under high-voltage power lines are an example.

"People have begun leasing that land and turning it into commercial garden space where each participant gets a little plot. People in condominiums and apartment houses can grow a lot of their own food that way.

"If all available vacant land in metropolitan L.A. were used for food growing, we could meet a significant portion of our food needs locally.

"Our present food distribution system wastes an enormous amount of non-renewable resources and causes a great deal of pollution."

Lack of information

Gibbons blames a lack of good solid information on how to get started for keeping a lot of people in this country from starting their own kitchen gardens or trying out edible landscapes.

He uses himself as an example of becoming self-taught. When he was growing up, near Monroe, Wisconsin, his parents gave him a 1.5 acre plot on their 80-acre farm. He prepared it, planted it and managed the garden all by himself. And it produced: vegetables, and apples from a couple of trees, he recalls.

Jim Gibbons also found his future growing there. He went on to become a certified nurseryman, and headed for California, where the growing season is long and usually bountiful and a fellow with a green thumb stands a good chance of finding regular work.

Today, after more than 15 years, Gibbons hasn't stopped learning or building on what his experience has taught him about plants, their health, and their productivity. He reads a lot and he networks with others with similar interests.

"Particularly the old-timers," he says with a chuckle.

Learn the soil

Successful gardening has to include being aware of local soil variations and climate. There's a year-around growing season in Southern California, and uncommonly fertile land in the San Fernando Valley area where Gibbons lives. But in other locations where folks might yearn to try their hand at growing their own edible landscape, there will be specifics to learn about pests and nutrients and watering.

"Books give basics, but you need to find someone with local experience if you're going to succeed."

If there is a secret, Gibbons says, it is to carefully prepare the plot before planting. For city dwellers, he suggests intercepting some of the leaves and grass clippings neighbors consign to the trash collector, and turning them into free compost.

When the plot is properly enriched and prepared, plant heavily, maximize the space, and diversify, says Gibbons.

One benefit from intensive early "ground work" is that, with good culture practices, the home gardener has no need to consider using petroleum-based broad spectrum herbicides, fungicides or pesticides, according to Gibbons.

"These chemicals obviously do not add anything of value to our food, but can harm us. As more and more of us are beginning to realize, many of the chemicals used on our food against pests and diseases are toxic to us, too. This is an unnecessary assault on our health and well-being. Growing our own food organically protects us and our environment from this assault."

Plant a poly-culture

Insects and disease are kept at a minimum in Gibbons' own garden by good care of the soil and its fertility, and by planting a diverse poly-culture, he says. He avoids chemicals, or even natural pesticides, relying on a garden hose to wash away infestations on the rare occasions they happen.

"In Southern California, we get our rain all at one time in the winter. I conserve water by using a drip system on my fruit trees, with a timer and an emitter at each tree. I water (when needed) one to two times a week."

Gibbons has written about his experiences and philosophy on edible landscape gardening for Ecolution, the newsletter of the Eco-Home Network in Los Angeles (4344 Russell Ave., Los Angeles, CA 90027, (213) 662-5207). He also talks about producing a television program, first for the local public access cable channel, then perhaps expanding it into a more widely-distributed videotape or televised series.

Gibbons believes edible landscaping and community gardening are "growth ideas" in 1994 and can be a profitable business venture when it comes to making an independent living, particularly in or near a metropolitan area.

An acre is enough

"You can make a living on as little as an acre, especially by raising specialty fruits and ethnic foods," he says. "It's happening all over the country. Look at the growth in community supported agriculture, where you grow food for subscribers who may pay, say, $100 a share in order to share all summer and fall in fresh fruit, berries, herbs and vegetables. If I were going into that business, I'd plant 50 to as much as 100 percent excess, in order to cover crop losses or drought. You can always sell the excess at the local farmer's market."

About three-quarters of the cityfolks Gibbons has helped get into edible landscaping want to work alongside him, in order to learn. For the remainder of the clients and customers of Gibbons Landscaping, he does all the work, land preparation, planting, cultivation and harvesting.

"I charge by the project for my services. It works out to about $35 an hour gross," he volunteers.

A self-reliant backwoodser ought to be able to live on that. ∆

Some information sources:

By Vern Modeland

Megan Hughes, horticulturalist at Meadowcreek, a sustainable living research and education center near Fox, Arkansas, agrees with Jim Gibbons about the value and rewards of growing your own edible landscape. She also recommends a couple of books:

The Complete Book of Edible Landscaping; Home Landscaping with Food-Bearing Plants & Resource Saving Techniques, by Rosalind Creasy. (800 pages) $22.00 plus $5 S&H from Sierra Club Books, 730 Polk Street, San Francisco, CA, 94109.

Designing and Maintaining your Edible Landscape Naturally, by Robert Kourik. (400 pages) $16.95 from Rodale Press, 33 East Minor Street, Emmaus, PA, 18049.

One free catalogue source is Edible Landscapes, P.O. Box 77, Afton, VA, 22920. (800) 524-4156.

Megan Hughes can be reached at Meadowcreek, P. O. Box 100, Fox, AR 72051, (501) 363-4500.

Specialized information also can be located through state agencies, county extension agents, your local library, and the Kerr Center for Sustainable Agriculture, Inc., P.O. Box 588, Poteau, OK, 74953, (918) 647-9123. ∆

A Backwoods Home Anthology

SELF-SUFFICIENCY

Muzzleloaders — art, science, and a piece of history

By Gene Willis

I don't know about you, but for me the word "muzzleloader" conjures up visions of the Continental Army fighting the Redcoats, or Daniel Boone exploring the frontier. And of course I can't forget to mention those rugged individualists, the mountain men.

Muzzleloaders are a connection with the past. Just think for a moment of the freedom and self-sufficiency that was won with the black powder weapons of yesteryear. People who were able to hunt for their own food and protect themselves and their families found a great deal of freedom and self-determination. Black powder firearms played a part in the development of our nation, and we can be informed and inspired by the study of days gone by.

Shooting a muzzleloader is both an art and a science. It is an art because there are many hand/eye skills used. The weapons themselves are often works of art. Many of the most popular models are available in kit form, with all the machining and fitting of metal parts done, so the owner can apply his own woodworking skills and creative embellishments.

Black powder is also a science because of all the variables involved in the ballistics of shooting these guns. For instance, if you fire a .54 caliber rifle using a 230 grain bullet twice, once with 100 grains of powder and once with 120 grains, the two bullets will not have the same velocity or range, or hit the same point. To shoot accurately, you must balance factors such as the weight of the bullet, range to the target, weight of powder, etc. You can get as involved as you want with the scientific side of black powder, or just follow the directions.

Rifles, shotguns, and pistols

The muzzleloader was the firearm used before the invention of the cartridge. Muzzleloaders are also called black powder guns because they use black gun powder for the propellant charge. There are black powder guns made for almost any use you may have for a gun. You can find single or double barrel shotguns, single or double barrel rifles, pistols and revolvers. There are several ignition systems to choose from, the most popular being the flintlock and the caplock (also called percussion).

Ignition

The flintlock uses a piece of flint attached to the hammer which strikes a steel, producing sparks which ignite the powder charge. The caplock uses a percussion cap (the ancestor of the primer in a modern cartridge) which ignites when it is struck by the hammer. The cap in turn ignites the powder through a nipple attached through the barrel.

Loading

Loading the powder charge and bullet into the muzzleloader is the same procedure for both flintlock and caplock.

First, always make sure there is no powder in the flash pan of the flintlock or percussion cap on the nipple of the caplock, and that the hammer is down in the uncocked position on both types.

Second, measure out the appropriate amount of powder for your gun and the range you are firing. Always follow the manufacturer's directions about the type and maximum or minimum amounts of powder to use. Different types and calibers of guns call for different burn rates and

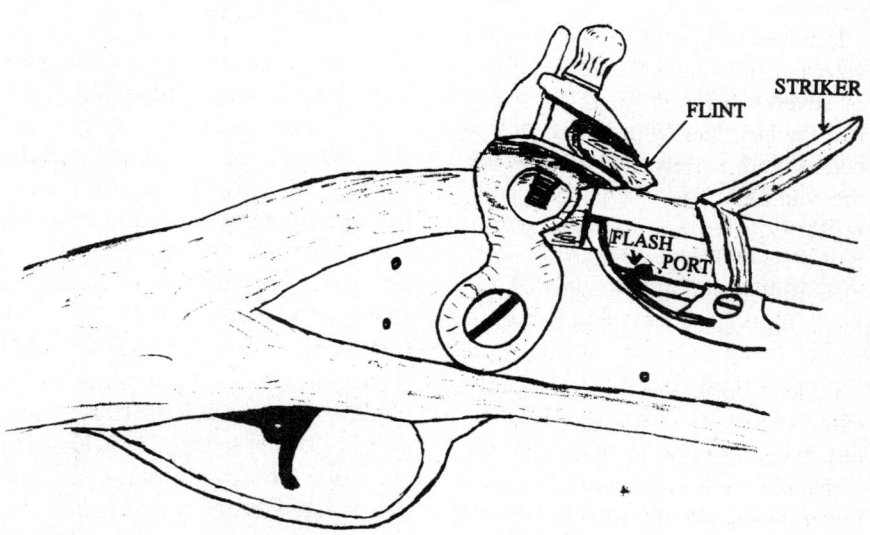

The firing mechanism of a flintlock rifle.

amounts of powder. Failure to follow directions can result in hazardous overloads, poor performance, or bullets stuck in the barrel. Do not pour powder directly from a canister or flask into your gun. Use a separate powder measure to prevent accidents.

After the powder charge is measured and poured down the barrel, the next step is the patch and bullet. There are several types of patches and bullets for use in muzzle loaded firearms. Again, you need to follow the manufacturer's recommendations.

sion cap on the nipple. For a flintlock, cock the hammer, and pour flash powder into the flash pan beneath the steel striker.

Take careful aim, slowly squeeze the trigger...KA-BOOM! Thunder and smoke reach out and connect you with the past.

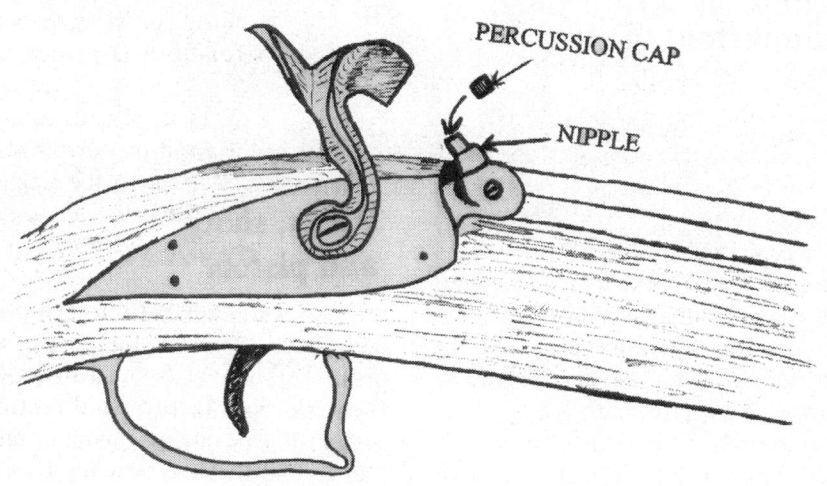

The firing mechanism of a caplock rifle.

Patches are purchased by caliber size and thickness. Patches are made of several different materials. I have had the best luck with the plain white cotton cloth variety. Bullets are either the round ball type or the cylindrical bullet type, called conical or maxi-balls. See the illustrations for examples. Bullets are made in different calibers, different weights, and different types.

To load the bullet, center the lubricated patch over the bore. You can buy patch lubricant or use the cheaper and more traditional saliva. Next the bullet is pressed into the muzzle opening. Then, use a ball starter to push the bullet and patch into the bore. The ramrod is then used to push the bullet all the way down to the breech, and tamp it down firmly. Now the gun is ready to be primed for firing.

To prime the gun, hold it horizontally, pointed in the direction you will be shooting. If you are using a caplock, cock the hammer and place a percus-

All of this might seem overwhelming to read about, and you might be tempted to just buy an AK-47, but it's actually fun, and you can always pretend you are Hawkeye (or Cora) in The Last of the Mohicans.

Pros & cons

Muzzleloaders do have both advantages and disadvantages. The disadvantages include limited range, only one shot on most of them, and they are a bit heavier than modern firearms of comparable power. Advantages would include the improved stalking and marksmanship you will develop. Most states also have special hunting seasons and higher bag limits for hunters who use muzzleloading arms. You may find you are allowed an extra deer per year with a charcoal burner.

There are many other facets to the art and science of shooting muzzleloaders. One of the best ways to learn safely is to join a black powder club or a group which does historical re-enactments. These folks are always looking for new members, and they will gladly share their knowledge of and passion for their interest with you. Many good books and magazines are available that deal with black powder shooting. Any large, and many small gun stores will have information about how you can find a club, and will have books and magazines about black powder guns for sale.

Give black powder guns a try. If you're quiet the next time you're in the woods, you might hear Daniel Boone blazing a new trail. Δ

A country moment

Jack Fazio builds a dock at Copco Lake, California.

Deer discourology

By Whitney M. Bollier

I had been battling the deer in my garden for vegetable and flower rights for many years. It wasn't until I discovered a simple solution to the problem that I started to enjoy my garden. Prior to this discovery I had tried just about every trick in the book. Many of the remedies that I tried are well known to most gardeners. Unfortunately I never had luck with any of them. I tried blood meal, which only seemed to attract the local dog and cat population during the day and marauding racoons and skunk at night. The blood meal didn't seem to bother the deer, however, because they kept on munching. I then tried expensive big game repellents made from lion urine and other stinky stuff but the deer kept on munching. I even tried tying little cloth bags filled with hair clippings from the barber shop to the plants in hopes that would do the trick, but the deer kept on munching. Even the fancy new ultrasonic devices designed to keep large pests such as dogs and cats from the yard didn't work. I finally resigned myself to planting just those plants that deer are not supposed to eat.

The deer left the oleander alone, of course, and didn't touch the euryops, a yellow daisy-like plant. However, they had a field day (night) when they discovered the agapanthus (Lily of the Nile) I had planted and mowed it down!

Then one day while returning home from a trip, I was reading one of those in-flight airline magazines, which had an article about how the US Forest Service was trying a new deer repellent they had accidentally discovered. The article went on to report that the new repellent had a long lasting effect which was what the Forest Service needed to protect seedlings when planted out on their own. The main ingredient in their new deer repellent was raw egg. The article didn't explain why the egg worked, other than just to say that it was effective.

So to make a long story short, when I got home I tried to make my own deer repellent from eggs and water with the bright idea that I could use it in my hose-end sprayer. After some trial and error I finally hit upon a formula of the right viscosity that worked.

The formula is a simple ratio of one raw egg per four cups of water thoroughly mixed in a blender at low speed (high speed if you don't mind a mess). Once the egg and water are thoroughly mixed, pour the mixture from the blender into a 2 gallon plastic sprinkling can (metal cans are hard to clean). Continue mixing egg and water until you have filled the sprinkling can two-thirds full to avoid spillage in the kitchen. A major word of caution: do not put the mix in a hose-end sprayer. It will work in the sprayer for a while, but you will soon have to buy another sprayer no matter how diligently you clean it.

Application: Lightly but evenly sprinkle the plants that you want to protect. Some plants do not take kindly to the mix being applied to their blossoms, especially mums and hydrangeas, so try to apply the mix to the leaves only. It is amazing how far the egg/water mixture will spread, because you don't need to saturate the plants to protect them. You may soon find after sprinkling your favorite plants that the deer might go after plants you had thought were safe. Don't give up. Just sprinkle everything and you will soon find that the deer will go elsewhere.

If you use an overhead watering system, this repellent, like any other, will be washed off and you will have to reapply it. The advantage of the egg/water mix is that it is ecologically sound, extremely inexpensive, does not stink (although the deer might think so) and will outlast most commercial products. But best of all is that it really *works*!

A word of caution: Once you have rid your garden of deer, you may become overconfident as a deer discourologist: you may have a rude surprise one morning if you don't continue to apply the egg/water mixture after heavy rains or watering. The deer are persistent in their search for food and will keep checking your garden for any new growth that you may not have protected.

For those of you who are plagued with large herds of elk, moose and other herbivores, give this formula a try . . . it might surprise you. ∆

Synopsis of sourdough

By Charles Bryant O'Dooley

Sourdough "starter," also known as "everlasting" yeast, was brought to the new world by American colonists in crocks and stone jars. When covered wagons moved westward, sourdough was brought along and guarded jealously.

Sourdough became legendary with the California Gold Rush of 1849. The sourdough "starter" was passed from neighbor to neighbor and was a common leavening in the days before packaged yeast became available.

San Francisco is famous for its sourdough bread, and tourists from all over the world who visit there make it a point to sample the wonderful flavor that's found in no other bread. Prospectors in the old west were often called "sourdoughs" because they always took with them a starter of sourdough.

Due to the expanding movement of people going back to basics, and with more and more homemakers baking their own bread, I decided to dig into my grandmother's trunk in the attic, get out her journal on bread making, and pass along to you her recipes for sourdough breads, cakes, etc.

I can still recall as though it was only yesterday when I used to come home from school on a cold winter day and open the kitchen door. The heavenly aroma of hot sourdough rolls fresh from the oven assailed my nostrils, and an appetizing smell wafted from the beef vegetable soup that had been simmering on the back of the stove all day. There were no school buses in those days, and I walked three miles to school and three miles back. After this long, cold trek, sitting down to hot sourdough rolls and soup was like dying and going to heaven.

Mother is gone now, and if I could be granted just one wish in this world, it would be as the poet wrote: "Time, oh time, turn back in your flight, and make me a child again, just for tonight." I hope you will experience the same joy when you try these recipes. I know one thing for sure: after you try them once, you will never go back to your old way of bread making.

Sourdough

The word "sourdough" always draws a mixed response. It passed from importance as a yeast product with the advent of commercial yeast. The yeast of today has many advantages, but it cannot give the flavor that sourdough does.

Yeast produces bubbles of gas as it grows. The flour mixture traps the gas, producing a leavened product. In order to grow, yeast needs proper food, and a sourdough starter provides this starch and sugar. Perhaps your grandmother called her starter a "sponge."

You can make sourdough simply by mixing flour with water, potato water or milk and exposing it to the air. Never add salt or a fat to your starter, as they don't provide food for the yeast.

Remember, sourdough is nothing mysterious. Basically the same principles are used to produce the yeast we buy in the store; they have simply been temporarily deprived of food and so are in a dormant stage.

Care and feeding of your pet sourdough

For best results, use glass or pottery containers and keep your starter loosely covered with waxed paper. The sourdough must be kept in a container which allows it "growing" room. Bean pots work well. Starter is meant to be used frequently, at least every two weeks, and can be kept in the refrigerator for that amount of time without replenishing, or indefinitely if used daily. The liquid will separate from the batter when it stands several days, but this doesn't matter. Just remember to feed your starter. And remember, a starter should be left out at room temperature until the mixture bubbles, at least 18 hours or overnight.

Milk starter

1 cup milk
1 cup flour
¼ cup sugar
1 tsp yeast

Mix together in a crock and let stand at room temperature uncovered for 2 to 4 days. Stir down 2 or 3 times a day. You can get a starter going with just the yeast in the air, but the addition of packaged yeast insures that you will get the best kind of baking.

To use the starter, take it out of the refrigerator at least eight hours before using and add another cup of flour, cup of milk and ¼ cup sugar.

Mix well and let stand in a warm place free from drafts. Save at least a cup of starter each time. If you want to bake several things and need more starter, you can double the recipe but let it sit out longer.

If you are not going to use your starter for several months, it can be frozen to keep it.

You can also make this water starter more historically "accurate." Mix one cup of plain flour and one cup lukewarm water in a scalded pot or jar and cover loosely, letting it stand in a warm place to "work" for four or five days. Stir down several times a day. It is ready when you smell the characteristic "sour" odor.

Sourdough bread can be made from a conventional bread recipe by using one-half the amount of yeast called for in the recipe and adding one cup of sourdough starter for each loaf of bread the recipe makes. Omit the liquid in the recipe. Crusty french bread can be made by brushing the loaf with salt water before and during baking.

Sourdough bread

> 5 to 6 cups flour
> 3 Tbsp sugar
> 1 tsp salt
> 1 pkg active dry yeast
> 1 cup milk
> 2 Tbsp margarine
> 1½ cups starter

To make dough, combine 1 cup flour with the sugar, salt, and undissolved yeast in a large bowl. Combine milk and margarine in a saucepan. Heat over low heat until liquid is warm. Gradually add to dry ingredients and beat two minutes at medium speed of electric mixer, scraping bowl occasionally. Add 1 1/2 cups starter and 1 cup flour or enough flour to make a thick batter. Beat at high speed two minutes, scraping the bowl. Stir in enough additional flour to make a soft dough. Turn out onto a lightly floured board. Knead until smooth and elastic, about eight to ten minutes. Place in a greased bowl and turn to grease the top. Cover and let rise in a warm place free from draft until doubled in bulk, about one hour. Punch down, turn out onto lightly floured board. Let rest 15 minutes. Divide dough in half. Shape loaf and place in greased loaf pans. Cover, let rise in warm place until double in size. Bake in hot oven (400°) about 30 minutes or until done. Remove from pans and cool on wire rack. Makes two loaves.

Sourdough biscuits

The night before add 1 cup of flour, ¼ cup of sugar, and 1 cup of milk to your starter. Beat well and let sit in warm place.

The next morning, assemble these ingredients:

> 1 cup starter
> 1 cup flour
> 2 tsp baking powder
> ¼ tsp soda
> ½ tsp salt
> ¼ cup shortening

Sift dry ingredients into bowl. Cut in shortening as for pastry. Add starter and mix lightly using all dry mixture. Knead five times. Make into thick biscuits. Let rise awhile. Bake at 425° for 10-12 minutes.

Sourdough corn bread

> 1 cup sourdough starter
> 1½ cups evaporated milk
> 1½ cups yellow corn meal
> 2 Tbsp sugar
> 2 whole eggs beaten
> ¼ cup warm melted butter
> ½ tsp salt
> ½ tsp soda

Mix the starter, milk, corn meal, sugar and eggs; stir thoroughly in a large bowl. Stir in melted butter, salt, and soda. Turn into a 10 inch greased frying pan and bake in a hot oven (450°) for 20 minutes or until they test done.

Note: Buttered corn stick pans may also be used for a delightful, colorful hot bread for a table. Fill each cup 2/3 full. Bake in a hot oven (425°) for 20 minutes or until they test done.

Sourdough french bread

> 1 cup starter
> ½ cup lukewarm milk
> 1 Tbsp sugar
> 2 Tbsp melted shortening
> 2 tsp salt
> 2½ cups flour

Mix ingredients together in the order given, working in the flour well. Let the dough rise in a greased bowl until it has doubled in bulk. Knead again and form into a long French loaf. Cut slashes across top of loaf and let rise again. Bake at 325° for 35 to 40 minutes. Take from the oven and brush the top with butter. (If your starter does not seem lively, add a teaspoon of dry yeast to starter and mix in before you begin.)

Sourdough whole wheat bread

> 2 cups starter (warmed overnight)
> 1 cup whole wheat flour
> 1 cup all-purpose white flour
> 2 Tbsp sugar
> 1½ tsp salt

Combine ingredients and mix well with a fork. The sponge will be soft and sticky. Cover with a cheesecloth and set in a warm place for 2 to 3 hours. Turn out on a warm, well-floured board. Knead 1½ cups white flour into dough for five to ten minutes. Shape into a round loaf and place in well-greased pie pan. Grease sides and top of loaf. Cover with towel and let rise until doubled in bulk (about 1 hour). Bake at 450° for 10 minutes. Reduce heat to 375° and bake 30 to 40 minutes. Remove, brush top with butter.

Special bread

> 6 cups milk (you can use part yogurt, sour milk, buttermilk, etc.)
> 1 stick butter or margarine
> 1 Tbsp salt
> 6 Tbsp sugar
> ¾ cup warm water
> 1 Tbsp sugar
> 3 pkg dry yeast
> 1 to 2 cups soy flour
> 2/3 cup unprocessed bran
> 1/3 cup wheat germ
> 1½ cups whole wheat flour
> 4 cups or more unbleached white flour
> 1 handful each: cornmeal, oatmeal
> 2 handfuls of your favorite wheat cereal, crushed

Heat milk, butter, salt, and 6 Tbsp sugar together to scald, and cool to lukewarm. Mix together warm water, 1 Tbsp sugar, and yeast, and allow to proof. Add yeast to milk in large bowl, and mix in grains, adding enough white flour to make a smooth dough. Knead well (10 to 15 minutes) and let rise until doubled in a greased bowl. Punch down, shape into loaves, and let rise again until nearly doubled. Bake for about one hour at 350°. Makes six loaves.

Sourdough herb bread

> 1½ cups water
> 1 cup cottage cheese
> ¼ cup honey
> 3 Tbsp oil
> 6 to 6 1/2 cups whole wheat flour
> 1 cup starter
> 2 Tbsp dry yeast
> 1 egg
> 2 tsp dill
> 3 Tbsp chopped onion
> 2 Tbsp chopped fresh parsley

Heat first four ingredients in a medium saucepan, until very warm (110° to 120°). Combine warm liquid with 3 cups flour and the remaining ingredients in a large bowl. Beat 2 minutes. By hand stir in remaining flour to make a stiff dough. Knead dough until it is smooth and elastic, about 5 minutes. Place in a greased bowl and turn around to grease all sides. Cover and let rise in a warm place until double in size. Punch down and divide into two balls. Shape each ball into loaves and place into two greased loaf pans. Let rise again until double in size. Bake 40-50 minutes in 350° oven.

Dill-onion bread

> 1 Tbsp dry yeast
> ½ cup warm water
> 1 beaten egg
> ½ cup cottage cheese
> 1/3 cup finely chopped onion
> 1 Tbsp butter
> 2 cups whole wheat flour
> 1/3 cup whole bran cereal
> ½ cup wheat germ
> 1 Tbsp honey
> 1 Tbsp dillseed
> 1 tsp kelp (optional)
> ¼ tsp baking soda
> 1 cup starter

Soften yeast in warm water. Combine egg, cottage cheese, onion, and butter; mix well. In another bowl stir together the flour, cereal, wheat germ, honey, dill, kelp and soda. Add cottage cheese and starter and yeast mixture, stirring well. Cover and let rise until double in size, about one hour. Stir dough down. Knead on a lightly floured surface one minute. With greased hand pat in a well greased 9-inch round baking pan. Cover; let rise until double in size, about one hour. Score top in diamond pattern. Bake 40 minutes at 350°. Remove from dish and place on rack to cool.

Sourdough banana bread

> 1/3 cup margarine
> 1 cup sugar
> 1 egg
> 1 cup mashed bananas
> 1 cup starter
> 2 cups sifted flour
> 1 tsp salt
> 1 tsp baking powder
> ½ tsp soda
> ¾ cup chopped nuts

Cream together margarine and sugar; add egg; stir until blended; stir in banana and starter. Sift flour, salt, baking powder, soda and add to first mixture; stir in nuts. Bake in greased loaf pan 350° for one hour.

Sourdough applesauce cake

> 1 cup starter
> ¼ cup dry skim milk
> 1 cup white flour
> 1 cup canned or homemade applesauce
> ½ cup white sugar
> ½ cup brown sugar
> ½ cup butter or margarine
> 1 egg
> ½ teaspoon salt
> 1 teaspoon cinnamon
> ½ tsp nutmeg
> ½ tsp allspice
> ½ tsp cloves
> 2 tsp baking soda

Mix the starter, skim milk, flour and applesauce and set covered in a warm place. Cream together the sugars and butter or margarine and add to the starter mixture. Add 1 egg, beaten well. Mix in the salt, cinnamon, nutmeg, allspice, cloves, and baking soda.

You can also add half a cup of chopped nuts and/or raisins, if desired. Combine all ingredients and beat by hand. Pour into 8-inch square pan. Bake at 350° for 30 to 35 minutes. Test for doneness, and allow to cool in the pan.

Pilgrim's bread

> ½ cup yellow cornmeal
> 1/3 cup brown sugar
> 1 Tbsp salt
> 2 cups boiling water
> ¼ cup oil
> 2 pkg dry yeast in
> ½ cup warm water
> ¾ cup whole wheat flour
> ½ cup rye flour
> 4¼ to 4½ cups unbleached white flour

Combine the cornmeal, brown sugar, and salt in a bowl. Stir the cornmeal mixture gradually into the boiling water. Add the oil. Cool to lukewarm. In a separate bowl, dissolve the yeast in the ½ cup of warm water. Add yeast to cornmeal mixture. Beat in the wheat and rye flour. Stir in the white flour by hand.

Turn onto lightly floured surface. Knead until smooth and elastic. Place in a lightly greased bowl, turning once to grease surface. Cover and let rise in warm place until double. Punch dough down; turn out onto lightly floured surface. Divide in half and knead a second time for three minutes. Shape dough into two loaves and place in greased pans. Cover and let rise again in warm place until double. Bake at 375° for 45 minutes.

Three-flour bread

> 2 pkg dry yeast
> 1 cup warm water
> 1 Tbsp salt
> ¼ cup vegetable oil
> ¼ cup honey or molasses
> 3 cups warm water
> 1 cup dry milk powder
> 1 cup rye flour
> ¼ cup soy flour
> ¼ cup wheat germ
> 4 cups whole wheat or graham flour
> 5 or more cups white flour

Dissolve the yeast in 1 cup of warm water and stir in salt, vegetable oil, honey or molasses, and 3 more cups of warm water. Mix in milk powder, flours, and wheat germ.

Turn out on floured surface and knead until smooth, adding more flour if needed. Place in greased bowl, turning once. Cover and put in warm place to rise until doubled, about two hours. Turn out onto floured surface, knead, and place in three greased 9x5 inch pans. Let rise until almost double. Place in a cold oven and set at 450° for 10 minutes. Turn down to 350° and bake 25 to 30 minutes. Makes three loaves.

Sourdough noodles

> 1 egg, well beaten
> ½ cup starter
> 1 cup flour
> 1 tsp salt

Mix together well. Add enough extra flour to make a stiff dough. Knead 8-10 minutes. Roll out to 1/8-inch thickness on well-floured board. Sprinkle flour evenly over the top of dough. Fold and cut ½-inch wide slices. Spread out and let dry overnight or eight hours. Use immediately or freeze. Cook the same as regular noodles. Δ

SPECIAL BUILDING ISSUE

MAY/JUNE 1994
No. 27
$3.50 U.S.
$4.50 CANADA

Backwoods Home magazine
...a practical journal of self reliance!

Woman Builds Log Retreat

**WIZARD OF WIND
THE FAMILY POND
GREAT BREAD RECIPES
THE WOOD COOKSTOVE**

My View

Self reliance — the key to happiness

The other night I had a dream I was working two jobs and earning a fabulous salary at each. The problem was I hated both jobs; in fact, I didn't even know what I was supposed to be doing at them. I went from one job to the other in a sort of no-man's land, sneaking down the hallways and wondering if I would be caught not knowing what to do. I didn't dare ask my bosses anything because I had been at these jobs for a long time and everyone thought I was an expert.

I suspected my uselessness would soon be detected and I would be fired. Not only did I not want to lose my big income, but I dreaded the humiliation of being exposed for the fraud I was. I wanted to quit before that happened, and it became the desperate goal of my dream to find a way to quit my job with dignity and without winding up broke.

I woke in a panic, and my wife asked what was wrong. When I told her, she said she had had a strange dream too. She said that in her dream I had taken my pocketknife and slowly and carefully made a cut around my left wrist. The knife went deeper and deeper until the hand fell to the floor. She gasped and asked me why I did it, and I told her not to get excited, that it was not that important. She became very excited and she said I tried to calm her. The hand has been pretty good to me all these years, I told her, but now I would get used to not having it. "It's not a big deal," she said I told her. "Don't get worked up over nothing."

You were so positive in the dream, she told me. "You know, like you always are."

I knew immediately what the dreams were about. For my dream, my subconscious had dredged up a ten-year period of my life that ended five years ago when I started *Backwoods Home Magazine*, and by coincidence my wife's subconscious had dredged up the five-year period of my life since I started the magazine. The ten-year period was full of self doubt and growing dislike for the succession of good-paying but unrewarding jobs. The five-year period was full of achievement and love of my job as *BHM's* publisher and editor.

The dreams brought home an important and eternal truth for me and, I think, for many readers of this magazine: **if you are not as happy as you think you should be, try taking total control of your life and doing what you really want to do. Try self reliance.**

For some of you that will mean doing what I have done: forsaking the cozy, secure, high-paying, but unsatisfying career and striking out on your own. You may fail or you may succeed, but you'll never know unless you try. If you succeed you'll be the envy of all those who were too afraid to try; if you fail you will simply go back to what you were doing.

I left Southern California's defense industry five years ago, at age forty-five. I left because I was growing increasingly afraid that I would not be able to keep a promise I had made to myself in my youth, namely that when I looked in the mirror at age fifty I wanted to be able to say, "Good work Dave; you utilized your God-given talents to the best of your ability, and you gave life the best shot you could have. Congratulations; you are a success."

Here's how I figure it; Life is a gift you should not waste. If you're lucky, you're alive for about 80 healthy years. That's the blink of any eye when compared to the couple of million years humans have been on earth, and it's an even quicker blink when you compare it to the millions of years that preceded humans and the millions that will follow them. So why waste this precios moment of life? Why throw it away on a job you hate, in a life that gives you little satisfaction? Why not go for it all?

Here's another way to look at it: Being born in itself is like winning the state lottery. Consider the hundreds of millions of sperm your father had and the several million eggs your mother's body produced. Somehow those two people met and the lucky combination that created you was one chance in billions. Talk about hitting the jackpot——just having the opportunity to be alive is an incredible gift.

So why waste this opportunity? Why not live up to your full potential to be a happy human being?

You won't be just doing it for yourself, but for your children too. We all want our children to be happy, and hopefully, to be successful at something. That's what our own parents wanted for us. By striving to do what makes us truly happy, we not only fulfill the dreams of our parents but we set the stage for our own children's success. They will learn from our example.

I know many readers already realize this and many have achieved happiness at their jobs and in their careers. Congratulations; you are already a success. But many of you are just as dissatisfied with your job and life as I was five years ago. You're the ones I'm talking to. You were drawn to this magazine, in part, for the same reasons I started it—a yearning for the country, in part as a symbol for the freedom from all that afflicts your life.

As it was for me, the country and its requirement that you become more self reliant may become your escape route to happiness. In the first couple of years of building my house, I also rebuilt my resolve to give life everything I had, whether I succeeded or not. You can too.

Relying on yourself—**SELF RELIANCE**—is the key.

Do I sound like a TV commercial? Well, this spiel will never make it to TV because there's no money to be made. It's free. All you have to do is decide that you want to be happy, and to muster the guts to pursue it.

I'm going to turn fifty in a few weeks, and I can now look into that mirror and say I've kept my promise. Fifty is no magic number either; it just happened to be my number.

Maybe yours if forty, maybe sixty. Whatever it is, use it to win the lottery of your life.

How to care for and feed the family pond

By Steven F. Minner

A well maintained pond can be the centerpiece of any homestead, as well as an excellent source of food and old-fashioned, family fun. However, like most other worthwhile things, pond maintenance requires some effort and a basic understanding of the healthy pond as more than a hole in the ground to catch water. A healthy pond is an eco-system all its own—one that lives and breathes.

Water level

The first concern of most pond owners is water level. If the pond is fed by a year-round creek, stream, or spring, water level concerns are secondary to other maintenance needs. However, many of us have to capture and store water in our ponds to prepare for summer, when many sources dry up. For example, my neighbor built a small containment pond "upstream" of his main pond to store water for later release into his main pond during extremely hot weather and low water levels. I have plans to build a small containment pond "downstream" of my larger pond to retain winter overflow from the larger pond. Eventually, that overflow will be pumped back into the larger pond when water levels are down, or into a cistern for watering our garden in the spring and summer.

For ponds with no year-round source, controlling leaks or seepage becomes critical in maintaining the water level. (In the hottest parts of the country, most fish species need at least 12 feet of water to protect them from the heat.) In ponds with raised-bank perimeters, leaks can often be spotted in the form of water or damp soil on the land side of the bank—or thick grass or other vegetation. Most old-timers claim that all ponds leak to some extent and that certainly seems true: it is rare to find a pond that doesn't have some leak or seepage.

Accepting that fact, the goal is to minimize leaks and seepage to maintain optimal water level. Several methods are common—all with varying degrees of success—depending mostly on the surrounding soil type.

I know of one family who successfully stabilized the water level in their pond by temporarily fencing pigs in the leaking section of their pond levee. Only the land side need be fenced: the pigs won't go out into deep water. Pigs, like cattle, will compact the hard bottom material and can often correct minor leaks and seepage. This method seems to work best when the livestock are given feed and fresh water (other than pond water) and straw is scattered around the area of the suspected leak. The animals trample the straw into the bottom, which helps stop leaks.

Others claim that leaks can be fixed by generously scattering chicken litter in the area of the leak. Apparently, the chicken manure breaks down in the water and fills tiny cracks; there it supports the growth of algae and other small plants that help to stop up leaks. Note: It's important to use dry, well-aged material, because fresh manure

can cause a troublesome "algae bloom" and oxygen depletion.

If these "natural" remedies fail, plastic liners can be installed over the leaking area. The obvious disadvantage is that the pond would have to be drained to expose the area of the leak. One of the newest innovations on the market is a spray-on plastic "barrier" that is applied to especially porous materials during pond construction or after the existing pond is drained. The obvious drawback to these latter systems is cost, but if cost is no concern, both "artificial" methods will fix leaks. For those of us with more modest means, "natural" remedies are generally successful unless the surrounding soil is extremely porous. Most local county extension services and Soil Conservation offices can provide advice on fixing pond leaks.

In the case of ponds with artificial levees, willows and other trees with "water seeking" roots must not be allowed to grow—especially on the side of the levee away from the pond. Willow roots will grow in a horizontal direction in search of water and can literally bore their way through the levee, breaking porous rocks and turning seeps into major leaks. Because of their extensive root systems, pine and evergreen trees growing on pond levees should also be cut and killed.

Water loss from seepage is generally secondary to water loss from evaporation in the summer months. Unfortunately, there is little that can be done about water loss from heat evaporation. However, wind breaks can be planted on the side of the pond from which the predominant wind blows to lessen the effects of evaporation. Some experts argue, however, that windbreaks are counterproductive, since the wind blowing over the pond's surface provides a free means of oxygen exchange and aeration.

Acid-alkaline balance

Once the water level is stabilized, maintenance efforts begin with an understanding of water pH levels that allow fish populations to thrive. Water has an acid-alkaline balance measured on a pH scale from 0 to 14, with the middle, or 7, representing a neutral condition. Numbers greater than 7 are considered alkaline; lower numbers represent varying degrees of acidity. Most species of fish will flourish in water with pH levels between 6.5 and 8.5. Water pH levels depend largely on the natural acidity or alkalinity of the surrounding soil and (obviously) on the pond's primary water source. Acid rain can affect the pH level, and it is a good idea to check the water frequently, especially in the winter and spring after rainy periods, since chemical runoff from fertilizers and other farm chemicals affects pH levels. Once the pH level is determined, acid or lime can be added to the pond to make necessary pH level adjustments. When adding acid or lime, it is important to accurately estimate the volume of the pond and add only the exact amount of additive needed. Volume is determined by multiplying the pond's acre-feet by the average depth. One acre-foot is 43,560 square feet of water one foot deep, or 43,560 cubic feet. As an example, a half acre pond with an average depth of five feet would have a volume of 108,900 cubic feet or 2.5 acre-feet. Since there are 7.48 gallons of water in a cubic foot, the volume of the half acre pond would be 814,572 gallons—give or take a few gallons.

The easiest and quickest way to test water pH level is to do it yourself with a testing kit purchased from a swimming pool supply company. The kits are inexpensive and represent an investment quickly recouped if only one fishkill is prevented. For the serious pond owner, a pH testing kit is a must in maintaining good water quality, and testing is very easy. A tablet or a few drops of test solution are added to a tube of pond water. The water will change colors and is then compared to a color chart or calculations provided with the kit. Alternatively, most county extension services and university agriculture departments offer water testing (or can provide information on water testing services) for a nominal fee. The obvious disadvantage is the time delay in waiting for test results to be returned via mail.

Oxygen content

Next to maintaining proper pH levels, adequate dissolved oxygen content is the most critical factor for fish population survival. Oxygen levels of at least 5 parts per million (ppm) need to be maintained for fish survival. Maintaining an adequate oxygen level is not as easy as adjusting the pH level, since oxygen content varies with the season and the time of day and is affected by weather conditions and the number of fish in the pond. Generally speaking, dissolved oxygen content is lowest during the early morning hours. Special attention should be given to dissolved oxygen content during lengthy periods of extremely hot weather when there is little or no air movement. If large numbers of fish appear at the surface and seem to be "gasping" for air, they probably are, and it is a sure bet that oxygen levels are critical. Corrective action must be taken immediately to avoid a fishkill. Unfortunately, such kills generally affect the largest fish, since they also have the greatest need for oxygen.

The most effective way to correct oxygen depletion is to install a commercial aerator. Unfortunately, aerators are not cheap, and it is easy to spend up to $1,000 on a commercial system—depending, of course, on the make, capacity, model, etc. Without question, it is better to own an aerator and never have to use it than to need one—even if only just once—and not have it. Used aerators are often available from commercial fish farmers but generally come with no warranty. If cost is not a concern, a commercial aerator is an excellent investment because of its efficiency. For example, a commercial aerator rated at 1/3 horsepower can pump a half million gallons of water in 24 hours and transfer 38 pounds of oxygen into the water—all for the cost of about 75 cents (assuming a 115 volt system and electricity cost of 6.5 cents per kilowatt hour).

Alternatively, many owners of larger ponds tout the efficiency of simply riding around in a small boat and stirring up the water with an outboard motor. My dad was a firm believer in "keeping the water stirred up" by riding around for at least an hour every day. He never used any other method of aeration and, interestingly, never experienced a fishkill from oxygen depletion. (And to think, we thought he just liked riding around in the boat.) My kids love to make "roostertails" in the water with a paddle as they ride around in our small fishing boat and, they are doing something good for the pond, too. Other pond owners mount outboard motors on permanent or semi-permanent mounting brackets and allow the motor to run unattended at the lowest possible speed that will stir the water and force an oxygen exchange. If a boat or outboard motor is used as the sole aeration method, oxygen levels should be checked frequently since the boat's operating speed, hull configuration, outboard motor size, etc., are all related factors in aeration efficiency.

After we experienced an oxygen depletion kill of about 250 fish (at a time when our outboard motor was in the shop), a neighbor loaned me a submersible swimming pool pump and connected the discharge side to a flat garden-type drip hose laid out along one bank and positioned so the spray went back into the pond. The pump had enough pressure to spray the water five to six feet into the air and once it was in place, we had no further problems with fishkill. Aside from the difficulty in determining the efficiency of that system (we didn't know if it was the new system or the reduced oxygen demand that actually prevented another kill), spray systems also pose potential water loss through evaporation—especially on hot or windy days. Other pond owners have installed submersible swimming pool pumps with the intake approximately six to seven feet below the surface. The discharge side consists of an "L" shaped PVC pipe that allows the discharge water to fall two to three feet back into the pond—a sufficient distance to create an oxygen exchange.

Aside from these "after the fact" remedies, one of the best ways to prevent oxygen depletion is to ensure that the pond is not overstocked. While it is tempting to overstock, there are definite limitations to dissolved oxygen content (and nutrients), and an overstocked pond is an invitation for a fishkill from oxygen depletion.

Water clarity

Muddy water and water clarity pose problems for all pond owners at one time or the other, and several simple

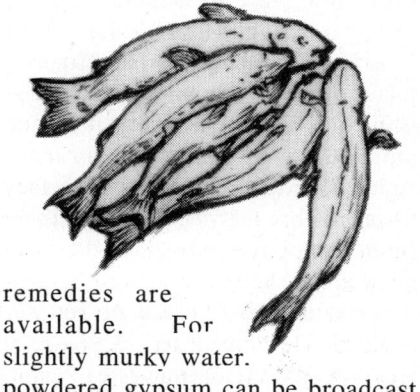

remedies are available. For slightly murky water, powdered gypsum can be broadcast over the pond's surface at a rate of 200 pounds per acre. For muddier water, as much as 800 pounds per surface acre may be necessary. Gypsum treatments can be repeated every 7 to 10 days until the water is clear. Gypsum treatments appear to work by bonding with suspended particles in the water and sinking them to the bottom.

Alternatively, a mixture of 75 pounds of soybean or cottonseed meal and 25 pounds of superphosphate can be broadcast over each surface acre of pond area. This method works by increasing the pond's microorganism food supply so fish don't stir up bottom mud while looking for food. This method can be repeated every 10 days but should not be used in hot weather as it can cause an algae bloom and oxygen depletion.

Finally, blocks of hay can be placed along the edge of the pond in shallow water. The hay attracts and absorbs particulate matter in the water. Hay should be applied at a rate of 7 to 10 "blocks" for each surface acre. After a while, the blocks will break down, settle on the bottom of the pond, and "disappear." Like the previous treatment, hay should not be used in hot weather as activated organisms in the hay may cause an algae bloom.

With these corrective measures in mind, it must be emphasized that the primary use of the pond will ultimately determine how clear the water may be maintained. Obviously, nutrient levels are of no concern in a pond used exclusively for swimming, and the water can be kept "crystal" clear. However, fish live on algae and plankton that naturally cloud the water and, in a stocked pond, water clarity must be compromised to a certain extent in the interest of maintaining adequate nutrient levels for the fish population. A good rule of thumb is that a white object should be visible to a depth of about 18 inches. If the object can be seen beyond that depth, nutrient levels need to be restored through fertilization. If fertilizer is needed, liquid fertilizer should be used when possible. Liquid fertilizer dissolves immediately, unlike granular fertilizer which settles to the bottom with very little of the fertilizer dissolving, according to researchers at Auburn University. Suppliers of liquid fertilizer claim that fertilization costs can be reduced as much as 60% as compared to the cost of granular (pellet) fertilizer. In any event, fertilization should begin in the spring (or when water temperature reaches 65°) and continue monthly through the fall, when water temperatures drop below 65°, with the "18 inch" visibility rule guiding the administration of fertilizer.

About swimming in your pond: I've discussed adding various materials to a pond, so let's consider which ones might affect the health and safety of swimmers. Many of them, like gypsum, pose no problem. During times when you have pigs or other livestock in the water, there may be contamination by manure, so don't encourage swimming at those times. If the water is murky, avoid swimming, since that will stir up silt. Fertilizer (granular or liquid) used in appropriate amounts is no problem for swimmers. And what about herbicides and fish poisons? I don't use anything stronger than chelated copper or copper sulfate, and then I wait a week to permit swimming. The chemicals will break down in the water. If you use stronger chemicals, like rotenone, wait a month. And there are other, stronger herbicides, such as chlorinated hydrocarbons, that could make swimming unsafe for an indefinite period. They do break down, but they break down into other dangerous compounds.

Weed control

Aquatic weed control represents an ongoing concern for pond owners. The best method of weed control may be a natural one—the stocking of hybrid grass carp. Carp should be stocked according to the following guidelines: light vegetation, 3 to 5 per surface acre; moderate vegetation, 6 to 10 per acre; heavy vegetation, 11 to 15 per acre. The goal is not to eliminate all aquatic vegetation but to limit it so that it feeds other species living in the pond without detracting from the pond's value. The carp are inexpensive ($3 to $5 each), have a reasonable life span, do not eat other fish species due to lack of jaw teeth and are not, themselves, susceptible to being eaten by other fish—provided they are eight inches or longer when stocked. We have had good success with White Amur Grass Carp as they consume three to five times their body weight every day during their early growing years. Amur prefer leafy, rooted aquatic plants, such as pondweed and coontail, but will also eat green algae, cattails and floating duckweed. White Amur can reach four feet in length and 100 pounds in their native habitats in Asia but usually mature at 25 to 40 pounds in pond environments. For the cost, they are well worth the investment.

Depending on the size of the pond, manual removal of aquatic vegetation is also a viable option. This method is labor intensive but only requires a good pair of gloves, boots or waders and a strong back. Once removed, aquatic vegetation is a great addition to the compost pile.

For those with less energy, there are chemical algaecides and herbicides on the market to control aquatic vegetation. Most are readily available at farm supply stores, effective on a broad range of aquatic plants, and can be administered in relatively small dosages. But like most chemical products, they are expensive (one commonly available aquatic herbicide sells for $240 per gallon) and frankly, many owners—the author included—don't like the idea of adding poison to stocked ponds, despite assurances from chemical manufacturers that they pose no threat to fish populations. Some suppliers warn, if a chemical algaecide or herbicide is used, a commercial aerator should be readily available for immediate use, since the reaction of many chemicals can greatly reduce the dissolved oxygen content of the water, which can cause distress or death to the fish population.

The key to aquatic weed control is to know your pond and to recognize when weeds begin to proliferate to unacceptable levels. I know of a once-beautiful pond—about a surface acre in size—about a mile from our farm that is covered from bank to bank by freshwater lilies because the owner let the problem get out of hand. Aquatic weeds, like rabbits, multiply at alarming rates if left unchecked and can render a pond unusable.

And speaking of pesky life forms, what about mosquitoes? There are two ways to keep them to a minimum: one is to make sure you have a healthy fish population (to eat the little buggers), and the other is to keep your water well-circulated and aerated. If you do have a mosquito problem, you might try the aeration methods I've discussed.

Mineral content

Finally, some consideration must be given to the mineral content of the water. Most pond owners don't give mineral content much thought and believe rainwater and other "clean" runoff has adequate mineral content. However, a mineral block for ponds is commercially available; the content appears suspiciously similar to blocks available for livestock. Some pond experts contend that a mineral block should be suspended in the pond and replaced once it is completely dissolved.

The rewards

Although it sounds as if pond maintenance is a full time job, the reverse is really true. All pond maintenance efforts are not done at the same time, and like other things on the farm, often coincide with the changing of the seasons. After you've fixed the leaks, tested the pH level, aerated, cleared the water, pulled all the excess vegetation and installed your mineral block, it is time to reap the benefits of your efforts. And what benefits there are in effective pond maintenance ...the thrill of catching a big mess of fish for supper, watching wild ducks make a late afternoon landing, going for a quick dip to get the dust off after a day of hauling hay or just seeing a child's sailboat on the pond. The benefits of effective farm pond management far outweigh the effort and truly represent one of the most fulfilling jobs on the farm.

Steve Minner is an active duty Navy officer who splits his time between his Navy job in San Diego and a small family farm in the foothills of the Arkansas Ozarks. His three-acre pond is home to catfish, bass, bream, a handful of grass carp, and various other critters. Δ

COUNTRY LIVING

Good-bye old friend

By Lucy Shober

Big Poney died today. He was 34 years old and had been going down pretty rapidly over this hot, dry summer. His bones seemed to poke out at every joint, and as much as I could feed him it never really made a difference.

He had been missing all morning. Following a storm last night, this was the first real day of crisp weather. Something seemed different about the way Poney was missing. Butterball, our other horse, seemed nonchalant enough, but he rarely left the side of his massive partner, and this morning he grazed alone. When I found Poney, my heart sank. He had lodged himself between two trees, and had obviously fallen, then struggled to get up all night . . . through the storm. He was mostly deaf, but when I yelled his name, he let out a deep, scared kind of whinny, and lifted his head. "Oh God, Pone, I'm so sorry . . . Oh, this isn't the way you were supposed to go . . ." He reached for my hand with his sweet old muzzle. His nubby teeth showed as he stretched his neck.

I phoned Charley, our neighbor, who it seems is always handy to help with the little dirty things that come up on a farm. "Charley," I started out in my strongest voice, "John's at work, and Poney is trying to die, and I can't use a gun. I've got a big favor to ask . . . ." Then of course I dissolved.

The first time we saw him was when, as a 25-year-old, Poney (whose official name was Rasputin) came to live with us. He had been a jumper for most of his life, then a school horse. His owner had figured that he would be dying soon, and wanted him to live out the year or two he had left in peace and quiet. He was a Frenchman. He ran a tight ship with his horses, you could tell by the way he walked with a click. John and I could hardly understand his speech, but just did a lot of nodding and smiling as he handed over the reins to this sixteen hands of solid horse. Our first horse.

I laugh when I remember that first evening, and the silhouette of John and Poney cutting a line first across one pasture, then another. We had to ride bareback, for the lack of a saddle. John was really flying. My heart swelled with pride, and when they finally returned, I ran to greet them. "When did you learn to ride so well? That was beautiful!" Poney was huffing, and John looked half dead. "What the heck are you talking about?" he almost swore at me. "I couldn't get off! That son of a gun has a mind of his own!"

It's true, Poney did have a mind of his own, but he used it well. He was a school horse, and after he had schooled us on how he was to be treated, his big-hearted gentle nature couldn't help but show through. When we rode him, we always seemed to follow *his* orders, going at his pace and in the direction he chose. If he decided to take a swim, we had to swim, too. If he wanted to take a path filled with briars, so did we, by golly. If on occasion we happened to slide off his unsaddled girth and end up on the ground, he would be right there sniffing to see if everything was OK, awaiting a remount.

On one occasion—a "Fairy Party" thrown by our three year old daughter Wren—he stood patiently while his hooves were painted purple and flowers were woven into his mane and tail. He even submitted to sporting a flowered red sheet and unicorn horn for the day. He knew when to behave. He would shuffle behind as fairy after fairy sat upon his massive back for a magic ride.

Those were warm days, those days of clip clopping along with the baby "June bug" riding contentedly in my lap, the deep comfortable smell of that big old horse wafting back to us. That seems like a long time ago today. The "baby" goes to school now, and he has a new baby brother. Wren lost a hard battle with leukemia, but spent long hospital hours weaving fantastical stories about "What Big Poney is probably doing right now."

It seems that in our family, we keep time by the animals we have known and loved and said good-bye to. Big Poney's death marks the end of an era. Our young era. Older isn't bad though, just more knowing and even a little more glowing. I like it, but I sure will miss that big black horse. So will his young hot blooded partner Butterball.

When Charley came, Butter was grazing quietly. I had locked him into another pasture. After the shot, all was silent. I thanked my good neighbor and we turned to leave when a shrill scream and then another tore out of Butterball. He raced across the field as if he had suddenly gone berserk. Back and forth along the fence line he just flew and kicked. I don't know how he knew, he couldn't even see the woods where Poney lay. But he knew, and he wanted to be with him. Clods of dirt hit my face as Butter rounded the corner into the opened gate. He stopped short, then quietly stepped up to his friend. He bit him sort of softly on the shoulder and made a gentle snorting sound. He's been down in the woods beside Poney for several hours now. I guess I'll let him stay all day. Somehow it doesn't seem like I have much right to intrude on what's going on with them there. ∆

A Backwoods Home Anthology

FARM/GARDEN

Raising water buffalo — are they better than cattle?

By Chris and Mike Braet

Would you believe . . . water buffalo? You might be surprised to learn that there are many advantages to raising water buffalo over cattle. Raising water buffalo costs about 25% less than raising a herd of cattle of comparable size. They are well adapted to surviving on marginal habitat. On scrub pasture, swampy areas, or poor soils, water buffalo continue to gain weight, while cattle barely survive. They are gentler and more docile than cattle, and they have a healthy respect for electric fences. Many water buffalo cows calve at annual internals for up to twenty years. (The gestation period is 10½ months.)

The flavor of the meat is comparable to that of beef in steaks as well as in processed meat products, but has only about half the cholesterol, and 20% less fat. Researchers at the University of Florida in 1986 completed comparative feeding trials and carcass evaluations between top quality crossbred beef cattle bulls and randomly-selected water buffalo bulls. Charts from these investigations testify to the ability of water buffalo to perform favorably in the production of quality meat.*

Their milk has an average of 8% butterfat and 50% more protein than cow's milk. It retains more water in the curd and loses more fat in the whey, making it ideal for soft cheeses like ricotta and mozzarella. It takes four liters of the buffalo milk to make one kilo of cheese, compared to eight liters of the thinner cow's milk. Water buffalo cows are usually milked for 16 to 18 years.

International recognition, demand, and trade in water buffalo meat is growing fast. Venezuela has more than 50,000 water buffalo. They raise the animals for meat and milk. Venezuelans are known for their buffalo cheese, queso blanco and mozzarella. Cheeses made with buffalo milk are a pure dazzling white, with an incomparable flavor. Italians who come to Venezuela pronounce it equal to or better than the best mozzarella sold in Italy, since most Italian producers find buffalo milk too expensive and cut it with ordinary cow's milk.

Water buffalo were first brought to the US in 1975. Dr. Hugh Popenoe, Director of International Programs in Agriculture at the University of Florida, purchased the first five from a Toronto zoo. Since then, more animals have been brought in from Guam (1978), and Trinidad (1981 and 1991). The world population of water buffalo is about 150 million, with over half found in India.

There are now around 3000 water buffalo in the US, but strict quarantine regulations are making it difficult to bring more animals in. Water buffalo have 48 to 50 chromosomes and cattle have 60, which makes cross breeding impossible.

There are two main types of water buffalo, and over 18 varieties. The swamp type is found mostly in China and Southeast Asia. They have broad, wide horns, a chevron on the chest and bigger hooves. The river type is found mostly in India and Pakistan and is used primarily for milk and meat. Their horns are more tightly curled and the head is carried higher.

The more we learn about the water buffalo the more impressed we are.

It's easy to work with the docile water buffalo.

Their temperament makes the animals a true joy to work with. Most of us have seen the pictures of the water buffalo and small children in Vietnam and in the Philippines. At first, it was thought that they would do well only in the warmer Southern climate. We have since learned that they are likely to survive just about anywhere with proper shelter. They are used in Bulgaria to pull sleds in the snow. With proper care and management, we feel the water buffalo could adapt anywhere.

The American Water Buffalo Association was established in 1986 and is based at the University of Florida. The dues are $25 a year. Currently we have members from 19 countries and 29 states. Anyone interested can write, AWBA, P.O. Box 13533, Gainsville, FL 32611. Anyone interested in learning more about these wonderful animals can contact either Springhill Farm, P.O. Box 51, Sheridan, OR 97378, 503-843-7175, or Turkey Creek Co., Rt. 18 Box 314Y-2, Texarkana, AR 75502, 501-772-1064 or 3510. We will be glad to answer any questions.

*Comparative Performance of Buffalo (Bubalus bubalis) and Beef Cattle for Meat Production —J.W. Carpenter, J.S. Eastridge, W.S. Cripe and J.K. Loosli. ∆

Nightmare No. 4

*I never met him
But his daughter said
His last night
He lay in bed
Trying to die,
Screaming
For her husband
To bring the gun.
"I'm glad he didn't
suffer long,"
She said.
But now he
Screams endlessly
Like a late night rerun I
can't stop
Inside my head.*

*John Earl Silveira
Ojai, CA.*

Moon over Bogus Brook

By Dory Hulburt

I wish I had thought of it, but the truth is we really do live in a township called Bogus Brook in Minnesota. (The brook is about two miles east of us, and it looks pretty genuine to me.)

As an emigré from the city, I knew life would be different in Bogus Brook. I didn't realize how different until the day I had to swerve to avoid a dead pig in the middle of County Road 4.

You don't find many specialists out here. You've got to be good at a few things in order to subsist. In the nearest urban center, population 1000-some, the barbershop is also the dry cleaners. The bank is also the driver's license bureau. This is confusing for the newcomer. But service is good and misunderstandings are readily resolved.

The personalized attention is not always welcome. I didn't appreciate the cashier who handed me my husband's dry cleaning and said pointedly, "Somebody had better do something about the lining in that sport coat, quick." Fortunately, we don't have much call for dry cleaning anymore, as we have eased out of full-time jobs and into self-sufficiency.

While service excels here, inventory is notoriously unreliable. We have learned to dread the words, "We can order it for you." It's the kiss of death in the midst of a home improvement project.

I once visited three local groceries before finding lasagna noodles, and another time, the 24-hour grocery was out of eggs. Worst of all, no one stocks Häagen-Dazs ice cream.

We have overcome these problems by learning to make our own noodles, raising our own chickens, and eating homemade ice cream.

It is the Police Report in the local paper which best underscores the difference between city and country life. We left an urban area sadly experiencing its first wave of drive-by shootings and a rape at the co-op only three blocks away.

Some criminal activity cited recently in the local Police Report included a squirrel caught in a woodchuck trap at a city building. (Police released the squirrel unharmed.)

A resident reported a skunk in a garbage can. (The police officer put a lid on the can and turned the matter over to the resident.)

At the high school, crime peaked when someone punctured the pump on a pair of Nike Air Challenger tennis shoes.

My favorite write-up, however, involved a high school football player who was reported by an outraged passing couple for baring his buttocks out the school bus window. My husband dubbed the news item "Moon over Bogus Brook." ∆

Here are 5 simple things that make our life easier

By Marjorie Burris

We've lived in the back woods going on 14 years now, and although we will be the first to tell you its a good life, we also have to admit it is a lot of work. We are always on the look-out for ways to cut down on our work and for ways to cut down on expenses. Here are five things we have either developed ourselves, or have learned from others, that have helped us. I hope they help you, too.

1. Telephone book paper towels. Paper towels are so very helpful; they are also expensive. Our city friends save their old phone books for us, and I always have a book of white pages on my kitchen counter. Husband keeps the yellow pages hanging draped over a clothes hanger by his work bench in his shop. The yellow pages are a bit stiffer than the white, but are good to wipe up paint and grease spills, wipe off the dip stick when checking oil, wipe up mud off the shop floor, clean greasy tools . . . well, you name it.

In the house, I use a handful of white pages to clean the top of my wood burning cook stove and my black iron skillet and dutch oven. Three or four white sheets individually crumpled put a nice shine on a window pane. I use a white sheet to wrap an apple or a tomato for long term storage, to clean off muddy shoes, or to wrap nut shells before burning them in the stove. Like newsprint, phone book sheets will leave a black smudge on some things, so I occasionally do use a "real" paper towel, but my phone book paper towels are used the most.

We do not use the phone book in the outhouse, however. The paper is too stiff.

2. Speaking of outhouses, we use a **coffee can toilet paper holder** in our outdoors toilet. A three-pound coffee or shortening can will hold a roll of toilet paper and the tight lid keeps out dirt and varmints. No more messy and costly toilet paper mice nests stuck around the corners of our privy. I labeled the can so guests know where to find the necessary item, and husband built a little shelf so we can set the can within easy reach of the occupant. Simple, effective, inexpensive.

3. Sometimes we can get rid of those mice and rats altogether with a **five-gallon bucket mouse trap**. To make the trap, fill a five-gallon bucket no more than half full of water. Make a cover for the top out of strong paper. I find a brown paper grocery sack to be just right.

Tie the cover onto the bucket firmly with heavy string or cord. Make a small cross opening in the middle of the cover with a sharp knife. Place a piece of light weight bait such as a piece of apple or a broken nut near the cross opening. Or smear a thick bait such as peanut butter or bacon grease near the center. When the varmint climbs onto the top of the bucket to get the bait, it will fall through the opening and drown. We have caught many pests, including large pack rats, this way.

I like this trap because we can use it in a barn or outbuilding as well as in the house. The trap is able to catch several mice in a night because it doesn't have to be re-set every time a mouse falls through and we don't have to check it every day. To empty, remove the cover, dump out the contents, and start over again.

We have found, however, that we have to either cover the bucket with wire or put the trap in a place where the dogs cannot get to it.

4. Plastic grocery sack shoe covers. You have to go in the house for one short minute; your shoes are wet and muddy; you don't want to track in mud; you don't want to take off your shoes. Sound familiar? Well, put a plastic grocery sack over each shoe, tie the handles around your ankles, and go on in the house without leaving tracks. Sometimes, if my boots have a lot of snow on them, I will "double sack," that is, put two sacks over each foot just to make sure the melting snow doesn't leak through. Saves a lot of time, energy, and frustration.

One word of warning: the sacks can be slippery on a waxed or tile floor, so walk carefully.

5. I keep a supply of grocery sacks hanging on the porch in an **old pants leg plastic sack dispenser**. To make a dispenser, cut off one leg of an old pair of pants starting at the fly and angling up to the pocket. Turn up a hem at the bottom of the leg and thread a piece of elastic through the hem, making a small opening through which you can pull sacks. The elastic opening will keep the sacks from falling out and will give you access to the sacks from either end of the leg.

Next, hem the raw edge at the top of the leg where you cut it off, and sew a hanging tab to the highest point of the bag. You will be surprised at how many plastic sacks you can stuff into your handy dispenser.

Perhaps you have some hints you'd be willing to share with your fellow backwoods dwellers. That's what *Backwoods Home Magazine* is all about—making life easier for one another. ∆

BUILDING

Determined woman builds distinctive vertical log studio

By Dorothy Ainsworth

When I graduated from high school in 1960, my father wrote in my autograph book, "When you get married and have twins, don't come to me for safety pins!" My role in our large family was Susie Homemaker, and sure enough, by age 21, I had fulfilled my destiny: two kids, two jobs, one husband. Later, to lighten the load, no husband.

For 15 years, I had put myself on the back burner. Hopes and dreams of security and independence had simmered. A notebook entitled "Wants and Needs in a Home" and a filing cabinet stuffed with log and timber-frame ideas revealed my yearning. An apartment-dwelling single mother waitressing in the big city was not my idea of the good life. Something in my genes insisted on a massive medieval fortress decorated in early pioneer. I wanted a house that the wolf himself couldn't blow down!

I diligently shopped around for a nice small town, secured a job and apartment in advance, loaded up my kids, Eric and Cynthia (along with his piano and her horse), and we were off. Happiness was Reno, Nevada in my rear view mirror!

It took a year in idyllic Ashland, Oregon, to find a suitable piece of land I could afford and secure a farm loan, and another year to drill a well and "get electricity." The third year I cut my baby (saw) teeth on remodeling a couple of old outbuildings into storage structures. Fraught with nothing but parallelograms, I learned harsh rule #1: "Plumb, Level and Almost Square," and tricky rule #2: "Measure Twice, Oops, Cut Twice." That summer the hand tools used me.

The dog would slink away when I donned my carpenter's belt and furrowed my brow in grim determination.

For a novice, there's no thrill like the tactile kinetic experience of driving a 16-penny nail home in three blows, then burying its head with two extra whacks for no reason. There was evidence of beginner's overkill everywhere. Electrical cord repairs looked like snakes that had swallowed gophers. A job wasn't finished until all the nails were gone. There were no gimmicks or shortcuts in the learning process. I sweated and strained and

Dorothy Ainsworth is shown holding the jig that helped her mark the birdsmouth notches on each rafter. The cupola frame rests atop the scaffolding behind her.

A Backwoods Home Anthology

The Fifth Year

133

Raising the log walls.

scarred. But the satisfaction of sawing a clean square cut with a hand saw rivaled sewing a fine seam or baking a perfect loaf of bread, and eventually the results became just as predictable.

It wasn't long before I discovered power tools with my Sears charge card. Yikes, that could mean twice as many mistakes in half the time! My circular saw was a new force to be reckoned with. It came with two blades: ripper and shredder. When I braced myself with gritted teeth and squinted eyes, the dog scurried out of sight.

Once in a while I'd take a break, sip a cup of coffee (liquid motivation) and gaze upon my 10 acres of star thistle and poison oak, envisioning a proverbial rose garden (without thorns) and a beautiful log home on top of the hill, surrounded by fruit trees in technicolor and kittens playing all around. For now, though, I'd enjoy the red-tailed hawk circling overhead and coyotes kiyiying at night. As a farmer creates his self-portrait in a freshly plowed

South view of the finished studio, showing the entryway, cushioned window seat, and deck. The window seat looks out at a view of Mt. Ashland.

field, I was driven to carve out an original relationship with this hilly, hostile chunk of land. There was no going back to the comfort zone.

I focused my energy and lucky things began to happen. Someone told me about lodge-pole pine logs available right out of the forest, for 3 cents a lineal foot. This economical option prompted some new possibility thinking. It confirmed my decision in favor of vertical-log construction for minimal notching and relative ease in handling and transporting. Inspired, I hastened down and bought a permit from the local ranger district of the U.S. Forest Service. I calculated gathering enough logs for one medium sized structure.

One day Eric was playing a Bach prelude; the next day his white knuckles were gripping a chainsaw and felling trees! After several excursions of terror and torture, we had stockpiled 180 logs for $42. Together we carried each 10" eight-foot green log 100 feet or more, stepping over slash piles, hobbling, staggering, grunting and whimpering. As my grip weakened with every step, I kept mumbling to myself: "Only 3 cents a foot, only 3 cents a foot." We loaded 15 at a time in the old Ford pickup and careened home, front-end floating.

Eric wanted an eight-sided piano studio (1000 sq. ft.) for good acoustics, and I wanted a barn-style house (1800 sq. ft.). The terrain dictated pier foundations. We decided to practice on the studio first. Flush-faced with enthusiasm, we sketched his "blue-print" on a napkin in a restaurant. Two heads are thicker than one, so we got a book from the library and set up the batter boards.

Upon one visit to the lumber yard, I spied a huge pile of large timbers in the back lot and my pulse quickened. It was love at first sight, and I bought them all as impulsively as a woman buys a pair of shoes. The salesman quietly wrote up my order for 10,000 board feet at $250/thousand (all my savings), looked up with one raised eyebrow and said, "Lady, do you know what you're doing?" I said boldly, "No, but I know what I want."

The stack included 30 huge pressure treated pilings salvaged from an old railroad trestle. I just happened to need 29 pilings for both foundations!

About a week later, a neighbor stopped by, curious about my timbers, and revealed that he owned a boom truck and a giant auger bit. After a brief discussion of both foundation plans (my favorite subject), he offered to drill the holes and set the pilings for $10 each. I seized the opportunity at once, and began the grueling labor of cleaning out six-foot deep holes by day and "slinging hash" at the cafe at night.

Setting one of the nine 12-foot-long foundation pilings. Each pressure-treated piling rests on a poured concrete pad at the bottom of a 6-foot-deep hole. Each piling was set plumb with tamped shale and gravel.

A Backwoods Home Anthology

By this time I was acquiring some major muscle, and I needed every fiber. There was no shade. Crow's feet turned into eagle's claws, hands into lobster claws. I kept whispering to myself, "Only $290.00, only one week's wages," (for the piling holes). I once read that you get rich by spending yourself. I was filthy, sweaty rich. My sister said I was *becoming* the man I wanted to marry!

Soon after the piers were set, the backhoe man I hired to dig a waterline trench just happened to have a laser-beam transit in his hip pocket. He vol-

Dorothy wrestles a log out of her pickup.

untarily marked all the piers level with each other. I cut them off and notched them to receive 4x12 rim joists for the piano studio and 6x12 girders for the house. I stood back and affectionately admired my big black pilings, spaced just so, jutting out of the stark landscape like Stonehenge. The time had come to contemplate the architectural overview of both structures and draw up the final plans, for county approval.

Logic told me to build within my capabilities, but aesthetics won out. "When ignorance is bliss, 'tis folly to be wise." Hence the piano studio was to be an octagon converging into a square cupola, with triangles and trapezoids dancing heel and toe on the roof. I was like a spoiled child who wanted everything on my list, except there were no elves to help and no Santa to deliver. I wanted archways and bay windows, vaulted ceilings and skylights, wide window sills and a cushioned window seat for reading magazines and eating chocolates on a rainy day.

But I would not employ a centerpost to support the roof! It would ruin the romantic notion of a nine-foot concert grand piano in the middle of the 30-foot room, with Chopin bouncing off the walls. The laws of physics have a way of humbling even the most deluded ego. I scratched my head while searching my memory banks. Eureka!

The window seat adds a touch of beauty to the home.

I remembered the "yurt principle." A hidden cable would defy gravity.

Yes, I wanted it all, completed in this lifetime, on a shoestring. Time and energy are the basic currencies of life; lack of money is merely an inconvenience. A sense of urgency gripped me.

What started out as "we" ended up as "me." Eric and Cynthia went off to college and met mates. Nature had its way. Meanwhile, back at the ranch, I was fluttering about creating a nest so there'd be something to be empty. Someday the chickens might come home to roost. I imagined future music festivals: spontaneous gatherings of diverse and harmonious spirits, and rosy-cheeked grand kids giggling and dancing about the room. Goals are dreams with a deadline, so I grabbed my hammer and got busy.

Building the floor was laborious but uncomplicated. Joists and subflooring were secured with screws—no creaking allowed. When I needed to "rest," I'd peel logs with my trusty drawknife. I documented all progress with self-portraits. Photography is my hobby.

The library was usually my best friend, but when it came time to square off the logs, there was no book.

Using a chain saw as a chop saw for squaring off logs. The bolt and handle must be equal distance from the wall (very important). The tapered end of the log is shimmed to make the imaginary centerline of the log parallel with the level bench.

With the optical illusions involved in staring at a gnarly tapered log, it's impossible to eyeball the cut. One can end up with a pile of firewood. After trial and error (and a little kindling), I devised a contraption using my chainsaw as a chop-saw and it worked beautifully! (See drawing).

Erecting the vertical-log walls kept me as busy as a Beethoven sonata. The general procedure was "Cut 'em off, stand 'em up, spike 'em in." Pre-drill like a drill sergeant. To get from here to there, hug a log real tight and waddle with lt. Who cares what the neighbors think? One sunny afternoon two bicyclists rode by and one yelled, "Hey look, they put the logs the wrong way!"

When the walls were standing and the headers in their final resting places, it was time to place the square cupola aloft. A gin pole put it there and scaffolding held it fast. Cutting the confounded compounded angles where three rafters met at the corners required some finesse with the 12" electric chainsaw. Next, to really challenge my capabilities, each birdsmouth had to be individually measured with a template and custom cut. After transferring the measurements to a 16' 2x12 rafter on the floor and making all the cuts, I pushed it up a long ladder propped against the scaffolding, one step at a time. Then I pivoted it on the top railing, using leverage to lower it slowly down onto its mark on the top plate, and fastened it to the cupola. When the birdsmouth miraculously seated in place, I sighed, "Ahhh, life doesn't get any better than

A BHM Writer's Profile
Don Childers

Don Childers is the artist who paints each of BHM's scenic covers. He has spent many years working for the Defense Industry, painting mock-ups of military equipment still in the planning stage. The stealth bomber and fighter, the HARPOON and TOMAHAWK cruise missiles, and a variety of other once secret weapons are among the many mock-ups he painted at various stages of their development.

He is also an amateur astronomer who has built many of his own telescopes, an amateur inventor of a graphic arts tool to sharpen exacto knives, and has illustrated various historical books. Many of his paintings have been sold to private collectors, and many more hang on the walls of admirals and generals around the country. The Dijon Museum in France exhibits one of his paintings, and several hang in English pubs.

this." The word "birdsmouth" still evokes a spiritual feeling in me.

The hardest job of all was going from the delicious solitude of the country to work at the cafe, where trying to get a bite to eat in 8 hours was like a giraffe at a watering hole with the lions coming. At home I had the freedom of a monkey, climbing up and down the rungs of the scaffolding. My goal was two rafters a day, 60 in all. I'd work right up to the last minute, then put on my war paint, fire up old Bessie, and speed to work, curling my eyelashes with one hand and steering with the other. I lost a few eyelashes that summer.

I glued and screwed every rafter, then drilled holes in their tails (just above the top plate) to receive the cable and four turnbuckles. I bushed each hole with annealed nylon. The moment of truth came with tightening the turnbuckles and removing the scaffolding. Nothing creaked, croaked, or settled. The structural integrity of my design was uncompromised!

Eight of the main rafters, like spokes, are true 2x12's, the rest

"Flatting" a log to create a flat, even side. Here Dorothy is making one of many shallow kerf cuts down to snapped chalk lines. Later she cut off the pieces formed by these cuts to create the flat side.

2x10's, to provide a 2" recessed nailing surface for the 1x12 pine ceiling. With age, pine mellows to a warm and wonderful patina. I helped it along with a coat of semi-gloss lacquer.

Now and again people would happen by offering advice—armchair experts. I never had to ask for a second opinion; dozens came, unsolicited. I discovered that common sense is not so common. Gullible ears will be filled. After pursuing a few wild geese, I became a skeptical inquirer. "Why don't you just....," was the quickest phrase to make me surreptitiously roll my eyes at the dog and feign snoring, then try to get back to work. In all my brief encounters, I never met a man who hadn't once lived in a teepee and built a log house—a curious phenomenon indeed.

An old friend taught me how to use clamps as a "poor-man's assistant." With auxiliary "hands," the roof plywood went on fast. I topped it off with shingles just before the first rainfall of autumn.

I furred out the inner walls with 2x4's, hid the wiring and insulation, and covered it all up with sheetrock. With the garden sprayer, everything on the outside got a dose of the old boatbuilder's recipe (linseed oil, marine varnish and turpentine) whether it needed it or not. The overspray restyled my hair!

Drilling the holes for the steel cables. The hole locations were carefully measured so that the cable makes a perfect circle centered on the axis of the building. This precision ensures an even distribution of tension on all the rafters.

A Backwoods Home Anthology

Partial interior view of the finished studio. Note the open vaulted ceiling.

I chinked the logs with 1½" foam pipe insulation, sanded and painted brown, then glued in place. I caulked with 50-year silicone seal (dark brown) and smoothed out each bead manually. For one month I was the self-appointed "Caulking Queen of Ashland," as evidenced by the splayed out middle finger of my right hand.

Since the walls were a foot thick, I made the window framing to accommodate. I used 1½ boards (one whole and one ripped in half) of pine 2x10's splined together, screwed and plugged in place. I ordered double-paned glass to fit each opening and secured the windows with my own molding. Simple brass casement adjusters open some of the smaller windows for cross ventilation. Built-in sliding windows in the cupola and a ceiling fan whisk out hot air.

This is the steel cable that keeps the weight of the roof over the uprights by preventing the rafter ends from spreading outward. This cable eliminates the need for a centerpost and allows an open, vaulted ceiling.

The Fifth Year

A Backwoods Home Anthology

Spatial relationships reign in the palisaded palace. Windows in clusters of threes, and tile work in the entryway, hearth, and bay window, repeat themes for visual appeal. To me, archways are the crowning glory in a home, perhaps hearkening back to my ancestry in a cave. I built them out of 2x10 "splined-pine," by cutting the curves on my band saw, then laminating to the right thickness. I glued and screwed and clamped, butcher-block style, and sanded the attractive end-grain until smooth. The stout arches lend support in spanning the doorways. I covered the 1" subfloor with 3/4" particle board and cozied it all over with carpet.

I tallied my expenditures. The cost of the piano studio came to $15,000, the sum total of "tips" I earned and spent daily. I was debt-free.

Three years had whizzed by and I was putting the finishing touches on my "baby." I sat down on the deck to rub sawdust out of my bloodshot eyes and pet the dog, when Eric appeared like an apparition! After piano-tuning school and a three-month hike on the Pacific Crest Trail to "round out his education," he came back to visit mom and his piano. I cleared the sawdust out of my ears and asked him to play. When I heard beautiful Mozartian trills wafting out the Dutch door and across the sunlit hills, it was all worthwhile . . . a labor of love.

Eric is now a tuner, teacher, performer and composer in Ashland. Cynthia is a model, actress, and photographer in San Francisco (and she still loves horses).

Having served my apprenticeship, I was ready to get started on the main house. New dreams beckoned. As serendipity would have it, I met a huge and handsome hunk (Kurt) at the fitness center and he whispered the magic words in my ear, "Let's go get your logs." We did, 300 of them, for $72. This time I was in love and feeling no pain. We laughed and giggled and sighed while laboring through the summer. When I couldn't lift my end, Paul Bunyan carried the whole 300 lb. log on his shoulder! I swooned and snapped photographs.

The winter of 1991 I built a model of the house to manifest the joinery inherent in my design: mortise and tenon joints, connecting girts and knee braces (all out of logs). I would use the timbers as ridge beams, top plates and cantilevered deck supports.

Kurt was not a carpenter; he had his own career. I wanted to tackle this new project myself, so we agreed he would help me with the logistics of raising the frame and any task impossible to do solo. He comes running only when he hears a blood-curdling scream.

The first year of actual construction (1992) was spent building the floor

The entryway.

and peeling logs; this second year (1993) the frame and roof. The pay as-I-go method (estimated from the piano studio) will ultimately cost $15/sq. ft. ($27,000). Though I pause to write, I'm in the process of roofing with barn-red metal, trying to beat the fall rains again.

When I purchased 2200 square feet of steel panels, 4000 screws and all the trimmings, the salesman commented, "This is definitely a two-man job." I thought....gulp...., "How about one woman?" It's been a little scary, flirting with the undertaker on a 6-in-12 pitch, 18' up, but affordable. This winter, as the rain patters down, christening the new roof, I'll be working inside with a Mona-Lisa smile on my lips, so glad to be on level ground again!

I still blow-dry my hair on the way to work with the windows down, but I have a brand new bumper sticker: Caution, Driver Applying Makeup. ∆

Dorothy hanging from the rafters.

The basic timber-and-log frame of the main house, now under construction. Dorothy has promised to write us a future article on this project.

A Backwoods Home Anthology

SELF SUFFICIENCY

Choosing and using a wood cookstove

By Mary Pipes

I've had a special friend for over 13 years now. She is a little on the heavy side, but it really makes her very attractive. She is old enough to be my mother and equally as gray. My husband and children love her as much as I do. Her name is Miss Home Comfort, 1923. She is my wood cookstove.

We bought her in the summer of 1979 from a man who had three. We wanted to experiment with being more self-reliant and this seemed like a good thing to do. So, four months pregnant with our second child, I really got brave and said, "Take out the gas stove." I figured that if I couldn't get her to work there are lots of things you can eat in the summer that you don't have to cook. But it wasn't that hard to figure out how to use her, so we didn't have to give up hot food after all.

There are several reasons to consider owning a wood cookstove. In an emergency, they can provide a source of heat and a way to cook. You are not dependent on outside utilities, just your own ability to obtain wood or coal. Even more rewarding is the feeling you can get from them. I can look at my stove and wonder who has cooked on it, whose child bathed in front of it, and who used it to warm up chilly hands and faces on a cold day. I can also think of the memories we have made around it—the Thanksgiving turkeys and fragrant cakes and pies that have come out of it. I appreciate it for making me more self-reliant, but I love it for letting us share in its history and continue the warmth of its traditions.

If you don't already own one of these beauties but would like to, there are some things to look for. First, check the grates in the firebox on the left hand side of the stove. This is

(Drawing by Jason Pipes, age 13.)

what the fire sits on as it burns. If they are gone or pieces of them are missing, make sure you can find a replacement for them before you buy the stove. This is the heart of the stove, because without the grates there is nowhere to build the fire. The grates should also turn to empty the ashes into the ashbox. There should be a square knob sticking out the front of the stove below the firebox. Take the grate handle, which is a handle with a square hole in it, place it on the knob and turn. Watch the grates move and make sure they don't bind.

Second, look at the cooktop to make sure it is fairly level and not warped. Also check to see that the support pieces and the lids (those round things on top) fit together well. Any large gaps will smoke.

Third, look inside the oven for holes in the wall. If it is rusted through anywhere you'll have a great smokehouse, but it won't do much for your cakes and pies.

Many cookstoves also come with warming ovens or shelves and/or water reservoirs, which are great but not essential to their operation.

142   *The Fifth Year*

As with any wood burning stove, proper installation is vital to your safety, happiness, and the success of your new cooking experience. You should check local building codes to insure that you are in compliance in order to avoid an unplanned housewarming.

Wood cookstoves work on a very simple premise. You make a fire in the firebox and the heat travels beneath the cooktop on its way up the chimney. As it does so the cooktop gets hot. If you want to use the oven, you close the damper which sends the heat beneath the cooktop and around the oven before going up the chimney. This heats the oven. The only big adjustment comes when you realize you can't set the burner on high or medium and you can't set the oven for 350, wait 5 minutes and bake. With a regular stove, you start preparing the food, then turn on the heat. With a cookstove, you start the fire, then prepare the food.

All cookstoves have the firebox with a draft below it and an ashbox below that to catch the ashes. There is also a lever, either on the top or the right side, which controls the oven damper. There may also be a draft control in the stovepipe. When starting the fire, make sure eveything is in the open mode. Double check so you don't end up with a kitchen full of smoke. Turn the grates to empty the old ashes and pieces of wood into the ashbox. Empty the ashes in the ashbox into something fireproof and place it on something non-combustible. I melted my floor by putting what I thought were cold ashes into a plastic bucket on a vinyl floor.

Most cookstoves will burn wood or coal, but using coal will cut the usable life of your grates down substantially. If you can get replacement grates easily, go ahead and use coal if you want to. But if you have to scavenge parts off another stove to replace your grates you'd be better off just using wood.

Start the fire using good, dry kindling. Don't start with pieces that are too big, unless you enjoy stirring sooty pieces of wood around. Take the lids off over the firebox to lay your fire. Light the kindling (I use newspapers underneath) and put the lids back on before your ceiling ignites. When the basic kindling is burning nicely, open the firebox door and carefully lay on larger pieces of wood.

The type of wood you use will determine how long it takes your fire to get hot. Hardwoods (oak, fruitwood, etc.) are harder to get burning, but once lit burn hotter. Softwoods (pine, aspen) light more easily but burn up quickly. I like to use the end pieces from 2x4s or 2x6s (or other dimensional lumber), split with a hatchet, to start my fire. Then I add oak or juniper to keep it going. Occasionally I'll throw in some more kindling if the fire is kind of slow.

You can begin cooking on the top of the stove fairly soon after starting the fire. High is on the left, medium is in the middle, and low is on the right, farthest from the firebox. Start on high and move your pan around to find the right spot. When the fire is burning well, adjust the draft to conserve wood and control the heat. Closed burns cooler, open burns hotter.

By the way, cast iron cookwear can't be beat on a cookstove. It heats up well, holds the heat, gives off trace amounts of iron, and will have your biceps looking wonderful (it's fairly heavy). Keep your eyes open at swap meets and garage sales for used, already seasoned ware. Or you can buy new at hardware and other stores.

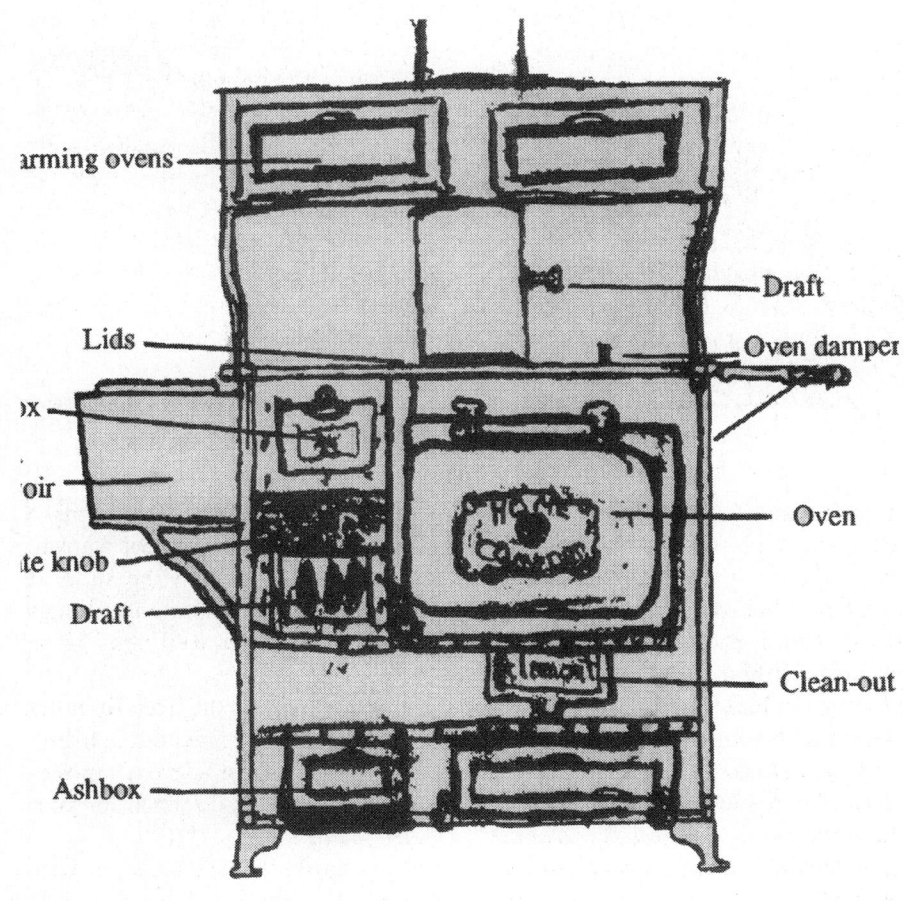

(Drawing by Ben Pipes, age 12.)

Keep an eye on the fire and add wood as needed. If you want to use the oven, let your fire get burning well, then close the damper on the back or side, allowing the heat to circulate around the oven. You may have a gauge on the oven door that tells you the inside temperature. I don't completely trust mine, so I use an inexpensive oven thermometer. Be patient—the oven can take awhile to heat up. Just grab a copy of *Backwoods Home Magazine* to read while you wait. Place an old pan on the bottom of the oven and fill it with water before you bake. It will help keep your baked goods from burning. In the oven, the left side is hotter than the right side, so you may want to turn things around half way through the baking time. The temperature won't stay constant as in an electric or gas oven, but if it's close you shouldn't have a problem. Once you have reached the temperature you want, use the draft below the firebox to control it.

You will have to clean the stove every so often. The frequency will depend on what type of wood you use and how often you cook. Using it full time and burning mostly pine, every one to two weeks is about right. If it seems like it takes *forever* to heat up the top of the stove, it's probably time. Wear old clothes and find something to keep everyone busy for half an hour. Once you get started you don't want to have to stop, if possible, because you will be having so much fun playing in the soot. When the stove is cold, remove the cooktop and brush the soot off the pieces. I do this over the stove so I only have to scoop the soot once. Push all the soot to the right hand side so it falls past the oven wall. There is a clean-out door someplace on the outside near the bottom of the oven door. Use a clean-out tool, which is a little rectangular piece of metal attached to a long handle, to pull the soot out. Put papers on the floor and get something to catch the soot. Close the doors and windows close by so your house won't be peppered with killer soot balls. Scrape out as much soot as possible, using the clean-out tool. Shine a flashlight in the clean-out door to check the far corners for soot. By now at least your hands, if not much more of you, is completely black. This is always when friends will come to visit or your neighbor down the road will show up.

Once everything is soot-free, this being a relative term, reassemble the cooktop. You are now ready to go again. With practice, this cleaning will become easier each time you do it.

Wood cookstoves are very "user friendly." I have found that with practice you can cook anything on a cookstove that you can on a regular stove. The only thing you need to remember is that food cooked this way is rarely "fast food," but the trade-off for taste and the feeling of accomplishment is well worth it. You will come to know your stove in a way that is impossible with modern day appliances.

I would truly consider it a tragedy if I had to part company with mine, and friends like that are hard to find. If you should choose to travel this same road to self-reliance, I hope your experience will be as warm and enduring as mine. ∆

A country moment

Paul Boos of northern California gets set to cut new lumber on a sawmill.

A BHM Writer's Profile

Mary Pipes

A homesteader at heart her whole life, Mary Pipes has been raising animals and growing gardens for the last 20 years in Arizona and Utah. For awhile she authored The Homestead Gazette, a self sufficiency newsletter. She loves to sew, quilt, and cook on her wood cookstove. She and her husband, Jim, homeschool their six children, and they raise chickens, cows pigs, and milk goats in Manti, Utah.

PROFILE

A Backwoods Home Anthology

Mick Sagrillo — Wizard of Wind

By Vern Modeland

Gentle breeze or gale force, wind is the fundamental output of the world's weather machine. People were harnessing the wind to work for them in the 1100s. Wind power became the energy source that brought electricity to many a farm before Rural Electrification Administration (REA) trucks came down the back roads.

The wind also seems to have pushed Mick Sagrillo on a course he really hadn't started planning yet when he was growing up in the 60s in Chicago, becoming someone who loves to teach and who, even more, loves to tinker.

Sagrillo today is in demand as one of two people singled out as leaders in the area of hands-on expertise when it comes to wind-powered electrical energy systems and their components. Sagrillo is the founder and owner of Lake Michigan Wind and Sun, a company that builds, re-builds and repairs wind generators and components. It has customers in 43 states and 18 countries.

"They're the kind of people I like to work with—people who are willing to get their hands dirty," he says of his clients.

Windpower resource

Sagrillo has collected what he describes as the largest patent library in the world specifically related to wind-powered electrical generation. He also has accumulated information, and the resources, to keep those old pre-REA Jacobs systems and Winco/Wincharger devices whirling and charging. His company sells newer technology too: wind generators and systems, towers, electronic

Mick Sagrillo

controls and inverters, and airfoils. It stocks replacement parts, or will make them, for numerous brands of wind systems. Lake Michigan Wind and Sun also consults, answering questions about location, system sizing, towers, interfacing with utilities, and other details that come up when looking into wind-generated electrical power systems.

"We don't do installations or on-site repairs," says Sagrillo. "We work here."

Here is a five-acre self-reliant homestead at the base of the Door Peninsula, that part of Wisconsin that peels away into Lake Michigan to shelter Green Bay. It's about 30 miles southwest from Sagrillo's home to the city of Green Bay.

Fleeing the city life

Mick and Lynn Sagrillo were early into the self-reliance movement. They first decided on getting away from the big city back in 1972, seeking a better environment in which to raise their new daughter, Jenny.

On Mick's teacher's salary of about $8000 a year, they managed to save almost $2500, keeping their needs simple, eating and preserving a lot of home-grown food, and utilizing Mick's inherited handyman abilities.

He found a job in the suburban Fox River area, teaching environmental studies, biology, and earth sciences for grades Kindergarten through 12 at Woodstock, Illinois. He also managed to talk his way into developing an environmental studies program for the entire school district.

"I was intensely interested, and anybody can become an expert," he says. With him, that's basic philosophy.

Lynn returned to school and got an advanced degree so that she, too, could teach. And in 1978, Lynn Sagrillo found a teaching position at

The Fifth Year

the University of Wisconsin at Green Bay.

Mick decided the time had come for him to become a house-spouse.

Finding a fixer-upper

Finding the right house in which to spouse took a while, he recalls. Eventually, he was able to convince one real estate agent that he meant what he said about wanting "an old farmhouse, in the middle of nowhere, one with no plumbing and no electricity."

The real estate agent called one day to describe a place that had been built in 1871 and added on to in the early 1900s. It had a scattering of out-buildings on five acres that included a very old log cabin and a three-hole outhouse. There were two electrical outlets in the house, three overhead lights, and an electric water heater.

The place was a consummate fixer-upper, perfect for the handyman in Mick. The Sagrillos drove up to look at it on a Saturday and made an offer on Sunday.

That first winter, they lived with cold winter winds whistling through exposed clapboards. But today, it's become a much-remodeled, super-insulated, passive solar, comfortable home for Mick, Lynn, and Jenny.

That is, when they all can be at home. Lynn is now a busy college lecturer who also is finishing up work on a Ph.D. at the University of Wisconsin, 165 miles away at Madison. Their daughter is in her fifth year of college studies, following her parents into teaching as a profession.

Sagrillo's first fix-up priority was to put in a septic system and some plumbing to replace the bucket he found was the end of the line for waste water beneath the kitchen sink.

He hopes for a greenhouse. He knows about greenhouses. His first one was built on a third floor porch of the apartment house in which they lived in Chicago in the early 70s.

One outbuilding, a 65-by-30-foot, brick-walled machine shed and granary, was remodeled to become a wind-powered shop and office for Lake Michigan Wind & Sun and his other interests.

Preserving the look

Preserving the exterior appearance of the old Wisconsin farm house as much as he could, Sagrillo gutted the structure. A new floor plan left just two rooms downstairs.

"There's a bathroom and everything else. If you want to have radiant heating, you have to have an open floor plan."

A wall of south-facing glass brings in the sun's warmth in winter. Lots of glass allows ready viewing of gathering storms.

"That's sort of humbling," Sagrillo says.

Today, the house has expanded to afford 3,000 square feet of living space.

"Cedar beams, oak floors, and lots of brick. The cabinets are walnut and oak and butternut. It's all locally-cut wood.

"I heat with wood, and we raise all our own pork and beef [and chickens and fruit and garden produce—selling enough to pay for what they keep]. It was a sustainable homestead until about two years ago."

Two years ago was about when the wind power business and his other work in renewable energy began absorbing a major portion of Sagrillo's time. The Public Service Commission of Wisconsin had picked him to serve on a Wisconsin Demand-Side Management Panel to oversee expenditure of up to $100 million on electrical utility consumer demonstration projects. He had become a founder and director of RENEW Wisconsin, a coalition of business, government and university professionals whose aim is to develop and foster the use of renewable energy in that state. He was called on as an expert witness in the area of wind power for the Wisconsin PSC at planning meetings. And there was his involvement with the Union of Concerned Scientists' Initiative on Renewable Energy. It is a group examining the potential for using readily renewable sources such as wind, solar, and water, to generate electricity in the Midwest.

Father of fair

Sagrillo also helped start the Midwest Renewable Energy Association and he is one of the founders of the Midwest Renewable Energy Fair held each June at Amhurst, Wisconsin. In four years, that event has grown to attract enthusiastic crowds, exhibitors, and media attention from all over the country. More than 6,500 people braved nasty weather to attend in 1993, to mingle and listen to folks who are living with renewable energy or someday hoping to.

The cost of harnessing the wind to generate electricity is competitive in 1993 dollars, according to the U.S. Department of Energy, particularly in the northeast and western parts of the U.S. A utility industry report claims that non-polluting wind generators could today be cranking out 10 percent or more of the electrical power being consumed within 40 of the 51 states. And the Great Plains states have the potential to *export* wind-generated electrical energy. A commitment by the power utilities to wind-generation there could turn out up to 10 times the demand in those states!

All this potential leads to why Mick Sagrillo is getting to be much busier than he'd like to be. He teaches an intensive week-long Wind Workshop for Jordan College at Grand Rapids, Michigan. And he heads off annually to Carbondale, Colorado, to teach at the Solar Energy Institute.

In between, he writes articles on wind power for various magazines, including *Backwoods Home* (Nov/Dec 1993). His activity hasn't gone unnoticed or unrewarded. Sagrillo won the 1992 Renewable Energy Pioneer award from *PV Network News / Solar Electricity Today* magazine. This year, he received the Environmental Achievement Award from the Wisconsin Greens, an environmental preservation group. And Wisconsin Secretary of State, Douglas La Follett, has nominated him for the prestigious John Ericsson Award given out by the U.S. Department of Energy.

His heroes

Who does such a man look up to? "Two of the very dear heroes in my life are my mother's father and my father's mother," says Sagrillo. His grandparents came from Yugoslavia and Italy to settle on a few acres in central Indiana where they raised their families and their food in a self-reliant old-world fashion that made a lasting impression on Mick Sagrillo.

"And there was my father. He's another of my heros. He was a putterer, a jack of all trades.

"I guess what I learned from them is that you can do, and you can be, anything that you set your mind to."

Mick Sagrillo is trying to pass on the real importance in that. Δ

Subscribing to Backwoods Home Magazine has never been easier

Just call our TOLL FREE number

1-800-835-2418

(This number is for ordering only. All others, please call 1-530-459-3500)

and use your Visa or Mastercard.

It costs a lousy $19⁹⁵ a year.

Three great bread recipes

By Richard Blunt

Homemade bread is one of my favorite foods. I've been making it the old fashioned way (by hand) for ten years. There are machines that will mix it, knead it, bake it, and probably eat it for you. But feeling the dough at each stage of development is part of the unique pleasure I experience when I make my own bread.

If you're fortunate enough to have developed an appreciation for good home cooked food, but you're still buying your bread at the grocery store, you're denying yourself one of the most rewarding experiences home cooking can offer.

The aroma of bread baking in your oven, followed by the delight of sitting down to a slice of fresh homemade bread and a good cup of coffee, a glass of milk, or your favorite beer, ale or wine is hard to beat.

We take bread for granted. We go to the grocery store and buy those tasteless, spongy loaves and somehow convince ourselves that this is as good as it gets. Or maybe we think it's the best we can afford or all we deserve. The truth is, good commercial bread is hard to find. Like many other foods, if you want it good, you have to make it yourself.

However, good bread is not only easy to make, it's fun.

In this month's column, I'm going to give you three good recipes. But first I'm going to give you a little technical information so you'll know what part each ingredient plays in the making of the bread as well as what's happening at each step along the way. With this, you'll be on your way to making the best bread you've ever tasted. If you're a newcomer to bread baking, these recipes will give you a great opportunity to make an excellent loaf on your first try. But, even if you are an old kitchen hand, give these recipes a try. I think you're going to like them.

The equipment

First, let's examine some of the equipment you're going to need. Although bread can be baked in two ways—free form and in loaf pans—we're going to use pans. There are several different sizes and each has a specific use. The most common, and the one we'll be working with here, is 9"x5"x3". This size pan will hold from 22 to 26 ounces of dough.

If you've read my earlier columns, you know I make big use of a food thermometer. When baking bread, the temperature of the liquids to be combined with the yeast must be measured. You'll want a good food thermometer for this. Liquid that's too hot will kill the yeast, but if it's too cold, it will slow the yeast down and the bread won't rise properly.

A good bread knife is as important as a good bread pan or thermometer. The wrong knife will tear fresh bread apart instead of slicing it. Take my advice; buy a good bread knife with a serrated blade. You won't regret it.

No matter how new or expensive your oven is, it's quite possible that the temperature settings on it are not accurate. When baking bread it is important that the oven temperature be accurate. To check this, buy an oven thermometer. They're not expensive. Set your oven to a medium temperature, like 300 degrees, and heat it with the thermometer in the middle of the oven. Check the thermometer in about fifteen minutes. If the set temperature does not agree with the thermometer, either use the thermometer to determine oven temperatures or call a repairman and have your oven calibrated.

Bread is best when baked in an oven that produces a steady and evenly diffused heat. Most gas or electric ovens produce radiated heat which can produce hot and cool spots. You can compensate for this by turning your loaves around once or twice during baking. But there are two more reliable solutions. One is to buy a baking stone and place it on the lowest rack in the oven. Better yet, buy a half dozen 5 1/2" square unglazed quarry tiles from your local building supply store. Place these on the lowest rack in your oven. They are less expensive than a baking stone and work just as well. I have been using my quarry tiles for ten years with excellent results.

During the rising process the dough must be covered. A good cloth dish towel will do the job.

Finally, when mixing bread dough by hand, a good sturdy wooden spoon is worth having. Bread dough can get quite stiff before all the required flour is added and the spoon will make mixing easier.

The ingredients

Now, let's briefly examine the ingredients you need to make bread dough and what part each plays.

First there's the flour. Flour is the backbone of any bread. There are several flours available for bread—white, whole wheat, barley, corn, oat, and rye flour to name a few. But we will use only the white and whole wheat here. Hard wheat bread flour and all purpose flour are the most common white flours used in bread. The hard wheat flour is used by professional bakers but is available at the supermarket. It has a high percentage of protein and gluten, which makes it a first choice for bread.

When the flour is mixed with water this protein is activated and makes the dough strong and elastic. A strong elastic dough will hold the gas generated by the yeast so the bread will rise. All purpose flour does not have as much gluten as bread flour and will not rise as reliably.

There are several types of whole wheat flour. There are stone ground and pumpernickel, which are coarse grinds, and graham which is finely ground. All whole wheat flour is made by grinding the whole kernel including the bran and the germ. (The germ is the sprouting section of the kernel and contains fat.)

There are several leavening agents used in baking. Yeast is one of the most important. Yeast cells feed on sugar in the bread mixture to produce carbon dioxide which is the reason the dough rises. You can find three varieties of yeast in the store—dry granulated, fresh cake, and fast acting dry granulated. I'm going to recommend the use of dry granulated for these recipes because it is easy to use and stores well. "Proof" your yeast before you use it. Proofing is done by mixing the yeast with some sugar and a little water that has been heated to between 110 and 115 degrees. Proofing lets you know if the yeast is active. In about 5 minutes a layer of foam should appear on top of the mixture. If you don't get the foam, the yeast is not active and you must start again with fresh yeast.

Sugar, in the form of refined white sugar, honey, or molasses impart sweetness as well as flavor to bread. It also helps the crust to brown. Because it feeds the activity of the yeast, sugar in some form is included in most bread recipes.

Salt accents the flavor of other ingredients and helps to control yeast activity. A lot of people, in baking bread, under salt. This doesn't do the bread any good but if you feel compelled to do so for health reasons, go ahead.

Fat contributes tenderness to the loaf and lubricates the gluten, helping the dough to rise. Butter, margarine and lard contribute unique flavors to bread. My preference is margarine because it is low in cholesterol. However, salad or vegetable oil can be substituted in any recipe calling for melted butter, margarine, or lard.

Many liquids are used in bread making, but milk is by far the most popular. Milk contributes a velvety grain and browner crust to your bread. It also adds vital nutrients and additional flavor. I use non-fat dry milk because it has the qualities mentioned above without adding fat to the loaf.

Measuring the flour, mixing the flour with the other ingredients, kneading the dough and rising (proofing) the dough are the four procedures that determine the success of your bread.

Flour does not need sifting when used for bread. When measuring flour for bread dough, use the "scoop and level" method. Scoop the flour from it's container with the correct size measuring cup, then level the flour to the top of the cup with the straight side of a knife or spatula. This is how all of the flour was measured for the recipes in this column. Don't tamp the flour down.

Because flour is not consistent with moisture content, even with the same brand name, the recipe that takes six cups this week may only require five cups next week.

For this reason I have given only approximate measurements for bread flour in the recipes. Also, the assembly instructions call for only a portion of the bread flour to be added when first mixing it with other ingredients. The remainder can be added a little at a time during kneading. When you have added enough you'll know by the feel of the dough.

Kneading

Kneading is where you get the first indication of what sort of adjustments will benefit the outcome of the recipe. If the dough feels too dry, it can be returned to the bowl and a little more liquid added. The dough should be a little sticky when you first start kneading. This allows you to add flour a little at a time until the dough feels just right. Sufficient kneading is necessary to get proper rising of the dough. Kneading consists of three routine steps and one occasional "fun" step. The routine steps are push, turn and fold. The occasional fun step is called, "slam". After sufficient mixing of the dough, sprinkle a little flour on the work surface and remove the dough from the bowl to this area. Form the dough into a ball, adding more flour to the work surface to prevent sticking. Push down on the ball with the heels of your hands. Pull back on the dough, give it a quarter turn and fold it. Now repeat this for ten to fifteen minutes - push, turn and fold. Every few minutes, pick up the dough and "slam" it down on the counter. The dough loves this treatment and will reward you with excellent bread. Kneading is complete when the dough no longer feels sticky and has developed an elastic texture.

To determine if kneading is complete, make an indent in the dough with your finger. If the indent springs back, you're done.

Proofing is when the yeast cells take over. This is a quiet period when the yeast does its act and the dough rises. Proofing should be done in a well oiled straight sided bowl, large enough to allow the dough to double in bulk, without coming over the top. The dough has risen enough when it has doubled its bulk. Test this by making another indent in the dough. If the indent remains, the dough has risen enough.

Well, let's get to the recipes. The first one is for the all time favorite "white bread." After seeing my first successful loaves of white bread come out of the oven, I became hooked on home made bread. I make four to six loaves a week to keep my kids from running away.

Classic White Bread

> 1 pkg (¼ oz.) dry granulated yeast
> 1½ Tbsp. white sugar
> 2 cups warm water (110 to 115° F)
> 4 Tbsp. melted butter or margarine
> 5 to 6 cups bread flour
> 1/3 cup non-fat dry milk
> 2 tsp. salt

Preparation

1) Mix the yeast and sugar with 1 cup of warm water and set aside to proof.

2) Melt the butter or margarine and allow it to cool.

3) Combine 4 cups of bread flour with the non-fat dry milk and salt. Blend this mixture.

4) Combine the proofed yeast with the remaining cup of warm water and the melted margarine or butter. Do this in a bowl large enough to mix in the flour.

5) With a wooden spoon, stir the flour mixture into the yeast one cup at a time until all 4 cups are mixed in. Continue adding the remaining 2 cups of flour until the dough becomes firm. The flour not used at this time will be used during the kneading process.

6) Sprinkle some of the remaining flour onto your work surface and remove the dough to this surface.

7) Start kneading as I explained earlier. Continue to add flour to the work surface to prevent sticking. Knead until the dough is not sticky and has developed a smooth and elastic texture.

8) Transfer the dough to a well oiled bowl, cover it and allow it to rise until it's doubled in bulk. Depending on the temperature, this will take from one to two hours.

9) When the first rising is complete, punch the dough down to remove the air. Transfer the dough to a lightly floured work area and knead for five minutes.

10) Divide the dough into two equal size balls and allow them to rest for five minutes. Shape these balls into loaves and place them into two well oiled 9"x5"x3" loaf pans. Cover these and allow them to rise until they double in bulk.

11) Bake in a 375 degree oven for 40 to 45 minutes or until each loaf sounds hollow when tapped with your knuckles. If you desire more color and crispness in the crust, remove the loaves from the pans and place them back into the oven until you have the color and crispness you want. Caution! This should only take about 3 to 5 minutes. Bread put back this way is just like a big piece of toast.

12) When the loaves are done and removed from the pans, set them onto wire racks to cool. Do not cut the loaves while they are hot.

This next recipe is for the Whole Wheat bread that has become a standard in my house. Give it a try. I think it may become a standard for you also.

Whole Wheat Bread

> 2 pkg (¼ oz. each) dry granulated yeast
> 2 tsp. sugar
> 2 cups warm water (110-115° F)
> 3 Tbsp. melted butter or margarine
> 2½ cups whole wheat flour
> 2½ to 3 cups bread flour
> 2 tsp. salt
> ½ cup non-fat dry milk
> 1 Tbsp. honey
> 1 Tbsp. molasses

Preparation

1) Combine the yeast, sugar and warm water. Set aside to proof.

2) Melt the butter or margarine and mix with the honey and molasses.

3) Combine the whole wheat flour with 1 1/2 cups of bread flour, salt, and non-fat dry milk.

4) Combine the proofed yeast mixture with the melted butter or margarine mixture in a bowl large enough to mix in the flour.

5) With a wooden spoon, stir the flour mixture into the yeast, one cup at a time, until it is completely mixed in. Continue adding the remaining 1 cup of bread flour until the dough becomes firm. Use what is left during the kneading.

6) Remove the dough to a floured work space and knead as I described earlier.

7) After kneading, transfer the dough to a well oiled bowl, cover it and allow it to rise until it doubles in bulk.

8) When completely risen, punch the dough down and knead for 5 more minutes. Then cut the dough into two equal size balls and allow it to rest another five minutes.

9) Shape the balls into loaves and place them into two 9"x5"x3" loaf pans. Cover and allow to rise again until they double in bulk.

10) Bake in a 375 degree oven for 40 to 45 minutes or until each loaf sounds hollow when tapped with your knuckles. Remove the loaves from the pan and place them back into the oven for a couple of minutes. This will add color and crispness.

11) Set the bread aside on wire racks to cool

The following recipe is a mixed grain bread that has an interesting texture and a wonderful taste. It is one of the breads I eat without anything on it.

Mixed Grain Bread

1½ cups regular oatmeal (uncooked)
1/3 cup Wheatena (uncooked)
2 tsp. salt
2½ cups boiling water
2 Tbsp. melted margarine or butter
½ cup molasses
¼ cup honey
2 pkg (¼ oz. each) dry granulated yeast
½ tsp granulated sugar
1 cup warm water
4 cups bread flour
2½ cups whole wheat flour
1/3 cup non-fat dry milk

Preparation

1) Combine oats, Wheatena, and salt in a bowl then mix in the boiling water. Set this mixture aside to thicken for about ten minutes. When the cereal has absorbed the water and become thick, add the butter or margarine, molasses and honey. Set this aside to cool to about 115 degrees F.

2) When the cereal mixture has cooled, combine the granulated yeast, sugar and warm water. Mix and set aside to proof.

3) In a separate bowl, combine 3 cups of the bread flour with the 2 1/2 cups of whole wheat flour and non-fat dry milk.

4) After the yeast has proofed, combine it with the cooled cereal in a bowl large enough to mix in the flour.

5) Mix the blended flour into the yeast cereal mixture, one cup at a time, until completely incorporated. Continue to add part of the remaining 1 cup of bread flour, a little at a time, until the dough becomes firm. Use the remaining flour during kneading.

6) Knead the dough until it's smooth and elastic and not sticky.

7) Transfer the dough to a well oiled bowl, cover and allow it to rise until it doubles in bulk. When the first rising is complete, punch down the dough, remove it from the bowl and knead it for another five minutes.

8) Divide the dough into two equal size balls and allow them to rest for 5 minutes.

9) Shape the dough into two loaves and place each into well oiled 9"x5"x3" loaf pans. Cover the pans with a clean cloth and allow them to rise until they double in bulk.

10) Bake them in a 350 degree oven for about 1 hour or until the bread sounds hollow when tapped with your knuckles.

Well, that's it for this time around. I'll see you in next issue's column when I introduce you to some of the secrets of real Oriental cooking that you can incorporate into you own daily cooking with great results. Δ

A BHM Writer's Profile

Ilene Duffy

Ilene Duffy is the business manager for *Backwoods Home Magazine*, but she also has written articles and book and video reviews. As the main proofreader for each issue, she is responsible for the remarkably low number of typographical errors that appear in BHM. A former bilingual kindergarten and first grade teacher for nine years in California, she originated BHM's very popular "Just for Kids" pages.

Ilene gave up teaching to become BHM's business manager shortly after she married the magazine's publisher, Dave Duffy. She says the biggest benefit of working with the home-based magazine is being able to stay at home with her three young sons and to raise her family in a quiet, country setting.

Quick and easy veggie food

By Jennifer Stein Barker

You're in the middle of building your house, and you want something quick and easy to fix for dinner, something that will satisfy those hearty working appetites without taking you out of the action for too long. When you're building a backwoods home, everybody has to participate, and you just don't have much time or energy for cooking; but you still want to eat a balanced diet!

If the weather is sunny, you can just throw something together and put it in the sun oven (and I'll discuss some sun oven recipes in the next issue), but if you want nutritious, easy recipes for your stovetop or campstove, you'll find some handy ones here. These recipes are designed to take no more than 45 minutes in the kitchen, from start to finish (even if your kitchen this year is a trestle table under the pine trees).

Tomato sauce Napolitano

This is a substantial sauce that will satisfy the heartiest appetite. Tempeh is usually available in the freezer case at health food stores.

Serves 4:

> 12 oz. uncooked pasta (shells or spaghetti)
> 1 onion, diced
> 2 Tbsp. olive oil
> 2 cloves garlic
> 1 - 8oz. pkg. tempeh, crumbled
> 2 Tbsp. tamari
> 2 - 1 lb. cans diced tomatoes
> ½ cup tomato paste
> ½ cup chopped olives
> 4 tsp. fresh basil, or 2 tsp. dried
> 1 tsp. rosemary (fresh or dried)
> ¼ cup dry red wine
> grated Parmesan cheese (optional)

Have a large kettle of boiling water ready to cook the pasta. Heat a large, heavy-bottomed saucepan over a medium-high burner. Cook the onion and olive oil (with a little water if necessary) until the onion is transparent. Add the garlic, tempeh, and tamari, and continue cooking, stirring frequently, until the tempeh and onions begin to brown well, about 3 to 5 minutes.

Add the tomatoes, tomato paste, olives, basil, rosemary, and red wine. If you are using fresh herbs in the sauce, add the pasta to the boiling water now. Continue cooking the sauce until the pasta is done and drained, then toss the sauce with the pasta (if you have shells), or serve the two separately (if you have spaghetti).

If you are using dried herbs, cook the sauce about 10 minutes before starting the pasta. Cook and combine as above.

Italian-style bulghur

The diced cheese makes little nuggets of surprise throughout the dish (although it's almost as good without it). This is basic fare around our house.

Serves 4:

> 2 cups bulghur
> 4½ cups water
> 2 cloves garlic, minced
> 2 Tbsp. tamari
> ¼ tsp. Tabasco
> 6 Tbsp. tomato paste
> 2 carrots, grated coarsely
> 1 large branch broccoli
> ½ tsp. basil
> ¼ tsp. oregano
> 3 oz. jack or mozzarella cheese, diced ¼"

In a large saucepan, combine the bulghur, water, garlic, tamari, Tabasco, tomato paste, and grated carrots. Remove the florets from the broccoli, and set them aside. Peel the stems and dice them, and add them to the pot.

Bring the pot to a boil over medium-high, then turn the heat down and simmer, covered, stirring occasionally, for seven minutes. Add the broccoli florets and the basil and oregano, stir, and simmer gently until the broccoli and bulghur are tender and the liquid has been absorbed by the grain. Turn the heat off and let it sit for a minute. Remove from heat, add the diced cheese, stir briefly to distribute it evenly, and serve.

Oriental-style bulghur

The bright colors and flavors really jazz this dish up.

Serves 4:

> 2 cups bulghur wheat
> 4½ cups water
> 2 cloves garlic, minced

(continued on next page)

> 1 tsp. fresh ginger, minced
> 2 medium carrots, grated coarsely
> 1 cup chopped red cabbage
> 2 Tbsp. tamari
> ½ tsp. Tabasco
> 2 tsp. toasted sesame oil
> 1 cup frozen peas

In a medium saucepan, mix all the ingredients except the peas. Simmer gently, covered, until the water is absorbed and the bulghur is tender, about 20 to 25 minutes.

Add the peas, turn off the heat, and let the bulghur sit on the burner for 2 more minutes. Serve hot.

Curried potatoes, mushrooms, and peas

This dish doesn't need any rice, but if you want to serve it with a little on the side, it will serve 6.

Serves 4:

> 3 lbs. yellow potatoes
> 2 Tbsp. peanut oil
> 1½ cups diced onion
> 2 cloves garlic, minced
> 3 tsp. minced gingerroot
> 8 brown mushrooms (about 6 oz.)
> 2 tsp. turmeric
> 1½ tsp. cumin
> ¾ tsp. coriander
> ¼ tsp. cayenne
> 2 Tbsp. tamari
> 1 cup frozen peas

Scrub and dice the potatoes (do not peel), and cook them in a steamer basket over boiling water until tender. Clean and halve the brown mushrooms, and slice them thinly. Set aside. Meanwhile, heat the peanut oil in a heavy skillet and add the onions. Braise and reglaze until the onions are transparent. Add the garlic, ginger root and mushrooms, and the turmeric, cumin, coriander, and cayenne. Stir to coat the ingredients in the pan and "toast" the spices for a few minutes, then add the tamari and enough water to keep the ingredients from sticking. Simmer gently until the mushrooms are tender, then add the peas. Simmer another minute, then check the potatoes. They should be steamed tender by now—if they're not, just cover the curry pan and set it aside for a few minutes. Add the potatoes, stir to coat them with the curry, and serve immediately.

Good garnishes: chutney, yogurt, raisins, nuts. ∆

> *"I told her
> I wanted the divorce,"
> He said,
> And took another drink.
> "I had to get away from her
> Even though I still loved her
> For two more years.
> God, I loved her.
> But I couldn't tell her
> That.
> Do you understand?"
> He asked,
> Looking like an animal
> That had gnawed off
> Its leg
> To get out of a trap.*
>
> **John Earl Silveira**
> Ojai, CA

A country moment

Margaret Boos of northern California fastens a chain to lift timber.

Learn the basics of wall framing

By Robert L. Williams

If you are interested in adding a room to your house, or partitioning an existing room, you will need to know something about wall framing. This is a somewhat complicated element of house building or carpentry, but virtually anyone who is motivated can learn to do it quickly and well.

To start, learn the names of a few basic aspects of wall framing: the sole plate, top plate, top cap, stud, cripple stud, corner post, rough window or door opening, sill, and rough opening. You also need to know the difference between a load-bearing and non-bearing wall.

A **load-bearing wall** is one that helps support the ceiling and roof; in other words, it helps support everything that is above it. A **non-bearing wall** is one that supports nothing but its own weight.

The **sole plate** is the long timber that is laid upon the subflooring and along the exterior boundary of the house or room. This sole plate is usually a very long 2x4 that is marked for 16-inch on-center stud placement.

The **stud** is the upright 2x4 that is nailed between the sole plate and the top plate and gives the wall its basic strength and rigidity. The **top plate** is the corresponding timber to the sole plate. This sole plate is on the bottom of the wall frame and the top plate, as its name implies, is on the top.

To frame a wall, start with a sound, straight, and strong 2 x4 that will reach, if possible, from one corner of the house or room to the other. Lay the sole plate and the top plate side by side upon the subflooring. Make sure that the ends of the two timbers are aligned.

At this point you can mark off the stud placement on both timbers at the same time. If you are not familiar with the basic carpentry tools, use a mea-

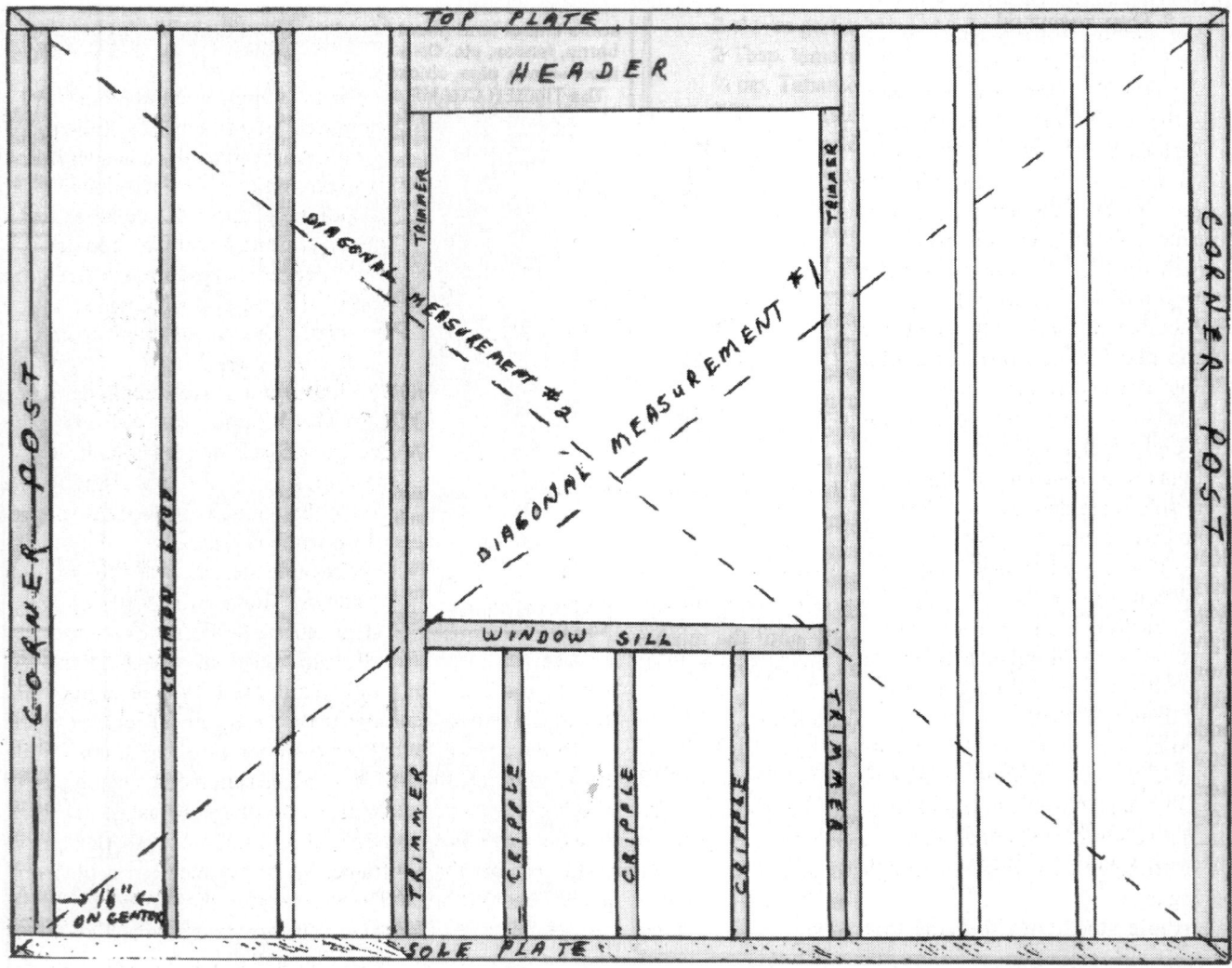

suring tape, preferably one that is 25 feet long. Notice on the face of the tape that every 16 inches the marking is in red. Some tapes have the word *stud* printed at the 16-inch intervals. When you speak of studs being placed 16 inches on center, you mean that from the center of one stud to the center of the next one, the distance will be 16 inches.

So even if you are uncertain in math, when you see the red marking at 128 inches, for instance, you know that a stud should be placed at that location. As you stretch the tape along the sole plate and top plate, mark the stud locations.

Remember that 2x4 is the nominal size of the lumber, not the finish size. A finished or dressed 2x4 is usually 1.5 inches x 3.5 inches. When you lay off the stud locations, use the tongue of your framing square, which is 1.5 inches wide, and mark on both sides of the metal. The space between represents the exact spot where the stud will be located.

In some modern construction, the stud placement is 20 inches on center, but many local inspectors insist on the 16-inch on-center spacing. Check before you do too much work.

Remember to mark both sole plate and top plate at the same time. Now separate the two timbers and lay the studs between them.. A stud is nominally eight feet long, but the actual length takes into account the thickness of the sole plate and the top plate, so the stud will actually be only 93 inches long if you want an eight-foot ceiling. When you are buying, ask for studs, rather than 8-foot 2x4s. Otherwise you will either need to cut each timber or you will have a ceiling higher than eight feet.

Examine your house or room plans. If there is to be a window or door in the wall, mark the location and indicate that you will need either a cripple stud or trimmer stud within the rough opening area.

A cripple stud is a short one that reaches from the bottom of the rough window opening to the sole plate, or to the ceiling over the window framing. A trimmer stud fits inside the rough opening and actually governs the size of the opening. It is nailed to the side of the regular studs between the header and the rough sill.

Nail in all the regular studs. Naturally, you'll have the plates and studs tipped up on their narrow (1.5") sides, rather than their wide 3.5" sides. Because the wall frame is lying flat, you can nail through the top of the top plate and the bottom of the sole plate and into the ends of the studs. At the rough openings for window or door,

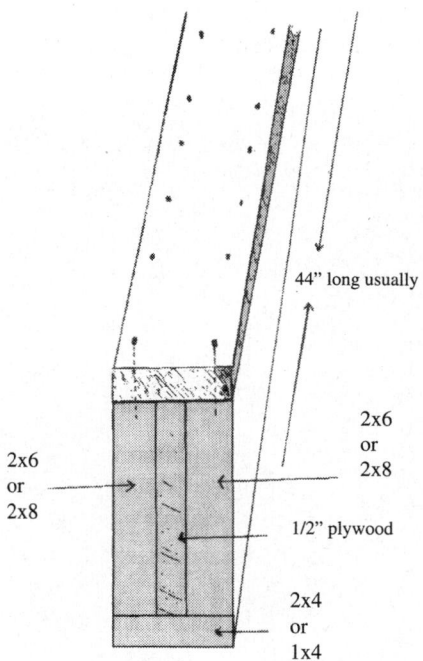

Header construction

determine from your plans how high the rough sill (the bottom of the window rough opening) should be and cut cripple studs to fit the space.

Lay the sill timber in place and check measurements and location carefully. (You can double the rough sill for added strength.) Now nail in the cripple studs, which are spaced exactly like the regular (or common) studs. Nail a trimmer stud against the inside face of the studs at each end of the rough opening.

Lay the rough sill in place and nail it securely by driving nails through the common stud and into the end of the rough sill. Then nail in all cripple studs under the rough sill.

It is time now to construct a header. The header is two 2x6 timbers nailed together with half-inch plywood spacers nailed between them. The spacers provide added width so that the header will be the same thickness as the wall frame. Cut trimmer studs to reach from the sole plate to the point where the header will rest. Nail in these trimmers. When they are in place, position the header in place and nail it by driving nails through the face of the common studs and into the ends of the header. As a rule there are no cripple studs over the rough window opening. It is easier to build a wide header that completely fills the space rather than cutting and installing short cripple studs.

For the rough door opening, use a trimmer stud on each side of the rough opening and then build a header to rest atop the ends of the trimmer studs. Depending upon space above the door, you may want to construct a wide header that will reach from the top of the rough door opening to the top plate. You can also nail in cripple studs if you prefer.

When headers are installed, notice how the trimmer studs support the weight of the header and how the header supports the weight of all above the window or door. Most people do not realize that the longest unsupported stretch of a wall is above windows. This is why well-constructed and strong headers are essential.

Before you think about raising the wall frame, use a long tape and measure from the lower left corner to the upper right corner of the frame. Write down the measurement. Then measure from the upper left to the lower right, again diagonally across the entire frame. Write the measurement down. The two lengths should be exactly the same. You are permitted a slight tolerance, but if the measurements are off by an inch or more, you need to double-check and make needed corrections while you can still do them.

When it's square, you can raise the wall frame. Have some bracing timbers handy and ready to install as soon as the wall frame is raised. To prepare for the bracing, you can nail foot-long lengths of scrap 2x4s to the subflooring about 10 feet from the wall. Have at least two braces ready to nail up as soon as the wall frame is raised. Gather your helpers. Several people can lift the wall frame and shove it into rough position. Some builders nail a temporary upright 2x4 to the floor header or joist so that the wall frame won't slide too far.

When the frame is roughly correct, nail the braces to the sides of studs and lay the free end near the floor bracing units. Someone with a sledge hammer can tap the sole plate until the bottom of the frame is perfectly positioned along the subflooring, and as soon as it is correct, another worker can nail through the sole plate and into the joists under the subflooring. This nailing keeps the sole plate from moving while the rest of the framing is completed. When you are ready, apply a level to the end stud. If it is perfectly vertical, nail through the stud and into the other elements of the wall frame, if any.

If this is the first wall, be prepared to brace it completely. As soon as you get a vertical reading, nail the bracing in so that the corner of the wall will be held in place. Go to the other corner and repeat the process.

When all the bracing is done and other frame units are completed and raised, you will be able to install the top caps. These are more 2x4s that are nailed on top of the top plate. The top cap laps over the top plate of the wall that adjoins the other walls. In this fashion you tie together all of the wall framing for added strength.

The basic wall framing is now complete. You are ready to move on to other facets of your construction. ∆

Visit our web site
http://www.backwoodshome.com

It's an easy way to...

- e-mail staff members
- buy an anthology or book
- re-read articles from back issues
- subscribe or renew your subscription
- link to other self-sufficiency web sites

SELF SUFFICIENCY

A Backwoods Home Anthology

Health care begins at home

By Dynah Geissal

I have raised three children. They are now 21, 23, and 26. When the oldest was 10, I had all the kids at the pediatrician's office for their checkups. After they had been examined, the doctor asked me to have them play in the waiting room and for me to come into his office. He said, "You know, in all these years, you've never brought your kids in for anything except their checkups. How do you do it?"

The way I cared for my children's physical needs seemed natural enough to me, but after talking with the doctor, I began to realize how much healthier my kids were than most. When they did get sick, they recovered quickly and easily without any need for antibiotics or outside intervention. There are many aspects to health, of course, but here I will discuss the physical features.

Let me stress the importance of regular checkups for everyone, preferably with one doctor. It's difficult for a doctor to know the progress of your child if you go to a different one each time. In order to be your child's primary healer you must be calm, positive, and strongly believe in the natural healing ability of the body.

Food

Nutrition is a key element. Each meal should consist of a whole grain, a protein source, and milk. There should be a fruit in every meal, with at least one raw and one citrus. One fruit may be in the form of juice. There should be two meals that include a green or yellow vegetable and one of these should be raw. A starch, such as a potato, may be served with any meal. There should be one food that is high in iron, such as peanut butter, each day.

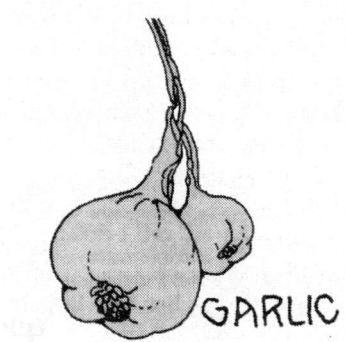

Sleep

Adequate sleep is important for the body's regeneration and maintenance. Each child should get plenty of sleep every night and should not be distracted from this by television, older siblings or anything else.

Exercise

Plenty of exercise is another necessity. Two to three hours of outside activity every day is essential. Be careful not to overdress children, and let them sleep in a moderately cold room—55° is not too cold.

Illness

Illness can be frightening to a parent. You can overcome your fear by educating yourself about illness. Symptoms are the body's efforts to correct an imbalance in the system. Avoid treatments that suppress symptoms. Fever, for example, creates an environment that's not conducive to a virus. When drugs are given, the body does not learn to heal itself. It becomes dependent on outside intervention. Ninety-five percent of childhood illnesses require no treatment other than raising the basic level of health.

It is amazing how many parents take their sick kids visiting or on errands with them. This should be avoided if at all possible. Have a rule that children with fevers are not welcome at your house or around your children. Some children seem to have sniffles and mild viruses almost constantly. I wouldn't worry about your kids being around this sort of thing, but I would definitely draw the line at an illness that is serious enough to cause a fever. There is enough to worry about concerning children's health without having someone else's sick child around yours.

When your own child has a fever, keep her in bed until the fever has been gone for 24 hours. She may feel better temporarily and the fever may recede, only to return later. If you allow your child to get up too soon, the illness may last much longer. So make it a rule about which there is no argument. Getting up too soon may result in chilling or overexertion. At the very least, the body won't get maximum benefit from the rest and rejuvenation that it should have had.

I consider a child to be feverish when the temperature is 101 or greater. There are a number of reasons that the temperature may be elevated, but only an illness will cause it to be as high as 101. If it reaches 104, I would contact a physician.

In most cases, a child becomes ill and within a couple of days begins to recover. Recovery will usually last a maximum of five days. If your child continues to get worse or does not seem to be making any improvement after a couple of days, consult a physician.

If your child is sick, he should be in bed. His body should be dealing only with healing itself, not in distractions in the rest of the household. The couch in front of the TV is not the place to be. The child should be in a quiet, private place where he can rest and fall asleep easily whenever his body requires it. This is very important. Here again—no arguing. When you're sick, you're in bed. Period!

The body learns to heal itself by doing so without the "aid" of drugs. There are certain nutritional and

The Fifth Year

herbal remedies that will help when your child is sick, but the main thing is to determine the cause. If half her classmates have the flu, the cause of your child's illness is fairly obvious. Usually I have found extenuating circumstances connected with most illnesses such as stress, improper diet or inadequate sleep. For example, maybe a child spent the weekend away from home, got very little sleep and ate mostly junk food. Or an older child may be excessively concerned over an upcoming test.

Aspirin should not be given for colds or flu. It brings down the fever, which is not usually desirable. It works against the body's natural healing. It is not a healer, it is a symptom reliever. Antibiotics and over-the-counter drugs are also usually counterproductive. Children who are routinely medicated when sick, get sick more often and become less able to heal themselves. It seems to have a snowball effect.

I will give you a list of remedies that I have used and have found effective for simple illnesses. With all of these, give plenty of fluids to prevent dehydration and to promote healing. Keep the child evenly warm and avoid drafts. Milk and other bland foods are good if the child desires them.

- **Colds:** At the first sign, start giving 1,000 mg vitamin C (this may be in the form of 4 rose hips) 4 times a day with ½ cup milk, and 5 times a day give 10,000 units of vitamin A. This works so well that a cold will usually only last 2 days or 3 at the most. It is important to catch it early.
- **Cough:** Lemon juice and honey, either as it is or with hot water added if that is more appealing. (Editor's note: children under two years of age should not be given honey.)
- **Diarrhea:** Clear liquids—water, fruit juice, broth. This gives the bacteria nothing to feed on but prevents dehydration.
- **Earache:** Apply hot towels or drop in lukewarm oil.
- **Flu:** Slippery elm.
- **Sore throat:** Clove tea, chewing cloves, gargling salt water.
- **Stomach ache:** ½ t. baking soda, ½ t. lemon juice in ½ cup water, chewing caraway, fennel, anise or dill seeds or chewing a prune pit after eating the prune.
- **Stuffy nose:** Salt water nose drops or hot onion soup.
- **Swollen glands:** Chicken soup, especially when the gizzard is included.

There are a few other conditions I would like to discuss, in case you would like to treat them at home. I have used all of these remedies successfully.

- **Backache:** Massage, stretching exercises, relaxation exercises and large quantities of greens and grains for healing.
- **Burns:** Cold water and aloe.
- **Cold sores:** Peroxide followed by cornstarch.
- **Impetigo:** Neosporin—not natural, but works miracles.
- **Pink eye:** Lemon juice diluted with water applied 3 times per day until cleared—about 3 days.
- **Ringworm:** Apply lemon juice 3 times a day.
- **Skin problems** (pimples, acne): Whole grains and yellow fruits and vegetables.
- **Stress:** B vitamins. I give this routinely to teenagers. It really does make a difference.
- **Warts:** Aloe vera applied regularly.
- **Worms:** Garlic and mint tea.

Being your family's primary healer is extremely rewarding. You will find that it feels wonderful to work with nature for your children's health. You will grow in confidence with experience and will feel a harmony with the natural process of life. In addition, and most important, your family will thrive and glow with health! ∆

Live free...

Support the

Libertarian Party

the party of individual responsibility and personal freedom

For information call:

1-800-682-1776

or write:

**Libertarian Party
2600 Virginia Ave. NW
Suite 100
Washington, DC 20037**

BUILDING

Build a fieldstone chimney

By Eric and Birney Dibble

Back in the days when Northern States Power Company sang a cute little song, "Electricity is penny cheap from NSP," we built a small summer home in northern Wisconsin and heated it with baseboard electrical units. We supplemented the heating with a large fireplace.

Then when we put a wood-burning stove in the basement, we wanted to vent it without using the existing fireplace chimney. So we built another fieldstone chimney right alongside the first one. This is how we did it, and how you can do it, as well. Total cost was $175.

Stone and blocks

Find your own field stones by looking in old river beds, farmers' fields, gravel quarries and along the roads. Try to pick them after a rain so you'll have an idea what they'll look like once you've cleaned them with hydrochloric acid and sealed them. Buy your blocks, tile, and other materials directly from a wholesaler. Do your own hauling to avoid the high labor costs.

Footings

Dig a hole about 20 inches deep and fill it with 12 inches of gravel and rocks. Pour your concrete footing 3' x 3' x 8" (see Fig. 1).

Laying blocks and tile

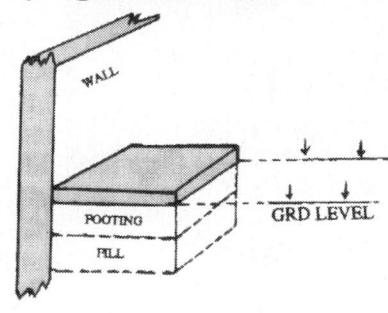

Figure 1

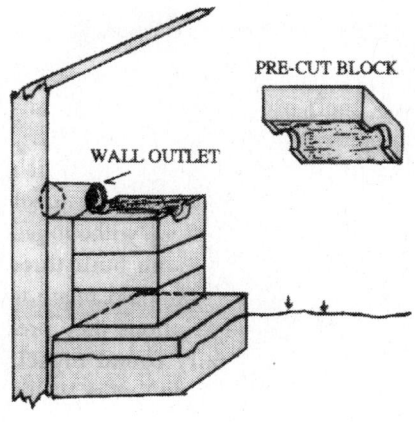

Figure 2

Lay and mortar blocks about eight to ten feet at a time (see Fig. 2). Use hollow or solid blocks. Hollow blocks are less expensive and easier to handle, but check fire codes to see if they're permitted. Determine where the wall outlet will be and line up the pre-cut

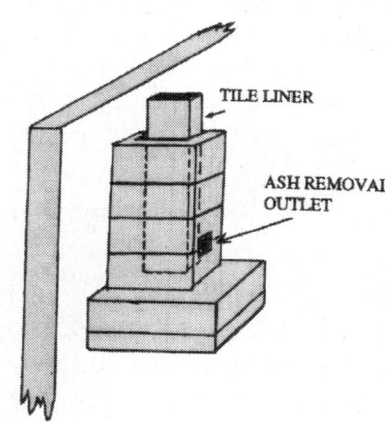

Figure 3

block to fit it. Tile may have to be cut also. If the outlet is close to the sill, be sure to insulate with tile. As blocks are laid upwards, the tile can be placed inside them. Remember to keep seams in the tile clear of mortar, as they must expand and contract with changes in temperature. The ash removal outlet should be cut out at this point (Fig. 3), and should be located one or two block courses from the bottom. Metal doors can be purchased from any wholesaler for very little money, and will save time and expense in the future.

Securing chimney to foundation

Drill holes in the building foundation to fit ¾ inch lag bolts (see Fig. 4, inset). Cement lag bolts in the foundation with large washers inside, then line them up and mortar them into seams between the chimney blocks. This should prevent future tilt.

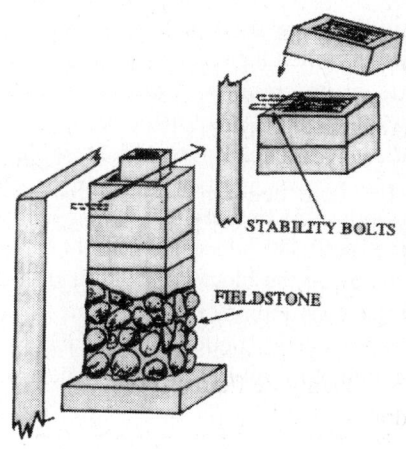

Figure 4

Laying fieldstone

Begin on the footings along the first fireblock and lay stone only three to four feet at a time, allowing five to six hours for setting before laying more stone. The mortar mixture should be approximately one part lime to seven parts sand and gravel, with some cement added for elasticity. The gravel should be fairly coarse. After one hour, smooth out and remove excess mortar with a coarse paint brush. The stones should protrude at least one inch from the mortar to protect the mortar base and prolong the life of the chimney. Place a good grade of polyethylene between the mortar and exposed wood to prevent damage to the wood. This is especially important

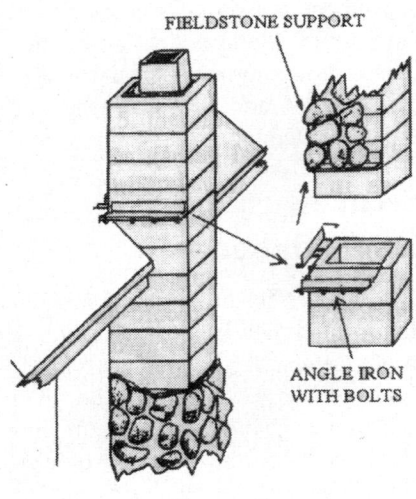

Figure 5

on buildings that have over-hanging eaves which have to be cut in order to fit in the chimney. Because of their weight, stones should not be laid directly on the eaves. Weld several bolts to an angle iron to form a shelf (see Fig. 5), and lay more stone above the shelf. This places the weight of the stones on the blocks instead of on the wooden building. Flashing is a must, to prevent ice buildup and damage to chimney or roof. Aluminum sheeting cuts easily and works fine for this purpose. Make sure that there is plenty of material under the shingles and that the aluminum is free of holes.

Topping the chimney

The chimney top should be at least two to three feet above the highest point of the roof (see Fig. 6). Where the block and tile meet, fill in well with mortar. Once the fieldstone is laid up to this point, concrete should be smoothed on top to make an angled edge. An optional chimney top can be placed to prevent moisture from collecting inside and to prevent birds and animals from going down the chimney.

Sealing

When all the fieldstone is laid and set, brush it down with hydrochloric acid to wash off extra mortar and clean the rocks. Then apply a good grade of masonry sealer to protect the mortar/stone seams and bring out the beauty of grain in the stones.

There is nothing complicated about this project, and doing it yourself will give you decades of personal pride every time you look up at your own chimney. ∆

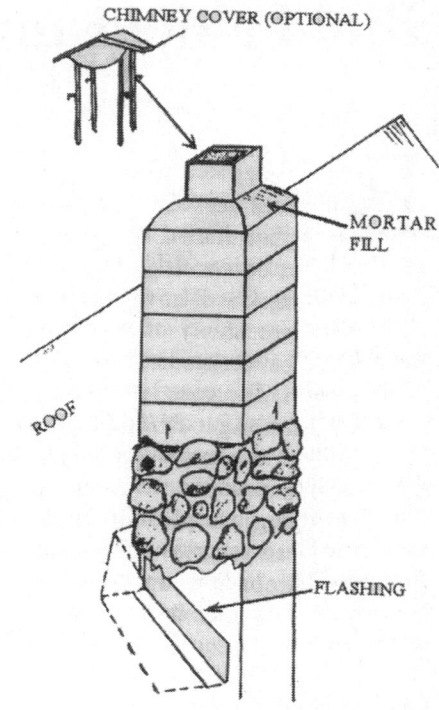

Figure 6

A BHM Writer's Profile

Chris Braet

Some people refer to Chris Braet as "Buffalo Gal", but she prefers to be called Chris. She and Mike have been raising water buffalo for six years, four years in Sheridan, OR. She has a married daughter, Erin, who has one child; and another daughter, Megan, who is at Southern Oregon State University. Mike is a Portland Firefighter and Chris is a farm wife.

Their farm consists of 156 acres, with 100 acres in hay production. They raise half for themselves and the other half is sold. With 60 animals it seems there is always something to do. They have the water buffalo divided into two groups— bulls and cows. Now that winter is here, they have the animals in their winter pastures and feed them twice a day. They feed out over a hundred tons of hay.

In the summer they are outside almost every day, and the winter is when Chris spends time on hobbies. She likes to read, knit, quilt, paint, and cook. She loves her life on the farm where the buffalo reign.

MAKING A LIVING

A Backwoods Home Anthology

Start a home-based food business

By Kristen Rogers and Randy Atkins

Whenever we needed cash to keep the farm running, we used to have to go outside to work. By the time we paid for the babysitter, transportation costs, and the cost of decent clothes to wear to work, we discovered that it was barely worth working for the returns we received in terms of cash flow.

But, even though our return was negligible, we still needed that extra income. That's when we decided to take something that we both enjoy doing—cooking and gardening—and turn it into a profitable home business.

Start small

We started very small. Taking just a few jars of jellies and jams to our local farmer's market, we sold enough each week to convince us that a small market did exist for the types of foods we enjoyed. Specializing in exotic and unusual foods, we started out with an item called Mango Chutney, which is a sweet and hot sort of sauce that tastes almost peachy, for those of you not familiar with mangos.

The Mango Chutney was a hit, even though we did have to educate our local customers on what to do with it. "Died and gone to heaven" on cream cheese and snack crackers was our first description. As we grew, our satisfied customers returned to us with other suggestions. "Use it as a marinade," suggested one customer. "Try it on whole wheat raisin bagels with cream cheese," said another.

Listen

Well, we're a lot of things but foolish isn't one of them, so we paid attention to what our customers told us. We passed the suggestions along to our other customers and prospective customers, and we were soon selling several cases of mango chutney each week.

One of our other popular products is Hot Pepper Jelly, which we make with no additives or food coloring, as with all of our other products. People who were not familiar with Mango Chutney often bought the more familiar Hot Pepper Jelly, sometimes taking our suggestion to put a jar of Mango Chutney together with the Hot Pepper jelly as a hostess gift.

Our small company grew very slowly to where we could afford printed labels and jars in bulk from a local wholesaler. As the season drew to a close, we began to look for other outlets for our products. We expanded our line to include freshly baked specialty breads, such as banana, pumpkin and cranberry bread, sold at wholesale prices to local stores.

At this point, 6 months into the actual business, the Gourmet Gardener is self-supporting, even making a small profit. It is a long way from anything more than a part-time home business, but it does help pay the monthly bills.

Much of what we make has also been the basis for some very successful bartering for items for the farm. Over the course of the summer we've traded for hay, other forms of produce that we don't grow ourselves, even two young rabbits to form the basis of meat production on a small scale for our own home use.

Do what you know

One of the hardest parts of starting a small business of your own is simply deciding what to do. For us, a business that had to do with food and cooking seemed only natural.

You, or you and a partner may have similar strengths and areas of expertise. If you know that there are areas where you don't exactly excel, you may find it helpful to take a course to develop these skills, or carefully explore the possibility of forming a partnership with someone who has the skills you lack.

Go it alone

In all honesty, we can't say that we recommend partnerships. As a general rule, partnerships can quickly degrade into sparring matches and power struggles between even the best of friends, even between spouses. So, unless you have a very clear definition of who does what, and you are willing to stick with that definition or modify it together, we recommend working alone. A sole proprietorship essentially means that you are responsible to no one but yourself.

Trial and error

Once you have settled on the type of business you'll start, and then decided if you'll work alone or with a partner, you need to develop product. We did this very slowly, basing it simply on what sold best at the farmer's market. As we kept going to the market, we'd try taking one or two new things, or we'd change the pricing or the containers. We played with it, experimenting until we had a product we were pleased with, packaging that we found attractive, pricing that allowed us to make a respectable profit and a small but solid customer base.

You may also eventually have to decide if you'll expand your business into a retail/wholesale operation, as we did. When the end of the summer, and the end of the season for the farmer's market drew near, we knew that if we didn't develop a different clientele and a larger customer base that come September, we'd be out of business.

Pricing

Bearing that in mind, we developed wholesale prices which basically reflected double our base cost to produce a product. For example, if

The Fifth Year

banana bread cost 65¢ to make, we charged 1.50 for it wholesale, which works out to be more a little more than 100% mark-up. We recommend that when you set prices you charge fairly but high enough not to have to be continually making price changes on the same products. It confuses the customers and will even confuse you when it comes time to do your bookkeeping.

When we first started, we set our price for apple butter at $2.50 for a pint jar. We discovered that for our market this was a ridiculously low price. We eventually increased our price to $3.50 for 8 oz, increasing our profit margin and our customer base. How does increasing the price and decreasing the size increase customer base? Apparently, people felt that even though the jars were smaller, the product had to be something special for that price, so they bought more and faster than at our original lower prices.

While this was a very amusing and profitable strategy for us, be careful not to price yourself right out of the market, making your product too expensive to be more than a fling. Our goal, and yours too, if you intend to be around long, was to provide a product that was so good that people came back regularly for more. Anyone can make one sale, but if you're going to be serious about building a business you need repeat sales. Repeat sales, at least in our part of the backwoods, are not made by offering the occasional extravagant gift.

Familiarity

Even if you specialize in slightly exotic cuisine such as ours, you may find that offering one or two more common items is a good idea. When we started to make the change into wholesale marketing to small, "Mom & Pop operations," we offered our usual line of unusual goods, but we also offered common foods that people were more familiar with. Typical examples are banana bread, cranberry nut bread, chocolate chip cookies, brownies and so forth. A good brownie is hard to find, and any true brownie lover especially one who works, lives alone, doesn't want to bake or just can't get it right, will develop a real loyalty for your product if you can meet his or her standards consistently.

Be consistent

Consistency is a major point in this line of business. Your customers need to know that they'll get the same moist, chewy brownie, the same rich, banana flavor in their bread, the same spicy pungence in their chutney every single time, no matter how many times they buy. So, you need to do everything you can to ensure "quality control." The product must consistent in taste, texture, size, and packaging every single time.

Remember that every customer who is dissatisfied with your product influences dozens of other people not to buy, according to Jay Conrad Levinson, author of the extremely helpful <u>Guerilla Marketing</u>. Develop your recipes and methods of baking so that the product is always the same. Carefully expand your recipe measurements into commercial sizes and stick with it every time you cook. Measure out products by weight, not volume. One and a half cups of batter in a pan can vary greatly, but measuring batter or fluids by weight is infinitely more accurate.

Appearance

Once you've developed your product and can produce it consistently, you need to pay attention to its appearance. Not only must your foods taste great, every time, but they have to look great, too. Looking great entails everything from garnishes and decorations on a fruitcake or bread to the type of packaging you use to contain it. What types and sizes of jars, what colors and types of lids for sealing...all are important considerations which by themselves seem insignificant.

Labels

Consider what type of labeling you'll have. Will you have handwritten labels, as we did at first, or will you jump right in with printed labels? The label design should reflect the type of company you are, how people should think about you. We are not talking so much about conveying an "image," as the advertising execs would call it. We're talking about your identity, showing people through your packaging and artwork and labels what kind of people run this little company. Our own labels are very homespun, though a little more upscale than the masking tape stickers we started out with.

When you have all these factors together, and you can do them consistently, you need to re-estimate your pricing structure. Every time you consider a product, you will work out its viability based on what it costs to produce in terms of cash and time.

Market testing

For a product to make it as far as printed labeling and packing in our company, it has to be proven. We sell it for a while on a temporary trial basis. At the Gourmet Gardener, this is easy and not expensive, kind of like a "market survey." If our customers like it enough to keep buying it, we keep producing it. If not, we stop. In our production and everywhere we can at the Gourmet Gardener, we follow the rule of KISS (Keep It Simple, Stupid).

Basically, that's all there is to it. You will set up books, as does every small business, and as you go along you'll learn how to best deal with your customers and keep them happy. And happiness is what it's all about. Stay loose and have fun. Those are the two most important keys to success in any business. ∆

Making your own sourdough yeast

By Judith Blucher

In spite of what many books will state, (and I sometimes wonder if they tried the process at all), you don't need some kind of commercial yeast or starter for sourdough. Come on now, you really didn't think those old sourdoughs of Yukon fame sent off to San Francisco for a little crock, some yeast granules, and instructions, did you?

Yeast

Yeast is a living organism and is present in the air, most probably already in your kitchen. Almost any house, especially older ones or those newer ones made of natural materials, will have any number of yeasts living in the kitchen.

Catching these wee beasties isn't that much of a hassle either. Simply mix a couple of cups of warm water with about the same amount of flour, preferably unbleached white, and put the mixture in a 75-85° warm spot. The mixture should be covered with a piece of cheesecloth or loosely woven muslin, and in four or five days you will notice little bubbles coming to the top of your mix. These are the yeast spores working, and they will impart a distinctly alcoholic aroma to the flour and water.

If for some reason you can't seem to "catch" the spores or want to speed up the process, try this. Find a juniper tree replete with its greenish blue berries. Pick about a cup and put them into a mason jar or plastic container. Add around a cup of water and shake gently for a minute or so. The powdery substance on the berries will yield a yeast which will enhance, or "kick off," the development of your sourdough.

Don't shake too vigorously, however, as the berries might split and flavor the water. Although some folks appreciate gin, not too many want gin flavored bread. At least not on a regular basis.

If you can't find juniper berries, Oregon grape berries are said to work well, although I have never tried them. Strain the berries from the water, and use the water with flour as before.

Be sure to use a large enough container when working with sourdough, or you might stroll into the kitchen some bright morning and find that the vigorous mix is creeping down your stove and onto the floor!

One of the best "warm spots" I have found to start the dough is in an oven with a pilot light. The warming oven on the side away from the firebox on a wood stove works well, too.

When the starter is brewin', either use part of it for bread making or put it in a cool spot and use some at least every two weeks. If you use it this seldom, the refrigerator is probably the best place to keep it.

Do not use a glass jar with a tight lid for storage. The fermentation continues, albeit at a slower pace, and might shatter or crack the jar.

The longer you keep and use your mix, the more fragrant it becomes. If liquid separates from the more solid mass, simply mix together. You should probably label this container. A friend of mine was away from home for an emergency appendectomy, and when she returned home found that her husband had helpfully cleaned out the refrigerator, throwing out the starter because he thought it was something spoiled.

The starter, once brewing well, is very hardy. Like all commercial yeast, temperatures above 95° could kill it.

When you are ready to get down to the actual breadmaking, here is a sample recipe. You might want to develop your own once you get familiar with the process.

Sourdough white bread

Ten to twelve hours before the actual breadmaking take:

```
1 cup primary batter (your original flour and
    water mix)
2 cups warm water
2 to 2½ cups white flour
```

Mix well and let sit in a warm spot for ten or twelve hours, covered with plastic wrap.

After that time, stir the mixture and remove one cup of this new primary batter to put back in the storage container.

To batter left in the bowl add:

```
A small pinch sugar
2 tsp. salt
1½ cups warm, reconstituted, non-fat, dry milk
2 Tbsp. melted butter or oleo
About 4 cups flour
```

Mix the flour into the wet ingredients until the mass is too stiff to stir. Flour your kneading surface and add about 1½ cups more flour. Keep kneading until the dough becomes smooth and does not readily stick to the board.

Oil a 4-6 qt. bowl and place the dough in the bowl. Turn the dough so it is completely covered with oil. Cover with plastic wrap, then with a towel. Return the dough to the warm spot until it has about doubled in bulk. Rising time will be about 2 to 2½ hours.

When the dough is double in bulk, punch it down again. Return it to the bowl and let it rise again for 30-45 minutes.

Turn the dough out onto the kneading surface and cut into two equal portions. Shape loaves by the usual method. (Pound out, stretch, fold ends over, and fold sides to middle. It helps to let the two pieces rest about five minutes after cutting, as it relaxes the dough and makes it easier to shape.) Grease, don't oil, two medium bread pans. Put in the dough and brush with butter if desired. Let rise in a warm spot for about one hour.

Bake at 375° for about 35-45 minutes, or until the loaves are nice and brown. When done, take from the oven, shake from the pans, put on a wire rack, and butter tops. For a softer crust, cover with a dish towel.

If you can resist, allow to cool before cutting. Enjoy! ∆

Dad

I used to wonder where the love went
When he beat her.
Did he carefully package it up
And hide it under the bed
Where it was out of mind,
But safe,
So he could still take it out
And show it to her again
At night?

John Earl Silveira
Ojai, CA

Make a lifeline before you need it

By Ralph LaPlant

If you live, work, or play around water, this may save a life. If you have tried to throw a line, you will appreciate that it can be difficult. Perhaps the rope does not have enough weight, or it tangles while being thrown, or it's not available when needed.

Easy to make

First of all, get a bleach bottle with cap. Next get a 50 to 70 foot section of 1/4" braided nylon rope. A useful option is a grommet large enough to allow the rope to pass freely but small enough that a knot in the rope will stop it.

Make a hole in the center of the bottom of the bleach bottle. If available, place the grommet over this hole. Thread the line through the bottle until you have about 2 feet sticking out the hole in the bottom.

Tie a figure-8 or other stopper knot in the line at the top of the bottle and pull it into the bottle until it is snug against the hole in the bottom and on the inside of the bottle.

The end which is sticking out the bottom of the bottle is tied in a loop, so it can be easily grabbed or looped around a piling or post. A bowline is a good strong knot for this. This knot should end up by the outside of the hole at the bottom of the bottle.

Make a hole in the center of the cap just large enough for the line to pass freely. Thread the line through the cap. Make another loop like the one at the bottom of the bottle in the other end of the rope.

Thread the line into the bottle and screw the cap on. Your lifeline is ready to use, though I would further suggest painting it with a "lively"

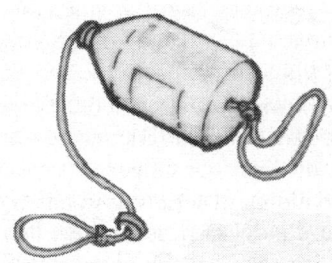

color or wrapping it with reflective tape.

Easy to use

When the lifeline is needed, all you have to do is unscrew the cap, hold the loop at the top of the bottle, and throw the bottle.

It's better to throw it past someone and pull it back to them than to have to repack and throw again. A little practice will get fast results.

This device is easily made and is inexpensive, but it can only be useful if you make it before you need it. ∆

Build an earth-sheltered log cabin

By Tok Thompson

Over a period of three summers, for a total of five months, I designed and built an earth-sheltered, passive-solar cabin. The structure is 12x30 feet, with the main room being 12x20 feet. Besides the main room, I have an ample-sized bathroom and a "mud room" entryway. The cabin is sunny, comfy, and easy to heat. The total cost? Under $1,500.

In essence, the design is a sod igloo, perfected over thousands of years by northern-dwelling indigenous peoples. The main function of the earth-sheltered design for them was the heat efficiency. Whatever heat seeps out of an above-ground house is whisked away by the wind, but in an earth-sheltered dwelling it is kept next to the house, dramatically slowing the heat loss process.

For someone to build a similar house for a similar price would not be that difficult. Of course, I scrounged for building materials as much as possible. I purchased, for a mere $80 at a moving sale, enough metal roofing to entirely surround the cabin, along with a large front window set for $20. The window was initially too big for the hole, so I widened the space with a chain saw to make it fit. Lumber for the foundation, floor, and roof totaled $1100. I was able to barter for the use of a bulldozer, which otherwise would have been very expensive. Someone was throwing the front door away at a local dump, and they were only too happy to have it put to good use. Where I live, trees are free or freely given by neighbors, which is what prompted my use of them as my main building material.

The biggest problem with sod igloos is their tendency to leak water and, after leaking, to eventually rot. In fact, nowhere in all the literature on earth-sheltered construction did I find any log-based plans, which is due, I'm sure, to these very considerations. To counter the problems, I relied on modern technology, including surrounding the house in metal siding, and coating the outside of the logs in copper napthalmate. It is a noxious substance, but good at stopping rot. A more eco-friendly way would be the old Norwegian method of curing the logs in salt water, or just using driftwood. For additional insurance, I installed PVC pipe both inside and outside the house to drain any water down and out beneath the floor. I may have done more than minimally necessary to keep our house nice and dry, but I didn't want to take the chance that I might have to dig out the walls later for repairs!

I had cut and stripped all the logs the fall before, to give them a year to cure and dry. Preparing the logs was actually the most strenuous part of the process. It took me a month and a half of constant work, and along the way I learned a few things.

First of all, there are several ways to make sure the logs are cured. One way is to kill them while still standing by peeling off the bark all the way around the tree and waiting until they dry out before cutting them down. Another way, which is the one I used, is to cut them down, take off all the bark and branches, and prop them up off the ground to dry. Still easier, however, is to use trees which are already dead, especially those that are still standing. Around the area where I live there is a kind of tree beetle that will kill spruce trees without harming much of the wood. Since things rot so slowly in Alaska, these trees often stand for years, drying and curing naturally. Towards the end of my building project, I used some of these and was amazed at how easy it was to debark them.

If you decide to cut fresh trees and debark them as I originally did, however, be prepared for some work. Most log builders recommend using a drawknife, which has two handles, for stripping off the bark. For me, it proved easier to use my machete, which I could grip on both sides while wearing a glove, and which had the added benefit of a point for use in working on tough spots. The machete also made hacking off branches or other obstructions mercifully easier for me. The only other tools I used in this process were a chain saw and a log-turner.

Assuming you have the site and the trees, the first job in construction is digging the hole. Although a backhoe would be ideal, you can make do with a bulldozer, as I did. Digging the pit by hand, although possible, would be a monumental task. Before you dig, however, be certain the proposed pit is situated on the site exactly as you like it. For maximum sun, the front should be pointed south, although I chose to compromise between sunshine and the best view of the lake. A slight rise to the north is ideal, and be sure to have a good sand or gravel base.

Laying a foundation

There are several ways you could build a foundation for your cabin. Poured concrete or chemically treated beams seem to make the most sense for this project. The adventurous could forego this step and rely on treated logs. I chose treated 2x12 lumber, two thick, creating the net effect of 4x12 wood beams. After carefully leveling these, I lay thick Visquene (polyethylene) over them, to act as another moisture barrier between the house and the ground below, and then built a subfloor of 2x6 lumber and CDX plywood.

I ran a 2x6 header board lengthwise along the house and nailed the 2x6 support joists into it. If I had been building the cabin any wider, 2x6 lumber would not have sufficed. As it was, I still placed several supports in the middle of the expanse. A viable alternative here would be a concrete floor, which would have the extra advantage of acting like a solar battery to trap the sun's heat during the day and radiate that heat back out at night. Personally, however, I prefer the look and feel of wood flooring.

Putting up log walls

When the subfloor was done, it was time for the logs. To move them to my building site, I used the bulldozer again, first pulling them with a chain, then using the blade to push them into the pit. One of the advantages of my underground design was that I didn't have to lift any logs. Although it was occasionally awkward to position them, this step was remarkably easy for me. Before pushing a log into the pit, be sure to plan ahead how you will roll it into place! If it is balanced just right, it is truly amazing how a person can maneuver even a 2x40 foot log with one hand.

Joining the logs together is a little like playing the guitar. You can do all right without knowing much, or you can spend a lifetime devoted to your craft. While the more you know and do will always show in the results, an airtight fit is simply not as necessary with an earth-sheltered design. The gaps between the logs can be filled with concrete (mixing it with sawdust gives it better flexibility) or store-bought log chinking (though this can be a bit pricey, if economy is an issue). Since most of the outside walls are covered with metal sheeting and buried underground, small gaps do not mean there will be holes into the outside air. More care should be taken with the few logs that will not be covered and buried, but by the time you get to those you should be getting the hang of log work. I recommend laying insulation between the logs, especially if you are not doing any elaborate fitting techniques.

My fast-and-easy approach consisted of cutting slices with a chain saw where the notches were to be, and then knocking them out with a sledge. When the next log was to be fitted on top, I would position it for the least amount of gap space, and occasionally I'd use the chain saw to improve the fit by removing bumps and other obstructions. It is also important to alternate the large and small ends of the logs or you will end up with one side of a house much higher than the other.

Roofing the cabin

This design includes a shed-style roof, which provides for maximum sun exposure and is, incidentally, very easy to build. To provide the slant, simply stop alternating the log ends and use the thicker ends exclusively toward the front of the cabin. The front wall thus becomes higher than the back wall. I began to build the slant about halfway up the wall although, in retrospect, I realize I could have used a bit more slope. Variations in the level at which you stop alternating will also depend, of course, on the shape of your logs. The more tapered they are, the longer you may wait to stop alternating log ends.

One of my prime motivating factors in choosing the shed roof design was the fact that winter was quickly approaching. Since this design involved lumber, it was the most expensive part of the house. There are alternative methods that would be cheaper, but they would also require much more skill than construction with lumber and plywood does. First, I placed a center beam across two walls so that it traversed the middle of the cabin and gave support to the roof. Then pairs of 2x6 boards were nailed together, much as when laying the floor, using two-foot spacing boards along two walls, and plywood was nailed over the top of them.

I laid aluminum roofing on top of that, as well as over the portion of the log walls that would be buried. I put insulation between the 2x6s from underneath and stapled Visquene underneath that. This, combined with sod and snow on top, provides excellent insulation.

A rather large front overhang is a good idea for two reasons. It keeps moisture away from that part of the front wall that is above ground. And it also cuts out hot summer sun, when the sun angle is high, while not interfering with the low-angle winter sun. The winter after I finished the roof, Alaska had the heaviest snowfall in 50 years and many buildings in the area collapsed, but my cabin pulled through just fine and I never had to shovel the roof the entire time. After that, I felt more confident about my little igloo.

As I mentioned earlier, this roofing method was easy but a bit expensive. A cheaper alternative might be pole roofing, with the poles covered first by chicken wire and then by concrete, which could be water-sealed. I was looking at this method when the imminent snowfall forced my decision.

The finishing touches

The next summer I returned from a honeymoon trip up the Alcan highway, and my bride Katie valiantly joined the project, helping me put aluminum siding along the sides of the cabin and fill in the pit with gravel. After those two jobs were done, all that was left were the little things—moving in a Franklin stove, installing windows, doors, floorboards, and so on.

It's been hard work, lots of fun, and in some ways a dream come true. Future plans include a full-service bathroom with hot and cold running water and a combination solar- and steam-powered electrical system. I have the plans now, and will write more later to let you know how they work out! Δ

SELF-SUFFICIENCY

Handguns are useful tools for the homesteader

By Christopher Maxwell

There are times when you will have your hands full, chopping wood, tending the garden, working on your house, or doing other things that would make it impossible or unreasonable for you to carry a rifle or shotgun. If you only see game, snakes, barn rats, predators or other pests when you are busy doing something else, you may want to consider acquiring a handgun.

I covered .22 caliber rimfire handguns in issue 12, (page 473 of the Best of the First Two Years), so this article will deal with centerfire handguns.

Bigger is better

Large caliber centerfire revolvers can be useful for those who keep livestock or have a problem with predators or feral dog packs. As a general rule, the larger calibers are more versatile. It is easy to make or buy a mild recoiling, less powerful load for a .44 magnum. But you cannot safely make a .38 or .357 magnum load more powerful than the factories make.

The most powerful handgun cartridge commonly available is the .44 magnum. The most powerful factory load for the .44 magnum propels a 240 grain bullet at about 1300 feet per second. This is not a load for beginners. From a three pound handgun this is more recoil than many experienced shooters want anything to do with. The .44 special cartridge can also be fired from the same gun. This cartridge sends a 246 grain bullet away at under 800 feet per second in the most common loading, and is very mild to shoot from a large revolver.

Several other loadings are available in both .44 special and .44 magnum that make this handgun suitable for any use from small game hunting and pest elimination to deer hunting and protection from large and dangerous animals. No other handgun is so versatile.

The traditional round nose lead bullet in .44 special is the least useful type and should not be purchased unless you can't find anything else or unless you find some very cheap for practice. It will take small game and eliminate pests and small predators.

This was the only .44 special ammunition made for many years, but now many improved loads are available. .44 special loads with flat tipped or semi-wadcutter bullets are more useful for small game and pests. The .44 special Silvertip load from Winchester will serve well for predators, both four- and two-legged.

CCI-Blazer makes an aluminum case .44 magnum round which is more powerful than the .44 special factory loads but less powerful than the full power .44 magnum. This load may be useful for those who want longer range and more power than the special, but aren't ready for the recoil and blast of the full power loads.

The full power lead bullet loads should be avoided, unless your idea of fun is scrubbing lead out of your rifling. The 180 to 200 grain jacketed hollow points are very effective on predators and large feral dogs but are too destructive for anything edible, and do not penetrate deeply enough for large dangerous animals like bulls or bears. For deer you want 240 grain jacketed soft points or very hard cast semi-wadcutters. For large dangerous animals, very hard cast semi-wadcutter bullets are needed.

With six chambers in the cylinder, you can load a shot load for snakes, a few .44 special small game or pest loads, and a few .44 magnum maximum loads for protection from large animals or a lucky encounter with a deer. All you need is to remember your loading order, or mark your cylinder in some way so you can rotate the right load for the job at hand into firing position.

Colt, Ruger, Wesson Arms and Smith & Wesson all make good large frame revolvers for the .44 magnum cartridge. I have always preferred Smith & Wesson revolvers over all

Smith & Wesson stainless .44 magnum revolver

others, but this is a matter of personal taste. Several of the large caliber revolvers by Smith & Wesson and Ruger are available with integral scope mount bases for hunters.

Similar versatile loads can be made for other large caliber revolvers such as the .45 Colt and the .41 Magnum, but you will have to take up handloading to enjoy the same versatility offered by the .44 Magnum/.44 Special. There is some variety of loads offered by the factories in those calibers but not nearly as great as for the .44 magnum.

Medium frame revolvers

If your hand is not big enough for the large frame revolvers, you can do all the above except deer hunting and protection from large dangerous animals with a .357 magnum revolver. The .357 will also fire .38 special ammunition, so you have a wide selection of power levels and bullet types available.

The .38 special wadcutter target load is very mild and is a good training load as well as an effective and not very destructive small game load. Semi-wadcutter .38 loads work well for small game and pests, but lead bullet loads in .357 leave too much lead behind in your barrel. Jacketed hollow points from 90 to 125 grains in both .38 and .357 offer destructive performance on thin skinned pests and predators but do not offer good penetration. 140 to 160 grain jacketed soft point bullets offer better performance on larger animals.

The .357 is at its best in barrels 6 inches or longer, so the bullet will reach its full velocity, but the shorter barrels can be effective if used with skill.

Ruger, Colt, Wesson, Taurus, and Smith & Wesson all make good revolvers for the .357. The Colt and Wesson are larger frames, almost as large as the .44 frame guns. One advantage of the Wesson Arms revolver is interchangeable barrels in different lengths. You can get several barrels and carry the shorter barrel for convenience when you don't need maximum power, and switch to the longer barrel when you do need more power.

Ruger, Taurus and Smith & Wesson make .357 magnum revolvers on the .38 size frame, which will be good news to those with small hands. I like the Smith & Wesson for its smooth trigger pull and fine accuracy, but suit yourself. They all work well enough.

Small revolvers

Smaller revolvers intended as personal protection weapons are made for the .38 special cartridge. I know of several people who use the little five shot Smith & Wesson as a farm gun to take small game and to eliminate pests and small predators when the opportunity occurs. This requires considerable skill and is probably too ambitious for a novice shooter. Though the potential accuracy of these small revolvers is remarkably good, they are very difficult to learn to shoot well.

One problem is the sights. These guns are usually equipped with "fixed" rear sights, actually just a

Smith & Wesson stainless 5-shot .38 special revolver

notch cut into the frame. This is adequate for self-defense at confrontation distances but better sights are required for field use. These revolvers can be ordered with adjustable sights, and should be if you want one for utility purposes.

Another problem is the grips. The issue grips simply do not give you enough to hold. Most people who buy these guns are more concerned with concealment than function, so the issue grips are as small as possible. The "LadySmith" versions of these revolvers offer a better selection of factory grips, or you can simply buy a replacement aftermarket grip like my favorite, the Pachmayr Compact. I don't like the factory supplied grips on any revolver; all of mine wear Pachmayr's.

Hunting with handguns

Hunting with a shotgun or rifle is not enough of a challenge for some hunters. Many states now have special seasons and licenses for hunters who want to try to take deer, bear, or other game with a handgun.

The Thompson Center Contender is one of the pistols made for these people and one that some country dwellers have found useful. It functions somewhat like a break open single shot shotgun. Many interchangeable barrels are available in calibers from .22 rimfire to .45-70. There are barrels available for .410 shotgun shells, which will also fire .45 Colt revolver ammunition. Many different barrel lengths are available including a kit with a long barrel and a shoulder stock to turn the pistol into a carbine.

I should mention here that while it is legal to buy the longer barrel and stock for the pistol frame, both the longer barrel and stock must be used together. Using the stock with a barrel under 16 inches or using a barrel over 16 inches with the pistol grip is considered an unlawfully short rifle.

If you buy the Thompson Center Contender carbine, you may not use the pistol grip or a barrel under 16 inches, or both in combination. It is legal to convert a pistol to a rifle, but to convert a rifle into a pistol requires some Federal paperwork, and may not be allowed by the laws of your state.

If you might need something like a .410 shotgun or a .30-30 rifle, and will have your hands too full to carry a long gun, the Contender is an option you should consider.

Several other single shot handguns are made but they are not as common or as versatile as the Contender and are beyond the scope of this article.

Automatic pistols

Centerfire self-loading pistols are usually designed as self-defense weapons rather than utility guns. While they have several advantages over revolvers for self-defense, the revolver's versatility makes it a better utility gun.

Automatic pistols will only function with ammunition within the narrow range of power required to work the action. Bullet shapes are restricted by the fact that the bullet must feed up a

Thompson Center Contender pistol with ten inch barrel

ramp and into the chamber. You cannot readily select from different types of ammunition in the magazine, you get whatever the next cartridge happens to be.

The only centerfire automatic pistol I have found useful as a farm or ranch gun is the 1911 model .45 automatic.

If you already own one, and don't handload your own ammunition, the best loads for large predators and small game is probably the Frontier 230 grain flat point FMJ. The standard 230 grain round nose jacketed bullet is prone to ricochet on hard surfaces, overpenetrate small animals, and is not too effective on large animals.

The CCI-Speer 200 grain jacketed hollow point may not feed from the magazine in many pistols without extensive work but I know of people who have taken deer with it at close range. It is also a very accurate cartridge in every gun I have tried. I have not shot any small animals with it but I suspect it may be too destructive for edible small game.

CCI and Remington both make shot loads for .45 auto. Both makers claim their loads will cycle through the magazine.

Small caliber automatics

Small caliber centerfire automatic pistols are just not very useful as farm or utility guns. They don't have the power for larger predators or the accuracy for small pests. They don't have the ammunition versatility of large caliber pistols or revolvers.

You could defend yourself quite well with your .44 revolver, but even an expert would have a hard time bringing down a deer with a 9mm pistol or hitting a coyote at 50 yards.

Most centerfire pistols of 9mm and smaller caliber are specialized self-defense weapons. As far as their usefulness as defense weapons, any firearm available can serve as a deterrent if it is available when needed. But no handgun has the power or hit potential of a rifle or shotgun. Any handgun is last choice as a defense, and should only be used if nothing else is available.

Skill and safe technique are essential to successful use of any firearm, and especially handguns. The best basic pistol instruction is available at low cost from the training division of the National Rifle Association. For a list of certified pistol instructors near you, write to the NRA Training Division, 11250 Waples Mill Rd., Fairfax, VA 22030, or call (703) 267-1000. ∆

Trading your city house for a country homestead — will it be a taxing move?

By Atty. Sandra R. Bullington, CPA

Assume you sold your house on its city lot and you're headed for the rural homestead of your dreams. The $150,000 you got for your house put $60,000 in your pocket after the $80,000 mortgage and $10,000 of sales costs were paid. Since you paid $95,000 for the house and have done nothing other than make your mortgage payments and live there, you've done well—well enough in fact to invest in a mortgage free homestead.

But as in any financial matter, there's always the Internal Revenue Service (IRS) to consider. Will you owe taxes? If you think you've got a handle on how tax laws work when it comes to buying and selling a house, try your hand at this quiz based upon the above facts.

1. What is the gain you've realized on the sale of your city house?
   a. $60,000
   b. $70,000
   c. $45,000
2. Is it possible to avoid paying taxes on the sale of your city house?
   a. Yes, gain on the sale of a personal residence is not subject to income tax.
   b. No.
   c. Yes, it is possible to postpone paying tax through the purchase of another home, provided certain requirements are met.
3. How much must you spend on your homestead in order to avoid paying tax on the gain?
   a. $60,000
   b. $80,000

   c. $140,000
4. Are there any time limits on when you must buy your replacement home?
   a. No, there are no time limits.
   b. Yes, your replacement home must be purchased within two years of selling your old home.
   c. Yes, your replacement home must be purchased (or built) and you must occupy it within two years before or after the date of sale of your old home.
5. Can you replace your city house with a working farm and avoid paying taxes on the sale of the house?
   a. Yes, if the farm is less than 100 acres.
   b. No.
   c. Maybe. It depends on the cost of the house located on the farm.

If you answered "c" to all of the above, you've got a good idea of how our tax laws apply to the sale and purchase of homes. If you got any of these answers wrong and are planning on replacing your urban house with a homestead, you should learn more about the tax consequences before you undertake such a move. The last thing you want to find out is that you owe substantial taxes when you weren't planning on paying any—especially if you've invested the cash from your house sale into a homestead. Before we move on to what type of homestead will qualify as a replacement home, however, it helps to understand how taxable gain is computed and how this tax law works.

Cash settlement doesn't equal gain

If you answered "a" to question #1, you're probably confusing cash flow with gain. You're also not alone as many people confuse the two. However, this can be dangerous to your financial health. The cash you receive at settlement can't be equated to the gain on sale—in fact it's possible to sell a house, receive either no cash or even have to pay to sell, and still have a substantial gain.

The gain on the sale of your house is computed as follows:

> Selling price of house
> Less selling expenses
> Less adjusted basis of house
> Equals
> Gain realized on the sale of the house

Your "adjusted basis" is what you paid for your house, increased by the cost of improvements, additions, and special assessments, but reduced by any gain postponed on prior homes, insurance reimbursements for casualty losses, deductible casualty losses not covered by insurance, payments received for right-of-ways or easements granted, and any depreciation allowed if your house was used in business. While this seems complicated, for most people their adjusted basis is what they paid for the house plus the cost of any additions or improvements (such as adding rooms).

Mortgages are usually the biggest factor affecting the cash you receive at settlement. If you remember that mortgages don't always arise from the purchase of a house, it helps to understand why cash received doesn't equate to gain. In the example above, assume you took out a second mortgage of $20,000, the proceeds of which were used to buy a boat. At settlement you would have received $20,000 less—instead of receiving $60,000, you would have left the settlement table with $40,000. Since the funds weren't used to improve the house, this mortgage doesn't affect your house's basis or cost, and consequently it has no effect on gain. Your gain would still be $45,000, but the cash you cleared would be less than your gain. This is just one example where cash received has no bearing on gain.

Section 1034

It's possible to sell your house and not pay tax on the gain. In fact, if you buy a replacement home which costs at least as much as the "adjusted sales price" of your old home, and other requirements of Internal Revenue Code section 1034 are met, you're automatically covered by that Code section and no tax is due on the sale of your home. While this is a simplification of the law, it gives the basic framework.

In order to figure out how much you must spend on your replacement home in order to avoid paying income tax, you must know the adjusted sales price of your old home. The IRS defines this term as "the amount realized minus any fixing-up expenses you might have." This definition requires that the terms "amount realized" and "fixing-up expenses" likewise be defined.

The "amount realized" is the selling price less selling expenses. In the above example, the amount realized is $140,000—the selling price of $150,000 minus the $10,000 of sales costs. Fixing-up expenses are decorating and repair costs paid to sell your house, but these expenses must:

1) Be for work done in the 90-day period which ends on the date you sign the sales contract
2) Be paid within 30 days after the sale
3) Not be deductible in determining your taxable income
4) Not be used in figuring the amount realized
5) Not be capital expenditures or improvements

In the example above, there were no fixing-up expenses, so the adjusted sales price is $140,000. Thus, in order to avoid paying tax on this sale, you'd need to buy a replacement home costing at least $140,000.

The purpose of Internal Revenue Code Section 1034 is not to penalize taxpayers who sell their home and then purchase a more expensive home—after all, this has been the American way of life. But this "tax-free exchange" is not accomplished by forgiving the tax on the sale of the old home, but through postponing the tax by decreasing the tax cost or basis of the new home. If the new home is later sold and not replaced, that is when the gain will be taxed.

To show how the postponement of tax works, using the example at the beginning of this article, assume your replacement home cost $160,000. Even though you paid $160,000, your basis or tax cost of the house will be $115,000—the cost of $160,000 less the $45,000 of gain not taxed on the sale of your prior house. If you later sell this second house for $160,000 and don't buy a qualifying replacement house, you'll recognize and pay tax on the $45,000 of gain postponed from the sale of the first house.

One of the requirements of Section 1034 is that the replacement home must be purchased (or built) and occupied within two years of selling your house. This means that you can acquire a replacement home two years before as well as two years after you sell your house. It also means that you must physically live in the replacement house as your main home within this period.

There are exceptions to this two year replacement rule for people who move outside of the United States, but these generally don't apply to those merely moving from an urban to a rural location.

What did you pay for your house?

The example at the beginning assumed that the cost of the house was $95,000. In real life things aren't this simple. If the contract price of your house was $95,000, it's likely that your tax cost or basis is more than $95,000, as many settlement costs are included in determining the original basis of your house. Legal and recording fees you pay increase the basis of your home as do the following:

1. Abstract fees
2. Charges for installing utilities
3. Surveys
4. Transfer taxes
5. Title insurance
6. Any amounts the seller owes that you agree to pay, such as back taxes or interest, or sales commission.

Often these costs are substantial and shouldn't be overlooked. If these costs are paid on your old home, they increase the basis of that property and if paid on the new home, they increase the cost of that property.

Will the IRS let you move tax-free?

The postponement of tax is allowed only if both homes—the one you've sold and the new one you've acquired—are your "principal residence." This is where country-bound homeowners may run into problems.

According to the IRS, your principal residence consists of the house and the land upon which it sits. You shouldn't have problems with your old home on its subdivided lot, but your homestead may be more than just a principal residence. How much acreage comes with your homestead? Do you plan to farm part of it? The answers to these questions could make the sale of your old house taxable.

If you buy a replacement home situated on 7½ acres intending to farm 6 acres, only the cost of the house and the 1½ acres will count as the cost of your replacement home. This is what the U.S. Tax Court decided in such a case. The cost of the 6 acres used for farming wasn't considered as part of the cost of the replacement home.

How does this affect you? If you sell your urban home at a profit, you'll have taxable gain (resulting in income tax) if your replacement home doesn't cost as much as your prior home. This may result if you have to exclude part of the cost of your new homestead.

The size of your homestead may also present problems. If you purchase a house on 100 acres, in most cases the IRS isn't going to let you use the full purchase price as the cost of your replacement home. Clearly, 100 acres transcends anyone's notion of land necessary to accommodate a residence. In between the 100 acres and the home on a small lot is a gray area. In addition, an intent to farm (versus a personal home garden) or operate a business on a portion of your land should affect you the same as the taxpayers in the Tax Court case—that is, only the land not used for farming or business will count as part of your replacement home.

Talk to your tax advisor if you plan to sell your city house and avoid paying tax on the gain by purchasing a country homestead. The facts and circumstances of your individual case affect the tax results and there are time requirements which must be met to roll-over gain on one home into a replacement home. If you are over 55, you may be able to use your once-in-a-lifetime $125,000 exclusion, which may solve any tax problems you have. For more information, you can obtain from the IRS, free of charge, Form 2119 Sale of Your Home, instructions for form 2119, Publication 523 Tax Information on Selling Your Home and Publication 551 Basis of Assets by calling 1-800-829-3676. Publication 523 contains several worksheets to help you figure the tax consequences of your move to the country. ∆

A country moment

BHM publisher Dave Duffy and friend Paul Luckey dig a shallow well at BHM's Oregon office.

BUILDING

A Backwoods Home Anthology

How to build a low-cost log lifter

By Robert L. Williams

When you are sawing logs for a house or other building purpose, it is necessary to get the log off the ground in order to keep from dulling your chain every time the tip hits the soil or rocks under the log. But how do you get the heavy log off the ground and onto sawing blocks?

There is an easy answer to the problem. You can build, for only pennies and a few minutes of your time, a log lifter that is capable of lifting, to a modest height of six to ten inches, the heaviest logs you will encounter.

Your needed materials include a chain saw, a length of chain or strong rope (up to 6 or 8 feet), a chisel, a long bolt with washer and nut or a 100-penny nail or similar spike, a drill with a quarter-inch bit or another 100-penny nail, and a long, slender length of wood to be used as a handle.

Start by cutting the base block, which can be as short as one foot or as long as you want it. The shorter it is, the easier it is to handle, of course.

Cut the log chunk (which should be at least 10 inches in diameter) so that it has two squared-off ends. Then move to the mid-point in the chunk and measure and mark two inches each way from the mid-point. Saw where you made the two marks. The cut should be one-third of the way through the log chunk.

Now use a hammer and chisel to chip out the section of wood you have just marked by sawing the two grooves. Your next step is to locate a long, slender length of wood to be used as a handle.

Wild cherry saplings work extremely well for this purpose. The big end of the pole should be about four inches in diameter, and the entire lifting pole should be at least 6 feet and, even better, 7 to 8 feet.

Lay the end of the pole into the space you just created with the chain saw and chisel. The end of the pole should align roughly with the outer edge of the cut.

At the center of the pole end drill a hole ¼ inch in diameter and let the drill bore into the chock log beneath the pole. Remove the drill and drive a fluted spike or 100-penny nail into the handle and into the chock log.

If you are using a bolt and nut, use a ½ inch bolt long enough to reach all the way through handle and chock log. Push the bolt through and add the washer and nut on the bottom.

Move up the handle now to a point 18 inches or so from the chock log. Drill a hole through the handle. The hole should be parallel with the chock log. Push the second bolt or spike through the hole so that at least four inches of the spike will stick out on each side.

Lay the handle into the chiseled-out space in the chock log and drill or bore a hole through the end of the handle and the chock log. You will later run a bolt or spike through the two pieces of wood.

When you are ready to use the log lifter, shove the chock log and handle tightly against the log to be lifted. Hold the handle nearly straight up while you wrap the chain around the log and around the handle spike or rod as well. Keep the chain tight as you begin to lift.

Now you are ready to work.

When you are ready to lift the huge log, push the chock log and handle as close to the log to be lifted as possible. Hook one end of the chain or rope to the spike or 100-penny nail. Run the other end of the chain under the log and across the top side and back to the other side of the handle.

Pull the chain tight and hook it to the other side of the spike or bolt. Be sure that the chain will not slip loose when you start to lift.

Now stand facing the log and put one foot against the chock log to keep it from sliding until you have pressure on it. Pull down on the end of the pole, and as if by magic, the huge log will roll toward you and onto the top of the chock log as you push the handle all the way to the ground.

Now have someone—if you have a helper—push the saw block against the side of the chock log and handle. Let the handle rise slowly, and the log can be eased on top of the saw block.

Go to the other end and repeat the process. Your log is now off the ground, and you can saw without worrying about the tip of your chain saw bar and chain.

If you must work alone, you will not be able to hold the handle down while you put the saw chock log under the log to be sawed. But there is a way you can handle the job.

Two ways, in fact.

The first way is to lean the saw chock log against the log to be lifted. As you lift the log and roll it away from the chock saw log, the shorter chock piece will slide down the side of the log and will fall into place while you lower the log onto it.

The second method is to find a way to anchor the handle while you place the saw chock log in place. One way to do this is to have a short length of heavy log within reach. When the handle is on the ground, roll the short length toward you until it covers and anchors the end of the pole.

Another way is to drive a stake into the ground at the point where the end of the handle will touch the ground. Have a short length of modestly strong cord handy, and when the handle end is one the ground, tie the handle to the stake.

This may sound like a lot of trouble, but it takes only seconds; and it is far better to use a few seconds than it is to nurse an injured back for weeks or months. ∆

A BHM Writer's Profile

Lucy Shober

Lucy Shober was born and grew up on Lookout Mountain in Tennessee along with 11 brothers and sisters. She had three children and was lucky to be living out her childhood fantasy—"to live on a farm with lots of room for any animal that needs a place to stay, have roly-poly babies that play in the dirt, and have a husband who loves her anyway." Perhaps the foundations of her dreams were laid during her childhood on Lookout Mountain, Tennessee, where she and her brothers and sisters kept pet monkeys, goats, pigeons, and coons.

Lucy majored in art in college, but worked in wildlife rehabilitation and environmental education. She began writing children's columns for local newspapers and soon found herself splitting her time between working the farm, writing and illustrating for Backwoods Home Magazine and other publications, and working part time at a child care center, alongside her two-year-old, roly-poly, dirt player.

She and her husband John ran "The Flying Turtle Farm" in Cloudland Georgia, where they raised and sold organic vegetables, minor breeds of poultry, and Irish Dexter cattle. Lucy had told us she liked to wander around among cattle, sheep, pigs, goats, horses, all manner of poultry, cats, and a three-legged dog who can still hit 20 mph after being caught in the garbage.

Lucy recently died of leukemia, at age 44. She will be remembered by all BHM readers who loved her columns.

FREE $500 KIT

JULY/AUGUST 1994
No. 28
$3.50 U.S.
$4.50 CANADA

Backwoods Home magazine
... a practical journal of self reliance!

Special Independent Energy Issue

RAISING FISH

ASIAN COOKING

KEEPING TEENAGERS AT HOME

BULK RATE
U.S. POSTAGE
PAID
COLUMBUS, WI
PERMIT NO. 73

The beast is at the door again

As our important holidays like July 4th approach, it forces many of us to reflect on the freedoms the people of America still enjoy, but it also makes us look sadly upon the freedoms we have lost. We are still the most free country ever, but our freedoms have been gradually eroded since the time those enlightened men drafted that great doctrine that protects us from Government: The Constitution.

Notice I said protects us from Government. Today all the talk is protecting us from crime, from drugs, from AIDS, from guns, and from—you name it—everything from inadequate health care to second-hand smoke.

But those framers of so long ago never had any intention of protecting us from things like second-hand smoke. They knew who the real enemy was. They were students of history, and they understood that the great evil that had stalked mankind throughout the ages had not been plagues or criminals or even invading armies. It was a people's own Government, which had always been more master than protector.

That's why men like Thomas Jefferson and James Madison and the rest of our founding fathers are so revered. They solved mankind's most ancient and critical dilemma by figuring out how to keep Government at bay and guaranteeing lasting freedom to the people. They did it with a carefully worded document that placed all power with the people and allocated only certain powers to the Government. It wasn't a perfect document, but it was close.

But as many of us have sadly come to realize in this modern era, Government is back. In an effort to respond to various groups' demands that "the people" be "protected" from the many plagues that afflict modern society, Government has gleefully responded.

Here's a short, very incomplete, list:

To respond to crime, Government has built prisons so that the United States now has the highest per capita incarceration rate in the world, much higher than much maligned second place South Africa.

To respond to drug abuse, Government has waged a war on drugs that has included "no knock" laws, seizure of private property without due process, and massive corruption of public officials.

To respond to AIDS, Government has decided that public schools will give our children condoms and sex instruction without the consent or approval of parents.

To combat inadequate health care, Government is attempting to institute socialized medicine, along with what it says is a central computer databank with records on not just our medical needs, but every aspect of our personal and monetary status.

To combat guns, Government is passing new restrictive gun laws against guns (they call them assault rifles) that are seldom used in crimes, and they want to register all gun owners. Their intention clearly is to confiscate all guns, the second Amendment be damned.

Dave Duffy

Everyone remembers the Government's two most recent and notorious attempts to control guns. One was at Ruby Ridge in Idaho and the other near Waco, Texas.

In Idaho undercover Government agents convinced Randy Weaver to sell them an illegal gun. We used to call that entrapment, but now the Government calls it an excuse to invade an individual's home. The Government invaded Weaver's home, shot his wife through the head, his 14-year-old son in the back, and put Weaver on trial. Weaver was acquitted, but his wife and son are still dead.

Near Waco, Texas, the Government went after guns at the Branch Davidian compound. I won't recount the horrible details, but we all saw the fire that killed 86 people, about half of them innocent women and children. The survivors were put on trial but were acquitted of any serious charges.

And the Government has just begun. It intends to go much further.

In an effort to combat what Government fears is too much criticism of itself, mainly by the hundreds of small conservative talk shows that have cropped up across the country to criticize Government erosion of our constitutional rights, Government, under the guise of a misnamed law called the "Fairness Doctrine," is actively considering regulating radio to allow "opposing" views to be aired.

Sounds scary?

As it has always done, somehow Government, like some monster from the past, has again outwitted the freedom-loving masses and has convinced them that they don't need protection from Government, but from everything else. And so the age-old beast our founding fathers had tamed is once more banging at our door.

It's a frightening prospect that it will get inside our homes again because it may take hundreds of years before enlightened men like Jefferson and Madison come along again to rescue us. Δ

INDEPENDENT ENERGY

A Backwoods Home Anthology

For a truly independent energy system, your choices are solar, wind, and water

By Larry Elliott

Just as the words "backwoods home" conjure up images of farmhouses, livestock, woodstoves, tractors, and gardens, the words "independent energy" bring to mind a whole new set of images, like solar panels, windmills, hydro electric generators, inverters, and batteries.

According to Webster's Dictionary, the word "independent" means to be self governing, not easily influenced, and showing self reliance, while "energy" is described as the capacity to perform work. These qualities of self reliance and work go hand in hand with a backwoods home lifestyle and the use of independent energy.

Anyone who is seriously considering a move to the country should become informed about energy and its proper use and production, the same as one would learn about raising livestock, growing a crop, or making a living.

When great grandpa or your great-uncle Joe settled down on his 160-acre government-granted homestead, independent energy was perhaps an ox, a mule, seven healthy children, or better yet a prairie windmill. Today we have much better choices of equipment, but the idea of producing your own energy from your own source and having it do useful work is still the same.

For more than 20 years I have been involved in the use of independent or "alternative" energy and the design or modification of related equipment, as well as sales and service of off-the-shelf equipment. Years of fielding customer questions on energy production and consumption have led me to the conclusion that for most people energy is not a subject they feel comfortable dealing with.

I suppose a lot of this comes from the fact that the average person has never had to deal directly with energy beyond paying a utility bill. I have also found that many of these same people have a somewhat unrealistic view of what an independent energy system can and cannot do, so they have a hard time selecting the proper equipment to suit a particular task. For many there is a romantic appeal to the idea of being completely free of utilities; this can get them into trouble without proper guidance.

It would be equally unrealistic for me to attempt to cover such a detailed subject as independent energy in a simple article, so this article is hopefully going to answer some of the most often asked questions and try to give some rule-of-thumb guidelines that will be helpful.

If you truly wish your source of energy to be independent, there are only a few choices: solar in the form of solar electric panels, hot water panels, and passive heating; wind generators for electric production and windmills for water pumping; and hydro electric generators.

I can hear all those living on gas or diesel generators letting out a moan, but in reality these generators should be used strictly as backups to an independent system or for occasional heavy use. If you have a good solar, wind, or hydro source or a combination of one or all, a fossil fuel generator as sole source just doesn't pencil out economically, and it certainly can't be seen as independent because of the fuel source.

There are areas of the country where these generators will be the only practical source though, and one simple rule should be followed in their use: It rarely makes economic sense to use the generator as sole source without the use of an inverter/charger and storage batteries. Even the smallest generator will spend most of its time running loads far below capacity with overall efficiencies as low as 5 or 10 percent.

An inverter running from batteries charged by the generator will not only increase the overall efficiency to its maximum and save a lot of money, but the reduction in maintenance and noise are well worth the extra effort.

Pump water sensibly

As most people I'm sure are aware, the most important thing in having a successful backwoods home experience is a source of good clean water.

For all of those readers who are blessed with a shallow spring, streams, or lots of gravity-fed water, skip to the next section, but for anyone who has to pump water from a well of any real depth (100 to 700-plus feet) read on.

The one item that causes most people a lot of headaches when living on solar, wind, or hydro power (unless the system is very large and supplies are abundant) is water well pumping.

Most off-the-shelf water well pumping equipment was designed without much consideration for power consumption and efficiency.

When using any independent energy source, the key to success is to limit the peak demand the system must supply, even for short periods, to a minimum. This rule dictates that pumping at slow (fewer gallons per minute) rates for long periods (hours) makes far more sense than pumping at a high volume for a few minutes and shutting off. (Note: This rule, of course, does not apply to those who pump water directly using a generator, since it is always best to load a generator to near full capacity in order to maximize efficiency.)

This leads to the second rule, that a successful system should include a cistern or large (1000-plus gallons) storage tank. This not only allows the use of a smaller, less power-demanding pump, but it also gives you a reserve supply in case the pump fails.

You can easily open a tank and dip out some water temporarily, but water that's still several hundred feet down a small hole can be a problem.

You will need a second small pump to draw water from the cistern and pressurize it, but this redundancy is countered by the fact that a small shallow-water pump can deliver far more water in gallons per minute on less power than even most large deep-well pumps.

For depths of 50 to 300 feet, a good low voltage DC submersible pump can supply all the water needed by the average household, even when watering gardens if first pumped to a cistern.

To give an example of how much advantage a storage pumped system can be, let me tell you about a solar electric system I just installed. The customer has a 150-foot deep well that would easily be pumped by a small DC submersible. Had she installed a cistern her pump power demands would have been around 100 watts. This pump could have easily run all day and delivered over 800 gallons.

> **It rarely makes economic sense to use the generator as sole source without the use of an inverter/charger and storage batteries.**

Since she had some unrevealed reason for her objection to a cistern, a 1/2 horsepower 110-volt alternating current (AC) pump was installed. This pump draws over 1500 watts and requires a large inverter. At this rate she is limited to around 100 gallons per day to avoid depleting her system. This is a 15-fold increase in power with an 8-fold decrease in water delivery.

Even the best AC submersible pumps are less than 25% efficient when run through an inverter and only slightly more efficient when on the grid or generator. They are generally a poor choice to be included in an independent energy system. A second very good choice for deep well pumping on an independent power source is a jack pump. See *Backwoods Home,* issue #25, "The solar powered silent partner," for more details.

Here's a word of caution to all those who may be drilling a well and selecting a pump system. Beware of pump dealers and installers who insist on sizing your pump using an industry standard formula called the seven-minute demand rule.

This rule is supposed to determine how many gallons per minute your pump should deliver based on a total of some hypothetical delivery rates for various household fixtures.

I have found these rates to be very excessive and size my pump systems to less than half of these published figures. I have yet to hear a customer complaint due to a lack of water.

I think this rule was set up for the convenience of the installer, not the economy of the customer. Use a stop watch and a gallon container to get a feel for your own household water needs before making a decision.

Conservation is key

I can't stress enough the importance of conservation in the successful use of any independent energy system.

Although conservation by itself is not a true energy source, in a round about way it can be seen as one. Every watt you don't use is one you don't need to produce.

It takes dollars in the form of equipment to generate any form of energy.

This does not imply that you need to live a Spartan, harsh life and deny yourself certain advantages to use an independent energy source, but it does mean changing some of the bad habits acquired when living on the grid.

Unfortunately, efficiency is an afterthought in the design of most American appliances and household devices, which makes their use in an independent energy system a little more difficult, but not impossible. Most of my customers are amazed at how little energy their systems produce when first living on it, but how in just a few months they find it producing all they need.

Reminds me of Mark Twain's story of how when he was 13 he felt his father was as dumb as could be, but by the time Mark Twain had reached adulthood, he was amazed by how much his father had learned.

A good rule of thumb is that once you eliminate the use of electricity for space heating, water heating, and cooking (electric stoves), most any house can be operated successfully from a solar, wind, or hydro system.

A very frequently asked question from potential customers is: "What size system do I need?," or "How much does it cost to supply enough power for an average house?" My reply is always the same: "Houses don't use energy; people do."

This gets to the heart of the fact that there is no "average house" and that each household is unique. Two different households may have the same number and ages of occupants, the same appliances, and the houses may be of the same square footage, but one may heat with wood and have a mountain spring as a water source, while the other may have a forced air gas furnace and a very deep well. These differences will mean that the house with the forced air gas heat and deep well pump will have a far greater power demand for heating and water, but may have a smaller demand overall if the occupants of the other house are constantly wasting energy.

I don't mean to make the installation of an independent energy system seem ominous and overly complicated, but I use these examples to illustrate the fact that proper planning and the help of a qualified designer and installer can mean the difference between success and failure. At best it will mean a system that works poorly versus one that gives years of satisfying and independent service.

The term "independent energy system" usually implies the use of electrical energy derived from an independent source, but a really well thought out and logically planned system should be more than that. A household energy system will involve using more than one source of energy for more than one end use, and if energy efficiency and conservation techniques are not incorporated throughout the system, the advantages derived from an independent source may be reduced.

Heat your house sensibly

As an example of this, let's look at space heating. Unless your backwoods home is located in a very mild climate, just about everyone in North America needs to heat his or her house at some time.

A very common heat source for many is the woodstove. In most cases this is sufficient, but I see a lot of peo-

A good rule of thumb is that once you eliminate the use of electricity for space heating, water heating, and cooking (electric stoves), most any house can be operated successfully from a solar, wind, or hydro system.

ple who see heating with wood as somewhat of a free lunch.

Wood may be gathered for little or no money, but energy in the form of human effort must be expended to cut and gather it, as well as fuel used to run the chain saw and haul it. When you look at the time spent in gathering, cutting, hauling, and stacking wood—and if you value your time to do other things around your homestead—it makes sense to be sure your home is as energy efficient as possible.

This is especially true if you use blowers to move the heat in the home. A large blower fan (or one that runs a lot) can add up to a significant amount of electrical energy that your independent system must provide.

A very wise choice you can make when selecting a heating system regardless of the fuel source is to use hydronic or water-based heating, either a baseboard or a radiant in-floor system. The amount of electrical energy needed to move heated water throughout the house is a fraction of that needed to run a blower.

You will also eliminate the dry, dusty air and drafty cold spots associated with other systems.

In most cases the size of your solar, wind, or hydro system can be reduced by as much as 50%. Remember that you will be placing maximum demand on the system at a time of year when the energy source is at a low point when using a solar energy system. While we are on the subject of space heating, I must mention the use of a passive solar greenhouse as a heat source. There are few areas of the country where the greenhouse can't supply some portion of your space heating needs and give the added benefit of fresh vegetables almost year round or at least be a good place to start plants for the spring planting.

Luxuries and such

I can think of only a few people I have known who made the move to the backwoods and didn't take along most of their habits and desires acquired while living in the city or suburbs. Most of this baggage is very quickly shed when they find them impractical and for the most part unnecessary.

Things like Cadillacs and Volvos are soon traded for Chevy pickups or jeeps when it's discovered that hay bales and goats, barbed wire and fence posts, and muddy roads and potholes are real killers of fancy cars.

A few desires most country transplants still retain and really don't have to give up are "luxuries" like hot running water, refrigerators and freezers, entertainment centers, and computers.

A word of caution to anyone who is looking to install a solar, wind, or hydro system and wants to be sure that appliances you purchase for your move to the country are compatible. Don't buy any gas range that doesn't have a true electronic ignition system. Ask the salesman if it has what is called a glow bar igniter. If it does, keep looking. These igniters are real energy hogs and will be a real nuisance.

I can't think of any good reason why a solar hot water system shouldn't be included in a backwoods home, even if money is short. A few rolls of black plastic pipe laid out on the roof makes a handy heater. Reliable and super efficient refrigerators and freezers are available that run on most any independent energy system. The cost of these appliances is higher than average, but even a propane gas refrigerator is expensive to purchase and can burn as much as two gallons of propane per week. What happens when propane isn't available or you lack the money to purchase it?

Even the smallest independent energy system can power a stereo or TV.

Yearning for independence

All of the advice I have given so far has been directed toward helping make the use of independent energy a pleasant and, most importantly, a liberating and self reliant experience. This experience I feel is unique and can lead a person to look beyond energy needs to even greater self reliance.

It amazes me how many people move to the country to "get away from it all," but still have the umbilical cord of city or suburban life attached.

Recently I made a call on a cattle rancher several miles east of my place to see about installing some solar water pumping equipment and to talk with him about weaning his ranch from the grid.

It took half an hour of driving through endless stretches of sage brush and juniper trees to get to his ranch house. I could see the house from at least seven miles away, and what really struck me was the thin single electric line running to the ranch house on pole after pole. In reality this line probably ended at the turbines on the Columbia River about 150 miles to the north.

This rancher is fiercely independent and feels very little connection to the suburbs of distant cities, but because everything on his ranch depends on that one thin umbilical cord and the willingness of some corporation to supply the power, his real self reliance and independence is diminished.

He has decided that the technology of independent energy and the need to preserve and enhance his own independence have matured at about the same time. He will soon be free of the grid. Perhaps it's now your turn.

(Larry Elliott is the owner of Solar Tech, 27250 Willard Rd., Bend, Oregon, where he designs and installs independent energy sytems. Phone: 503-388-2053.) ∆

A BHM Writer's Profile

John Janetos

Janetos was living in Chicago at the time he wrote his last article for *Backwoods Home*. He was paying off his catfish farm before moving down to Arkansas, so that he wouldn't be burdened by a monthly payment while trying to get his business off the ground. It proved to be a good plan. When he moved to Arkansas he was able to devote all of his time to the business, and at present he is raising about 30,000 pounds of catfish per year while supplementing his income with other projects.

He has tried his hand at various types of livestock, cattle, goats, sheep, pigs, rabbits, and various types of poultry and waterfowl. The livestock wasn't worth the effort for the return he was getting, so he got rid of all the livestock. The birds were much less labor intensive, so he stuck with them.

Janetos now has a small commercial poultry and waterfowl hatchery business that does well. He raises several breeds of chickens, turkeys, guinea fowl, emus, geese, royal mute swans, black australian swans, several breeds of exotic ducks, and pea fowl. He also raises Rhodesian ridgeback dogs. These are lion hunting dogs from Africa. They make great guardian dogs for the homestead, in addition to being exceptional hunting dogs.

He raises and sells loofa sponges, fruit, and vegetables and he planted 100 black walnut trees, 25 pecan trees, and 200 Christmas trees 3 years ago. The Christmas trees are almost ready to sell.

He has been writing articles for various back to the land type magazines because he enjoys sharing his experiences with others who are interested in the country lifestyle. If anyone would like additional information on his projects, they can write to him at: Lazy J Ranch, P.O. Box 454, Maynard, Arkansas 72444

COUNTRY LIVING

A Backwoods Home Anthology

The great cow caper

By Edie L. Norling

When I found myself the owner of a 34-acre farm, all I had going for me was 48 years of city experience, the desire to become countrified, and about 32 "how-to" books. The closest I'd ever come to farm stock had been those Sunday afternoon "drive bys" that city dwellers occasionally engage in. I had always been fascinated by pastures filled with those peaceful looking creatures called cows, quietly standing around eating, waiting for someone to go by so they could all turn and stare! Why they do that is still a mystery to me.

Ignoring the advice of my current do-it-yourself book, which told me to start small, I decided that my chickens needed a companion. So the hunt for a housecow began.

Now being a city person I had no idea exactly what housecow meant, and even a few of my farmer neighbors gave me "A *what?*" on that one. I think that the word was made up by the author of my do-it-yourself cow book.

That very same book suggested starting out with a Jersey cow, unless you wanted to take milk baths, in which case a Holstein cow was called for.

Using my super-city thinking I went about this quest very logically: I bought papers from every town within my area code and pored over the farm sections.

Then one weekend there it was, the ad I had been waiting for:

For sale, Jersey cow, good producer.

Paper in hand I ran to the phone saying to myself, "I hope she isn't sold yet," and dialed as fast as my fingers would go. The phone was answered by this soft-spoken woman, and when I asked to speak to the owner of the cow, she giggled and said I had her.

I had intended to bring my "cow book" to the phone so I could ask some intelligent questions, but in my

excitement I'd left it in the other room so I just asked her to tell me about the prize that was for sale.

She informed me that the cow was "bred back" just as if I would know what that meant. In keeping with the tradition of the knowledgeable buyer, I never let on that I was quite puzzled. We made arrangements for me to come and meet this cow, and I frantically wrote down the directions.

I then called my son to have him borrow his mother-in-law's stock trailer and pick me up so we could go see. The fact that we had to drive 76 miles to see this cow is of no consequence, because at that point I would have gone 176 miles.

I should probably mention that I am lousy at directions. Whenever I write them down, I tend to use abbreviations that have yet to be invented. After driving around aimlessly for over an hour, we stopped and phoned for new directions.

We finally found the right road and the right drive. Around a curve was a pasture full of Jerseys, and yep, you guessed it, they all turned to stare at us as we drove by. They all looked identical to me and I wondered how would I recognize the "bred back" one?

As I went up a freshly painted porch to the door, I thought to myself that anyone who would keep their porch painted had to be honest and wouldn't sell me a bad cow.

I rang the bell and this very attractive gal in jeans and a blouse answered and said "You must be the lady that phoned for more directions a little while ago." I was too embarrassed to say anything so I just nodded, and she came out and invited me to join her in the feed lot.

There were about 20 Jersey cows in the feed lot and I asked which one was for sale. She pointed to one cow and said her name was "Wheezy." I looked to where she pointed and darned if I knew which one she meant. Remember when I said that all cows will stare at you? Well, they had done it again. She said the name a little

The Fifth Year

louder and one of the cows began to walk toward us.

She was beautiful, with big brown eyes and the longest eyelashes I had ever seen. It was love at first sight, and I knew that I had better ask my memorized cow questions before I forgot everything and said "I'll take her!"

I fired these at the owner one-by-one, and the answers came back just as fast. I was in awe of this gal—she seemed to know everything about cows.

Well, thinking that I had really impressed her with my questions, I blew it all by asking, "What is 'bred back'"? That one broke her up, and when she stopped laughing she explained that when a cow is bred back it simply means that she is "with calf." Well I thought, what a concept! That meant I would be getting two for the price of one, and that settled that, so I said "Sold!"

She led "Wheezy" out of the lot toward the trailer while I went to wake up my son. I told him that he needed to help get the cow into the trailer.

Now, experienced cows don't mind being handled, don't mind being milked, don't even mind being led around, but they do mind going up into a dark box, and this cow was no exception. Our planning was cut short when my son announced that he wasn't going to have anything to do with the back end of a cow, so he opted to go in the trailer and pull while the owner and I pushed from the back.

My first lesson in cows did not come from the do-it-yourself book but from hands-on experience. Before the owner could tell me not to push from directly behind the cow, I found out myself why it was a good idea to push from the side. My love affair with Wheezy almost ended right then and there as manure squished down my jeans to my white tennis shoes!

Well, we pushed and pulled for a few minutes with me squishing all the while and then the owner remembered that this particular cow did not like men. Since my son fell into this category, we decided that there was no way she was going to climb into a closed trailer with him. My son consented to trade places with me, figuring that the cow was out of ammunition. And, viola, it worked!

The enormity of what I had just done didn't hit me until we drove out of the drive . . . I had just spent $700 on a cow that I knew nothing about!

I must have made my son stop about 50 times on the way home so I could get out and check the trailer to see that my investment was still there. By the time we pulled into the farm yard at home, my son had given new meaning to the expression "mumbling under your breath." With all the stops it took us twice as long to get home. Boy, was I ever tired.

When we got out of the pickup it hit me: cows don't have reverse. How were we going to get her out with the halter on the other end? I asked my son for suggestions and all I got was a dirty look.

I have to admit that all the excitement and sense of adventure that I had started out with was at low tide and I did a little mumbling of my own. I stalked to the back of the trailer, threw open the door, squished my way past Wheezy, and untied the rope. I then grabbed each side of the halter and stared her right in the eyes and said, "Look cow, you're going to get out of this trailer one of two ways, on your own or as roast beef; it's your choice!"

Then I nudged her back and out she went, dragging me with her. Seems that she was very tired of being shut up in the trailer and very anxious to get out, because off she ran with me hanging on trying to apply the brakes.

I yelled to my son to help stop the cow, but he was laughing too hard. When he finally stopped laughing he helped, and the cow was installed in the barn.

Now some would say there are easier ways to purchase farm stock, but few would be quite so memorable as to be funny years later. Those famous do-it-yourself books have stood by me in many an experience, and I have blessed the authors many times over, but that is another story. ∆

Writing

I write at work
(changing the screen
when the boss comes this way),
While driving
(the steno pad
braced against the wheel by my left hand, I write with my
right, steering with my knees, flying down the freeway at
seventy-five miles per hour in a Honda Civic—Death himself
smiles as I go by),
In the shower
(chanting verse like a mantra to remember every word until I
can dry off and find a pencil and paper),
Making love
("Is there something wrong?" she asks. How can I tell her
my soul stepped out for a poem?)

John Earl Silveira
Ojai, CA

COUNTRY LIVING

A Backwoods Home Anthology

Lucky duck

By Dynah Geissal

Every year when the irrigation ditch is opened in order to flood the fields, we see a huge influx of raptors. Seeing five bald eagles sitting on fence posts near the barn is always a thrill to me. The five had been around for a couple of weeks when three decided to move on.

Apparently the pickings were getting slim, because after a couple more days, I noticed one eagle flying low over the creek. I watched for a few minutes, hoping to witness a successful hunt.

To my amazement, it began to hover over my domestic ducks. Previously, the raptors had shown no interest in any of my domestic fowl or livestock.

Suddenly it plummeted, and as it emerged from the water, it was indeed grasping one of my white ducks. As I watched, it beat its wings harder and harder as it attempted to carry off the duck. After a few minutes, it began to tire and the wings slowed.

It apparently decided to try another tactic and began to move toward the shore, towing the duck in its talons. The eagle succeeded in dragging the duck onto the bank, but by that time, it must have been exhausted. It let go of the duck and in an instant the duck had dived into the water.

The duck stayed under the water for as long as possible. I have read that eagles never kite or hover, but this eagle stayed over the spot where the duck was until the duck came up for air. The eagle plunged, but the duck was too fast. It ducked.

This spectacle went on for 15 minutes. Eventually the eagle flew away. I didn't see it again. Amazingly, the duck was unhurt as far as I could determine. ∆

A BHM Writer's Profile

Dory Hulburt

Raised in Chicago and small-town Wisconsin, Dory Hulburt was in her thirties when she moved to a farmstead in east-central Minnesota.

She is bemused to be, in mid-life, learning a new, and better, lifestyle. Who knew that a rooster could survive a window falling on its neck ... that a worm curled around a connection could stop a well pump from working ... that asparagus is best in spring and squash in fall!

After moving to the country, she was able to give up her day job and make a living writing. Things fall into place when you're following the right path.

The Fifth Year

FARM/GARDEN

Raising fish in the farm pond

By Steven F. Minner

One of the most fascinating and rewarding aspects of pond ownership is stocking and raising fish—either for fun or as a food source. Stocking and raising fish in a farm pond is not difficult, but a working knowledge of the most common fish species is necessary to ensure a thriving fish population over the long term. Special attention must be given to the size of the pond (and therefore, the number of fish it can support), minimum and maximum depths, available habitat for the fish, and personal or family preferences about the different species as food sources.

Most farm ponds are stocked with varying combinations of the following fish species: channel catfish, hybrid bluegill, largemouth bass, black crappie, and white amur grass carp. Other species which are less popular but equally suited for introduction into farm ponds include redear sunfish, Florida bass, and the hybrid striped bass (a cross between a male white bass and a female striped bass). Commercial fish suppliers, state hatcheries, and county extension services can provide information about stocking rates and combinations of these less popular species.

Catfish are generally considered the best food species in the pond because they grow fast, are durable and clean, and do not prey on smaller fish of other species. Although there are many species of catfish, including white, blue, channel, black bullhead, Yellow bullhead, and brown bullhead, channel catfish have become the most popular species for farm ponds. Channel "cats" are greenish-gray in color with deeply forked tails. They have no scales, and as "fingerlings" have spots which generally disappear with age. Catfish have four pairs of "whiskers"—actually called *barbels*—which help them find food.

Among their most distinguishing (and dangerous!) features are the bony spines in front of their pectoral and dorsal fins. I accidentally stepped on a small catfish and had a spine literally

Channel catfish

staple my shoe to my foot. After removing the shoe, about ½ inch of the spine was still imbedded in my foot. Therefore, I recommend extreme caution when handling a catfish or fishing for them. When caught, their spines become a real weapon as they struggle to escape. Because the spines can easily puncture human flesh, a pair of thick, leather working gloves is necessary when cleaning or taking catfish off the hook.

Catfish feed naturally on insects, frogs, and minnows, and without supplemental feeding, grow one half to one pound each year. Supplemental feeding with commercial feed will double that growth rate. Some species of catfish can reach weights of 400 pounds, although pond-raised fish don't reach that size. A 40-pound pond-raised catfish is rare.

The average life span for a channel catfish is six to seven years, with some fish occasionally living more than 10 years. At weights of even one to three pounds, they are a real challenge on lightweight tackle, but once landed, their white meat is more than worth the fight.

With commercial food and clean, adequately aerated water, channel catfish develop excellent flavor, and two to three "average" size catfish (three to four pounds) with trimmings make a complete meal for a family of four. Catfish fingerlings (four to six inches long) cost $33 per hundred in my area of the country from a commercial supplier; six- to eight-inch fingerlings cost $45 per hundred and are, in my opinion, worth the extra cost, as they are that much closer to harvest weight and less susceptible to predation by larger fish. Channel catfish can also be obtained from many state game and fish commission hatcheries at considerably less cost than the commercial prices quoted above.

Catfish do not generally reproduce in ponds because of a lack of suitable habitat for laying eggs. In the wild, catfish lay eggs in tree stumps and under rock ledges and guard the opening to prevent other fish from eating the eggs. To encourage reproduction in an otherwise open farm pond, suitable habitat must be provided. Otherwise, periodic restocking will be

Floating catfish cage

necessary as the mature fish are harvested.

I purchased plastic five-gallon buckets from an ice cream company for a dollar each and cut oblong holes in the lids just large enough for an egg-laying female to enter. We put several small rocks in each bucket and then sank them in our pond to provide breeding habitat for our catfish. We've seen the first catfish "yearlings" in our pond, so we know our "catfish condominiums" (as my kids call them) are working. If buckets or other artificial spawning containers are used, they can be periodically checked for the presence of eggs. They should be checked late in the morning, since most spawning occurs at night; checking in the morning will minimize disruption to the laying fish.

The spawning containers should be checked quickly and the egg mass, if present, should not be exposed to direct sunlight. Experts recommend that spawning containers for catfish be placed in four to five feet of water for best results. In a pond that does not have a year-round water source, spawning containers must initially be placed in slightly deeper water to account for summer droughts and lower water levels during hot weather.

Raising catfish in cages

Some pond owners opt to raise catfish in floating cages. The obvious benefit of this method is the ease of monitoring growth rates and ultimately harvesting the mature fish—they are simply scooped out of the cage with a large net. The disadvantages are an increased chance of infection and disease (from overstocking and the stress of confinement), susceptibility to poachers (the two-legged type), the need to have a boat to check the cage, and a requirement to feed the fish daily.

However, with proper stocking rates and close monitoring, raising catfish in cages can be very successful. Catfish cages must be anchored with only one anchor so that the cage can swing freely with the wind. Otherwise, a strong crosswind can overturn a cage anchored in two directions. Walter Robinson, a research assistant at the University of Arkansas at Pine bluff, has designed one of the best floating catfish cages I've seen; his plans are included as part of this article for those interested in raising fish in cages.

Bluegill

Largemouth bass

Hybrid bluegill

Hybrid bluegill (a cross between a male bluegill and a female green sunfish) vary in color—even in the same pond—and range in color from pale yellow-green to almost black with some having orange or orange and blue tints. Most have dark vertical bars and a darker area at the base of the dorsal fin.

Hybrid bluegill will grow four to five times faster than the normal bluegill strain because they continue to feed actively after the water turns cold. Hybrid bluegills will mature at a weight of two to two and a half pounds. They are strong and aggressive and will bite the hook when other species won't. Once hooked, the hybrid bluegill provides a challenge for young and experienced anglers alike—especially on ultralight tackle.

A national commercial fish supplier sells 100 hybrid bluegill fingerlings (one to three inches long) for $40. Like other species, many state hatcheries sell hybrid bluegill stock for considerably less. Prices vary, so it is best to shop around.

Largemouth bass

The largemouth bass is unquestionably the most popular gamefish in North America and an exciting species to stock in the farm pond.

Largemouth bass are greenish in color with a silver underside. Their most distinguishing characteristic is a darker lateral stripe down each side. They thrive in ponds with good water quality and prefer quiet water rather than streams.

Largemouth bass eat insects, frogs, salamanders, minnows, and small fish, but have been known to feast occasionally on small snakes and even low-flying birds that venture too close to the pond. Largemouth bass grow one half to three quarters of a pound per year with an adequate food source, and can reach a weight of two pounds or more (and lengths of 10 to 14 inches) within three years of stocking.

Black crappie

They are very effective in controlling other, unwanted fish species and may live 10 years or longer.

Largemouth bass are relatively expensive to purchase from commercial sources; 100 fingerlings (one to three inches long) sell for $73 in my area. Largemouth bass are also available from many state fish hatcheries for much less.

Black crappie

Black crappie are the largest of the "pan fish," i.e., bluegill, hybrid bluegill, redear sunfish, longear sunfish, and pumpkinseed. They do very well in farm ponds but must never be stocked in ponds less than two acres in size. Optimally, they should only be stocked in ponds larger than five acres. They reproduce easily and should be stocked with largemouth bass to offset excessive reproduction.

Black crappie are silvery black in color and covered with a pattern of small, dark scales. In some parts of the country, black crappie are called "calico bass." They are aggressive, bite easily and are especially popular with young anglers. The average growth rate for this species is one fourth to

Per acre stocking rates

(Without supplemental feeding)

	All species	Bass & bluegill	Catfish only
Amur grass carp*	3- 15	3- 15	3- 15
Largemouth bass	100	150	---
Hybrid bluegill	400	600	---
Channel catfish	200	---	300
Black crappie**	50	---	---
Flathead minnows***	10 lbs.	12 lbs.	10 lbs.

(With supplemental feeding)

	All species	Bass & bluegill	Catfish only
Amur grass carp*	3- 15	3- 15	3- 15
Largemouth bass	100	200	---
Hybrid bluegill	600	1,000	---
Channel catfish	400	---	700
Black crappie**	50	---	---
Flathead minnows***	10 lbs.	16 lbs.	10 lbs.

* White amur grass carp are stocked according to need. Ponds with more aquatic vegetation will require more grass carp for vegetation control.

** Black crappie should never be stocked in ponds of less than two acres in size.

*** Flathead minnows are recommended as a forage base for all other species.

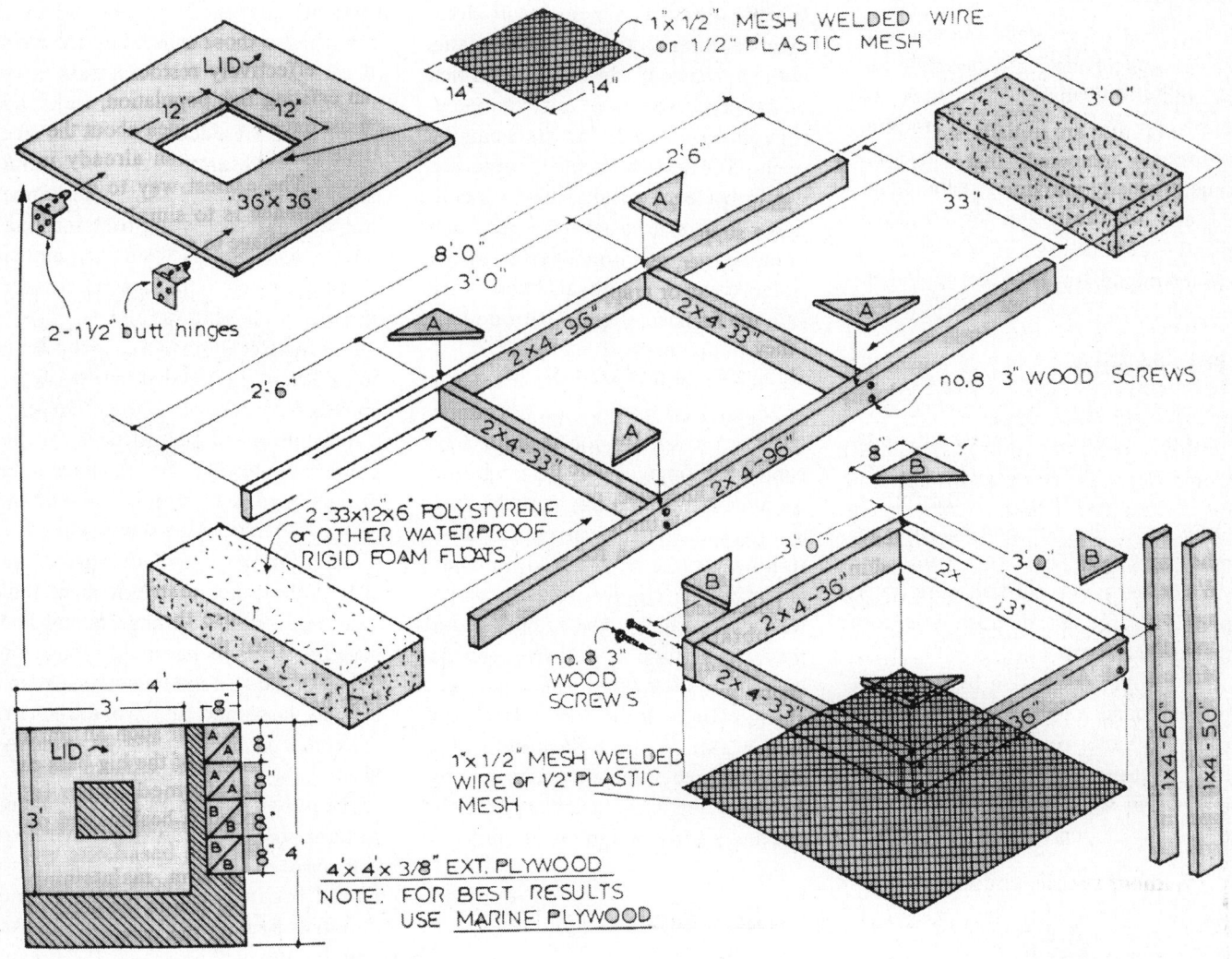

Parts and dimensions for constructing a floating catfish cage

one half pound per year; they mature at approximately two to three pounds.

Black crappie have a normal life span of two to three years but occasionally live as long as seven years. Prices vary for black crappie fingerlings—again, depending on the source—but as of this writing, 100 fingerlings (one to three inches long) are selling for $74 in central Arkansas from a major commercial supplier.

White amur grass carp

White amur grass carp control excessive aquatic vegetation by consuming three to five times their body weight each day. White amur grass carp do not prey on other fish species because they lack jaw teeth. For that same reason, they must tear plant vegetation from the top downward rather than rooting it up and muddying the pond.

Grass carp are exceptionally strong swimmers and are attracted to flowing water; fish barriers (preferably made of plastic netting) should be installed to keep them in the pond. My neighbor welded a removable wire "basket" (with very small netting) that fits into the end of our overflow pipe as a barrier for our grass carp. For ponds with a spillway, an inexpensive barrier can be constructed with steel fence posts, a livestock (or pig) panel and tightly woven wire poultry netting—as long as the gaps in the wire will not allow a fish to pass through.

There are two varieties of white amur grass carp: the diploid white amur and the triploid white amur. The diploid variety can reproduce but generally doesn't do so in ponds because of a lack of optimal breeding conditions. The triploid variety is genetically altered and cannot reproduce. These fish can reach weights of 25 to 40 pounds in ponds. White amur grass carp sell for three to five dollars each and should be six to eight inches long when stocked.

Stocking rates

The goal of an effective stocking program is a balanced fish population. For initial stocking, the process is simple—just adhere to proper stocking ratios and stock all species at the same time. The table provides recommended initial stocking rates for a one-acre pond—depending on whether the owner intends to provide supplemental fish food.

Tempering

When fish are initially stocked, they must be "tempered," that is, they must be gradually introduced to the temperature of their new environment. Otherwise, the fish can be shocked and may not survive. When we stocked our pond, our fish were transported in large, plastic trash cans from the state hatchery.

We tempered the fish by gradually pouring pond water into the trash cans until the water reached the temperature of the water in the pond. One major fish supplier recommends that one quart of pond water be added to the bags which the fish are shipped in. Water can be added in one quart increments at three to five minute intervals until the water in the bag reaches that of the pond. After the water temperature is equalized, the fish can be released. The fish should be released gently by lowering the shipping container or bag fully into the pond and opening it or turning it over on its side. To avoid additional shock, small fish should never be dumped or thrown into the pond.

If the pond has never been stocked or contains no mature bass or crappie, there are no special considerations for habitat for fingerlings—although they should be fed floating "catfish" food as a supplement to their regular diets. If, however, the pond already contains larger bass or crappie, suitable habitat for the fingerlings must be provided or they will be little more than expensive baitfish for the mature fish.

Fingerlings should be introduced into a part of the pond containing brush and other aquatic plants for protection. Otherwise, cedar trees can be cut and sunk throughout the pond to provide protection for the fingerlings from mature fish.

Discarded Christmas trees are easy to obtain, free and can be easily weighted with a rock or brick and some wire (if necessary) to ensure they do not resurface. We cut several large cedar trees and sunk them in the deepest parts of our pond for fish habitat, and judging from the number of fish we catch in those areas, fish are attracted to those trees.

To effectively restock a pond with an existing fish population, the owner must have a good idea about the relative numbers of fish already in the pond. The easiest way to determine this balance is to simply go fishing. (Honey, I have to go fishing again. It's a tough job but somebody's got to do it!) If the pond is balanced, it will yield both small and large bream and bass in excess of ten inches long. On the other hand, if the bream are exceptionally large and the bass are small, the pond probably has far too many bass.

The most common stocking problem in farm ponds is an overabundance of the regular strain of bluegill (also called bream in many parts of the country) because they reproduce so readily. When this occurs, the bream will be exceptionally small and the few bass in the pond will be very large. In ponds with such an imbalance, catching one of the big bass can "lure" the uninformed owner into thinking the pond is healthy and producing big fish.

Over the long term, maintaining a proper balance of fish in the pond will depend largely on the owner's ability to keep accurate records about the number of fish caught annually (including size), the species and number restocked and the amount of commercial food fed.

With the exception of black crappie, all the species discussed in this article can be stocked year-round. Black crappie are more sensitive to heat and

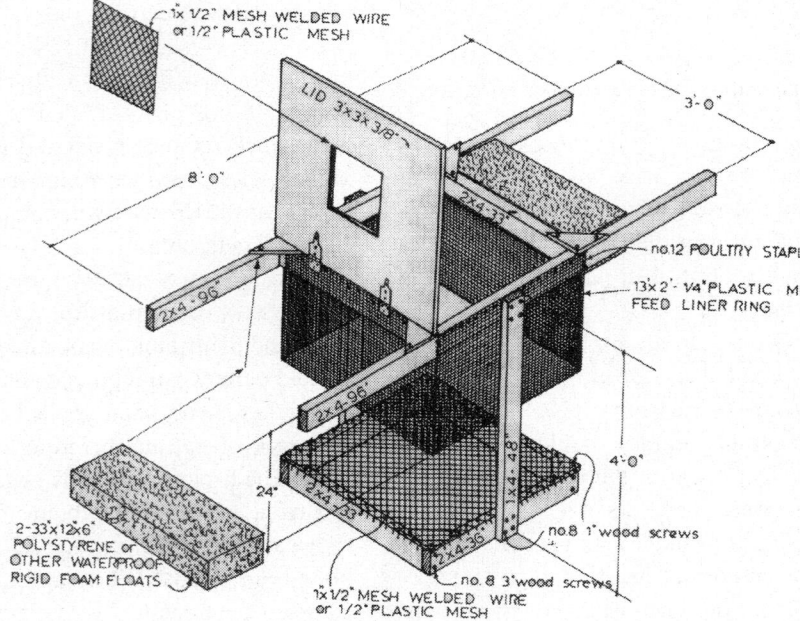

Cage near completion

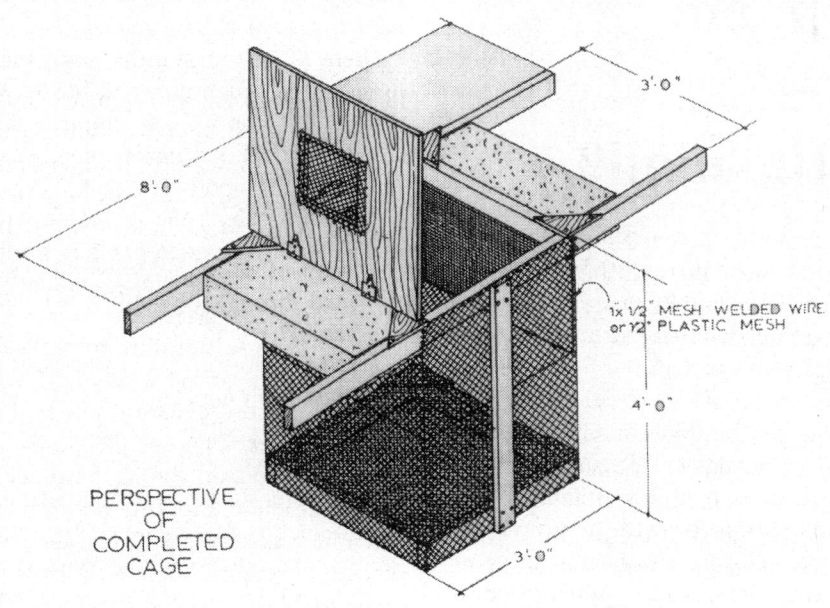

Perspective of completed cage

must be stocked only in the fall, winter, and early spring when both the weather and water are cool.

Feeding your fish

In the spring or after the water reaches approximately 65°, fish can be fed floating feed. During the winter months, however, fish are much less active (due to slower metabolism rates) and will not seek out floating food as readily as they do when the water is warmer. Therefore, they should be fed "sinker" food during winter months. Commercial fish food costs seven to nine dollars per 50 pound bag, depending on the time of year purchased and the brand. I've compared most of the commercial brands in my area and found prices can vary as much as $2.50 per bag, even though all seem to have about the same protein content (32%). Our fish are not discerning enough to know the difference between the seven dollar a bag variety and the well known "Fish Chow" brand that costs in excess of nine dollars in my area.

Even if commercial food is fed, fathead minnows should be periodically stocked as a forage base for largemouth bass and crappie. They should be stocked in new ponds and restocked in established ponds every six months—unless schools of minnows are seen regularly in shallow water around the pond's perimeter. Fathead minnows range from olive to pale tan in color with non-distinctive black markings; they mature at approximately three inches in length. There are approximately 250 minnows per pound and they sell commercially for six to nine dollars per pound depending on the supplier.

Fish (and especially channel catfish) can be easily trained to respond to a feeding "call." One major fish supplier recommends that fish be fed two cups of feed per day for six to seven days in a row—even if the fish do not initially find the food. After that, the fish should feed actively and should be fed all the feed that they can completely eat in 15 to 20 minutes.

We trained our fish differently. My dad and I initially offered them two or three, three-pound coffee cans full of commercial fish food. Just prior to broadcasting the food from our small dock, we lowered the end of a four-foot metal pipe into the water and tapped on the other end with a hammer about eight to ten times. Call it good luck or Fish Psychology 101, but it worked for us—beginning the second day we did it—and now our fish come quickly when called for feeding. We have found that fish prefer to eat the same time of day and at the same place in the pond. Also, a regular feeding routine helps in training fish to eat all the food they are offered.

Turtle problems

Turtles pose special problems for fish owners. They love fish food and unfortunately, respond to a "feeding call" just as fish do. If left unchallenged, turtles become very bold and can easily eat 10% of all commercial fish food. Over a feeding season, that can be expensive.

Turtles sometimes eat small fish, but more critically they disturb the beds in shallow water in which fish lay eggs, and therefore interfere with natural fish reproduction. Also, turtles compete with fish for oxygen. The easiest way to eliminate turtles is with a small caliber rifle or pistol. If that method isn't an option, commercial turtle traps are available. These floating traps allow turtles to be captured alive for release elsewhere.

For many folks, the ultimate reward for stocking the pond is a meal of fresh fish with all the trimmings. For others, it is simply the pleasure of wetting a hook as the sun goes down and feeling an aggressive fish tugging on the other end of the pole. And, for yet others—the author included—there is nothing like the daily fascination of seeing big, healthy fish feeding and thriving in the farm pond. Δ

How ya gonna keep 'em down on the farm — after they've seen the mall?

By Robert L. Williams

In the May/June issue of *Backwoods Home Magazine*, there was a letter from Cindy Gibson of Knoxville, Tennessee. Mrs. Gibson wanted to hear from parents who had ideas on how to keep the young folks happy while living away from malls and crowds.

Well, Mrs. Gibson, the problem you are addressing is a vital one to anyone who wants to enjoy a life far removed from city problems of crime, vandalism, and other unsavory elements. And while my family does not profess to have all of the answers, we have found workable solutions.

We have a 17-year-old son, Robert, who is dedicated to staying at home, even though he has full permission to come and go as he pleases (within reason, of course). He has available to him a pickup truck, car, and money—in case he wants to go off and sow his wild oats. Happily, although he has a very full social life, he truly enjoys—and prefers—staying at home.

Why would any young man prefer the company of old fogies (like us) when the real "scene" is only a few miles away? Why would he prefer the company of adults to that of his peers? And why would any young man prefer working to seeing a movie with his friends?

To get some answers (who knows what *the* answers are?) we started by asking our friends who have also found that their young ones actually enjoy staying at home. We are happy to share their responses with *Backwoods Home* readers.

The first consideration, as we see it, is to take proper steps to make home an attractive place. Now, how does one do that? By painting, adding a room, or installing a pool? The best answer that we found was to make the people who live in the home attractive.

This can be done in several ways. First, if parents are constantly cheerful, cooperative, understanding, and simply fun to be with, many young people will want to remain in the company of such people. When a child (and throughout this article the term "child" refers not to a tot but to the offspring of the parents in the home) finds that when he makes a mistake, the parents are willing to help clean up the mess or help him prevent repeating the mistake, he will find that they are really pretty nice old coots.

If the kid (no matter what the age) breaks a dish, scratches the furniture, or challenges your equanimity in any of the infinite ways kids have of shattering anvils and dispositions, keep under control and handle the incident with no more reaction than is necessary. Don't scream and yell. Don't lose control. Don't try make him feel that he is a criminal. And don't point out how flawless you were at his age.

When the glass of tea spills, say something like, "Kid, this is the biggest mess I have seen since I accidentally dumped dishwater in the preacher's lap at the church social." Then grab a cloth and start to clean up the tea. Toss him one so that he can help. By admitting that you, too, are less than perfect, he won't have to feel that he is expected to be ideal.

If he goofs on some special activity, rather than showing him all his defects, point out that baseball, for instance, is the Great American Game because it is the one sport where you can foul up (pun intended) two out of three times and still be great.

There is an old popular song that urges us to accentuate the positive, and by doing so we can eliminate the negative. If the kid makes one *A* and five *F*s on his report card, make such a positive fuss about the *A* that he will reason that if one good grade is worth so much, how much more would *more* good grades be worth?

Don't keep telling him how he is failing by comparison with you. Keep in mind the old chestnut about the father who asked his son the Pertinent Question: "Son, do you have any idea what Abraham Lincoln was doing when he was your age?" And the son replied, "No, but I know what he was doing when he was *your* age."

Be positive in all matters, when humanly possible. When the gremlins and glitches strike, stress to your child (and to yourself) the quote by Henry David Thoreau: "Let us spend one day as deliberately as nature, and not be thrown off the track by every nutshell and mosquito's wing that falls upon the rails." Imagine a huge locomotive being de-railed by something as tiny as a mosquito's wing. Yet we allow matters of infinite smallness to disrupt our mornings, our weeks, and our lives. And we then pass on the discontent to all those around us.

Another major element of making the home attractive is that of pleasant responsibilities. Chores are necessary, and more often than not, several people must complete the work.

If our children rebel at the idea of working in the yard, garden, or house, possibly we have given the work a highly negative association by complaining so much about it. We have all heard the bit that starts, "Every day of my life I work my fingers to the bone, slaving for you, and what thanks do I get?" No one knows what comes next, because kids automatically tune us out at that point. If the responsibility is pleasant, there is no need to use that line of faulty persuasion.

Building a storage house for tools and equipment

But how can chores be made pleasant? First, why not, if time and circumstances permit, work *with* the child rather than send him out to do the work alone. Let it be understood that if he will help you with the dishes, you will help him with the wood chopping.

When mowing the grass, if the job is dreary, cut sections at a time. Set short-range goals in all things. Set your sights on the big weed 20 feet ahead. When doing the dishes, talk together.

This does not mean lecturing. Ask the child questions that are provoked by positive and wholesome interest, not nosiness. Ask the child what his suggestions are. Ask him what he prefers to do that day in order to make chores more pleasant. Show him that you really do care about his ideas and suggestions.

Earlier I mentioned showing respect for our children. Nothing turns a child off faster than the attitude that we often give that says, "Yeah, yeah. You kids know it all. Well, you want to know something? If brains were dynamite, you couldn't blow your nose."

Why not take another tack and say, "Good thinking, Humbert! Your idea is better than mine. Let's try it and see how it works."

Then make it work. Let him see that he did in fact have the solution all along. Help him to realize that you not only respect his suggestions and ideas but that you respect him as a human being, as a friend, and as a child and member of the family.

Keep violence out of the home at all times. If we hit a grown man or woman, we have committed a crime. But if we hit a child, we say we are disciplining him. Why hit anyone, when there are happier ways of solving a problem?

We have a rule in our house that we will not say anything to each other that we would not say to our worst enemies. Think about it. If our worst enemy spills the iced tea, we will assure him that it's perfectly all right and no harm was done. If the person we love most in this world spills the tea, we leap all over him in anger and frustration. Isn't there something wrong with that picture?

Now, what about practical and workable solutions? When we needed a riding lawn mower, we found the one we wanted and made plans to buy it. Robert, age 14 at the time, looked lustfully at the shiny new machine, and we asked if he would like the new mower to be his very own personal equipment. He was delighted, and he liked it so much that he couldn't wait for the grass to grow so he could cut it. And he still has that mower, and he performs all the maintenance and repairs on it, and a blade of grass in our yard doesn't have any more chance than a sheet of clean paper in Steven King's house.

When our house was destroyed by a tornado and we set out to build a new one ourselves, using only a chain saw and a few basic tools, we asked our son to help with the design of the house. We let him pick where his room would be, and we also let him choose the wall covering, light fixtures, furniture, and arrangements. The result was that he worked like a dynamo on the house. After all, it was his house, too, not just ours.

When the house was built, he wanted a log tool shed for his own equipment. My back was breaking from sawing logs for the house, but we cheerfully went to work. And when he saw how interested we were in helping him have the things he wanted, he

Working together

became equally interested in helping us to realize our personal goals. (And now that he has his own gardening supplies, he can't wait to work in the garden as well as the yard!)

Another suggestion that we have found to be really useful is to make the necessary work pay off. In money, I mean.

When we needed a deck, I told Robert (then 14) that when the deck was built, we'd write and sell a story about how to build a classy deck for nearly nothing. I told him he could have a percentage of the money from the article to put into a savings account, so that when he was ready for his own truck he'd have a good start made on paying for it.

Since that time he has been my official writing assistant. He takes the photos, does some of the writing, helps with addressing envelopes, and mails the packages . . . and we split the money.

I asked him to come up with a way to split wood that would cause it to burn slower, put out more heat, and last longer. It was a tough assignment, but he jumped all over it. And now he has a method of splitting wood that requires no extra work, but we get up to twice or even four times the heat and burn life from wood that we were getting earlier. This, of course, means using less wood, which means less work, and he has now completed an article which will be mailed to *Backwoods Home Magazine* shortly. If the magazine buys it, the money will be used for the truck fund.

We all like to hike, and we decided that hiking could also be profitable. So we made arrangements with a newspaper and with a small magazine to write stories about favorite hiking spots. My wife Elizabeth does some of the writing, and Robert and I do the rest. The result is that we have earned literally thousands of dollars and now have a contract for a book on our favorite hikes.

We read books together. We talk about the books. We relate the characters to people we know. We apply historical problems to our own community or even our personal lives. The result is that Robert recalls with astonishing detail the events that occurred in historical settings or in famous novels.

When he studies physics, we find practical applications for what he has learned. We travel together, and the trips are more meaningful because we have read about the sites (and sights) we will see and we know that the trips will pay, not cost us.

Perhaps most important, we stress that our house belongs to all three of us, and Robert has as much right to invite his friends to visit as we have to invite ours. He has the right to plant his own garden, and we help him, just as he helps us.

As to family regulations, I told Robert years ago that he could say anything he heard me say and do anything he saw me do (unless there was physical danger involved). We believe in setting examples, not in insisting on standards that we cannot hope to reach. We have our friends in, and we visit in their homes. Robert has his set of friends and looks forward to spending time with them each week. It is understood that if we find fault with his friends, he can find fault with ours.

So, in brief, here it is: make work pleasant; make the home (and its residents) attractive; create mutually profitable outlets for work and recreation; allow each person his private space; let everyone be a contributing member of the family and a sharing member in the rewards; demonstrate trust and understanding; show patience and help rather than becoming critical and irritated; just like each other; and encourage positive traits.

Most of all, let love and mutual respect for each other and for each other's rights and privileges set the tone for the family life. Encourage self-reliance, creativity, and initiative.

These suggestions are not all-inclusive; and they will not solve every problem. But they have worked wonders for us. ∆

Father and son on the rail

| INDEPENDENT ENERGY |

Independent energy runs *Backwoods Home Magazine*

By Dave Duffy

Backwoods Home Magazine is a business situated in the forested mountains of Southern Oregon, about five miles from the nearest utility power line. Because we are so remote, it was more cost effective for us to generate our own electricity rather than pay the utility company to bring lines in. Here's a look at the way we generate and use electricity.

Our requirements

We needed enough stable electricity to run a 2500-square-foot building housing our five computers, printers, scanners, and other equipment necessary to put out a magazine.

Computers are sensitive to surges and dips of electricity, so the stability of the power was a main concern.

Our main computer, a two-gigabyte Novell Local Area Network (LAN) file server, has the capacity to store 154,000 camera-ready magazine pages, which is equal to 1,540 issues of the magazine, which means we have enough storage capacity to keep us in business for 256 years. Just thought I'd throw that in for all you lifetime subscribers.

Since I don't like the noise of a generator, and since this site lacks the adequate water and wind resources to produce enough electricity, I decided to install a photovoltaic (solar panel) system with a diesel generator backup.

We have about $20,000 invested in our system, but it is fairly large. My nearest neighbor, by contrast, has only a few thousand dollars invested in his modest home system, but it is adequate for his needs.

Our system consists of 24 photovoltaic panels—12 Hoxan and 12 Solarex. Solarex and Hoxan are among the excellent American, Japanese, and German modules on the market. Most of the brands are very durable, and it is fairly typical in the industry to give a 20-year warranty with them. As a precaution, however, we mounted the panels on towers within our garden area so Annie's horse, Buddy, and the company donkey, Donna Quixote, wouldn't bump them as they mowed the meadow.

Tracking the sun

Because you can significantly increase the power output of solar panels by keeping them perpendicular to the sun, we mounted our modules on two solar trackers that follow the sun as it travels its east to west course throughout the day. The 12 Solarex modules comprise a solar array that sit on a Zomeworks tracker, and the Hoxan modules make up an array on a WattSun tracker.

The trackers work differently. The WattSun tracker uses an electronic sensor that controls motor-driven actuators that move the tracker on both its horizontal and vertical axes, keeping its photovoltaic array perpendicular to the sun. The sensor is powered by a small battery pack that is charged by the panels.

The Zomeworks tracker uses no motors or sensors, but relies instead on two steel tubes partially filled with Freon that are mounted on the east and west sides of the frame. The frame is angled towards the east-west path of the sun, and it works by gravity. Reflector shades on the outside of the tubes cause the morning sun to shine only on the western tube, causing the Freon to boil and rise in the tube, thus making the bottom of the east tube heavier and forcing the tracker to swing so the array is facing the rising sun. Throughout the day the heat of the sun keeps the Freon alternately boiling and rising in one tube, while liquefying and falling in the other, letting the weight at the bottom of the tubes orient the tracker to the sun. Is that clever, or what!

Inverters and voltage

Only a few years ago many people with their own independent energy system stored their power in 12-volt batteries, so had to use 12-volt lights and other 12-volt appliances, which were often both expensive and poorly made. But with the development in recent years of reliable inverters, which are devices that convert 12 or 24 or 48-volt battery voltage into the standard 110-volt house electricity the utility company provides, most people who build their own independent energy system today include an inverter.

We use the new Trace 4000-watt pure sine wave inverter, which is a true marvel of engineering. Only a few months prior to writing this article, *BHM* operated on two Trace modified sine wave inverters, which are great inverters and were standards in the industry, but its modified sine wave was not acceptable to our LaserJet printer, on which we produce camera-ready pages.

To solve this problem, we had purchased a DeskJet printer, which was much slower and less clear than the LaserJet but which accepted the modified sine wave. We used it to print rough drafts of articles. But for camera-ready copy we still needed the LaserJet so had to install a special plug near the printer that led to the diesel generator shed outside. Every time we ran that LaserJet, we had to fire up the generator. A real pain!

Batteries

The batteries for an independent energy system are the weak part of the system, considering how reliable all the other components are. You need large batteries—golf cart type or larger—to store power properly. We use 16 Trojan L-16s, which have a total storage capacity of 1400 amp-hours. In layman's terms, we have enough juice to run all our equipment in our 2500-square-foot building for about two days. Both our photovoltaic array and our batteries are wired at 24 volts.

If the sun doesn't shine for about two days, however, we must start up our backup diesel generator to recharge the batteries and provide us with power.

Diesel generator

We use an 8000-watt China Diesel generator as a backup. We chose a China Diesel because, like most other diesels, it runs at a slow rpm (revolutions per minute) and is built like a truck diesel, that is, for the long haul.

We use the China Diesel intermittently during winter. It is located in a sound-proof generator shack, which we built according to Skip Thomsen's book, More Power to You.

The key to making any generator live a long and productive life is to change the oil frequently, and we do. Like your automobile, changing the oil is 80% of the maintenance that needs to be done.

Controls

One convenient piece of equipment installed in the battery room is an Ananda Power Center, a power control and distribution cabinet from Ananda Power Technologies. It contains the PV system controls, metering, and overcurrent protection in a prewired, preassembled, tested, and certified cabinet for a safe and code-approved installation.

A handy feature of the Ananda cabinet is a digital amp-hour meter which lets you know at a glance just how much electricity you have taken out of or supplied to your batteries. It's an important feature that allows close monitoring of the condition of the batteries, which is important to extending their life.

Conserving

It's easy enough to generate electricity using an independnet energy system like photovoltaics, but it's important to conserve it.

The sensible independent energy system uses batteries to store the electricity for later use. But the typical large batteries like the L-16s we use only give a few days storage. If the sun doesn't shine for a week, you're going to run out of stored electricity.

So if you're going to be successful with an independent energy system, you have to use lights and other appliances that do not suck up all your electricity fast.

That means using fluorescent lights. They use 20% of the power of their incandescent counterparts, and their life expectancy is measured in years rather than months. We must have 50 fluorescent lights installed here.

It also means non-electric heat; we use two air-tight, high tech woodstoves that burn very clean.

And it means using sensible refrigeration, since the typical household refrigerator accounts for 20% of the power consumption in the home. Good alternatives are the new energy-efficient electrics or the excellent new propane models, which we have opted for.

So that is our story in a nutshell. It is a brief and fairly superficial overview, and it is only one of many ways to arrange your indepenent energy system. This issue and the dozens of articles we've printed in the past contain many variations of independent energy use. ∆

---

*Restore
the
Bill of Rights
with*

FULLY
INFORMED
JURIES

Find out how ordinary people, as trial jurors, can repair years of legislated special-interest damage to our rights, simply by saying No to bad laws!

Phone

1-800-TEL-JURY

for a free
Jury Power
Information Kit!

AMERICANA/HISTORY

Looking behind the *Declaration of Independence*

By John Silveira

The phone rang and I counted the rings as I raced across the house to answer it. Two...three...four rings. I got to it just before the answering machine picked it up. "Hello?"

"Just talked with Duffy," a man said. It was a familiar voice but I couldn't quite place it. "He says you went and quit your job."

"Mac," I yelled. "How're you doing. I haven't seen you in months." It was O. E. MacDougal, the poker player who's good friends with the fellow who owns and publishes *Backwoods Home Magazine*, Dave Duffy.

"I'm fine. It's nice to be back. So, is it true? You quit your job?"

"Yeah."

It was true. I'd just quit my job the Friday before. Not my job with *BHM*. I'd spent the last 15 years working for various defense contractors in Southern California. Fifteen years I can never have back. But that's over, now. I'm out of it.

"Kind of your own declaration of independence," he said.

"That's a nice way to put it."

"It's appropriate for the next issue."

"What d'ya mean?" I glanced at the calendar. The July/August issue was coming up.

"The Fourth of July is coming up," he said.

"Oh, yeah, Independence Day."

"So, what are you doing today? I'm going to be up your way. I was thinking of dropping by if you're not too busy."

"Come on up. I'd love to see you."

"Got coffee?"

"I'm putting the kettle on, now."

"Then I'll see you when I get there."

He hung up.

I went back to my computer. I still work for *BHM* part of the time. Half-time, to be precise. The rest of the time I'm trying to make it as a writer.

I know, lots of people have tried to do this before, and starved. But I have something going for me most of them didn't—I'm 20 pounds overweight. I'll last weeks before I starve to death.

Half an hour later, I was working on my novel and I heard a familiar rap at my front door. I went to answer it and there stood Mac, a bag of tortilla chips in one hand and a plastic bowl in the other.

I stepped aside. "Come on in. I just put the kettle on."

He went into my kitchen and I followed.

"I brought some salsa," he said.

He sat down at my kitchen table and one of my cats, Doggy, was in his lap in seconds. Doggy doesn't like anybody. She doesn't even like me. Mac stroked her a couple of times and she put her head down and went to sleep.

"I think this is where she left off the last time I was here," he said.

"You've been among the missing for the last few months," I said. "Where've you been?"

"Travelling." He plays in a lot of private poker games here in Southern California, but often he travels and we don't see him for months.

I moved some of my stuff off the table as he told me where he'd been on the East Coast. He played up in Boston. Fished in Florida. Did a lot of sight seeing. He likes museums. Went to several symphonies in various cities.

"How've you been?" he asked.

I nodded. "Okay."

"Making your bills?"

I cringed.

He smiled.

"So, you're going to try to make it as a writer."

"That's what I'm trying to do. Everyone's telling me I'm crazy."

"What are they saying?"

"Oh...they're telling me the odds are against me."

"They are," he laughed. "They're overwhelmingly against you. They're terrible."

My heart sunk. "Do you really think so?"

"I know so."

He opened the bag of chips and the plastic bowl. "This is great salsa," he said and added, "But writing's what you want to do. So, do it."

"Are you being sarcastic?"

"No. You've got to try it. Forget the odds. What do you think the odds were against me making it as a poker player or Dave making his magazine go? Everyone who's made it as a writer started out with the odds stacked against him."

"I guess that's true."

"It's no guess. Anyone who starts out trying to do something on his or her own starts out with bad odds. You're in good company."

"I don't always think of it that way."

"And you're still working for Dave?" he asked.

"Yeah."

"That'll help you pay the bills. But I haven't seen anything by you in the last few issues."

"I didn't have time. That was part of the reason I quit my other job. Like you said this morning, it was my declaration of independence."

"That's good."

The kettle started whistling. Mac put Doggy on the floor and went to get us each cups while I scooped up some of the salsa with a chip. "Hey, this is great stuff. Where'd you get it?"

"I'll leave you the recipe."

"You made it?"

He nodded.

"By the way, what brought the other one about?" I asked.

"The other what?"

The Fifth Year 195

"The real *Declaration of Independence*."

"1776 and all that?"

"Yeah," I said.

Colonists wanted rights

"Well, in the beginning, it was that the American colonists just wanted to be treated like Englishmen."

"Englishmen?"

"Sure. You've got to remember, the colonists were English. But they didn't think they were getting the full rights accorded the Englishmen living in the British Isles."

"I guess I think of them as the original Americans, so I forget they were Englishmen.

"By the time they got around to adopting the *Declaration of Independence*, they forgot too. In fact, by then I think they realized they had not been Englishmen for a long time."

He went to the stove and started making us both coffee while I ate more of his salsa. You grind your own beans and make coffee one cup at a time at my house.

"You know," I said, "this would be great with steak or something."

He nodded again.

"So, what happened to make them think they weren't being treated like Englishmen?"

"Do you want the graduate course or the, 'let's have a cup of coffee and shoot the bull about it,' explanation?"

"Make it short."

"It started because the King needed more money to pay for the French and Indian War which had just ended."

"What was the war about?" By this time I had picked up a pencil and I'd started taking notes.

"It was actually part of a larger war being fought in Europe where it was called the Seven Years War. The principals were Britain and France. In North America, they were each trying to kick the other off the continent."

"I take it the English won."

"Yeah. Anyway, as Americans have come to learn, wars cost money and the King had incurred an enormous war debt."

"So he needed taxes."

"That's right. But because of the English Constitution the King couldn't levy taxes without the consent of Parliament and they said, 'No.' They'd been taxed enough.

"So they looked around for other sources of revenue, and his advisors suggested he get it from the colonies. And that's where the trouble started—though neither the King nor Parliament anticipated them.

"Various acts were enacted, starting with an unpopular tax called the Sugar Act in 1764."

"What was that?" I asked.

"It levied duties on a variety of items in the colonies including sugar, rum, molasses, various foods, and lumber."

He brought us each a cup of coffee and sat down. Doggy got back up in his lap. She looked at him as if checking to see if he was going to stay put this time. Then she put her head down and went back to sleep.

"The colonists didn't like the Act for two reasons. First, they obviously didn't like shelling out the money. Second, to enforce the Act—in other words, to ensure the taxes were paid—a system of customs houses, staffed by British officers, were set up and those accused of evading the tax were tried in a vice-admiralty court. This amounted to a trial without jury. Not that there were that many trials. But, still, it rankled the colonists."

"Trial without jury?"

"Sure. It was tantamount to a military trial for civilians."

"So, what did they do?"

"At first, the colonists acquiesced. But a year later the King imposed another tax, the infamous Stamp Act. It forced the purchase of a stamp that had to be affixed to all publications and documents to make them legal. This was to help pay the cost of maintaining troops in the colonies."

"The troops were there to...?"

"To discourage further French influence, the Spanish, Indians, and to collect taxes from the colonists."

"And they took a dim view of the new tax," I said.

"Sure. And not just because it was a new tax. The Sugar Act was a tax on goods but the Stamp Act was a tax on documents, and that was quite another matter. It was a tax on wills, it was a tax on ideas—books, newspapers, and pamphlets—and it interfered with the conduct of trade and business because every contract and every bill of lading had to have a stamp to be legal. It also struck at the most influential people in the colonies—merchants, lawyers, newspapermen, and what have you. And it was a harder tax to evade. If you wanted to bring a contract to court or review a will, the first thing they checked was to see if the tax had been paid. Still, many refused to pay it, and in some cities, there were protests and even instances of riots."

"What did the colonists do?"

No taxation without...

"It was 1765 and the Revolutionary War was still 11 years away. But two colonies, New York and Massachusetts, called for a Stamp Act Congress to protest. Nine of the colonies sent representatives. When they met, they adopted what was called the Declaration of Rights. It established the first opposition to taxation in the colonies without representation. It also opposed trial without jury in the Admiralty Courts. The colonists insisted that, as freeborn Englishmen, they were entitled to trial by a jury of their peers, just as Englishmen in Britain were. As a result, Parliament backed down. But they agreed to repeal the Act only on the provision that the Declaratory Act was passed, in which Parliament reaffirmed its authority over the colonies and declared its power to pass binding legislation over the colonies. It was passed—the same day. There was rejoicing throughout the colonies when they learned the Stamp Act had been repealed. But, as John Adams pointed out, armed with the Declaratory Act, Parliament would impose new taxes on the colonies in the near future.

"Did they?"

"You bet they did. Still, with the Stamp Act Congress, something had been established that I think made the eventual move to independence easier, though I don't think anyone thought too much about it then and you don't hear too much about it now: the colonists for the first time showed they could present a united front."

"So, what happened?"

"The King's bills didn't go away and Parliament was still reluctant to allow the King to raise taxes in England. In 1767, Parliament tried a new set of taxes on the colonies. They were the Townshend Acts. These were import duties on tea, paint, glass, and other things the colonists could not produce—or could not produce readily—for themselves. The result was, pay the import tax or do without. But there was something more ominous: to facilitate in collecting the tax, the Townshend Acts also authorized general search warrants."

"General search warrants?"

"Armed with a general warrant, a British official could search your home or business on the pretext of looking for things to tax."

"I'm going to guess that this didn't set well with the colonists."

"No, they not only protested again, but many colonial merchants refused to import British goods and other colonists refused to buy any goods from England. This didn't set well with the merchants in England. They pressured the King and Parliament to resolve the issue. In the meantime, there were some riots, particularly in Boston, and it was while trying to enforce the Townshend Acts that British troops fired into a mob killing five in what we now call the Boston Massacre.

"Finally, after another three years passed, all the taxes—except the tax on tea—were repealed. The tax on tea was kept for symbolic reasons: The King and Parliament still wanted to show they could levy a tax."

"It sounds like the Revolution came about over money"

"What do you mean?"

"Well, it just seems like we fought the Revolutionary War over money instead of ideals."

"Do you have a problem with money?"

I didn't answer.

"Let's see what money represents: it's work, it's time, it's a better standard of living, it's what religious organizations ask for to feed starving children overseas, it's what governments use to solve problems—money for wars, money for social programs, money for the homeless. And though many government officials whine about the rich and the so-called greedy, what do they want to take from the rich and the greedy? Their money. The poker games I play in are not played for trophies..."

"They say, 'Money is the root of all evil,'" I interrupted.

"The actual quote, from the Bible, is, 'The love of money is the root of all evil,' and no one loves money more than the government."

"Okay, so what happened next?"

"It wasn't just the taxes that bothered them. They didn't like the threat of trials without juries, they didn't like the way the King and Parliament could impose laws without the colonists' consent, and they didn't like general warrant searches.

"And there were more ominous signs of the possible loss of freedom. In New York, the British demanded citizens provide quartering for their troops. The colonial assembly refused and Parliament threatened to disband the assembly. Although the King had intervened in the colonial affairs before, this was the first time Parliament had attempted to do so.

"Then, there were even more problems. Have you ever heard of the East India Company?"

"Yes, but I can't remember why."

Boston Tea Party

"It was a British trading consortium that really had nothing to do with the American colonies, but they had run into financial trouble. To bail them out, prime minister Lord North gave them a legal monopoly on tea in the colonies. What this did was make illegal the importation of tea by colonial merchants who, incidentally, were smuggling it in to avoid the tax.

"There were more protests, more acrimony, and then, just before Christmas, on December 16, 1773, a band of Bostonians, dressed as Mohawk Indians, boarded several ships in Boston Harbor and dumped about £10,000 worth tea into the water.

"This not only offended Parliament, it caught what friends the colonists had in Parliament by surprise. Even the other colonies were shocked. Protest or not, dumping the tea was the destruction of private property. These weren't supposed to be the L.A. riots, you know.

"In retribution, Parliament closed the port of Boston, suspended the colonial charter of Massachusetts, and appointed a council to replace the one the colonists had elected. The other colonies realized that if it could happen to one of them, it could happen to them all."

"Then?"

1st Continental Congress

"Then, the colonists realized, if they were to resist these abuses, they would have to act collectively, just as they had in 1765. So, in 1774, they called for a Continental Congress to meet in Philadelphia."

"Why Philadelphia?"

"It was centrally located and it was the biggest city in the colonies."

"Bigger than New York?"

"At that time it was."

"Did they all attend?"

"Every colony except Georgia sent a delegation.

"When they met, one of the first things they did was to affirm that Englishmen in the colonies were entitled to the same common law rights as Englishmen in England."

"Like protection against general warrants and the right to jury trials?"

"Sure. So you see, it was more than money issues. One of the important things to come out of the Congress was the Virginia delegation's instructions, which were composed by Thomas Jefferson and later published in pamphlet form under the title of, *A Summary View of the Rights of British America*.

In it he argued that Parliament had no authority in the colonies. What was Parliament? An elected body. But elected by whom? Certainly not the colonists.

"Following his lead, John Adams published a series of letters in a Boston newspaper in which he not only argued that Parliament had no authority over the colonies, but he went a step further, arguing that the King didn't either."

"Them's fightin' words," I said.

"More than you know. But what they were trying to do was force Parliament and the King to redress the colonial grievances, to assure the colonists the rights due them, and to resume the harmonious relationship that had existed before."

"Just by protesting?"

"They had mapped out a strategy of nonimportation and nonconsumption of British goods along with a decision not to export any goods to England after the rice harvest had been exported.

"But there was already talk, especially among the delegates from Massachusetts and Virginia for independence."

"Were they pushing hard?"

"No. It was mostly talk and when the Congress ended, most of the delegates were sure the problems could be resolved and they'd remain within the Empire.

"Still, in case things didn't work out, they made provisions for a Congress to meet the following spring.

"Obviously, the issues weren't resolved to the colonists' satisfaction," I said.

"Bingo. The following spring the Second Continental Congress convened in Philadelphia. By this time, the Battles of Lexington and Concord had been fought. There were still those who hoped to avoid war, but whether they liked it or not they were on their way to the *Declaration of Independence*.

"The British still had a chance at conciliation but passed up the chance. They were sure they could quell the insurrection by a show of force. Instead, they alienated many of their colonial supporters who wanted to stay in the Empire.

"In August of 1775, the King declared the colonies were in rebellion and all trade with them was banned.

"The colonists now hoped for aid from some of Britain's enemies, like France. But they had to make a demand for independence if they were to get it."

"Why?"

"Why would the French care about a bunch of British colonists in the New World who just wanted better treatment within the Empire? However, if the colonists were to actually break away in armed rebellion and weaken the British, particularly in North America where the French hoped to reestablish themselves, they had something.

"But keep in mind, France was still a monarchy, as were almost all the other countries in Europe so supporting a popular revolution was a dangerous thing for any monarchy."

"You said some of the delegates still opposed independence."

"Sure, some opposed separation—but not for the reasons you'd expect. John Dickinson of Delaware wanted to set up a central government and secure foreign aid before taking the step.

"Like, from France."

"Or other enemies of Britain: France, Spain, Holland, and Russia."

"Russia? Even then?"

"Czarist Russia was looking for a warm water port. The western Europeans, especially Britain, along with the Ottoman Empire, were frustrating them. Three quarters of a century later, this issue would rear its ugly head in the Crimean War and bring with it Balaklava, Tennyson's, *Charge of the Light Brigade*, and a bunch of bad movies.

Call for independence

"On April 12, 1776, North Carolina authorized its three delegates to vote for independence. Then, on May 15th, Virginia authorized its delegates to put forward the motion for independence.

Ironically, it was Richard Henry Lee who was selected to offer the motion."

"What was the irony?"

"The son of one of his cousins was the greatest military leader this country ever produced. But he's best known for leading troops against the very country his family had fought to create."

"Robert E. Lee?"

"Yes."

"Was Richard Henry Lee still alive when the Civil War was fought?"

"Oh, no. He'd been dead over 60 years.

"Anyway, the previous December the Congress had already denied the sovereignty of Parliament over the colonies. Then, on May 10, 1776, it denied the authority of the King."

"Why wasn't independence achieved earlier, then? Like, when Lee introduced the motion?"

"The times. Communications were slow. Few of the delegations had yet received authorization to vote for it."

"How slow were communications?"

"Before the advent of the telegraph, very slow. Thirty-eight years later, in the War of 1812, the final battle of that war, and the most decisive American victory, actually took place six weeks after the war was over because communications were so slow."

"So, in Revolutionary times..."

"Messages went by horseback, carriage, boat, or foot."

Democracy vs. liberty

"But it was no longer just a tax issue. The colonists now knew they had to have a broad range of rights to ensure their freedom. They not only wanted democracy, they wanted liberty."

"What's the difference? It seems, if you have one, you have the other."

"There's a difference between democracy and individual liberty. The two are not synonymous.

"How do you mean that?"

"In a pure democracy, with no guarantees of personal liberty, the individual is always in danger of the tyranny of the majority.

"When he wrote the *Declaration of Independence*, Jefferson summed up what we now regard as American freedoms in the first two lines of the *Declaration of Independence*.

"If you think about it, the first line ultimately led to the Constitution and the second line led to the Bill of Rights."

"Can you explain that?"

"The first line of the *Declaration of Independence* is a collective reference that says one group of people has the power to—and here I quote, *'When in the Course of human Events, it becomes necessary for one People to dissolve the Political Bands which have connected them with another, and to assume among the Powers of the Earth, the separate and equal Station to which the Laws of Nature and of Nature's God entitle them, a decent Respect to the Opinions of mankind requires that they should declare the causes which impel then to the Separation.'*

"The first half of the second line asserts individual rights. *'We hold these Truths to be self-evident, that all Men are created equal, that they are endowed by their Creator with certain unalienable Rights, that among these are Life, Liberty, and the Pursuit of Happiness'*

"The last half of that line ties the first two ideas together. Jefferson was aware of tyranny of the majority and the failures of pure democracy in ancient Greece. He wrote, *'That to secure these Rights, Governments are instituted among Men, deriving their just Powers from the Consent of the Governed, that whenever any Form of Government becomes destructive of these Ends, it is the Right of the People to alter or abolish it, and to institute new Government, laying its Foundations on such Principles, and organizing its Powers in such Form, as to them shall seem most likely to effect their Safety and Happiness.'*

These lines discuss first, our collective rights as a people and nation, second, our rights as individuals, and third, how the two are related. They are the foundation of the American philosophy. They are evidence of the collective genius of the people who founded this country and, in particular, of Thomas Jefferson who penned the lines."

"What comes next?" I asked.

"Are you really interested in this?"

"Yes."

"Well, in the third line, they said that governments long established should not be changed for light or transient causes. He was saying that a revolution should not happen without good reason.

"In the fourth line, he asserts that when there are legitimate reasons, it is not only the right but the duty of the oppressed to revolt against the government.

"From there on, the *Declaration of Independence* goes off to show how the English King had violated the principles those lines embody and how the colonists were entitled to break the bonds."

"Why didn't they cite Parliament, too? It seems they were the ones passing the tax levies."

"There were two reasons. First, the colonists still hoped for support from some of Parliament's members. Second, since the colonists had no representation in that body, they felt Parliament had no legal authority or power over them."

"That makes sense."

1st American document

"The *Declaration of Independence* is the first official state document of the fledgling United States and it expresses the new and wholly American philosophy as seen through Jefferson's eyes."

"Reading those lines, it also becomes clear why the Constitution of the United States, when it was drawn up in 1787, addresses only the first line of the *Declaration of Independence*, and why there was a push for a bill of rights, which is embodied in the second line."

"We did an article on the Bill of Rights," I said.

He nodded. Then I remembered the whole article arose from a conversation with him. (Editor's note: see Issue No. 12 November/December 1991)

"Even in those days there were those who failed to grasp the importance of the first two lines and how fundamentally different they are from each other."

"Give me an example of someone who didn't get the connection."

"Alexander Hamilton, for one. He, and many others who made up the Federalist Party did not see the Bill of Rights as necessary. They reasoned that the government had no right to make laws abridging individual freedoms, therefore, a bill of rights was meaningless. They also reasoned that the people would not impose laws abridging their own freedoms.

"Of course, history has shown they were wrong.

"But, keep in mind, there have been very few instances in history where the individual has been accorded a station as high or higher than the state. The *Declaration of Independence* and the Bill of Rights both do that. In fact, by asserting that the government obtains its legitimacy only from the consent of the governed, it elevates the individual to a higher status.

"The Bill of Rights is vitally important to our freedom. If you consider its implications, the words make us somewhat less than a true democracy. It means there are things the individual is entitled to which, at least according to our Constitution, cannot be denied him—even by majority vote.

"By comparison, in the first democracy of which we know, Greece's, the average Athenian was nowhere near as free as the average American is today. The concept of written, guaranteed rights did not exist.

"There are those, even today, who want a pure democracy, one that is instantly reponsive to the so-called 'will' of the people.

"To these people, it is the majority will that is important. To them, the Constitution should be easily and readily ammendable.

"Our Constitution is not. It requires time and much more than a simple majority. They find that objectionable. But it is all that protects the individual from tyranny by majority vote—democratic or not.

"If you'll recall from your article on Jefferson and Adams, on June 11th, the Congress chose John Adams, Thomas Jefferson, Benjamin Franklin, Roger Sherman, and Robert Livingston to draft the declaration proclaiming independence from Britain.

(Editor's note: see Issue No. 16 July/August 1992)

"By July 1st, it was presented to the Congress and nine of the delegations voted for independence. It was adopted the next day, with 12 of the delegations ratifying it. New York ratified it on the 15th when its delegation received its instructions. Then, on August 2nd, the delegates still in Philadelphia signed it."

"You're kidding. I always thought that they signed it on July 4th."

"No. On Monday, July 8th, it was read publically."

"Is that Jefferson's handwriting in the *Declaration of Independence*?"

"No. Today, we think that what Jefferson wrote was transcribed onto parchment by a guy named Timothy Matlock from Philadelphia. That was the copy they signed."

"Was Matlock a delegate?"

He shook his head. "Just a hired pen.

"John Hancock was the first signer. His name is centered, right after the text of the document, with a large flourish. It is the most conspicuous name on the document. In signing it, he said something to the effect that he wanted King George to able to read it without his spectacles."

"Was he an important delegate?"

"Yes and no. He was President of the First Continental Congress and, once the Revolution started, he hoped to be given command of the Continental Army. The command was given instead to George Washington. Years later, he hoped to be nominated to the presidency of the United States if Washington declined the position. Obviously, he didn't."

"I suppose you know who signed it last, too."

"Yeah, Thomas McKean. He didn't sign it until 1777."

"The next year?"

He nodded.

"Is there anything you don't know, Mac?"

"There are lots of things I don't know, John."

"Well, tell me, what took him so long?"

"He'd been there to debate it and vote on it. He just wasn't there when they started signing it. Several other delegates weren't, either. They also signed it later."

I was still writing furiously.

"John," he asked, "do you know anything about fly fishing?"

"No."

He woke Doggy as he put her back on the floor.

"I've got two rods out in the car."

"I've got to do an article for Duffy."

He shook his head. "You've got to go fishing."

"There's no way."

"Yes there is."

That evening, Doggy, Mac, and I had trout for dinner. ∆

The Thinker

Have you missed columns by some of todays most influential and interesting libertarian and conservative writers? Find the best of them—Dave Duffy, John Silveira, Vin Suprynowicz, P.J. O'Rourke, Walter Williams, George Will, Jeff Jacoby, and others **free** on the web at:

http://www.gis.net/~dmann/

Chinese cooking

By Richard Blunt

What's your first thought when Chinese food comes up in conversation. Quick, now.

For most folks it's their favorite Chinese restaurant. Was it yours? Think "Chinese food" and we think "Chinese restaurant." It's that simple. But, in this issue's column, I'm going to convince you that you can make Asian food at home and it will match or surpass any you have had, even that in the finest of Chinese restaurants.

The Asian connection

Notice I said "Asian" food. The reason is that all the ethnic foods on the Asian continent, from India to China, are somewhat related. India, China, Cambodia, Vietnam, and Thailand, just to name a few, have been exchanging food ideas for centuries. The two with the greatest influence are India and China. Over the years, while each has developed distinctive foods with unique aromas, tastes, and presentations, each has incorporated new flavors and preparation concepts by borrowing from their neighbor across the Himalayas. China and India even use a similar cooking utensil to fry food. In India it's called a kanhai and it's primarily used for deep frying. In China it's the familiar wok and it's used for everything from deep frying to stir frying and steaming.

The other, smaller, Asian countries have also exchanged ideas with their neighbors and all—large and small—have benefited as a result.

In this country, we have been attracted to the wonders of Indian and Chinese food for decades. However, since the Vietnam War, we have also discovered a whole world of new flavors and delights as we have explored other Asian food concepts. This is demonstrated by the increasing success of Vietnamese, Cambodian and Thai restaurants in this country.

But there is another feature that has made Asian food attractive to Americans. For health reasons we have become very cautious about the amount of fats and calories we consume. As a result, we eat less meat and have greatly increased our daily consumption of vegetables and starches.

But this has been the standard fare in Asia for many centuries. In most of those countries, the proportion of meat in the diet is very low. The result is a diet that is low in fat, cholesterol, and cost. Not only that, but the common method for cooking vegetables in eastern Asia is stir-frying which retains all of the flavor and vitamins. In this country we boil our vegetables which does just the opposite.

Another aspect of Asian recipes that makes them attractive to Americans is that they're very high in preparation fun and eating pleasure. I would like them for that reason alone.

Chinese recipes

For this issue, what I've included are Chinese recipes. In each recipe I have added a couple of flavoring ideas of my own which are optional. But what these ideas will do is help you to vary the recipes to suit your own tastes.

Incidentally, if you find the concept of Asian food, as opposed to just Chinese food, interesting, let me know and we can begin a culinary tour of the Asian continent from our own kitchens, in future columns.

Learning the hard way

I learned to prepare Chinese food the hard way. I started by going to the best restaurants I could find in Boston and New York and eating. How did I know they were the best? That was the easy part.

When I was younger and lived in Brookline, Massachusetts, I had a neighbor who knew I was an aspiring chef. Her name was Ann and she took me under her wing. She knew more about European and Asian food than many well known and certified chefs in the Boston area. Whenever I scraped enough money together and was planning a visit to a first class Chinese restaurant, I'd go next door and have a cup of coffee or a shot of Glenlivet with her. She would advise me where I should go and what I should order. She would also describe the characteristics of the food I would be eating and tell me how to look for the subtleties in them. After a couple of years talking with her and following her advice (sometimes she would go with me on these excursions), I could walk into any restaurant and know exactly how the food I ordered should smell, look, and taste. I tried something new every time I went to one of these restaurants and kept detailed notes on my experiences. I also purchased a couple of books Ann recommended and started to experiment at home. I have been experimenting ever since.

After my first month of preparing Chinese food at home, I realized it was not the mystery I had believed it to be. And if you introduce yourself to Chinese/Asian food by preparing it at home, you'll open up a whole new, adventuresome, and seemingly endless world of exciting food options, especially if you are on a weight reduction diet. All you need to succeed is a reasonable amount of diligence and a few good recipes. As soon as you understand the basics, you'll be able to go to your refrigerator and, depending on what you find there, make your own recipes.

I believe the real difference between Asian food and other foods around the world is the subtle combination of natural flavors combined with simple preparation methods. Simply put, you get Cordon Bleu results without having to use Cordon Bleu rituals. Caution! Chinese/Asian food can become addictive when you discover how easy it is to prepare.

Equipment

Now, let's talk about the equipment you'll need. In the beginning, if your kitchen is outfitted properly, it won't be much. It has always been my practice to try to use the equipment available in my kitchen when introducing myself to a new concept. Chinese food was no exception. For stir frying and other wok functions, a 14-inch teflon-coated saute pan served me at the beginning. I suggest you buy one even if home cooked Chinese food is not in your future. You'll quickly see it has many other uses. On the other hand, if you decide to prepare Chinese food more frequently, consider buying two.

For cooking rice I use a 1½ or 2 qt saucepan with a tight fitting lid. The heavier the pot, the better it will cook rice. This is because the heavier metal distributes heat more evenly.

A steamer of some sort will be necessary for steaming vegetables and, in some instances, to complete entrees. Aluminum steamers with two levels are made in various sizes and sold in Chinese food stores and specialty food stores. The 12-inch medium steamer is the best all around unit. Directions for use come with the steamer.

A coarse meshed, long-handled strainer or slotted spoon for removing food from the wok, saute pan, or deep fryer is an important utensil. These can be found in the kitchenware section of most department stores.

Any well equipped kitchen should have a chopping board, a variety of sauce pans, a grinder for meats, and a pan for deep frying. A wok is an excellent deep frying pan. Because of its round bottom it requires only 4 cups of oil to reach the recommended 3-inch depth for effective frying.

Many cookbooks strongly suggest owning a Chinese cleaver if you intend to prepare Chinese food. I don't agree. Throughout my career, I have owned the same set of high-carbon stainless steel cook's knives. A 10-inch French knife, a 6-inch narrow blade boning knife, and a 3-inch paring and utility knife are all that I have ever needed or used. But knife selection should be a personal preference. Choose whatever feels comfortable to you and gets the job done.

So, as you can see, it will not be necessary to spend a lot of money on special equipment. I would not be surprised if you have most of the utensils in your kitchen right now.

Special ingredients

Preparing Chinese food requires the use of some special herbs, spices, sauces and vegetables. Since the recipes I have included here are meant to introduce you to this popular variety of Asian food, I have outlined only those required to prepare these recipes. We can talk in greater detail about others in future columns. But I suggest you buy the ones listed below before attempting to prepare any of the recipes.

Bean sauce is a spicy sauce that comes in cans or jars and is sold in Chinese food stores. It contains yellow beans, salt, flour, and vinegar. There are two other varieties, hot bean sauce and sweet bean sauce. At this time, you are only interested in the regular variety.

Curry paste is found most often in Thai and Indian food stores and can be found in several varieties. I have suggested red curry paste as an option in the barbecued rib recipe. The one I use is composed of red chili peppers, ground coriander seed, ground cumin seed, ground white pepper, chopped garlic, lemon grass, chopped coriander roots, Kaffir lime skin, shrimp, and chopped galangal. Galangal is a root that is unfamiliar to most Americans. It is in the same family of plants (rhizomes) as ginger, but it has a much lighter flavor.

Bean sprouts are widely available in two varieties, mung and soy. Both are low in calories and contain protein. Use mung sprouts at this time. They are easier to use and can be added to hot foods and salads.

Five spice powder is a spice blend containing Szechuan peppercorns, star anise, cinnamon, cloves, and fennel. It has a strong flavor and should be used sparingly.

Ginger root is the irregularly shaped rhizome root we are all familiar with. It has a very strong flavor and, used in small amounts, it will add a delightful flavor to many Chinese dishes.

Oyster sauce is a thick, brown, richly flavored seasoning that is a little salty. It is made from ground oysters and soy sauce. The best place to find it is in Chinese food stores.

Peanut oil is the preferred oil for most cooking in my house. It does not absorb flavors from or impart flavors to the food being cooked. For this reason it can be used up to four times for deep frying before being discarded. If you are avoiding saturated fat, safflower or canola oil are also good choices.

Plum sauce is made from plums, ginger, chilies and other spices. I have used it in the marinade for the spareribs. With this recipe you will experience one example of the sophisticated blending of flavors found in most Asian foods.

Dry sherry is a substitute for Chinese rice wine, but this description does not do it culinary justice. I prefer to use the sherry because I like the taste. Try both this and the rice wine and make your choice. The sherry sold as "cooking sherry," found in food stores, is garbage. Don't use it. Remember, if you can't drink it, don't cook with it.

There are two types of **soy sauce** on the market, dark and light. Dark soy is used most often and is actually thicker in texture as well as being darker in color. Light soy is thinner and is used most often in salads and marinades. The soy used in all of the recipes included here is dark (or regular). Once again, if you are curious, give both a try and use the one that appeals to you the most.

Hoisin sauce is probably one of the most popular of all Chinese prepared sauces. It's a mixture of sugar, water, soybeans, garlic, sesame seed, chili pepper, and various other spices. It has the widest range of uses in cooking, and it can be combined with other sauces you're making or used as a straight dipping sauce.

Canned **water chestnuts** are easy to find and easy to use. But they have little flavor or no flavor at all. They do, however, contribute a fresh crunchy texture to most recipes. Fresh water chestnuts are expensive and must be peeled before using and they are not always available in good condition. But they are incredibly sweet and have a delicate flavor much like raw coconut or apple. Do yourself a favor—if you are just beginning, use the canned variety to start. As you become comfortable with the recipes and basic procedures, go out of your way and find some fresh water chestnuts. I feel that this will help you appreciate them more.

Lemon grass is an indispensable herb in Southeast Asian food and has a delicate fragrance. It is actually a sedge and it can be found in specialty food stores and Chinese grocery stores. If you are inclined to use it a lot, you can even grow it yourself. But, if you live in an area that experiences frost, grow it in a pot and bring it indoors during cold weather.

Now, let's get started and turn some of this column into good eating.

First, review the following recipes. Decide which one you want to prepare and make up a shopping list.

Next, I want you to learn how to cook rice. Rice is a regular staple at the Chinese table and is served with most meals. Boiled rice is served even when fried rice is on the menu. Rice was cultivated in China at least as early as the 27th century B.C., and today 94% of the world's crop is still produced and consumed right there on the Asian Continent. So it stands to reason they have probably developed an efficient way to cook it. The following recipe is simple, foolproof, and works with any variety of long grain white rice. No salt is used because this is the tradition in China. Give this recipe a try, especially if you have had trouble cooking rice in the past. The recipe produces 3 cups of cooked rice.

Boiled rice

```
1 cup long grain rice
1 2/3 cup cold water
```

1. Place the rice and cold water in a 1½ qt sauce pan and cover.
2. Place the pot on a burner set to a high heat to boil.
3. When you see steam coming from under the lid, turn the heat to a low flame. Do not remove the cover.
4. Cook the rice for 15 minutes then remove it from the heat. Again, do not remove the cover!
5. Let the pan sit for 20 minutes.

There you have it, perfect rice. Remove the cover, fluff the rice with a fork, and serve.

Fried rice is the most popular version of cooked rice that I know, other than boiled rice. It is a popular way to use up leftovers and is one of the first foods in Chinese cooking to invite you to use your own imagination. This is a favorite recipe in my house.

Fried rice

```
3 cups cold cooked rice
¼ cup chopped ham, cooked pork, lamb, shrimp or beef
¼ cup slivered blanched almonds, toasted
1 egg (scrambled ahead of time)
```

Vegetable mixture

```
4 chopped water chestnuts
¼ cup chopped fresh mushrooms (choose your favorite
    type)
4 chopped scallions (cut off the root end and chop the
    whole stalk)
¼ cup fresh or frozen peas
½ cup fresh Mung bean sprouts
1½ tsp fresh lemon grass, chopped fine, or ½ tsp ground
    dried lemon grass (optional)
2 Tbsp peanut oil
```

Sauce

```
1 Tbsp dark soy
2 tsp oyster sauce
1 Tbsp dry sherry
2 Tbsp chicken or beef broth (fresh or canned)
```

1. Chop the ham, cooked pork, chicken, lamb, shrimp or beef, place in a bowl, and set aside.

2. Heat your oven to 325°. Toss the almonds in 1 Tbsp of oil so they are coated, then spread them evenly on a baking sheet and roast them until golden brown. This takes about 15 minutes. Shake the pan a couple of times to ensure even roasting. Remove them from the oven and combine them with the scrambled egg and set aside.

3. Chop the water chestnuts, fresh mushrooms, and scallions and combine them in a bowl with the peas, bean sprouts and lemon grass. Set this mixture aside.

4. Combine and mix ingredients for the sauce.

5. In your wok or saute pan, heat the 2 Tbsp of peanut oil over high heat. Do not allow the oil to get so hot it smokes. (As soon as the oil starts to smoke, it starts to become saturated.)

6. When the oil is hot, add the vegetable mixture and stir fry it for about 30 seconds. Now add the meat, eggs and almonds. Stir fry for another 30 seconds.

7. Place rice on top of this mixture, cover and allow to cook for 1 minute. Now remove the cover, add sauce and stir the entire mixture thoroughly and heat to serving temperature for about 3 more minutes.

8. Remove from the heat and enjoy.

This next recipe is a favorite of my wife's and it also gives you a lot of options to use different ingredients and still get an excellent end product. With a little bit of thought given to the options you have, the recipe can come to the table in several unique and distinct forms. Here are a few variations Tricia and I have enjoyed over the years. In the first, the recipe calls for chicken, though I have used various cuts of beef, veal, and pork, with the same marinade. Depending on my particular preferences at the moment, I have used almonds, cashews, pecans, or peanuts. (I don't use walnuts because some people have complained of the flavor.) The recipe calls for about 1¾ cups of vegetables. I have made substitutions to clean out my vegetable bin along with leftover canned vegetables that were used in other recipes. This has included fresh asparagus, fresh carrots that have been slant cut to 1/8 inch thickness, and blanched or fresh zucchini. I have also used frozen peas, green beans, and canned bamboo shoots.

Substituting oyster sauce for bean sauce is a good change if you are using veal or pork as the meat. Red curry paste (1 tsp.) is an excellent substitution for bean sauce when lamb or beef are used. This is an entree and goes well with both boiled and fried rice. I have also scored some points by serving it with spinach fettuccine at a party.

Chicken with bean sauce and nuts

Makes 4 servings:

1 lb. boneless and skinless chicken breast (raw). This is 1½ to 2 whole breasts depending on the size of the chickens.
4 Tbsp peanut oil for stir frying

Marinade

1 egg white (slightly beaten)
1 Tbsp corn starch
1 Tbsp dry sherry

Vegetables

1 tsp minced fresh garlic
¼ cup sweet red pepper (diced in ½ inch pieces)
½ cup fresh snow peas (washed and stems removed)
½ cup sliced fresh mushrooms
4 scallions (white and green parts)
½ cup sliced water chestnuts
½ cup nuts (almonds, cashews, pecans, or peanuts), coarsely chopped

Sauce

1 Tbsp dry sherry
1 Tbsp dark soy sauce
1 Tbsp Hoisin sauce
1 Tbsp bean sauce
½ cup fresh or canned chicken broth
½ tsp sugar
To thicken sauce:
2 tsp corn starch dissolved in 1½ Tbsp of water

1. Combine the egg white, sherry, and corn starch to make the marinade.

2. Dice the chicken breast into 1-inch pieces and add to the marinade. Refrigerate this for at least 2 hours.

3. Prepare the vegetables as follows and set them aside.

Combine and set aside:
    Minced garlic
    Diced red pepper
    Snow peas

Combine and set aside:
    Sliced mushrooms
    Diced scallions

Set aside: Sliced water chestnuts

4. Combine the dry sherry, soy sauce, Hoisin sauce, bean sauce, chicken broth and sugar. Set this mixture aside.

5. Combine the corn starch and water to make the thickener for the sauce. This will settle, so remember to mix it again before using.

6. Toast the coarsely diced nuts in a 350° oven for five to ten minutes.

Assembly:

1. Heat the wok or saute pan on a high heat and add 1 Tbsp of peanut oil.

2. Add the garlic, red pepper and snow peas. Stir fry for 30 seconds.

3. Add the mushrooms and scallions for another 30 seconds.

4. Add the water chestnuts and stir fry for another minute.

5. Empty the contents of the wok or saute pan into a serving dish.

6. Return the unwashed wok or saute pan to the heat and add remaining 3 Tbsp of peanut oil.

7. Stir the chicken pieces in the marinade and add them to the remaining heated oil. Stir fry the chicken until it turns opaque. Remove the chicken from the pan and set it aside.

8. Return the vegetables to the wok or saute pan along with the sauce, corn starch, and water.

9. Heat this mixture until it starts to thicken. Add the chicken back to the wok, mix and stir fry for about 1 minute.

10. Transfer the mixture to a heated serving dish.

11. Lightly mix nuts into meal just before presentation.

12. Serve immediately.

This next recipe is great if you have a garden. The possible combinations of vegetables are unlimited.

Stir fried vegetables

```
2 carrots, peeled
2 cups fresh broccoli
2 cups fresh cauliflower
1 large sweet red pepper
4 oz fresh mushrooms
2 cloves fresh garlic
½ cup snow peas
¼ tsp minced fresh ginger
2 Tbsp peanut oil for stir frying
```

Sauce

```
1 Tbsp bean sauce
1 Tbsp Hoisin sauce
1 Tbsp soy sauce
¼ cup chicken broth, fresh or canned
1 Tbsp dry sherry
1 tsp sugar
½ tsp rice vinegar
¼ tsp fresh ground black pepper
½ tsp fresh chopped lemon grass (optional) or ¼ tsp
    ground dried lemon grass
```

Thickener

```
2 Tbsp corn starch
2 Tbsp water
```

1. Slant cut the carrots 1/8" thick and set them aside

2. Remove broccoli flowers from the main stem. Cut 4 inches from the stem and slant cut the remainder of the stem and set aside. Cut the flowers in half and set aside.

3. Break off cauliflower flowers and cut to the same size as the broccoli and set aside.

4. Dice red pepper in ½ inch pieces and set aside.

5. Slice mushrooms and set aside.

6. Peel and mince garlic, set aside.

7. Wash and remove stems from snow peas, set aside.

8. Combine all sauce ingredients.

9. Mix corn starch and water. Remember to remix before use.

Assembly

1. Place wok or saute pan on medium high heat.

2. Add 2 Tbsp of oil along with the ginger and heat. Do not allow to smoke.

3. Add carrots and garlic. Stir fry for 1 minute.

4. Add broccoli and cauliflower and stir fry for about 3 minutes.

5. Add snow peas and stir fry for 1 minute.

6. Add mushrooms and peppers and stir fry for 1 minute.

7. Add sauce mixture, bring to a boil and cook for 1 minute.

8. Remix thickener and add to mixture. Stir until sauce thickens.

9. Transfer to a heated serving dish and serve immediately.

The only thing that I will say about this last recipe is pick a Friday night when you don't have to go to work on Saturday to start pulling it together. Go out and buy your favorite beer or wine and get ready for some good eating on Saturday. When you buy your spareribs, ask your butcher for the young tender variety that have been trimmed of most fat.

Barbecued spareribs

1 slab of pork ribs, between 2 and 3 pounds.

Marinade

2 cloves fresh garlic, minced
1 tsp fresh ginger, peeled and minced
¼ tsp five spice powder
2 Tbsp dry sherry
3 Tbsp dark soy sauce
2 tsp plum sauce
1 tsp red curry paste (optional)
1/8 tsp Tabasco sauce
2 Tbsp honey

Assembly

1. Mix together all ingredients of marinade.
2. Brush meat on both sides with marinade. Combine whole slabs with marinade in a large pan. Cover and set in the refrigerator to marinate overnight.

Next day:

1. Preheat oven to 375°.
2. Pour 2 cups of water into a roasting pan.
3. Remove meat from marinade, place on a rack and set rack into roasting pan. Do not allow ribs to touch the water.
4. Place pan in oven. After 30 minutes, brush both sides of ribs with marinade and turn over.
5. After 1 hour, remove ribs from oven and turn up to 450°.
6. Pour off water from roasting pan, brush ribs on both sides with remaining marinade and return pan to oven.
7. In about 10 minutes turn the ribs. After another 20 minutes remove the ribs from the oven.
8. Cut into individual ribs and serve.

Well, that's it for this issue. I hope you enjoy what you prepare. If there's enough response from you, the readers, I'll take you on that kitchen tour of Asia in the near future. Write and let me know what you think. ∆

RETURN OF THE 3 FOR 2 SPECIAL! ONLY $39.90

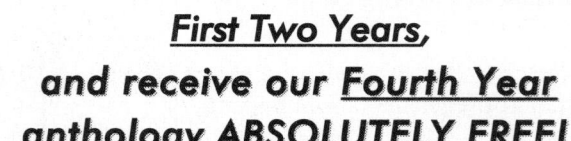

Subscribe (or renew) for a year, buy *The Best of the First Two Years*, and receive our *Fourth Year* anthology ABSOLUTELY FREE!

Backwoods Home Magazine

THE SELF-RELIANCE GOLDMINE!

Year after year, it's the information you need to achieve a self-reliant lifestyle for yourself and your family.

Send a check or money order, along with your name and address, to
Backwoods Home Magazine
PO Box 40
Montague, CA 96064

Or call toll-free: **(800) 835-2418** for credit card orders only. Others please call (530) 459-3500.

Just for kids — sun-kabobs and solar sizzle

By Lucy Shober

Picture yourself in this dreamy scenario: It's a hot summer afternoon. The sun is beaming through the shade trees as you loll in the hammock sipping fresh-made icy tea and nibbling tidbits from a home-cooked sizzling lunch.

Sound great? It will sound and taste even better when you find that you can create this scene yourself with no help! While it can be pretty dangerous to try and cook lunch on your mom's kitchen range, there's a safe and fun way to cook your own lunch with a heat source that's roughly 149,600,000 kilometers away. It's hard to burn your fingers on this stove! Our special oven (if you haven't already guessed) is that amazing cooker, our SUN!

You can produce the heat and water to cook a delicious meal just by using a little ingenuity and that big ball of fire in the sky. Follow the directions below for making a *solar still*. You can use the water that you produce to make that icy *sun tea* and to wash up with before lunch. To make your meal, you should follow the guidelines for a *solar cooker*, and the recipe for *sun-kabobs*.

Solar still

If you would like to use the water produced by the solar still for your picnic lunch, it's best to get started a few days early in order to collect enough.

To make the still, get permission to dig a hole in a sunny spot in your yard. It must be about twenty inches deep and forty inches across. Put a small bowl at the center of your hole. Now you must put a *clean* clear plastic sheet (about sixty inches wide) over the hole and secure it there with the dirt that you've taken from the hole. Just place handfuls of it all around the edge of the sheet, being careful not to get any into the bowl inside. Now find a little rock to place in the center of the sheet. This will weigh down the plastic with the low point being directly over the bowl. Don't let the plastic touch the bowl: it should be a couple of inches above it.

As the sun heats your still, the water contained in the earthy floor of it will evaporate and rise to the plastic. Soon that water will condense and form droplets which will drip down the plastic into your bowl. It might be a long wait, but your fresh water will be as clean as the driven snow! Remember this trick if you ever get stuck in the Mojave desert.

Place handfuls of dirt around the edges of the plastic sheeting that covers your solar still. (Color this picture!)

Sun tea

When you've collected enough water, find a large glass jar to make your sun tea. Put into it several tea bags (use herb tea, not caffeine tea) and maybe a spice or two. Cloves or fennel would be nice, but sift them out before drinking the tea. Cap the jar, and set it in a hot sunny spot. After several hours, check to see if the tea is dark enough, add ice, and thank your flaming friend in the sky for this refreshing drink.

Solar cooker

For this great project, you will need to have these items:

- Some black tempera paint or a large sheet of flat black paper
- An empty oatmeal box
- A large sheet of aluminum foil
- A small mirror
- A nice sunny day
- Scissors
- Good tape
- A *clean* thin dowel or long thin *clean* stick

First you should cut a rectangular hole in the side of the box. Leave about an inch at each end. (See picture.) Now cover the inside of the box with the foil, keeping the shiny side showing. Tape the edges to the box, then tightly cover the outside with dark paper (so the hole stays open) or paint it with the black tempera.

If you do your work outdoors, you will notice that the foil reflects the glare of the sun into your eyes, and that the black surface is much easier to look at. The black absorbs the sunlight and heat and the foil reflects them into your eyes...or onto the sun-kabob! The cooker will work from the inside and out to give you a good lunch.

Now, to get things cooking, poke the dowel through one end of the box and out the other. When you feel that it is sturdy enough, slip one end out and spear your delectable ingredients from the recipe onto it. (The recipe follows.) It's best to alternate fruits and meat so that the flavors will mingle. Now re-poke the stick into its hole, close up your solar oven, and find a hot sunny spot in which to set up your outside kitchen. You can secure the cooker by wedging pebbles under it, but make *sure* that it is facing directly at the sun. Slip the mirror into the box to reflect even more sun rays onto the kabob. Depending on the type of day you choose, you should have a meal in thirty minutes to an hour. Have fun, and watch out for Bowzer or Fido or *whoever* might want to steal your hard earned picnic lunch!

Recipe for sun-kabobs

You will need:

- One hot dog or some sliced pieces of ham
- Some pineapple chunks
- A few cherries
- Sliced oranges, apples or any other delectable fruit.

Chop these ingredients into bite sized pieces, put them in a bowl and pour any of the leftover juice from your fruit over it. If you are adventuresome, you can add a dash of cinnamon or nutmeg to this mixture before you cover and refrigerate it. You can let it sit in the refrigerator for a while, to let the flavors mingle, or use it right away.

Enjoy! Δ

A country moment

Theresa Dillard, 7, of Klamath Falls, OR, shows off

You can add a mirror to your solar stove to create more heat.

INDEPENDENT ENERGY

Designing for solar heating

By Don Fallick

How you plan for solar heating depends to a very great extent on whether you're building a new structure or adding on to an existing one, and on the method of heat transference. It might be said that these considerations loom so large as to virtually determine the design of the system.

Active systems

So-called "active" solar heating systems produce the highest temperatures. Their liquid heat-transfer fluids lend themselves best to integration with a conventional heating system. They are relatively easy to retro-fit to an existing structure, are not especially bulky, allow for traditional architecture, and can be modified, enlarged, or even removed, at any time. They also require expert installation, and are inordinately expensive to purchase, run, and repair.

"Active" disadvantages

Virtually all active systems require electricity to run pumps and controllers. Protection must be provided to guard against freezing of the circulating water, or to ensure that poisonous anti-freeze solutions remain isolated from the environment. Protection must be "fail-safe" against power outages during severe winter weather. Lots of systems failed in Seattle, Washington, in 1991 when a coastal city that rarely sees any snow caught over two feet in 24 hours. Much of the city was without power for several days during the coldest Christmas on record. Provision must also be made for emergencies caused by the failure of these "fail-safe" systems.

Active systems require direct sunlight to function, so there must be some way to store heat during cloudy periods as well as at night, and to recover the stored energy. All these requirements increase the cost of the system while decreasing its efficiency. The trade-off between reliability, cost, and efficiency has led many solar designers away from "active" systems, especially when designing for new construction.

Passive systems

Besides allowing a wider choice of building sites and orientations, new construction facilitates design of passive solar heat systems, which use sunlight to directly heat the building itself, or the air within it. Passive systems depend upon *convection* or *radiation* to circulate the collected heat. While some "passive solar" homes do use fans to assist circulation, most can function, at least minimally, without electricity.

Because they do not need to heat a liquid up to near boiling, passive systems are good at extracting useful energy from even diffuse sunlight. If your area is frequently overcast in winter, a passive, warm-air system may be your only solar option. Many solar "experts" who make a living selling active systems refuse to acknowledge how much energy such a system can extract from a theoretically "impossible" situation. (See "A house heating solar greenhouse" in *BHM* # 12.)

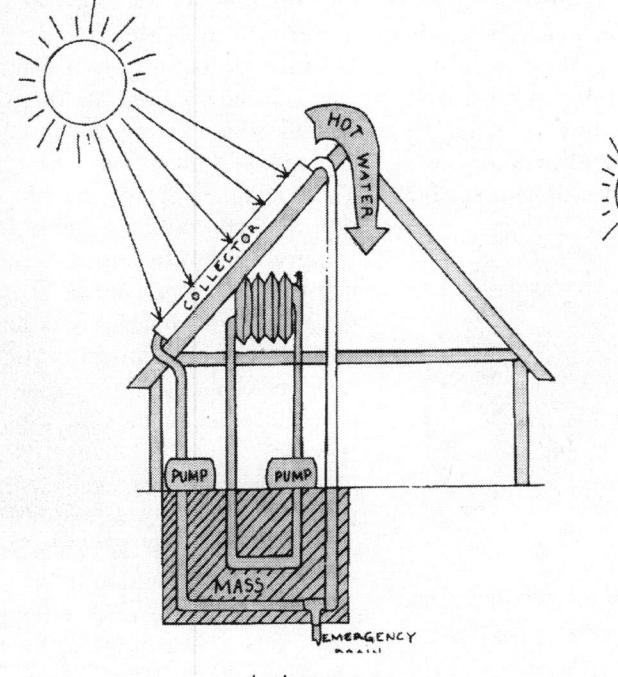

Active system

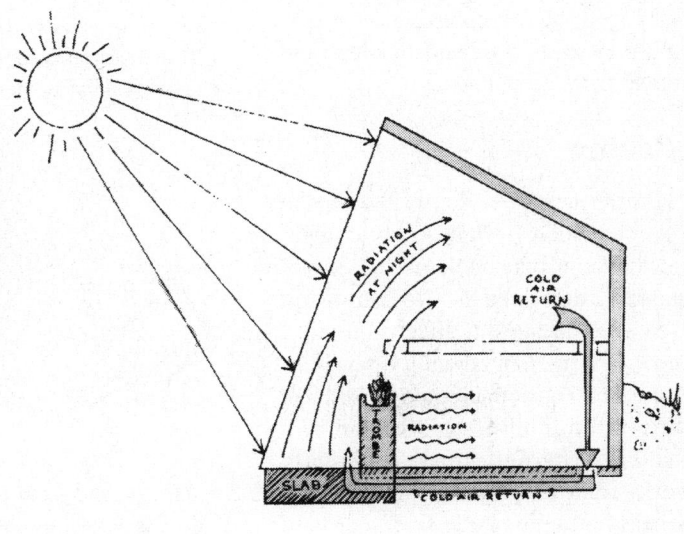

Passive system

"Passive" disadvantages

The disadvantages of passive solar stem from the same qualities as its advantages. Because passive systems operate on small temperature differentials, they require excellent insulation to retain those "extra" degrees of heat. Often, such houses are earth-bermed, or even built underground, to take advantage of insulation which is literally "dirt cheap." Because the house or the air is heated directly, the system must be built into the building, or at least be a major architectural addition.

The large areas of glass needed to capture diffuse sunlight make it impossible to disguise the nature of a passive solar heating system. Regardless of one's preferences in architecture, or the actual design, passive solar homes come in only one basic style. Worse, those large glazed areas can turn the building into an inferno in the summer unless provision is made for shading and ventilation.

To prevent nighttime heat loss, glazed areas must be covered with insulating shutters or blinds. Opening and closing shutters requires tedious daily attention. Owners of passive solar homes dare not leave them unattended more than a day or two. Many ingenious systems have been invented to solve this problem, and some work fairly well, but all complicate the system, add to its cost and upkeep, and detract from its efficiency.

Glazing

Glazing is indeed the weak point in a passive solar design. Many companies have introduced so-called "solar" plastics, designed not to cloud up, even after decades in direct sunlight. I know of none that actually delivers as promised. Those that come close have shown tendencies to weaken and weather. The only thing that really works right is tempered glass, which is heavy, fragile, expensive, and hard to seal permanently. **Do not use** ordi-

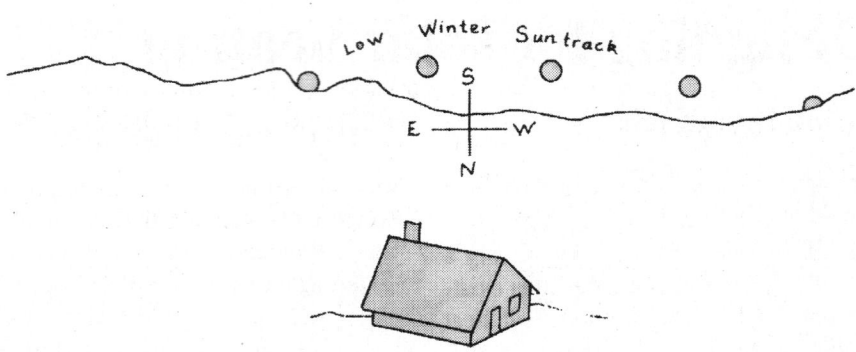

Taking advantage of a low spot on the horizon by orienting away from true south

nary window glass, which becomes deadly when shattered. Tempered glass isn't much stronger than window glass, but it breaks into rounded pieces or powder, instead of deadly, pointed missiles.

One of the most important advantages of passive designs is that they tend to use "low technology." If you're capable of designing and building a "normal" structure, you can probably do just as well designing and building your own passive solar home.

No free lunch

All solar heated designs must include provision for a backup heating system, for those periods when *insolation* (incoming sun energy) just isn't enough to overcome weather of extreme severity or duration. There are no 100% solar heated homes. How

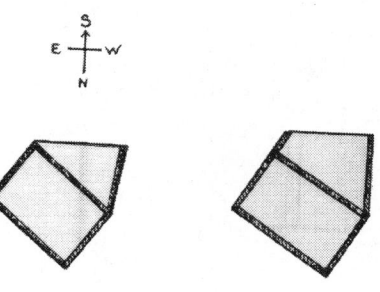

Two ways to add a south-facing greenhouse to a non-south-facing structure

close you come to 100% will depend on how much time, money, and expertise you have available to put into the project, as well as the weather.

There's no free lunch. A solar assisted home is one which receives less than 50% of its heat from the sun. The less you depend on your solar system, the cheaper and easier it will be to build.

An example

The house heating solar greenhouse mentioned earlier provided about 75% of our heat, at a cost of about $1000, including the use of lots of recycled materials and **no** hired labor. Convective distribution of heated air was assisted by floor grates, costing nothing. (See "Heat your upstairs by cutting holes in the floor," *BHM* #14.) These additions, plus a **lot** of insulation, helped convert a cold, drafty, century-old house into a fuel miser that used only one cord of hardwood to get through a bitter Wisconsin winter! We could have increased our "solar percentage," but the cost would have far exceeded the return in saved energy!

There are many contractors who will install a prefab "solarium" for you, usually for a stiff fee. These range from really good ones to strictly decorative units that leak more heat than they produce. One of the best national brands is sold by Four Seasons. They work, they don't leak water **or** heat, and they're guaranteed. They're not cheap, though.

Doing it yourself

The weak point of virtually all do-it-yourself greenhouses is sealing the roof glazing panels. "Sunlite" solar plastic by Kalwall is still the best solution, in my book. It will eventually degrade and need replacement—in 10 to 15 years. It costs nearly as much as glass. But you can get it in rolls, and stretch a single sheet over a 2 x 2 support grid, sealing it down with silicone seal and gasketed roofing nails. It's picky work getting it on right, but not difficult, and it leaves a glazed roof that can't leak, except at the edges. These can be sealed just like any glazing. The plastic is nearly 1/8" thick, lasts much longer than the corrugated stuff most of us are familiar with, and looks lots better.

Existing structures

Solar additions to existing structures can be practical, even if there is no south-facing wall to attach them to. The greenhouse need not be built parallel to the building wall. A triangular or irregular plan can work just as well as a rectangular one, as long as the ratio of the greenhouse volume to glazed area is kept around 9:1, plus or minus a bit. In my experience, ratios higher than 10:1 won't provide enough heat to justify the expense and trouble of construction, while ratios lower than 8:1 will be difficult to insulate at night.

Other orientation

It may not be necessary to orient the glass to face due south anyway. Generally, solar heating systems work best with a maximum southern exposure to the sun, but there are exceptions.

When the sun is low in the sky, the earth's atmosphere filters out much of its heat energy. That's one reason why it's hotter at noon than in the morning or the evening. Near the US/Canadian border, the winter sun is close to the horizon *all* the time, so there is less reason to prefer noonday sunlight. It may be possible to increase the total duration of direct "insolation" by orienting the building slightly away from due south, taking advantage of low spots in the horizon.

My house in Washington State did just this. (See <u>BHM, The Best of the First Two Years</u>: "Semi-underground, solar house has some ideas worth crowing about.") High canyon walls would have blocked the low winter sun, but the house was oriented to take advantage of a rift in the canyon rim, giving a boost to the total insolation, just when it was needed most.

The only way to tell if such "misorientation" will help is to compare suntrack charts for all sites under consideration.

Sky heat

Depending on your intended use, you may wish to orient a passive solar collector to take advantage of either morning or afternoon sun. "Sky heat," which is the primary source of the energy collected by warm air systems, is greatest in the afternoon, when the earth is re-radiating the solar energy it has soaked up in the daytime. Greenhouses intended primarily for house heating should be oriented to take advantage of sky heat, as well as the more direct sunlight around noon.

Sky heat may not be necessary for greenhouses intended primarily for raising plants. Seedlings need long hours of light. Heating them is secondary. In fact, a greenhouse optimized for heat may get too hot for raising plants, and require venting to keep from killing them!

Vertical glazed walls

It's easiest to build vents into vertical walls. Everybody "knows" that solar glazing is supposed to be angled to catch the sun as directly as possible. The angle usually recommended is equal to 90° minus the latitude of the site. For the continental US, this results in a glazed wall between 65° and 45°. Such walls are difficult to build, glaze, seal, insulate, and ventilate.

Fortunately, studies have shown that an identically glazed vertical wall loses only about 5% to 10% of its heat-gathering ability. Improved ability to shutter or otherwise insulate a vertical wall against nighttime heat loss may more than make up for the slight loss in heating efficiency.

But the real plus for vertical walls is their greater ease of ventilation.

Designing for maximum light vs. maximum sky heat

Screens, window cranks, and other technology are readily available and cheap. If you make most of your main glazing openable, you may not need any other vents. If you can't do this, as a rough rule of thumb, you'll need a ratio of about one square foot of vent to nine or ten square feet of glazing.

Vents should be placed so as to create a cross draft, with low vents facing the prevailing wind, and high vents on the downwind side. Greenhouse suppliers sell heat-operated, non-electric vent operators. I've seen them in use, and they work well and last forever. Check with your supplier before designing your vents, as they have weight limits.

Convection

Hot air rises. This is the basic principle behind convective heat distribution. If you can make the solarium the lowest part of the structure, with gradually rising living areas, natural convection will tend to distribute warm air from your passive collector without any other assistance.

However, you must also design in a way for the cooler air to return to the collector for reheating. In our house in Wisconsin, warm air from the collector flowed through the kitchen/dining room, up a step to the living room, then up the stairs to the bedrooms. The final bedroom had a floor register which allowed the relatively cool air to descend to the living room floor, where it was sucked across the kitchen floor and back into the collector. It did create a relatively cool draft across the floor, but the temperature differential was only about 10° F, so it wasn't unpleasant.

Convective solar additions frequently have problems like this, but designers of new structures can plan for convection to eliminate winter floor drafts.

Thermal mass

Solar heating systems are cyclic. They gather heat in the daytime, but use it primarily at night. To bridge the gap, there must be some way to store excess heat and distribute it later. Many methods have been tried, but all work on the same principle: moving a fluid such as air or water past a previously heated thermal mass, or *heat sink*. The mass adds inertia to the system, soaking up energy during the day and radiating it slowly at night.

Thermal mass can take many forms, but there are only two ways to get the heat energy into it. Active systems circulate high temperature liquids through or around the storage medium, heating it up. Because the storage mass is relatively small, it must be heated quite hot to retain enough energy to last the night. Heat transfers only from a relatively hotter medium to a relatively cooler one, so the liquid must be very hot indeed for the process to work. This is the source of all the problems with active systems.

Passive systems use a slightly different system. Instead of heating up a fluid and using it to transfer heat to the storage mass, they use sunlight to heat up the mass directly. If the mass is just large enough, it will hold just enough energy to radiate all night long, returning to its original temperature by morning. If the mass is too small, it won't hold enough energy to last all night. If it's too big, the mass will require more hours than there are in the day to reach the proper temperature. In other words, it will never get warm enough to function properly. Fortunately, a lot of mass is required to heat a whole house by radiation, so it's hard to build in too much.

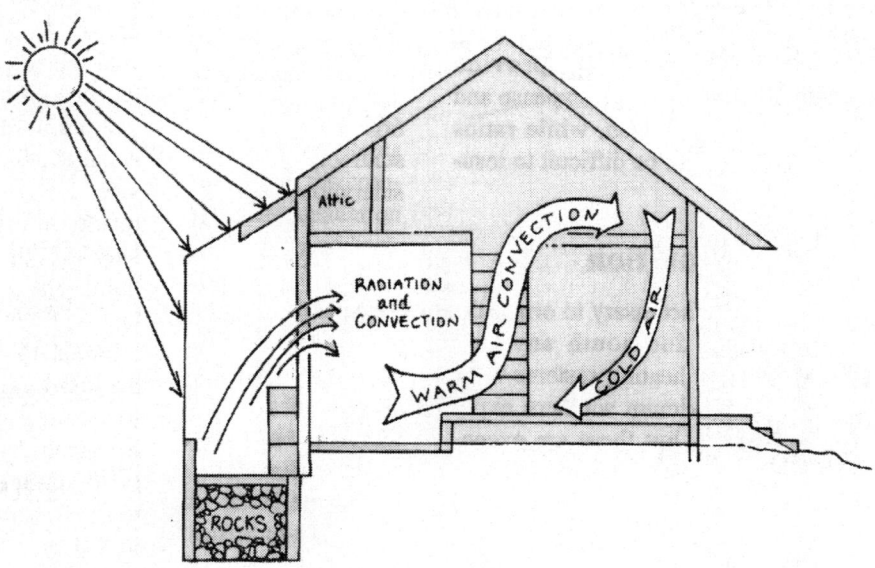

The author's solar-heated house in Wisconsin

The ideal place to put thermal mass is just inside the glazed area. Thick, concrete slab floors make excellent thermal mass, but must be well insulated from the cold earth beneath. They should be painted dark colors for heat absorption, or decorated with dark rock slabs, set well into the concrete for good conductance of heat.

Trombe walls

One way to add **lots** of thermal mass (without the disadvantages of concrete floors—see below) is to build in a short, **very** thick partial wall between the solarium and the rest of the house. This is called a *Trombe* (rhymes with "bomb") *wall*. It soaks up heat directly from the sun shining on it during the day and re-radiates it into the house at night.

Trombe walls are usually painted dark on the collector side, but may be any color desired on the radiation side. They are frequently covered with brick, to add yet more thermal mass, beauty, and additional radiation surface. Often there is a brick-enclosed planter on the wide top of the trombe wall. The earth provides yet more thermal mass, and the houseplants grown there disguise the solid nature of the Trombe.

The water Trombe

Concrete has two great disadvantages as thermal mass. It's very expensive in the quantities needed, and it's virtually impossible to add or subtract mass after it sets. Ken Kern, author of The Owner Built Home, invented the "water Trombe" to solve these problems.

A water Trombe is a wall consisting of stacked steel water barrels. Since water is only half as dense as concrete, a water Trombe needs to be about twice as thick as a concrete Trombe wall. This can be easily accomplished by stacking the barrels horizontally, on their sides, with one end facing the collector and the other facing into the house. Only the collector ends need be painted black.

Caution! A drum full of water weighs about 460 pounds. If you build a water trombe, **be sure** you build a rack that is strong enough to hold the weight. A 25-foot Trombe wall with barrels stacked in two layers weighs close to **five tons**. Be sure your foundation and footings are up to it. Because of these weight considerations, a Trombe wall of any kind is not something you can easily retrofit after the building is built. It is possible in some cases, but I wouldn't recommend it without the services of a competent architect. ∆

Live free...

Support the

Libertarian Party

the party of individual responsibility and personal freedom

For information call:

1-800-682-1776

or write:

Libertarian Party

2600 Virginia Ave. NW

Suite 100

Washington, DC 20037

Restore the Bill of Rights with **FULLY INFORMED JURIES**

Find out how ordinary people, as trial jurors, can repair years of legislated special-interest damage to our rights, simply by saying No to bad laws!

Phone

1-800-TEL-JURY

for a free Jury Power Information Kit!

The gosling that lived

By Dynah Geissal

The winters are long in Montana, and spring comes late. I always look forward to our first picnic, and most years we have it on Mother's Day. Even then there aren't many hours of warmth. This year Mother's Day definitely felt like spring. We loaded food and dogs into the truck in preparation for our picnic at the river.

The geese hadn't come to eat that morning. I had found them crowded around the dominant female who was setting on eggs. Geese are very protective of the young ones, and I knew that the eggs must be hatching. The adults were ready for their roles as guardians.

We had a great time on our picnic. Trees and grass were getting green, and birds were returning. The feeling of spring was exhilarating. After three or four hours, however, we were getting chilly. It was time for chores anyway, so we headed home.

I checked the goose nest first. The geese were gone. One egg was left unhatched and there, at the edge of the nest, was a dead gosling only half out of its egg. But wait, the eye was open and shiny. I picked the baby up. It was cold and limp.

I carried it into the house and kept it under my shirt while I built a fire in the cookstove. It stayed there during chores. Still there was no sign of life.

Later, my husband and I talked by the stove for about an hour. Suddenly I thought I heard something. I looked at the gosling. No sign of change, but still the open eye had not glazed over. I tucked her back in and then there was another sound. I was sure this time.

I looked at the gosling—and yes, a rasping gasp for breath, then one more! Then nothing. I couldn't detect a heartbeat or breath.

We went to bed and I took the baby with me, although it was still limp and apparently lifeless. Sometime during the night, I awoke to peeping sounds and a little body nuzzling against me. The gosling was very much alive now.

By morning she seemed to be as healthy as any newly hatched baby. Now I wondered if the other geese would accept her. They probably would, but had the gosling bonded to me? Would she know she was a goose?

When the geese arrived to be fed, I took the gosling from my pocket. The adults were being very protective of the other hatchlings, and I couldn't get too close. I put the baby down and backed up. She looked at me. The geese screamed. She looked at them. She looked back at me once more, and then she joined the other goslings in the center of the circle of geese. ∆

INDEPENDENT ENERGY

A Backwoods Home Anthology

Micro-hydropower — a working example

By Greg & Bonnie Chaney

The advantages of micro-hydropower installations are often mentioned in the literature about independent energy systems, but actual examples of working installations are rarely cited. This is probably because solar power is the current high-tech trend. Meanwhile micro-hydropower installations are restricted by their unique site-specific requirements.

There are numerous books on the topic of how to turn running water into usable energy, so the scope of this article is restricted to the story of our own installation. Anyone attempting to install their own hydro system will end up doing things differently, because every setup must be adapted to the local terrain; but the same series of decisions will need to be made.

The vital prerequisite for hydro power is an available water supply. The climate where we live near Juneau, Alaska, is extremely wet. We average two or three sunny days per month; the rest of the time it is usually overcast with a better than 50% chance of rain or showers. In our case, one of the requirements we had when we looked for remote property was that a ready water supply be available.

Measuring potential — volume, head, & friction

We purchased a four-acre beachfront lot. There is a small beaver pond bordering the upper edge of the property. I discovered that there are several small streams which flow into and out of the pond, which means that some water can be taken from the pond without draining it. I measured the volume of water flowing in one of the streams which fed the pond during the dry season to get a feel for the potential minimum water volume.

To measure flow volume, I used a stopwatch to time how long it took to fill a five-gallon bucket. The stream had a low flow volume of about 20 gallons per minute. This turned out to be lower than the total volume of water flowing in and out of the pond because I only measured the flow of one the streams which feed the pond, but it provided a good minimum figure. During the rainy season, you would be hard pressed to hold a five-gallon bucket in the stream without it

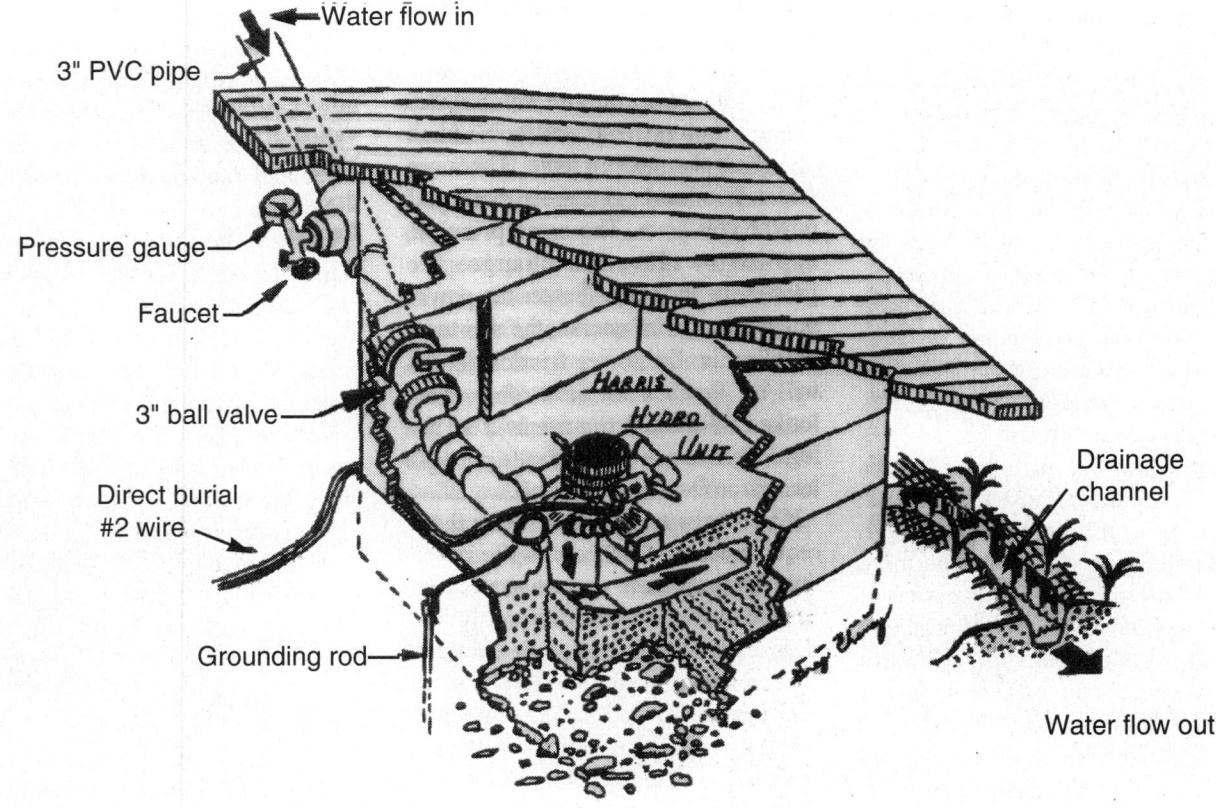

Cut-away view of our micro-hydro power shed

The Fifth Year

getting washed away. It is normal for water volume in streams to fluctuate wildly, so it's advisable to look at your water source during both wet and dry periods to get a feel for its seasonal dynamics.

The second critical requirement is that there must be a path for the water to run downhill to a lower elevation. The difference in elevation between where the water is taken into the system and the hydro generator site is called "head." Hydro power systems are generally divided into high head and low head categories. Roughly speaking, anything over 25 feet can be considered high head. Low head installations can often use traditional water wheels to good advantage, but high head situations usually employ pelton wheels to gain highest efficiency.

I tried to use a topographical map to determine elevation change, but due to its scale it proved to be too crude to be useful. In order to accurately determine the elevation difference between the pond and the generator site, we used a hand-held level and a 20 foot section of pipe. Although the tools were simple, we were able to measure a vertical drop of 93 feet from the pond to the generator site.

Another consideration is the distance the pipeline will run between the intake site and the point of use. In our case, the distance turned out to be around 500 feet. The pipeline distance is important because the farther water has to travel through a pipeline, the greater friction losses will be.

The amount of potential hydro power is related to how much water volume is available and how much elevation change you have. The more water you have, the more potential power you have. The same principle applies to elevation change: the greater the drop, the greater the power potential. And of course, the shorter a pipeline is, the lower friction losses will be. Perhaps the most often-overlooked additional requirement is the legal right to use water from a particular source for a hydro project.

If you have a site which meets these requirements, then comes the question: Do you have enough water and head to make it worthwhile?

Our system

In our case, we're drawing water from a pond, so we have a natural reservoir which buffers changes in stream flow. As I mentioned earlier, we have a minimum input to the pond of 20 gallons per minute, but this flow grows so high it can't be measured during the rainy season. Harris Hydro Company has put out a chart which lists the potential power available from various combinations of water volume and head. In our case, we have over 200 gallons per minute available water flow during the wet season and 93 feet of head. From the chart I figured out that we could generate about 1100 watts of continuous power.

Unfortunately, friction losses in the pipeline need to be factored in to bring things into focus. Power lost due to friction in a pipeline is something which can be compensated for by using larger diameter pipe. The larger the pipe, the lower friction losses will be. Unfortunately, bigger pipe costs more money. In our case, we bought the largest pipe we could afford, but friction losses reduced our maximum potential output to around 720 watts.

At first I was depressed by this lower output, but when I actually began to use the system I found that we got by very well with 400 watts continuous (300 kw hr/month) of power without any significant conservation effort. We have lots of lights, a VCR, computer, washer, propane dryer, stereo, and a 16 cubic foot freezer. We do have a propane range, propane hot water heater, propane dryer, and a wood stove. If we were running heating elements with electricity, we would need more power.

Our hydro system consists of several components. It starts with a six-square-foot intake screen on the edge of the beaver pond which borders the eastern edge of our property. This connects to 100 feet of four-inch schedule-22 PVC pipe which reduces to three-inch schedule-40 PVC for another 400 feet. The vertical drop from the pond to the beach is 93 feet, so the static water pressure is about 40 pounds per square inch at the bottom of the line. The end of the pipeline is near the beach by our house.

Where the pipeline ends, we have built a little shed which houses a Harris Hydro pelton wheel connected directly to a 24 volt high-output automotive alternator. This produces DC electricity, which is fed to a battery bank at the house. The battery bank consists of eight deep-cycle "Group 27" 12-volt batteries wired to produce 24 volts. The batteries are in a separate compartment vented outdoors. All positive battery cables which run out of the battery compartment are fuse protected.

We selected a 24 volt system for several reasons. Harris Hydro high output units are wired for 24 volts. 12 volt systems require thick wire to keep line losses down to a minimum. 24 volt systems transmit electricity more efficiently and therefore smaller diameter wire can be used. Trace 24 volt inverters have better performance characteristics. The only negative side to a 24 volt system is that there are very few appliances which can be run directly on 24 volts, while there are many 12-volt appliances available. In selecting a 24 volt system, we had to use an inverter to make it worthwhile. Our Trace 2460 inverter changes the DC power into standard 110 volt AC household electricity. The house is wired using standard residential components. This saved us a great deal of money over a 12-volt system, because the wire size is smaller and residential electrical components benefit from the economy of mass production.

Although the whole system sounds complicated, we received a great deal of design help from the staff at Real

Goods. The amount of electricity present in the system could be lethal or start a fire if the installation were improperly designed. I strongly recommend getting assistance from a competent source when designing an independent electrical system. You could be putting yourself and your family in grave danger if you approach the project like a big version of a car's electrical system.

Laying the pipeline

The most difficult thing by far turned out to be installing the pipeline. Everything we read concerning pipelines mentioned that burying a pipeline solves several problems including UV damage from sunlight, freeze protection, less potential damage from vandals or accidents, and stability. We decided to bury as much of the pipeline as we could, but when we asked the backhoe operator who was installing our septic tank if he could dig the trench for our hydro pipeline, he took one look at the steep, boulder-strewn, wooded slope and said, "Nope."

So we buried the lower half of the pipe by hand; the upper half lies mostly on the surface. Digging a ditch up a steep slope through rocks, roots and boulders proved to be a massive undertaking. We also installed a branch line to the house for a water supply. All in all, we spent lots of time standing in muddy ditches in the rain hacking at gnarled tree roots which were twisted between boulders.

Progress was excruciatingly slow, and there never seemed to be much to show for all the effort at the end of a day. Most of the time we measured progress in inches per hour or feet per day.

One day I was outside cutting the trench through bedrock with a pick. Our son Connor wanted me to wear a silly hat from my childhood trip to Disneyland. Well, there I was, swinging the pick for all I was worth, wearing this silly hat, and my wife Bonnie walks out. I finally had to take the hat off so she could stop laughing hysterically and get up off the ground.

Once the trench was roughed out, we put in the pipe. Even that turned out to be slow, because the PVC pipe must be dry when it's glued. So a makeshift tent had to be erected over every section before it could be glued. It is a real challenge to keep two pieces of pipe dry in a mud-filled trench in the rain! I hope we never have to do anything like that again.

Eventually came the time to pressure test the pipeline before burying it. I didn't have the proper pieces to cap the ends of the pipe to the house and the hydro shed, so I put a cap which was held on with a hose clamp on the end under the house and a plastic cap on the end by the shed site. Well, since I am going to the trouble of telling you this, you can guess what happened. The cap under the house blew off and for a little while we had a three-inch pipe blasting water into the underside of the house. It got my heart going, but there wasn't any damage and it's sort of a funny thing to look back on (although I don't ever want it to happen again). The pipeline held, and it hasn't given us any trouble so far.

Burying the pipe turned out to be almost as hard as digging the trench, because the rocks, roots, and muck we had dug out of the trench all rolled to the bottom of the slope. So when it was time to fill the trench in, we had the choice of carrying the rocks back up the hill or digging more out of the ground.

System testing — ours and nature's

November 15 was the first day we were able to test the system to see if it worked. Once the "big test" showed we had a success, we were busy cleaning up the yard when Bonnie spotted a pod of killer whales right in front of our place. There were several milling around in front of our place. As we watched, they drifted north. When they were about 100 yards north of our mooring buoy, they all started swimming right for the beach. At first we couldn't figure out what they were up to, then we saw the sea lions in very close to shore. The whales definitely wanted to eat the sea lions, but the whales couldn't follow the sea lions into the shallow water. The killer whales stayed by the sea lions for at least an hour. The whales were slapping their tails, spy hopping, and nearly jumping out of the water. It was quite a show. It eventually got dark and we didn't see any sea lions eaten.

A couple of days before Thanksgiving, the weather got pretty cold (mid teens) and a north wind came up which blew 50 knots. It was blowing very hard in the early morning, so I went outside to check on things. I saw and heard a large tree fall near the pipeline. It fell because we had cut its roots on one side. By the end of the day, four trees had been blown over and I was a nervous wreck. I couldn't help but wonder if a tree was going to fall on the house. We were very fortunate that the pipeline wasn't damaged by all the roots that were torn up by all the falling trees. It is hard to describe how relieved I felt once the winds subsided.

The winds died, but it remained cold. Things started freezing hard. The shut-off valve for the hydro plant froze in the open position, but water still ran through the pipe. Eventually the bathtub drain froze too. (I've put more insulation on it since then.) Large icicles formed on all the waterfalls in the area, and an ice sheet even formed on the hydro shed floor. Although things were very cold, the bottom line was that the pipeline did not freeze, the hydro plant still produced power, and the household water system worked fine.

We just experienced the coldest February in 15 years. Our system held up well until the last week. At that point the power output began to drop substantially. After two days of decreasing electrical output we had no power, but some water was still flowing through the pipeline.

I chopped a hole in the ice on the pond over our intake and found the screen covered with slush. Very little water was able to get through. Temperatures were near zero with sustained winds of over 30 mph. There was nothing to do but wait.

At the beginning of March, things warmed up to the 20s and low 30s. After the weather warmed up, our system turned itself back on. So a micro-hydro system can even work through a Southeastern Alaska winter, but the more insulation you have and the deeper you bury your pipeline, the better.

Cost comparisons

A word about cost. The components for our system cost us about $5000. We did all of the installation ourselves. If we'd had a contractor do the work for us, the cost would have been much higher. The biggest unexpected expense in terms of labor and money turned out to be the pipeline. This is probably the most site-specific aspect of any hydro power installation.

On the positive side, we do not have to buy fuel or listen to a generator droning away. Our friends with gas and diesel generators are constantly buying and hauling fuel and doing the required maintenance.

Our annual maintenance consists of changing the bearings and brushes, which costs about $20. If we compare our costs to electricity purchased in town, it will be 10 to 15 years before our system pays for itself. (Juneau's electricity is generated by hydro power and is relatively inexpensive.)

This comparison isn't very realistic because we don't have access to our municipal power supply. When we compare our cost to a gas or diesel generator based system, our system will pay for itself much sooner.

There are many good suppliers of independent energy products. The supplier we found for our system was Harris Hydroelectric Systems, 632 Swanton Road, Davenport, CA 95017, 1-408-425-7652.

(**For more information about using water to generate electricity, see** Backwoods Home Magazine's **three-part series on water power in Issues number 16, 17, and 18.**) Δ

A BHM Writer's Profile

Jeff Heikenfeld

Jeff grew up in Zion, Illinois, one mile from Lake Michigan. His father Gourden was an avid fisherman and camper so the family spent much time camping and fishing around Wisconsin and Illinois. At age 11 he joined Boy Scouts and earned the Eagle Scout award at age 17. His love and respect for the outdoors was learned through the scouting program.

Jeff says that his writing career really started when he was published in Backwoods Home Magazine. He took the article to the local newspaper, Perry County Times, and was hired as a stringer. The paper hired him as a writer/photographer and he stayed there part-time for two years.

Then he was hired by a much larger daily paper in the city, the Carlisle Sentinel. He had written over two hundred articles for the three Perry County newspapers (one owner) but it was scary to switch from a local weekly to a much larger daily paper. One week later he was asked to write the weekly automotive column for the Sunday paper. He had sold cars for three years and ended up doing the auto column for two years as well as writing feature stories.

Jeff enjoys meeting people and most of his writing is about country folks. He has written all sorts of articles from teaching chess to students with low self esteem and behavior problems to articles on environmental architecture, as well as speeches for a local county commissioner. He takes photos for most of his stories and enjoys song writing (blues, country) and at times poetry writing.

Jeff lives in a hand-hewn log home (circa 1800) with his son, Benjamin, and his daughter, Victoria Rose. His older daughter, Heidi, attends Susquehanna University. He has nine acres bordered by a stream where he raises goats and chickens. His hobbies include antiques and fishing. He also enjoys hunting and looks forward to teaching his children to hunt and fish.

INDEPENDENT ENERGY

A Backwoods Home Anthology

Here's a low-cost, low-tech refrigerator that really works

By J.D. Hooker

A friend was recently preparing to shell out well over $1000 for a kerosene-fired refrigerator. While these are useful and valuable devices in many circumstances, I didn't think he needed one.

He had a 4-inch, 200 foot deep well to supply the water needs for his household and livestock. After he examined my water-cooled refrigera-

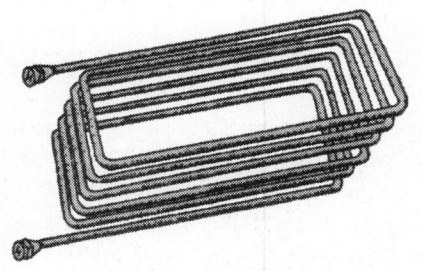

Fashion cooling coils from copper or plastic water line. Even garden hose would work.

tor closely, he built himself a duplicate the same weekend.

For inhabitants of many rural areas, a similar owner-built unit can offer the same cost savings and reliability they do for our households. There are no moving parts, no chemicals like freon, almost no maintenance, no operating cost, nothing to wear out, and they can be put together from salvage material in only a few hours.

Cold well water needed

The only real requirement is a deep well water supply, with a steady water temperature between 35° and 50° F.

In most of the country, deep wells have become a necessity for those out-

side the public water supply lines, due to lowering water tables, ground water pollution in shallow wells, and similar circumstances.

Check your water temperature by allowing the water to run for several minutes, emptying the lines and tank. Then fill a bucket with fresh water and insert a thermometer. If your water temperature is above 50°, you are probably one of the people who should look into a kerosene or LP gas refrigerator, or stick with electric.

It's simple

Really, the whole idea is extremely simple. At the point where the water supply enters your dwelling, the incoming cold water is routed through a coil of pipe or hose installed inside an insulated box before it goes anywhere else. Whenever water is used for dish washing, laundry, showering, flushing the toilet or whatever, fresh

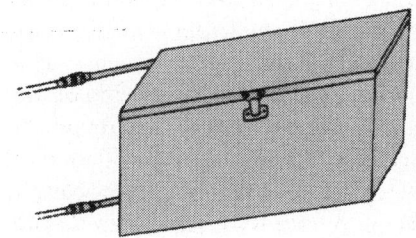

Install the cooling coil in an insulated box and hook it up to household plumbing. An old, worn-out chest-style freezer is ideal, but any sort of insulated box will work.

cold water circulates through this coil and cools the interior of the insulated box.

Construction

Any sort of well-insulated box will serve. Depending on your tastes, abilities, and what is available, you might opt for anything from an ultra-fancy oak and brass ice-box replica to something rigged together from plywood and sheet metal scraps.

For me, the best solution was to use a worn out chest freezer. I knew my wife would never go along with this

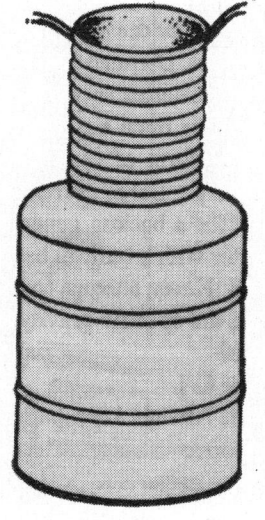
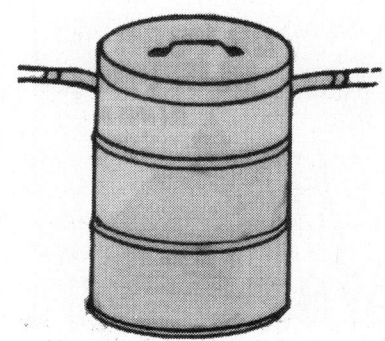

For a smaller cold storage space, wrap a 30-gallon drum with garden hose and insert it into a 55-gallon drum. Fill the space with insulation or very dry sawdust. Make a lid from styrofoam or other insulating material.

The Fifth Year

project if I didn't end up with something that looked like a normal and attractive household appliance. The chest type is superior to upright freezers because all your cool air won't spill out when you open the door.

The very first thing I did was cut off the power cord. The next step was to repaint the unit with appliance enamel. Then I cut a hole in the bottom and installed a PVC sink drain in case of spills or condensation.

Using a conduit bender, I then formed ½" soft copper tubing to match the interior dimensions of the compartment. Hard copper and sweat-on fittings—or even plastic pipe—would probably work just as well. I already had the soft copper tubing, so I used it.

After putting the unit in place, hooking it into the water line, and checking for leaks, we had to wait almost two days for the inside temperature to drop to 42°. Since then it has held that same reading for almost five years.

Cold water refrigeration is not a new concept. Nor is it adaptable to each and every situation. If, however, you are already drawing your water supply from a deep well with a fairly constant water temperature, why would you want to keep throwing your hard earned money away for electricity, kerosene, or any other fuel when you can refrigerate for free? ∆

The care of lead acid batteries

By Larry Elliott

Storage batteries are used in just about every independent energy system. The lead acid storage battery is a familiar sight in your car. Usually these batteries give years of trouble-free service and the average driver rarely has to be concerned about the chemistry of the battery, cycle life, or charge/discharge rates. The lead acid batteries used in an independent energy system are another story. If there is one item that is least understood or abused in these systems, it's the battery. If you follow the list of do's and don'ts outlined below, living with the storage battery will be a lot easier and less costly.

Rule 1. This comes as a shock to most people, but a 12-volt lead acid battery is almost dead when the voltage at rest (no loads or discharge) is 12 volts. Less than 25% of the battery's capacity remains. The voltage of a 12-volt lead acid battery will vary between 11.6 and 12.6 volts discharged and fully charged. This one volt range can be used as an approximate indicator of the state of charge and illustrates the need for an accurate digital voltmeter.

Rule 2. In order to obtain long life from your batteries they should be discharged to no more than 50% of capacity. This is not easy to accomplish, especially in a solar electric system in winter. A backup generator or, if you have the wind, a wind generator, can make this a lot easier to do reliably. Hydroelectric systems don't usually have this problem.

Rule 3. Don't use car batteries in an independent system. They are not made to be deep-cycled and will have an early death when used in this way. A good golf cart or forklift battery like the Trojan L-16 is a much better choice.

Rule 4. Never let a lead acid battery sit in a discharged state. Recharge as soon as possible. Every time you let them set for any length of time (even a few days) you will begin to accumulate lead sulfate on the plates that reduces their capacity.

Rule 5. If you live in a cold climate, be sure and provide insulation or a warm area for your batteries. The useful capacity and the batteries' ability to deliver power are greatly reduced in cold temperatures. Your batteries can also freeze when in a discharged state, so keep them warm.

Rule 6. Never draw large amounts of current from your batteries when in a discharged state. Damage to the plates can occur.

Rule 7. Batteries should have an "equalize charge" at least every other month or sometimes once a month depending on how severe the service. An equalize charge is a form of controlled overcharge that helps to place all the cells at an equal voltage. Large currents are needed to equalize, so once again you can see the need for a backup generator. An ideal method of equalization is to purchase an inverter with a built-in battery charger and an equalize function.

Rule 8. Never attempt to adjust the electrolyte level in the battery. Raising or lowering the specific gravity not only voids the warranty, but can ruin the batteries or pose an unhealthy risk of acid burns. Adding distilled water when needed should be as far as you go.

Rule 9. Always keep battery terminals and the tops of the batteries clean and free of corrosion. The batteries can self discharge rapidly, and badly corroded terminals can cause electrical problems, especially when drawing a lot of current.

Rule 10. Do some follow-up study on charge and discharge rates for your batteries. Consult a reputable battery dealer or the supplier/designer of your system as to the best way to treat your batteries. Nothing can kill a good set of batteries faster than improper charging and discharging. ∆

A subscription to
Backwoods Home Magazine
is always a great gift.
Call 1-800-835-2418
to order.

Sun oven cookery

By Jennifer Barker

Sun ovens are a wonderful labor-saving device for a backwoods family. The warm, sunny days of summer are when you least want to build a fire in your cookstove. In a backwoods home where everything runs from the sun and the woodstove, having a sun oven means freedom from having to deal with propane around the house at all. The sun provides the fuel without cost or effort to you! It's like having free fuel deliveries daily!

There are many different designs for sun ovens, but the basic theory is similar: the same rays that warm your face, when reflected to concentrate on a smaller area than normal, can provide enough heat to actually cook food. Insulation and weatherstripping can increase their efficiency. Some designs produce more heat than others, but all will simmer a hot dish on a clear day, and most will bake bread. Costs vary too. My favorite oven is the Sun Oven™, selling for around $150. Home-made ovens can cost as little as a few dollars if most of the materials are scrounged. While they may be a little less convenient to work with, and less weather-resistant, home-made sun ovens are every bit as effective to cook with as expensive commercial models.

Some basic hints for sun oven cookery: if you're baking bread (one loaf at a time works best), put a rock or two in the bottom of your oven as a heat-sink. When preheating an empty oven for baking, keep a close eye on it. It will rapidly reach a temperature hot enough to smoke the paint on the inside! If you're cooking a hot dish, a dark-colored casserole works best, and a clear glass one next-best. My favorite baking dish is a 2 liter amber glass covered Pyrex casserole. A wide-mouth jar painted black will do nicely for boiling water or rice-and-beans (make a small vent-hole in the lid, and use masking tape to leave an unpainted viewing-stripe up the side). If you have windy days where you live, the large reflectors of your sun oven may act like sails, causing your oven to tip over. Brace the oven well with rocks, put a few inside to weight it down, or even tether the oven to a rock or tree.

If you want to have a pot of rice warm and ready when you return home from work at the day's end, just put a measured amount of brown rice in your sun oven, along with twice that amount of water. Turn the oven to face where the sun will be at 2:00PM. The rice will cook as the sun passes by, and then stay warm but not have a chance to burn. When you are ready, just add a quick stir-fry from your garden, and you'll have an easy dinner! Or cook rice and lentils in the sun oven, and add a big fresh salad.

Some of the recipes I have used in previous *Backwoods Home* articles come out great when baked in a sun oven. Quick breads are delicious (*BHM* #16, 3rd Year Book), especially date-nut bread. Single loaves of yeasted breads bake well too. Don't be discouraged if they take longer to bake than the recipe says. Just start by preheating the oven to the correct temperature, and turn the oven every 20 minutes or so to make it face the sun and stay the hottest possible. Bake until the loaf tests done, and it will come out just fine. For hot meals, Italian and Oriental-style Bulgur (Veggie Fast Food, *BHM* #27) will cook up in an hour or less. Put all the ingredients listed in the covered casserole together, and stir them once or twice as they cook.

Here are some more good sun-oven recipes. You can cook any of these recipes on the stovetop or in a conventional oven, with minor adjustments to the amount of liquid, but somehow they taste best when cooked by the sun.

The compleat burrito

Don't feel limited by what's in the recipe: use any vegetables you have in the garden. Try substituting lentils for the black-eyed peas. This is supposed to be a simple dish that's adaptable to what you have! Serves 4:

> 2/3 cup brown rice
> ¼ cup blackeyed peas
> 2½ cups stock or water
> 1 Tbsp. chopped green chilies
> 1 medium carrot, grated
> ¼ cup tomato paste
> 2/3 cup sliced green beans
> ½ cup kernel corn
> 1 Tbsp. chili powder
> ½ tsp. cumin
> ½ tsp. oregano
> 1 clove garlic, minced
> ½ tsp. minced gingerroot
> 1 Tbsp. tamari
> 1/8 tsp. Tabasco
> 8 whole wheat tortillas

Combine all ingredients except the tortillas in a 2 quart or larger covered casserole. Prepare as follows: pick over and rinse the rice and black-eyed peas, and drain. Add the water. Use canned or fresh chili peppers. Grate the carrot coarsely. Add the tomato paste. Use fresh, canned, or frozen beans and corn. Add the spices (if using fresh oregano, use 1½ tsp.

chopped fresh leaves). Add the rest of the ingredients, except the tortillas.

Place the casserole in your sun oven, and cook till all the water is absorbed. Stir occasionally if you like, but it's not necessary. This dish usually requires turning the sun oven once or twice, as it should simmer at least an hour. Allow 3 hours for total cooking time.

Serve the filling wrapped in tortillas, garnished with your choice of the following: grated cheese, sliced avocado, guacamole, lettuce, tomatoes, salsa, olives, really hot sauce, fresh cilantro - you name it. Let your imagination be your guide!

Tempeh stew

This is a wonderful vegetarian stew with a savory miso gravy. Serves 2-3:

> 8 oz. tempeh, diced
> 2 cups water
> 2 carrots, diced
> 2 large potatoes, diced
> 1-2 turnips, diced
> 1 clove garlic, minced
> 1 tsp. prepared mustard
> 2 Tbsp. miso
> ¼ tsp. rosemary
> ½ tsp. thyme
> ½ tsp. marjoram
> ½ tsp. sage
> 1 Tbsp. arrowroot or 2 Tbsp. flour

In a 2 quart or larger covered glass casserole, combine the tempeh, water, diced vegetables, and garlic. Stir them together and cook in a sun oven until the vegetables are tender (this means about ½ hour of simmering, after everything comes to the boil).

Stir in the mustard, miso, and herbs. Simmer for about 10 minutes more. Dissolve the arrowroot or flour in ¼ cup of water and add it to the casserole, stirring well. Close the sun oven and bring back to the boil. Simmer about 5 minutes more, then stir and serve.

Allow at least 2½ hours total cooking time for this.

Sun-oven curry

This curry is easy to make and adaptable to a variety of vegetables. Serve with little dishes of homemade chutney, yogurt, coconut, and raisins on the side for an Indian feast. Serves 2-3:

In a 2-quart casserole, place:

> 3 medium potatoes, diced
> 3 medium carrots, diced
> 2 cloves garlic, minced
> 1½ tsp. minced gingerroot
> enough more vegetables to fill up the casserole
> try: broccoli stems, sliced
> mushrooms, sliced or quartered
> zucchini or crookneck squash, chunked
> green peas or snow peas
> green beans
> daikon (oriental) radish, sliced

In a small bowl, mix:

> 1 Tbsp. whole wheat pastry flour
> 1 tsp. turmeric
> ½ tsp. cumin
> ¼ tsp. coriander
> ¼ tsp. black mustard seed
> ¾ cup water
> 2 Tbsp. tamari

Stir the liquid into the vegetables until everything is well-distributed. Cook in the sun oven, in a covered casserole, until the vegetables are tender and the sauce is thickened (about ½ hour after it comes to the boil). Occasional stirring will make this come out better.

Sources: Heaven's Flame, a Guidebook to Solar Cookers by Joseph Radabaugh ($10) Available from: Home Power Magazine, POB 520, Ashland, OR 97520. ∆

Backwoods Home Magazine's

Web site

is easy to access on your computer.

Just type in:

http://www.backwoodshome.com

INDEPENDENT ENERGY

A Backwoods Home Anthology

Build a 12-volt power plant from the junkyard

By Edwin A. Towne, Jr.

I call this a "junkyard power plant," because I picked up most of the parts at the local scrap metal yard, one of my favorite places to shop. The parts and design can be changed to use whatever materials you have handy. My wiring diagram will only work for a Mopar (Chrysler) set-up.

Parts list:

1. Double pulley Mopar alternator, window type. These are usually higher amp than the single pulley type.
2. Horizontal shaft gas engine, five-plus horsepower. Eight to ten horsepower is good.
3. Early style Mopar voltage regulator.
4. Two replacement-type battery cable ends.

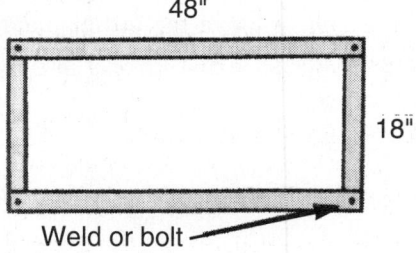

Figure 1

5. Automotive electric wire, 10 gauge.
6. Automotive electric wire, 16 to 18 gauge. Old lamp cord will work.
7. A house-type light switch.
8. V-belts. Length depends on how you build.
9. V-belt pulley. Same diameter as alternator pulley. Steel or cast iron.
10. Female spade terminals, 3¼", salvaged from a Chrysler vehicle, with an assortment of closed loop terminals.

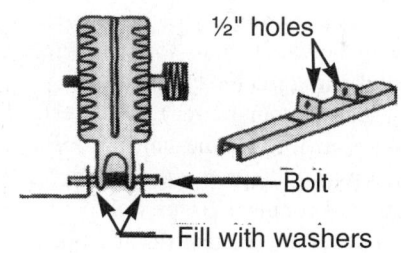

Figure 2

11. Two wheels, if you want a portable unit. I used old wheelbarrow wheels.
12. Sheet metal for a control panel. A piece cut from an old car body works fine. Size depends on your design.
13. Ford alternator rotor. Others will work, but Ford works best.
14. Frame parts. I used 2" angle iron, ¼" thick.
15. Bolts, nuts, washers to assemble frame. Or you can weld it.
16. Mopar alternator belt adjusting arm.
17. Ground strap, negative battery post to frame.
18. Three pieces of channel iron for motor mount and alternator mount.

Procedures

Lay out your engine and alternator with a belt connecting the pulleys. Measure the length of this and add the length of the battery or bank of batteries you want to use. The width will be at least the length of one battery. Mine was 48"x18".

Cut your angle irons to the sizes needed to form the frame and either bolt or weld the corners. Be sure the corners are square (see Figure 1).

The motor should be mounted in a corner of the frame with the starting cord facing outboard, where you will be able to reach and pull it easily. Cut two lengths of channel iron to fit the frame at the location you want your motor. Bolt or weld them to the frame, with the proper separation for the motor mount holes in the engine base. Put the motor on the channel irons to mark the location for the bolt holes.

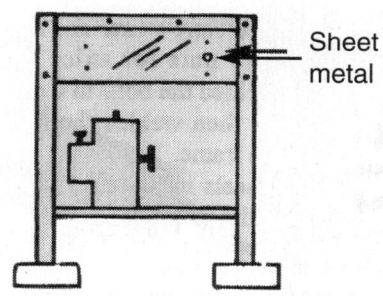

Figure 4: Rear view. Mount regulator and light switch on engine side of panel.

Remove the motor and drill holes in the channel iron.

Next is the alternator mount. For mine, I used two pieces of 3" angle iron, welded about 6 inches apart on a piece of channel iron, which was then welded across the frame. Drill ½" holes in the upright ends of the angle irons and use flat washers to shim each side of the alternator. The washers will allow for some adjustment in case your pulley alignment is not perfect (see Figure 2). Make sure everything is straight and square, and be sure the pulleys are in line and spaced the correct distance apart for the V-belt to connect them.

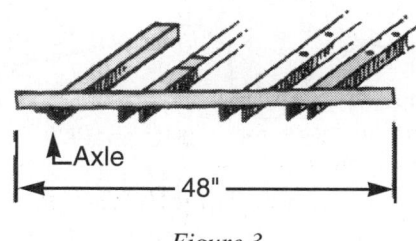

Figure 3

The Fifth Year

If you want the unit to be portable, you can mount wheels under the front. I used old wheelbarrow tires and rims, with bolts and nuts for axles (see Figure 3). I welded the bolts to a piece of angle iron, then welded the angle iron across the frame.

With the wheels in place, make the rear legs and the uprights for the control panel. I used 1" angle iron with Ford Alternator rotor halves mounted on the bottom. The irons must be long enough to form the legs and raise the control panel high enough that it will be out of your way when you are trying to start the engine. Raise the frame so it is level with the tires installed on the front. Measure the distance from the frame to the ground. Measure that same distance on the leg, and add the length of the teeth on the rotor half. When the teeth sink into the ground, the unit will be level. Weld or bolt the legs/uprights onto the frame.

Mount the engine, V-belt, and alternator on the frame. Adjust the alternator shims if needed. Loosely attach the alternator adjustment arm to the alternator. Make a bracket to bolt the other end to. I used a piece of angle iron welded to one of the engine mount cross pieces.

Weld or bolt a cross piece at the top of the rear uprights. Attach the piece of sheet metal to this cross piece. Drill ¼" holes to mount the voltage regulator, and attach it. Drill ¼" holes to mount the switch, with a ¾" hole midway between them for the toggle to stick through (see Figure 4).

Secure your battery or batteries in the frame. Wire the unit according to the wiring diagram (see Figure 5). Be sure all connections are tight.

I wired the engine throttle open and operated the choke by hand. You could install a regular lawn mower throttle cable, but the engine will run at full speed anyway.

To operate your power plant, first be sure the switch is in the *off* position. The switch should be off anytime the engine is not running to avoid burning out the voltage regulator.

Start the engine and allow it to warm up. Then turn the switch to the *on* position. You should hear your engine slow down as it picks up the load from the alternator. The alternator is now charging your battery. When the battery or bank is charged, the regulator will cut the power to the alternator field, which will cause your engine to race again. Turn the switch off and kill the engine.

I used one big Caterpillar Heavy Equipment battery, bought at the junk yard for $5.00. I only had to run the engine about half an hour in the morning and half an hour in the afternoon or evening to operate my lights, radio, 13-inch television, and other 12-volt appliances.

A few additional things to keep in mind:

An alternator will not charge a dead battery. It requires power to produce power.

An alternator will charge in either direction of rotation.

Mopar alternators use external-access brushes. (This makes for easy brush replacement.) They have internal fans.

A finger guard for children can be made from hardware cloth.

I have occasionally unhooked my power plant from my house to use it to start vehicles in cold weather. That's the reason for the wheels.

Welding two short pieces of 2-inch diameter pipe to the uprights gives you a place to insert wheelbarrow-type handles. They make it a lot easier to move the power plant around. Δ

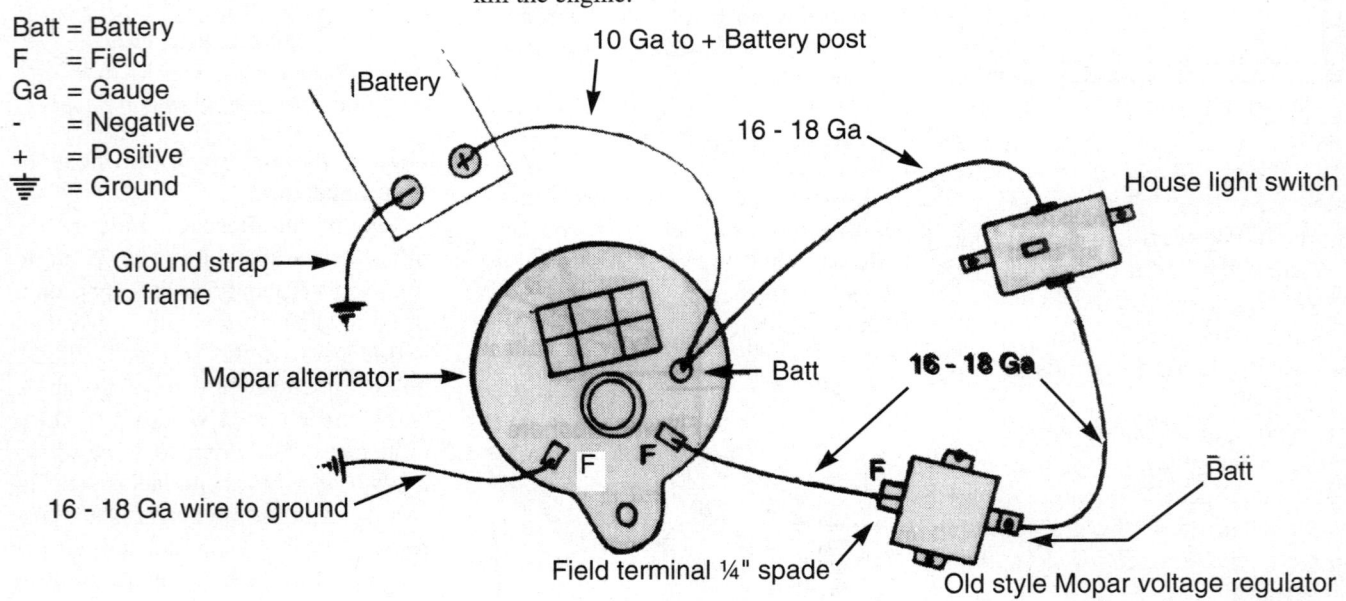

Figure 5: Wiring diagram.
It doesn't matter which F terminal is used for F or ground. All F terminals use ¼" spade connectors.

Firewood: how and what to buy

By Ray Lagoe

Like any business the firewood industry has developed a language all its own. For the novice wood buyer this terminology can be complicated and sometimes downright misleading. And like any profit-making business, there are honest dealers and those who are just out to make a quick buck. Your first line of defense is understanding the business and its language.

In the early '80s my wife and I fled the city and bought our dream home in the country. Soaring energy costs due to the energy crises coupled with our new found status as "country folk" convinced us to install a combination wood/oil furnace in the basement to heat our new home.

This led to my first experience in buying firewood, and it was a disaster. When I needed fuel oil, all I had to do was call and have it delivered — so why not the same with the firewood? Big mistake.

Delivery of my first load came while I was at work. My wife checked the truck, assured herself that it was what we ordered, paid the man and asked him to put it by the garage door. Did I mention that it was a dump truck? He backed up to the garage door, and you can guess the rest.

So here I am in the second week in December with the season's first big snowstorm filling my driveway with big snowflakes, and I have 6 cords of "green," wet, unsplit firewood blocking the garage door. And my snowblower, of course, is inside.

So after my crash course in the school of hard knots (sorry about that) I talked with a few old-timers, read up a bit, and familiarized myself with the firewood business. Hopefully this information can help you avoid some of the mistakes I made.

How it is sold

Firewood is sold in several different ways: cut and split, in chunks, as logs, and as slabwood. Cut and split is the least amount of work. Pieces are cut 12 to 24 inches long and split to a reasonable size, so all you have to do is stack it. Some dealers will even do that for a small additional charge. (You may have to do *some* splitting, depending on the size of your stove.)

Chunks (sometimes called billets) are pieces cut 12 to 24 inches long and delivered unsplit. These are usually a little cheaper to buy, but leave you with the task of splitting. Some people feel you get less wood per load this way, but I haven't noticed a big difference once it's split and stacked.

The most economical way to buy firewood is in log length. You have the advantage of cutting pieces to any lengths you want, and you save as much as 30 to 40% a cord. The disadvantage is the time, labor, and equipment involved. If you have the tools and are handy with a chain saw, this is the best way to go. A load of logs runs around $300 (prices vary by area) and will average around 16 face cord — less than $20 a cord. (I'll explain *face cord* shortly.)

Slabwood is the cheapest to buy — saw mills will sell it as cheap as $10 a pickup load. Slabwood is the pieces cut from the sides of the logs at the mill. They are two to four inches thick and of uneven lengths. This is usually a mix of hard and soft woods and makes excellent kindling and fuel for small woodstoves.

What is a cord?

The traditional measure for firewood is the *cord*. A standard cord measures four feet high, four feet wide, and eight feet long — an average of 128 cubic feet of wood and air space. The actual volume of split firewood in a cord is between 75 and 95 cubic feet, depending on how small it is split and the skill of the stacker.

Today the term *cord* often refers to a *face cord* (sometimes called a *run* or a *rick*)—a *face cord* is a pile of firewood cut 12, 16, or 24 inches long, stacked four feet high and eight feet long. This varies from state to state, and since there are no consumer laws regulating firewood, measurements can be very confusing to the buyer. If you don't know the dealer, ask for specific measurements.

For the remainder of this article, the word *cord* will refer to a *face cord*.

When buying more than a cord or two, you may be quoted a price by the size of the truck. A six-wheeler load (six-wheel dump truck) cut and split averages about five to six cords of wood. Unsplit chunks average closer to five cords and are a little cheaper.

If you buy wood in log lengths, you have two choices, ten-wheeler load or tractor trailer load. Jerry Graham, the foreman at Black Creek Lumber, says the average ten-wheeler load will be 15 to 16 cords of wood (when cut 16 to 20 inches long). A tractor trailer load will average about 24 cords cut the same length.

Jerry suggests finding a dealer that has a crane mounted on his truck so the logs can be stacked instead of dumped. Stacked logs are much easier to separate and cut. A ten-wheeler load of logs can get pretty tangled up and just about doubles the bull work.

Choices of firewood

(See the Nov./Dec. 1993 issue of *BHM* for an article on low cost firewood.)

Firewood is almost always sold as mixed hardwoods; a lot depends on the types of wood native to your area. Bottom line: the denser the wood, the better the heat (see chart) and the less trouble you'll have with soot and creosote build-ups in your chimney.

Most softwoods are lightweight and resinous, they burn quickly and produce few coals. The resins present in many softwoods (especially pine, fir, and cedar) create dangerous build-ups of creosote in chimneys and flues. These build-ups greatly increase the risk of chimney fires. If you have to burn softwoods, try to mix them at a two to one ratio (two hard to one soft) with hardwoods.

Never be afraid to inspect a load before it is unloaded. I once had a load of logs delivered that was almost 50% softwood. I refused to accept the load and sent it back. The dealer called the next day to apologize and sent a new load out the same day. Always be sure you get what you're paying for.

Stacking and drying

Half the weight of unseasoned wood is water. After seasoning under outdoor conditions it will be less than 20%. Check the ends of your wood: green wood will show growth rings and saw marks but the surface will appear solid. As the wood dries, it shrinks and cracks. If the cracks run from the center to the bark you can be pretty sure the wood is seasoned.

Some old-timers say you can tell if wood is seasoned by the sound it makes when you bang two pieces together. A soft dull thud means the wood is still green, a sharp crack means it's dry.

Firewood that is cut, split, and properly stacked will dry twice as fast as unsplit wood. Some stove owners like to cut and stack their wood a year in advance to ensure a good supply of seasoned wood. Properly stacked wood will dry in about four months.

The best way to stack your wood is in a long running row, but few people have that kind of room. If you have to stack your piles side by side, leave at least one foot between rows to allow for good air circulation. If you want to cover the pile, cover only the top, never the sides. Don't worry too much about rain and snow — sitting out in the snow will have little effect on the moisture content of your wood. The top and bottom layers may have damp bark, but any surface moisture will dry in a day or two once indoors.

A couple of final cautions: always remember "safety first"— wear safety equipment when cutting, splitting, and stacking. Gloves, steel-toed shoes, and eye protection are a must. Clean your woodstove regularly and never leave a woodstove unattended for long periods of time.

If you don't know your firewood dealer, pay him a visit and talk to some of his customers. Most of all don't be afraid to ask questions. Δ

Density of wood and heat produced by various tree species

An air-dried cord of these types of firewood produces the equivalent in heat of from 218.6 gallons of fuel oil (hickory) to 121 gallons (fir).

Species	Rel. density	BTU/Cord
Shagbark Hickory	72	32,800,000
Black Locust	69	31,400,000
White Oak	68	31,000,000
Bitternut Hickory	66	30,000,000
Chestnut Oak	66	30,000,000
American Beech	64	29,100,000
Laurel Oak	63	28,700,000
Northern Red Oak	63	28,700,000
Rock Elm	63	28,700,000
Sugar Maple	63	28,700,000
Yellow Birch	62	28,200,000
White Ash	60	27,300,000
Southern Red Oak	59	26,900,000
Black Walnut	55	25,000,000
Oregon Ash	55	25,000,000
White Birch	55	25,000,000
Black Tupelo	50	22,800,000
American Sycamore	49	22,300,000
Silver Maple	47	21,400,000
Sassafras	46	21,000,000
Yellow Poplar	42	19,000,000
Red Alder	41	18,600,000
Eastern Cottonwood	40	18,200,000
Black Willow	39	17,800,000
Quaking Aspen	38	17,300,000

Softwoods

Species	Rel. density	BTU/Cord
Tamarack	53	24,100,000
Western Larch	52	23,700,000
Douglas Fir	48	21,900,000
Bald Cypress	46	21,000,000
Red Pine	46	21,000,000
Hemlock	45	20,500,000
Cedar	44	20,000,000
Fir	43	19,600,000
Pine	41	18,600,000
Spruce	40	18,200,000

SEPT/OCT 1994
No. 29
$3.50 U.S.
$4.95 CANADA

FREE 5 YR INDEX

Backwoods Home magazine

...a practical journal of self reliance!

Making a Living

PRESIDENTIAL WIVES
HOMESCHOOLING
SOURDOUGH BREAD
BARTER NETWORKS

My view

Bad laws, good solutions

A letter from Charlotte Monte on page 88 of this issue suggests that a "revolt/revolution of some sort" may be needed to straighten out what is wrong with American government. That may be so, and John Silveira, in fact, is working on an article for *BHM* that will explore the history of revolts in America's past. You may be surprised at how often various American groups have actually engaged in revolts, so the precedent is certainly there.

But there are also a number of very good peaceful revolts many Americans now engage in. They are effective, sometimes legal and, in my opinion, almost always moral ways to corral government. Let's look at one illegal and one legal way to control our government.

Underground economy

America's underground economy is estimated to be between one tenth and one third the size of our regular economy. That's a lot of illegal activity, and just about everyone is engaged in it. If your babysitter didn't pay taxes on the last sawbuck you gave her, she is part of that illegal underground economy. If you fudged the figures on your last tax return, you too are part of it.

The reason why so many people are willing to take part in the underground economy is because they know they have the moral high ground. In spite of pronouncements by some church leaders that it is a moral responsibility to pay taxes, truly moral people understand that that just isn't true, that in fact morality and legality have nothing to do with each other.

Equating morality with legality is what the Nazis tried to do in their defense at the Nuremberg trials after World War II. We only followed orders, they said. Moral behavior prevailed, of course, and the allies told the Nazis they had a moral obligation to disobey legal but morally wrong laws that called for the killing of innocent people.

Americans today instinctively apply that same moral argument when they participate in the undergrond economy. They feel that their earnings are theirs and that the government has no right to take the fruits of their labor, at least not to the degree that today's government takes it from them. They consequently have judged many tax laws to be immoral usurpations of their money for purposes of furthering government programs they want nothing to do with, and they have either stopped paying taxes or cheat on them.

It is a moral high ground that is difficult to argue against, so the government doesn't even try. Instead they have imposed harsh penalties on tax evaders, especially well known tax evaders (remember Willy Nelson?) to send a signal that they will collect taxes, moral or not. "Fear is the foundation of most governments," John Ad
ms said in 1776, and it still is today in1994.

So how is the underground economy a good solution for bad tax laws? Ask the late great Soviet Union. By the time the Soviet Union collapsed, the only thing in the country that worked was their underground economy. As our own government grows larger and larger, so does our underground economy. It is a natural response to oppressive taxation and regulation, and it is a moral one.

Fully informed jury

The fully informed jury is a legal, as well as moral, way to corral government. A jury has the right to judge not just a potential violation of a law, but the law itself. This isn't a new discovery. An organization called the Fully Informed Jury Association (FIJA), which you can reach at P.O. Box 59, Helmville, Montana 59843 (Telephone: 406-793-5550), has a fairly large network of people, including an excellent newspaper you can subscribe to, that will tell you the details. (We ran a good article on it in Issue No. 19)

If you find yourself on the jury of, say, a tax evasion trial, you can acquit even if the evidence is overwhelming that the defendant violated a tax law.

That goes for any jury you are on. If you are on a jury considering whether or not a 20-year-old kid should go to prison for possession of a marijuana cigarette, you can acquit him and no one can do anything about it. If, as a juror, you want to acquit pro-life activists charged with blocking an abortion clinic, you can acquit also, with total impunity. Same with people charged with gun violations or failing to send their children to public schools.

Judges often try to use scare tactics against juries, telling them they have to rule a certain way if the law has been violated. That is simply not true; you have the right—and the obligation—to judge the morality of a law, just as those World War II Nazis did.

Fully informed—and morally responsible—juries are one of the main reasons why Americans in the past forced the government to repeal Prohibition; prosecutors could no longer get convictions. And it's one of the tools ordinary people used to help end slavery; juries stopped convicting those charged with harboring runaway slaves.

So there are two powerful weapons—the underground economy and the fully informed jury—at our disposal. One may be illegal but both are moral. If enough people use them, we could have a much needed, but peaceful, revolution in America.

By the way, Thomas Jefferson had something to say about rebellion: "I hold it that a little rebellion, now and then, is a good thing, and as necessary in the political world as storms in the physical."— in a letter to James Madison, Jan. 30, 1787. ∆

MAKING A LIVING

A Backwoods Home Anthology

Here are some home-based businesses that are worth trying

By Skip Thomsen & Cat Freshwater

Sooner or later, we all find that it is nearly impossible to run a homestead without a dependable source of income. Ideally, we would like to earn that income right at home. Not only would we enhance our feelings of independence and self sufficiency, but we could enjoy a valuable level of togetherness with our family.

We've seen a lot of folks pack it in and head back to town because they "couldn't find a job." Yet it seems somehow foolhardy to set off on a homesteading adventure when the whole show is dependent on finding a job in the nearest town. Especially when most small towns have one thing in common: significant unemployment. When a job does come up, it's much more likely that it will go to a local than to a newcomer.

We may well need some work to generate an income, but we do not need a job. It has been our experience that anyone who can do anything well can find work just about anywhere. Let's face it, if you've got what it takes to be a successful homesteader, then you've also got what it takes to be in business for yourself.

If it just happens that a job works out for you, that's great. But remember: any time you are working for someone else, your employer has to make a profit from your efforts if he's going to stay in business. If you are in business for yourself, your earnings (assuming you run your business in a businesslike manner) reflect the wage and the profit, not just the wage.

The number of people running successful home businesses is amazing. Some are just getting by, and others are earning as much or more than they did at straight jobs in the city. And all of them are having more fun than they would be if they were working for someone else.

Aside from the obvious need to know what you are doing in your intended field, the essential requirements for success in any self employment are self-discipline and the composure of a self-starter. When you're self-employed, there's nobody around to tell you to get it in gear, or to see to it that the job gets done properly and on time. Your reputation is what insures the next job coming your way, and your income is directly proportional to your effort. If you're considering working for yourself, this level of commitment should not be a scary concept.

Buy and sell used cars

Over the years, we have run several successful home businesses. Our first was buying and selling cars and trucks. We started out by buying a rig that needed some body work and general cleanup. It was to be our family car. After completing the repairs, we happily drove our new looking car until another bargain "mechanic's special" showed up. We bought it, repaired it and sold the first one for enough to pay for both cars and their repairs.

It didn't take too many more deals like these to convince us that here was a good home business opportunity. We went to all of the nearby banks and other money lending businesses and left our names as buyers of repossessions. We watched the classi-

The Fifth Year

fied ads for damaged cars or those needing repairs.

"Project" cars and trucks are notoriously hard to sell. Most people won't even bother to call when the ad says that the car needs help. We've bought less than perfect cars for half the price the seller was originally asking. We just went to look at the cars and left an offer with a phone number. They almost always called back.

After a while, it became obvious to us that we could do a lot better if we specialized in one or two makes of car. At that time (the late seventies), we decided on Toyota Corollas. All Corollas from '74 on up had lots of interchangeable body, mechanical, and interior parts. That interchangeability made it possible for us to buy an occasional wreck that had low miles but an unrepairable body. We could then install the fresh engine and interior in a high mileage car we bought for next to nothing and have an easy sale when done.

We soon established a reputation for selling excellent quality cars at reasonable prices. We also guaranteed what we sold, which was pretty easy with our available supply of parts. Besides, in all the years we sold Toyotas, the only repair we were ever asked to do to a customer's car was to replace a water pump.

An auto repair business at home may require that you live on a piece of property large enough for a shop and the storage of a few cars. It also requires that your zoning allows you a repair business on the premises. Again depending on your location, you might even need a license to conduct any kind of business that involves the selling of cars. Often this doesn't become an issue in a real low-key operation, but it's best to check before you jump right in. Some parts of the country are real picky about this sort of thing; others won't bother you if your business (noise, traffic, etc.) isn't bothering somebody else.

If auto repair is not your thing, you could apply the same concept to your own area of expertise. Perhaps you like repairing and refinishing furniture or rebuilding musical instruments. Maybe you're into heavy equipment; whatever your field, if folks can depend on you for an excellent product, you can go into business for yourself.

Publish books . . .

All of our auto dealing was done at our mountain homestead where we made our own power. We ran the shop, house and our office on our home-built power system for 10 years, and it worked so well that quite a few folks suggested that we write a manual on how to duplicate the system.

And that's how we got into the publishing business. We were getting tired of fixing cars about then anyway, and the idea of embarking on a whole new business venture sounded exciting. We wrote More Power to You! over a period of about a year. During that year, we sold the homestead and moved to a little community on the Oregon coast. We bought a little house, and immediately added a room for our new desktop publishing business. (See *BHM* #11.)

Our book was about ready for the press, so we had to decide how much of the printing and binding we were going to do ourselves. After getting several quotes on both the whole job and just the printing, we decided to have our first run of 1000 books printed at a small, local shop; we collated the pages and bound the books ourselves. We bought a machine to punch the pages and install plastic comb bindings, and with a couple days' work in our garage, we had the job done and saved close to $2000 in the process.

The first printing was selling quickly, and our local printer, who specialized in small runs, didn't want to do another of ours. And although 1000 books was doable in our garage, a run of 5000 would have been overwhelming. As it turned out, the price break for the larger quantity brought the finished price per book down to about what we had paid for just the printing of the first run. More Power to You! is now in its third printing and still selling.

. . . or a newspaper

We also took on another related business venture shortly after our move. We felt that the north Oregon coast needed an "art paper." We envisioned a tabloid size paper of about 20 pages, showcasing local writing and artistic talent, and listing the art, music, and other cultural events in the area. We proposed the idea to local merchants and asked if they would support the venture of this free quarterly paper with their advertising. The resounding "yes" we got from nearly everyone was all we needed to launch Elixir!

We did all of the layout and graphics for our advertisers, and the first issue of 500 papers paid for itself. The paper was distributed to many of the restaurants, stores, motels, hotels, and other businesses in our three closest communities. Subsequent printing runs were 1000 and then 5000 issues. We sent boxes of them to friends in Portland, Seattle, San Francisco, and other cities from which many of our tourists came; these issues were distributed mostly at coffee houses and restaurants. The paper was so well received that we started getting requests for subscriptions.

Elixir! eventually went on an indefinite hiatus because we couldn't get enough submissions. We asked for material that had something to do with life on the coast. And we published only the best that we received. We didn't have the budget to pay for submissions, but we were surprised that there weren't more writers eager to see their work in print. So, although Elixir! was earning us money, we had to fold it; we could no longer write the entire text ourselves. The point here is that local newspapers and specific-topic newsletters can be profitable businesses, and if your interests lie in this direction, they can also be a load of fun to produce. We sure met a lot of wonderful folks doing ours.

Since then, however, we have written and published two more books and have three more in the works.

Desktop publishing is a home business that can be done anywhere in the country. The only requirements besides your inclination and skill, are a good electrical power source and, in most instances, a telephone. Some business relationships will require that you send work via modem, but mailing diskettes still works in most instances. And at the ever-falling prices of computers and peripherals, the investment to get started is small.

Build homes

After moving to the coast, we entered yet another "home business" with excellent earning potential; but it requires either a friendly lender or a sizeable nest egg. Our little beach community was lacking well-designed, modest-sized homes for sale. The demand was high and the supply was low. Great environment for a builder, right?

We had already designed and built several homes in the past, so we had the tools and qualifications. We decided to try one there and see how it went.

With borrowed money and a carpenter/artist friend, we went to work. We bought a lovely, wooded lot, designed a home especially for that property, and went to work. It took about six months for us to complete our first "spec" house, an all-cedar showcase of labor-intensive woodworking. It sold immediately; and we made enough on it that we needed to borrow only a little for the second one. By the third house, we were on our own.

Does working at home sound like something you'd like to do? Before you chuck it all and decide to set up shop in your garage, you might want to take inventory of your skills and aptitudes. And don't forget commitment and self-discipline. Ours are only a few examples of workable self-employment.

Basically, most businesses fall into either of two categories: service or product oriented businesses. When you narrow down your choices to a few different areas that interest you, check at your local library for both books and magazines addressing the work-at-home side of each field. And to help you get an idea of the range of possibilities, here is a broad view of some endeavors that lend themselves to home business.

Desktop Publishing:
Newsletters:
    specific topic
    general interest
    local home school

Local jobs:
    letterheads
    business cards
    menus
    forms
    flyers
    sales brochures

Self-publishing:
    books, your own or others'
    booklets
        tourist information
        recipes
        how-to's
        local history/culture
    newspapers
        arts/music happenings
        happenings coverage
        tourist information
        political forum
        local news/events
        all of the above

Repair business:
    farm machinery
    auto/light truck
    computers*
    home electronics*
    appliances
    home-handyman stuff
    any combination of the above

*Strange to recommend for a wilderness home-based business? Word travels swiftly in the country. If you are good at something and charge reasonable rates, you will be surprised how many computers and related peripherals (for example) will appear out of nowhere.

Carpentry-related:
    framing
    complete building contracting
    concrete
    roofing
    remodeling
    painting

These aren't exactly "home" businesses, inasmuch as you won't be able to build someone else's home at yours. The business is, however, run from your home; you decide the hours that you work, and you call the shots.

Welding:
    At home in your shop
        repairs
        fabricating equipment and
        related products

Truck racks, utility trailers and related equipment, can be custom made-to-order or made-up-for-inventory and perhaps sold through a dealer in town

    With portable truck-mounted welder*
        on-site repairs at neighboring ranches/farms
        heavy machinery at job site

*We've seen "have welder-will travel" welders keep real busy in the country.

Furniture Building:
    sold through a dealer in town, an artist's co-op, or at your home-studio, if you are anywhere near a tourist area or even a good-sized city

Fine-arts or crafts goods:
    sold through nearby artist's co-ops, galleries, stores, or at various fairs and events (if you're willing to travel)

Sewing:
    alterations and repairs
    manufacture* of sewn goods, fabric or leather

*We had a neighbor who made custom-designed, belt-hung "holsters" for

equipment used by surveying crews. She researched the market and found a need to fill.

Bookkeeping:
    personal tax returns
    business accounting

Many business needs can be taken care of by modem on your home computer, too.

Computer-based businesses:
    setup
    training
    programming

These include working with a business in town (any town, anywhere) doing exactly what you would be doing if you were there, only doing it at home via modem. It is surprising how many computers there are around, and how few of them are used to their potential. There is a need almost everywhere for help in setting up programs and peripherals, teaching people how to run them, and just showing folks (including business folks) how to get the most out of their equipment. Magazines like *Home Office Computing* are valuable resources for home-business opportunities.

Heavy equipment operator:
We strongly recommend that if you need a job done, and find that you can buy the equipment to do it yourself for anywhere near the same price as having the job done, by all means, buy the equipment. This applies well to machines like dozers and tractors. Owning a dozer—and knowing how to operate it well—gives you an instant business opportunity. There is almost always someone nearby who needs some dozer work done, and the going rate in most areas of the country is around $30/hour for a small machine.

Tractor work:
    grading
    plowing
    disking
    mowing
    anything else your machine is equipped to handle

There are folks around who would love to plant that certain several acres every year if they could find someone reasonable to do the machine work. These are the people who don't have quite enough tractor work around to justify buying their own machine.

Baking:
We know several women who bake all sorts of scrumptious goodies at home and distribute them to nearby restaurants, delis and stores. This does entail frequent trips to town, so "nearby" becomes the operative word here.

Catering:
Again, this is an option for those who live near enough to a population center to make it work.

Homesteading school:
Don't laugh! This is recommended only for folks who have been homesteading long enough and successfully enough to be viable teachers. The demand for this information is increasing at a rate proportional to the government's revocation of our independence and individual freedom. If the day-to-day operation of your homestead would accommodate a school, be it one day or several, it's worth thinking about. The sessions can include meals and even lodging, produce an income for you, and provide a priceless, hands-on experience for would-be homesteaders.

Alternative energy:
    consulting
    sales
    installation
    service

If you are truly knowledgeable in the field of alternative energy and its application to the real world of homesteading, why not produce your income by helping others achieve independence. Design systems that best use available resources to fill your client's needs within his/her budget and, once again, word will get around. Assuming that there are no zoning regulations to prevent it, you can operate this type of business out of your home. Depending on your location and the general interest in your area, this can be a business that is environmentally positive and profitable, as well.

Child care:
If any of your neighbors still work in town, and if you have the disposition and skills to look after their little ones, you can supply them a service that provides you with a steady income.

Any of the business opportunities listed above (and lots more that aren't on the list) can keep you as busy as you want to be—if you are good at what you're doing, dependable, and charge a reasonable fee for your time. Reasonable doesn't mean cheap, either. You should charge whatever the going rate is for your trade.

Word spreads fast in a small community. If you are good at your craft and dependable, your reputation will find customers for you.

Being in business for yourself just beats the heck out of having a straight job. Your hours are your own, and your income is directly proportional to your effort. We've talked quite a few people into starting their own businesses, and without exception, they ended up making more money while working fewer hours than they did while at a straight job, and they had more fun. Of course, we've been very selective about whom we tried to convince. They were already self-motivated, independent folks; the kind that make good homesteaders.

We're still publishing, and still build an occasional house. And we've got this really nice Toyota pickup for sale...

(This article was excerpted from <u>A Modern Homestead Manual,</u> by Skip Thomsen and Cat Freshwater, which covers the planning, philosophy, realities, survival, and nuts-and-bolts of homesteading. Watch *BHM* for an upcoming review.) ∆

Use your own sawmill to cut lumber prices

By Robert L. Williams

One of the greatest shocks to the *Backwoods Home* audience in the past several years has been the sudden and shocking increase in the price of lumber. At present a 2-x-10 pine board 12 feet long costs $13. A 14-foot board of the same dimensions costs $16, a $3 jump in price for the 2 extra feet.

To feel the total impact of the increase, consider the cost of rafters or joists for an entire house. If you need 16-foot joists, each one will cost you nearly $20. Multiply the number of feet for the long side of your projected house. If the house is 52 feet long, you will have 624 inches on that one side only. If you divide this number by 16, which represents the on-center spacing of joists, you will find that you need 40 joists on each side of the house (counting the out-side joists or headers on each end).

That is a total of 80 joists, each costing roughly $20. The final bill is $1,600—for floor joists only. You will need ceiling joists and rafters, so you will more than triple the amount for the three areas of the house. That figure comes to $4,000, because the rafters must be longer than 16 feet and will cost even more than joists.

Then you must figure the cost of all the studs (a couple hundred of them for a modest house), subflooring plywood, sheathing plywood for the roof, and literally dozens of other locations where huge amounts of wood are needed. In short, you will need about $18,000 to $20,000 worth of lumber for a house of 2,500 square feet. But there is, for many people who are adventurous and willing to work, a way to alleviate a huge portion of the cost of lumber.

The startling truth is that you can actually eliminate all of the cost of lumber, over the long haul, and can in fact make a nice profit while doing so. The way out is to buy a used sawmill. Or, for that matter, a new one, although you can spend up to $30,000 for a new one. There are many, of course, for lower costs, and you will need to shop around if you want to get the best buy.

The reason for suggesting a used one is that, for most people, it may not be advisable to spend a great deal of money until you have tried milling and decided that you want to continue with the work. Then, if conditions warrant, you can invest in a new mill.

You can find a used sawmill, such as the 40-year old mill shown in the photos accompanying this article, for a reasonable price. This particular mill was bought by Mike Still for $7,500, and the price included several extras, in addition to the actual cutting part of the mill. Mike and his wife Alison often operate the mill as a team, and when Alison is tied up in other projects, Mike hires help for the gruelling work. Still, he says, he can operate the mill, pay the help, and still enjoy the work, along with a handsome profit.

And if $7,500 seems like a huge investment just to save a little money, you might find it interesting that in one morning in January this mill turned out 75 one-by-six boards, 34 two-by-fours, and eleven one-by-eleven shelving boards, in addition to a huge stack of edging boards. Figure the work of one morning as follows: $3 each for the two-by-fours; $14 each for the one-by-tens; $8 each for the one-by-sixes, and $8 each for the edging boards. A little arithmetic tells us that the studs are worth $102; the one-by-tens add $154; the one by-sixes add $600; and the edging boards are worth another $200 minimum. The total is $1,056 worth of lumber for one morning's work.

What about joists? You can saw a 2-x-10 or a 1-x-10 for exactly the same cost and with the same effort. A 6-x-10 timber costs no more to saw than does a 1-x-10 board. If you saw 100 2-x-10s for floor joists, each 16 feet long, you have saved about $1500 for the two or three hours needed to saw the lumber.

With most "portable" sawmills capable of heavy duty work, the longest board or timber you can saw is likely to be 20 to 24 feet. And if you saw 80 of them, the value of the lumber is about $1760.

To put it another way, if you work steadily and if you have a good supply of trees from which to saw your lumber, you can saw enough lumber to build a 2,500-square-foot house within two weeks—easily. If you push, you can do it in eight or nine days. And for two weeks' work you have enjoyed a return of $18,000 from your $7,500 investment.

Mike has made the first cut on this log, creating a flat working surface.

But what if you have no earthly idea how to operate a sawmill and have never been around the operation in any form? There are schools scattered around the country where you can enroll in a three-day course in sawmill operation.

If you are mechanically inclined, you can save yourself even more money by making your own repairs.

There are, of course, some severe considerations. First, you must have a way to handle the massive tree trunks that you will be sawing. If you have heavy equipment, you have no problems. If you do not have equipment, you may need to design your sawmill operation so that the rollers used to move the logs to the cutting area can be operated largely by gravity. In other words, be sure you can drag the logs to the sawing area and then let them roll, with the aid of a peavy, down a very gentle incline to the saw.

When you are making the purchase, ask the seller how much more he would charge to help you set up the sawmill for operation. He may agree to help you for a very modest amount, particularly if he has not had much interest from buyers and he wishes to move the mill quickly.

While you are shopping for a mill, look for one that has a blade 56 inches wide. Such a blade will allow you to cut boards, if you want, need, or have a market for them, up to 26 inches wide.

When you start to saw, you will make your first cut along the side of the log and only wide enough to remove the bark and leave a smooth, flat surface wide enough to meet your needs. You may want to saw two or three of these edging boards that can later be cut to remove the bark from both sides.

If you want to saw timbers eight inches wide, measure from the sawn edge of the log to a point eight inches across the log end. Then use the peavy to turn the log and then saw off slabs and edging boards until you have a thick log eight inches wide. Now lay the log flat on a smooth side and again saw off the slab. You are now ready to set the saw cut at two inches and you can slice off timber after timber, and each one will be eight inches wide and two inches thick. You can, in fact, cut virtually any dimension lumber that you want or need.

And the news continues to get better and better. For one thing, you can sell sawdust about as fast as you can produce it. An ideal price for sawdust is $10 for a pickup load and $25 for a one-ton truck load.

He can cut thin boards...or stout beams.

Then you can saw for other people. A fair price for the services of you and your mill is $100 per thousand board feet. You and one good helper can saw four to five thousand board feet in one good day's work, which will pay you $400-500 for your efforts. Of course, you must deduct the pay for your helper and the cost of operating the sawmill. Even so, you can still realize a profit of about $300 per day's work, depending upon many intangibles.

You can also saw and sell lumber to customers. In some states you must have the lumber grade-marked, which means that someone recognized as competent must inspect your lumber and mark it. Grade-marking costs about $30 to $40 per thousand board feet, depending upon your part of the country.

If you do not have a long-standing supply of trees, you may need to buy timber, which will cost, again depending upon the part of the country, $50 to $75 per thousand feet, standing.

You can also buy a used four-side planer and plane or dress the lumber so that you can get top price for it. Such a planer will do tongue-and-groove planing for finish carpentry work. And you can sell the shavings from the planer and get back part of your investment in that fashion.

If you want to eliminate subflooring and sheathing costs, you can cut your own boards rather than use plywood. Your floors and ceiling will be thicker, very strong, and highly economical (except for the sweat, sore muscles, and time needed for the operation).

If anyone tells you that sawmill work is easy, keep one hand on your wallet as you talk. It is very hard work, and in summertime it is excruciatingly hot, just as it is unbearably cold in winter. There will be days in which you cannot work, and you will be at the mercy of wind, biting and stinging insects, and snakes. But if you can take the work, the payoff is great! ∆

Backwoods Home Magazine's Web site
is easy to access on your computer.
Just type in:
http://www.backwoodshome.com

FARM/GARDEN

A Backwoods Home Anthology

Raising goats as a business is a profitable and fun venture

By Jayn Steidl Thibodeau

Question: What animal can be used for meat, milk, fiber, brush control, costs a minimal amount both initially and for upkeep, and not only will pay for itself the first year but actually make you a profit?

Answer: The much-maligned goat.

The goat has always been portrayed negatively, whether in Biblical reference or in conversation with the neighbor who chases the kid's pet nanny down the road by your house. In truth, the goat is an intelligent and affectionate animal, which in turn gets it into more trouble than the more easily handled sheep. But while the sheep industry is in a national decline, the profit potential in raising goats on your homestead is unlimited.

Different goats have different purposes. Dairy goats can be used for both meat and milk. A typical Spanish goat, on the other hand, is basically a meat goat that doesn't produce enough milk to make the chore worth your time. The Spanish goat, however, will have an undercoat of hair known as cashmere and can be shorn in the same way that sheep is shorn. The Angora goat is basically a fiber goat, although they have been sold for slaughter.

Using goats in any of these ways can produce a profit over and above the cost of the animal. We have been raising goats profitably for the last seven years, and although we have made every mistake in the book we are still in business, which must say something about just how much profit a goat sideline can give you.

Fencing can be easy

Fencing is the first step to raising goats. If you don't have the proper fencing, you don't have any business with a goat on your homestead. But fencing doesn't need to be expensive. Our fencing originally was free. We used the ever-popular wooden pallets from a lumber company to build a large lot around our barn. They were given to us for the hauling. Later, as we began to show a profit, we added an electric fence.

In training the goats to the electric fence, we discovered that the way to do this was to first put them in a small pen built of wooden pallets with three electrified wires that we ran inside the pallets for an interior fence. After two weeks of this pen, we were able to turn them out in a portable lot with only one electric wire, and they never crossed. Even goats that had been chronic roamers stayed home after this lesson.

The Fifth Year

235

Finding goats cheaply

To find the proper goat, you first need to know something about them. If you have a friend or neighbor, go and ask questions. If you don't, go to the local auction house and ask questions there. Find out what terms such as mastitis, foot rot, and smooth-mouthed mean. And touch the goats. Go in with them and feel the udders. A good bag will feel soft and pliable. A bad bag will feel lumpy or hard. You can't always tell by looking, so be sure to touch.

Don't buy anything from the auction at this point; you aren't ready. Auctions are where people go to unload their problem stock, and eventually you will know a good goat from a headache, but you just aren't smart enough at this point.

Ask someone to show you how to tooth a goat, or verify age by the teeth. This is relatively simple, and you must know this to progress to the next step.

Now that you aren't a complete moron about goats, let's go buy some.

While you were at the auction you listened to the market prices, and you know that goats in your area are worth a certain amount. This amount will change from season to season, with fall and winter being the cheapest time to buy goats and spring and summer the best time to sell.

So, listen to your friends and neighbors. Who bought goat kids for their children to raise in the spring, summered them, and doesn't want to bother with them now that the kids are back in school? This is a potential seller. Who didn't bother with fencing, instead staking the goat out all summer? Staking is harder in the winter, so there is another potential seller. Didn't the fellow down the road have three or four goats that have been out on the pavement twice last week? Get down there the next time those goats are out. You'll get them cheap. Watch for newspaper ads. Lots of goats are advertised, and most people don't keep up with the market price.

Some people don't want to spend the effort to winter their goats, but don't want to sell either. Offer to keep their nannies for them in exchange for the kids. Then return the nanny when the kids are weaned at four to six weeks of age. (Or raise them on the bottle.)

If you can't find any using your eyes and ears, all hope is not lost. Head back to the auction, but don't buy the stock yourself. Find a buyer (he'll charge about a dollar a head) and tell him what you want and how much you are willing to pay. Then stay at the auction. Watch your buyer at work. The best buys come at the end of the auction when all the public has gone and just a few buyers are left. Your buyer may buy you a lemon or two; no one is perfect, but his business is to keep his client happy, and he does know goats. And buy several goats. Goats are sociable and easier to handle as a flock rather than singly.

Making money with goats

Now you have your fencing and your goats. The most important thing to remember about making money with goats is that you have to keep them alive. When you bring them in, give them a round of vaccinations that will include tetanus, C&D, and whatever your vet recommends for your area. Don't skimp on the shots, but it is cheaper to give routine vaccinations yourself rather than having the vet do it. Vaccines are available through your vet or through a feed store.

Worm your goat as soon as it comes in, especially if you are in a high-parasite area. Don't overfeed for the first two weeks, which is about how long it takes for the C&D vaccine to be effective.

If you have purchased dairy goats, you have several options open to you. First, naturally, would be dairying. If you don't plan to have facilities to have a Grade A dairy, check with your state health department for regulations. In Arkansas, we are not required to be a Grade A dairy for the first hundred gallons per month. Some states may require a release form.

But dairy milk doesn't have to go for human consumption. You can raise a variety of baby animals on goat milk. Baby calves, lambs, and pigs all thrive on goat milk, and calves and lambs can, with supervision, nurse right on the goat. Or you can buy

Cody and Clint Carlyle

orphan kids and raise several on each nanny. Some enterprising people have even developed businesses with milk-based products such as soap or casein paints.

The Spanish goat

The Spanish goat has a different purpose. You can't raise orphan animals on her, but she will raise her own kids more easily than the dairy goat can, and she will be much more efficient at converting feed and browse than the dairy goat.

Her main purpose is meat production, so you will look for a nanny who raises heavy, fast-growing kids. Her secondary purpose is brush control. Many people who have trained their goats well lease them out when the kids are weaned to people who need a pasture or lot cleaned out. This saves your pastures if you have an overstock problem, but you need to be sure that you have a clear, written agreement about who pays for your animal if the clients' dog eats your goat. It is best to send a guardian along with the goats if you plan to leave them for an extended period.

The third purpose of a Spanish goat is to produce Cashmere. When you select your goats, push back the outer layer of guard hair. Underneath will be a fuzzy layer, which is cashmere. Your first goats won't produce much, but if you breed for this trait you will have a good crop in a couple of generations. Cashmere sells for a premium price, as not much is produced, and it may sell locally to hand-spinners. Any sheep shearer will shear your goats for a nominal fee.

The Angora goat is going to be targeted to hand-spinners. The kids just don't have a lot of meat on their bones. Don't go with Angoras if your pastures are full of brambles as it will ruin the mohair. And Angoras have been known to get entangled in brush and die before help comes. They are intended for clean areas.

Where to sell goat meat

Well, you could sell your goats at the auction, but if you want to make a little money you will invest some sweat into this enterprise. Goat meat has a ready market as chevon, and it is sold as such to gourmet restaurants and specialty meat shops. Individuals buy goats on the hoof for barbecues, and if you have raised your goat organically you can deal with organic food stores or individuals who will process the goat themselves. You can target a specific market such as an ethnic group.

The point is that there is an unlimited marketing potential out there for goat meat. Publicize the fact that you raise goats by donating a goat for a club barbecue or serving chevon at a church dinner. Once people taste this delicately flavored meat, you won't have to look for your buyers; buyers will come to you. One point, though: if you have targeted an ethnic group as your market, be aware of their special holidays and have goats ready. If you disappoint your customers, it is hard to keep them coming back.

What if my goat dies?

If you lose your goat, find out why it died. You can't learn from your mistakes if you don't know what the mistakes are. Invest the few dollars to have a post-mortem done by your vet. You may save the rest of your flock. Also, if you have a goat who dies of natural causes (old age, heart attack, etc.) there are body parts which can salvage the initial cost of the goat. I know this sounds morbid, but it actually can be the difference between losing money and breaking even. Hides can be tanned. Goat skins are a beautiful material and sell well at craft fairs. If the goat had horns, you are in luck. If you will take the time and effort to cure the skull, you have an excellent product which is much in demand for incorporation into the Western decor that is so popular now. I bought an old goat for $25 last year. The goat promptly died, but he was a breed with trophy horns. The skull brought $250. Just remember a piece of advice given to us by a local sage: If you can't afford to lose it, don't buy it.

I hope some of these tips will be of use to you. We have really enjoyed our goats and the visitors who come to our homestead to talk about or buy our goats. The goat market has been, for us, a really satisfying way to make an income from our land without having to go into town and work. With a little luck and a lot of sweat, it can do the same for you. ∆

Broken Family

I don't know
Who snapped the picture
Because we're all in it.

My parents have since divorced
(She's now grey,
He's dead)
And my sisters and I are grown
With children of our own.
There is nothing
From that day to remember,
Not even whose birthday cake
Sits on the table before us.
But everyone is happy and smiling.

The photo,
Cracked and peeling,
Is clutched in my hand.

John Earl Silveira
Ojai CA

You have to learn to shovel crap before you learn to be the boss

By Dave Duffy

Annie's horse, Buddy, and the company donkey, Donna Quixote, are the occupants of the one-acre meadow in front of *Backwoods Home Magazine's* office. In a month they make a significant contribution of fertilizer to our local ecology, so significant that every month we have to go out and shovel some of it up and wheelbarrow it to the garden compost pile.

The other day I asked Jasper, a local teenager who sometimes works for *BHM* and whose dream is to someday own his own business, to shovel it up for $6 an hour. That's a reasonable wage in these parts for unskilled labor, and I knew he needed the money. "Take all day," I said. "It's worth fifty bucks." But he declined, saying shoveling horse manure was a "crappy job." Instead he went down to the neighbor's house and helped clean a swimming pool for free.

So I asked Gertrude, a lady neighbor who also works on occasion for *BHM*, if she wanted the job. I knew she also needed money, and besides, she owed the company about 28 hours worth of labor for money I had advanced her. She didn't decline the job, but called it "very humbling" work. I didn't see her for several weeks after that, so I figure that was her way of saying no.

Since I had no takers, one Sunday I grabbed a shovel and wheelbarrow and started to clean it up myself. John Silveira, this magazine's senior editor, dropped by the office and saw me shoveling. "Want a hand," he yelled as he came into the meadow. "I grew up on a New Hampshire farm; I know how this stuff should be done."

He grabbed a rake and together we raked and shoveled horse and donkey apples for two hours. Not only did we clean the meadow, but we had a lot of fun cracking jokes about it and discussing life's philosophical questions.

The job also didn't cost me any money because it was a weekend, and Silveira had come to the office on his own time to work on magazine business he hadn't had time to complete during the week. So I saved the $50 I had intended to put into someone else's pocket, and as a bonus, we both got some exercise and good conversation. Not a bad day's work.

But I'm sure you can see the moral in this story. Silveira and I are willing to shovel horse and donkey crap for free, while Jasper and Gertrude are not willing to do it for pay. We understand that work is simply something that must be done, that it has no hierarchy; Jasper and Gertrude do not. The moral is: If you're not willing to shovel crap, you'll have trouble achieving success.

It is, I think, the most critical element of success a person can understand, especially if the success you are looking for involves running your own business.

Me and Larry Bird

Running your own business is like trying to win a basketball game. A lot of people think basketball is about slam dunks, tricky passes, and shots at the buzzer. But it really isn't; basketball is about winning the basketball game.

That's why a relatively ungifted athlete like Larry Bird is considered by many who understand the game to be the greatest professional basketball player ever. Although Bird could pass and shoot well, his real talent was that he was a hard worker at all the little things that mattered to win a game, such as practicing free-throws until they became automatic, studying his fellow players so he could read and anticipate their moves, and constantly adjusting his own game to take advantage of whatever was working for him and his teammates.

Bird didn't care about his own statistics, but about the numbers on the scoreboard. He knew that it wasn't the job that mattered, but the outcome. He would have been right at home in *BHM's* meadow shoveling horse crap with Silveira and me.

Artist Don Childers

Ilene Duffy with son Robby

You must bring to your business what Larry Bird and I have brought to ours: a willingness to do what it takes to succeed, regardless of how unglamorous you may think some of the tasks are. If you have to shovel crap occasionally, then by gosh you must be willing to shovel crap.

I'd like to tell you a bit about how I made a go of *Backwoods Home Magazine* as a way of illustrating how hard work and paying attention to the details work. Larry Bird and I have a lot in common—although he is slightly taller than me.

You are the janitor

I started *Backwoods Home Magazine* five years ago, as a vehicle to escape southern California's congestion, smog, and rotten environment and move to the country where I knew I could live a happier, more self-reliant life.

There were no investors for the magazine, no fancy office, no connections, and no money. Just me, determination, and work, 12-18 hours a day, 7 days a week, in a converted two-car garage where my daughter, Annie, and I both lived and worked. I was the publisher, editor, writer, typist, and janitor. Annie, too young then to play much of a role, was my cheerleader.

To supplement the newborn magazine, I became a part-time receptionist and errand boy for a local company owned by a friend. Not only did I not view being a 45-year-old errand boy as humbling work, but I am still grateful to my friend Kurt Warner who gave me a chance to earn a few extra bucks while I pursued my dream.

Now with *BHM* a success and housed in a real office all its own, I still take out the office trash, vacuum the rug, deliver the mail to the post office, and, I don't mind admitting, shovel crap for the four-legged lawn mowers in the meadow. To me these tasks are just part of what has to be done around here—and they serve as a reminder of the little things it takes to keep a business going.

A little talent necessary

Like Larry Bird, I came fairly well equipped to make a go of my business. My God-given ability to write and edit had been honed during the previous 20 years of on-again, off-again careers as a newspaper reporter and technical writer. Along the way I also picked up enough technical savvy to understand the topics this magazine's articles would be about.

So I had the basics down for my particular business, as you should too for whatever business you go into.

It is a fact of life, I think, that hard work is vital to make a go of a legitimate business, but it is also a fact of life that without some form of beginning skill, all the hard work in the world will be in vain.

If you lack that beginning skill, you must go out and acquire one. It's largely a matter of investing your time to educate yourself about something you think you'd like to do to make a living.

The family angle

Although you may be the perfect person for your business, sooner or later you will need help in running it. A mate who is willing and skillful is the best employee you can have. I have such a mate in my wife Ilene, who I met shortly after founding *BHM*. Her job is to pay attention to the details of the business, and she is extremely good at it. She does the bookkeeping, data entry, and proofing of each issue, all of which are critical elements of magazine publishing.

If you don't have a mate who is willing or able to help you, you will be at a serious disadvantage. Most of the successful small businesses that I know of include husband and wife teams at the top. It's one more good argument for having an intact family unit.

A family or home-based business is also about the best educational tool I know of for your children. My 12-year-old daughter, Annie, has not only learned what the nature of a business is by watching me struggle through the start-up and running of *BHM*, but she has learned many computer programs just by being around the office. As she grows, she plays an ever increasing role in the magazine, occasionally writing a children's article or doing odd jobs for a little pay that she spends on her horse. Your own business, then, doubles as an excellent hands-on homeschooling course.

Your family will also realize tax advantages with your own business. Part of your vehicle and its mileage, part of your house, and various "supplies" can all be deducted from the business. It's a neat way to keep some

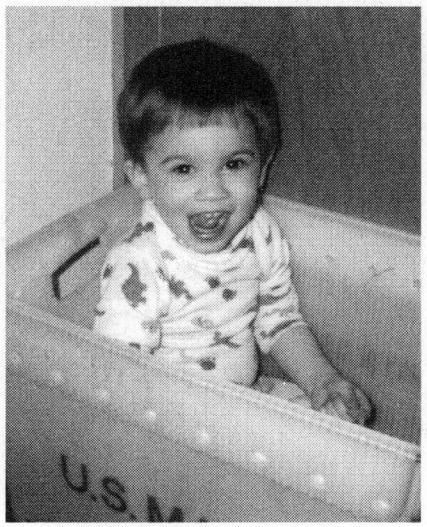

Jacob Duffy helps with the mail.

A Backwoods Home Anthology

of your money out of Uncle Sam's pocket. An accountant or business advisor will show you how to set things up.

A moral boost

If you don't have a mate capable of helping, you can still achieve success. A good substitute is a trusted friend or friends who can give you moral support and occasional help. Annie, age seven at the time I started *BHM*, was my first moral sidekick. Don't laugh. A seven-year-old cheering you on and helping with mailings is a tremendous moral boost. In the early days of a business, people who are important to you can sometimes make or break your spirit.

Beware of doomsayers

Which brings us to doomsayers. People who start their own business tend to attract a lot of wet blankets who want to discourage you from such a daring enterprise.

I attracted them. "You'll never make a dime at it," one seasoned relative told me in a fatherly advice session. I also took a lot of ridiculing smiles from former co-workers who thought there was no life outside their cozy 40-year careers at the company.

Even some of the people who gave me encouragement in the beginning later confided to me that they secretly did not believe I would make a success of *BHM*.

I'm not sure what it is that makes people fearful of attempting to run their own lives, but most people are. The biggest doomsayers you will encounter will be people who would never dare attempt what you dare.

Don't let these people get to you. Their discouraging comments and forecasts of doom for your business undertaking are really aimed at themselves. They doubt they would have the guts to attempt what you attempt, and you become the object of their self criticism. If you are successful they will congratulate you, ask for a job, and swear they were behind you all the time.

Listen to the people who encourage you. Fortunately, all the people who mattered in my life not only encouraged my attempt to start *BHM*, but many, like Ilene Myers, Jan Cook, John Silveira, Richard Blunt, Tim Green, and Don Childers, gave me many hours of free work to help me get off the ground. And, you know what, all of those people are now involved in some sort of personal business undertaking of their own.

Don Childers . . .

If your business grows you will eventually have to hire someone besides your mate to help out. Even Larry Bird had his big men, like Robert Parish and Kevin McHale, he could go to.

Hiring can be a dangerous step in running your own business because, like the five players on the basketball court, every employee must play a major role.

You're not a big corporation that can absorb some dead wieght; you're a very small business that needs full output from every employee. If you hire a dud, your business will suffer.

My first key player was Don Childers, a talented aerospace artist who was as fast at drawing as he was good. Don brought a talent to *BHM* that makes us stand out on the newsstand, namely original paintings for our covers.

He also provides illustrations that give graphic relief to pages that would otherwise be gray with print. Since most of our articles come from people who are not professional writers or photographers, we often get articles that are not accompanied by photographs, so Don's talent is important.

Don is part-owner of *BHM* but not yet a full-time employee. He paints the covers at home and often flies up here for the week preceding the printing of the issue.

Don is one of those people who gave me free time during the early days of *BHM*, making my dream part of his dream of doing something so special with his art that it would attract wide public notice. He's achieved that now; his covers—82,000 of them this issue—are on the newsstands of 14,000 stores in the United States.

From left, Meaghan Silveira, Buddy, and Annie Duffy

...and other key players

My first full-time employee was Christopher Maxwell, our managing editor, who I recruited out of Chicago, of all places. He had been a contributing writer of gun articles.

Maxwell isn't a great editor in the sense he is a master of grammar and punctuation. What he is is a great thinker who can see to the heart of a matter quickly, and he has the confidence in himself to make decisions without being afraid he'll make a wrong decision.

Believe it or not, the courage to make a decision is a fairly rare trait in business. The brains to make a correct one is even rarer. The delays caused by indecisive managers is probably a prime reason why so many small businesses fail. Keep that in mind when you hire a key player in your business.

Maxwell is also a voracious reader who admits he even reads the cereal box when he's eating breakfast, and he's an eager learner who studies the magazine, its readership, and their wants and needs. With such a large number of article submissions to *BHM*, I needed someone like Maxwell who could read an article quickly with understanding, see what it's about, ascertain if it fits the purpose of *BHM*, and make a decision on whether or not we should use it.

It is a crucial role he plays because it frees me to do other things. But I do not give him total independence. As you should do with your small business, I keep my hand in the article selection process, and Maxwell and I work closely together.

John Silveira, my senior editor, is similar to Maxwell in that he is somewhat weak with punctuation and grammar. But like Maxwell, he is smart and a great thinker. He is also a thorough researcher and talented writer who brings a unique writing style to the magazine, not to mention a good poet who adds a touch of class and controversy (see the letters in this issue).

An NBA coach once explained the great value of seven-foot-tall basketball players by saying, "You can't teach tall." That's also true of your key employees. In the case of Childers, Maxwell, and Silveira, I needed smart, talented people to make my magazine stand out from my competitors. As on a basketball team, one or two gifted people have a major impact. And just as you can't teach tall, you can't teach smart or talent either.

It's something to keep in mind no matter what business you start. Your key people, especially early on, are important to your continued success. Don't hire your unemployed friends and relatives unless they can contribute significantly to your business. They may just end up draining your cash and helping you go out of business, so they and you will have no employment in the end anyway.

However, also don't overlook talented relatives. My older brother, Hugh, was invaluable to me during the first six issues of the magazine. Hugh is a lawyer, but—and I know this sounds impossible for a lawyer—he speaks, thinks, and writes clearly. The unsung hero of the first six issues, he critiqued them from cover to cover and advised me as to what was working and what was not. In some cases it was a simple validation of what I suspected worked; in others it was a caution about what I suspected didn't.

My daughter, Annie, is another example. She has talent beyond her years when it comes to design and layout. In fact, she was instrumental in designing the layout and selecting the photos for this article. She also works cheap.

The rule of thumb? Hire talented people who will also shovel crap.

Be creative when hiring

Also be creative when you hire your key people. The so-called experts may not be the people you need. You, as the business owner, must often use your gut feeling when searching for the right person to hire.

Let's go back to Maxwell and Silveira's suspect skills in grammar and punctuation. You may think that an odd handicap to have as an editor; I know most other magazine publishers would. But it's not. In fact, it is an advantage.

John Silveira, senior editor

Here's why: Your typical small magazine reads like one or two editors edited all the articles. That's because your typical editor has no field of his own; he is an editor or would-be writer, period. The articles end up over-edited and take on a monotonous similarity of style, with key ingredients often edited out.

Maxwell and Silveira have their own fields (Maxwell is a locksmith and Silveira a mathematician), so they are used to solving problems in the real world. Writing was something they did on the side until I hired them.

Since a key reason for the success of *BHM* is that we rely on people with real knowledge to write our articles and not professional writers who try to write about something they heard about, Maxwell and Silveira are ideally suited to edit people who, like themselves, have their own field. They have developed a respect for people with true knowledge.

Also, one of the ways *BHM* differs from other magazines is that we have many different voices in the magazine, because the real secret to good editing is to edit as little as possible so the original writer's voice remains intact. Maxwell and Silveira are looking for a writer's knowledge and clarity of presentation, not his or her ability to turn a phrase or place a comma.

Neither editor has any formal education as an editor, and that is also to the magazine's advantage. The college-degreed journalists who wind up as most of the nation's magazine and newspaper editors usually never really graduate from the academic world. In a sense, like many politicians, most have never worked for a living, and they do more harm than good. All you have to do is read your daily newspaper to see the type of largely useless articles that result.

Quality control

Speaking of useless garbage, make sure your business doesn't create any. That means you must practice quality control, which necessitates having some sort of system in place that checks the quality of the product.

In the case of *BHM*, our quality control extends to the relevancy and accuracy of our articles, to the careful handling of our database so readers get their subscription sent to their correct address, and to the mail room so customers get the books they ordered.

That's where Lenie, Terrell Hemingway, and Jennifer Hoie are most valuable.

John Silveira and Jennifer Hoie take a break from work to feed Buddy.

Lenie, of course, is the key player in quality control. She has the ability to see the little things that go unnoticed by most other people. So not only does she get to maintain the accuracy of our database, but all articles must be read by her so she can catch typos and grammar slips. Luckily, she knows grammar, because nobody else around here does.

Lenie has so much to do she can't do it all, so Terrell Hemingway, a teacher who will have returned to teaching as this issue hits the newsstand, is her assistant. Terrell also has a natural eye for detail, so she gets to enter new subscribers into the database under the ever-watchful eye of Lenie.

Terrell's job is inherently a critical quality control function, because one incorrect address entered into our database tends to multiply itself many times, resulting in an angry call or letter from a subscriber and someone scurrying around here trying to mend the broken fence.

Another quality control role is played by Jennifer Hoie, our advertising manager but also our order filler. She sends out and stamps all outgoing mail. Like a misplaced subscriber address, one wrong book sent tends to cause many headaches. She seldom makes a mistake.

Jennifer's other function as advertising manager is also key and relates to quality control. She is our main contact with the people who have a lot of money to spend, namely the advetisers, and boy do we want their money. Jennifer has the perfect match of personality and businesslike manner to make the sale without giving away the store.

Quality control is essential in all businesses but absent in most. It's something we stress heavily at *BHM*. Not only does quality control minimize the number of costly mistakes your business makes, but it is also good public relations for your business.

It's a matter of perception for many customers. I know we do a good job with the articles we print, but all an article needs is a few typographical errors, and many readers will assume that *BHM* is a sloppy outfit given to mistakes and misinformation. That's a reputation a small business can't afford.

Learn technology

A lot of people shy away from technology when it comes to bringing it into the country, but *BHM* doesn't. We encourage people to learn the new technologies like photovoltaics that help bring a comfortable standard of living to remote locations.

Technology can also help your fledgling business. An understanding of the new computer desktop publishing technology has helped us maintain a professional look at a price we can afford. That professional look, coupled with the high quality of our content, enables us to compete successfully with magazines that dwarf us in size.

If there is affordable technology available that can give you a leg up on the competition, by all means go out of your way and learn it.

Persistence/desperation

Motivation coupled with a plan are a powerful combination for the entrepreneur. Without them you're liable to give up as soon as the going gets bumpy.

Starting a business is always a struggle. That's why not everyone is in business; the failure rate is high. It's sort of like living in the country; if it were easy to stay in the country, everyone would be here and it would turn into a city with all the city's problems. The country is sparsely populated—and nice because of that—because it takes a certain type of person to make it here. Same with your business.

Backwoods Home Magazine was a struggle for about two years, but I had a good plan and I had strong motivation: I wanted to be able to live in the house I had already built in southern Oregon, and I had made a vow to myself that I would go on skid row before I went back to the rat race. Sounds drastic I know, but that's the way some of us Irish are. If necessity was the mother of invention, desperation was the mother of this magazine.

Thrift and the long haul

BHM has had its ups and downs. Every time I think we are on a roll, we get a cash flow problem. The government tax collector is always there with his hand out if you succeed, but you won't find him anywhere but at the welfare office if you fail.

You must count every penny, in good times as well as lean times. Save for a rainy day, the saying goes, and it's a true saying.

Also, don't go for the quick buck, but for the long haul. If you follow fads, your business will fail as soon as the fad goes away. The environmental movement is an example of a fad. Most of the environmental magazines now on the market are in financial trouble because the environmental fad, once strong and able to support them, is starting to wane. Thank God.

Have fun

Succeed but have fun. Besides the obvious monetary advantages in having your own business, there are many non-monetary advantages. And like winning the basketball game, the point of owning your own business, for me at least, is not to make a big success out of the business, but to be a winner at the game of life. That means making a good life for you and your family.

For me and Lenie, owning our own business has allowed her to stay at home with the kids as she works. To Lenie that is the best benefit of all.

When we have a lull in business, such as after each issue goes to print, we can take a few days off and go to the Oregon Coast for a vacation.

Publisher Dave Duffy installs photovoltaic panels.

With our own business, we also work for our future, not that of someone else. When I put in a 12-hour day, or when Lenie stays up until 3 a.m. typing in classified ads, we are the ones who benefit.

I make a point of telling all my employees that their future is not in working for me, but in getting their own business going. I'll hate to see them go, but they'd be crazy to stay.

In the meantime, I'm working on my fall-away shot at the hoop by my office door, just in case Larry Bird comes out and accepts my challenge to see who is the best one-on-one player on my two-and-a-half acres. Δ

The Thinker

Have you missed columns by some of todays most influential and interesting libertarian and conservative writers? Find the best of them—Dave Duffy, John Silveira, Vin Suprynowicz, P.J. O'Rourke, Walter Williams, George Will, Jeff Jacoby, and others **free** on the web at:

http://www.gis.net/~dmann/

Visit our web site
http://www.backwoodshome.com

It's an easy way to...

- e-mail staff members
- buy an anthology or book
- re-read articles from back issues
- subscribe or renew your subscription
- link to other self-sufficiency web sites

Subscribing
to Backwoods Home Magazine
has never been easier

Just call our **TOLL FREE** number

1-800-835-2418

(This number is for ordering only. All others, please call 1-530-459-3500)

and use your **Visa or Mastercard**.

It costs a lousy $19.95 a year.

(Or use the order form at the end of this book.)

MAKING A LIVING

Grow an independent living with a cut flower business

By Vern Modeland

An investment of as little as $200 for seeds and soil mixes planted on 500 to 1,000 square feet can blossom into several thousands of dollars worth of cut flowers, according to Jim Gibbons, who makes his living growing everything from vegetables to flowers.

Gibbons' cultivates all the organically grown vegetables, fruits, and herbs his family eats.(See his story in *BHM* Issue No. 26.) Lately, cut flowers are expanding their home business income substantially.

"I got some tips from other people in the horticultural business that flowers are really an easy thing to market. And from what I've seen it's true. In California, cut flowers are a yearround product. Elsewhere in the country, you might need unheated greenhouses, then you could extend your growing season quite a bit.

Growing cut flowers commercially can be very labor intensive, Gibbons said.

"They are perishable. They don't keep. Probably the best thing to do is to first develop your market. The production part isn't hard at all.

"A few flower plants we found were not real easy to grow here, but because we had such a diversity it really didn't matter. If you have a couple of dozen varieties, you don't have to worry about one or two that didn't make it.

"This year I've experimented with about 80 different types of flowers. I'm trying everything and I'm finding nothing is really hard to grow. Sweet Peas are one of the most popular of our cut flowers.

"You can sell to supermarkets and the little corner store. You can make arrangements with small family run markets if you have the volume. Basically the best way is to make the contacts yourself, be the distributor and the grower. Try to start your marketing close to where you are growing them. You may have to go to nearby

Linda Gibbons puts the final touches on an arrangement.

Seedling flats in the greenhouse

towns but try to market as close to home as possible because it is a perishable product. If you have a route where you are supplying several different areas with impulse items kept near the cash register, you don't want the physical distribution to become a grueling aspect of the business, especially when you are the entire staff.

Costs and prices

"If you invest, say $75 in seeds and maybe another $50 or $60 in starting soil mixes to get 'em going, you could have as little as a couple-hundred dollars invested, and if you have the demand available nearby, you could grow several thousand dollars in cut flowers.

If you're doing it yourself on your own time, as far as overhead, you don't need much. The main cost would be distribution, in driving them to Farmers' Market, or having a jobber route from store to store to deliver arrangements or little bundles of flowers to display. Florists are kind of stuck in a way because they rely on this big wholesale distribution network and usually have to go into the Flower Market in each city and take whatever is there. But florists are creative people and will likely take whatever is unusual or different.

"Pricing is tricky. When the flowers are ready, you have to move them. You either have to hold out for your price and let a large percentage spoil and accept that, or you can drop your price and go for volume. On a real small scale, you're better to hold out for your price and if people don't take 'em they're not an expensive item. Even if you threw 50 percent away, you shouldn't have any loss. You can make money on whatever you sell.

"You want to go for top quality, always, and build a reputation for having a quality product. Flowers are a real quick thing. You cut flowers that will last a week and you have to keep good track of what is aging. If they only have a couple days left, throw them out and replace them with fresh ones so they will last a week. You'll build up repeat sales if people know you are really consistent with your quality and effort.

"Flowers should be cut in the morning in the cool part of the day. We try to cut them and put them immediately into a preservative. We take it right out into the patch in five-gallon buckets. Sometimes we take vases out and fill them in the field. Vases are inexpensive and you can do arrangements and have no more than $2 in the whole thing. You can find the sources of vases at wholesale in trade magazines such as the horticultural magazines like *Nursery Manager*, which will have a source book annually that includes everything you would possibly want.

Marketing ideas

"It's not hard to sell to women but men generally think flowers are what you buy on Valentine's Day and Mother's Day. Have your own stand in a good location and work the major holidays and you'll net a couple of thousand dollars in a couple of days.

"I would say the best thing to do is become your own retailer rather than be a wholesaler. In the flower business, the big growers grow 30-40 acres of one flower. If you happen to grow the same thing at the same time, they are going to be selling these things at 25 cents a stem and you might want to get 50 to 75 cents a stem on the same flower and there'll be no way you can drop your price to meet theirs, and there is no reason a dealer will buy from you anyway if you have the same product. There is no reason for a retailer to go out of their way to buy the same thing from someone else who is a small guy just getting into it. But if you have something different, that's a different story."

Once you have a cut flower business started, there is profit potential in creating and maintaining cut flower gardens for other people, Gibbons has found. And the kind of customer who wants a flower garden isn't necessarily only the up-scale. He says he's found most people to be interested when the idea is properly presented to them.

"They say, 'You actually do that?' They like the idea of going out and cutting flowers and putting them in the vase and leaving the rest to you.

"After you have a raised vegetable bed and you have an orchard, what else is really worth having in your yard? The concept of a cut flower garden is proving to be real popular among my landscaping customers. It doesn't need to be a real big area. They can actually cut quite a few flowers from a small area if the bed is developed like a raised bed of vegetables, where you enrich the soil properly and do a really good job of taking care of the ongoing needs of the plants.

What to change

"I never charge by the hour; I always charge by the job. You need to know the time you have involved and the cost of your materials. Then charge, say, $65 a month for spending

45 minutes there. When you tell people hourly rates, they usually won't like that because your hourly rate likely will seem to be high. They'll ask, 'how come?' People are generally more comfortable with a lump sum. It's best to never discuss hourly rates.

"I quote what it costs to put in a garden, and then what I charge to maintain it per visit or once a month, which is adequate if you did a real good job of establishing an enriched base with lots of compost and organic fertilizer so that the flowers grow really strong.

"I treat flower beds the same as I treat raised bed vegetables, and I go to the extra expense in creating the garden so that down the road it becomes very easy to maintain."

Make up a photo album

Jim Gibbons' expansion into the cut flower garden business has grown mostly from word of mouth endorsements within his network of present landscape customers.

To explain his work, he put together a photo album filled with color pictures of specialty cut flowers and blossoming garden plots.

"You need color photos. I use a photo album with examples of what I grow so they can simply point at it and say, 'This is what I want' or 'I don't like that flower.' Basically, all flowers are pretty popular."

The photo album has advantages over a brochure, Gibbons points out, particularly for someone who is just getting started. Mostly, it's less expensive and more flexible in the startup stage.

"All you have to do is shoot a couple of rolls of film, and its a great marketing tool you can show people."

Intellectual capital

You don't have to invest much money to try the cut flowers business, Jim Gibbons says. In fact, he thinks it is better not to.

"I always look to start a new type of service or business with no money. You need intellectual capital rather than cash. Once you figure out what it takes in your mind and you know what you are trying to do, then everything seems to fall into place and you keep costs under control.

"When you're getting started, don't worry about the technical problems of growing cut flowers; worry about the technical aspects of marketing them. The growing aspect is really pure enjoyment and is easy. There is no problem growing flowers anywhere. The problem is always going to be how are you going to sell them to make a profit.

"That's the whole key, and that is where you have to put 80 percent of your energy."

Sources

Here are some names and mailing addresses of leading trade periodicals in the cut flower and flower garden business:

Flowers, 12233 West Olympic Blvd., Suite 118, Los Angeles, CA 90064.

Floral & Nursery Times, Box 8470 Northfield, IL 60093

Floral Edition, 120 St. Louis Ave., Fort Worth, TX 76104. This is a buyers' guide for mass market floral buyers.

Floral Mass Marketing, 549 West Randolph, Chicago, IL 60611.

Florist, 29200 Northwestern Highway, Box 2, Southfield, MI 48034.

Florists and Florists-Wholesale, American Business Directories, 5711 South 86th Circle, Box 27347, Omaha, NE 68127. These two directories list United States wholesale florists and the sources of supplies.

Flower News, 549 West Randolph, Chicago, IL 60611.

Nursery News, 549 West Randolph, Chicago IL 60611.

Nursery Digest, 1601 North Palm Ave., Suite 303, Pembroke Pines, FL 33026.

Nursery Manager (Southern Florist), 120 St. Louis Ave., Fort Worth, TX 76104.

Additional help can be found at your local university or county extension office and at the library. Δ

A country moment

The Zeman boys—Skyler 5, Quincy 9, and Jason 7, of Hornbrook, California, go on the warpath.

FARM/GARDEN

Here are three ways to build a stanchion

By Knight C. Duerig

As Nancy Hogg of Porthill ID pointed out in the March/April *Backwoods Home Magazine*, most barn designs do not have any plans for stanchions included. I checked out all of the books I've got that include barn plans and though several of them show a cow in a stanchion, none of them show how to build one.

With some deeper digging I managed to find a couple of drawings in some old USDA Extension Service material. The plans for the hanging stanchion (Figure 1) can be used if the design of your barn has crossbars in the right area or you can put a crossbar where you need it. The calf/cow stanchion (Figure 2) can be built as a separate unit and then anchored where it is needed.

Hanging stanchion

As shown in Figure 1 the hanging stanchion is hung by chain from a crossbar and it is also anchored to the floor with chain. If you want more than one they should be set so that there is about 26 inches between them. Although it's not shown in the drawing I'd put a turnbuckle in the top instead of a chain. That way you can tighten the whole assembly instead of having it sway from loose chains.

Calf/cow stanchion

The calf/cow stanchion is designed so that it can be built for use with either calves or cows. The main difference is that the calf stanchions are built with 1x6 material and the cow stanchions are built from 2x6 stock. Of course, if you have a supply of used 1x6's, you can always make your own 2x6's. There is also a slight difference in the overall dimensions.

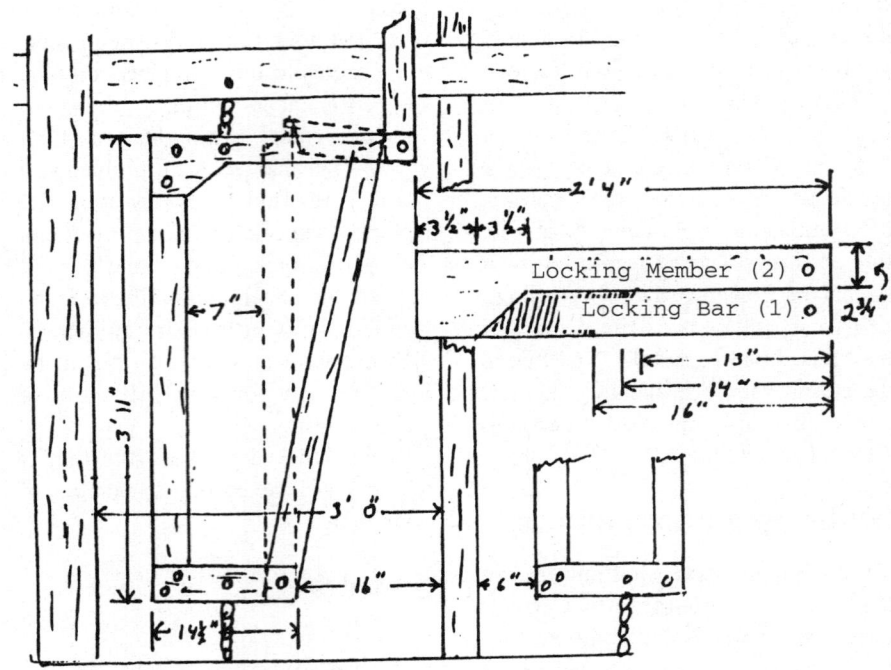

Figure 1. Hanging Stanchion

Bill of materials per stanchion

Locking Member	2	2'4" (cut as shown from Locking Member)	2x6
Locking Bar	1	1' 2 1/2"	2x4
Bottom Members	2	4'1"	2x4
Vertical Member	1	3'11"	2x4
Vertical Member	1	3/8" x 5 1/2"	
Machine Bolts	8	1 1/2 x 1/4" as needed	
Chain			

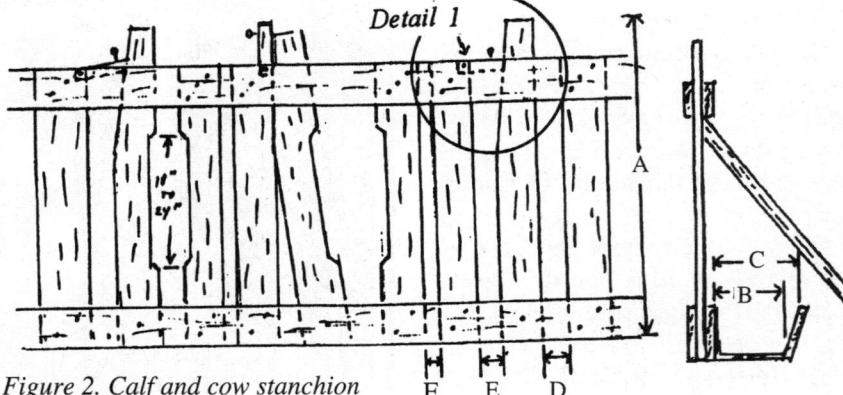

Figure 2. Calf and cow stanchion

Bill of materials per stanchion

	Calf	Cow
Uprights	1'x6'x10'	2'x6'x12'
Crossbars (4)	1"x6"x28"	2"x6"x34" (extend as needed)
Machine Bolts (11 ea.)	1/4"x3"	5/16"x5"
Screw Eyes (1)		

Measurements

	Calf	Cow
A	3'6"	4'
B	10"	10"
C	12"	12"
D	4"	7"
E	4"	7"
F	2"	2"

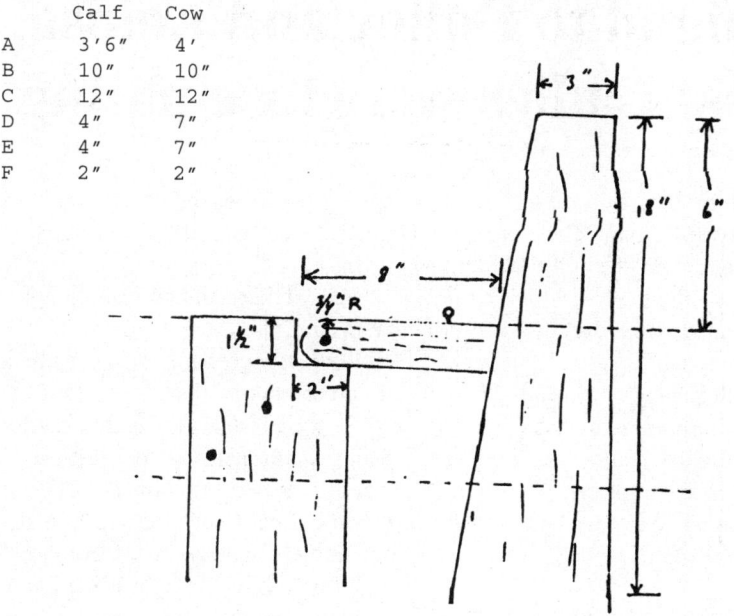

Figure 2. Calf and cow stanchion (Detail 1)

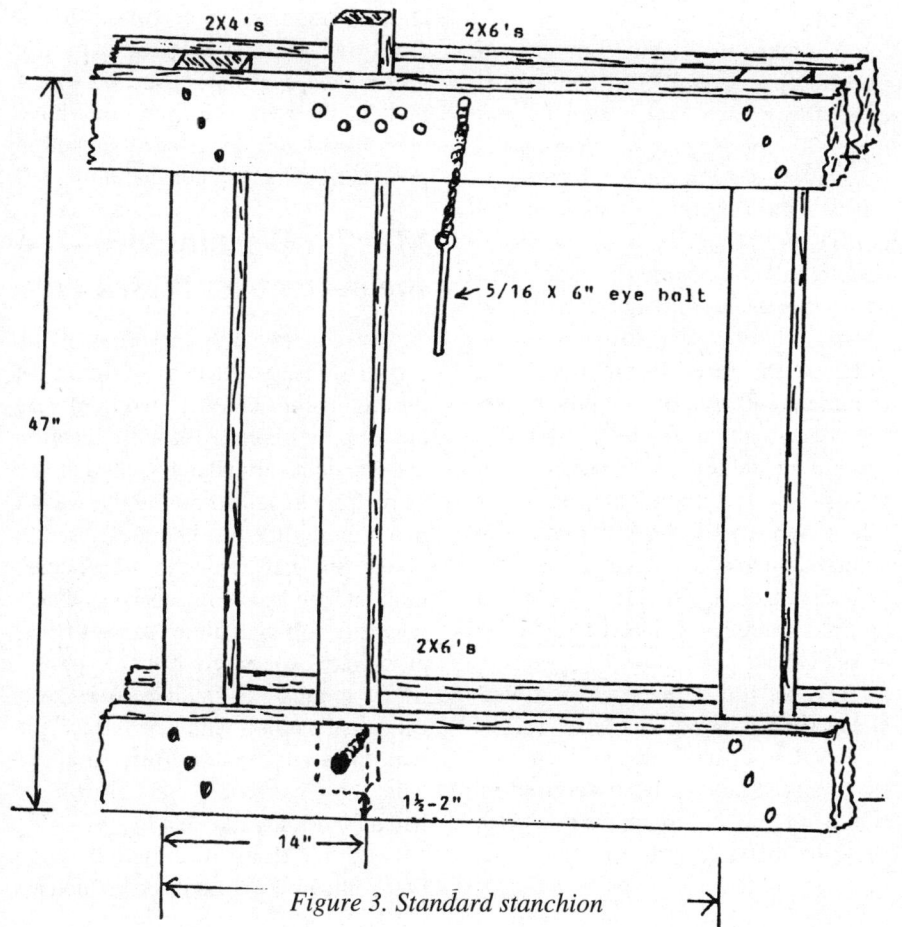

Figure 3. Standard stanchion

A Backwoods Home Anthology

Although the uprights are spaced 4 inches apart for the calf stanchions, you can vary this space by notching the inside of each upright from ½ to 1½ inches, to allow for growth in the calves. I'd leave them all at 4 inches to start, and only notch them as needed.

The feeding/hay trough on the far side of the stanchion is built from 1x10 and 1x12, cut to the length of the stanchions, or you could build them as 24 inch wide boxes, one per stanchion.

Another way to build the stanchions is shown in Figure 3. Use 2x4 uprights; one 47 inches long and one 49 inches for each stanchion, with 2x6 crosspieces. Screw or bolt the short upright in place, then set the longer upright about 2 inches above the floor and drill for a single pivot bolt, at least 5/16x5. Across the top, drill a series of 3/8" holes completely through both 2x6's and the 2x4 upright. Space these holes about 1 inch apart, and stagger them. These holes allow you some adjustment in the tightness of the stanchion, just by where you place the eye bolt to hold the upright.

Use bolts & nuts

You'll notice that the plans call for the stanchions to be built using machine bolts instead of nails. This will cost a little bit more, but you'll appreciate having gone to the added expense the first time you have to remove and replace a broken upright. Also, you can save money on the bolts by going to a farmers' co-op and buying them by the pound.

Now that you know the critical dimensions for the stanchion openings for cows and calves, you can design your own if none of these fit your requirements.

(**Knight Duerig** writes and publishes the *Non-Consumer's Digest*, a monthly six to eight-page newsletter about re-use, recycling, repairing, and rebuilding things. The cost is $1 for a sample or $12 for a subscription. *Non-Consumer's Digest*, P.O. Box 403, King Hill, ID 83633. ∆)

A Backwoods Home Anthology

AMERICANA

From Martha and Abigail to Dolley and Louisa, America's earliest First Ladies were fascinating

By John Silveira

It was the best of times, it was the worst of times . . . wait a minute, it was the worst of times. I was getting ready to head for Oregon again, driving through central California, from south to north without an air conditioner. On a good day in February a trip in an unairconditioned car up through the middle of the state can leave you somewhere between medium-rare and well-done.

I packed my cooler, one of those cheap little styrofoam jobs I'd bought for $2.99 at the supermarket. I filled it with ice, tossed in a bunch of fruit juices and sodas, some cream cheese spread, a bag of grapes, and four oranges, and I wedged it on the floor between the passenger's seat and the dashboard of my little Honda Civic. The cooler squeaks no matter how I put it in there. Seven hundred miles of squeaking.. I'm used to it and I've almost stopped talking to myself.

I put my computer on the floor behind the passenger's seat, the monitor and my notebooks on the backseat, my boom box and CDs (there's no radio in this car) on the passenger's seat. Then I stood back and tried to think of what I was forgetting.

The sun had not yet risen from behind the hills that lie east of my house. If I got on the road early enough, I could be in Oregon before nightfall.

From behind me I heard a short toot from a car on the street.

I turned and saw a strange van pulling to the curb. I thought it would be someone looking for directions, but when the door opened out stepped O.E. MacDougal, the poker player who's a friend of Dave Duffy, the fellow who publishes this magazine. I looked eastward again. The sun was about to break over the hills. I didn't have time for a visit.

He walked up my driveway and looked into my car.

"You're all packed," he said. There was disappointment in his voice.

"I want an early start," I said. "I've got a long trip ahead of me."

"I was hoping to get up here before you got on the road."

"Why?"

"To see if you wanted to ride up with me."

"With you? I'm going to Oregon."

"Dave was supposed to tell you I'm going up there too. You want to ride with me?"

It had taken me about 30 minutes to pack my car. I emptied it and loaded everything into Mac's van in just under 90 seconds and we were on the road before the sun cleared the hills.

It was the first time I was going up north with company. Now I had someone to talk to besides myself, and Mac's cooler doesn't squeak. And did we talk, about everything—sports, politics, the three Punic Wars, the imminent collision of the Shoemaker-Levy 9 comet with Jupiter.

We even talked about presidential wives. Not the presidents, but their wives. Who would have thought they could be interesting? Right as we were passing through Stockton, I made a comment about the latest one in the White House.

"Have any others been as controversial as she?" I asked.

"First Ladies have always been controversial. They've been accused of wielding too much influence with their husbands, immoral behavior, spying, even insanity . . . and sometimes the accusations were true."

"Insanity?"

"Mary Todd Lincoln was thought to be insane"

"Well, it's probably still a great job if you can get it," I said.

"Being First Lady? I don't know. Some women loved it, quite a few hated it. When Franklin Pierce's wife found out he'd been elected President, she fainted—and it wasn't from joy."

"I would have thought it's a job any woman would want."

"I'd say, as a rule of thumb, the younger they are when they get there, the better they like it. Otherwise, there aren't a lot of generalities to be made about them. They've been as different from one another as people in any group have ever been. And on top of that, in the two centuries there have been First Ladies, the lot of women in general has changed considerably.

Martha Washington — the perfect 1st First Lady

"Just consider the very first of the First Ladies, Martha Washington. In the eighteenth century, women were not usually given a formal education and the education she got, though she came from a well-to-do family, wasn't much more than just being exposed to books. She was trained to run a household and to deal with servants. That's what her job was going to be. It was all society expected of her.

"So, though she could read, it never became a passion with her. In fact, she was an atrocious speller. Imagine what the press would make of it if we had a First Lady like that today?

"Another thing to consider when you compare First Ladies of 200 years

250

The Fifth Year

ago with First Ladies of today is how death figured into their lives."

"Death?" I shuddered. I've been accused of having a morbid preoccupation with death.

"Yes. Nowadays, death is almost an unusual event. But 200 years ago it was always at the door."

"Really?"

"Sure. In 1962, when Jacqueline Kennedy gave birth to a baby boy that died in less than 48 hours, it became part of the media circus. But in the early days of this country there was barely a First Lady with children who didn't lose one or more before they were grown.

"And in a day when divorce was almost unheard of, the leading cause of broken families was death of a spouse.

"For example, George wasn't Martha Washington's first husband. She'd been married when she was much younger. But almost all women married young then. She was just 17 and the man, Daniel Custis, was in his thirties. They both came from well-to-do families and they had settled comfortably into marriage. But, when she was 25, he died. Not only that, they had had four children, only two of whom survived infancy, and one of those, a girl, died while still a child. The other, a son, died soon after the Revolutionary War, and George and Martha raised his children.

"Just remember that death played a much bigger part in the lives of the early First Ladies—as it did in the lives of all women in those days—and you'll have a deeper appreciation of them. I find it amazing that families functioned when so many of the children died. Today, there are people who don't know anyone who's experienced the death of a young child."

"How'd she meet Washington?" I asked.

"She'd been a widow about a year. She was one of the richest widows in Virginia, and a mutual friend introduced them. George was a colonel in the Virginia militia. He was tall, imposing, and sociable; they hit it off—to use a current term—and they got married and settled into a very comfortable life on her plantation."

"Love at first sight?" I asked.

"No. History has told us that Martha wasnt his true love. Sometime before, he'd fallen in love with Sally Fairfax, the wife of a friend. It was a love affair of the heart only; none of the hanky-panky Hollywood drools over. Sally was probably the only woman he ever romantically loved.

Martha Washington

"Of course, we'd never have known any of this because history would have forgotten the Washingtons, except for one thing—the Revolutionary War. He was chosen to lead the newly formed American army and went off to war. And she followed. She joined him each winter when the army made winter quarters, and she joined him not as a spectator, but as a participant."

"Participant?"

"Though one of the richest women of her times, she nursed the wounded, sewed for them, and generally took care of them. At least once, she was mistaken for a servant by soldiers who did not recognize her, and many of the women who came to meet the wife of the Commander-in-Chief were surprised to find her sewing clothes for the troops while she entertained. It was not something these other women would ordinarily have done, but they pitched in when they saw her doing it. And please remember, she wasn't doing this for photo opportunities as a First Lady might do today. She just did it."

"You sound as though you admire her."

"I admire several of the First Ladies."

"Okay, but tell me, how'd she like the public eye?"

"There was no public eye to speak of in those days. But, as with so many of the women who followed her, there's no reason to think she would have liked it."

"How did the people in Washington, D.C. see her?" I asked.

"She never lived in Washington, D.C. In fact, she's one of the only two First Ladies who didn't."

"Who was the other?"

"William Henry Harrison's wife. He died before she got a chance to move there."

"So, where was the capital?"

"The very first presidential home was in New York City. But there's no reason to believe she liked New York. Nothing against New York or New Yorkers. It's just that she'd been born to, and belonged on, a plantation. The capital moved to Philadelphia in 1790."

"How did the guy-on-the-street perceive her?"

"The guy-on-the-street didn't know who she was. She spoke publicly just once, and that was on her way to her husband's first inauguration."

"What moved her to speak then?"

"As she went through Philadelphia, she was so moved by the crowds that supported her husband, she spoke to express her appreciation. But she never spoke to the public again."

"She wouldn't be able to get away with that nowadays," I said.

"Stumping was not a woman's job then. None of the wives of any of the early presidential contenders did it. In view of the times, it would have cost votes."

"Why?"

"It was just something women didn't do."

"Did she like being First Lady?"

"No. The Washingtons were not great socializers and made it a habit to retire early each evening—even during his Presidency.

"Still, there probably couldn't have been a better First Lady than she, anymore than there could have been a better first President than her husband. No one knew how a democratically elected President or his wife should act. Virtually all of the world's leaders of the time were some sort of autocrats.

"George dispensed with all the trappings and pretensions of royalty, and Martha, by being herself, influenced the behavior of all the First Ladies who followed her."

"Did she know any of them?"

Abigail Adams

"She knew several of them. She and the second first lady, Abigail Adams, were good friends and she assisted in the wedding plans for the First Lady who was destined to become the most famous of them all—Dolley Madison.

I hardly noticed as we passed through Sacramento around noon.

Abigail Adams — political, influential

"Abigail Adams was the next First Lady, right?"

"Right."

"What was she like? Anything like Martha"

"No. She was very literate. It's not that she was better educated than Martha. Both of their educations consisted of home tutoring, but her temperament was different and she developed a passion for books and all things intellectual. It made her unlike most other women of her time.

"She is also very important to historians. A lot of what we know about the early history of the United States comes from a lifetime of correspondence between Abigail and her husband, John. She also corresponded with the third President, Thomas Jefferson.

"Martha, by the way, wrote letters to her husband, too, but destroyed them all before she died. So there are things we'll never know about there relationship.

"Abigail, however, through her letters revealed herself to be well informed, very political, and extremely perceptive. We now know she was an extraordinarily capable woman. For 10 years, while her husband served in various official positions, she ran the family farm in Quincy, Massachusetts, hiring the help, renting to tenants, buying and selling land, and tending to all the financial management.

"And in her correspondence with John, she always voiced her opinions on the affairs of the day.

"Did she influence him?"

"Absolutely. But he didn't always heed her advice."

"Why?"

"Some of her opinions were too controversial for their day. We know from one of her letters that, while the Continental Congress debated whether to call for independence, she warned her husband that the the men in attendance should remember women would not hold themselves bound by any laws in which they had no voice or representation. She said women might rebel."

"What was his reaction?"

"He was unusually patronizing toward her. It just wasn't something men were ready for yet."

"But otherwise they got along?" I asked.

"Sure. She was both a good match and a good foil for him. He was cold and often arrogant and didn't win friends easily. She was charming, tactful, and favorably impressed almost everyone that met her.

"And remember what I said about death? Things happened in those days that you would never see happen today."

"Such as?"

"People usually died at home back then and Abigail missed her husband's inauguration because she stayed home to tend his mother who was sick and busy dying."

"What did the folks in Washington think of her? . . . did she ever live in Washington?"

"The Adams's were the only First Family to live in all three capitals: New York, Philadelphia, and Washington, D.C. And apparently, the Washingtonians of her day liked her just fine. She was, by the way, the only woman, so far, to have been the wife of one President and the mother of another."

"That's right, the Adams' son was John Quincy Adams. But let's hold off on his wife. Who was the next First Lady?"

Did Thomas Jefferson have a black mistress?

"Well, the next President was Thomas Jefferson. He was the first of many men to go to the White House as a widower. His wife, Martha, had been dead for 18 years when he was elected, and he never remarried.

"He, on the other hand, was her second husband. She'd first married when she was 17, but she was widowed when she was 19. Four years later she married Jefferson. Ten years after that, she was dead after giving birth to their sixth child.

"So, there was no First Lady during his term?"

"No First Lady per se, but there were White House hostesses who filled the roll and could be considered First Ladies."

"What do you mean?"

"Two of their six children survived to adulthood . . ."

"Just two?"

"Yes. They were both daughters and, as was often the case in those days, when they married they married men who were their cousins.

"These two daughters served as hostesses, along with a future First Lady, Dolley Madison, whose husband was Jefferson's Secretary of State."

"Why didn't Jefferson remarry?"

"I don't know. Maybe he would have, if he'd had a choice, but he felt he couldn't. For the rest of his life, there were rumors and accusations that he took one of his slaves, Sally Hemings, as a mistress and that she bore him five children."

"Did he?"

"I don't know, and I don't know if anyone else is sure. But there is the possibility that this is the woman he loved after Martha and that she bore him children. But, times being what they were, there's no way they could have any more than the secretive relationship that's been speculated about."

"So, if attitudes were different, there's a chance we could have had a black First Lady."

"If the rumors are true, I suppose it's possible."

"So, who's next?" I asked.

Dolley Madison — First Lady for the ages

"Well, Dolley Madison was the very next First Lady."

"And you said Martha Washington had a hand in her marrying James Madison?"

"Yes, and Dolley was another young widow, just as Martha had been. She'd married a Quaker, John Todd, at the age of 22. They had a son together, but three years later an epidemic of yellow fever swept through Philadelphia and killed both her husband and son."

"Was she another rich widow?"

"No."

"How'd she meet Madison?"

"She was just 25, and was catching the eye of many of Philadelphia's bachelors."

"Philadelphia?"

"It was still the capital."

"Okay."

"One of the men was a 43-year-old Congressman from Virginia, James Madison. Their marriage was encouraged not only by Martha, but by Aaron Burr, the man who would eventually kill Alexander Hamilton in a duel."

"So, at 25, she already knew a lot of important people."

"That's right."

"If she was just 25 and Madison was 43 . . ."

"She was a lot younger, also taller and heavier. He wasn't a big man."

"Anyway, his political star was rising and he was well regarded by his peers. She married him, and six years later, when Jefferson was elected President, he appointed Madison his secretary of state and they moved to the new capital, Washington, D.C. But the District was still an undeveloped marshy wilderness with a serious housing shortage so Jefferson invited them to live in the White House—which wasn't called the White House, yet; it was called the Executive Mansion—and they spent their first three months there."

"Is that how she started helping with the hostessing duties at the White House?"

Dolley Madison

"Yes. And she didn't impose. She acted as official hostess at Jefferson's insistence."

"How was she received when she became First Lady in her own right?"

"She was one of the few women who really seemed to enjoy it. During her husband's administration, when she hosted White House dinner parties, she sat at the head of the table. Madison, the chief architect of the Constitution and, along with George Mason, one of the two forces behind the Bill of Rights, as well as a great debater, didn't like to lead the conversation."

"You're kidding."

"No, I'm not. He left that to Dolley."

"Wasn't there something about her saving some valuable stuff from burning in the White House?"

"It was during the War of 1812, which took place during Madison's administration. British troops invaded Washington, D.C. and, while her husband took command of some troops and rode off to meet them, Dolley was left in charge of the White House.

"No one knew until it was too late that the British were coming her way to perhaps capture the President and burn the Executive Mansion. When she realized this, she took it upon herself to save several of the national treasures including the original draft of the Constitution, the Declaration of Independence, important cabinet papers, and one of Gilbert Stuart's famous portraits of George Washington.

"The British got there right after she left and torched the place, burning it to only a shell. It wasn't habitable again until Monroe's administration, and the Madisons spent the rest of their time as the First Family living in various houses around the District.

"When the Madison administration ended, they moved back to the family estate, Montpelier, in Virginia. Nineteen years later James died and she moved back to Lafayette Square, which is in the District. That was 1836. A year later, for the third time, another widower, Martin Van Buren, took office."

"The third widower?"

"Yes, first Jefferson; then Andrew Jackson, who preceded Van Buren; then van Buren."

"It's funny," I said, "but because of public relations, it's very unlikely that we'd ever elect another unmarried widower to the presidency."

"I think you're right," Mac said.

"Did Van Buren ask for Dolley's help?"

"No. But when she offered it, he accepted it. She was already an icon in Washington, and she often served as hostess throughout his administration along with Van Buren's daughter-in-law, Angelica, whom Dolley introduced into his family.

"But Van Buren served only one term and was succeeded by William Henry Harrison. Harrison's administration lasted just 30 days. He died of pneumonia brought on by standing in the rain during his inauguration. But his successor, Vice President John Tyler, was also a widower and though Tyler's daughter-in-law served as First Lady, Dolley was always there to give assistance, assurance, and advice."

"No wonder she was so famous."

"Her story doesn't end there. Later, when Tyler left office, James Polk became President and, though Dolley and Polk's wife, Sarah, became best of friends, the Polks were not into entertaining. In fact, Mrs. Polk didn't even allow alcohol in the White House. But once again Dolley filled the role. After many White House functions, guests often went to her residence in Lafayette Square for something stronger than what Sarah Polk served."

"So, how many years was she associated with White House functions?"

"Not quite half a century. She became, in her time, one of the best known figures in Washington. She served as either First Lady or the official White House hostess longer, and for more Presidents, than any other woman ever has or likely ever will. When she died, at the beginning of Zachary Taylor's administration, she was 82 and she was given what amounted to a state funeral."

"Wow. Why don't they teach this stuff in grade school?"

"They did at one time. They just don't anymore."

"Did she have much influence on the First Ladies that followed her?" I asked.

Elizabeth Monroe — "la belle Americaine"

Mac let out a sigh. "The two most difficult reigns as First Lady were probably Martha Washington's and Elizabeth Monroe's."

"Why's that?"

"Washington's because there had never been a First Lady before. There were no traditions and no precedents. Martha was First Lady when no one knew whether she should behave like royalty or a commoner. She managed by just being herself."

"But Elizabeth Monroe had a tougher job. She had to follow Dolley. Though history is slowly forgetting her, Dolley was really the most successful White House hostess ever.

"But Elizabeth Monroe had one thing going for her."

"What was that?"

"She came to the White House as a heroine."

"Really?"

"Her husband served several years on diplomatic assignments in Europe, particularly France. While there she acquired a taste for French clothing, French furniture, and other things French which became part of her mark on the White House. But it was also in France that she acquired the reputation as a heroine."

"What'd she do?"

"Her husband served as U.S. minister to France during the French Revolution. The aristocracy was shaking in their collective boots. King Louis XVI, Marie Antoinette, the famed chemist Lavoisier, and a parade of others had gone to the guillotine. It seemed no one, regardless of their station, was safe in France. In fact, the higher your station, the more likely you were to feel the kiss of the guillotine, and among those who appeared destined for the blade were the Marquis Lafayette and his wife."

"Wasn't Lafayette a hero in our own Revolution?"

"That's right. And at the height of the French Revolution, with mobs running in the streets and members of the aristocracy queuing up for their turn to be beheaded, Elizabeth Monroe would cross the streets of Paris in a carriage to visit the imprisoned Mdme. Lafayette. The French admired this kind of courage, and because of it they released Lafayette's wife and gave Elizabeth the sobriquet, 'la belle Americaine.'"

"What was she like as First Lady?"

"She did some things future First Ladies appreciated. Martha Washington had established the tradition of returning the calling cards of all who had visited her. As a result, First Ladies spent their days dashing about Washington.

"Even Dolley Madison didn't dare veer from this tradition.

"Elizabeth Monroe stopped it and, though it earned her criticism in Washington social circles, it no doubt won her the thanks of every First Lady to follow her because, suddenly, First Ladies were no longer slaves to the Washington social scene."

"I guess today, what with all the people who would love to get the President's or the First Lady's ear, it's a godsend," I said.

"True, but it probably happened more because Elizabeth wasn't inclined to assume all the duties of a Washington hostess. And she didn't. She and her husband allowed their married daughter, Elizabeth Hay, to plan and conduct many of the White House functions.

"This daughter, raised and educated in Europe, counted among her friends Hortense Beauharner, a relative of Napoleon and, for a time, Queen of Holland. She knew that Europeans still regarded Americans as somewhat backward, and it was her ambition to make the White House more European. But she neither impressed the Europeans nor did she win the appreciation of her fellow Americans. The result was that, between her and her mother, White House functions were less than fun.

"Oh, there's something else you might want to add: It was during Monroe's administration that the presidential mansion became known as the White House. It was then that they painted it white to cover the burn scars and soot left over from being burned by the British.

"What color was it before that?"

"Brown, I think."

Louisa Adams — a tragic heroine

"Who was the next First Lady?" I asked.

"John Quincy Adams's wife, Louisa."

"What was she like?"

"In some ways she was like her mother-in-law, Abigail Adams. She was bright, literate, and articulate. She

Louisa Adams

was also an accomplished harpist and pianist. She wrote poetry and was fluent enough in French to translate French literature into English."

"Sounds brilliant."

"She was. But here the similarity ends. Where Abigail was strong willed, Louisa Adams was weak and meek. And where John Adams was warm and loving—at least with Abigail—John Quincy was cold and dominating with Louisa. John frequently referred to Abigail as his partner. There was none of that with John Quincy and Louisa.

"If any First Lady was treated worse by her husband, I don't know who it was."

"She'd been born in London to an American father and an English mother. She met John Quincy when he was visiting London. His idea of courtship was to give her a study plan to prepare her for marriage, then leave after telling her he'd be back within seven years."

"She bought into this?"

"They got married in 1797. In their first 13 years of marriage, she was pregnant 13 times. But only three of the children lived.

"When they returned to the United States, he was elected to the Senate from Massachusetts.

"Then, in 1809, he was appointed minister to Russia. He told her she had to go with him, that she had to leave the two eldest children in Massachusetts, but she was to bring the baby to Russia.

"When you went to Europe in those days, you had to plan on being gone for a long time, and she knew it would be a long time before she saw her children again."

"So she didn't do it, right?" I asked.

"Yes, she did."

"Didn't she miss her kids?"

"Of course she did. Not only that, but she was miserable in Russia. They didn't have the money needed to entertain and they had few friends. While there, she also gave birth to a daughter, but she died."

"Talk about bad times."

"It gets worse. When they left Russia, John went on alone to Paris. He ordered her to follow him. She left with her son, who was then just six, a French maid, and a small escort of Russian soldiers. It was winter. During their trip, their water and wine froze. Ice on frozen rivers often threatened to break up and swallow their carriage, and when rumors reached them that Napoleon had escaped from Elba, all the soldiers deserted—all except for a 14-year-old boy."

"A 14-year-old soldier to protect her?"

"That's right."

"Men letting her down. It sounds like the story of her life."

He laughed. "Hold on, it gets worse."

"It can't," I said.

"It does. At one point, they were attacked by French soldiers. They were dragged from their carriage and the soldiers were about to murder them—and probably rape her— until Louisa, speaking to them in French, screamed things like 'Viva Napoleon' and convinced them she was American."

"Are you making this up?"

"No. But just listen; there's more.

"When they reached Paris, John Quincy met her. He was on his way back from the theater, and he gave her hell for arriving late."

"That's all he had to say?" I asked.

Mac smiled and nodded.

"Has anyone ever made a movie about this?"

"Nope. She's one of the great tragic female figures in American history. But not one person in a thousand, now alive, knows she ever lived."

"I hope things got better when she was First Lady."

"Nope. The election of 1824 was a four-way race. Among the contenders were her husband; the ever popular hero, Andrew Jackson, whose fame was the result of his victory over the British at the Battle of New Orleans; the perennial presidential contender—the Harold Stassen of his time—who had the nickname the Great Compromiser, Henry Clay; and a man named William Crawford.

"Jackson finished with the most popular votes and the most electoral votes. But he didn't win a majority of the electoral votes, and that's what it takes to win the presidency. In accordance with the Constitution, the election was thrown into the House of Representatives.

"But in the House, Clay unexpectedly threw his support to Adams, and it was just enough for Adams to win the presidency. But right after the inauguration, Adams made Clay his Secretary of State, which in those days was considered a stepping stone to the presidency. In fact, of the seven presidents to follow Washington, five had served as Secretary of State."

"Wow."

"By the way, you might want to add this to your Gee Whiz file: of the 34 presidents since, only one has been Secretary of State."

"Who was that?"

"James Buchanan."

I wrote it down.

"So how did that affect Adams's presidency?"

"The public never felt good about it. Suspicion surrounded his administration, and he became a tremendously unpopular President. Without many friends, he and Louisa were often alone at the White House. Their marriage, already unhappy, became quarrelsome and Louisa's life became even more unbearable.

"To top it all off, when the Monroes left the White House, they took their furniture with them and the Adamses, who as you should recall couldn't afford to entertain in Russia, didn't have enough money to refurnish it."

"Doesn't the President get expenses for stuff like that?"

"Nowadays, but not then. As a result, the White House always looked shabby while they lived there."

"What did this woman do for relief?"

"In spite, or maybe because, of all of her experiences, she became an early champion of women's rights. Late in her life, in an effort to understand a woman's place in the world, she studied the Old Testament and found evidence that equality of the sexes was intended.

"She also corresponded with feminists of her day.

"And when she discovered her mother-in-law's letters . . ."

"That was Abigail . . ." I said.

"That's right . . . when she discovered the letters, and became aware of the impact Abigail had had on the birth of the United States, she took the letters to heart and treasured them for the rest of her life."

"Why didn't she just divorce Adams?"

"It wasn't something you did in those days."

"Anything else she ever did we should know about?"

"She once bought a slave."

"Come on. First you make her out a tragic heroine, then you spoil it all by telling me she bought a slave."

"That's right. And no self respecting New Englander would have bought one. But, she bought title to a black woman, then freed her. It was one of the last significant acts of her life."

"So she did it just so she could set her free. She did something for another that she couldn't do for herself."

The signposts said we were closing in on Willows. I thought about Louisa Adams for awhile. But Mac was still talking.

Tarnished reputations

"I said earlier that Andrew Jackson was a widower when he assumed the White House. His wife, Rachel had died in January of 1828, just a few months before his inauguration."

"So she never filled the role of First Lady," I interrupted.

"No; she was, however, an interesting figure in her own right."

"Tell me something about her."

"Jackson wasn't her first husband."

"She was another widow." I said presumptuously.

"Nope. She was the first First Lady to be divorced."

"I didn't think anyone got divorced in those days."

"Not usually. When she was 17, she'd married a man named Lewis Robards. He was a violent and jealous man. For six years she endured in a marriage, no part of which was made in heaven. When she was 23, he left her and told her he was filing for divorce. A year later she married Jackson. But as it turned out, Robards hadn't divorced her at all and in 1793 he sued her and Jackson for adultery.

"To make a long story short, the divorce was finally settled and a year later she married Jackson again. But the story became grist for the scandal mills and it followed them for the rest of their lives. Some think it was the scandal that wore her down and ultimately killed her."

"So who filled in as First Lady for Jackson?"

"The Jacksons had no children of their own but they adopted one of the twin sons of one of Rachel's sister-in-laws and renamed him Andrew Jackson, Jr. They also raised another one of her nephews. This one later married one of his cousins . . ."

Angelica Van Buren

"Like Jefferson's daughters married cousins?"

"Right . . . and they lived at the White House for most of Jackson's two terms."

"What was her name?"

"Emily Donelson. She was just 21 and a mother of one when she began her reign as hostess. She had three more children while a White House hostess, and Jackson, who loved kids, loved having her and her family there."

"Nice job for a 21-one-year old," I said.

"It didn't go well at first. Jackson's Secretary of War, a guy named John Eaton, had married a woman who, like Rachel Jackson, had what they called a 'tarnished reputation.' Washington women, Emily included, shunned her. Jackson, remembering the grief that scandal, rumor, and gossip had caused in his own marriage, and the effect it had had on his wife, insisted Emily accept the woman.

"To make another long story short, when she refused, he sent her packing back to Tennessee. But it didn't last long. He missed her, and he missed her children, so he asked her back."

"What about Eaton's wife?"

"Jackson appointed Eaton governor of Florida and—zoom—the Eatons were out of Washington."

Angelica Van Buren

"Who's next?"

"The next President was Martin Van Buren. He was the third man to assume the presidency as a widower. His wife, Hannah, had died 18 years earlier and he raised their four sons—all of whom, by the way, survived childhood."

"So this time the mother died but all the kids lived," I said.

"That's right. The stories of the First Ladies are filled with both tragedy and irony. Anyway, he was elected to the presidency and five men moved into the White House.

"For the first time, it appeared there would be no First Lady. But Dolley Madison was still alive and, as I said earlier, she arranged to introduce a young lady into their midst—Angelica Singleton. Angelica was a cousin to Dolley by marriage.

"The Van Buren men took to her immediately and one of the sons, Abraham, married her so America had another official White House hostess.

"Incidentally, Angelica was one of the women who loved being a White House hostess. But, of course, she was young."

Anna Harrison — widowed too soon

I saw another road sign telling us we were approaching a town called Orland. The miles were melting away like butter on a hot griddle.

"The next President was William Henry Harrison, hero of the Indian wars and son of one of the signers of the Declaration of Independence," Mac said. "He was 68 when he took office and there would not be a first-term President older, until Reagan.

"His wife, Anna, had stayed home, too sick to attend his inauguration. The inauguration didn't go well anyway. The weather was bad and he contracted pneumonia.

"A week later, Anna had recovered from her own illness and was packing for the move to Washington, when word came to her that her husband had fallen ill. Then, when she was actually ready to leave, the news reached her that he was dead."

"So she never lived in the White House," I said.

"No."

"Anything you can tell me about her?"

"Let's see what I remember. She had had 10 children, all of whom she home-schooled. She would probably have been another reluctant First Lady because she had opposed her husband's candidacy for the presidency. And she was the only First Lady to be the wife of one President and grandmother to another."

"Okay," I said. "Who's next?" Δ

(Next issue John Silveira will explore the lives of more of America's early First Ladies. They will include two who never left the upstairs family quarters; two who were related through marriage to the only President the Confederacy ever had—Jefferson Davis; the First Lady whose advice could have gotten her husband reelected, if he'd taken it; the first one with a formal education; and the First Lady who was more than 30 years younger than her husband.)

Making sourdough bread

By Richard Blunt

Yesterday I came across a letter from a reader who asked about sourdough bread. The woman, from Oregon, wanted help finding a recipe for Sheepherders Sourdough Bread, the best of which she said is found in the area of Bishop, California.

In our March/April issue, we published an excellent article on sourdough bread titled *Synopsis of Sourdough*, by Charles Bryant O'Dooley. The article piqued my interest in fermented baked foods and I've made several loaves of sourdough bread a week since I read it. Until then, I had for years agreed with James Beard who said making sourdough is "a most fickle process that is most overrated." Well, my family has enjoyed enough sourdough bread since I read that article that it's changed my outlook entirely.

For one thing, the making of sourdough is a food subject that is fun to read about. But more importantly, some cooks, me included, develop a passion for creating unique tastes in their home-baked breads, and sourdough offers great opportunities. Many of us have several pots of bubbling starter going all the time. I'd like to share with you some of the starters I use, along with my version of Sheepherders Sourdough.

Desire for bread has always increased during times of hardship and decreased during times of plenty. However, great breads of the world have managed to sustain a constant popularity, whether peace and plenty or famine and war. Making bread is an ancient craft, and sourdough is perhaps the most ancient of breads. It is what I call a pioneer bread—like corn pone, rye 'n' Indian, and Johnny Cake—and it continues to find popularity in the kitchens of those learning to cook from scratch.

The first step in making a loaf of sourdough bread is to prepare the starter. This is the most interesting and critical part of the whole process. Almost anything that has fermenting ability will make a starter. But, once you've created it, whether the starter is worth using or not is another matter. There are many varieties of starter. All have unique flavoring qualities and affect the finished bread in a number of different ways. It is also possible to control the amount of sourness found in the finished product.

Let's start with the basics. What is a starter? Well, through the engineering of hungry humans, flour, liquid, sugar, yeast, and bacteria (wild yeasts and bacteria or factory created) are mixed together and allowed to become familiar at loosely controlled temperatures for a period of time. For a flour, you can use white flour, rye flour, graham flour, whole wheat flour, or any other processed grain like

corn meal or barley flour. The flour is combined with a liquid—like water, milk, or even beer, and some form of sugar—which could even be honey. With a little time and patience, your starter has begun. The most important requirement in this is to have as much control over the outcome as possible. Most starters require a boost of processed yeast in the beginning, which is what I mean by control. Trying to start by capturing one of the many forms of wild yeasts can be tricky and unpredictable, though not impossible. It is most certainly the way the very first sourdough was created and, to some people, it is probably still the only way to create a starter. But in my opinion adding processed yeast does not hurt the validity of the starter, and adds a wonderful flavor. I suggest you give both methods a try. If you enjoy baking, you'll find the process to be fun.

Before we get down to the production of the various starters, let's look a little closer at the chemistry. Don't worry, this isn't going to give you flashbacks to the high school chemistry class you've spent the last 20 years trying to forget. Sourdough bread is easy to make and success does not require a master's degree in chemistry. But it's not going to hurt you to know what's going on when you make your starter, and it's my column and I want to tell you. Essentially, bacteria that are present or are added to the starter work on the carbohydrates to form lactic and ascetic acids. The amounts and mixture of these acids determine the level of "sour" taste in the bread. On the other hand, yeast feeds on the sugars present to produce carbon dioxide gas which leavens the bread. There you have it, taste and leavening action, all in this little microbe farm you're going to keep in your kitchen.

The flavor of a sourdough starter varies greatly with environmental conditions. Because of this, professional bakers use commercially prepared cultures to maintain uniformity. For example, a commercial sourdough rye that I am familiar with is prepared as follows: A starter is prepared from rye flour, water, and a dried culture of acid forming microorganisms and set aside to ferment at controlled temperatures for about 24 hours. The fermented starter is then added to a mixture of white and rye flour, shortening, yeast, sugar, liquid, and flavor additives. From this point on, the dough is handled the same as regular yeast fermented dough.

Sourdough French bread is a true example of just how interesting this craft can be. A variety of this bread, that has been produced in San Francisco area for more than 100 years, is especially interesting. The leavening and acid development both come from a completely natural "mother" starter, or "sponge," as it is called. Attempts have been made to develop this starter in other parts of the country. All efforts have failed, even with the use of the "mother" sponge from San Francisco. This is unfortunate because the starter contains a particular yeast and an unusual form of acid producing bacteria that have a unique relationship. This chemical teamwork creates a bread that can only be purchased in that area. But keep in mind that it is possible for you to create a bread unique to your kitchen only. I don't know about you, but the thought of this excites me. So let's get started.

As I said before, we're going to be working mostly with starters in this issue. The recipe for Sheepherders sourdough is my own sourdough formula of Sheepherders bread. This wonderful bread is a contribution to the world of baking presented by Basque sheepherders and can be purchased in several areas of California, from Santa Monica on the coast up to San Francisco and from Fresno to Bishop in the central part of the state. Unfortunately, that recipe for Sheepherders sourdough is a classified formula, so I am offering my own recipe for your review. Give it a try and let me know what you think. If you find it to be off-base, send me a note with your corrections and your own recipe. With all of the food knowledge that is connected with this magazine, I know that there are some fine recipes out there.

Starters

Welcome to Blunt's Sourdough Club. The only requirement to maintain your membership is to enjoy baking and give a name to each one of your starters. I have three and they are named Arrogant Dave, Persistent Gert, and Strong Trish. Each displays the character of the folks that they are named after.

There are a few basic things you should keep in mind to maintain a strong and healthy starter for a long time.

1) Once your starter is active, store it in a container that is large enough to allow it to expand.

2) Use glass, ceramic, plastic or stainless steel with a lid that fits so as to allow gases to expand. Because of chemical reactions that will affect the leavening ability of the starter, do not use any other kind of metal other than stainless steel.

3) If you have not separated a wooden spoon to be used only while you are baking, do so now and use only this spoon to stir your starters. Don't use it to stir soups, or cake batters, or to scoop ice cream. This is your "starter" spoon and it will help you to prevent unwanted flavors and bacteria from getting into your mix.

4) Always keep your starter refrigerated when not in use.

5) I use each one of my starters at least once every two weeks and, when I do, I replenish what I've used with equal amounts of flour and low fat milk or water. To do this, I heat the milk or water to 90° F. If you have not used your starter in two weeks, you'll have to "sweeten the pot" to keep the culture alive. To do this, simply remove the starter from the refrigerator and allow it to come to room temperature. Next, pour off half of mixture and replace it with equal amounts of warm low fat milk or water and <u>all purpose</u> flour. Mix, and allow the starter to sit at room temp and start perking again. I let mine stay out over night. If a clear liquid forms at the top, just stir it down. This liquid eventually rises to the top of all starters and has an alcohol content of about 15%. If you want to get the same feeling experienced by a frontiersman when he was snowed in a wilderness cabin, fresh out of booze, take a taste. If you don't find it to be ambrosia, then you are no frontiersman with a love for "hooch,". I personally think the stuff is terrible and would rather drink sump water through a dirty sock. But there were mountain men who used it to get a buzz.

Now, onto the starters.

Arrogant Dave

This is a starter that is very unpredictable. It can be difficult to get going in the beginning, but once you do, look out; it can try to control your kitchen. It gets yeast from the many wild airborne organisms. I personally feel that this wild yeast starter is not necessary to make an authentic bread. But, for the purists who want to give it a try, here it is.

Where you live may greatly affect the success of this starter. I was lucky and activated mine on the second try. There are others who live in the same area I do who have not been as fortunate and a few are still trying to achieve my success as I write this.

Ingredients

> 2 cups low fat milk
> 1 ½ cup all-purpose flour
> ¾ cup whole wheat flour
> ¼ cup rye flour
> 1 ¼ tsp honey

1. Pour the milk into a glass, ceramic, or stainless steel bowl. Cover it with a double layer of cheese cloth and allow it to ferment at room temperature for at least 24 hours. The next day the mixture should smell sour.

2. Blend the three flours together with the milk, then add the honey and mix well. If the weather is warm, cover it

again with a double layer of cheese cloth and set outside sheltered from direct sun and wind. What you are trying to do is to capture wild yeasts. I leave mine out about 24 hours, then bring it inside and set it in a warm place and allow the wild yeasts to activate. If this is going to happen at all, it'll happen in about 3 to 5 days. If the starter turns black, green, or pink, throw it away and start again. I mean, **throw it away**. You may be dealing with food poisoning if you don't. But, let's assume it hasn't turned color on you. When the starter starts to bubble and swell in size, it's ready to use. I know you'll enjoy the breads you make with this starter.

Persistent Gert

This starter is boosted by prepared dry yeast. It's both dependable and easy to work with. You can hear it fermenting clear across the kitchen during the first two days of chemical change. Then, it falls silent. This is enough to make you think that there is no life left in it. But take my word for it, this starter and the person it is named for have life and energy that will be with us for a long time.

Ingredients

> 1 pkg active dry yeast
> 1 ½ cups all purpose flour
> ½ cup whole wheat flour
> 2 tsp honey
> 2 cups warm water (90° F)

1. Combine all ingredients in a large glass, ceramic, or stainless steel bowl. Cover the bowl loosely with plastic wrap and set it aside in a warm spot for 3 to 5 days. We're using plastic wrap here, instead of cheesecloth, because we're ensuring that no wild yeasts get into the starter. Each day stir the mixture down. When it's bubbly and smells sour, it's ready to use.

Strong Trish

This is my favorite starter. It's contributed well to every sourdough item I've applied it to. It has a wonderful flavor and you'll love all of the breads you make with it. The secret is yogurt. It's been discovered that yogurts—the ones that contain active cultures—have at least six lactic acid forming bacteria. Lactic acid is at the heart of the flavor in sourdough. In addition, yogurt has three other flavor producing bacteria as well. Yogurt has also recently been reported to help lower cholesterol, break down lactose (a sugar that many of us have trouble with) into digestible sugars, and possibly it even aids in lowering the risk of developing breast cancer. What more can you ask for. Eating this bread is like a trip to the doctor.

Ingredients

> 1 cup low fat or skim milk
> 3 tbsp unflavored yogurt with active cultures
> (Read the label to make sure it states it contains live or active cultures.)
> ¾ cup all- purpose flour
> ¼ cup whole wheat flour

1. Very carefully heat the milk in a sauce pan to 95° F. After removing the pan from the heat, stir in the yogurt.

2. Pour this mixture into a glass, plastic, or stainless steel container that takes a tight fitting lid and set it covered in a warm place until a curd forms. This should happen in about 24 hours.

3. Once the curd has formed, remove the lid, stir in the flour, then transfer the mixture to a container large enough for the contents to expand, loosely cover it as you did with the other starters, and set it aside in a warm spot. Let it ferment for 3 to 5 days. If a clear liquid forms, stir it back into the starter. Remember, if any of those off-colors appear, throw it away and start over.

Well, there you have it, three starters that should keep you busy for awhile. Try them with a couple of the recipes that appeared in the March/April issue, or give this next adventure of mine a try and let me know what you think.

Blunt's Basque sheepherders sourdough (Northeast variety)

Sponge batter

> 1 ½ cups starter (take your pick, I like the Strong Trish)
> 1 ½ cups bread flour
> 1 cup warm water

Leavening

> 1 pkg dry yeast
> 1 cup warm water (100° to 110° F)
> ½ tsp sugar

Dough

> 2 cups sponge batter
> 1/3 cup melted butter (not margarine)
> 1/3 cup sugar
> 7 to 9 cups High Gluten Bread Flour
> 2 tsp course salt

1. About 8 hours before you want to make the bread remove your starter from the refrigerator and measure 1 ½ cups of starter into a bowl. (Remember to replenish the

starter as described earlier.) Add 1 ½ cups of bread flour and 1 cup of warm water. Mix well with your wooden spoon, cover with a double layer of cheesecloth and set aside to ferment for 8 to 12 hours.

2. After the fermentation period, mix together the yeast, 1 cup of warm water and ½ tsp sugar. Set aside for yeast to proof—about five minutes

3. While the yeast is proofing, measure out 6 cups of flour and mix in a large bowl with the salt.

4. Melt the butter and combine it with the sugar, 2 cups of sponge batter, and yeast mixture. (Return the remaining sponge batter to the container containing the basic starter and return it to the refrigerator. This will maintain your starter for later recipes.)

5. Combine this batter mixture with the 6 cups of flour. Mix with a wooden spoon until you form a thick batter. Continue to add the remaining flour one cup at a time to form a stiff dough. This should be about another 2 ½ to 3 cups of flour. The dough should remain on the soft side but not sticky. Remember, this a french bread, too much flour makes it dry.

6. When the dough becomes to hard to handle in the bowl, turn it out on a floured board or counter and knead until smooth, adding flour as you find necessary. This should take about 10 to 15 minutes. Place the dough in a greased bowl with straight sides, cover and allow it to sit until it doubles in bulk. This will take about 1 ½ to 2 hours.

7. After the dough has risen, punch it down and form it into a smooth ball.

Baking (Unique to Sheepherders Bread)

For this you will need a 4 ½ or 5 quart cast iron or cast aluminum Dutch oven with a lid.

1. Cut a circle of aluminum foil to fit the bottom of the Dutch oven. Grease the sides of the Dutch oven, and the foil on the bottom, using a solid shortening. Grease the inside of the lid, also. Place the dough in the pot, cover with the lid and let the dough rise until the dough starts to push the lid off of the oven. This should take about an hour.

2. Bake with the lid on in a 375º F oven for about 15 minutes. Remove the lid and continue baking until the bread is an even medium brown and sounds hollow when tapped. Remove the loaf from the oven, turn the loaf out of the Dutch oven, and place it on a rack to cool.

Let me tell you that this is a large loaf of bread, it is impressive to serve at a party with a selection of cheeses. (For the not so daring, there is also enough dough with this recipe to make four loaves of bread using medium 8x4x2 inch bread pans.) But the way I make it, though not easy, gives me a great deal of satisfaction. Give it a try and let me know what you think. ∆

A BHM Writer's Profile

Annie Duffy

Annie Duffy, 15, is Backwoods Home Magazine publisher Dave Duffy's daughter. Besides writing a popular teen column for BHM, she maintains the magazine's internet web site (http://www.backwoodshome.com) and troubleshoots computer and software problems.

Annie is a sophomore in high school, and she likes to sing, sew, act, and work with computers. She is your typical teenage girl: her room is always a mess, she keeps changing her hair style and color, she sleeps all day on Saturday, and she'll do anything to avoid doing the dishes. But she's a hard worker when she's not goofing off.

Internet users can reach her at annie@backwoodshome.com.

Old-fashioned desserts

By Jennifer Stein Barker

Do you remember when desserts were warm, comforting, and satisfying? They were full of hearty flavor, too, and nobody worried about fat because most of the desserts were based on grains and fruits. A little ice cream for a topping, well, that never hurt anybody....

The recipes that follow are modern versions of those old-fashioned desserts. They have been updated to use whole grains, natural fruits, and lower-fat dairy products. You can eat these hearty desserts without guilt, in the knowledge that you are getting good nutrition along with that old-fashioned happy-tummy feeling.

Indian pudding

This New England classic is *soooo* comforting on a winter evening after a dinner of hearty vegetable soup. For a surprise, try it after a curry, too. It's not the same kind of "Indian," but it works!

Serves six hungry Indians:

> 3 ¾ cups milk
> ¾ cup cornmeal
> 1 egg, lightly beaten
> ½ cup honey
> 1/3 cup dark molasses
> 1 Tbsp. fresh ginger, finely minced
> 1 tsp. cinnamon

Preheat the oven to 325°. Lightly oil a 1½ quart baking dish.

In a medium sized saucepan bring the milk to a boil. Lower the heat and sprinkle the cornmeal over the milk, whisking all the while. Whisk and cook slowly until the mixture has thickened, using a spoon to scrape the corners of the pan occasionally. Remove the pan from heat and let cool for 10 minutes.

Whisk in all the remaining ingredients until well blended. Pour into the prepared dish. Place this dish in a pan of hot water that comes halfway up its sides, and bake for one hour and 45 minutes or until a knife inserted in the center comes out almost clean. Let cool for 10 to 15 minutes before serving.

Serve warm, plain or with maple syrup or ice cream.

Apple pandowdy

A classic New England dessert, rich with molasses and spices.

Makes one 9 x 13 pan:

Sauce

> 6 or 7 large apples
> ¼ cup dark molasses
> ¼ cup honey
> 1 tsp. dried orange peel
> ½ tsp. cinnamon

Biscuits

> 2 cups whole wheat pastry flour
> 2 tsp. baking powder
> ¼ tsp. cinnamon
> ¾ cup milk
> 2 Tbsp. honey
> ¼ cup oil

Wash, core, and slice all but two of the apples. (Leaving the skins on adds flavor and texture, but you may remove them if you like.) You should have about eight cups of sliced apple. In a medium saucepan, combine the molasses, honey, orange peel, and cinnamon. Add the sliced apples and cook over low heat until the apples are very tender and the mixture is the consistency of applesauce.

While the apples are cooking, prepare the biscuits. Sift the pastry flour, baking powder, and cinnamon together into a medium bowl. In a small bowl, mix the milk, honey, and oil. Add the liquid all at once to the dry mixture and beat just until evenly mixed. Turn the dough out onto a floured surface and knead four or five times, then pat it out ½" thick. Use a glass or biscuit cutter three inches in diameter

---

It's easy to subscribe to
Backwoods Home Magazine.
Just call us at:
1-800-835-2415

to cut out eight biscuits (you may have to pat the last one together from the scraps).

Preheat the oven to 375°. Now wash, core, and cut the last two apples into ½" chunks. Add them to the sauce and spread it in a 9 x 13" glass baking dish. Arrange the biscuit dough over the sauce in two rows of four biscuits. Bake for 30 minutes, or until the biscuits are golden and the sauce bubbles up around them.

Serve warm. This is very good with ice cream or frozen yogurt.

Vanilla ice cream

A treat best saved for special occasions. Try this with rum or liqueur, or over one of the desserts in this article.

```
2 cups light cream
2 cups low-fat milk
2/3 cup nonfat dry milk
¼ cup honey
1 stick cinnamon
2 eggs
1 Tbsp. cornstarch
3 Tbsp. vanilla
```

In a medium saucepan, bring the cream, milk, nonfat dry milk, honey, and cinnamon stick to a boil. Remove immediately from the stove. In a glass or metal bowl, whisk together the eggs and cornstarch until the cornstarch is completely dissolved. Whisk in the hot milk mixture. Return to the pan and heat gently on "low" until the mixture thickens. Remove from heat, add the vanilla, and refrigerate until thoroughly chilled.

Freeze, following directions with your ice cream freezer.

Steamed fruit pudding

A modern version of the classic way of using up stale bread!

Serves eight:

```
2 Tbsp. oil
1/3 cup honey
2 1/3 cups bread crumbs
2 beaten eggs
½ - ¾ cup milk
½ cup chopped figs, dates, raisins, or mixed dried fruit
```

Mix all ingredients. Use enough milk to make a mixture the consistency of soft ice cream. It should mound up a little in the bowl. My favorite dried fruit combo is figs and raisins and pineapple, but use your own imagination.

Oil a medium-sized pudding tin, the kind with the tube up the middle and a snap-on lid. Use a stockpot large enough to put the tin in, and cover with a lid. Pour enough boiling water into the pot to come one third of the way up around the sides of the tin. Simmer, covered, on medium heat for three hours. When the pudding is done, it will be firm, springy, and moist. Spoon or slice into dishes and serve with hot fresh lemon sauce (below).

Fresh lemon sauce

```
1 cup water
4 tsp. cornstarch
¼ cup honey
4 Tbsp. fresh lemon juice
grated rind ½ lemon
2 tsp. brandy
freshly grated nutmeg
```

In a small pan, dissolve the cornstarch in the water. Bring to a boil, stirring constantly, and boil five minutes or until thick and clear. Remove from heat and add honey, lemon juice and peel, brandy, and a sprinkle of nutmeg. Serve warm over cakes or puddings. ∆

A country moment

Jason and Skyler Zeman play on the slopes of Mt. Shasta, California.

Odd-jobbin' can be a country goldmine

By Don Fallick

Country folk are known for doing things themselves, so one might suppose that small towns and rural areas would be poor prospects for the free-lance handyman. The fact is, this just isn't so. Many elderly ruralites try to stay on the old homestead long after their youthful strength has deserted them. In many cases, their children have flown the nest, too, and may live so far away that they can't help ma or pa with the difficult tasks needed occasionally in any home.

Cleaning out garages and barns, hauling trash, washing windows, painting, tilling gardens, even cutting the grass may be chores beyond the strength or agility of the elderly. Blindness or arthritis may prevent them from maintaining their own cars, lawn mowers, or utilities. Elderly women may not know how to do any of these things. Their husbands may no longer own a pickup truck, a tiller, or other equipment needed. All this can make money for you. If you are a jack-of-all-trades, you can make $8 to $10 per hour or more, and feel good about doing it.

What to avoid

One of the best parts of odd-jobbin' is the opportunity to pick and choose your jobs. If you don't like to work on ladders, for example, you don't have to. But there are some jobs you should choose to avoid, because they can get you into legal hassles.

1. Don't do major electrical work, unless you are a certified electrician. If you ignore the regulations requiring certification, you may be liable in the event that someone is hurt or killed, even if you know your work didn't cause it. Personally, I won't do much more than replace lamp or dryer cords, or replace regular 110 volt switches or outlets that have gone bad. And always shut off the electricity at the breaker box or fuse box before working on any circuit.

2. Take similar precautions working with natural gas or propane lines. If you're not certified, you can still change furnace filters, and even shut off and clean out some gas appliances. Do not shut off the gas at the main service valve, unless you smell gas and can't locate the leak. Legally, you need to be a certified tech to turn the gas main back on. And never monkey with a gas appliance that has been red-tagged.

3. Plumbing is rarely life-threatening. If you're willing to see a plumbing job through to completion, and you know what you're doing, there's no reason you can't make minor plumbing repairs. Remember, though, once you take on a job, you are honor bound to finish it. Nothing will lose you customers as fast as biting off more than you can chew.

4. Ladders may not scare you, but power lines should, especially if your ladder is aluminum. I don't do jobs that require me to come close to power lines with such a ladder.

5. In general, if a job is unsafe don't do it. As a private contractor, you are responsible for your own safety and your own on-the-job injuries. You're also responsible for any damages caused by your activities, deliberate or accidental. Think before accepting a job.

Tools needed

A **truck with racks** for the bed. You can tie ladders and stuff to the outside of them or use tarps over the top and sides when hauling trash. Overload springs are helpful, as is a trailer hitch. A good, long logging chain and/or a pair of come alongs can be handy too.

Lawn and garden tools. You'll want a full complement of shovels, rakes, and hoes. A good rototiller can pay for itself. You'll also want tools for digging out stumps and bushes, pruning trees, and trimming hedges. A good garden cart is vital.

Ladders. Much of your work will come from people who are afraid of ladders. Really high ones (up to 40 feet) can be rented, if you don't already have one. But you will want to own at least one good, general-purpose ladder. It should be fibre-glass so it won't conduct electricity. I also recommend a 20-foot extension ladder.

Ladders are rated by the weight they will safely hold. Yours should take your weight, plus as much weight as you are likely to be carrying up or down it. I recommend 250 lbs. minimum. Shingles, tool boxes, etc. can be awfully heavy and the ladder's safety rating will deteriorate as it ages.

Protective clothing. Gloves and a good pair of boots for starters. It's not a bad idea to have a pair of junky coveralls and a hat handy for messy jobs. I've found a pair of rubber Wellington boots real useful, too.

A good telephone answering machine. You don't want to lose a new customer while you're out helping an old one. The best machines give your callers an unlimited time for their response. I have "call answering" service through my local telephone company. This works just like an answering machine, but is much more flexible. I never have fuzzy tapes, and I never lose messages due to lightning strikes or power outages. I can call and get my messages from any phone, and the service lets me know if I have messages every time I pick up the receiver. It costs about $6/month.

Pricing and estimating

There are two main methods to determine pricing. If you're just starting out, call another handyman in your area and find out what his rates are. By doing this, you know your rates won't be out of line with the prevailing wages in your area.

Whether you can make money with these rates is a different story. The other way to determine pricing is to figure your cost of doing business and add what you feel is a reasonable hourly wage to that. This works better for some jobs than others. For example, if you're hauling junk to the dump, you know what the dump fees are, how many truckloads, and how far it is. If the dump fee is $10, it costs you $.21/mile to drive your truck, and you have to go 30 miles round trip to the dump, your business cost is $16.30.

If you figure it'll take you 45 minutes to load the truck, 15 minutes to unload it at the dump, and 30 minutes to drive there and back, you need to add an hour and a half's wages for yourself. At $8/hour this comes to $12, for a total estimate of $28.30.

Figure up a few jobs like this, then call your local handyman and get his estimates. This will give you an idea what other folks are actually paying themselves.

Only you know what your time is worth. Personally, I charge a higher hourly rate for doing things I dislike, and a lower hourly rate for easy jobs. For example, I charged only $5/hour for cutting a lawn with my customer's riding lawn mower, but $10/hour for cleaning out horse stalls. My point of view is that, if they are not willing to pay the higher price, I can find another job more to my liking.

Pricing structures can include flat rate fees for various jobs. Some handymen include a flat rate service call as part of the fee. The cost of getting to the job either comes out of your wages or you must charge for it. I figure I'll have to travel to work no matter what my profession, so I take it out of my wages.

Rather than repeat complicated calculations for jobs I do often, I have developed flat rates for some of them. For years I charged a flat fee of $20 per truckload for dump runs. Then they closed the county dump, and I had to haul trash to the new waste to energy incinerator 40 miles away, where they weigh you in and out, and the disposal fee varies with the net weight.

When my cost of doing business varies like this, I use a cost plus rate structure. I charge $.21 per mile, plus the dump fee, plus $7/hour. Most customers are satisfied with this. For those who want an estimate of the total, I have enough experience to know that most truck loads usually cost about $35 to $45, and the mileage usually runs around $8. My time depends on what I'm loading, whether I have help, etc. This gives the customers an idea of whether they can afford my services but protects me in case their trash turns out to be really heavy or includes items the trash plant charges extra for, such as drywall and auto batteries.

Taxes and licenses

State taxes range from Oregon, which doesn't even have sales tax, to Wisconsin, which taxes just about everything. Some states don't tax services. If your state is not one of these, you'll need a state sales tax number. But just about everywhere, you need a business license from your county to be legal.

A business license tells the state who is responsible for the activities of your business and tells you what taxes you need to collect for the state and how and when to pay them. There is a nominal fee which varies from state to state and sometimes with the type of business. Mine cost about $20. State taxes are arranged to be as painless as possible for the business person, because the state wants businesses.

Federal Income taxes are another matter. If your income from your business is more than nominal, you'll have to file a quarterly tax return. Even if you don't, you'll still have to file a much more complex annual return than most folks who are not self-employed. You'll have to pay a self-employment tax in lieu of Social Security and file a Schedule SE, along with a long form 1040 and maybe others as well. The best thing to do is call or visit the IRS (I know it hurts) and ask what forms you are required to file and how often you have to file 'em. The IRS has a stack of handy little starter kit for folks just starting in business. The kit contains answers to most of your questions, it's free, and it's available just by calling or writing your nearest IRS office and asking.

Not all states have income taxes—Washington has none, for example. But those that do mostly require the same kinds of shenanigans from the self-employed that the Federal tax men do. State and Federal tax offices can be found in your White Pages telephone directory, under United States Government or under the name of your state. Information about local taxes can most likely be found at your county assessor's office. There's no getting around it—paying your taxes, even if you are willing, is at best a difficult, frustrating experience. In some cases, it can be almost as bad as being on Welfare.

Painful as it is, you really must not skip any tax reporting requirements. Even if it later turns out that you didn't actually owe any taxes, the IRS can still shut you down, impound your tools and vehicles, even fine you or jail you, just for not touching all the bases. You would think an organization like the IRS would have bigger fish to fry than some poor, rural handyman. Remember, all those giant corporations that are defrauding the tax collectors have lots of accountants and lawyers on their payrolls. It's easier for the tax men to come after you.

Record keeping

Even in this day of big government, they still can't require you to be an accountant or even to hire one. Still, it's a good idea to know at least a little bit about bookkeeping, if only so you will know (and can prove) whether you're making a profit or not. If you're ever audited, you'll need these records.

Accounting is basically keeping records of how much money you were paid (income) and how much you paid out (expenses) for things directly related to your business. Your business expenses will probably be things like gas for the pickup and rototiller, repairs, advertising, business cards, tool rentals, and so on.

If you maintain an office or workshop in your home that is mainly used for business purposes, you can count a proportional part of your mortgage payment, utility bills, etc., as business expenses. Frankly, this has never helped me very much, but what can you expect when your house payment and utility bills amount to less than $400/month total?

The IRS will require you to keep books, but these can be very simple; just a daily list of income and expenses, with monthly totals. They will throw a lot of technical terms at you, but the two you simply must understand are cash basis and accrual basis.

These are the two basic ways of keeping track of money. Cash basis does not mean that you don't accept checks or credit cards. It means you don't count income as income until you've actually been paid. And you don't count bills as paid until you've paid them. This is the common sense way of bookkeeping that everybody does intuitively. Unless you just love difficult mathematics for its own sake, its the method you'll use.

Some businesses whose size or extremely uneven cash flow makes cash basis accounting impractical use another method called accrual basis. They count money as income the moment orders are received, and bills as paid as soon as they are authorized. You can see that this could be handy for a mail-order book club, for example, but for ordinary folks it's a disaster. That's about as much of it as I understand.

One reason I like to be paid by check is that it simplifies my bookkeeping immensely. I save all my old bank statements and check registers, and I can prove, even years later, just how much profit (or loss) I made.

I buy cheap receipt books at the grocery store for less than $2 and use them too. I keep the carbon copies. Save everything. If you are ever audited, you'll be glad you did. I know lots of folks who just throw all their statements, paid bills, etc. in a shoe box all year long, then gobble aspirin like

candy every April trying to figure it all out.

A better way is to use two shoe boxes, one for income and the other for expenses. At the end of each month, staple, clip, or rubber band that month's income and expenses into separate bunches then fasten the bunches together. At tax time, your records will be divided into monthly records of income and expenses, neatly fastened together.

Insurance

You are responsible for any damage you do while on the job, or any damage caused (even years later) by any service you furnished. For example, if you prune someone's tree and 5 years later it dies, blows down in a storm, and destroys someone's roof, you could be held responsible. Of course, you know your neighbor wouldn't sue you for such a ridiculous chain of circumstances, but what about her heir's insurance company?

Considering the price of being wrong and the cheapness of business liability insurance, I think it's foolish not to have it. In some places it's illegal to do business if you're not insured, but in any event, a minimal $100,000 liability policy will probably cost around $100/year, and can save you a lot of grief.

Insurance rates vary widely from company to company, and depend on many factors, but especially on three:

1. Do you have any employees? Even one employee who is not a member of your family can greatly increase your rates. Helpers who are members of your family are not usually counted as employees.

2. What is your main type of business? Hazardous activities naturally cost more. Some companies want to limit you to only the activities listed in the policy. If you're doing anything not specifically listed, you're not covered, period. Others only want to know your main line of work. If you are doing something else, as part of your regular business, you're still covered. It's a better deal but, of course, it costs more.

3. Coverage. This includes things like total dollar amount per claim, deductible amounts, etc. Some policies include damages to you and your possessions, rented tools, etc. Others do not. This is where you need an insurance agent. Reading and understanding all the fine print before you sign is vital. If there's something you don't understand, and your agent won't explain it to you, get another agent.

Advertising

The best advertising you will ever get is word-of-mouth. In small towns and rural areas, a reputation as a hard worker is better than any amount of paid advertising. I always ask my customers to refer me to their friends, and give them my card. But if you're new to the area, it can be hard to get noticed at all. Here are some tactics I have used:

— **notices on bulletin boards** in supermarkets and community centers. These can be hand-written. Make a fringe of tear-off strips along the bottom, with your name, phone number, and the word "handyman" (or whatever you call yourself) on each strip. Stress that you are hard-working and fair priced.

— similar **notices at senior citizen centers**. You might consider offering a senior citizen discount of 5% or 10%. I try to court senior citizens, as I have found them to be pleasant to work for, when treated respectfully, and almost

universally honest. I've never gotten a bad check from a senior citizen.

— similar **notices at farm supply dealers, grain elevators, auctions**, etc.

— a small notice in the **classified section of your local weekly newspaper**. Potential customers look here first if they don't know who to call. Don't make it fancy, or people will be suspicious..

— **ask for work**. I was buying milk at a local dairy farm one wet, muddy spring when I noticed the farmer was having trouble with his spring planting. I asked if he needed any help and ended up milking for him for 3 weeks while he got his crops in.

Barter

A nice thing about owning your own business is that you can accept payment "in kind."

I once traded 100 hours of labor at a ranch for a horse. Another time, I bartered 150 hours of work for down payment on a house. You can often make a better deal bartering for your work than working for money. But remember, it costs you money to do business, so subtract your expenses from the value of the item you are being offered before making your decision.

Avoid barter fever, though. If you're offered something you weren't already planning to buy, it may be best to work for money.

Another problem with barter is that you must usually complete the whole transaction. If I had only completed half of those hundred hours at the horse ranch, I would have had a hard time getting paid half a horse. Working 50 hours and getting paid even minimum wages would be better than working 50 hours and getting nothing. Moral: be especially careful when bidding a barter job.

Hiring help

There are some jobs that are just too big to be done by one person, or at least to be done safely or efficiently. A strapping, teenage son or two can come in real handy here, but don't neglect your daughters. A painter I know has three daughters working for him. One of them is his best, and fastest painter. I've known women and girls who milked cows, fixed cars, did carpentry, and just about any other so-called man's job. But even with all the home grown help you can get, there may come a time when you need an employee.

Legally, if you hire someone to work for you, you are responsible for paying worker's compensation insurance, Social Security tax, Federal and State income tax, and filing enough paperwork to drown an accountant. Fortunately, there is a way out of most of this. Hire your temporary workers as "contract labor."

If you are the employer, you must provide all those benefits. If you hire another company to subcontract the labor, that company is responsible. The contract laborer is that other company. Of course, the contract laborer may elect to break the law and keep all the money you pay him for himself. The main function of the contract is to protect you from future prosecution or lawsuits should something go wrong. I know of no case where this has been tested, so I can't say whether it's legal or not, but I know a lot of plain folks who think it is.

The common alternative to doing it the (prohibitively expensive) legal way, or the semi-legal, risky way, is to pay your help under the table. This is the cheapest way to go in the short run, but also the riskiest. If your illegal employee is hurt on the job or causes damage to your customer's property, your insurance will certainly not cover it. They may even cancel your coverage. Furthermore, if the government finds out, you can face hefty fines, or even a jail sentence.

The few times I've needed to hire an extra pair of hands, I've done it by hiring another self-employed handyman to work with me, setting up a temporary partnership. It does complicate bidding. But the handyman I usually work with is my neighbor Jim, who frequently trades work with me in this way. We've agreed to pay each other the same wages, and not worry about minor differences. This simplifies things immensely, and makes bidding on two-man jobs practical for both of us. We keep in touch, and almost never end up bidding against each other.

Bad debts

In rural areas and small towns, you're not too likely to get burned by bad checks. If someone's check does bounce, it's almost never deliberate. It's just too difficult living in a small town with a bad reputation. I have had checks bounce. Every time, when I called up the customers, they insisted on paying me in cash immediately. I've never had to send a check back to the bank.

Working odd jobs in the city (I've done that too!) is not so secure. I have been burned by city customers. Trust your instincts. If you aren't sure that the customers check is good, demand cash. To avoid offending the customer, you must make it clear to him that you want cash, before you begin work. Customers will probably figure that you're not reporting all of your income to the IRS. This is common enough in rural areas, and most folks won't be offended.

I prefer to be paid by check as it helps me keep records of my income and expenses. I don't worry about reporting my income to the IRS as it's low enough, and I have enough kids, that I never end up paying taxes anyway.

Odd job opportunities

I have done some mighty odd odd jobs, but mostly they fall into five distinct areas. Here are a few things I have learned about each.

Hauling. The main thing I haul is trash. In the country, garbage trucks are a rare sight. Most folks store up their trash in the garage for the monthly dump run, or until the dogs start getting into it. If they don't have a truck or a utility trailer, they may call you when it starts to get ripe.

With stake sides on the back, I can get 30-40 bags of trash in my pickup. This means I can haul trash for several customers in one trip. With a full truck, I can make $50 profit in one dump run, even after paying the high rates at the incinerator.

Sometimes, hauling trash means someone has cleaned out a shed and has a whole truckload to haul. Often enough, I get paid to clean out the shed and load it into the truck, plus a dump run fee on top of that. Cleaning out garbage can be hard to bid. It's never as easy as it looks like it's going to be. The worst garbage jobs are ones where you can't park the truck close to the trash. This doubles the amount of work, but lots of folks don't want to pay double the price.

I charge extra for hauling appliances. If I have to move a refrigerator or washer, I almost always have to hire help. I don't begrudge paying Jim for his help in loading and unloading heavy items, but it galls me to have to pay him for riding in the truck with me for 2 hours. I know he feels the same about me.

Many states have recently enacted laws requiring all loads to be covered. You'll need a tarp of the right size to cover your truck, with and without stake sides installed. Too large a tarp can be as much a problem and too small. In some states, it's also illegal to haul wood with nails in it. I know a guy who did it anyway and suffered for years from flat tires in his driveway. No, it wasn't me.

In some states it may be illegal for you to haul trash. In Washington, the whole state is divided up into sanitation districts. Each district is licensed to one company only. In return, that company is supposed to serve all customers in the district, but most find it uneconomical to serve those who do not live in town. In theory, you must have such a license to haul trash in Washington. In practice, nobody much cares whether you do or not, and the state ignores small haulers who keep a low profile. Unofficially, it's OK to service the customers the big companies don't want. Just don't rub their noses in it by trying to compete with them directly.

Demolition. When an old building needs to come down, the handyman is the first one most folks call. There are two things to beware of: safety . . . and safety. If you haven't ever torn down a building before, get experienced help. In demolition, there's no substitute for experience.

First, check the building for stability. If you have to, brace it so it won't fall down on you while you're working on it. Some buildings will be so unstable they may have to be pulled down first. It will take a long time to tear apart a building that's already down. I tried it once. Never again! If it's possible, try to demolish the building in the reverse order of construction. This means furnishings, cabinets, windows and doors come out first, then interior wall surfaces. Leave the floor, so you have something to stand on. Take the roof off. Most old roofing is not worth saving. Stand inside the building and knock out the siding with a sledge. Then take the walls down, one at a time. Before you start, make sure you have a contract with the owner specifying how far the demolition is to proceed. Three friends of mine took down a barn for a local farmer, just for the materials. Were they ever surprised to learn that he expected them to break up the concrete foundation and haul it away, too! Get it in writing first.

Protective clothing is a must for demolition. I won't work without a good hard hat, leather gloves, goggles, and steel-toe boots. My life has been saved by wearing a hard hat, my hands by gloves, my eyes by goggles, and my foot by the boots. Demolition is hard, hot, dirty, dangerous drudgery, and the protective clothing makes it even more uncomfortable. But it's not as uncomfortable as eye surgery, or wearing a cast for two months. If this scenario does not appeal to you, don't do demolition.

After the building is down, it still must be de-nailed, loaded, and hauled away. Don't forget to include these very time-consuming operations in your estimate. Frankly, demolition is so very labor-intensive that most employers won't pay enough to make it worthwhile. I used to do quite a bit of it but now I leave it to the young fools who don't value their time.

Home maintenance. This includes painting and clean-up, as well as minor repairs. I have four favorite products that I use to make this work fast and easy. The first is Trisodium Phosphate, or TSP. Used according to the directions, it cleans years of gunk off of exterior walls in a jiffy and helps paint to stick.

The second product is Fixall patching plaster. Actually, any good brand of plaster of Paris will work but I like Fixall the best. Besides filling small holes in drywall or wood, it's handy for filling the grain of old wooden siding or trim prior to priming. The more you stir it, the faster it sets, so add water cautiously and mix no more than you can use in five minutes. Its one real disadvantage is that it's terribly hard to sand, so work as fine as you can.

Another favorite product is "stain-hide shellac" made by Kilz or Bullseye. It is pricey, but it covers stains that'll bleed through any other paint. It's available in spray cans or liquid. If you've got a surface that just seems to drink primer without ever getting sealed, try this stuff. I've never had to use more than two coats on anything.

My other favorite product is grabber screws. These range in size from tiny drywall screws to huge decking screws, and come in a variety of finishes. They can't be beat for patching BIG holes in plaster or sheetrock. For old, lath and plaster walls, remove the plaster from the broken area, screw a piece of sheetrock in its place, and tape and finish like drywall. Drywall grabber screws will hold directly to the wooden laths.

To patch big holes in drywall, cut out the broken area in a rectangle and screw 1 x 2 furring strips to the inside of the sheetrock, so it will support the edges of the patch. Cut a rectangular patch, just the right size to fit, and screw it to the furring strips. Voila! Ready to tape and finish!

A smaller hole can be patched by gluing an oversize piece of sheetrock to the inside of the wall. A couple of grabber screws stuck into this backing piece make it easy to handle inside the wall. To hold it tight while the glue dries, lay a stick across the hole and run a longer grabber screw through the stick and the backing. After the glue dries, remove all the screws, glue a proper size patch to the backing, tape, and finish.

Yardwork & gardening. This is your bread and butter. Lawn mowing, hedge trimming, etc., provide the day-to-day work that pays most of the bills. This stuff requires little expertise, just the patience to do repetitive tasks and keep doing them well. This is also your best advertising. People do compliment each other's pretty lawns and gardens. If you're responsible, your name will get passed around.

You may not agree with the way the customers want their grounds kept. If they want you to use Weed n Feed, and you're an organic gardener, you owe it to them to do it their way. Save your advice for times when they ask for it, especially when working for farmers or the elderly. The only time I make an exception to this rule is when I know something that can save the customer money. Few people mind advice of this sort, even if they decide not to take it. Even so, unless you are on very good terms with the customer, phrase your advice as a question: Did you know there's a sale on grass seed right now at the Grange?

Agricultural. Every rural area has its own special seasons when good money can be made by those who are lucky enough to be hired. In my area, the big chance for agricultural work comes during the wheat harvest. Wheat truck drivers get around $100/day, working seven days a week for five or six weeks. If you've done good work for the farmer or his mother, and he knows you're a reliable, hard worker, you can make a bundle every harvest. I know ex-handymen who've retired to working the harvest. They make $4000 in six weeks and loaf the rest of the year.

Not all agricultural work is so rewarding. I've shoveled out horse stalls, milked and fed cows and goats, strung fences, pulled stumps, loaded hay, and other odd jobs around the farm. Perhaps the oddest job I've ever had was agricultural. I once planted 2000 dahlia bulbs in one day. It was back-breaking work. But it paid money, I learned more than I ever guessed there was to know about dahlias, and I made a friend. Not bad for one day's work! Δ

Help your children to read by teaching them the phonic basics

By Barbara Sorensen Fallick

I always intended to homeschool. My children were bright, avid learners from the environment. I read to them daily and they loved books. I expected that they would absorb reading from the environment as they had absorbed spoken language.

Perhaps it would have happened had there been enough time. After my divorce I was forced to place my children in school while I worked to support the family. I trained in the Montessori method and later became certified for Kindergarten through third grade. I then realized that, though I had been a college graduate and an avid reader as a homeschooling parent, I had not really known how to help my children develop the skills for reading.

Later I remarried and became the step-mother of five children who had been homeschooled. I saw that some of these children had in fact just learned to read from the environment and from self-teaching, but others had not.

Some had reached the age where they really wanted to read well, but had not mastered basic skills they needed to quickly become masterful readers. They needed and wanted specific guidance.

Here are some specific techniques parents can use to help their children develop a basic understanding of phonics and beginning phonic reading. They include games aimed at mastering the short vowels, and beginning to read using those vowels and all of the consonants. Begin playing pre-reading games when the child is very young. The games can be adapted to an older beginning reader.

Learning the sounds

Chants:

Teach a young child of 2-3 the sounds as a traveling game, waiting in the doctor's office, or at nap or bedtime. Put these to a simple melody or to a rhythmic chant, such as: 'What does the B say? Buh-buh-buh." "What does the C say? Kuh-kuh kuh." Add words with the initial sound to the chant: 'What does the B say? Buh-buh-buh. Banana! Bear! Box! Bed!" Alter this with different words according to the child's interest, experience, and mastery.

Vowels:

The vowels are a special category because one letter makes several sounds. I personally prefer to teach the short vowels first, then the long vowels, and then alternate spellings for the same sounds, and finally, any vowel sounds which do not fall within the above categories.

The short vowel sounds are: a as in apple, e as in elephant, i as in invitation, o as in octagon, and u as in umbrella. Use the same format for a chant for vowels, "What does the a say? a, a, a. Apple! And! Avalanche!" Similar chants need to be made for each of the vowels.

Sound boxes:

Make small containers of miniature objects for each sound. Use small boxes such as check book boxes, drawstring bags, or baskets cheaply obtained at thrift stores as containers—one for each of the sounds. To visually teach a difference between vowels and consonants, use one color of container for vowels and a different color for consonants.

No verbal teaching of the difference between them is necessary at this stage. Place approximately five miniature objects which begin with the initial sound in each container. For instance, in a container, place an ax, apple, ant, antelope, and axle.

I find my names of objects by going through the dictionary. I find my miniature objects in Lego sets, Barbie doll sets, and craft stores. Sometimes I make them myself such as a miniature envelope or invitation.

Initially, teach the child the names of all of the objects of one given sound—a great vocabulary expander.

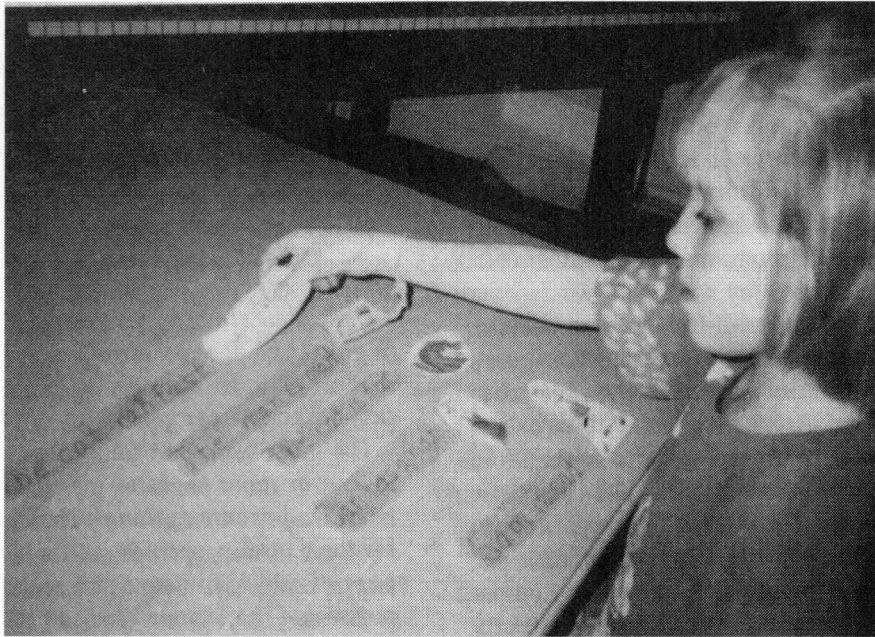
Mary Evette Stoutner matching sentences and pictures

Then, mix the objects from three to five sounds together and have the child sort by initial sound.

Dictionary:

Have the child make a picture dictionary of beginning sounds. Alott a separate page for each vowel sound and one for each consonant sound. Give the child magazines in which to look for pictures of things beginning with his special sound. Magazines can be cheaply bought at thrift stores.

The child cuts out the picture for his sound and glues it on the page. Print the name of the object by the picture.

Associating the sounds with written letters

Many teachers teach all of the sounds, associating them with the written letter, before beginning to read.

He can read 'at' by learning only two sounds. Add "c" and he can read "cat." Each time a new sound is introduced, he can read new words. I deliberately introduce sounds which will make words when used in combination with sounds he already knows.

It is always appropriate to teach the child any sounds s/he asks about. Also, teach sounds important to the child such as the sounds in his name.

I base the sequence on which I teach the sounds on the *Phonics Practice Readers* published by Modern Curriculum Press (see sources). This is simply because the child can read a book as soon as he has learned all of the sounds in the book. The first book in the series introduces words using the short vowel a; the consonants m, x, c, t, s, n, d, b, r, f, h, p, and the sight words "the" and "is." The rest of the games used in this article will be based on these sounds.

Flashcards:

Make flashcards for each sound. Stay consistent with the colors you have chosen for vowels and consonants. Introduce 3-5 sounds initially. The child says the sound the letter makes when s/he sees the flashcard.

As s/he masters these five, add one or two more. Each time a new sound is added, put in the pile several copies of the flashcard for the new sound but only one copy of each of the mastered sounds.

If a child has mastered a, m, x, t, and s; and h and p are being introduced, show him flashcards in an order such as h, a, p, m, h, x, p, h, t, p, h, s, p. This way, s/he gets lots of drill on the new sounds/letters and quickly masters them. Sing the chant or song as each flashcard is shown. Introduce the sight words on flashcards as well.

Sandpaper letters:

Make a sandpaper letter for each sound. Begin using only lower case (small) letters. Again, mount the vowels and consonants on the appropriate colors. Use these in conjunction with the object boxes. Tell the child the sound the letter makes and show him how to trace the sandpaper letter with his/her finger making the strokes in the same order s/he will later use in writing it. S/he feels the letter, and says the sound. Then s/he takes one object from the object box and names it.

Combine the name of the letter with the object box minatures, saying "A says a. Apple." The child traces the lower case a and takes the minature apple from the box. Use a small piece of fabric for the child to lay the objects upon. Again, use one color of fabric for the vowels and a different color for the consonants. Felt works very well.

Have the child retrace the letter for each object in the box, repeating the procedure described. The tracing of the sandpaper letters gives the child muscular memory of the letter. His kinesthetic sense is being used. Thus he not only sees, hears, and speaks the sound; he also feels it.

Beginning reading

Once the child has learned all of the sounds in the first book of the phonics series, s/he is able to read that book.

Other games to reinforce these sounds are listed below.

Cards and objects:

Place minature objects whose names use only the sounds already learned in a container. Examples: a man, a cat, a hat, a pan, and a bat. Each name is written on a seperate card. The child matches the name with the object. Again, a small felt piece helps delineate working space.

Objects and movable alphabet:

A movable alphabet is one where all of the letters are separate and can be moved to any order to spell a word. They can be made by writing one letter on a piece of paper. Montessori sources sell wooden ones.

Some educational sources will have the alphabet letters available in cardboard, plastic, or magnets. The child uses the movable alphabet to spell the names of objects or spell other words using the sounds s/he knows.

Cards and pictures:

Glue pictures of objects using the learned sounds to a piece of poster board. Write corresponding words on separate cards. Place the words over the pictures as the child reads and identifies each word.

Word lists:

Lists of words using the sounds are compiled and read by the child: rat, ram, tax, fax, tap, sap, fact, past, had, sax, fan, dab.

Flip charts:

Make a sectional flip chart. The initial or ending sound changes by flipping a card but the other sounds remain the same to construct new words. An example of words with the initial sound changing is mat, cat, sat, fat, pat, bat, hat. In a flip chart, it is not necessary that each combination of sounds actually makes a word since many multi syllable words use syllables which are not words in and of themselves. For instance, hap is not a word but it occurs as a syllable in the word happen.

Sentences and pictures:

Write sentences with words using the initial sounds. Then draw pictures which illustrate these sentences, or cut them from magazines or discarded school books. Write the sentence on one piece of paper and mount the picture on another. The child matches the correct sentence with the picture showing its meaning. Sample sentences are: Dan has a hat. Sam is sad. The cat is fat. The cat ran fast. The man is mad. In the sentence "Dan has a hat," the word a is a new sight word and would need to be taught.

Further development of reading skills

The games listed above apply to all of the letters of the alphabet. In the *Phonics Practice Readers*, there are 10 books in the Series A, two for each short vowel sound. The child will have learned all of the sounds for all of the consonants and all of the short vowel sounds once s/he completes the series.

Phonetic farm:

One further Montessori method for beginning readers who have learned all of the sounds is a phonetic farm. Many farm animals' names are phonetic such as dog, cat, ram, duck, rat, and pig. These animals can be assembled in a container. Also in the container on separate pieces of paper are names of the animals.

Use one color paper for the nouns, and a different color of paper for phonetic verbs or sight words which have been introduced, such as ran, run, sat, is, had, put, set, sit, fed. Use yet another color for phonetic or sight word adjectives the child knows, such as bad, sad, red. Use another color for each of the other parts of speech used: prepositions, conjunctions, adjectives.

At this point, no specific teaching is needed about why the different colors are used. You could say, however, all of the words on the pink papers are called adjectives. When the child suggests a new word, you might say, "That is a verb. We will need to write it on the yellow paper."

If the child suggests any words, phonetic or not, write them on a paper of the proper color. The child will quickly learn the words he suggests as sight words because they are important to him. The child uses the phonetic farm by constructing sentences with the words and putting the animals through the motions suggested by the sentence.

Writing and reading

Many children develop their writing skills simultaneously with their reading skills or even learn to read through writing. Children who are ready to write should be encouraged to do so. Ready is pretty much defined as children who enjoy writing.

Give the child writing materials. Suggest s/he try to write the letters after finger tracing them on the sandpaper letters. Suggest s/he write the names of objects or write sentences to go with pictures, or the child can draw his own pictures. Always accept invented spelling from a child. It can greatly reduce a child's writing output if s/he is required to spell correctly from the outset. However, if a child asks how to spell a word, tell him.

Help develop his skills further by asking questions like, "What sound do you hear at the first? What other sounds can you hear in the word?" If the child does not like this type of questioning, don't do it.

Making it practical:

Obviously, this can become quite a bit of work to produce and/or purchase these materials. Also, a child using these materials can move through the beginning reading stages quite rapidly and the materials would no longer be needed. Suggestions below are ways to make it practical to make these materials available for a family.

Sibling help:

You might find it tedious to make and play all of these games with your little one. A reading sibling of 7-10 would probably find it fun. Even homeschooling children like to play school. One of the older ones can be the "teacher" for the younger one.

Homeschooling support group:

Even if your child does not have an older sibling, perhaps there would be children in the support group who would enjoy and learn from tutoring your child.

An active homeschooling support group is a tremendous way to develop the materials. Different families can develop the materials for different games. A group library can be established where the materials can be borrowed back and forth so that well-made materials can serve many beginning readers.

Sources

The Learning Crew, Songs for learning phonics and other beginning reading skills. 1-800-477-5551.

Phonics Practice Series, Modern Curriculum Press, Inc, 13900 Prospect Road, Cleveland, Ohio 44136. These are also frequently available at educational stores. ∆

A country moment

Rich Perrigo and Robby and Jacob Duffy smelt on the Pacific coast.

MAKING A LIVING

A Backwoods Home Anthology

PV as a country business? — if you're a jack-of-all-trades

By Larry Elliott

Just rolled into the driveway after spending the better part of two days setting up an independent energy system for a client, only to get a call from Dave to hurry up and get this article finished. As I write, a knock on the shop door tells me a customer has delivered a generator that needs a new shaft welded and machined. The phone rings and, as I listen to a woman tell me she thinks there may be a problem with her solar system, I look down at a note left on the desk asking me if I would be willing to make some repairs on an electric car. The rest of the day was pretty slow and uneventful, but this scenario is pretty much repeated most days as I go about trying to earn enough money to stay financially solvent while living out in the country.

Be a jack-of-all-trades

This article is titled *"PV as a country business?—if you're a jack-of-all-trades"* because, as you can see, I do everything from machine shop work to writing. I think most people who "succeed" out in the country pretty much fall into the same category as I do. You must be a "jack-of-all-trades." Not that you have to develop hundreds of different skills before moving to the country, but you must be willing to try most things and put your best effort forward in what you do try.

For anyone contemplating getting into an independent energy type business that can provide you and your family a living in the country, I will outline some of the things I have done to do just that.

The most obvious first step would be to do a little research in your chosen area to see if you have the resources to support a business. Find out if your area has adequate sun, wind, or water resources. Is the population density great enough to support your business? What competition do you already face? Are you willing to cover a lot of territory to obtain enough business? Do rural electric lines already extend everywhere?

Offer personal service

If after doing this research you determine that it looks favorable, ask yourself if you possess the skills that are necessary to do a good job. There are many good reputable catalog companies that can sell your potential customers just about anything except the most important ingredient, and that is personal service. It will be your ability to deliver good, on-site help on warranty repairs. And troubleshooting will be your ace in the hole.

Remember that you are not only getting into a new business for yourself, but the business itself is new. Everyday there are new products coming on line with changes in specifications and price. Codes and regulations change continuously and even customers' needs will change.

Are you willing to put up with "tire kickers"—the people who will use up a lot of your time just exploring the possibility of buying something from you? Will you be able to modify and improvise out in the field, sometimes miles from the nearest hardware or electrical store? Just like any business it can take several years to build up a clientele that can support you. Many independent energy dealers have been in business for years and still must rely on income from sources other than the energy business. Another very important point I need to make and that I feel is critical is to limit as much as possible your monthly need for income. Don't go into this with a lot of debt. If there is one thing that has helped me to be successful, it is my lack of debt. When sales fall off, and they do, I can still get by. As a matter of fact in most parts of the country sales are somewhat seasonal, with summer months being the busiest times.

Most elements of good business practice are generic to any business, but being in the independent energy business requires at least one special element and that is patience with the customer and being willing to bend over backwards to make something work. Remember, if all of this is new to you, what do you think your customer feels like? Every effort is made by manufacturers to build in reliability and serviceability, but once in a while things happen that can be quite annoying to a customer. For most systems, you will end up babysitting them for at least a year free of charge. Fortunately, most equipment is reliable enough that you don't have to spend a lot of time, but occasionally it can be a pain in the butt.

I'm sure most people have said—at least to themselves—that they would like to start their own business and be their own boss. In some ways you are your own boss when working for yourself, but in reality having your own business can be a lot more headache and responsibility and work than punching a clock. Those who choose to move to the country do so to get away from that rat race and get off the treadmill. In spite of the headaches and hard work, your own business will allow you to live a better life. ∆

The Fifth Year

A Backwoods Home Anthology

MAKING A LIVING

Here's how to start a part-time, one-person mail order business

By Michael Simmons

After getting laid off from a lab job in a circuit breaker factory in central Illinois, I decided to get into business for myself. I had had a gut full of unreasonable supervisors and uncooperative co-workers and felt it was time to establish a one-man company of my own. The severance pay was substantial as I had been there several years, so I decided to invest that into my enterprise rather than fritter it away while taking a chance on another similar job to open up.

I knew practically nothing about true entrepreneurship, so I pored over library books to learn what I could realistically do with minimal risk. Mail order greatly appealed to me as it would mean no store front, no set hours, no dress code, or any other of the usual constraints of business. I concentrated there.

I loved to write and worked toward being self-published, making my own booklets, but found that after a few unproductive starts I would have to go that direction much later. Having inventories of things to sell via mail order can be expensive and if you wind up with something no one wants; you are out of a lot of hard-earned money. So I had to be rather careful about what I could invest in.

Looking for possibilities

I had read that the beginner mail order businessperson would do well to investigate the possibilities in their own hobby, and that it would pay well to search through old issues of magazines devoted to such hobbies for ideas. The good possibilities could be items that did well then, but were no longer available because the business vanished, changed product lines, or whatever. That turned on a light on my head.

I had been a ham radio operator for years, and I knew full well that hams would spend money on things for their radio shacks even if they were broke. All I had to do was to find some product that had done well previously, was no longer available, but could be re-introduced with relatively little expense. I didn't know if it could be done, but I was determined.

I spent several days at a local university library going through one ham radio magazine after another looking at hundreds of ads. Finally, I saw something that had been advertised month after month (which meant it had been selling well) in a small ham magazine, something that I could definitely sell.

It was simply a very fancy certificate to which a ham radio license could be attached to make it look more like a diploma rather than a plain dollar-bill sized piece of paper. It had sold for just a few dollars apiece, and had apparently been discontinued in the 1970s. The picture of it in the ad reached up and slapped me right in the eyes.

I could do that. To get started, it would only require a local printer to reproduce it, some large envelopes and protective cardboard sheets for mailing, and a little office equipment.

About a week was spent at my computer and ink-jet printer to come out with just the right layout to be placed on a custom-made certificate put out by the Goes Company. Then the work was presented to a local printer who agreed to print 250 certificates for $45. I made my own mailing labels using computer printer labels and bought mailing supplies from a wholesale business office supply store. Everywhere I could I made do with the cheapest items and doing things myself, when possible, to save money. Even a cent or two saved on each shipment could mean an extra dollar total earned each day.

How to advertise

I decided I would place a good-sized classified ad in one of the small ham radio magazines, as by then I was running short on cash. Previous experience indicated that a small classified ad was false economy because of too few responses. It's always better to spend a little more money to get many more responses. The ad rates were only 35 cents per word, and if the ad response was good I would move to the bigger magazines with more expensive ads. I also had printed small flyers which I would mail free to all inquiries which wanted to see what the certificate looked like before sending money. This is standard practice in mail order. If you can only run a classified ad instead of a much more expensive display ad, you should offer free literature to further explain your product or service to prospective customers.

I would like to say that after my first ad the money and inquiries overflowed from our mailbox, but it didn't. A number of orders did come in, but only somewhat more money was earned over expenses. There was little to brag about. I got discouraged. But, I did keep running ads, and the money did keep coming in and even began to increase a little. Repeating ads helps build business.

Nonetheless, I kept wondering if I was wasting my time and effort which could prove ultimately "unworth it." Yet, in the back of my mind I kept remembering that the previous seller had run display ads with pictures of the item. But such ads were expensive to run and if the item didn't sell well a person could lose hundreds of dollars. I didn't know what to do.

However, that was due primarily to a lack of mail order experience. A

274

The Fifth Year

ham in Wisconsin had positively loved this certificate and had offered to buy my "business." I thought: Is there something to this that I am not catching onto? Could there be more of a market to this than I knew of?

Finding free advertising

About six months later I noticed something in a larger ham magazine that I should have known about before having ever sent in the first ad. It was called a New Products column. Any new product was featured in this column, usually with a picture, which would be the equivalent of a $400 or $500 display ad. I thought, what the heck, I'll send in a sample of my product to the editor in charge of that column and see what happens.

They ran it in the July issue of 1992. It consisted of a beautiful ad with several column inches of text plus my mailing address and phone number. For free. Three days later the mailbox was running over with orders. I even had letters from Canada and Germany. I had phone calls around the clock.

I had to make emergency runs to the printer and business supply store to restock. I laughed, I cried, the depression left. I was making money; up to $100 a day. And so far I had only spent about $80 total to get started. What was really uplifting was all the thanks for offering such a product that was "very timely" and "my friends love it, here is another order." Such praise was used as testimonials in future sales literature.

The profits impressed my ever-patient wife who had been making most of the money up until then. Some of the money was plowed into a laser printer for other mail order ventures and publishing efforts. With a new book binder, I was able to print small orders for specialized books, particularly for my wife's nursing home business which could pay handsomely for technical publications. Other small businesses liked ordering a hundred or fewer flyers printed from the laser printer using inexpensive but quality desk-top software.

Although I wasn't pulling in big-time money, I was finally my own boss of a modestly successful mail order business selling a product that has never suffered a complaint or refund request. I learned a great deal about starting my own business, dealing with customers and never letting mistakes hold the business back. I almost gave up several times, but with the encouragement from strangers and a loving wife, I pushed on to some success.

I did not get rich with the business, but I did earn a respectable living and had a great deal of fun doing it. Some of the more important truths that were learned, which are not always in the popular how-to books follow:

Research: Spend a great deal time at a public library studying everything you can get your hands on regarding being self-employed, running a small business, particularly the mail order business.

Money: Don't count on a bank or a savings and loan company to loan you the necessary capital, no matter how good your idea is. The Small Business Administration may be able to help, but you may not want the government staring down your back either.

Do not use credit cards to finance your business unless you are very sure your business can succeed. If you need finances, try to build up small and slowly, with trusted friends investing money to help you. Get a good lawyer to draw up the legal documentation to protect all involved in such an investment scheme.

I built up my business with no loans at all and I am glad I did it that way. There are no banks telling me how to run my business. If necessary, take on a second part-time job to finance the project. This may mean putting your business on hold for awhile, but it is worth being debt free.

Keep at it: Persevere, learn and improve. Doubts and doubters will be plentiful to tell you that you will never make it. Surround yourself with successful people who can encourage you, and constantly read literature that can also spur you on. You may have to work at your business for a few years before a profit shows, but you will be very glad you pushed on once your accounting books start showing in the black.

Quality: Push for the highest quality work you and your suppliers can give your customers and yourself. Quality sells and ensures happy customers which, in some markets, is extremely important for repeat business and referrals. If you have to pay extra to get the highest quality, do so because you will never regret it.

Speed important: In mail order, speed is vital. Many customers will be impressed by your prompt attention to their inquiries and orders and some will give you loyalty when you respond promptly. This is very important. True, by law you must deliver within 30 days of receipt of an order, but shipping the same day or within 24 hours will mean repeat orders.

Service: Customer loyalty can be greatly enhanced by giving them personal attention along with what they requested. Slip in a note of thanks, especially to any compliment they have paid you. Many customers like having their fur stroked and it pays nice dividends.

Credit cards? Being able to accept credit card orders can mean sales, but experience has shown it is an aggravation and it is only worth it on relatively large orders. My advice: don't mess with it unless your customers start asking to use their cards constantly. Your bank can help you with details on how to get set up with credit card sales and whether or not it would be worth your efforts. Typically, the credit card companies will take four percent of the sale amount for their own, and ask that you have at least 10 sales per month on credit. A credit card machine to process the sales will cost around $25, and if a customer contests a sale, the credit card company will withhold your money until you can prove the transaction did take place legitimately.

Records: Keep very good records of transactions. The post office demands it, and good bookkeeping is vital to any business.

Don't get sued: Don't ever sell something for which there is the possibility of being sued. In other words, don't even think of selling something like booklets on making explosives. If someone gets hurt using the information or product, you can be successfully sued for millions of dollars. Something similar to this happened to Soldier of Fortune magazine several months ago.

Bogus opportunities: Don't try to get started with the "Business Opportunity" junk in most classifieds. Most of these are totally bogus and some are downright illegal. When you first start advertising, expect junk mail galore to glut your mailbox. They almost always state: "This is not a chain letter" (yes, it is) or "Here's something that can make you millions." Bull, if that person made millions, then why bother with this ad? Trash them or start your log fires with them.

Be flexible: Be ready to change products or markets when it appears when your present market is saturating.

Recipes: Don't try selling recipes or "special reports" by mail order. You'll be extremely lucky if you manage to break even.

No instant riches: Don't expect to become rich soon. Most one-person mail order businesspeople make a few hundred dollars a week. If you can equal that, you have done well.

Work long hours: Expect to work many hours a day getting started. A number of "business opportunity" ads claim you could work for only an hour or so a day and get rich. If you are a crook, true. If you are honest, 12 hours a day can be considered normal.

Competition: Don't ever start into a market in which there are already two or more businesses fighting for their share. If there is only one other business doing something, you can compete if your quality is better and less expensive. If you can be the first to come out with a particular item, success will be much more likely.

This should be enough advice to help anyone to get a good start into a home-based mail order business. There can be much more to learn, but the above is very important to follow, and is almost never in books. The rest you can learn along the way. Δ

A BHM Writer's Profile

Dave Duffy

Dave Duffy is the founder, publisher, and editor of *Backwoods Home Magazine*. He built his own home in a remote area of the Siskiyou Mountains of southern Oregon while launching the magazine, and that home served as *BHM's* first office. Since the home was 10 miles from the nearest electric utility pole, Duffy installed a photovoltaic system to produce sun-generated electricity to run the computers and printers to publish the magazine.

Duffy has since moved the magazine 11.3 miles down the road, across the Oregon border and into northern Calfornia.

Born in Boston, Duffy spent his first 29 years there, where he worked as a journalist for several daily newspapers. He then moved to Nevada and California, working as a journalist for newspapers and later as a writer and editor for the Department of Defense.

Unhappy with working for others and living near cities, he spent several years of vacations and long weekends building his hideaway in southern Oregon. He eventually fled the rat race for the woods. In 1989 he started *Backwoods Home Magazine* to help others do the same.

SELF-SUFFICIENCY

Try an ex-military truck for rugged, reliable service

By David Jensen

Most of the time I was growing up, my father owned a 1941 Dodge weapons carrier. It was a flatbed and could haul more than the ½ ton it was rated. My family moved a lot. We'd fill the truck and a big military trailer with everything we owned and head on down the road. With the hubs pulled and tin cans pressed in for dust covers, the front end was freed up. Top speed was 45 miles per hour and it got 14 miles per gallon, whether it was pulling a load or not. It was kind of relaxing to watch the lines flip by on the freeway and hear the mud tread on the tires howl.

When we settled on our place in Montana, the Dodge pulled the hay rake and mower, hauled lumber, skidded logs for the house, turned the wheat grinder with a shaft from the power take-off (PTO), and drove us to meet the school bus in the winter. When it got cold, sometimes 40 to 50 below, Dad got it started by building a fire in a stove made from a two-gallon oil can and putting it under the truck. The smoke rose up under the hood and through the floorboards, warming the engine and driving the mice out of the headliner.

When he had bought it, the frame was broken and welded in spots and the engine block was cracked. He put Stop-Leak in the radiator and ran it that way for 15 years. I've never seen a vehicle abused more and survive. We broke a lot of cable pulling logs. We also broke an axle, a U-joint, and tore off a brake line, all minor repairs considering the abuse. With a frame we got for $75 and another engine, scrounged from a parts rig, it is still a solid truck with the original running gear.

I've since owned several military-type Dodges and have been consistently impressed with them as solidly-built work trucks. They aren't perfect for every situation, though.

The first point to think about is if you really do need a truck. Maybe you just need four-wheel-drive transportation. In that case, something lighter and faster would take care of you. If you just want to haul things on roads that aren't too bad, or in dry fields, then there are a lot of good deals around on old farm trucks. Those big two-wheel-drive trucks are handy. I've got a 1946 1½-ton flatbed and we use it for a lot of things, but it's

My brother's restored 1942 ½-ton carrying a 1-ton load

parked right now because the roads are too muddy and it's a hard vehicle to get unstuck.

Best choices in trucks

The fact is, we invariably get into situations where we need a four wheel drive that can haul more than just passengers, something that can be worked hard without hurting it. If that sort of a truck interests you, there are four options to choose from in the Dodge military "family:" 1941-42 ½-ton weapons carrier, later model ¾-ton weapons carrier, the Dodge Power Wagon, and the ¾-ton M-37.

The weapons carriers from 1941 and 42 were built lighter than the ¾-ton versions, which were built from the last part of 1942 on. The later models had a better body and a two speed transfer case. The older versions get around pretty well, but a two-speed transfer case gives you an extra-low gear which is nice to have on rough ground.

From 1946, Dodge sold a one-ton civilian truck that had a lot of military left in it. Even though it had the same six cylinder L-head engine, Dodge called it the Power Wagon. The drive train is essentially the same as the military Dodges. It was built through 1971 and sold in the U.S. until 1968. The Power Wagon looks very similar to a military Dodge. The wheel base is longer and it has an eight foot bed which is good for hauling 4 x 8 sheets of something. The hood stretches out straight instead of slanting down like the early weapons carriers.

Power Wagons tend to sell for higher prices than the military trucks. You can generally find a running weapons carrier for around $1,500. A Power Wagon in the same condition will usually go for $1,000 more in our area.

The next in the family of Dodges was the M-37, which was built for the military from the 1950s through 1968. Much like the ¾-ton weapons carriers from the 1940s, the M-37 is short and boxy. It had the same engine, a two-speed transfer case, 9.00/16 tires, etc. Later years had synchros in the transmission. The transmissions in earlier trucks were well-built, but they are called crash boxes because that's what they sound like until you learn the fine art of double clutching.

M-37s are sold for about the same price as the old weapons carriers. They aren't as antique-looking (the hood is one piece and opens from the front), but since they are newer it's easier to find one that isn't too rusty. Rusty bolts and parts can be a real nuisance on the older trucks. Surplus M-37s were used by a lot of fire departments, school districts, road departments and such. A lot of these trucks have been maintained fairly well and garaged. They're usually sold through a bid process.

Twelve and 24 volt electrical systems were common on the M-37. An M-37 with a 24 volt system seems luxurious after you've driven an older weapons carrier with 6 volt lights. You just need to be more careful with the wiring since 24 volts isn't good for your body and you have to buy two batteries. The added starting power and brighter lights are worth it.

The M-37 cab can use either a canvas top or a metal one provided in an arctic kit. The arctic kit is a good option if you can find it. A lot of M-37s have fiberglass tops, which work better than canvas. A good heater makes up for the drafts.

The only disadvantage with the M-37 is that it has a short bed (like earlier weapons carriers) and the wheel wells stick into the bed too far to allow a 4 foot sheet of plywood to slide between them. As with the other Dodges, there were body styles for various purposes. Ambulances are fairly common. A lot of farmers have simply put on a flatbed, stripping whatever bed or body might have come with the truck. After all, it's better for hauling hay.

As good as the Dodges are, the cabs on the early weapons carriers and Power Wagons were not built as well as some of the other makes. The rest of the sheet metal, fenders and such, are plenty tough, but the cab leaves a lot to be desired. The doors are often rusty in the corners and didn't take the wear and tear very well. The gauges are tough to work on if the studs on the back are rusted since the dash isn't removable. The Power Wagons in the mid-1950s had different gauges, but the cabs are still not built as well as, say, International pickups from the same period. The ¾-ton weapons carriers and M-37s had a better ride and a sturdier, if uglier, design for the cab and sheet metal.

Buying tips

To some people, an old Dodge is a religious object and should be considered reverently and spoken of in hushed tones. Some of these people won't sell their truck to you, even if they advertised it, unless you know what you're about. Other than dealing with that, checking a Dodge out before making an offer on it is pretty much the same as with any other vehicle. First, ask all the questions you can: How did (does) it run? How long have you had it? Where did you buy it? How many miles? Any problems? Any alterations? Do you have the title? Is it in your name?

Things to check over include: Coolant? Very green is a good sign. None can mean one of two things, either the coolant was drained (this is good, although it might mean a leaky radiator hose) or else it wasn't and the water froze, cracked the block and leaked into the engine (this is not good). Look the engine over for crack lines or leaks. Check the oil, feel it. Any metal shavings? Brown or creamy means water, which means a cracked block or blown head gasket. If the engine hasn't been run for awhile, the water will have settled to the bottom of the pan, but should show some droplets on the dipstick. Hairline cracks in the engine block that you miss initially are not always the end of the world. They can be welded, or a lot of times just some Stop-Leak in the radiator will take care of the problem. But try to see if there are any before you make an offer. It's hard to find a little crack on a greasy engine. Check the ridges of the water jacket along the block. This is usually where the cracks will be.

Get under the truck and get greasy. Make sure the major components are all there. I've seen more than one truck with the transfer case or a drive line removed. Look for cracks along the frame. Rust is dangerous when it has eaten enough metal to create holes in, or weaken, the frame or other important parts. If moisture has gotten into moving parts, such as piston or brake cylinders, the rust can fuse them into immobility. Take a screwdriver and poke around. Surface appearances can fool you. Check the gas tank and lines for corrosion or leaks. Look for broken springs. Check the tires' tread and inspect the sidewalls for cracks or oil damage. Oil splatter around the sidewalls indicates a seal needs to be replaced. Too much oil on tires (or hoses) over time and the rubber deteriorates.

Get inside the cab and watch out for wasp nests. Missing headliner and rotten seats are not a big deal. Broken gauges are an inconvenience and something to gripe about when haggling over the price. See if the doors close tight and work smoothly. Do the windows roll up? How much of the glass is broken?

Look for welds, bailing wire, and places cut with a cutting torch. Some alterations, such as a PTO winch from another type of military truck or a professional-quality conversion to a V-8 engine, can add enough in usefulness to make up for whatever they detract from the truck's value as a collector's item. But a power-steering gear box welded to the frame or a GM transfer case crammed in at an angle that eats U-joints is a sign that a lower intelligence has been touching the truck. An alteration should be useful, and removable. For example, a flatbed bolted to the frame is preferable to something welded on. Ninety percent of the major alterations I've seen have changed a workable truck into a parts rig that's missing some parts. The only way to be safe is to look over a few trucks and get familiar with the standard components. Look also for bolt heads where the edges have been rubbed off. This isn't always a bad sign, it just shows where someone has been working.

My first truck

When I was 15, I bought my first truck for $400. It was a 1942 Dodge command car an orchardist had made into a flatbed, but was otherwise original. It had been parked in front of his house for about four years, but he said he had driven it to where it was parked. We pulled it to get it going and drove it home. It burned oil, and ran rough at first. After a few miles it ran a lot better.

I worked on it through high school. It wasn't a restoration, I drove it regularly and fixed it when it needed fixing. There were millions of little problems, pine needles in the gas line and bad wiring for instance. I drove it out to Utah from Washington state when I started college, a 1,600 mile (round trip) road test. I had three problems: a leaking gas fitting, a dragging brake, and the generator finished eating a bearing as I pulled into Provo, Utah. Frustrating? Not really. It had become satisfying to work on a vehicle so simple that I could solve its problems on my own. I had the tools and I had the time. Those minor repairs took a few hours but cost less than $20. The total cost of the truck and parts I put into it was $850, and to my way of thinking that's a good price for a heavy-duty four wheel drive that can get you across some rough country, or even down the highway, if a little slow.

Buying a running truck in good condition is the best way to go, but it's more expensive and the fact that a truck runs well is not always a sure sign that there won't be any problems in the future. Sometimes it takes a little persistence to get someone to sell that treasure in their back yard. A guy in our area has a Power Wagon parked on his land with a sapling growing between the body and a fender, but will he sell it? Not this month, and I ask every month.

It took six years to convince one fellow to sell me his Power Wagon that was parked in a vacant lot, year after year. Some people are ready to sell right away, whether they advertised or not, and most people will eventually sell a truck that they aren't using. Either that or they finally die, and then you get a second chance. A lot of these trucks have been sitting more than 5 years. I figure that if a truck was running when it was parked it ought to run again, but I'd expect more problems with a truck the longer it has been sitting, particularly in a damp climate. Of course, a truck that has been parked was not being otherwise abused during that time.

Starting an old truck

People advocate various measures before starting a truck that has been sitting, ranging from a preliminary cussing before rolling it down a hill to a frame-up restoration.

If I had to give some advice, I'd say: Tow it home and dismantle it. Tear the engine down and rebuild it. Have the frame sandblasted before painting. Rebuild the rest of the truck by cleaning and painting each part before reassembly. Replace worn parts. Rewire it with new wire. You'll probably need an air compressor and a paint gun. If money is an issue, I'd recommend industrial enamel paint. It oxidizes a little faster and scratches easier, but for $20 a gallon, you can't beat it.

Having said that, here is how we do it: Check for coolant and stop the leaks. Get air in the tires. Take off the air cleaner, if there is one, and clean the cobwebs and wasps out of the carburetor throat. Make sure the choke works and isn't sticking. Pull the spark plugs and clean them off. Dip the ends in gas, just the gap that produces the spark inside the engine. Check the gap on the plugs if they don't appear to all be gapped the same. Pour some light oil (some people use diesel) into each cylinder to lubricate the valves. Most of them will stick anyway, but the initial lubrication seems to help them loosen up.

With the plugs back in, put in a battery and turn the key on, watching for shorts in the wiring (smoke, sparks, etc.) Remember that the electrical ground will be positive unless someone has changed the electrical system. Prime the carburetor with a little gas and turn the engine over. The older trucks have a starter button on the floor above the gas pedal.

Brakes will always need attention if the truck has been sitting more than a year or so. I usually have just put brake fluid in the reservoir and bled the brakes initially. The emergency brakes work well, usually, but it's better to save them for emergencies. The slave cylinders will often be corroded entirely up, that is, not rebuildable. The master cylinder is usually rebuildable.

The scenario for every rig I've owned has been this: Put in brake fluid and bleed brakes before driving the truck home (I wouldn't go more than 20 or 30 miles, preferably on back roads like this if the truck had been sitting more than a year). Get truck home with no brake troubles. Notice some fluid leaking from master cylinder (located low and to the front of the firewall on the Power Wagon and under the floorboards of the M-37). Usually it has not been a bad enough leak to worry about immediately.

After a few days, at least one brake will start dragging and I'll notice brake fluid on the back of the rim. The brakes will gradually drag more and more. You park your truck and it won't move when you try to move it again. You have to pull the wheel off and get the brake shoes loose. Usually the fibre pads are swollen from the fluid and need to be cleaned and dried. If the cylinder is not too rusty you can rebuild it, otherwise replace it. It can happen with one wheel after another until you've done all four. It's easier to look at them all at once. Expect to work on the brake system and budget a couple of hundred dollars for parts. Once it's fixed it's fixed, unless you leave the truck parked too long.

After making all the preparations, which includes getting the brakes working, I usually try turning the engine over with the starter a few times. This is mostly ceremonial, but if you can get a backfire it's reassuring. The backfire happens because the valves are sticking. If you want to watch which valve is sticking, remove the valve covers located on the block under the manifolds. A valve sticking open will allow the engine to run but it will probably backfire or run rough. A valve sticking closed will not allow the camshaft, and therefore the engine, to turn.

We usually start out towing the truck in a mid-range gear (3rd or 2nd) in four wheel drive. This gives you more traction which equals starting power, and a good speed to make the engine turn over. As long as the engine is turning over, you don't need to tow the truck very fast, a couple miles per hour is fine. Starting out, let the towing vehicle take up the slack on the cable and then start out with the clutch in until you get up to speed. To start out with the towed vehicle in gear and the clutch out is going to be a little abrupt. Letting the clutch out

An unrestored ¾-ton M-37

after you're moving is smoother for everybody.

The truck is going to run rough at first, until the valves begin breaking loose. Keep an eye on the gauges to see what's happening with your oil pressure, temperature, and amps. A wildly jiggling ammeter, or one showing a heavy discharge, needs attention and temperature over 190° F is getting too warm. It isn`t unusual for the oil pressure to start at 40 to 60 pounds and drop to 25 while idling after being warmed up. As long as you're not losing oil and your rods aren't knocking, it just means that your engine is worn. Once the truck runs good enough to move under its own power, we start driving home. As the valves break loose it starts sounding better and better. After 15 miles, my Power Wagon sounded great. The valves stuck for a few minutes after starting for the next few days.

Dealing with problems

There are horror stories about gears and bearings in the running gear being corroded badly in a truck that looked sound otherwise. One of our parts trucks had a transfer case full of water and it didn't sound good turning.

Other than having to replace a few bearings, we haven't had many drive train problems from trucks sitting. Engines have given us some heartache though.

I eventually put another engine in my first truck to replace the original oil burner. The engine had been sitting for years. We put it in and tried to get it started as described above. A valve had been corroded and broke off, pounding its way through the number five piston. It was a bit traumatic since we'd been working in a lean-to with no lights or heat, but there was no damage to the cylinder walls. A new piston cost $40, and with a valve job the truck ran well for 10 years until my brother, Jake, finally put in a new engine.

My M-37, had been sitting for several years, but had been started occasionally. It ran well and I drove it home. My brother, Eric, bought it and drove it from Utah to Washington state. I had paid $2000 for it because it was in great shape. It had a PTO winch and 18,000 miles on the odometer. Before my brother got half way home the rods were knocking because someone working on it previously had bent the oil pick-up tube from the oil pump. The point is, paying more and having something immediately driveable isn't always the best way to go. Also, take off the oil pan and look things over, even if its just cleaning out the sludge in the bottom of the pan, before doing any extensive driving. An oil change is needed anyway, especially if you've put diesel down the carburetor or spark plug holes, so all that pulling the pan will cost you is an oil pan gasket.

Wheels & tires

One difference between the earlier weapons carriers and the later models was the wheels. The older rigs ran on 5 hole bud rims and 7.50/16 tires. The later models used a slightly wider rim with the same bolt pattern and had 9.00/16 tires. The older trucks can run duals on back (or front), but the rims are too narrow for the bigger tires. Sometimes you can make a taller tire fit, but it balloons out the sidewalls.

The wider rims don't allow you to use duals, but heavy duty 9.00/16 tires can take a good load. The advantage is that you get more ground clearance and better road speed from the taller tires. The rims from the later models will bolt right onto the older trucks. For the cost of rims (around $30 each) and tires (around $100 each) you can give your older truck a better ride and more clearance. Of course this gets a lot cheaper if you can find someone parting out a truck, or better yet, if you can get a good deal on a parts rig with good rubber.

The scalloped military tires that came stock on the Dodges aren't real impressive, but they do function and their sidewalls are tough. With chains all around, they get meaner since the smooth surface puts more chain to the ground. Whatever kind of tires you run, the big rims make balancing crucial. Just a rough balance on a bubble balance works, but I've had shimmies on unbalanced wheels that could almost bounce you off the road if you took a curve faster than 30 mph.

Something to remember is that the lug bolts have right hand threads on the passenger's side and left hand threads on the driver's side. R and L are stamped in the end of the lug bolts and it's good to look before you put a wrench to them. A lot of times the wheels haven't been taken off in years. Start out by spraying WD40 and a little oil on the lug bolts. If the ends have been painted over, wire brush the paint off first. If it's not urgent to get the wheel off, keep the lug nuts soaked for a couple of days. You will probably still have to use a cheater bar on the end of your lug wrench handle. It is possible to break a lug bolt off, in which case you'll have to pull the brake drum, punch out the broken part and put in a new stud. Once I had to stand on the end of a 12-foot cheater bar and jump up and down on it to loosen some lug nuts. Before you put the wheel back on, put a little oil on the dry threads, and don't use a 12-foot cheater bar to put the nuts back on.

Parts & information

For any of these Dodges, you need a source of parts and information. Engine parts aren't a problem. You can get them at any good parts store because the same six cylinder L-head engines were used, with differing bores over the years, in civilian cars and trucks too. In fact, any of those engines will fit in a Dodge military truck, except for the larger Chrysler six cylinder that looks the same but is a few inches longer (compare engine lengths before making a swap). There are a number of businesses that sell parts for prices comparable to what you'd pay for any other kind of truck. We've never had to use any of these outfits since we've built up our own bone yard of parts trucks and know some people in the area willing to sell parts. Cultivating local sources is one of your best options. A magazine called *Military Vehicles* (P.O. Box 1748 Union, NJ 07083) is a good source of information, although it does cater to collectors of all sorts of vehicles, not just Dodges. Another magazine is the *Power Wagon Advertiser* (R.R. 1 Box 59, Norway, Iowa 52318). Through advertisers in these magazines, you can get just about any manual or part you want to buy. The December 1992 issue of *Four Wheeler* had several good articles on Power Wagons and a restorer's guide to parts and sources for Power Wagons and military Dodges. The May 1987 issue of *Country Journal* had an article on Power Wagons by Donald McCaig. I've met several collectors who have McCaig's piece memorized and will quote it word for word, without citing the source, naturally.

Caution

I've praised the simplicity of the military-type Dodges' design and even claimed it was satisfying to work on them. I hope I haven't made it seem either too easy or too difficult. My first truck was as much a form of education as it was transportation, and I would be polishing the truth to say it was painless. Mechanical work can be a brutal and confusing confrontation with physics and chemistry. If you know how to adjust valves or troubleshoot a starting problem, you are probably already familiar with that world. If you don't have that kind of background, an old Dodge could be a rough way to get it.

In all truth, a restored military-type Dodge truck for $5,000 to $6,000 is a reasonable option. But even for a good-running truck at half the price, I'd have to spend a lot of hours doing some other kind of work to pay for it. I'm not saying it's easy or risk-free. It takes time and energy. But if you can put a small investment into a carefully chosen truck and solve its problems with some tinkering and a few parts, the satisfaction you get from doing it yourself is almost as good as the feeling that you saved a few bucks. ∆

Install a remote telephone line

By Phil Wilcox and Serena Somers

We live on a remote 20 acres in Northern California that is 6 miles from the nearest town and 1½ miles from the nearest paved road. Until about two years ago, there were no power or telephone lines out our way. Then a local gold mine decided that they wanted both power and telephones and had the lines run from town, along the paved road past us, to the mine.

We had no interest in obtaining electrical power, as we are satisfied with our solar electrical system. With it and propane and plenty of good oak wood to burn, we were doing fine. But we did decide that it would be convenient to have a telephone in our cabin. Both of our mothers are elderly and live thousands of miles away. It would be nice to keep in closer touch with them. It would also be good in times of emergencies, such as injury or fire, to be able to summon help rapidly. We have a CB radio, but rarely find anyone on the other end. Besides, the trip to town to use the pay phone was becoming a burden—sweltering in summer, freezing and often wet in winter. So, in February of 1992, we started talking about and investigating the various options open to us. We thought the project would be complete by the end of summer.

Several of our neighbors were using cellular phones, but their reception was not always dependable and the monthly expense was beyond our means. We looked at several radio telephones, but they proved to be quite expensive and depended on line-of-sight views to some other residence where telephone service already existed. This turned out to be almost impossible due to the hilly terrain where we live.

Choosing the hard line

One by one, we eliminated the possibilities other than running a hard line from the paved road to our cabin. This is the way we finally decided to go, and about one year after we started, we now have our phone! Hence, this story.

It was not an easy task. There were many tears, much sweat, and, yes, even some blood (minor scrapes and cuts).

We live at 2000 feet above sea level and the nearest phone service (at the main road) is about 1300 feet elevation. So, we had a difference of elevation (hills!) of about 700 feet to contend with. Not just down or up *one* hill, mind you, but up and down, around trees, through creek beds, across vehicle access paths, etc. Also, of course, the wire would be laid across property belonging to others. Permission had to be obtained.

Next, we had to find out what kind of wire and equipment to buy, where to buy it (living rurally, one doesn't always have access to materials), what the cost would be, how much was needed, etc.

First, Phil walked the distance a few times to try and pick the best route to follow. Then, with the help of a friend, they measured the route to see how much telephone line would be necessary (4900 feet). They tied pieces of plastic surveyor's tape on trees and bushes to mark the route.

The wire

Then all our friends were consulted to see if anyone knew of any used wire available. We found several coils of wire many hundreds of miles away and finally arranged to have it delivered by another friend who was headed our way. We did not know if it was wire that would be acceptable to the telephone company (Pacific Bell), nor did we know how many feet of wire were in the coils.

A piece of the wire was shown to the telephone company engineer in our area and, after finding out that it was acceptable, we started to unwind the wire to measure it. There, the fun began! This was heavy, Rural-C, 14 gauge, copper-coated steel wire (one pair) that acts like a tightly wound spring. Once you undo the tape holding the coil together, it decides to unwind itself into one giant tangled mess! Those of you who fish and have ever had a huge mess of fish line to untangle can appreciate our problem—only this was much longer and heavier wire. With help from good neighbors and many weeks of intermittent work, we finally wound up with eight separate pieces totalling about 4100 feet, the longest piece being about 1400 feet.

We needed at least another thousand feet of wire, so we tried calling the source of the original batch of used wire and were told that there was no more wire available. The telephone company would give us no leads as to where to find any or any other assistance. They do not seem to like "Farmer Lines," which is what they told us we were getting ready to install. This means that they will install and maintain their line to a readily accessible point and the customer installs and maintains their own line from that point to their residence. We had attempted, along with three other neighbors, to get the telephone company to run a regular line up our road to serve all of us, but their insistence on about $8,000 in advance soon put a stop to that idea.

We did find a local resident who sells rural telephone equipment, but he wanted about $200 per 1000 feet for the telephone line, plus very high prices for the splicing equipment, junction boxes, etc., that would be needed. Eventually, we did find a company (Greybar) that would sell us the wire at about $75 per 1000 feet plus delivery charges, and we ordered a roll. It had to be shipped from Illinois and took time to reach us.

Stringing the wire

We originally planned on stringing the wire from tree to tree over most of the distance, with only a small portion actually lying on the ground. But we either could not find the proper devices to use on each tree or it was too costly. Again, the telephone company was no help. So we decided just to lay the wire on the ground. Not having had it there for very long, we don't know if that was a good choice or not. We suppose that it will be subject to abuse by deer, gophers, motorcycle riders, etc., but we'll have to wait and see.

We finally finished laying out all the wire, and with a couple of friends, walked the line again soldering and weather-proofing each of the ten splices as we went. Almost done, after a long and tiring day, we were confronted by the owner of one of the pieces of property we had crossed. Although he had previously given us a tentative "okay" to do so, he now made it clear that no telephone wire was going to cross his property! No amount of pleading could get him to change his mind. So, we assured him that we would remove the wire from his property and go around a longer route. Of course, this meant more work, more wire, more cost, and more time.

Then the rains came! And stayed! It was wet and miserable (and muddy) for weeks and weeks. Finally, with better weather and the land having dried somewhat, we managed to cut the line and started over to string the wire around the borders of our neighbor's property. The terrain was much rougher and steeper—hence, more sweat and tears! It was hard work. We knew we would not have enough wire and, indeed, did not. So, we had to measure the amount we were short and then order another 1000-foot roll, the minimum size available. It again seemed to take forever to arrive.

Phone company surprises

Meanwhile, working with one of the few telephone company personnel who handled "Farmer Line" installations, we completed the necessary paperwork. There are all sorts of extra costs associated with such installations. There is the regular installation charge, of course, but they also tack on many extras, including an annual

Phil wrapping a splice in the telephone line

charge of some $78, the purpose of which is never explained.

Until now, we have had our own telephone and answering machine located in the tack room of a friend's horse ranch closer to town. We asked to have this same telephone number transferred to the "Farmer Line" and that seemed to present no problem. We set a date (January 15, 1993) to make the switchover. When we realized we had to order more telephone line, we asked if that date could be postponed for a couple of weeks. No problem! Oh, yeah? Come January 15, the telephone company disconnected our telephone and anyone calling us was told that it had been disconnected. A call to our "Farmer Line" representative brought disbelief. She had not told anyone to do that! Besides, she discovered that all the information pertaining to our old and new line had been erased from the telephone company computer! She was afraid we would have to start all over again. But luckily, she found a way to circumvent that. So, we agreed on a new date to make the switchover, January 27.

On January 27, we discovered that the old telephone line had been disconnected (and callers were so informed), but that the new line had not been connected. Rather, a new and different telephone number had been assigned to us, but no one had bothered to inform us. In fact, we eventually received a bill from the telephone company showing the charges on our old location up to the date of the disconnect. And later, we even received new calling cards for this new telephone number they had forgotten to tell us that they had assigned!

All of this necessitated more phone calls to our "Farmer Line" contact. (She really was trying to help us, but nothing seemed to go right!) She cancelled this strange new number and promised that we would have our old number back. After conference calls with the repair service, central office, computer center, etc., she said that all their information showed our new line installed and working. I informed her that, contrary to what she said, there was no dial tone at their junction box down at the main road. When I dialed the new number they had temporarily assigned us, I got a disconnect message. When I dialed our old number, it just rang and rang. She promised they would investigate.

The same thing happened the next day. The telephone company said the line worked. I told them it did not.

The following day, the telephone company sent out a repair man; I was down at the road, watching for him. He discovered that there was, indeed, a problem in their line and confirmed to me that our line was fine—no shorts or grounds. I asked him how this could be, since all of their computers, etc., showed that the line was, in fact, working. He smiled as he explained that you can't always know what's going on by sitting at a desk one hundred miles away. "Sometimes," he said, "a human being has to go out and check on things." He promised that the problem would be fixed that day. And it was!

Parts and accessories

Rural line wire (CR2) is available from Greybar Electric, which has offices in many large cities. We got ours out of South San Francisco (415-871-7000). Try and talk to a sales person who is familiar with telephone supplies. We used one pair (2 wires) wire, but multiple pair is available (6 pair wire would serve six lines.)

Greybar also has other devices, such as clamps, splicers, etc., but a knowledgeable salesperson is imperative. They carry drop wire clamps for tree-to-tree connections, but our rep could not find them in the catalog.

Radio Shack has all the materials necessary for interior wiring. Get a copy of their large catalog. They also have an outdoor phone wiring box, part number 279-343.

If you live on 12 volt DC power, a good answering machine is no problem. Several are available. Check the power rating on the label. Ours is a Panasonic Model KX-T1450. Simply cut off the 120 volt AC to 12 volt DC transformer and replace it with whatever connector you need for your 12 volt system.

Our telephone is in and working. We have mixed feelings about it. It has been nice not hearing that "ring" for several years now, but is sure is nice to have closer contact with our friends and family.

The only problem now is that all outgoing calls beginning with the prefix "1" are intercepted by either Pacific Bell or ATT, asking us what number we are calling from. I got so tired of this one night, that I asked why this was happening. I was informed that it was because we are not in their computer. I called our contact, who told me that it was going to be that way from now on because that's the way "Farmer Lines" work. I don't believe it has to be that way and have thought about objecting, but, as Serena says: "It's better to put up with it than to have no phone!" I guess she is right.

We will gladly answer any specific questions you have. Just send a SASE to: Phil Wilcox, 20560 Morgan Valley Road, Lower Lake, CA 95457. ∆

NOV/DEC 1994
No. 30
$3.50 U.S.
$4.95 CANADA

NEW RECIPES

Backwoods Home magazine

... a practical journal of self reliance

Great American Food
BARBECUING GOAT
COOKING SQUIRREL
BUILD A LOG HOME
ELECTRIC CARS

DON CHILDERS

A Backwoods Home Anthology

> **Note from the publisher**

Liquid apple pie and Fred Johnston

This is usually the last page written for each issue, so I'm often drinking a celebratory beer or ale as I write it. I just finished a bottle of Rogue "Dead Guy Ale," which lived up to its name, and am now on a bottle of Rogue "Ashland Amber Ale," which is so smooth it makes you wonder what it must be like to live in Irish Heaven.

Last night, as Silveira, *BHM's* senior editor, and I put the final touches on the rest of the issue, we drank Liquid Apple Pie, a blend of Everclear and other secret ingredients that would probably kill most normal people. Vernon Hopkins, my 82-year-old trapper of a neighbor, bought the recipe for $50 in 1993 at a trapper's convention. He was sworn to secrecy upon handing over his $50.

All this good brew got me to thinking about what a bad rap booze in general has taken in recent years. Alcohol, mixed with the right stuff, can be made into a fine beer, ale, wine, or other brew like Liquid Apple Pie, and the best of these mixtures ranks among the finest food known to the human race. And yes, I know it doesn't mix well with driving and that a lot of morons abuse the stuff, but there are morons in every aspect of human endeavor.

A good glass of ale such as I'm drinking now is a cause of celebration, just as many of the fine food dishes in this issue are. And it has just struck me like a left hook that there are no ale, beer, wine, or other alcoholic recipes in this issue. Egad! How did I let it happen?

Both Silveira and Blunt, the food editor, are excellent cooks and appreciate a good glass of spirits. In fact, we have all, at one time or another, made our own beer and wine, and some of it turned out great.

The last time I made beer was in 1975, two years after I moved from Massachusetts to California. It was with my good friend, Fred Johnston. Fred and I were newspaper reporters at the Ventura County Star-Free Press in Southern California, and it became our habit to get shaky with coffee in the morning as we worked through various deadlines and stiff with beer in the evening as we wound down. It is a trait shared by many of the nation's media people.

Fred and I followed a good beer-making recipe pretty carefully, until it came time to add the sugar, which is the ingredient that yeast turns into alcohol. We decided to add more sugar, even though the directions said we could be making a bomb due to excessive carbonation. Remembering that my oldest brother, Bill, lost partial use of his thumb when an exploding Royal Crown Cola bottle blew up in his hand as he worked at a bottling plant in Massachusetts, I decided we had better store the 20 or so 6-packs we made behind a sheet of plywood in my garage. Every time we

Dave Duffy

reached for one of those home-made beers we tapped the bottle with a screwdriver or whatever was handy to see if it would blow up. None ever did, and the beer tasted lousy. Total failure. So much so we just let the beer sit there for a year, until Fred was tragically murdered in Los Angeles in 1976.

Tragedy that it was, his fiancée, Kate Acosta, told me that Fred had once said that if he were to die he wanted to be mourned at a rip-roaring Irish Wake. So we had an Irish Wake, at my house.

It was one of the greatest parties you've ever seen. About 200 people did what Fred would have wanted: They talked about how great he was, how funny he was, how they used to do this or that with him. I've never seen so many people laugh like hell while remembering Fred, then go outside and ball their eyes out. Even I did it. But Fred was a special guy; he was worth crying over.

As the party progressed, I asked Fred's father if he'd like a glass of the beer Fred and I brewed. He said sure, and I tapped and opened a couple of bottles of— surprise to me— the best damn beer I've tasted— to that point. It was the closest thing to a miracle I've ever been a party to. I broke out bottles for everyone, and what an Irish Wake it turned into. We polished off all the beer Fred and I had made.

Since then, however, I have had an even better brew. It was made by Blunt, who has been my close friend since we were both age 13. It was back in the early '80s, while I visited him in Boston, that I first savored several incredible ales he had made. They remain the best brew I've ever had, either store-bought or homemade.

So today I called Blunt, who still lives on the East Coast, and asked him if he'd duplicate those ale recipes for a future issue of *Backwoods Home Magazine*.

"How about the March/April issue?" he said.

"We'll dedicate the whole issue to Fred Johnston," I said.

Blunt, who had never met Fred, asked, "Who was he?"

"Never mind," I said. "You'd've liked him." ∆

My view

Politics, self reliance...

I got a letter from a reader recently protesting that my personal political views that often find their way onto this page have no place in a self-reliance magazine. It's not the first letter I've gotten like that, and I assume there are quite a few readers out there who feel the same way.

So what! Since this issue coincides with what I consider to be the most important political elections in decades, namely the off-year national elections in November in which all of the U.S. House of Representatives and roughly one-third of the U.S. Senate is up for election, I thought I'd take the opportunity to explain why I think politics and self reliance are inseparable.

The Greek philosopher Plato said it well in the 4th century B.C.: "The punishment of wise men who refuse to take part in the affairs of government is to live under the government of unwise men."

Ignoring politics is like ignoring the coyote who roams out back by the chicken coop, or the osprey who perches in the tree above your trout pond, or the owl who waits by your house for nightfall so he can pay a visit to your cats. I'm not sure what each of us would do to prevent the coyote, osprey, or owl from acting against what we'd like to protect, but we'd be foolish, even irresponsible, to ignore their threats. The politician is also a predator who needs to be guarded against; otherwise he will take everything you have—personal possessions, personal freedom, even the right to bring up your children the way you want.

Like the coyote, osprey, and owl, the politician is not by nature an evil creature; he just acts the way that comes natural to him. And I know some readers are saying, "But it shouldn't be that way." But it is that way, and a study of history shows us that it's always been that way, no matter what group in society—church leaders, aristocrats, or peasants—had political power. Even the hard-headed communists with their utopian beliefs have finally learned that (except for the ones on American college campuses).

That's why our founding fathers set up the country's political system the way they did. History had taught them that powerful political men always wanted more and more power, and that even democracies such as Plato's ancient Greece always seemed to deteriorate into tyrannies.

America's political system, on the other hand, is like no other in the world, past or present. It grants all power to the people, and the people grant to the state certain delineated powers. Even today the great democratic republics of Western Europe are based on the premise that the state possesses all power, but it grants certain rights to the people. The United States' system is just the opposite: the people possess the power, and the state is allowed only the power that we grant it. It's all in our Constitution, a wonderfully clear and wise document that was written by wonderfully clear and wise men.

And we, as a people, have generally been fairly wise during the 200 years since our Constitution was put into effect to guard our freedoms against predatory politicians. We began to let our guard down in the 1930s when we let the federal government, then in the hands of President Franklin Roosevelt, assume broad powers to "rescue" the country from the Great Depression. Ironically, World War II and the post-war economic boom revived the economy, but the expanded government took the credit and it has continued expanding ever since.

...and Bill Clinton

So here we are today with Bill Clinton, the consummate predatory politician, in power. Behind him is a U.S. Congress that is controlled by the President's own political party. And on the agenda of President Clinton and the Democrat-controlled Congress are the most sweeping expansions of federal power since Roosevelt presided over the Great Depression. President Clinton feels he has a historic opportunity to expand federal power and right the wrongs he sees in society. (Never mind that the rest of us don't see them.)

Inadequate health care for all is one of the wrongs he sees, so his national health care plan proposes to transfer one-seventh of the nation's economy to the control of the federal government. Environmental degradation is another, so more and more we live in fear that an environmental bureaucrat may show up on our homestead doorstep. It's like waiting for the Gestapo.

My premise for talking politics in a self reliance magazine is simple: the federal government is about to grow so powerful in so many areas under President Clinton that none of us will be able to hide from it. Self reliance means nothing unless you have the freedom to practice it; if you want to rely on yourself, but the government insists instead that you rely on its mandates of how you should run your life, then what meaning has self reliance?

You cannot hide in the backwoods from predatory politicians. Not only will they find you, but if they decide they don't like the way you are living your life, they will forcibly stop you.

In this November's election, Americans who want to stop the federal government from growing larger than our foundding fathers ever could have imagined, have a chance to stop it. You can't vote out Clinton, but you can vote out his source of power—the Democrat-controlled Congress.

That's what I'll do.

American food—it's as varied as the melting pot

By Richard Blunt

Oftentimes, I stop and wonder what people ate in the early days of this country. We cooks do that sometimes. And it's at times like this that I often remember how, years ago while I still worked with and was being trained by old Sully, he spoke several times about Thomas Jefferson and the influence he had on improving food served at the White House. He often joked that he thought Jefferson's main reason for becoming President was so he could eat and serve guests gourmet foods made by professional chefs. When he said things like that, they didn't mean much to me until years later, after cooking French, Italian, Chinese, and other dishes and I started asking myself, "Exactly what is American Food?" I knew it wasn't hot dogs, Big Macs, and take-out chicken.

So, in my spare time, I set out to get an answer to my question. In the end, I found there was no simple answer to what I initially believed was a simple question.

What I found, however, was that over the centuries there have been many contributions to "American" foods that not only made interesting eating but interesting reading as well. I'm going to share some of the things I've learned, and by the time we reach the end of this article I'll discuss some ideas and recipes that concern the most "American" meal I can think of—Thanksgiving.

But I should tell you that even with this original American meal, there are things that may surprise you. Turkey is now the established main course served on this wonderful family day, but it apparently wasn't even on the menu that first Thanksgiving dinner in 1621. From what the Pilgrims themselves wrote about the first Thanksgiving dinner, it consisted of venison, roast duck, roast goose, eels, and clams for entrees. There's no report of turkey being served. What had been served, however, was a significant improvement over what they had been eating. For, up until the harvest, the travelers on the Mayflower had been living on salt horse (actually dried beef; I don't know why they called it salt horse), hardtack, beer, dried fish, and cheese.

English influences

For years to come, most of the settlers in the eastern part of America came from England or the English colonies and their tastes in food reflected this. At that time, British tastes called for a limited amount of seasoning. The seasonings that were available were pepper, mace, clove, and ginger. And that was in Europe. In the New World colonies, even those seasonings were available only to the luckiest or wealthiest families. For the most part food in this part of the world could, at its best, only be considered as fair and unimaginative.

The American Indians

However, to make use of some of the native fair in North America, English housewives started to draw upon the centuries of experience the Indians had acquired using native plants and meats. And the Indians taught them a great deal. Indian cooking placed a great emphasis on the many uses of corn. The colonists were quick to learn the value of cornmeal as well as wheat flour to make their breads and gradually many fine and lasting recipes emerged. Johnny cake, corn pones, hoe cakes, hush puppies, and hawg'n'hominy (a mixture of hulled dry corn cooked with salt pork) are just a

few examples. Another corn dish the Indians made, one they called msickquatash, included dried beans. They shared this dish with the Pilgrims who quickly developed about 12 variations as it spread across the country. Today we call it "succotash."

Another secret they shared with the Pilgrims, but which we have little regard for today, is that corn should be cooked within an hour of being picked. Nowadays we know this is because 90% of the sugar in corn turns to starch in a short time. The Indians, and later the Pilgrims, boiled their water in the fields so they could cook and eat ripened corn as soon as it was picked. When's the last time you did that? If you have your own garden or know where you can buy fresh picked corn and have it cooked within an hour, I strongly recommend you give it a try. You're not going to be disappointed.

The development of "American" food seemed to be on a good track for a number of years, but sometime during the late 1700s, it started to get some mixed reviews. Here are a couple of examples of some of what was happening. In 1796, the first truly American cookbook, called American Cookery, was published. The author was listed as "An American Orphan." Her real name was Amelia Simmons. The book was published in four editions and gave the first professional directions for making Indian pudding and johnny cake. An American mode of cooking can be seen when later editions presented recipes that included Independence Cake and Federal Cake.

Food was available in great variety and abundance during this time. A visitor to a New York city market recorded 63 kinds of fish, 14 varieties of mollusks and shellfish, 52 types of meat and poultry, and 27 kinds of fresh garden vegetables. Compare this inventory with that of your local market today.

Unfortunately this abundance did not promote culinary excellence. An English seagoing novelist, visiting this country during this period said, "God sends the meat, the devil sends the cooks," and "plenty of good things for the table in America, but . . ." And the "but" was not flattering. This bad reputation continued until French and Spanish influences were felt.

French influences

In the beginning, French haute cuisine and the Puritan English did not get along very well, and French culinary sophistication had little influence in this country for a long time. But the seeds of change had been planted. A Virginian named Thomas Jefferson followed Ben Franklin as U.S. envoy to France and spent five years in Paris. He became addicted to French food, and when he became President he hired the first French chef to serve in the White House. By 1896 the slow but consistent blending of French food concepts in this country became apparent when a cookbook, The Boston Cooking School Cookbook by Fannie Merritt Farmer, was published. This book described the meaning of cooking as the capacity to combine English thoroughness with French art. This proved to have a great influence on what American food was to become.

Spanish influences

However, that was in the east. The French had little influence in the southwestern and western parts of the new country. There, the Spanish influence was felt, all the way from Florida to the coast of California. The Spanish brought hot peppers, like cayenne and Tabasco, north—culinary delights they had pilfered from the Indians of Mexico, Central and South America. In Louisiana, the use of these peppers, in combination with another indigenous vegetable, the tomato, became the standard formula to change standard recipes into Creole variations. Bean dishes—the bean is another native plant—are characteristic of the Spanish influence on American food. Foods like chili and guacamole

(made from the avocado, a native fruit) were also brought here by them. Today, guacamole is so popular in this country that dictionaries now recognize the word as a part of our language.

Barbacoa is a Spanish word first applied in the New World after Spanish explorers had observed the outdoor grilling of meat by Haitian and North American Indians. The English adapted the word as barbecue.

As the Spanish developed their successful ranchos in New Mexico and Arizona, they further developed and refined the techniques of the barbecue. Many barbecue sauces were developed by them at this time and they're still popular across this country today.

Pennsylvania

Germany has also contributed a great deal to "American" food. The Pennsylvania Dutch (actually, Deutsche) are ancestors of German speaking refugees who came here from the Rhineland and other parts of German speaking Europe. Also settling into Pennsylvania were the Quakers from England and Wales, the Amish from Switzerland, as well as many others. It did not take long for the word to spread that good food was to be had in Pennsylvania. If you have ever had a sample of good sausage scrapple with your breakfast, you know what I am talking about. My mother

was born and raised in Altoona, PA, so I can tell you that these folks brought good food ideas to this country.

By the way, one thing Jefferson could not convince people of, and which was not widely recognized until years after his death, was that the tomato was a versatile and nutritious food source. Back then, there were those who thought tomatoes were poisonous. Among its other names was "the devil's plum." In the early nineteenth century Pennsylvanians added tomatoes to succotash, and that variation became a popular standard.

If I can ever get my mother to give me some of her Pennsylvania recipes, I'll share them with you. She has a recipe for hot potato salad that is wonderful.

The African connection

You've probably never heard anyone cite the contributions the African slave made to "American" food. Let me be the first to tell you about them. Nowadays, it is common to describe what the slaves ate as "soul food." It was poor people's food—but it was good food. It came about because, back in the 1800s, while the rest of America was entering its era of food abundance, the plenitude was not available to the slaves. What they often subsisted on was what their masters would not eat. In spite of this, they made lasting contributions to the way we eat.

When the slave ships landed, they brought more than just the slaves. They also brought some unique African cooking traditions. For example, one of the foods familiar to the slaves was the peanut. A century before the English settled in North America, African cooks were using peanuts in their cooking. These legumes had arrived on the African continent aboard Spanish ships which had brought them to the Guinea Coast and the Congo.

To the slave, brought here in chains and strangers on a continent they didn't even know had existed, the peanut was a familiar sight, so one of the first things they shared with cooks of European ancestry was how to cook with it. Soon after the first slaves appeared in American kitchens, the first soups made with peanuts were served. I have heard that peanut soup is to Virginia what bean soup is to Boston. Later, thanks to George Washington Carver, a man who had once himself been a slave, the peanut became a standard source of food to almost everyone in the world.

But the inventiveness of the black cook goes beyond peanuts. Poverty made it necessary for them to rely on items that were in great supply but of little use to others. Pig fat was one such item and the black cooks developed a talent for deep fat frying. All varieties of fish were cleaned and coated with corn meal and fried to a crisp state. My grandmother fried mackerel so crisp you could snap it in half and eat the fish bones and all. Do yourself a favor; give it a try.

Sesame seeds were already familiar to cooks with European backgrounds, but black cooks did things the Europeans never thought of. Sesame was known on the Niger River in Africa as "benne." Once they were brought here, slaves would pound sesame seeds into a paste, as they had done in Africa, and they mixed it with hominy, for both the flavor and nutritive value. By substituting them for peanuts and combining them with oysters, they also developed an interesting cream soup that is enjoyed even today.

Few other American cooks, then or now, know more about the barbecuing of wild game than the experienced black cook. This is probably because, quite often, meats like possum, squirrel, and raccoon were all that was available to them. Today, however, examples of the early negro recipes for these are hard to find.

The cooking methods developed by the slaves were good, simple, and required no frills, but they were so consistent that if you eat fried chitterlings or candied yams in New York City or San Francisco today, they are the same as anywhere in the South, today or 150 years ago.

The Italians

Between the end of the nineteenth century and the beginning of World War II, Americans "naturalized" Italian food. Italian restaurants have been around at least since 1849 in California. There, during the Gold Rush, you could get a good tomato and pasta dish in most mining towns. Ever since, Italian food has continued to gain popularity. Sometime before World War I, Kansas farmers started growing durum wheat, the type of wheat necessary for making good pasta. At about that same time, canning companies began producing canned tomato sauces. The lasting influence of this taste in food was sealed.

Many talented Italian farmers settled on the west coast. This greatly influenced the produce industry and did much to influence "American" food. The first commercial growing of bell peppers, eggplants, broccoli, and many other vegetables can be traced to Italian farmers. Most of us have our favorite Italian recipe or restaurant. In my house, when we're looking for good food that's reasonably priced, Italian often comes to mind.

The religious societies

The nineteenth century seems to be a time when America's food experienced many changes and sophistications. Breakfast foods, as we know them today, were the result of a series of events that happened during this period. Many religious societies were started during this time with the idea of improving their members' lifestyles. One of the earliest was the Shaking Quakers. Basic and wholesome food was one of their primary tenets. They advocated the increased consumption of fruits and vegetables and less use of meat. They were among the first in this country to use the whole wheat kernel when grinding flour. They actively protested the removal of the live germ from the kernel by commercial mills. These protests were supported by a young man in Connecticut named Sylvester Graham. A Presbyterian minister, Graham preached that all bread should be cooked at home and baked with whole wheat flour. This didn't make him popular with commercial bakers, and on more than one occasion he required police protection to hold meetings.

He attracted many followers. People like Bronson Alcott—father of Louisa May Alcott, the author of Little Women—were influenced by Graham's preachings. Leaders of the Seventh Day Adventists also adopted many of Graham's food ideas. This set in motion some interesting events:

The Seventh Day Adventists, in Battle Creek, Michigan, believed that any Adventist who suffered indigestion should be treated in a private sanitarium. To this end they awarded a medical scholarship to a man named John Henry Kellogg, and the Battle Creek impact on the American diet was set in motion. Kellogg had some strong ideas about breakfast foods. Two years after he was put in charge of the Seventh Day Adventist health sanitarium, he developed the first Battle Creek health food—Granola.

Another supporter of Graham's food ideas was a chronic dyspeptic named Henry Perky. Perky owned a vegetarian restaurant in Colorado and, in his spare time, developed what we know today as Shredded Wheat.

Meanwhile, one of Dr. Kellogg's patients at the sanitarium, C.W. Post, developed another breakfast cereal that today we call Grape Nuts. Kellogg and Post started the breakfast food industry and both died very wealthy men.

Other food pioneers

Another man, Gustav W. Swift, helped develop the use of refrigerated trains to ship beef across the country, and as a result fresh meat was available on American tables anytime of the year.

Early in the 1900s, another man, Clarence Birdseye, quit his government job to perfect a fast freezing method to preserve food for commercial purposes.

This century also saw the development of commercial canning in France. But after it was brought to this country, Americans quickly began canning more food than all the rest of the world combined.

There are many other countries, religions, and individuals that have made significant contributions to what has become "American" food, and the process continues to this very today. To cover everything, I would need about 200 more pages, and as soon as I was finished the article would be obsolete because the process keeps going on.

In future articles I will cover foods from Greece, Japan, and the Scandinavian countries. But as you can see, although there is no cuisine that can be distinctively identified as "American," we have somehow created a multiplicity of foods that now form the American food experience. I believe this is what makes cooking in this country so interesting and in part explains why the art of cooking has attracted talent such as Julia Child, Craig Claiborn, Paul Prudhomme, and James Beard, just to name a few. I hope to be sharing with you my ongoing answer to the question, "What is American food?" for a long time to come.

It's recipe time and the most American food I can think of is served on Thanksgiving Day. Here are some of my family favorites.

Roast turkey with johnny cake and sausage stuffing

Everything served in our house on this day is made from scratch, so I carefully check inventories on the weekend before, so that I will not be caught short on a day when most stores are closed. Make sure you have an ample supply of homemade stocks.

Johnny cake:

This is a cornmeal bread that, in combination with the sausage recipe that follows, forms the basis of this stuffing but both the johnny cake and the sausage can be served alone or used in other dishes.

> 1 cup flour
> 3 Tbsp sugar
> 2 Tbsp baking powder
> ½ tsp salt
> 1 cup yellow corn meal
> 2 eggs
> 1 cup whole milk
> 2 Tbsp melted butter
> 1 Tbsp bacon fat

Method
1. Mix together flour, sugar, baking powder, salt, and corn meal.
2. In a separate bowl beat the eggs and mix them with the milk, butter, and bacon fat. Now add this to the flour and mix gently with a wooden spoon until liquid is incorporated. Be careful not to over mix. This batter does not have to be lump free.
3. Grease a 9x9 inch baking pan, then evenly spread the batter in the pan.
4. Place in a preheated 400° oven and bake for about 45 minutes.
5. Remove from the oven and set aside to cool.

Homemade sausage: (This should be prepared the day before.)

> 12 oz rindless salt pork diced into 1 inch pieces
> 2 lbs lean pork diced into 1 inch pieces
> ½ lb smoked ham (whatever you prefer, I like Cure 81)
> ¼ cup brandy (I like Apple Jack)
> ½ tsp ground nutmeg
> ¼ tsp ground mace
> ½ tsp summer savory
> ½ tsp dried thyme leaves
> ¼ tsp allspice
> ½ tsp fresh ground white pepper
> ½ tsp dried basil leaves

Method
1. Simmer the salt pork in water for 5 minutes and drain.
2. Pass the pork, smoked ham, and salt pork through the coarse screen on your meat grinder, then through the fine screen. If you do not have a meat grinder, I strongly recommend that you get one before attempting this recipe.
3. Place the ground meat in your mixer's largest bowl and incorporate the remaining ingredients using the paddle.
4. Saute a small amount of the sausage and taste it. Adjust the seasoning to meet your tastes.
5. Cover and refrigerate overnight. This allows the seasoning flavors to penetrate.

Stuffing:

> 1 lb fresh homemade sausage
> ¾ cup diced Granny Smith apples (peeled and cored)
> 2 cups chopped onions
> ¼ cup chopped celery
> ½ cup diced walnuts that have been lightly browned in the oven
> 2 tsp marjoram
> 1 tsp dried thyme
> 1 Tbsp dried sage
> ½ tsp Fennel seed
> 1 tsp salt
> ¼ tsp nutmeg
> 7 cups johnny cake diced into ½ inch chunks
> 2 eggs well beaten
> 4 oz butter or margarine
> 2 cloves fresh garlic finely minced

Method
1. Saute the sausage over medium heat until all the pink color is gone. Remove the cooked sausage from the pan and set it aside. Leave the fat in the pan.

2. Add the apples, onions, and celery to the pan and saute over medium heat until soft. Remove from the pan and drain off the excess fat.

3. Combine the walnuts, marjoram, thyme, sage, fennel seed, salt, and nutmeg with the sausage.

4. Combine sausage mixture with the johnny cake and the cooked apple- onion- celery mixture, lightly mix and stir in the beaten eggs.

5. The mixture should be moist but not heavily wet. If more moisture is needed, use your homemade chicken or turkey stock to moisten to your satisfaction.

Stuffing and roasting the turkey:

> 1 18 to 20 lb Bird
> 1 qt. water
> 1 medium onion
> 2 carrots
> 2 stalks of celery
> 1 bay leaf
> salt and freshly ground pepper

Method

1. Remove the neck along with the liver, gizzard, and heart and place them in a sauce pan with about 1 quart of water, 1 medium onion cut into quarters, 2 carrots that have been cut into quarters, 2 celery stalks cut into one inch pieces, and a bay leaf. Simmer this, covered, over a low heat for about an hour. The result will be a broth you can use for your gravy. You will be using your own gravy recipe but this gives the entree your personal touch.

2. Wash the turkey then dry it, inside and out, with paper towels. Rub the inside of the turkey with a light sprinkle of salt and fresh ground black pepper.

3. Stuff the neck cavity with about 2 cups of stuffing. Pull the neck skin back and fasten it to the turkey's back with skewers.

4. With the breast side up, fold the wing tips under turkey and stuff the main cavity with about 6 to 7 cups of stuffing. Do not pack tightly, it should remain loose. Before placing the bird in the oven, cover the exposed stuffing with a heel of bread or aluminum foil. This will keep it from drying out while the turkey is roasting.

5. Tie the drum sticks and the tail together with twine.

6. Rub the outside of the bird with softened butter.

7. Preheat the oven to 325°. Place the turkey on a roasting rack and put it in a suitable size roasting pan. Now place the turkey in the oven, breast side up.

8. Roast the turkey for 4 ½ to 5 hours.

9. Test doneness by sticking a fork in the thickest part of the thigh. If the juices run clear the turkey is done. If using a meat thermometer, stick it in the same part of the thigh without touching the bone. When the thermometer reads 180° the bird is done.

10. Remove the bird from the oven and allow it to rest for 30 minutes before carving.

Glazed carrots with peas and onions

This is a favorite in my family anytime of the year and it's quick to make.

> 1½ lbs. sliced fresh carrots
> 1½ cups chicken or beef broth
> 6 Tbsp butter
> ½ cup diced fresh onions
> 1 tsp brown sugar
> 2 tsp honey
> 1½ cups fresh or frozen peas
> ½ tsp salt
> ½ tsp freshly ground black pepper

Method

1. Simmer the carrots in the broth over medium heat until just tender. Drain and reserve the broth.

2. Melt the butter in a suitable size skillet and saute the onions over medium heat until tender.

3. Add the brown sugar, honey, and ¼ cup of the reserved broth and stir until the sugar is dissolved. Add the carrots and peas and continue to saute until the vegetables are glazed.

4. Add the salt and pepper and serve.

Here are 2 pie recipes that have become favorites with my family on holidays. They are both made in a 9" pie dish and use my Never Fail Crust recipe.

Never fail crust

The following crust is for the two pie recipes that follow.

> 3 cups all purpose flour
> ½ tsp salt
> 1 cup shortening
> 9 Tbsp ice cold water

Method

1. Measure the flour into a mixing bowl by scooping the flour from the container and leveling to the top of the measuring cup. It is not necessary to sift.

2. Add the salt and mix well.

3. Using a pastry blender or two knives, cut the shortening into the flour until the mixture looks like a bunch of little balls the size of small peas. To spite what many so called pros will tell you, this can also be completed very efficiently using your fingers. You must work quickly though.

Remember that shortening melts next to heat and your fingers mean heat.

4. Add the ice water to the flour mixture and press the mixture until the flour absorbs the water and forms a moist ball then press this ball together with your fingers keeping in mind that your fingers still mean heat, so don't hold this ball for a long time. The less the dough is handled, the more flaky and tender it will be.

5. Place the dough in the refrigerator to chill for about 30 minutes.

6. Divide the dough into two balls, making one ball slightly larger than the other. This larger ball will be the bottom crust.

7. Roll the larger ball on a lightly floured counter into a circle about 1/8 inch thick and 2 inches larger than the size of the pie dish. Now fold the crust in half (this makes it easier to lift and move), place it in the pie dish then unfold it to fit the dish.

8. Gently press the dough to fit the contour of the pie dish. There will be about one inch of the dough hanging over the dish. Lift this up and fold it in half to make a standing rim around the pie dish.

9. Roll the second ball of dough to the same thickness but only about 1" larger than the pie dish.

There you have my Never Fail Pie Crust.

Now for the pies.

Blueberry pie

Wild blueberries are found in Europe and North America. Cultivated blueberries were developed in New Jersey and are the most available blueberry today. This is a favorite fruit in my house. The following recipe is my wife's "Birthday Cake."

> 6 Tbsp margarine or butter
> 5 Tbsp all purpose flour
> 1¾ cup sugar
> ½ tsp salt
> ½ tsp fresh ground nutmeg
> 2 tsp quick cooking tapioca
> 1 Tbsp lemon juice
> 6 cups fresh or frozen blueberries
> 1 Never Fail Pie Crust
> 1 egg, lightly beaten

Method

1. Place the margarine or butter in a small sauce pan and set on a medium heat to melt. After this melts, stir in the flour to make a smooth paste. Cook this paste while stirring for about 5 minutes. Remove from the heat and allow to cool. You have created a flour roux.

2. Combine sugar, salt, nutmeg, tapioca, and lemon juice and mix with a spoon.

3. Add the flour roux to the sugar mixture and mix well.

4. Combine this mixture with the blueberries and mix very gently. Try not to break the berries.

5. Preheat your oven to 375°.

6. Follow the recipe for preparing and rolling the pie crust and place the bottom crust in your pie dish.

7. Spread the filling evenly in the pie dish.

8. Carefully fold the top crust in half and place it evenly over half of the pie dish, then unfold it to cover the other half. Now seal the two crusts together by fluting the outer edge of the crust with your fingers. Fluting is simply a process of crimping the dough together by pressing with your fingers or a fork. Trim off any excess crust with a knife.

9. Cut 4 X's around the pie and one in the middle.

10. Brush the crust with the lightly beaten egg and place in the preheated oven to bake for about 45 minutes to an hour. The pie is ready to come out when the crust is evenly browned and the filling is bubbling in the middle.

Old fashioned apple pie

This is my favorite food. To me, this "is" American food, Amen.

Use tart, crisp, and fresh apples when preparing this recipe. I use Cortlands, Granny Smiths, or Macouns. You will need about 10 apples that are peeled and cored to get the 2 lbs. required for this recipe.

> 3 Tbsp butter
> 2 Tbsp flour
> 1¼ cups sugar
> 1 tsp cinnamon
> ¼ tsp nutmeg
> 1 tsp salt
> 1 tsp lemon juice
> 2 lbs sliced fresh apples

Method

1. Melt the butter in a small sauce pan over a medium heat. Add the flour and cook, while stirring, for about 5 minutes. Remove from the heat and set aside to cool.

2. Combine the sugar, cinnamon, nutmeg, salt, and lemon juice. Mix thoroughly, then add the flour paste and mix again.

3. Toss this mixture with the sliced apples and set aside while you prepare your crust.

4. Spread the filling evenly in the pie dish and follow the same procedure outlined for the blueberry pie. This pie may require more or less time in the oven, depending on the condition of the apples. Older apples are soft and cook faster.

Well, that's it folks. I'll catch you next issue and we'll continue our ongoing journey through the American food experience. ∆

AMERICANA

Collecting old phonograph records is fun and educational

By Don Fallick

It takes a pretty sophisticated alternative energy system to guarantee electric power all year round. Those two- or three-week cloudy periods can be downright inconvenient when you want to play your favorite music, especially if you're not musically talented yourself.

My family solved this problem by acquiring a hand-cranked, vintage phonograph. It was made in 1931 by the Brunswick Balke Collender Company, and has such "modern" features as automatic shut-off and user-regulated turntable speed. Best of all, records rarely cost me more than a dollar, which is about what they cost new nearly 100 years ago. So much for inflation.

Free records

Most of my records cost me nothing at all. When friends and relatives hear that I have a "Victrola," most offer to give me all the old 78 rpm records they have in their attics. Often these are records they inherited and have no means to play themselves. Records I don't care to keep I trade with other 78 rpm collectors or donate to a thrift store. Some I keep just because of their importance in the history of music. For example, I have a recording of the composer Rachmaninoff playing his own Prelude in C Sharp Minor. I'm not terribly thrilled by the piece, but I'm not likely to trade it. I'm not real hot on opera, either, but I'm hanging onto my one-sided recordings of Enrico Caruso, too.

Getting started

It is not necessary to own a hand-crank phonograph to get started. Really old records need a soft steel needle to avoid damaging the record grooves. But there were *lots* of records produced in the 1950s which can be played by any electric record player with a "78" setting. Such players can frequently be found in thrift shops for less than $50. "Recent" vintage records are much thinner and more flexible than the old stiff, thick ones made in the first half of the century, and may have the word "unbreakable" printed on them somewhere. If it says "78 rpm" on the label, you can be sure it's modern. Early records did not say "78 rpm" for the simple reason that virtually all early records played at that speed.

Edison's phonographs

The first record players were invented by Thomas Edison a century ago. They played shellac cylinders, not the flat disks we are used to. It quickly became apparent that the fragile cylinders were too hard to store and too easy to break, so Edison switched to disks, which originally played at 80 rpm.

Unconfirmed stories circulated by record buffs say that another company invented their own machine that played at 78 rpm, but had an adjustable speed regulator. Thus, Edison records could be played on their machines, but not vice versa. After fruitless attempts to defend his patents, Edison abandoned the field to the Victrola and its many clones.

I have not found real evidence for this story, but something caused Edison to abandon a lucrative field, and it changed the "standard" phonograph speed from 80 to 78 rpm.

Serious antique collectors have run up the price of really old machines in good condition. Fortunately, you're not looking for the same machines they are. Relatively "newer" machines from the 1930s and '40s probably play records better than their older cousins and cost lots less. If you don't mind owning a phonograph that looks its age, you can buy a perfectly functional one in most big city antique shops for around $200. It will play all the old records, as well as the newer ones. If you know what to look for, you can buy one from a private party or an estate sale for even less. Here's what to look for:

The turntable mechanism

Phonographs are really simple machines. There just aren't many ways they can break. There are three main parts: the turntable, the sound system, and the cabinet. The turntable is powered by a spring motor, just like an old alarm clock. If you're considering an old phono, and the turntable doesn't turn, either something is stuck or the drive spring is broken. Remember, you have to wind it up and turn it *on* first. Wind it up just until it feels hard to turn the crank, to preserve the antique spring. Let it unwind when you're all done, for the same reason.

There will be a brake that stops the turntable so you can change records, with a lever near the turntable that releases the brake, and sets it. A screeching sound when the brake is set is normal. "Modern" phonographs have a second lever for setting the automatic shut-off, so it trips at the correct time. You can probably live with a non-functional auto shut-off, but the start and stop lever has to work.

If the turntable won't turn, lift it off its spindle and oil the mechanism with sewing machine oil. There should be two or three oil ports, usually covered or with screw "stoppers" to keep dust out. Allow the oil five or ten minutes to penetrate, then top off the oil ports and try again. This will frequently free a stuck turntable. If the spring is broken, it may cost more to fix it than to buy another machine. Consult an antique restoration specialist.

The sound system

The sound system of an old "Victrola" consists of a megaphone (or *horn*) and the tone arm. The tone arm is really part of the horn, with one pivot that allows it to follow the record grooves and another to allow the head to be raised. On the head is a replaceable needle, a set screw to hold it, and a diaphragm of "isinglass" or some other plastic material covering a small soundbox. That's it. Microscopic wiggles in the record groove vibrate the needle, which transfers the vibration to the diaphragm. Air in the soundbox resonates with the diaphragm, producing sound, which is amplified by the megaphone. This was Edison's ingenious, mechanical method of reproducing sound.

Until the 1920s, recording masters were made the same way, in reverse. Someone shouted into the megaphone, causing the needle to make wiggly grooves in a soft plastic disk. Records printed from such masters don't have nearly the volume or clarity of later, electrically recorded disks.

Checking the sound system

To check out an old phono's sound system, bring along a test record, and if possible a steel phonograph needle. An antique dealer may be able to furnish one, but at estate sales, what you see is what you get. Often, old phonographs may only need a new needle and some sewing machine oil to be playable. New needles can be purchased by mail order (see "Sources" at the end of this article) and may be available through local antique dealers or repair shops.

If you can't find a real phonograph needle, you can still test the sound system, using a sewing needle, a sewing machine needle, or even a cactus needle, but *don't* play your record with it. You'll ruin the record. Just screw the needle in place, then scratch your finger across the tip. If you get sound, the sound system works.

Tone quality . . .

The quality of the sound you get may surprise you, especially if you have a new needle and even a halfway decent record. The tone arm is so heavy, even "bad" scratches won't affect the sound. In fact, some of my "best" records are cracked from the hole to the rim, yet they play well, with no audible click. Other than an actual chip out of a record, about the only thing that can make it sound bad is a dull or rusty needle. If the tone sounds "fuzzy," stop the record and replace the needle right away.

Some of my friends are amazed at the way I grip my records, instead of holding them gently by the edges. I don't worry about getting a little bit of finger grease on the records, as I would with LPs. No one will ever know it's there. But I *am* worried about dropping them. These records were amazingly fragile even when they were new. A tumble onto any surface can mean disaster. I teach the kids how to handle the records, then try to be philosophical if one breaks. The kids quickly learn to be very careful! I've lost only two records to mishandling in 13 years.

. . . is in the wood

The wooden "horns" of some quality phonographs were made as carefully as violins, and they impart a mellow sound to the records played on them that can't be duplicated by even the finest CD players and speakers.

Some old phonos were gorgeous pieces of furniture, while others had plain "box" cabinets intended only to hide the works. If possible, get a player with a lid that covers the tone arm while the record is playing. This will largely eliminate the scratchy sound often associated with Victrolas. If you are good at it, you can buy a beat-up but "fancy" phonograph and re-finish it for a profit. There are antique buffs who make good money doing this.

Collecting for enjoyment

There are also serious collectors who scour the country for "important" or "collectable" records, but my philosophy is different. These records, and the machines to play them, were made to give enjoyment by being played, not hoarded. When I shop for records at thrift stores, I make sure to tell the clerks that my family is going to listen to the music, and that we aren't connected to the power lines. I almost always get a big discount on the price.

My kids love the old jazz and boogie-woogie records I bring home, and they're developing a taste for more "serious" music. They're also learning history from a different perspective. We study the Great Depression, the World Wars, the Dust Bowl, and other aspects of American history by listening to the songs that were popular at the time, played on the actual records of the time. It's a real "hands-on" learning experience. Some of my records have stories connected to them about the friend or relative who gave them to me, and my kids always want to hear the story along with the record. I find I enjoy cataloging my collection and learning about the composers and artists mentioned on the labels.

Living history

We also enjoy taking the Brunswick to our local nursing home and playing records for the residents. The old folks love hearing again the songs of their youth and telling the kids about their lives. And the kids get a real sense of history by listening to people who were young when the records were new. History and biography consist of much more than the stories about generals and presidents we read in school.

At our house, history not only lives, it sings.

Ten years ago, I paid 10¢ for a 10" diameter record at the Salvation Army store, and 25¢ for a 12" disk. Now I pay 25¢ for the smaller records and 50¢ for the big ones, and up to a dollar for a popular record in mint condition. I even paid $5 once for a rare record I especially wanted.

Collecting and playing 78 rpm phonograph records is lots of fun, educational, and good exercise too. Besides, where else can you buy a genuine antique in mint condition for less than a buck?

Sources

- **Phonographs:** Antique dealers. Check local newspapers for estate sale notices and bankruptcy auctions. Yard sales rarely have usable machines.

- **Records:** Friends' & relatives' attics, Goodwill, Salvation Army, and other thrift stores. At estate sales and auctions you can sometimes buy them by the boxfull. Sometimes available at yard sales, usually overpriced. Check to make sure they are not broken, and that all disks of a set are present, or the price goes down. Be firm—many people mistakenly think all old records are valuable antiques.

- **Needles:** Available from Antique Restorations, 920 W. Jewell Avenue, Salt Lake City, UT 84104. Also old piano rolls.

- **Information:** Most "big city" libraries have references like these:

<u>Olde Records Price Guide, 1900-1947 Popular and Classical 78 RPM's</u>, by Peter Soderbergh, ISBN 0-87069-297-6. Wallace-Homestead. Second Printing 1980. Best all around reference for a beginner I know of. Arranged chronologically, with lots of historical notes and pictures of "important" record labels for each time period, and price ranges of records.

<u>The Record Collector's International Directory</u>, by Gary S. Felton. ISBN 0-517-540010 (cloth) or 0-517-540029 (paperback). Crown Publishers, 1980. Record dealers who buy and sell records, with addresses. ∆

A Backwoods Home Anthology

RECIPES

Try traditional early American fried squirrel

By Rev. J.D. Hooker

If you really want to, you can take a whole lot of short-cuts with this recipe. It would probably still taste just as great. However, you really would miss most of the enjoyment, and couldn't possibly find the meal nearly as satisfying. I hope that you'll just take my word on this, because if you skimp on the preliminaries, you'd probably enjoy eating at one of those fast food chicken places just as much.

Ingredients:

```
1 energetic youngster
1 .410 shotgun with shells
1 adult
1 squirrel rifle (a .22 rimfire is fine, but a .30 or .32
    muzzle loader is more traditional.)
1 squirrel call
1 one-or-two-foot section of ½" plastic pipe
1 pocket-full of small stones
1 small carry-along cooler with ice
5 fox squirrels, or 6 gray squirrels
2½ cups of white flour
1¼ cups of cornmeal
3 large (or 4 medium) eggs
2¼ cups milk
1½ tsp. baking powder
1 tsp. salt
½ tsp. black pepper
1½ cups beef tallow
½ cup applejack whiskey (if unavailable, either
    bourbon or sour-mash whiskey will do)
```

Preparation time: Approximately 12 hours

Instructions:

To begin with, you'll probably need to get out of bed an hour or two earlier than usual, because you'll want to be out in the woods right about daybreak, or even a trifle before.

Let the kid use the .410, while you handle the rifle.

You know, there are quite a lot of people who might argue that a shotgun is really an unsportsmanlike weapon for hunting squirrels. If you happen to be one of those people, all I can say is that you need to try collecting a limit of squirrels with a diminutive little .410 bore yourself. It really requires considerably more skill than most folks would imagine. Really, this tiny gauge is more of a specialist's

weapon, with its tiny shot charge and limited range. That is undoubtedly the reason it's been recommended for teaching youngsters to hunt for so many years: it actually forces them to acquire a much higher level of skill than another firearm would. In fact, I've found that I'm not the only squirrel hunter around here who likes to use adapter shells. These allow the use of 2½" .410 shells in my side-by-side 12 bore.

Here in Indiana, the season on squirrels opens in mid-August, when (normally) it's not just warm, but downright hot. So—at least early in the season—a small cooler filled with ice is a real necessity. Without it, your hunting efforts can all too easily be turned into wasted time, as the game you collect spoils at an accelerated rate in such temperatures.

Take turns with the youngster, one of you staying prepared to shoot, as the other attempts to call your quarry into range. Here's where that section of water pipe comes into use. Use it sort of blow-gun fashion, shooting the small stones into the air, so that they'll rustle a lot of tree leaves in their descent. If you'll alternate between using the pipe and using the squirrel call, you'll soon have every bushy tail within hearing range convinced that one of their kindred has stumbled on to a feeding bonanza. They'll think they hear him happily barking away, as the husks and shells from the nuts he's feasting on fall from the tree top.

During hot weather, it pays to clean each squirrel as it's taken. Add the meat to the cooler before moving on to another part of the woods to begin calling again.

You might want to think about letting the kid save the tails from the squirrels you collect, because Meps, the fishing tackle people (who probably made some of the best lures in your tackle box) will still buy them. They don't pay a whole lot, and I doubt if you could ever make any real money at this—but if neither of you miss too often, selling the tails should pretty well pay for your ammo. And that's not a bad lesson for a kid to learn, either.

Once you're home again, with your firearms cleaned and put away, clean the meat more thoroughly, picking off any bits of hair, etc., and removing any pellets from the .410. Rinse the meat under cold water, then cut it into frying sized pieces. Refrigerate until time to prepare dinner.

Preparation:

Place the meat in a pot, and cover with lightly salted water. Bring to a rolling boil, then reduce heat and simmer until tender. When the meat is tender, add the applejack (or whiskey) and simmer about five more minutes.

While the meat is simmering, mix together the flour, cornmeal, baking powder, salt, and pepper You can just dump all of these dry ingredients into a paper sack, fold the end closed, and shake real well to mix.

Once the meat is tender, remove from the heat and use a slotted spoon to dip the pieces of meat from the liquid. Set the meat aside to cool slightly.

As the meat cools, mix the eggs and milk together; use a fork for very thorough mixing. Then melt the tallow in a heavy skillet. (You can substitute any sort of shortening you like, but at least once try using the tallow—you'll love the extra flavor!)

Once it's cooled enough to touch, dip each piece of meat into the milk-egg mixture, then dredge in the flour mixture. Fry a few pieces at a time over moderately high heat, turning once, until golden brown. Drain on paper towels.

Add enough of any remaining milk mixture to what's left of the flour mixture to form a very stiff dough. If you have to, add just a little more milk to form the dough. Bring the broth remaining from simmering the squirrel to a boil again. Drop the dough, by tablespoonfuls, into the boiling liquid. Cook for about fifteen minutes, and serve these boiled hushpuppies with the fried squirrel.

If you can add some fresh sweet corn, cooked on the cob, maybe a salad of fresh garden produce, and some ice cold sweet cider, you'll have a traditional American feast, one that's actually *too good* to serve to a king. (But if you can get any of your liberal friends to come to dinner, you might just be able to change their whole outlook on firearms and hunting. Fried squirrel suppers are highly addictive, after all!)

Hopefully you'll have included the youngster who helped to collect the meat for the meal in its preparation as well. Maybe you ought to let him, or her, be the one to ask the blessing before you enjoy it as well. I mean, they've earned the right, by this point, to enjoy the adult-sized privilege/right of expressing gratitude to their Creator.

And hopefully you'll also do your part in cleaning up after dinner, just to show your own good upbringing.

For dinner conversation, you might want to make certain that the youngster you've spent the day with really understands the true traditions of American squirrel hunting. Especially the part about how a bunch of early American farmers, craftsmen, clergymen, and shop owners, with their aim honed by years of squirrel shooting, took on the most powerful military force on earth, and drove the British army into the sea!

Anyway, this is absolutely the very finest fried squirrel recipe that I've ever tasted. If you'll prepare it exactly according to the directions, I'm positive that you'll agree. Δ

A BHM Writer's Profile

Carole Perlick

Carole Perlick works for the magazine primarily on the order desk and mail room. Shortly after starting at Backwoods Home Magazine Carole began writing book reviews and has done several articles for the magazine.

Before retiring to the country six years ago, she worked as a nurse for 18 years, ran a 72-unit aprtment building, and managed a grocery/liquor store for her husband. While raising five children, she was deeply involved in church activities, scouts, and athletic programs.

Carole currently is active in her community, serving as an EMT, volunteer firefighter, and member of the Copco Lake Fire Board. She also teaches religious education at her church.

She enjoys her home in the country, her family, travelling, and putting her thoughts down on paper.

A Backwoods Home Anthology

RECIPES

Barbecue a whole goat (and more) in an imu

By Don Fallick

The South Sea Islanders have developed a technique for easily cooking even large animals like goats and pigs whole. It's called an *imu* (pronounced *ee-moo*)—a hole in the ground lined with hot rocks. Though the actual techniques are simple, preparation of the food and timing can make or break your meal. Here's how my family prepares a luau for about 60 people, using our favorite Polynesian cooking method.

It generally takes two people to prepare an imu—one to prepare the food, and the other to dig the hole and prepare and tend the fire. Don't plan on doing anything else for a while.

Killing the goat

An old wether is ideal. Imu cooking will tenderize virtually any meat. If you start with a naturally tender doe or kid, the meat may dissolve by the time you unearth it. Even an old buck will work fine, if you take proper precautions in butchering: remove the head and testicles immediately after killing, and don't allow even one hair to touch the meat. I've even known some folks to castrate a buck just before killing it, but I think this is unnecessary and cruel.

For this to work, you must be able to drop and kill the buck with one shot. Buck goats have notoriously hard heads, but any gun that can drop a deer should work equally well on a goat. I've even used a .22, though it's certainly not my preferred gun. The trick is to feed the goat a bit of grain in a pan on the ground, then scratch him behind the horns with the muzzle of the gun. When he relaxes and starts to eat, with the gun still in contact with his skull (*behind* the thick part)—shoot. This is not messy. The front of a goat's skull is so thick that the bullet will be trapped within it. Done correctly, the goat dies instantly, while eating grain and being scratched in his favorite spot.

Immediately castrate the buck, place a block of wood under his neck, and chop off the head with a felling axe (a hatchet will take too long). This removes two of the three sources of "buck scent" that will otherwise make the meat taste rangy. The other is the buck's hair.

String up the carcass and clean and skin as you would any other domestic or game animal of similar size, but pay particular attention to keeping the hair off the meat. I've found it useful to have a helper hose off the meat while I clean out the innards. Save the heart, kidneys, and liver for later use. Organ meats don't do well in an imu, as they tend to disintegrate.

It's not necessary to hang goat meat, though some of my neighbors insist on it. If you're going to imu the goat, you'll never know the difference anyway.

We marinate the goat overnight in home-made barbecue sauce:

Marinade

Ingredients

> 1 pint vinegar
> 1 pint catsup
> 1 pint sugar (brown sugar preferred)
> 2 pints tomato juice
> 1 cup oil
> ½ cup inexpensive prepared mustard

Simmer ingredients together about 10 minutes, add enough water to cover meat, stir well, and soak overnight in a porcelain bathtub. Do not use a galvanized laundry tub, or the meat will taste like sheet metal. Cover with a clean cloth to keep off flies.

"Stuffing"

We stuff our goats with five or six whole chickens or rabbits, and about ½ peck each of apples, potatoes, tomatoes, green peppers, carrots, a dozen ears of corn, and half a dozen "Spanish" or "Walla-Walla Sweet" onions. These are the big, white, mild onions. All except the potatoes and corn are for flavoring the meat, and will most likely disintegrate in cooking. Any that survive will be delicious, however. If you want to make sure that some survive, you gotta wrap 'em in aluminum foil. Baked apples make a wonderful dessert. Wrap some of them, and the potatoes and corn, individually in aluminum foil, too.

Even an old buck will work fine, if you take proper precautions in butchering: remove the head and testicles immediately after killing, and don't allow even one hair to touch the meat.

Final preparation

When all the "goodies" are neatly arranged inside the goat carcass, wrap the whole thing in about 12 layers of clean, old fashioned burlap bags (*not* plastic feed bags) which have been soaking overnight in water, diluted barbecue sauce, or marinade. Then wrap the whole thing in at least two layers of new chicken wire fencing. This will allow the goat to be fished out of the hole after it's cooked, without falling apart in the dirt. I like to wire a coat hanger "handle" near each end, just to be sure. This much food is heavy, and the meat will be falling off the bone when it's done. Use clean hay hooks to lift it out of the hole, and wear leather gloves. The metal will be very hot.

Preparing the imu

Make the hole about 1½ feet larger in every dimension than the stuffed and wrapped goat will be. Line the sides of the hole with stones about half the size of a brick. Leave the bottom bare at this time. Sometimes we prepare a big pot of pre-boiled beans, with all the trimmings, to go in a "bean hole" in the bottom of the imu.

The sides of the imu must be fairly straight to work well, so don't try it in sandy soil. Rocky soil works very well, but beware of tree roots, which can carry your imu fire a long distance. And be sure to drown your fire thoroughly when you're done. Just burying the fire with earth won't work, as the hot rocks can keep it smoldering underground a long time. We had one imu re-ignite itself *three days* after we thought it was out.

The secret of an imu is in the fire. Span the hole with two six-inch-diameter poles, and lay up a "criss-cross" fire directly over the hole. Build it in layers, and add a layer of stones above the third layer of wood. There should be enough stones to cover the bottom of the hole. If necessary, add another layer of stones above the fourth layer of wood. All stones should be roughly the size of half a brick.

Light the fire in several places and keep it burning until the stones are white hot, and stones, fire, and all have fallen into the hole. Keep adding wood for two or three hours, until the hole is half filled with burning coals. I like to burn fruitwood, or even old cedar fenceposts (*without creosote*) the last hour or so, to give the meat a nice tang.

Working quickly, and wearing leather boots and gloves, shovel out any remaining chunks of burning wood, and about half of the coals. Level the stones and coals in the bottom of the hole, and throw in about a peck of moistened sweet leaves (grape, maple, gum, sycamore) or vegetable tops. Then add your prepared goat. Shovel the remaining coals around and on top of the goat and cover with an old piece of sheet metal, to reflect the heat back into the hole. Cover the entire thing up with dirt until no steam escapes.

Cooking

Leave it in the ground 8 to 12 hours. It will start to smell wonderful long before then, but remember, once you pull it out, you can't put it back if it's not done. It takes a certain amount of courage to do your first imu. It's foolish to go to that much trouble and cook that much food for only a few people, so you'll find yourself inviting more people for dinner than you've ever fed before. The first time we did it, we invited our whole church, and 60 people showed up. It kinda makes you nervous when you start to uncover the food, not knowing whether it's done or not.

Tell 'em to bring hearty appetites.

I've done this several times, and it has always worked. If you're chicken about it, though, have five or six dozen ears of corn soaking, so you can roast 'em over a fire if anything goes wrong, or if too many show up, or just for a change of pace.

Roast corn

Soak in water for 20 to 30 minutes: five dozen ears of corn with husks intact.

Roast over hot fire or burning coals, until outer husks are brown on one side.

Turn and roast other side till brown.

Strip husks back (be careful of steam) and slather with butter and garlic salt.

Feeds 60 adults. Double the recipe for teenagers. Δ

It could probably be shown by facts and figures that there is no distinctive native American criminal class, except Congress.

Mark Twain

A Backwoods Home Anthology

RECIPES

Your throw-away fish can be keepers if you know how to prepare them right

By Richard Blunt

With the price of all kinds of fish constantly on the rise, do you fish with idea of eating your catch? If so, read on. I have some ideas that will help you increase your fishing pleasure. I'm going to give you some tips on how to prepare fish, especially the ones you might have thrown away in the past.

Years ago, when I was growing up in Boston, fish was a large part of my diet. I was fortunate to live in an area that offered the opportunity to fish both salt and fresh water. Not only that, but like me, my mother loved fish and was an expert when it came time to cook what I caught. Between my ability to catch them and her talent to cook them, we enjoyed some delightful meals.

At the end of a fishing trip, I often brought home cod, haddock, pollack, mackerel, flounder, blue fish, or stripped bass from the ocean, and trout, salmon, yellow perch, bluegills, and largemouth or smallmouth bass from the lakes and streams of New England. With this variety, fish meals were always an adventure at our house. Take my word for it, no local restaurant could match the variety of fish we ate.

Caring for your catch

But, before you grab that fishing rod, you should know how to care for your fish from the time you pull them out of the water to the time you put them on the stove. These are the points you should keep in mind:

- Fish spoils quickly. Whether you buy or catch them, make sure they have clear eyes, red gills, and a fresh clean odor before you consider them eatable.
- From the moment you land them, fish are best preserved when kept alive or cold.
- Large fish—in the 15 pound or larger range—should be killed, field dressed, and put on ice immediately after catching. The flesh on these monsters tends to bruise severely if allowed to thrash around on the bottom of a boat or on the dock.
- On extended fishing trips (two days or more), maximum chilling techniques should be employed. I use an ice-salt mixture that's similar to the mixture I use when I'm making homemade ice cream. I mix four ounces of course ice cream salt with five pounds of crushed ice. Then, as I catch and clean my fish, I preserve them by placing a layer of this ice mixture on the bottom of a suitable size cooler. Next, I tightly wrap my cleaned fish in plastic and place it on top of the ice. Then I cover it with a second layer of ice. As I catch more fish, I clean them, wrap them in plastic, place them on the ice, and cover them with ice. If you use this technique, try to remember to keep the lid of the cooler closed as much as possible.

Panfish

I have often watched people catch bluegills, crappies, yellow perch, or other small fish and toss them away. Even many experienced fisherman do this because they feel these fish are not big enough to fillet or steak. But these fish are quite a treat when cleaned and properly prepared. Pan dressing is the most efficient way to prepare them for cooking. To pan dress means to remove the head, scales, fins, and tail. However, I leave the tail on because I like the taste.

Small catfish or bullheads are another fish I keep, and they are best cooked whole, after cleaning and skinning. All my large fish I fillet, then cut into steak or chunks.

Most cookbooks will address the preparation of large fish and disregard pan fish. So, here I'm going to talk about fish that are primarily pan size. With this in mind, I'm going to share with you three of my favorite recipes for pan frying and barbecuing these fish.

The first recipe is a new one that I discovered over the winter. Because outdoor barbecuing is very popular at my house, but impractical during the winter months, I started work on some different ways to achieve a "barbecue" effect indoors.

Here's a recipe I've often used when cooking chicken, and I discovered it also works well with many varieties of fish.

302

The Fifth Year

Bullheads, marinated and "barbecued"

Mustard marinade:

> ¼ tsp salt
> ½ tsp fresh grated white pepper
> 1½ tsp Dijon mustard
> ½ tsp dried thyme leaves
> ½ tsp fresh grated nutmeg
> 1/8 tsp Allspice
> ½ tsp ground ginger
> 1 clove finely minced garlic
> 1 tsp vegetable oil

Method
1. In a bowl, combine and mix all of the marinade ingredients.
2. Rub this marinade on the fish and set them aside for 30 minutes to one hour.

B.B.Q. sauce:

> 1 tsp vegetable oil
> ¼ cup finely minced onion
> 1 clove finely mince garlic
> ¾ cup apple cider
> ¼ cup fish stock
> ½ cup light red or rose wine
> 1 Tbsp worcestershire sauce
> 3 Tbsp white vinegar
> 5 Tbsp tomato paste
> 2 Tbsp brown sugar
> 6 to 8 whole bullheads, 10-12 inches or 4-6 catfish fillets, 6-8 ounces each

Method
1. Over medium heat saute the onion and garlic in the vegetable oil until soft but not browned.
2. Combine the cider, fish stock, wine, worcestershire sauce, vinegar, tomato paste and brown sugar.
3. Mix and add to sauteed vegetables. Bring the mixture to a light boil over medium heat and reduce heat to low.
4. Simmer, stirring occasionally until the sauce thickens, about 20 to 30 minutes, but longer if a thicker sauce is preferred.
5. Set aside to cool for 30 minutes.
6. When the sauce has cooled, arrange the fish on a greased baking pan.
7. Brush each portion on both sides with sauce and place in a preheated 400° oven to bake.
8. Bake for about five minutes and baste again with the barbecue sauce. Continue to cook until the fish flakes easily at the thickest part. This should be in 15 to 20 minutes.

Fish stock

During the years that I worked with Chef Sully, I was given the job of filleting the many pounds of whole cod and haddock that were delivered to the restaurant. That was because I made the mistake of telling him about some of my fishing experiences. These tales included my proficiency in skinning, filleting, and steaking fish. What Sully taught was that if you purchased ten pounds of fish, you must try to use ten pounds of fish. After removing the fillets, there were several pounds of heads, tails, and bones left. According to Sully, this meant rich fish stock that had many uses. As you have noticed, I include it in the first recipe. I also use this stock in soups, chowders, quiches and other items that benefit from the rich taste that the stock provides. Here is my standard recipe.

When I say fish bones, I mean back bones with tail and fins removed and head with gill cover and cheek assembly removed. The head adds much of the stock's rich flavor.

> 2 to 3 pounds raw fish bones
> 1 small onion
> 1 medium carrot
> 1 stalk celery
> 1 small bay leaf
> Enough water to cover. Depending on the size of the heads this could be 1 to 2 quarts.

Method
1. Rinse the heads to remove any slime. Cut skeleton into small pieces.
2. Peel onion and carrot; cut into small pieces along with the celery.
3. Combine the fish bones, vegetables, and bay leaf in a suitable size saucepan.
4. Add enough water to cover this mixture and bring to a boil over medium heat.
5. Reduce the heat and simmer for about one hour, covered. Check every 20 minutes and add water if necessary.
6. Remove from heat, separate stock from bones, bay leaf and vegetables.
7. Strain stock through cheesecloth and return to pot.
8. Bring to a boil over medium heat and simmer until it reduces to about half the volume.
9. Remove from heat and cool as quickly as possible. I freeze stock in one to two cup batches. This makes it easy to thaw and use in small amounts.

Blunt's fried panfish

This includes bullheads, trout, perch, bluegills, crappie and any other fish of this size that suits your taste. I do not recommend frying salmon or large trout. It is my experience that these fish are oily and retain more natural flavor when baked, broiled or poached.

    6-8 panfish less than 1½ inches thick
    Vegetable oil—enough to cover the bottom of the frying skillet with about ¼ inch of oil
    1 cup all purpose flour
    ½ tsp salt
    ¼ tsp freshly grated black pepper
    ¼ tsp dried basil leaf
    ¼ tsp dried thyme leaf
    1/8 tsp garlic powder

Method

1. Cover the bottom of the skillet with oil, at least ¼ inch deep.
2. Preheat pan over medium heat.
3. Wipe the fish with paper towels to remove excess moisture.
4. Create a seasoned flour by combining the flour, salt, pepper, basil, thyme, and garlic powder in a bowl.
5. Coat the fish on all sides with the seasoned flour, and place in the heated pan.
6. Cook for about five minutes on one side and turn to cook on the other side. This should take about three additional minutes.
7. Remove from the pan and place on paper towels to drain for a couple of minutes.

Eat it, enjoy it, and may they always be biting when you're fishing. ∆

RETURN OF THE 3 FOR 2 SPECIAL!
ONLY $39.90

Subscribe (or renew) for a year, buy <u>The Best of the First Two Years</u>, and receive our <u>Fourth Year</u> anthology ABSOLUTELY FREE!

Backwoods Home Magazine

THE SELF-RELIANCE GOLDMINE!

Year after year, it's the information you need to achieve a self-reliant lifestyle for yourself and your family.

A Backwoods Home Anthology: The Fourth Year

384 PAGES! A FABULOUS COLLECTION!
This book contains an incredible volume of information that will still be helping you for years to come!

Send a check or money order, along with your name and address, to
**Backwoods Home Magazine
PO Box 40
Montague, CA 96064**

Or call toll-free: **(800) 835-2418** for credit card orders only. Others please call (530) 459-3500.

COUNTRY LIVING

A Backwoods Home Anthology

David and the D-4
...a story about growing up

By Marjorie Burris

I've been reading with interest the many letters to *Backwoods Home Magazine* from people who are wanting to make a move to the country, and I especially relate to those who want to raise their children in a rural setting. I want to encourage you; I've been there.

As it turned out, my husband and I were not able to move to our backwoods homestead until after all our boys had grown and left home, but all three of our sons still tell us the time they spent here was the biggest influence in their lives. Here's the story of our son David, not because it is the most unusual or important, but because he is the oldest, and I start with the first. Our other sons have their stories, too.

"Dad, this is ridiculous. I'm not doing this anymore!" David, barely 15, threw down his shovel and glared at his father. The rest of our pick and shovel crew—myself and sons Duane, 13, and Don, 8—straightened up and stood still. We felt the same way. It was unusual for one of our boys to rebel with so much vigor, but after all, David *was* a teenager and he was entitled to express his feelings. My husband put his arm around our oldest son's shoulders and called for a family conference. We left our tools by the side of the road and trudged back to our old log house to talk this over.

We had bought our old remote 40-acre homestead about a year before. It had been in bad shape: not a window in the house was intact (thanks to vandals), an old broken down barn and sheds needed to be cleared away, the meadows were eroded from being overgrazed, and the 2½ mile road into the place had big gullies which made it nearly impassable. But the homestead had a good spring for water, we had bought the land for a reasonable price, and our family was not afraid to work.

Although we could not yet afford to give up our jobs in the city and move

The Fifth Year

305

here, our whole family eagerly came to the "ranch" as often as possible, and we worked together to restore the old place. We'd made good progress: the house was tight and comfortable, the barn and sheds had been made into firewood, and now we were working on the road. With hand tools. We had to: it was all we had. It was an almost impossible job, even for five good laborers.

After we had settled down with hot cocoa and cookies, my husband Hubert looked at David and asked, "Well, son, if you refuse to work on the road with pick and shovel, what do you propose we do? We've got to fix the road."

"Dad, I'm going to buy a bulldozer." David stuck out his chin with determination. The rest of us gulped. We couldn't afford a **bulldozer.** Besides, none of us, Husband included, knew anything—zilch, zip, zero—about heavy equipment. A four wheel drive truck was our limit. We thought.

"Tell us how you are going to do that." We found out David wasn't just dreaming. He had it all planned and he'd been looking at bulldozers. "I'm going to take the twenty-five hundred I've saved from my paper route for a down payment. I've found a good used D-4 Caterpillar for five thousand. Dad, I can make the payments on the rest of it." This kid was only two months into his fifteenth year. Whew, I thought to myself, most kids want a *car* when they are sixteen.

We talked seriously. Hubert and David took a knowledgeable friend to inspect the dozer. The owner admired David's spunk so much he knocked $500 off the price without being asked. Hubert agreed to pay the owner the rest of the price, and he and David drew up and signed a contract for David to work on our road at so much an hour until he paid back his father. Our backwoods place had presented David with a problem and had given him the incentive to find a solution.

We hired an 18-wheeler to bring the Cat from Phoenix to the little town nearest our ranch, but since the big truck could not maneuver the last 10-mile stretch of dirt road into our place, the driver off-loaded the dozer and left Hubert, David, and me standing looking at the yellow beast. David was going to have to "walk" the Cat in, and the only time he had even been on a piece of big machinery was the 20 minutes when the previous owner had instructed him the week before.

David climbed up into the driver's seat and I heard him mutter, "Let's see, how do I start this thing?" Fear gripped me. I yelled, "Just be sure you know how to **stop** it." I started to climb up beside my son, but my husband beckoned me aside. "That was good advice you gave David, but I think you should ride in the truck with me. This is David's trial, and his victory will not be so sweet if his mother tags along at his elbow." Wise Husband.

Hubert and I hurried ahead of David to open a cattle guard gate, waited until he passed through, then closed the gate and dashed on to the next gate. We were often out of sight, but always stayed close enough to hear the dozer coming along the road. Up and down the twisty mountain road, through a creek, over a narrow pass, he plodded on at two miles an hour.

At dusk, five hours later, grimy and tired, he reached the ranch. As he rolled through the gate, he stood up and made the V-for-victory sign, triumph in his eyes. It reminded me of a newsreel I had seen when I was a girl during World War II; when Patton's men rolled into Berlin they had the same look and made the same sign.

David became a good Cat operator. He had to: crawlers don't make money standing still. He became a competent grease-monkey. He had to: crawlers need maintenance. And he became an expert welder. He had to: crawlers break. He fully paid his father with work, and one summer, before he graduated from high school, he and his brother used the dozer to haul logs for a sawmill.

When David graduated from college, he wanted to go to medical school. Among other schools, he applied to the Uniformed Services University of the Health Sciences, a medical school in Washington, D.C., that educates doctors for the armed forces and public health. Entrance requirements were tough. Some questions on the application were, "What university did you graduate from: West Point, Annapolis, Harvard, Yale or Other? What books have you authored? What public office have you held? Have you chaired a charitable organization?" His answers, "Other, None, None, and No," didn't look very impressive. After all, he was only 21 years old. Then he came to the last question: "What other experiences have you had that make you feel you would be a good candidate for this school?" David groaned in despair.

"Tell them about your bulldozer and how you learned to solve problems in the backwoods," I suggested. David shrugged and started writing. It was all he had to offer. It was enough. Out of 3,000 applicants, he was chosen by the army to fill one of the school's 97 places.

A few weeks later, Second Lieutenant Burris attended a reception for the new enrollees of the school on the grounds of Bethesda Naval Hospital in Washington, D.C. It was a glittering affair: military brass, congressmen who supported the school, professors from the school, the Surgeon General of the United States—an intimidating affair for this young man who had been raised in the backwoods of Arizona.

When it came time for David to be presented to the officer in charge of the Selection Committee for the school, two silver oak leaves, one on each side, escorted and announced him to the general. "Burris? Burris? Ah, yes, from Arizona. The one with the yarn about the bulldozer."

Our lowly second-looie drew himself up to full height, looked One-star straight in the eyes, and said, "Sir, that was no yarn—that was the truth." Oak-leaves drew audible breaths. One-star's eyes narrowed; he started at David's head and slowly, slowly looked him over down to his toes, then slowly, slowly he looked him up again to his eyes. He found the young man not defiant, nor arrogant, but simply telling the truth and as unwavering as cold, hard steel. A smile crept into One-star's eyes and he stuck out his hand. "Welcome to the Army Medical Corps, Burris. We need young men like you!"

Later, I asked David what he was thinking during that eternity of scrutiny. "Promise you won't poke me, Mom?" he smiled. I promised. "I was thinking that if One-star wanted to become a two-star, he needed to take lessons from my mom on how to back a guy up against a pine tree and do a **real** stare-down." I was sorry I'd promised.

All during his four years of medical school, and during his year of internship, when David got tired or discouraged, he would lean back in his chair, close his eyes and relive some of our escapades at the ranch. It gave him strength to "carry on."

After internship, David was assigned command of a small army clinic just outside Heidelberg, Germany. He was appalled when he learned the medics under him had only studied how to rescue wounded from manuals; they had never had hands-on, practical training. David knew how hard it was to climb around on big equipment carrying heavy tools, let alone how hard it would be to quickly extract and carry off a limp, wounded body.

He moved the entire unit out into the field and made them practice, first by carrying awkward sand bags, then by carrying one another. He drilled and drilled and kept on drilling, even after he became unfondly known as "Ol' Bulldozin' Burris." Later, some of the corpsmen David trained were called upon to use that training in the Gulf War.

Today, David is a Lieutenant Colonel. He is a surgeon and a Fellow of the American College of Surgeons. He is also Board Certified in Trauma Surgery and Board Certified in Trauma Intensive Care. He is stationed at Walter Reed Medical Center in Washington, D.C., where he does surgery on both active and retired army personnel, their families, congressmen, and anyone else eligible to be admitted to Reed. He is also assigned on a rotating basis to do surgery on the emergency patients admitted to one of the city hospitals in Washington.

There, he is on the forefront of a very real war—a war the young people of our inner cities are waging on one another. His heart is broken by what he sees. He has told me over and over how much he wishes those young, aimless, and angry inner-city kids could be transported to the backwoods, even if it were just for a few weeks or a summer, and be challenged by a big interesting world without drugs and gangs. David does what he can to counsel those who are his patients, but by the time they come to him, most are too hardened to listen. He keeps on trying, though.

David phoned me yesterday. He was waiting to operate on his fourth trauma patient of the morning. He was tired, so he put his feet on his desk and let his thoughts wander back to the ranch. "What are you and Dad doing?" he wanted to know. As it happened, we were just getting ready to go out and service the bulldozer. We have become the grease-monkeys— we had to, our sons are all grown and gone.

"I'm glad you called," I told him, "we are having trouble taking a filter loose. How do you do it?" He explained over the phone, long distance, how to get to the filter.

"Well, Mom, I've got to go. Just got paged, my patient is ready." There was a brief pause. "Mom?"

"Yes?"

"Thanks for the time we spent in the backwoods."

"You're welcome, David." Δ

A BHM Writer's Profile

Edie Norling

Edie Norling lives outside a small town called Montello in Wisconsin. Besides writing she works as an office nurse and chiropractic assistant.

She and her husband, who is also a writer, live on a 35-acre farm, and all experiences she writes about happened on the "farm." She enjoys organic gardening, crafts, reading, and messing around with things she hasn't done before.

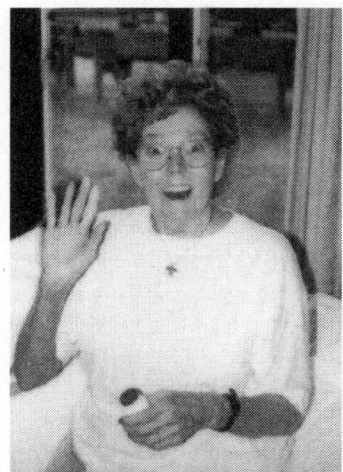

A Backwoods Home Anthology

BUILDING

Building an expensive log house—the cheap way

By Robert L. Williams

(Note: This is the first of two articles that will explain how you can build a comfortable and superb log house for an incredibly low price. In this first lesson you will learn how to cut the logs for the outside walls for less than $100, and then you will learn how to build the walls.)

Anyone planning to build a log house is in for at least two major surprises, one great, one not so good. The not so good one is that a log house is a lot of hard work, uncertainty, frequent problems, and considerable expense, if done the usual way.

The great surprise is that there is a way to build a terrific log cabin or house with very little work, virtually no problems or disappointments, and only a fraction of the cost of building the traditional log cabin, if you use our way.

When we built our log house, we used full-length logs that were 60 feet for the front and 40 feet for the sides. Total cost of all of the outside logs was $132.64. Your cost will probably be much less. Most people do not want a log house as large as ours.

The finished product of our log house construction project: 4,300 square feet—the equivalent of 25 rooms and two decks—and all at a cost of $20,000.

The key to the whole job is that your major implements are a chain saw, a chalk line, and a four-pound hammer. You will need some of the other basic tools, but with the three mentioned above you can build most of the actual log part of the house.

Basements, foundation walls, and chimneys will be dealt with in a future article, but for now, we'll concentrate on the part of the structure that will be composed of logs.

Assuming that the foundation wall or other underpinning is already in place, that whatever sub-flooring you plan to use is installed, and that all you need at this point are the log walls themselves, here's what you and your chain saw can do.

Cutting the logs

First, discard the notion that a log house must be built with an adz and other pioneer implements. Rest assured that if the hardy pioneers had owned a trusty chain saw and had access to fuel, they'd have dumped the axe and the adz and all the rest in a flash and started jerking on the starter cord.

Determine the size of logs you need for the walls and set about sawing them. Let's settle on logs that are ten inches high and eight inches thick.

Find the straightest, truest, longest, and most knot-free tree trunks you can find that are approximately the size you need. If you plan to have outside dimensions of (for talking purposes only) 40 feet by 28 feet, then you can calculate the number of logs needed. Be sure to allow two extra feet in length for each log. In other words, the logs will extend one foot past the corner at each of the four corners.

If you want ceilings eight feet high, you will need ten logs on each wall: that is a total of forty logs, half of them 28 feet long and half of them 40 feet long, with deductions for windows and doors. At these parts of the walls you can use shorter logs.

Now determine from your working plans how many full-length logs you will need. For many log houses, there

Use a square and a level to mark off the exact size of the timber you want for the house.

308

The Fifth Year

Sometimes even the worst-looking logs will emerge as beautiful squared timbers for the log house. Notice the outline of the finished log on the end of the uncut log.

is a need for full-length logs only above the door framing. A very simple way to deal with the log numbers is to use eight 10-inch logs, and your door frame will be 80 inches high. If you want a lower door frame, use seven 10-inch logs and one eight-inch log for a 78-inch door frame.

You will then need only one or (at most) two full-length logs to take you to the top of the wall. So locate two or four full-length logsthat are 40 feet long and two or four 28-foot logs. These logs can be of pine, poplar, or any other type that meets your basic requirements.

Don't be afraid of poplar. It is very strong and durable, as long as it is kept off the ground or concrete, and it hardens to the point that it rivals many other hardwoods. In the Great Smoky Mountains, there are poplar log houses that have stood for over 200 years and are still in super shape.

Now you are ready to begin sawing. Locate a tree that will be at least ten inches in diameter at the small end. Drop the tree and cut off everything longer than 42 feet. That allows two extra feet for squaring and miscalculations, and allows for the log to extend one foot past the corner, as indicated above.

Use pry bars or poles to raise the log until it is at least six to eight inches off the ground. Place a short length of log under the 40-foot log so that it is off the ground along its entire length. This is so that your saw will not dig into the dirt and dull the chain as soon as you start to cut.

Saw along the cut line by first cutting a two-inch groove and then following the groove along the entire length of the log.

Square the ends of the log and lay off the dimensions of the finished log. Do this on both ends of the log.

To mark the cut lines, use a square and a level for marking. (You can make both of these within minutes with a chain saw if you don't want to spend the money.) First, go to the small end and hold the square to the top edge of the log where you will have at least 10 inches across. Mark along the line horizontally.

Now use the square to mark vertically from each end of the horizontal line. Mark the horizontal line for ten inches and then drop the two lines. Then measure down eight inches on both lines and mark another horizontal line.

When you have finished, you will have an eight-by-ten log outlined. It is important that the top and bottom lines be perfectly horizontal. You must have a true rectangle if the log is to be straight and true.

Now go to the large end and repeat the process until you have another perfect rectangle. Center the rectangle on the end of the log, just as you did on the first end.

Drive a nail into the top left corner of the first rectangle or have someone hold a chalk line at that point. Stretch the chalk line across the top surface of the log to the other rectangle, where you will hold the line at the same corner. Snap a chalk line along the entire length of the log.

Now it's time to crank the saw. Be sure that the chain is sharp and go to one end of the log and pull the tip of the saw bar along the chalk line until you have cut a groove (or *kerf*) that is about two inches deep. Be sure to stand on the side of the log that is opposite the cut line. By doing so, you will be well out of the way in case the chain slips from the kerf, because there is no way you will accidentally cut through a log that is a foot or more in diameter.

When the entire log is grooved, go back to the starting point and cut deeper, pausing from time to time to

As you finish slabbing one side, turn the log and slab the other side. Keep the saw as straight as possible as you cut. If you allow it to slant, your cut will damage the timber.

see that the saw is following the vertical line on the end of the log. Hold the saw as level, from left to right, as you can. Continue cutting until you have cut all the way through the end of the log.

Once you have made a true start, it is easy to keep the rest of the cut true. Don't try to force the saw. Tilt the saw downward until the bar is in the first groove you cut. Be sure that the bar stays in the groove the remainder of the way. If you do so, you will have a smooth and straight cut for the first side of the log.

You may have to stop and brush away sawdust so you can see the groove. Do this rather than let the saw run out of the cut line. When the first side is slabbed, roll the log over so that the flat side is facing down. The log will now remain stable and motionless for the next two cuts.

Repeat the chalking for the next cut and then saw off the slab. Then cut the other side. You now have three straight cuts. Roll the log so that you can make the final cut just as you made the first three.

The first cuts will be slow and awkward, but as you learn better how to handle the saw and its way of cutting through the particular wood you are using, you will pick up speed. The first log will seem to take forever to cut. You may spend an entire day on that first log, but you will quickly learn how to speed up the work, and you will soon be able to cut a log in an hour or so.

Leave the log where it is and cut the other top logs until you have everything from the door up to the top of the wall. Now decide where you want the doors and mark the rough door openings. Measure from the outside of the rough opening to the end of the wall. Allow for an extra foot or 18 inches.

If it is 18 feet from the rough opening to the corner of the house, make the logs 20 feet long or so. Cut all the logs that will be used from the foundation wall to the bottom of the windows. You may want to vary the dimensions of the logs, if necessary, so that the top of the log will correspond with the bottom of the window frame. If you want the bottom of the windows to be at 40 inches, use four 20-foot logs ten inches high. If you want the window bottom to be 36 inches, use three logs 12 inches high.

If there are to be windows between the door and the corners, measure and mark off the rough window openings. Then cut the logs accordingly. Some of them will be only four to six feet long.

As you cut the logs, leave them all on their blocks so that they can begin to dry out. While they are drying, you can begin work on the basement or foundation walls.

Installing the sub-floor

When you've got the logs ready to stack into walls, you must first build your floor framing, just as you would if you were building a traditional frame house. Install the floor joists 16 inches on center and then prepare to cut out for basement stairs or any other irregularities in the floor plan. (Remember, we'll cover the foundation in a later article.)

Next, install your sub-flooring. The usual and best way is to use 5/8-inch or one-inch plywood (whatever your local building code requires). To install the plywood sub-flooring, nail the panels in place at right angles to the floor joists.

Start the first panel and line up the outside edges of the panel with the outside edges of the floor framing timbers. The first panel will stretch across six joists, including the first framing timbers, which will be doubled. In other words, the eight-foot panel will cover the first or outside framing timbers and four more, for a total of 96 inches.

Let the sub-flooring panel end halfway across the top edge of the floor joist. If you do so, the next panel

When the first cuts are made, roll the log over to make the final cut. The result is a timber like this one, that was cut in little more than an hour and at a cost of less than one dollar.

A Backwoods Home Anthology

If your logs are large enough, you can split them down the center and make a timber out of each side. Or, if a log is too small to use for timbers, you can split it to make the ramps on which you'll slide the wall timbers.

will also have nailing room on top of the joist.

Some builders prefer to start with a half-panel; that way, the panels are staggered, and no two rows of panels will end at the same joist. Such a nailing arrangement will assure you the greatest strength and stability for the flooring as well as the floor joists.

Moving the logs

Then it's time for fun. You are ready to start stacking logs to form the walls. If you have a fork lift or other equipment that will lift the logs for you, the work will be simple and easy, but most families living in backwoods areas do not have access to such equipment and must improvise. Here's how to improvise:

If you must move logs, there is a reasonably easy way to do so. Use a pry bar and fulcrum to lift the front end of the log, and while the log end is in the air, place a short length of log under the log. This short log should be three to four feet in length and at least ten inches in diameter. Next, go to the far end and repeat the process. Add a third short log in the center of the long log.

Now fasten a chain around the end of the log and use a pickup truck, garden tractor, or other machine to pull the log until it is parallel with the front side of the house. Keep the log at least six to eight feet from the base of the foundation wall.

When you are ready to lift the log into position, work out a sliding arrangement. This means that you locate a log ten inches in diameter and rip it down the exact center. Then take the two log halves and stand them so that they lean against the foundation wall. They will serve as ramps, and you will slide the wall logs up them and onto the platform. The top end of the log halves should extend ten inches over the edge of the foundation wall and sub-flooring, while the lower end should be grounded firmly in the soil in front of the house.

You should drive a stake at least a foot long into the soil in front of the lower end of the ramp log so it can't slip and slide off the foundation wall when you start sliding the constuction logs up and onto the sub-flooring.

Before you start sliding and prying the log upward, be sure to have nearby a hammer and a small block of wood (a six-inch block of 2 x 4 works well) to use as a chock block. The best possible chock block is made of a 2 x 6 that is cut diagonally so that it resembles a triangle.

Start a nail into each of two chock blocks, so that when you need them, all you have to do is drive the nail into the ramp log that the full-size log is sliding on.

You are now ready to manhandle the first log into position. Use a pry bar to raise the first end of the log two or three feet. When the log end is as high as you can reasonably get it, place the chock block in place and drive the nail into the ramp log, so you can release the log end and it will not slide back downhill.

Go to the other end and lift it as you did the first end. Slide the log up as you did before, but this time you can take the end two feet or so higher than you did the first end. Install the second chock block at that point.

Keep jockeying the log upward, driving in the nails of the chock blocks at each stop. When you reach the top, slide the log gently off the ramp logs and let it down easily onto the sub-flooring.

Now work the log across the floor surface to the place where it will be installed. The easiest way is to use two or three very small round sticks. Broomsticks work wonderfully. Use a crowbar to pry up the end of the log and insert the first broomstick or sapling under the end. Let the end only rest under the log and let the long part of the stick extend toward the wall where the log is to be installed.

Do this at both ends and in the middle. When you are ready, you can push one end of the log at a time until you reach the end of the sticks. Lift the log by prying with a crowbar and re-insert the sticks and repeat the process. Keep doing this until the log is at the desired position.

The Fifth Year

Building the walls

If you plan to use anchor bolts, these should be installed before you start to secure the first logs.

You must now fasten the log in place, once you have shifted it so that one foot of log extends past the corner limits of the foundation framing. If you plan to have a rough door opening on that wall, now is the time to mark off the rough opening. The end of the log should reach to the rough opening mark.

Align the exterior side of the log with the floor framing and the foundation wall and sub-flooring. Then begin to spike the log into position.

Use fluted spikes. These are foot-long spikes with spirals on them, almost like giant screws. As you drive these into the wood, they turn and screw their way through the wood. The result is that they are almost impossible to pull out.

At one point, we had spiked two logs together and found that we needed to remove the top one. After prying with all our might and using all the leverage we could manage, we finally succeeded in removing the log—but only after the head of the spike pulled through the whole log and out the bottom. The fluted part of the spike remained in the bottom log.

What this tells us is that it's going to take a tremendous force to pull these logs apart once they are properly spiked. That makes for a strong house. You can buy fluted spikes from several suppliers. If you cannot locate them, use 100-penny nails. These do not work as well, but they are far better than whatever is in third place.

You will find that it is difficult to drive the fluted spikes without bending them. Your best bet is to use an electric drill with a quarter-inch bit to drill a pilot hole through the log. Then use a one-inch bit to drill a larger hole for countersinking the spikes. Depending upon what you use for countersinking, you may be able to get by with a 5/8 inch drill bit.

Once the pilot hole is drilled, drill the countersink hole half-way through the log, or at least four inches deep. Use a four-pound hammer to drive the spikes down to the top surface of the log, and then start to countersink.

One of the best homespun methods of countersinking is to use a large bolt. Stand the bolt so that the small or threaded end rests atop the fluted spike. Then hit the flat head of the bolt with the four-pound hammer until the

You can slab a log in just a few minutes. In the background you can see the rising log wall and the rough openings for a window and a door.

spike is driven through the remainder of the log and into the wood below it. In this manner, the log is now securely fastened to the floor framing and sub-flooring.

Complete the first wall length now. If there is a rough door opening, start the next log at the far side of the rough door opening and continue the log to the next corner. When this is done, you have the first log course for one wall.

Complete all the spiking now. You should drive in one spike every two feet along the entire length of the log.

Now you have completed the first course on the front wall. Next, do the same thing with the back wall. Repeat all the processes as described before.

When you are ready for the end walls, measure carefully and cut the end logs so that they fit exactly. If you are uncertain of your measuring skills, lay the end log so that it spans the two front logs. Then mark along the inside of the two installed logs and along the inside edge of the end log.

Use a chain saw to under-cut the end log along the lines you just marked. Place blocks under the end log so that it will not crash to the floor when the cut is made.

When you are ready, slide the end log into place and drive in the fluted spikes as before. Now, however, you need to drive one spike from the outside edge of the front and back logs and into the ends of the end log. You now have the logs tied together securely. Do the same with the other end log.

Then start the second course by using the system known as the *butt-and-pass* method. This is a very simple and useful method that is an alternative to the more traditional (and difficult) dovetail corners. Dovetail cuts are tricky, and it is very easy to ruin a log. This is a minor disaster, because you may have to cut an entire new log to replace the one you mangled. The butt-and-pass system is so easy that it is virtually impossible to foul up.

When you start the second course of logs, start with an end log, rather than front or back. This time the log will lap over the front and back logs and stick out one foot past the outside edge of each. Use the fluted spikes again every two feet, and always use two spikes, one in each direction, at the corners of each course.

When the end logs are installed, slide the front and back logs up and maneuver them into place. These will slip between the end logs on this course. For the third course, install the front and back logs first and then cut the end logs so that they fit between them, as you did before. Alternate this pattern all the way up the wall.

When you reach the proper height, end the logs where rough window openings are marked. You can build in rough window and door openings as

A Backwoods Home Anthology

This view shows the wall risen above rough openings for windows and a door.

soon as at least two logs are in place. To build the rough opening framing, use 2 x 8 lumber and a square to get true square corners at all points. Use 60-penny nails to drive through the framing timbers and into the ends of the logs. Use 20-penny nails for the corners of the framing rectangle.

Keep a level against the rough opening frames until you are totally positive that you have correct vertical and horizontal readings on all timbers. Then nail braces to the framing and to the logs. Run other braces from the inside of the rough opening frames to the sub-flooring. The purpose of these last braces is to keep you from letting the walls get out of true vertical (or *plumb*) position.

As you approach the top of the door or window frames, keep a constant check to see that the final log along the side timbers of the framing will end very close to the top of the framing. The log that crosses the rough opening frames should fit flush along the previous course of logs and also flush along the top of the rough opening framing.

At the end of every two courses of logs, use a line level to run from end to end and from front to back to see that you are keeping the walls even. If you do not keep them as accurate as possible, you will encounter great difficulties when you are ready to install roof rafters.

When you cross the window and door rough openings, your wall will be nearly high enough. If the rough door opening is 80 inches high, you have six feet and six inches in ceiling height at that point. When the next log is installed, you will add ten more inches to that height, making a total of seven feet and four inches. So you can see that the log that crosses the rough door opening plus one more will give you adequate height for a ceiling.

You will see quickly that the higher you go, the more difficult it is for you to get the logs onto the floor area. The split log used for sliding the logs into the area will work well for the most part, but you may need to go to longer log ramps when you reach the fourth or fifth course.

An excellent method is to use a log at least 14 feet long, so that you have as much sticking up over the log wall as you have on the outside. When you push the log up as high as possible, go to the inside and then pull down on the ends of the logs. You will achieve a sort of see-saw effect, and as you lower the log ends, the construction log will slide slowly down the incline.

A second method that works is to use two more short logs on the inside of the cabin. When the log reaches the top of the wall, insert the ends of the short logs under the wall log and then pry downward, and again the log will slide slowly and gently down the shorter logs.

When you reach the final course and your line level tells you that all walls are the same height, you are in excellent shape. If you find that one wall is too low, make little chock blocks to put under the top log. Make the blocks thick enough to raise the top log to the proper height, wide enough to reach across the top of the support log, and a few inches long.

Next: Wall framing, chinking, and roof construction. ∆

A country moment

Clamming on northern California's Pacific Coast

The Fifth Year 313

A Backwoods Home Anthology

INDEPENDENT ENERGY

Making and using a solar cooker

By Joe Radabaugh

Solar cooking is a delightful alternative to conventional cooking methods. The solar cookers available today really work and they deserve serious evaluation by a much larger audience. For 40 years, small groups of people have been using and refining some very good designs. But these designs have, for the most part, gone unnoticed even by those involved with alternative energy. With such a lack of support, you'd think they would have vanished from view long ago. But they haven't.

The people who have taken the time to integrate solar cooking into their lives find the motivation to keep refining the designs comes from the tools themselves: solar-cooked foods taste delicious and the ovens are fun and easy to use.

My own involvement with solar cooking began in the mid-seventies. I found myself drawn to the alternative energy movement. Those were idealistic and innocent times, but they were also serious and important times.

Started as a hobby

It was during those days that I saw my first solar cooker and began the hobby that led to the cooker described in this article. I started out building the most efficient styles I could come up with. Later, while keeping this efficiency, I strove to simplify the building process, the materials needed, and the actual use of the cooker. The cooker is now basically cardboard, aluminum foil, and glass. Yet, because of the design, it is remarkably efficient and durable.

It looks so simple now, but you should realize that this simplicity took years of effort and many accidental breakthroughs. The testing for this cooker is now complete.

What I have included here is a very good starter model that can lead you and your family to a lifetime of enjoyment without threatening your pocketbook. A solar cooker can easily be built for under $10.

Gathering materials

The solar cooker aimed at the sun

The first step involves a search for cardboard boxes in your local grocery and department stores. For the oven box, you are looking for two particular boxes. These can be rectangular (easier to find) or square (their collectors work better). The smaller of the two boxes becomes the inner box, so it defines the cooking area and the power of the cooker. For a medium size cooker, the area of opening of the inner box (length times width) should equal 120 to 160 square inches, and it should be 9 to 12 inches deep. The larger box, the outer one, must be two to three inches larger in all directions.

For collectors, find four flat pieces of regular (not double strength) cardboard from appliance or bicycle stores. These should be about two feet by three feet. And gather five to seven more boxes which you will cut up for insulation.

Other things to gather:

1. Eight ounces of white paper glue (such as Elmer's™).
2. One small roll of 18" wide heavy duty aluminum kitchen foil.
3. A piece of double strength glass ½" larger than the length and width of the inner box (about $2 to $3 at a glass store). Buff the edges of the glass by rubbing a rock or metal over them, so they're not dangerously sharp.
4. A small amount of flat black paint.
5. (For square oven only:) One yard of elastic band material, say 3/8" wide, from a sewing store.
6. A baking tin that fits in the inner box, preferably one that puts a slight pressure on the sidewalls, to form a rack.
7. Some cotton cloth from recycled clothes.
8. Some string.

The oven box

Take the outer box and cut up cardboard pieces to fit in the bottom (cut the cardboard with a mat knife, being careful not to cut yourself). Make these layers thick enough so that, when the inner box is placed in the outer box, the top rim of the inner box is one inch lower than the top rim of the outer box.

The outer box must have two opposite flaps left sticking out. Tuck the other two between the inner and outer boxes. The inner box must have all of its top flaps bent out and all the way back so that they fit between the inner and outer boxes.

Now cut more pieces of cardboard to stuff between the inner and outer boxes until the inner box is wedged tightly. Doubled-over pieces look nicer.

The tops of these filler insulation pieces must be arranged so that, when the glass rests on the top rim of the inner box, it makes a good seal. (That is, you don't want big gaps where the heated air will escape.) Also, it must

314   *The Fifth Year*

A Backwoods Home Anthology

Side view of the solar cooker in action

be easy to slip a finger under the glass for easy removal.

In use, the cooker will be tilted toward the sun. Therefore, the side-

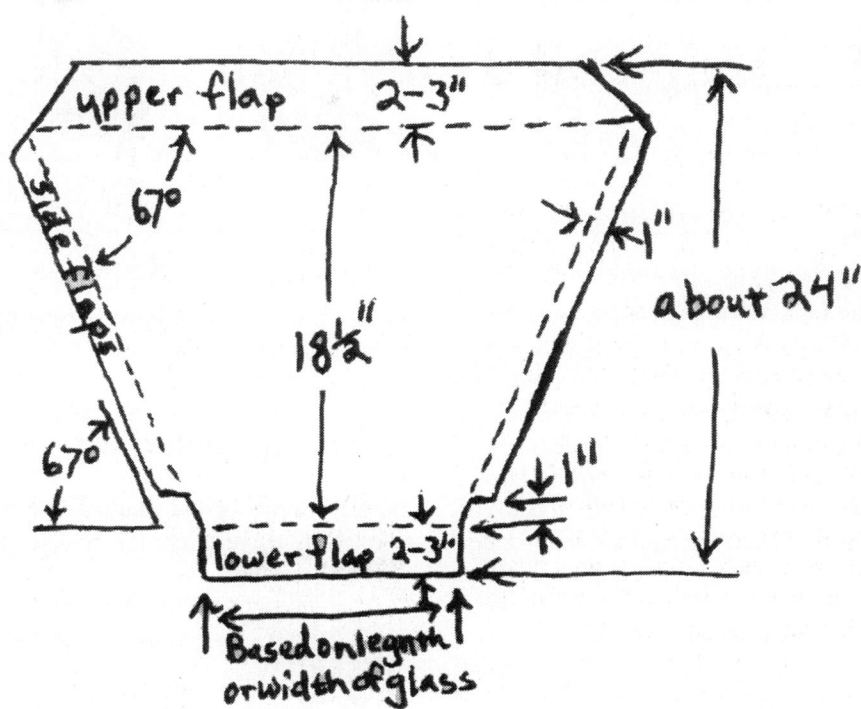

Here's the pattern for the collectors. The dimensions will depend on the dimensions of your box.

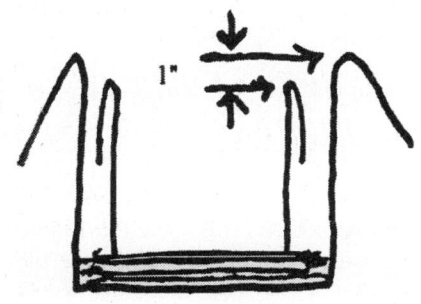

The top rim of the inner box must rest one inch lower than the top rim of the outer box.

wall, which will be lower when it's tilted, must be arranged so it will support the glass in position.

Now paint the inside black. Optionally, you may cut handholds in the outer box and squirt glue under the cuts to keep them from tearing out.

Note for later: The box will smoke slightly during the first couple of times it is heated up, but this is just a curing process. Also, cardboard shrinks slightly when heated, so you will have to repack later to keep the inner box tight.

The collectors

Draw the collectors, as shown, on the four flat pieces of cardboard. A square cooker will have all four collectors the same size, while a rectangular cooker will have two sizes, based on the length and width of the glass. The 67° angle can be found using a protractor, or by folding a piece of paper like an airplane, as shown in the diagram.

Cut out all four collectors. Then take a tool with a blunt point and crease a line along the dotted lines. Bend in on

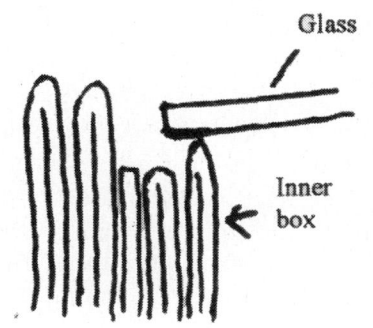

Arrange the filler pieces so the glass rests on the top rim of the inner box, and so you can slip a finger under the glass to remove it.

the crease lines. Next, bend the upper and lower flaps all the way over and glue them down. Press with weights until the glue dries.

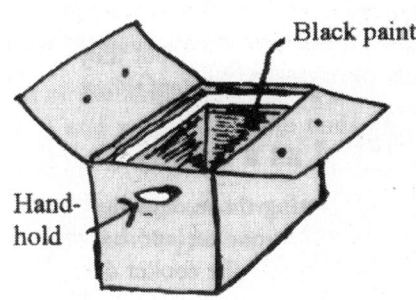

Leave two of the flaps on the outer box out, so you can tie the collectors to them when it's windy.

Gluing aluminum foil to the collectors

Roll foil over the collectors, and rub your finger over the side flap bends to show where to cut. Cut the foil so that it does not quite reach these bends; it will be easier to center later. Do not cover the side flaps.

The Fifth Year

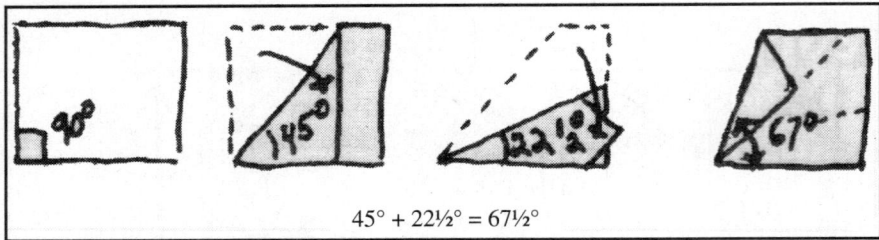

You can find the 67° angle by folding a piece of paper as shown here.

Smear a glue mixture (two parts water, one part white glue) over the dull side of the foil, using a piece of cloth and two to three tablespoons of glue mix. Line up the collector and lower it onto the foil, tap it lightly, and turn it over. Apply the foil to the side of the collector that is *not* glued to the bent-over upper and lower flaps. Being a little off center is okay, but if it's off too much, peel off the foil and try again. Press on the edges of the foil and pull out large wrinkles. Take a clean cloth and rub outward on the foil to smooth it.

Connecting the collectors

For a rectangular cooker, set collectors out as they will fit on the box and glue the side flaps together on two opposite corners. When the glue has dried, poke holes in the side flaps on the other two corners, placing holes near the cardboard bend, and tie these corners together with a cotton cord. When it comes time later to fold the collectors flat and pack them away, the rectangular collectors will be untied and separated into two sets of paired collectors.

For a square cooker, glue two opposite sets of side flaps together, as below. Then lay them out as they will fit on the oven box. Cut off the side flaps from one of the unattached corners. Connect this corner by laying

The side flaps are glued together with the foil sides facing each other.

these two collectors next to each other (about ¼" apart), with the foil sides down. Now cut a cloth about 18" x 4" and glue it over this corner, as shown. When the glue is dry, fold inward on this cloth hinge and arrange the collectors so that the unattached side flaps are on the outside and line up with each other. Poke holes near the bends of the side flaps, and tie the two segments tightly together with elastic material. This will allow these corners to separate slightly when the collectors are folded flat, but pulls the corners together when unfolded.

The slip-in piece

A slip-in piece made from cardboard and cloth is attached to the upper collector. This slips between the cardboard filler pieces of the upper sidewall for quick attachment of the collectors to the oven box.

To make it, cut a piece of cardboard 16" one way and the length of the glass the other way. Crease two lines and bend as shown. Then cut a piece of cloth six inches one way and the length of the glass the other way, and glue three inches of the cloth inside

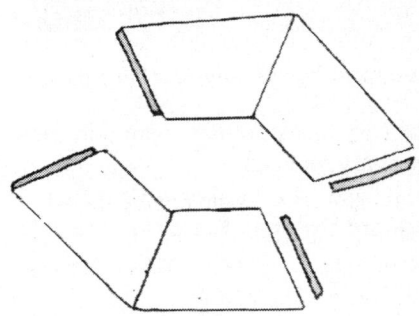

To make a cloth hinge for the collectors: First, cut off the side flaps from one corner.

the folded cardboard (leave three inches outside), as shown. Next, glue the cloth that was left out to the upper collector (glue it to the doubled-over lower flap of the collector). On square collectors, this would be to the right of the cloth hinge.

Finishing up, setting up

The rack: A dark baking tin is used for a rack to hold food and catch boil-over. It's nice if the rack puts a slight pressure on the sidewalls, for stability. If the baking tin has handholds, these may be bent for a better

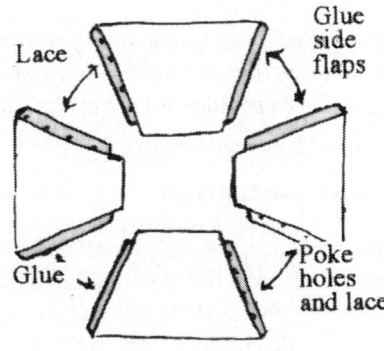

Connect the collector panels with glue and with laces.

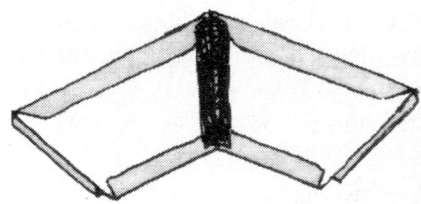

Next, glue the cloth to the panels.

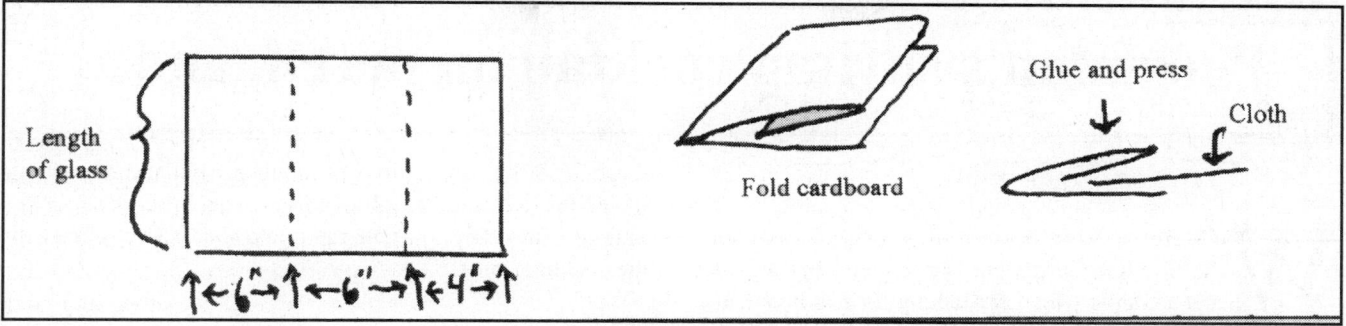

Making the slip-in piece

fit. You can also build a rack from wood, or by bending sheet metal.

The glass: Check again to see that it rests on the top rim of the inner box with no large air gap. The glass will become hot, so handle it by the edges or use a cloth. Keep the glass clean. Remember to buff the edges so they're not sharp.

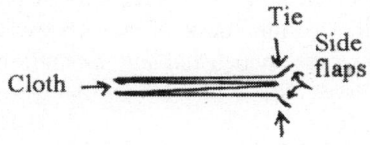

Hinged collector panels in the folded position

Propping the oven toward the sun: Use rocks or other objects in front and back. If you use only one, the wind easily tips the cooker.

Aiming: Use shadows created by the cooker to orient it; don't look at the sun. Approach the cooker from behind, checking shadows on the sides for east/west adjustments. Touch the oven box and see where the shadow line from the collectors crosses your arm for up/down adjustments. Aim the cooker in front of the sun's path.

Wind: Poke holes in the flaps left out of the oven box and also in the collectors on the top and bottom. Tie collectors to flaps with cotton cord.

Cooking

Jars: Boil and steam food in recycled jars, half-gallon or smaller in size. Painting them black will reduce cooking time, but leave a clear strip to see food by using tape when painting.

When cooking, don't overfill jars with beans and grains, as these foods expand. You can poke a hole in the lid or leave it on loose to avoid pressure buildup. If food is actively boiling, open jars slowly to release any built-up pressure. I've never broken a jar because of pressure buildup. If a lid sticks, tap around the edge, or pry up under it, to release any vacuum pressure. It should then open easily.

Learn to cook with more than one jar at a time. Start with the longest-cooking food, and when it is boiling, add more jars. Learn which foods (grains, potatoes, squash, lentils, etc.)—and what quantities of them—you can cook in one pass, so you can

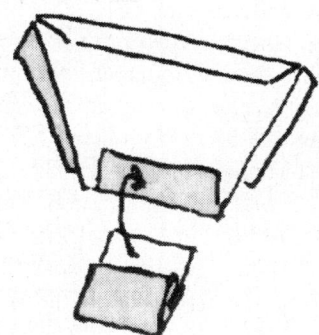

Attach the slip-in piece to the upper collector.

cook when you are gone all day. Learn cooking patterns that fit your lifestyle.

Beans: Use 2¼ cups of water for 1 cup of beans. If you boil them actively over a long time, add more water. Pintos take the longest.

Grains: Most grains cook better if you preheat the water in the solar cooker for an hour or so. Use a two-to-one water-to-grains ratio. Long grain rice can be put in the cooker in cold water.

Vegetables: These cook in jars with little or no water, or they can be added to beans and grains. Potatoes and sweet potatoes cook well on the rack, if lightly oiled. Otherwise, put them in jars. Winter squash cooks in its own skin. Corn on the cob steam-bakes in its own sheath.

Bread: Bread cooks best in dark, one-pound coffee cans. Oil the cans. Let dough rise in the cooker without collectors attached, then add the collectors when you're ready to bake. Bread shrinks, so it will come out of the cans with a gentle tapping when it's done.

Pizza and pies: Bake the crust first.

Etc.: Try jams, cinnamon rolls, cake, corn bread, cookies, and other munchies, as well.

When the food is cooked, you can fold the collectors down over the glass. This provides good insulation, so the food stays hot until you are ready to eat. Δ

Backwoods Home Magazine
has a Web site
that is easy to access
on your computer.
Just type in:
http://www.backwoodshome.com

Poor man's shrimp cocktail on perch, and...

By Pat Ward

We were working our cows by Copco Lake near the Oregon-California border one day and we met a couple who were fishing for perch. We had always referred to perch in that lake as trash fish until we tried the way they fixed them. So, this first recipe was their wonderful idea.

Poor man's shrimp cocktail on perch

> ¾ cup Catsup
> 1 Tbsp horseradish
> 2 tsp Worcestershire Sauce
> 1 Tbsp lemon juice
> Tabasco to taste
> about 2 lbs. of filleted perch

Mix the catsup, horseradish, Worcestershire, lemon juice, and Tabasco in a bowl and place the mixture in the refrigerator to let the flavors marry. Clean the perch by removing the heads and internal organs. Place the cleaned fish in a frying pan, in a single layer, with enough cold water to just cover them. Heat the fry pan over a high heat until the water just starts to boil then remove the pan from the heat and let it sit for one minute. Pour off the hot water and rinse the fish under cold water until they are thoroughly cooled through so they are no longer cooking. Skin and remove all the bones (a miserable job). Chill the fish in the refrigerator until you're ready to serve them and then serve them with the cocktail sauce.

Zucchini with green chilies

> 2 lbs. zucchini, cubed into ½ in. thickness
> 1 large onion, diced
> 2 Tbsp olive oil
> 1 6 oz. can of diced green chilies
> salt and pepper to taste
> 1 lb. jack cheese sliced in ¼ in. thick slices

In a frying pan, cook the zucchini and onion in olive oil until most of the moisture has been cooked out of the zucchini. Pour off any excess liquid. Add the green chilies, salt, and pepper and stir well. Use the slices of jack cheese to cover the squash then cover the fry pan and let it sit until the cheese has melted, and serve.

Zucchini melts

This was originally made for me by a friend who used eggplant. But the kids didn't like eggplant so I substituted some large zucchini that were running amok in my garden They loved it. I have since used it, as a one-dish meal, for the grandkids and adults alike.

> 2 eggs
> ¼ cup milk
> 1 large zucchini
> 1 cup flour
> olive oil for frying
> 1 large onion sliced ¼ in. thick
> 2 large tomatoes sliced ¼ in. thick
> 1 lb. cheddar cheese sliced ¼ in. thick

Preheat the oven to 350°. Gently beat the eggs and milk together until they're blended. Slice the squash into ½ inch slices and dip the slices in the egg-milk mixture then coat each one with flour. Fry these slices in the oil, a few at a time, until they're tender. Place the fried slices on a cookie sheet and on the top each piece place a slice of onion, a slice of tomato, and a slice of cheddar cheese. Place the cookie sheet in the oven and heat until hot and the cheese had melted.

Spaghetti chicken

This recipe was put together one night when I had a lot of unexpected company and nothing "ready" to feed them.

    8 chicken legs separated into thighs and drumsticks
    olive oil for frying
    garlic powder to taste
    1 large (32 oz.) jar of spaghetti sauce with mushrooms
    2 or 3 small cans of mushroom stems and pieces,
        drained
    salt and pepper to taste
    2 lbs. angel hair spaghetti

Fry the chicken in the olive oil until it's just browned on the outside. Drain off all the excess fat and sprinkle the garlic powder onto the chicken pieces. Pour the spaghetti sauce over the chicken and simmer it for ½ hour. Pour the mushroom pieces on top.

In a separate pot, cook the angel hair spaghetti according to the package directions. Drain. Pour the spaghetti onto a large platter, arrange the chicken on top of it, then pour the sauce over it. Sprinkle a line of freshly grated parmesan cheese in a row down the middle.

Habañero-apricot jam

This jam was introduced to me by a couple from Klamath Falls, Oregon. I loved the jam so much that they gave me two habañero pepper plants to raise my own peppers. Since I got the plants in the winter, there were no bees to pollinate the blossoms. So, I robbed a small feather from my Quaker parrot, Max, and used it to hand pollinate them. They produced small, beautiful, bright orange peppers that are considered by many to be the absolute hottest peppers around—as much as 800 times hotter than jalapeño peppers.

To make the jam, follow whatever recipe you use to make home canned apricot jam with the additional step of adding to the fresh chopped fruit two teaspoons of pureed habañero peppers and proceed with the recipe from there.

I puree my peppers, seeds and all, in a small amount of water. Another friend purees his along with several apricots. However you do it, be very careful when handling the peppers, the oil is very irritating to the skin, as well as the mouth.

My next kitchen experiment will be to try the peppers in other fruit jams. ∆

> The lonelies are out tonight
> Sneaking through my house
> Looking for me in the darkness
> They know I'm lying here awake.
>
> John Earl Silveira
> Ojai, CA

A BHM Writer's Profile

John Silveira

John Silveira is the senior editor of Backwoods Home Magazine and has written for it since issue No. 1. He is also the author of Sex and Sins in the Cemetery, a book of poems published by Backwoods Home Magazine in 1996.

Silveira grew up on a farm in New Hampshire. He says his father, in order to teach him how to shoot with accuracy, would give him one 22-caliber bullet a day and send him out hunting small game. He became a deadly accurate shot.

He has known BHM publisher Dave Duffy for 33 years, ever since they met at Suffolk University in Boston, Massachusetts, when the two of them would go into classes drunk and have to leave in the middle of some to go outside and puke. "Those were great days," Silveira recalls. "That Irishman could outdrink me then, but I can hold my own now."

Silveira is a mathematician by training and a historian by avocation, but his heart has always been in writing. He has been able to bring the mathematician's keen eye for accuracy to his writing and create authentic and very popular historical articles for the magazine. His articles are often used in homeschooling curriculums, or are reprinted in the alernative small press media.

Silveira is also a fiction writer and is working on several novels, some of a science fiction nature, and each one is weirder and scarier than the next. If you'd like to know how scary that can be, read Silveira's poetry.

Sourdough with substance

By Jennifer Stein Barker

This article is to follow up Richard Blunt's discussion of sourdough in the September/October (Issue No. 29) issue of *BHM*. Since I'm writing it, though, it's going to be on *whole-grain* sourdough, or as I call it, "sourdough with substance." These basic breads and pancakes will stick to your ribs and form a solid foundation for your meals.

My favorite starter is a combination of Richard's "Persistent Gert" and "Strong Trish." It combines the good qualities and flavors of both, and is extremely reliable. To make it, merely add one teaspoon dry yeast to the Strong Trish recipe. Do not cover tightly, as this starter is going to be very active for several days. If you are like me, and don't have an all-purpose flour around the house, use half-and-half whole wheat pastry flour and bread flour. (Using all pastry flour will produce a starter which will not hold its bubbles, while using all bread flour will produce one with so much gluten that you can't stir it). Once your starter has settled down and smells good and sour, you are ready to feed it and work with it. It will develop more flavor and become more reliable over time.

To feed, take your starter out of the refrigerator and bring it to room temperature. Look at the recipe you intend to use, and decide how much starter you need to make. Add warm (95°) water or milk, and flour, in equal parts. Figure that one cup each of liquid and flour will make 1½ cups of additional starter. Add the required amount of milk and flour, and set the starter in a warm place until it has bubbled and soured. If liquid separates out from the starter, this is perfectly OK. Just stir it back in, then remove the amount required in the recipe and store the remainder in the refrigerator.

Hint: If you do not have a warm place in which to sour your starter, try putting the container in a box with a towel on the bottom and a few jars of 95° water tucked in with it to keep it warm. Place a pillow or towel over the top to keep the heat in.

Another hint: I like to keep an extra two cups of starter in the refrigerator container so that I can have sourdough pancakes on impulse. It saves having to think of feeding the starter the evening before I want them. A one-quart yogurt container with a tiny hole punched in the lid is the perfect size for this.

Sourdough whole wheat bread

This basic whole wheat bread is given a delicious flavor by the addition of sourdough.

> 1 Tbsp. dry yeast
> 2 cups warm water
> 1 Tbsp. honey
> 1½ cups starter
> 3 Tbsp. oil
> 2 Tbsp. dark molasses
> Approx. 7 cups whole wheat bread flour

Dissolve the yeast and honey in the warm water and let sit in a warm place for about 10 minutes until it foams up. Add the starter, oil, and molasses to the yeast mixture. Add the first three cups of bread flour and beat the dough well until it looks smooth and satiny and comes together in glutenous strands. Add more flour ½ cup at a time, beating well with each addition, until the dough is stiff enough to knead.

Turn the dough out onto a floured board and knead 8 to 10 minutes, until the dough springs back vigorously from an impression. Place the dough in an oiled bowl, turning once to coat the top. Cover and place in a warm spot to rise until doubled in bulk (about 1 to 1½ hours). Punch the dough down and let rest a minute, then turn out of the bowl and form into two loaves. Place each loaf in an oiled 5x9" bread pan. Cover and let rise until doubled in bulk.

Preheat the oven to 375°. When the loaves have risen, bake them for 35 to 40 minutes, until the loaf sounds hollow when removed from the pan and tapped on the bottom. Remove from pans immediately and cool on a wire rack. When completely cool, they may be stored in plastic bags in a cool place.

Country French bread

This crusty, moist, slightly sour-flavored bread goes well with soups and stews. Makes one large oval loaf:

> 1 cup sourdough starter
> 1¾ cups warm water
> 6 cups whole wheat flour
> 1 Tbsp. yeast
> ¼ cup warm water
> Coarse cornmeal

Put the sourdough starter in a bowl with the 1¾ cups warm water. Add 2½ cups whole wheat flour, and beat well to form a thick batter or "sponge." Cover and let it sit overnight in a warm place to sour.

In the morning, dissolve the yeast in the warm water, and stir it into the batter. Fold in more flour ½ cup at a time. When the dough is too thick to stir in more flour, turn it out on a floured board and knead 8 to 10 minutes, until it is smooth and very springy. Place the dough in an oiled bowl, turn, and cover. Set it in a warm place to rise until doubled in size, about 1½ hours.

Sprinkle cornmeal on a baking sheet. Punch the dough down, knead it a minute on the floured board again, and shape it into an oval loaf. Place it on the baking sheet, cover and let rise until almost doubled, about 30 minutes.

Preheat the oven to 425°, and place an empty pan on the bottom shelf to preheat. Brush the top of the loaf with water, and make several cuts in the surface of the dough with a sharp knife, about ½" deep and 1" apart. Place the bread in the oven and pour a cup of hot water in the empty, hot pan. Bake for 35 to 40 minutes, or until the crust is golden-brown and the loaf sounds hollow when tapped on the bottom.

Pumpernickel

(*Asterisks flag ingredients changed in variations below.)

> 1 Tbsp. dry yeast
> 2 cups warm water*
> 1 tsp. honey
> 1½ cups sourdough starter
> ¼ cup dark molasses*
> 3 Tbsp. oil
> 2 Tbsp. caraway seed*
> ¼ cup cornmeal*
> 3 Tbsp. gluten flour (optional)
> 3 cups rye flour
> 3 cups whole wheat flour
> Additional wheat or rye flour as needed

Dissolve the yeast and honey in the warm water and set in a warm place for 10 minutes or so, until it foams up. Then add the starter, molasses, oil, caraway seed, cornmeal, and gluten flour (if used). Add the rye and whole wheat flours in alternating half-cups, starting with the rye flour and beating well after each addition, until the dough is stiff. Turn the dough out onto a floured board and knead for 10 minutes. This dough will not be as springy as an all-wheat dough, but it should stand up well when it is formed into a ball.

Place the dough in an oiled bowl, turning once to oil the top. Cover and put the dough in a warm place to rise until doubled, about 1½ hours. Then punch the dough down and let it rest a minute. Shape into two oval loaves and place on a large cookie sheet that has been oiled and generously dusted with cornmeal.

Preheat the oven to 350°. When the loaves have risen to double, brush the tops gently with water and bake them for 50 to 60 minutes, until they sound hollow when tapped on the bottom. Remove immediately from the pan and cool on a wire rack.

Swedish rye

*For the 2 cups warm water, substitute 1 cup warm water, 1 cup orange juice, and 1 Tbsp. grated orange peel. For the ¼ cup dark molasses, substitute 2 Tbsp. honey. Omit the caraway seed and cornmeal.

Sunflower rye

*For the ¼ cup molasses, substitute 1 Tbsp. honey and 2 Tbsp. dark molasses. For the caraway seed and cornmeal, substitute 1/3 cup chopped sunflower seeds.

Sourdough pancakes

A tangy way to start the day. This basic pancake recipe can be altered in texture and flavor by the substitution of rye flour or rolled grains for the whole wheat flour. Try adding a mashed banana or blueberries, too. Be adventurous! Makes about 16 four-inch pancakes:

> 2 cups whole wheat sourdough starter
> 1 egg
> 2 Tbsp. oil
> ¾ cup whole wheat flour (all-purpose, or a blend of bread and pastry flour)
> 1 tsp. soda
> Approx. ½ cup milk or water

Whisk together the starter, egg, and oil. Add enough milk or water to make a runny batter, whisking well to blend. In a small bowl, stir together the flour and soda until thoroughly blended. Combine the two mixtures, whisking until completely combined. It is not necessary to beat down the bubbles that form. If the batter is too thick to spread on the griddle, it may be thinned with additional milk or water. If it's too thin, just add a little more flour.

Heat a griddle or skillet on medium-high until a drop of water thrown on the surface will sizzle. Oil the griddle lightly, then pour or ladle batter on the griddle to make pancakes the size you want. Cook each pancake until bubbles form on the top, and the edges begin to set up. Flip and cook on the other side until golden on both sides.

Serve immediately with warm honey-maple syrup.

Honey-maple syrup

Mix real maple syrup and light honey in equal proportions (example: 1 cup maple plus 1 cup honey). Serve warm. ∆

How to keep those excess eggs

By Anita Evangelista

Chickens have no sense of timing. In early spring, a small flock can crank out bushel-baskets of sparkling white or toasty brown ovoids. Unfortunately, by then all the winter baking has become a mere memory, and a chicken-keeper is liable to become hopelessly swamped with the seasonal overproduction. And when baking season rolls around again, the hens have gone on vacation. In spite of lights, timers, and genetic manipulation, no one's found a way to completely fool the birds....so it looks like this over/under abundance problem will be with us for some time.

By a stroke of good luck, there are a handful of ways to keep eggs on hand even when the hens lay off. You may freeze eggs, put them in a solution of waterglass, or pickle them. The first two methods allow you to use "fresh" eggs long after they have been laid; the last method makes the edible goodies instantly available for snacks and hors d'oeuvres.

Freezing

Your home-grown eggs can rest comfortably in the refrigerator or cold room for a month to six weeks without losing too much quality. If you find the dozens piling up, consider freezing the excess. Here's how:

Whole eggs—Wash the egg in cool water until free of dirt. Crack eggs, one at a time, into a small bowl and inspect for bits of shell or other unwanted materials and remove. Pour the egg into a larger bowl. Continue in this fashion until all your eggs are opened. Carefully mix yolks and whites using a fork. Avoid beating air into this—it will leave you with tough end results.

At this point, some people add either salt or sugar (corn syrup or honey may be used) to the egg mixture. Salt is added at ¼ teaspoon per three eggs, and is used when you plan to use the eggs for main dishes or omelets. Sweetening, added at ¾ teaspoon per three eggs, is included when the eggs will be saved for baking. The addition of either salt or sugar helps to keep the frozen eggs free of lumps—but I've frozen eggs without either additive. I never seem to know in advance how I'll use the eggs later.

Next, pour the egg mix into ice cube trays, or place three tablespoons of egg per muffin cup into oiled muffin pans. Freeze until rock hard. Empty the frozen "individual eggs" into plastic bags or put inside freezer containers. Label and put into the deep freeze. When you want to use a single egg for cooking, just pull out one of these egg cubes and thaw until soft. Then treat it just like a fresh egg.

You can also freeze a number of eggs mixed together for using in special dishes. Be sure to label with quantity of eggs in the mix, and what the planned use will be.

Egg yolks—Separate white from yolks. Mix the yolks very lightly. If you wish, add 1½ teaspoon sugar or ¼ teaspoon salt to each half cup of yolks. Freeze in single tablespoon quantities, representing one egg yolk—or in larger quantities to fit your recipes. Label carefully!!

Egg whites—Separate white from yolks. Don't mix or beat these at all. Freeze individually at two tablespoons per ice cube tray section, or as a quantity. Thawed whites can be as stiffly beaten as fresh egg whites. Frozen eggs keep for nine to twelve months.

Water glassing

This is one of those old methods of egg preserving that Granny probably used when faced with an egg excess. Old crocks often show the tell-tale white film around their interiors which is characteristic of water glassing.

Water glass is actually sodium silicate, a sealing compound which is still in use—though hard to find. Our local plumbing supply shop has been unable to come up with a supplier for two years, and gets many calls for the stuff anyway. If you can locate water glass, it's relatively inexpensive and quite efficient at sealing the holes in egg shells for long term preservation. It will also seal your plumbing shut, so don't pour excess into plumbing!

Use a large jar, canning jars, or crock. Food grade five-gallon buckets may also work, though I've never tried them. Pour boiling water into your container and clean thoroughly.

You will be using three cups of water to each 1/3 cup of sodium silicate. Using an approximation suitable for your containers, boil and cool a sufficient quantity of water—this provides a fairly sanitized liquid to be used for storage.

Fill your container about half full with the cooled water, measuring as you go. Then, stir in the appropriate amount of sodium silicate.

Next, using a long spoon (avoid too much hand contact with the water glass), lower eggs into the solution one at a time. When your container is filled, leave about two inches of water glass above your eggs. Cover and date. Store in a cool place.

That's it! Water glassed eggs will gradually become watery and lose their high yolks and firm whites—-but can be stored safely at room temperature for four months, and up to a year if refrigerated or kept in a cool environment.

To use water glassed eggs, pull out an egg with a slotted spoon and rinse in cold water (rinsing your hands as well, if you've handled the solution). Crack the egg into a cup or small bowl. If it looks and smells acceptable (no sulfurous odor), it's safe to use.

Should an egg break in your water glass, don't try to use it. The remaining eggs will still be safe, although the

A Backwoods Home Anthology

solution will become progressively more smelly. Other eggs may absorb the odor, so it's best to remove them from the solution. Store those eggs in the refrigerator or a cold place and use as soon as possible.

Pickling

Pickled eggs are a rather expensive delicacy these days (check your supermarket and prepare for a shock), but they are exceptionally easy to make at home. They can be stored at room temperature, and make delightful additions to salads, on canape trays, for deviled eggs, sliced on ham sandwiches—and as a straight snack. What more could we ask for in a stored egg?

Use eggs which are at least a week old, though ten days to two weeks is better, otherwise they won't shell easily. Boil the eggs until hard boiled (a good ten minutes at hard boil), then quickly dunk the eggs in cold water. Shell.

Sterilize quart canning jars by rinsing in boiling water, or pour boiling water into your preferred container. Place shelled eggs into hot jars (a quart jar holds up to a baker's dozen). For each quart, add a teaspoon salt.

Prepare a pickling solution, using your favorite unsweetened recipe or this one:

Mix three and a half cups any type of 5% (or stronger) vinegar to each half cup of water. Add a quarter cup or so of thickly sliced onions. Bring to a boil. Remove onions.

Pour this basic solution over the eggs. If you are using canning jars, dunk your lids into boiling water, put onto jars and seal. Invert the jars to slosh vinegar solution on lids.

Then, let the jars cool. If using another kind of container, be sure eggs are completely covered by solution. Cool. Date and label.

If your vinegar solution was boiling hot and your eggs were still heated after shelling, the canning jars will seal. If your jars fail to seal, it's not a major worry—the pickling solution is strong enough to protect the eggs for some time. Keep unsealed jars in a cool place or in the refrigerator, and use first. I've kept pickled eggs for well over a year.

With any of these three methods, we can keep loads of excess eggs for a good long time. We'll show those chickens who's boss. ∆

Subscribe to *Backwoods Home Magazine* by calling

1-800-835-2418

The Fifth Year

COUNTRY LIVING

Some thoughts about my wood cookstove

By Dynah Geissal

I had just finished reading a short article of nostalgia about the Model T. It was written by two elderly gentlemen born in the last century. I closed the book and got up to take a shower. Checking the fire in the cookstove on the way, I mused that for a person born after World War II, there really isn't much that elicits such reminiscences.

A minute later I had to laugh at myself. What was I thinking? True, folks in town may not have much fondness for the thermostat on the wall, the furnace in the basement, or the kitchen range that heats food with a flip of a switch. To them, those things are taken for granted as necessities, and paying the power company is just another bill they must earn money to pay.

But a woodstove, now that's a different animal. It's almost a part of the family. I need ten cords of wood a year for our stoves and there are five months in which to get them. Stocking up on wood is like stacking the hay for the livestock for the long winter ahead. It's just a part of life—hard work, but a labor of love.

The cookstove provides heat for the kitchen as well as for cooking all our meals. Our summers are short and all our mornings are cool, so even in midsummer the cookstove heat is welcome. In those few weeks of heat I do all the day's cooking in the morning when it's possible.

I was given an electric pot, but I've never used it. Starting up the cookstove is the first morning chore and is as much a part of the early routine as brushing teeth and feeding baby chicks. By the time the first livestock chores of feeding and watering are finished, the water is boiling for tea and the kitchen is warm.

The cookstove is also our only source of hot water. In lieu of an electric or gas water heater, the pipes travel through the firebox and by convection fill the tank with hot water. There's plenty of hot water for dishes,

laundry, and showers. I have to admit, though, that when three adolescents were trying to shower before school it was a bit difficult—but that's been a while back.

The water jacket burned out many years ago and we replaced it with black pipe. We've replaced the grates several times, as well as the handle for the oven. But that old baby still works as well as when it was first made.

When the stove was given to me 20 years ago, the top had been sold for scrap metal. I had no trouble finding tops, but I could not find one with the correct dimensions. In the end, I used my saber saw with a metal cutting blade and fashioned one to fit (and ruined the saw in the process).

No other type of stove could be a part of my life like that wood cookstove is. Something is always cooking: soups or stews, of course, but also other things that would seem pretty weird on another kind of stove. Today, sap from our box elder is cooking down on the cool side of the stove, and bread is rising above it. In the fall, a huge cauldron cooks the pig heads. Most days find a large pot of water with a two-gallon bucket of milk inside, turning the day's goat milk into cheese.

In the late summer there is almost daily canning and blanching of vegetables for freezing. Huge pots of tomatoes that are being converted into tomato sauce, hot sauce, chili sauce, and catsup are nearly permanent fixtures during that season. And there's always a pot of water boiling, just waiting to make someone a cup of tea.

No, I never had a Model T, but that Monarch cookstove…I could write a book about that sweetheart. With a few minor replacement parts fashioned at home, that stove will last a lifetime. I like that. I could write a similar paean about wood heat stoves, but I'll save that for another time.

The point is that those of us who choose a simple country life surround ourselves with the things that are simple, functional, and meaningful in our lives. ∆

COUNTRY LIVING

Preventing and surviving stove and chimney fires

By Don Fallick

The great danger of a stove fire is that it may become a chimney fire or house fire. If the heat in the stove causes it to draw too fast, it can become uncontrollably hot, and warp, crack, or burn through the stove, stove pipe, or the flue, allowing the fire to escape into the house. Or the stove or flue may become hot enough to ignite nearby flammable materials. Finally, the hot gasses erupting from the chimney may carry sparks, or even burning chunks of wood, to the roof or the area outside the house.

The best way to cope with any of these disasters is to prevent them—at the beginning of the burning season—by checking all parts of the stove and flue for proper installation, cracks, thin spots, and especially for highly flammable creosote build-up in the chimney. Most of the "luck" traditionally associated with chimney sweeps can be summed up in one sentence: A clean chimney is less likely to burn your house down.

Increase your "luck" by cleaning the chimney several times during the heating season, by keeping the stove and flue in good repair, and by burning only dry, bare wood in your stove. Painted or treated wood, cardboard, old Christmas trees, and paper with gasoline, kerosene, or oil residues may burn hot enough to ignite any creosote not removed by cleaning. Avoid them.

Basic safety equipment

Basic safety equipment can sometimes spell the difference between a problem and a disaster:

• **Heat detectors** work better than smoke detectors in wood-heated houses. They cost a little more, but won't go off every time you open the fire door to load fuel.

• **Insulated gloves** should be kept near the stove for emergencies.

• **Fire extinguishers** in two types: a flare type (such as Chimfex, manufactured by Standard Railway Fuse Corp., Boonton, NJ 07005), for putting out the fire inside the stove, and a CO_2 or dry chemical type, for putting out any fires that may escape into the house. You'll need both kinds, as they are not interchangeable.

• **An emergency ladder** available in every upstairs room.

• **Fire fighting instructions**. Post copies of the following instructions near the telephone, the door, or other conspicuous places away from the stove. You don't want them damaged or made illegible by smoke, heat, or fire, and you don't want to be reading them next to a runaway stove. ∆

Fire Dept. phone:_____
Ambulance phone:_____
Chimney sweep:_____

If you have a stove fire

1. Alert everyone in the house to get out. Another adult or older child can do this while you're coping with the fire, then stand by to call the fire department or help fight the fire.

2. Close all stove doors and air inlets. If you catch it early, this step alone may extinguish the fire. **Never** throw water on a hot stove—it may cause the stove to crack! Use your flare-type extinguisher. Check for flare and fire-fighting instructions near the telephone.

3. Call the fire department. If your first efforts to fight the fire aren't immediately successful, call the fire department immediately, so they have time to respond. If you live in a remote location, or if roads are bad, it may take them longer to reach you. Every second counts.

4. Move flammable materials away from the stove and flue. If the fire hasn't spread, and if you think it's safe, search the house with your fire extinguisher in hand, checking for hot spots and removing endangered materials. Don't forget to check outside the house and in the attic, too. Children, pets, and the elderly should be out by this time.

5. Hose down the roof, to prevent the fire from spreading there. If there are overhanging trees, hose them down too. It's a good idea to keep a ladder available for this job.

6. Wait for the fire department. If all the above has failed to control the fire, there's little more you can do. Don't put your life in danger saving material possessions, when there's help on the way. The safest place to wait is outside. Make sure everyone is out of danger, and keep children calm and controlled.

7. After the fire is out, and the stove and chimney have cooled down, check them thoroughly for damage, and repair them before relighting the stove. Check all extinguishers and detectors and replace or recharge any that need it. Clean the chimney. Stove fires and chimney fires rarely burn off all the creosote present. In fact, they just dry it out and make it more flammable. Get it all out. If you don't have the equipment or knowledge to do it yourself, hire a professional. Δ

A BHM Writer's Profile

Dorothy Ainsworth

Dorothy Ainsworth likes to write for BHM because the readers may be people just like her—possibly squeaking by on little more than minimum wage, but with a big desire for shelter, self-sufficiency, and the peace of mind that ultimately comes from being true to oneself.

As a waitress and single mom rearing two kids on her own, she fiercely wanted security without being beholden to anyone. At 40, with no previous building experience, she bought a piece of land with a farm loan, read stacks of how-to books, and started in building her house. Her most powerful resource was drive. On a shoestring income she learned to use any cheap or free natural materials she could get her calloused hands on. With logs, stones, straw, and mud, an energetic person with imagination and research can create a home with his or her artistic signature in every touch.

Any discomforts of living on the barest necessities for a while were totally offset by indescribable feelings of fulfillment that came from everyday accomplishments.

Dorothy is now 54 and has 10 structures under her carpenter's belt: pumphouse, water storage tank, root cellar, barn, shop, storage building, small guest cabin, piano studio, and 2 log homes (rebuilt main house that burned). The average cost was $15/sq.ft. and, except for her land payment, she's debt free. Tunnel vision paid off and the journey was worth it.

Her future plans include writing a waitress book about her humorous experiences serving over 1 million people in 38 years. She also hopes to find time to indulge in her lifelong hobby and first love—photography. Meanwhile she's in the process of editing the videotapes she took of building the original house.

Venison recipes

By William Shepherd

Cooking wild game isn't as simple as preparing domesticated meat. Hunters don't have the option of hand picking tender cuts from the local supermarket. For instance, deciding which way to cook venison is as integral to successful cooking as is the actual preparation. Venison doesn't have any inner marbling fat to baste the meat while it's cooking, so it can easily be overcooked. Meat of this density should be cooked medium-rare, that is, brown on the outside, pale red in the middle. Cooked this way, most venison will be tender and juicy and have a meaty flavor. The same cut of venison, if cooked well-done, will be evenly browned from the outside to the center, but it will also be dry, tough, and flavorless.

Many people will wince at the idea of medium-rare venison, simply because they have been brainwashed for years by people telling them that it's not safe to eat venison unless it's fully cooked. Where this idea originated I have no idea, but it's simply a myth.

The key to cooking venison is suitable cooking methods. Just remember, venison is naturally lean, so tenderizing is often necessary. One of the best methods is marinating with milk, wine, and citrus juices. Overnight marinades tenderize and leave a very distinctive taste that will flatter the venison's flavor.

Braised peppersteak

Ingredients

- 1½ pounds venison steak shoulder or round steak
- 2 Tbsp cooking oil
- 1 4-oz can mushrooms
- 1 cup water
- 1 beef bouillon cube
- 2 Tbsp soy sauce
- 1 Tbsp sugar
- ¼ tsp garlic salt
- ¼ tsp pepper
- 1 green pepper, cut in strips
- 1½ Tbsp flour
- ¼ cup water

Marinate meat overnight, remove from refrigerator, cut steak into ¼" thick strips, brown meat in cooking oil. Add mushrooms, one cup water, bouillon cube, soy sauce, sugar, garlic salt, and pepper. Cover and cook five minutes. Add green pepper strips, cover, and cook an additional three minutes. Mix flour and ¼ cup water, add to skillet and stir until thickened. Serve over noodles or rice. Serves 4.

Crown roast of venison

Ingredients

- 1 venison roast, about 4 lbs
- ½ tsp garlic salt
- 1/8 tsp pepper
- ½ lb bulk pork sausage
- 20 oz can apple slices with juice
- 1/3 cup apple cider
- 10 slices bread, dried and cut into ½" cubes
- 2 Tbsp raisins
- ¾ tsp cinnamon
- ½ tsp cardamon
- ¼ tsp allspice

Mix garlic salt and pepper together, rub mixture into all sides of the roast. Place roast in covered roasting pan. Cook sausage in skillet until brown, drain excess grease. Combine next eight ingredients with sausage, stirring enough to moisten bread. Pour this mixture over roast; cover with lid. Insert meat thermometer into center of roast. Bake at 325° for two to three hours or until meat thermometer reads 135° to 140°. Time will vary. Garnish with cranberry sauce.

Venison pan fried steak

Ingredients

- 4 steaks, sirloin or rib, ¼" thick
- 3 Tbsp butter or margarine
- 4 medium onions, sliced thin
- 4 green peppers, sliced thin
- 2 Tbsp Parmesan cheese
- 1 cup mozzarella cheese, grated
- ½ tsp garlic
- ¼ tsp black pepper

Place butter or margarine in large heavy skillet, turn heat to medium. Add onions and green peppers, saute until tender. While onion mixture is cooking, combine remaining ingredients in small bowl. Remove cooked onion mixture from skillet; set aside. Add steaks to skillet. Fry one minute each side, turn heat to medium low. Spread onion and cheese mixture evenly over steaks. Cover and cook until cheese is melted. Serve hot on fresh bread. Serves 4.

Fried finger steaks

Ingredients

- 1 pound 1½" boneless venison steaks cut from the round sirloin or backstrap
- 1 tsp lemon-pepper seasoning
- ½ tsp salt
- ½ cup buttermilk
- 1 egg
- 1 cup all-purpose flour
- ¾ cup vegetable oil or shortening

Marinate meat overnight in lemon juice. Remove from refrigerator and sprinkle with lemon-pepper seasoning and salt. Cut into strips. Mix buttermilk and egg in small bowl. Dip strips in mixture and dredge in flour. Preheat iron skillet, add vegetable oil or shortening and brown steaks on both sides. Serves 3 to 4.

Broiled tenderloin

Ingredients

- 2 whole venison tenderloins, about 1¼ lb each steak.
- 1¼ tsp garlic salt
- ½ tsp pepper
- 2 Tbsp soy sauce
- 1 Tbsp ketchup
- 1 Tbsp vegetable oil
- ¼ tsp crushed oregano

Mix all ingredients except tenderloins in large container. Add meat, cover, and marinate four hours in refrigerator. Remove tenderloins from marinade. Briefly sear both sides over hot coals or under broiler. Continue broiling until desired doneness is obtained. Remove from heat, slice thinly and serve while hot. Serves 4 to 6.

Pan broiled chops

Ingredients

- 6 venison rib chops
- 2 Tbsp bacon fat
- 3 medium onions, sliced
- 1½ pounds fresh mushrooms, sliced
- 1/3 cup all-purpose flour
- 1 cup beef stock
- 1 cup milk
- ½ tsp salt
- ¼ tsp pepper

Lightly brown chops on both sides in bacon fat, using iron skillet over moderately high heat. Transfer chops to shallow pan; retain drippings in skillet. Broil chops at high heat five inches below heating element. Turn and broil till medium-rare. In the drippings in skillet, gently cook onions and mushrooms until lightly browned. Blend flour, stock, milk, salt, and pepper. Add to pan. Cook, stirring constantly until thickened and bubbly, about four minutes. Serve onion and mushroom sauce over chops while both are hot. Δ

A country moment

Jerry Henscher, of Lakehead, California, shows off a clam he dug out of the Humboldt Bay mud.

INDEPENDENT ENERGY

Converting your gas car to electric is no shocker

By Shari Prange

A small sedan, such as this VW Rabbit, is a practical electric family car.

The old advertisement said, "Your car is your freedom," but sometimes it feels more like indentured servitude. Actually, buying the car is only the beginning, followed by the registration, insurance, and inspections.

Then there's fuel. It seems like every time you get into the thing, it's thirsty. There isn't a gas station on every corner any more, and if you need diesel, you may have to hunt even further. This is especially inconvenient if you enjoy the solitude of life away from towns and cities.

Of course, you can put in your own fuel tanks at home. However, they can be as much hassle to refill as the car. And there are all the regulations about monitoring the tanks for leaks.

Then there's maintenance and repairs. An acquaintance of mine once said that you buy an internal combustion car over and over again—one piece at a time. And the newer cars are getting harder and harder for the home mechanic to work on.

The simple alternative

There is another option that can end your servitude: an electric car.

An electric car simplifies your life in many ways. The most obvious one is fueling. What can be more convenient than coming home and plugging in the car? No muss, no fuss. You don't have to go out of your way to find gas or diesel, and you don't have to deal with the regulations connected to home tanks.

Another beautifully simple aspect of the electric car is its maintenance—or lack of it. Say goodbye to the auto repair shop and the parts store. An electric car needs very little care, and what maintenance there is can be done easily by the owner.

An electric car can simplify your paperwork, too. If you live in a state that requires smog inspections, you don't have to participate any more. Once the state classifies your car as "electric" on its main computer, you are exempted from smog inspections.

As a final bonus, an electric car is a pleasure to drive, because it's so smooth and quiet.

Electric cars today

The electric cars available today are conversions. A small number are new cars converted to electricity by manufacturers. These range in price from $25,000 to $150,000, and are generally sold to fleets, such as utilities.

For the average person who wants an electric car, a more economical option is to convert a used car, or have the conversion done by a mechanic.

So just what is involved in converting a car to electricity? First, you remove everything related to the internal combustion system: engine, exhaust system, fuel system, and cooling system.

Then you add a charger, battery pack, speed controller, motor, and a few other small bits and pieces. Let's take a minute to tour a typical conversion, and see what each part does.

The charger

The electricity comes into the car through a charger. The car doesn't care where the electricity originates—a public utility, a small generator, a solar array, or even a wind generator.

The most common chargers use 110 VAC (volts alternating current)/20 amps input. These are popular because the charger is small and light, and 110 volt power is readily available. If the car has used up its entire capacity, this charger will bring it back to a full charge in about 12 hours. Typically, this means overnight. If the car is only partially discharged, it will come up faster.

There are also 220 VAC/30 amp chargers available. These will charge the car in six to eight hours. However, they are more expensive, some of them are large and heavy, and 220 volt power is not as readily available.

If you want to feed juice to your charger from a solar array, it will need to be a large stationary array. Solar panels on the car itself are not cost effective. Covering the entire roof of the car with panels and letting it sit in full sun all day would only provide about five miles worth of electricity, at a cost of about $3,000 for the panels.

Batteries

From the charger, the electricity moves into the batteries. The typical conversion has a 96 to 120 volt battery pack. The size of the pack is constrained by two factors. Any less than 96 volts, and the car won't have adequate speed and acceleration to be streetworthy, nor will it have much range. Above 120 volts, compatible components have not been available (although 144 volt components are now coming out). Also, the added bulk and weight of the extra batteries tends to negate the gains in power.

The batteries most commonly used are 6-volt lead acid traction batteries, the same kind used in golf carts. Typically, they are rated at 230 amp/hrs, and weigh about 67 lbs. They are 6-volt batteries because there has not been a suitable 12-volt traction battery available until very recently. There are some 12-volt traction batteries now on the market, but they are too new to know yet what kind of performance they will give.

They are lead acid batteries because any other kind of battery, at this point in time, suffers from one of two drawbacks. Either it is still available only as a laboratory test model, or it is several times more costly than lead acid. Gel cells require low current charging to avoid internal damage. Standard chargers commonly available do not provide the appropriate charging profile for gel cells.

Finally, they are traction batteries rather than starting/lights/ignition (SLI) or marine batteries. SLI batteries can provide high current, but cannot stand up to repeated deep discharges and charges. Marine batteries can take the charge/discharge cycle, but don't last very well when required to provide high current. A traction battery is intended to move a vehicle down the road, and it can handle both deep discharges and high current draws.

Key and throttle

Turning the key turns the car "on," just like a gas car, but nothing happens until you depress the throttle. Then a main contactor closes and electricity flows from the battery pack to the speed controller. A potentiometer, called a *potbox*, is connected to the throttle pedal. It sends a signal to the controller based on how far the pedal is depressed. The controller releases energy to the motor in proportion to the signal from the potbox.

Most controllers in conversions today are sealed solid state units which are very reliable and durable. They are also very efficient, quiet, and smooth in operation.

The controller operates by "chopping" the voltage from the batteries. It functions like a switch that turns the electricity on and off 15,000 times per second. How long each "on" pulse lasts is determined by the throttle pedal and the potbox.

Motors

From the controller, the electricity flows to the motor. In the old days, this might have been an aircraft starter or generator pressed into service in a car. These made great aircraft starters and generators, but lousy car motors. They were designed to operate at much lower voltages and higher rpm. In an automotive application, they were fragile and highly inefficient.

Fortunately, today there are reliable, efficient motors available that are manufactured specifically for electric cars. The most popular for conversions is the series brush DC (direct current) type motor. This motor operates well in the rpm, voltage, and current range of a passenger car. It combines efficiency with affordability, making it very practical for daily driving.

Permanent magnet motors show up most often in ultralight solar race cars. Although they are very efficient, their efficiency is limited to a narrow rpm band. This makes them suitable for endurance races at a constant speed, but not for the ups and downs of daily driving.

Brushless DC and AC units are also available, but at a significantly higher price. The motor itself may not cost more, but the complex control system it requires is much more expensive. These systems are generally only found in production cars or high-budget, high-performance race cars.

Other exotic motors, like exotic batteries, tend to be unavailable or unaffordable for the average person.

Adapter & transmission

The motor is mounted to the original transmission using an adapter. Typically, this adapter comprises one or two precision-machined aluminum plates, and a steel hub. The safest, most reliable hub type is the taperlock. This will not work loose like a setscrew hub.

Conversions are manual transmission cars. The clutch is maintained for safety reasons, and because it provides a much smoother ride.

Why no automatics? There are problems with power losses, delayed throttle response, and mismatched shift points in automatics that produce inferior performance.

What about direct drive? Many production cars use direct drive. However, in order to get acceptable speed and acceleration, they require battery packs of 300 volts or more. This puts them out of the reach of the average person.

From the transmission, the power goes to the wheels, just as it did in the gas car. The drive wheels can be front or rear with equal ease. What is not practical at this time is four-wheel-drive, due to the complexity and cost involved.

Performance

Okay, so here's this electric car. What can it do? Typical range for a 96 volt sedan is 60 to 80 miles. Some of the high-performance sports car conversions can stretch that to 80 to 100 miles. These miles are typical daily driving: some stop and go, some freeway, average speed about 40 mph. The top speed on a typical sedan is about 65 mph, and on a sports car it's about 85 mph.

Night driving is not a problem. A DC/DC converter taps the main battery pack for a few amps to charge a 12 volt accessory battery for lights, horns, etc.

Cold weather is not a problem, either. There are various types of passenger compartment heaters available. Both the cold temperatures and the heater will diminish performance somewhat, but probably only about 15%. There are happy electric car drivers in Maine, Quebec, Alaska, and even the Yukon.

Can they climb hills? You bet. For long continuous climbs, or very steep hills, or hills that require freeway speeds, a high-performance conversion is recommended: a light, aerodynamic body, with a large motor and at least a 120 volt system. For intermittent climbs of a mile or less on a mild grade at reduced speeds, a typical 96 volt sedan is adequate. Climbing hills will reduce the car's range, under severe conditions (we're talking actual mountains here) by as much as 50%.

What about going downhill? Can that energy be harnessed to recharge the batteries? This concept is called *regenerative braking*. Although much experimentation has been done on it, there is not yet a satisfactory system available commercially. Some systems, like connecting a small alternator to a second motor shaft, simply aren't very effective. Others are not compatible with the available motors and controllers. Others are bulky and complex, and have a potential failure mode of full acceleration (not a good thing when you want braking action).

Also, for a great many people, regenerative braking would not fit their driving patterns. Most people live up high, and their main downhill stretch comes when they first leave home—and the battery pack is fully charged. The ideal application for regeneration would be a long downhill in the middle or at the end of the drive.

Time & money

What does it cost to convert a car to electricity? The cost in dollars is inversely proportional to the cost in time. On the low end, you can buy a bare-bones kit for around $4,000, add another $1,000 or so in batteries and miscellaneous materials, and spend about 200 hours of your time installing it. In this scenario, you will be responsible for designing the component layout and designing and fabricating things like battery racks and boxes, various mounts and brackets, and a wiring loom. You will also need to make any necessary suspension modifications.

This is the kit for the rugged individualist who wants the feeling of accomplishment that comes from creating the car with his own brain and hands.

On the high end, you can buy a completely prefabricated kit for about $7,000, and add about $750 for batteries and 40 hours of your time. This is the kit for the person who has other outlets for his creativity, and simply wants to get the car finished and on the road.

Once it's built, it will save you about 60% on operating costs. A conversion typically uses about 0.4 kwh (kilowatt-hours)/mile of electricity. The only other maintenance expense is replacing the battery pack at about four to five year intervals, and replacing the motor brushes at 80,000 miles.

There are also various tax benefits available. These change from state to state and from day to day, so check for the current information in your area.

A typical conversion uses 16 six-volt batteries, some located under the hood and some in the rear of the car.

Electric cars tomorrow

In the past four years, public interest in electric cars has increased enormously. With the increased public interest has come increased manufacturer interest. Where will it go from here?

Major manufacturers

The state of California has mandated that in 1998, 2% of the cars offered for sale must be zero-polluting, and that number increases to 10% by 2003. All of the major manufacturers have electric car programs in progress in order to meet this mandate.

American manufacturers, while publicly trumpeting their programs, have been fighting tooth and nail behind the scenes to overturn the mandate. They are concentrating their reluctant programs toward supplying electric vehicles to fleets in the hopes of meeting the mandate without really having to address the public market. With the exception of the GM Impact, these programs are producing production conversions of existing gas cars, light trucks, and vans.

They tend to use AC drive systems, direct drive or automatic transmissions, and very high voltage packs of unusual batteries. All of this contributes to price tags from $50,000 to $150,000.

Quite probably, foreign manufacturers will be the first to offer production electric cars for the mass market. Peugeot and Fiat already offer such cars in Europe. The Japanese and Korean manufacturers are also developing mass-market electric cars. Potential prices for these are unknown, but are likely to be much closer to the $15,000 to $20,000 range.

Initially, all of these will be electric versions of existing gas cars, simply due to the time and expense required to tool up for a completely new chassis. As the market grows to support the effort, cars designed from the ground up will appear.

Will private conversions continue? Of course. Americans have a genetic need to modify their cars. The hot rod controller will simply replace the hot rod carburetor.

An electric motor mounts to the original transmission through an adapter plate.

Components

It seems likely that there will be two parallel tracks of electric vehicle technology for some time. The major manufacturers are concentrating on AC systems and exotic batteries. Due to the difference in cost, grassroots efforts are likely to continue to use DC systems and lead acid batteries.

This is not to say that there will be no improvements. Motors, controllers, and chargers that can handle DC systems up to 144 volts are now coming available. Also, as the market expands, prices will come down.

DC motor technology has been around for a long time, and has been refined to the point where efficiency differences between DC and AC motors are negligible. There are not likely to be major breakthroughs in DC motors.

Where the improvements will come will be in matching the motor to the overall system. There are trade-offs between rpm and torque, speed and efficiency, and many other factors. With a systems approach, the motor can be engineered to provide the best match with the controller and the performance needs of the car.

Controller manufacturers are also looking to match their components better to the motors and the overall systems.

The debate in controller technology today revolves around MOSFETs (metal oxide semiconductor field effect transistors) and IGBTs (insulated gate bipolar transistors, pronounced *igg-bits*). These are the pieces that actually turn the electricity on and off inside the controller.

IGBT proponents claim higher efficiencies. IGBT controllers are also easier to manufacture, because fewer IGBTs are needed than MOSFETs to do the same job, and production can be more easily automated.

MOSFET proponents question the higher efficiencies in systems under 144 volts, which include most conversions. While fewer IGBTs are needed, each one is much more expensive than the MOSFETs. IGBT controllers tend to be bulkier and noisier, since they operate best at lower frequencies than

MOSFETs. They also require more cooling.

It's too early to call the results on the MOSFET/IGBT debate, although it may evolve into parallel tracks like the AC/DC debate. At this time, the MOSFET technology is the more proven and established system.

Batteries

Everyone wants to know, "When will they come up with a better battery?" Like motors and controllers, the battery debate divides into parallel tracks.

On one track are the exotic batteries: sodium sulphur, nickel metal hydride, silver zinc, lithium polymer, and more, too numerous to mention. Each has its proponents. In fact, the U. S. Advanced Battery Consortium was formed to examine and sort out these technologies and develop a better battery to meet the California mandate. The energy-to-weight goals set by the USABC eliminate lead acid from consideration.

There is considerable debate regarding whether any of the exotic technologies can be developed to a marketable stage in time for the mandate, and whether "marketable" is measured by the fleet market or the public market.

On the other hand, there is the Advanced Lead Acid Battery Consortium. This is a group of lead acid manufacturers who have pooled their research efforts to show that lead acid is a more viable immediate alternative.

There are a great many advances being made in lead acid technology. These include new grid alloys for longer life, super-thin plates to minimize heat problems, and radically revised architecture that may give us batteries shaped like thermos bottles.

While the advanced lead acid batteries can't approach the energy-weight goals of the exotic batteries, they may provide the same energy as traditional lead acid batteries at half the weight—and about the same cost.

Like the motor and controller manufacturers, battery manufacturers are looking at how their product interacts with the whole system, especially the charger. In addition to developing lighter batteries that last longer, they are developing batteries that can

An electric motor mounts to the original transmission through an adapter plate.

accept a charge faster, and the chargers to match.

Battery charging time is limited by heat. Fast charging produces heat inside the battery, which shortens the battery's life. Gassing is caused by built-up heat literally boiling the electrolyte.

New battery designs can accept higher charging currents—briefly—without heat problems. New charger designs accommodate this by pulsing the charging current, giving the plates a brief rest between pulses. The charger may even insert a tiny discharge between charge pulses. This kind of technology is still experimental, but is expected to be in production within four years.

With pulsed quick charging, the car would still be charged primarily at home, overnight. Most people would rarely need the quick charge, but when they did, they could stop at a charging station and recover up to 80% of the battery's charge in 15 minutes or less.

(The last 20% of the charge is the most difficult to do quickly without damaging the battery.)

The big picture

In the immediate future, for the average person, electric cars will primarily be conversions using improved versions of traditional DC and lead acid technology. Foreign manufacturers will probably be the first to offer mass produced electrics for the general public, with domestic manufacturers limiting their focus to fleets.

The performance of today's technology is adequate for most people's driving needs. However, as new technology becomes available, today's cars can be upgraded. Every time the battery pack is replaced, it will have more energy per pound and a longer lifespan than the pack it replaces.

The electric car is the only car that runs better the longer you own it.

Resources

For a list of businesses supplying conversion kits and components, conversion services, books and videos, and turnkey cars, contact:

Electric Vehicle Industry Assoc.
P.O. Box 59
Maynard, MA 01754
(508) 897-6740

For the location of an electric car club near you, contact:

The Electric Auto Association
(800) 537-2882

For information on tax incentives and legislation relating to electric cars, contact:

Goldschein & Gomez
Alternative Energy Consultants
221 "G" Street, Suite 207
Davis, CA 95616
(916) 753-8057 ∆

A Backwoods Home Anthology

Just for kids — some pioneer recipes

By Lucy Shober

When I was a little girl, I used to visit my grandfather's home town in Edgecombe County, North Carolina. He filled my head with tales of how things were done when he was a boy. One of my favorites was his story of the making of Brunswick stew. As I nestled into the musty back seat of my aunt's huge black Packard car, he would begin the tale. We would rove through the miles and miles of dusty tobacco fields, the tall yellowing plants surging up on either side of the road, and he would drone on. The more he talked, the hungrier I got.

According to his memory, the farm hands would work in the fields harvesting those massive leaves from dawn 'til way after dark. Along about sunset, someone would kindle a fire and set a great black pot of water on it. Several of the fellows would then take to the woods and shoot up some rabbit and squirrel, perhaps even a wild turkey. Someone else would chip in a bunch of onions brought from home, and maybe a wife would have packed her husband off that morning with a basket of butterbeans and tomatoes from the garden. Several ears of pilfered corn might have finished off the recipe. These ingredients would be left to bubble and stew as the workers returned to the fields.

As the men picked and packed the great leaves, the delicious aroma of that Brunswick stew wafted through the fields, finally beckoning them to supper. As I listened to him spin his story, I always wondered, but never got around to asking . . . did they bother to take the skin off those squirrels? I would picture that lovely vat of bubbling stew, and my mouth would ache for a taste of it—until in my imagina-

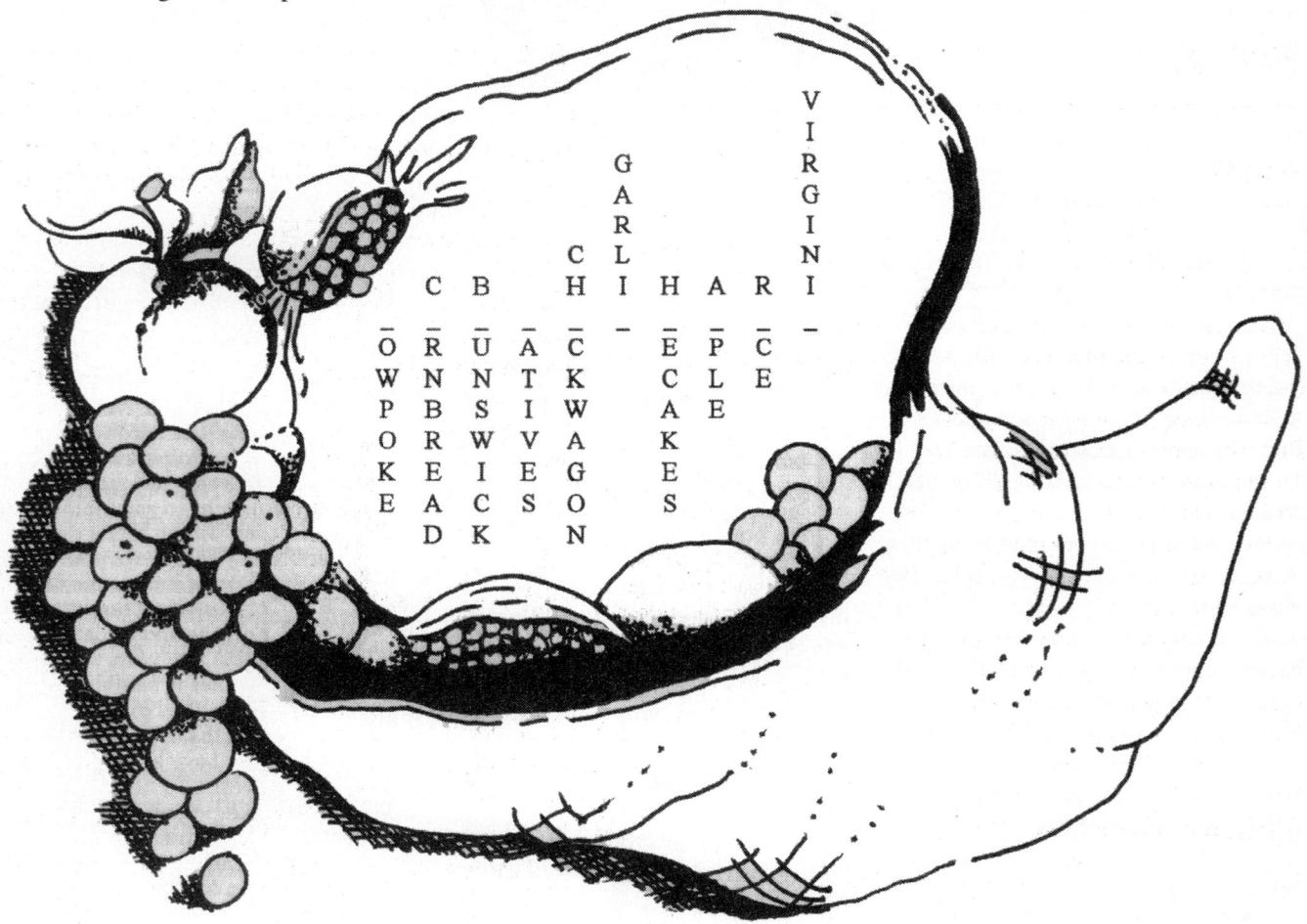

Find the secret word!
Fill in the blank spaces with letters from words in the article. The answer is a symbol for peace and plenty.

tion, a soggy wet squirrel tail would pop to the surface of the pot. It wasn't until many years later, when I actually tasted Brunswick stew (there were no tails, feathers or ears.), that I discovered how very delicious it is.

When you think of how available most foods are to us today, it can sometimes lead you to wonder how our pioneer ancestors could have survived. With no refrigeration and few (or no) grocery stores close by, they had to rely on common sense, imagination, and the land around them for most of their daily menu. It might be fun sometime to pretend backward into history, and try the diets of several of our forefathers. Depending on the section of this country that you would like to visit, and the time in history, you could come up with meals ranging from the most bland to the most delicious. Why not plan a historic supper for your family? Have an adult help you build a campfire, then follow the recipes below. Read the explanatory notes for each one. These notes will tell you the *reasonings* for the *seasonings*. (All of these recipes are adaptable to oven or stovetop cooking. You will need an adult to help you with them either way, but that's a big part of the fun.)

Mud apples

This is a variation on a Native American cooking method.

You will need

> 4 large apples
> A bucket of mud

Coat the apples with about an inch of mud on all sides, being sure that the mud is of a nice thick consistency. When the fire has burned long enough to make some coals, have your adult help you to scoop some of the coals to the side. Bury the apples in the coals, and leave them there for about 45 minutes. Scrape away the cooled coals. Knock the dry cooked mud off of the apples and discard the skins. Spoon up the sweet steamy pulp for a surprising treat.

Some groups of Native American people used a mud coating on their food as a sort of oven. The steam from the mud would keep fresh-caught fish moist, and as it dried and became clay-like, it protected the food from burning. When the mud was peeled off, it took a lot of the fish scales with it. A delicious instant meal.

Chuckwagon beans

This is a cattle trail recipe from the Midwest. Although this was originally done on the campfire, it might be best if you bow to modern convenience and do the cooking on a stove top.

You will need

> A 16-ounce package of dry pinto beans
> 9 cups of water
> Two large onions, peeled and chopped up
> 2 teaspoons of salt
> ½ teaspoon of oregano
> ½ teaspoon of garlic powder, or two cloves of sliced garlic
> ¼ teaspoon of pepper
> 1 tablespoon of brown sugar or molasses (add this last, and put in a little more if you like.)

Wash the beans and heat them along with 6 cups of water 'til they boil for five minutes, then turn the stove off. Let them sit for an hour. Add three more cups of water and boil it all again. Now add everything else, stir it up, and cook it for about an hour.

Cowpokes on the drive west had to settle for foods which were portable. That meant a basic menu of beans and lots of meat. For a treat, there was cornbread, biscuits, or a sweetened rice dish. Pinto beans (which are small and spotted when raw, like a pinto pony) seemed to be the favorite. When cooked, these beans swell up and turn a sort of pinkish white. They were first given to the settlers by the natives on the Mexican border.

When you eat beans with rice or corn, the two foods mix up inside your body to create an important type of protein which is like the protein in meat. (Your body is made largely of protein, and so you need to eat a lot of it.) That's why the native Southwestern people were so healthy with a diet of mostly beans and corn and not much meat.

Baked pocket yams

These were "handy" during the winter months, and not particular to any one area of the country.

Take several sweet potatoes, individually wrap them in foil, and surround them on all sides with mounded hot coals. Occasionally turn the potatoes. Cook till the sweet steam pipes out of the foil (about 45 minutes). Poke into the potato with a clean sharpened twig to check for doneness (the center will be soft).

When the potatoes are done, DONT EAT THEM YET. Let them cool a bit, then slip one into each pocket to be used as hand warmers. These will keep you comfortable while you chat around the campfire. Pioneer mothers used to send their children off with these in the winter months to keep their hands toasty on the long walk to school. Then the kids would eat them for lunch. When you eat yours, you might want to use a dish and slather them up with butter.

Rice cakes

These were eaten all along the East coast.

Ingredients

> 1 egg
> 2 cups cooked rice
> 2 spring onions, chopped

Mix indgredients and fry on an oiled skillet. YUM.

A ship sailing from Madagascar in about 1685 was hit with bad weather and had to make a forced docking in Charles Town, South Carolina (now Charleston). The captain made friends with a local man, and as a present, he gave him some of the ship's cargo . . . a bushel of rice. From that small gift was born the rice industry in America.

Rice needs the lowland swampy terrain that our coasts provide. That's why in states like Louisiana and the Carolinas, tasty rice dishes are so common. Rice was (and is) easy to store and mixes well with lots of other ingredients. This recipe was (and is) simple to make, filling, and nutritious.

Brunswick stew

This version of the stew is as easy as 1-2-3. You don't need to find a tobacco field to enjoy it.

Ingredients   (All cans are the 16 ounce size.)

> 1 can of lima beans
> 1 can of corn
> 1 can of chicken broth
> 1 can of chicken, or 1 pound of fresh cooked chicken
> 1 squirrel tail (optional)
> 2 large onions, chopped up
> 2 cans of chopped tomatoes
> 3 cooked, peeled, and chopped potatoes
> A dash of pepper, garlic, brown sugar, and salt
> Cooking oil
> Hot sauce to taste

Put the onions and a tad of oil into the pot first and cook them 'til they turn clear, then add all the rest. Depending on the amount of juice from the vegetables, you might have to add a little water. Keep it bubbling, and stir it for about 20 minutes.

Two or three eastern communities with the name of "Brunswick" like to claim this stew as their own concoction, but generally, Brunswick County, Virginia, is given the credit. It is thought to have come about in the early 1800s.

Hoe cakes

These are a Southern tradition.

Ingredients

> A pot full of water
> 3 cups corn meal
> 1 teaspoon of salt
> Shortening

Put a pot of water on the stove to boil. Mix corn meal and salt in a large bowl. Slowly add boiling water 'til the batter becomes mushy but not stiff. Let this sit while you heat up some shortening in a skillet. When the shortening is hot but not smoking, drop several heaping tablespoons of the corn meal mixture into the pan. Keep the corn "cakes" separate so they don't run together. Turn down the heat a little, then flip them over and cook the other side. They should be flat and crispy golden brown. That's it.

These are called HOE cakes because they were originally cooked over a fire on the flat part of a garden hoe. They are basically an African-American invention and are like those potato chips . , . you can't eat just one—especially if you drip butter on top. ENJOY. Δ

A country moment

Jake and Robby Duffy hold smelt caught at the beach in Orick, California

Pemmican — the all purpose food

By Bill Palmroth

Few foods have been around as long as simple pemmican. For centuries, it was a highly sought-after food of the frontier pioneers and plains Indians. Although buffalo was the preferred meat, just about any kind of meat would do in a pinch...deer, elk, moose, you name it.

As a one-time distributor of dehydrated foods, I frequently received calls from outdoor enthusiasts about various dried foods. When the subject got around to dried meats, I reluctantly had to tell them that my company offered nothing in the way of meats. Generally, I suggested that they try making their own pemmican.

Pounding the dried meat

There were, and still are, many advantages to making your own pemmican. It has long-term storage value, and because it is based solely on dried meat, it is highly nutritious. Once prepared, it needs no refrigeration and can be easily reconstituted by adding water.

Today, beef, deer, elk, and moose can be easily converted into pemmican. Ten to fifteen pounds is a good amount to start with. The first step is to cut the lean parts of the meat into long strips about ¾" thick. These are then hung to air dry. The Indians traditionally did this in the late fall, after a couple of early frosts had killed most of nature's insects.

The drying process can take several days or weeks, depending on the weather conditions. Modern man can set the kitchen oven at slow heat and let the meat dry that way, but there is some evidence that oven drying destroys certain amino acids and a less nutritious food results. However, if normal diets are maintained, there should be no problem.

Once the lean meat is dried, it is pounded into a powder or a string-like mass. The pounding further reduces the bulk and also drives off any remaining moisture. A log or small anvil can be used as a workbench to break up the meat fiber. The back of an axe or a wooden maul works well for breaking down the meat. In general, five to six pounds of lean meat will be needed to yield about a pound of dried meat needed for pounding, which is long and sometimes hard work.

Fat is the next most important element in the recipe. Beef fat is preferred. The fat from wild game is also excellent for this part of the recipe, and if there is not enough from one animal, beef fat can be added into the mix. The rule of thumb in pemmican making is to allow one pound of fat for every pound of dried lean meat.

Remove the fat from the carcass, place it in a pot, and slowly heat the mix until liquid. Once the fat is liquid, add it to the mix of pounded meat. Stir the contents into an even mix. Let the extra mix cool and harden. The final result is old-style pemmican.

Although native wild berries were sometimes added to early-day pemmican, it wasn't until much later that spices and dried fruits became regular additions to pemmican recipes. This was for no other reason than to please the white man's palate.

Modern recipes call for the addition of raisins, black currants, and even sugar (something I don't recommend). If wild berries are used, they need to be crushed and dried before adding them to the pemmican. Oatmeal and flour also have been added by some cooks, as have cornmeal and nuts. A number of spices—including salt, oregano, pepper, bay leaves, and garlic salt—have been advocated as ways of improving taste.

Pemmican can be stored in glass jars or in muslin or canvas sacks. It can also be frozen, but be sure to allow plenty of time for a chunk to thaw prior to taking it on a trip or hike. Under normal storage conditions, it will last up to two years.

The pemmican can be eaten as it is or reconstituted much the same way modern freeze-dried foods are soaked and allowed to take up water. Then it can be browned and tossed into a stew with dumplings, or water can be added to make a kind of meaty broth.

Old-fashioned pemmican will give any modern-day food a good run for its money. ∆

A Backwoods Home Anthology

AMERICANA

Former first ladies — beautiful, brilliant, crazy

By John Silveira

(When we left off last issue, O. E. MacDougal and John Silveira were travelling from Ojai, California, to Ashland, Oregon. Mac was talking about the First Ladies and White House hostesses of the late 18th and early 19th centuries, and had just finished telling about Anna Harrison, the wife of President William Henry Harrison, who served the shortest time in the White House.
— Editor)

"Who's next?" I asked.

Letitia Christian Tyler

"Well," he said, "Harrison was the first President to die in office. His vice president, John Tyler, succeeded him but no one really knew what a vice president was actually supposed to do when the President died. So, the first thing Tyler did was make it clear he wasn't just filling in while another President was chosen—he was now the President. It was an important precedent."

"So, what was the new First Lady like?"

"Letitia Tyler was a quiet, aristocratic southern woman. Her courtship with John lasted five years. And talk about slow engagements. She didn't allow him to kiss her until three weeks before the wedding, and then it was only on the hand."

"They sound pretty cold to me."

"It was the times. Once they got married, they made up for it. She had nine pregnancies, eight births, and seven of their children lived beyond infancy. Only one other First Lady, Anna Harrison, had more children.

"Throughout his political career, she avoided the limelight. But she was devoted to him and they were apparently very happily married.

"She was extremely competent, and it was only because of her shrewd business investments—giving the family financial stability—that made it possible for him to pursue a political career.

"But, when she was just 48, she suffered a debilitating stroke that left her an invalid. So, two years later, when he became vice president, he decided to spend the entire of his term at their home in Virginia to be at her side. But Harrison, as I said, died a month after taking office and Tyler had to go to Washington. He was the President, now. Letitia, the dutiful wife, accompanied him. But, because of her paralysis, for the next two years she almost never left her room in the upstairs family quarters of the White House.

Letitia Christian Tyler

"The stroke also left her unable to speak, but she regained that function. Her intellect, however, had been untouched. I mention this because her husband, by his own admission, never made an important decision without consulting her first."

"Who served as hostess since she was an invalid?"

"She had a 25-year-old daughter-in-law, a former actress, who served as hostess. But a little over a year into her husband's administration, Letitia died. She was the first First Lady to die in the White House, and once more we had a widower President.

Julia Gardiner Tyler

"But Tyler wasn't just the first man to become widowed while President; he was also the first to marry while President."

In her time, she was considered to be outrageously beautiful. Suitors pursued her on two continents— here and Europe.

"Someone he met at the White House?"

"Yes. His second wife was Julia Gardiner. In her time, she was considered to be outrageously beautiful. Suitors pursued her on two continents—here and Europe. Someone somewhere gave her the nickname, 'The Rose of Long Island,' and several businesses used pictures of her on their products—all without her permission, of course.

"They met about a year after Letitia died. Julia's family had just come back from a tour of Europe and they were invited to a White House dinner. A romantic would say it was love at first sight—for him, not her—and throughout dinner he openly flirted with her. Afterward, they all retired to another room and played cards and he continued to flirt. As the Gardiners left, he even chased her around the room and tried to kiss her good night."

"Wow, I could see the headlines on that one today."

"Oh, it's probably happened since. Several Presidents have been known for their attractions to women. But this was no one night's dalliance. The next day he began his pursuit in earnest. He saw her as often as he could. He wrote to her almost daily and, two weeks after he met her, he proposed as they danced at a Washington ball. But she turned him down."

"Why?"

"She was 23—he was almost 54."

"Now I can really see the headlines. But you said they wound up married. What changed her mind?"

"Later, she and her family accepted yet another invitation to be with Tyler. This time they took a cruise along the Potomac aboard the Navy warship Princeton. A new Navy cannon was to be tested and, while the crew readied the gun, Tyler, Julia, and many others went below decks. On the top deck the cannon was fired. It exploded and killed five people including her father."

"When the news came down below, she fainted. Tyler, himself, carried her unconscious from the ship. Later he ordered a state funeral for the dead and spent several weeks consoling her."

"During that time, her view of him changed. She saw more and more of him and several months later they eloped to New York."

"Wow, exploding cannons, romance, a president sneaking off to New York to get married; they didn't tell us about this stuff in school."

"And we're poorer for it, too. Think of how much more interesting history would have been."

"How'd they get along? I mean, the age difference didn't go away."

> *...exploding cannons, romance, a president sneaking off to New York to get married; they didn't tell us about this stuff in school.*

"It seemed the longer they were married, the more she came to love him. And she especially loved his letters to her. In fact, it was the letters he wrote right after they'd met that made it so difficult for her to stop seeing him. If he'd been any other man, the age difference would probably have doomed them, whether he was President or not."

"So, how long was she actually First Lady?"

"Eight months. He was nominated for another term in 1844 and accepted, but a short time later he changed his mind and didn't run after all. After they left the White House, they had seven children."

"That means he had 15 kids, altogether."

"That's right. It's the record."

"What kind of a First Lady did she make?"

"A good one. She was full of energy and kept a busy schedule. Washington society loved her and, among other things, she taught the Marine Band to play 'Hail to the Chief,' and it's been the standard accompaniment for the President's entrance ever since."

"She started that?"

"Yes. When they left the White House, they moved back to Virginia, his home state and, though she'd been born in the North, she adopted her husband's Southern sympathies. When tensions built before the outbreak of the Civil War, she made it clear she was supporting her husband's views, and her family all but disowned her."

"How much longer did he live?"

"She was just 42 when he died. Twenty-seven years later, when she died, it was in the same hotel where he had died."

"Is that important?"

"No. You can just put it in your gee-whiz file."

"Okay. Did she ever remarry?"

"No. No widowed First Lady would remarry until the twentieth century.

"By the way, years later, when secession of the Southern states became inevitable, her husband was elected to the Confederate House from Virginia, but he died before he could serve.

I watched a sign for towns called Proberta and Gerber go by. "I just can't believe he had 15 kids," I said.

Sarah Childress Polk

"You're still thinking about that, huh? Well, that's the Presidential record. But the next President and First Lady made up for it. They didn't have any."

"Who were they?"

"James and Sarah Polk. She was an unusual First Lady. Perhaps because they were childless, she dedicated her life to him and served as his personal secretary while he was in Congress, while he was governor of Tennessee, and later when he became President."

"Did they want kids?"

"I don't know but they didn't miss them. There's nothing in their letters or anything their contemporaries wrote to show they were anything but indifferent to children. And this was in a day when a woman's success was often measured by how they raised a family.

"She was, however, well liked by Washington society. Included among her best friends were the wives of

Julia Gardiner Tyler

some of her husband's political enemies. You wouldn't see that today. She also formed friendships with some of the most powerful and influential men of her time including the former President, Andrew Jackson, who had helped her husband's career; Franklin Pierce, a future President near whom the Polks lived when James was a Congressman; and there was Joseph Story, one of the Supreme Court Justices. Her circle of friends alone made her unusual in her time.

"But they were unusual times, anyway. The country was changing."

"What do you mean?"

"With Jackson's election, the old guard was gone from the White House. John Quincy Adams was the last man who might be called a Founding Father to be elected to the presidency.

"So, by Polk's time, all the original patriots were either dead or too old to be elected. There was a new criteria for attaining the presidency: you had to be popular. And Jackson was extremely popular. He was a 'peoples' president.

"Also, the lot of women was changing. More and more of them went outside their homes for jobs. The great mills of the Northeast were being built and women were a ready and cheap source of labor.

> *If some historian made a case that James Polk would have been nowhere near as effective as he was, or even that he wouldn't have made it to the White House, without her, I wouldn't argue. I think, quite possibly, she was the best First Lady we ever had.*

"Women's rights also became an issue. During Polk's administration there was a convention of women in Seneca Falls, New York. Those who attended demanded improvements in educational and job opportunities for women and they wanted more say in family matters. Married women of the time were considered just another possession of their husbands.

"What's ironic is that the most controversial issue at the meeting was suffrage."

"Why?"

"Many of them didn't think they needed the vote."

It sounded strange to me, but I didn't ask him to explain why.

"Anyway," he continued, "Sarah's husband is considered the first 'dark horse' president."

"What's a dark horse candidate, anyway?"

"It's someone who's not considered a contender but who suddenly emerges from the back of the pack to be among the leaders. It's a horse racing term. Polk was not one of the leading contenders for the Democratic presidential nomination in 1844. But he emerged as one, winning out over Henry Clay…"

"The man you called the Harold Stassen of his time."

"Yes…and also Van Buren, who had been the eighth President."

"Why was he chosen?"

"Clay and Van Buren opposed the annexation of Texas, which nine years before had seceded from Mexico and now wanted to become part of the United States. Polk not only wanted Texas, but he wanted the Oregon Territory, which was in dispute with Great Britain. Apparently, the American people wanted them, too, because they made him President.

"By the end of his administration, Texas, along with what was called the Mexican Cession, was annexed and the northern border of the Oregon Territories was settled along the line that forms the northern border of the State of Washington and runs east. The United States established claim to more territory under Polk than any other President before or since—almost 1.2 million square miles, one third of what is now the U.S."

"You're kidding. If you'd asked me who he was before this ride, I wouldn't have known."

He laughed. "You and tens of millions of others."

"What was Sarah like?"

"Many of her contemporaries thought she had too much influence on her husband. It could have been true. Polk was an incredibly effective President and Sarah was a big help to him. If some historian made a case that James Polk would have been nowhere near as effective as he was, or even that he wouldn't have made it to the White House, without her, I wouldn't argue. I think, quite possibly, she was the best First Lady we ever had."

"So, you're saying…"

"I'm saying, the United States might not be anywhere near as big as it is today if any woman, other than Sarah Polk, had become First Lady in 1845."

"How come I didn't know who the Polks were?" I asked.

He shrugged. We passed a sign that said Jellys Ferry Road. Someday, I'm going to drive down that road.

"She was a bright, opinionated woman" he said, "and not only James

Sarah Childress Polk

but other Washington politicians often discussed the issues of the day with her.

"She read all the correspondence and newspapers that came to James and she marked what she thought deserved his attention and passed them along to him.

> *...the United States might not be anywhere near as big as it is today if any woman, other than Sarah Polk, had become First Lady in 1845.*

"But, for all the support she gave him, she didn't like the expectations others had of her. She didn't want to be a White House hostess and she didn't want to entertain at parties. She didn't like the time these things took away from helping her husband.

"She also guarded him against the world and was vindictive toward anyone who criticized him. On at least one occasion, she intercepted and destroyed a White House invitation before it could be sent out because it was going to a man who had criticized him. Martin Van Buren's son also criticized him and she banished him from the White House guest list for the rest of James's administration. There were probably more instances of this.

"So, not everyone liked her," I said.

He shook his head. "Anyone as strong willed as she was has a way of making enemies.

"Nowadays, Polk's administration is remembered as having been dull, and about all Sarah's remembered for is having the gaslights installed in the White House. I suppose in some ways it was dull. The Polk's were teetotalers, and after White House dinners guests often went to Dolley Madison's house to get an alcoholic drink."

"I remember you saying that when you talked about Dolley Madison," I said.

"Also, though she liked music, she felt there were times when it was inappropriate—like on Sundays. In fact, at the inaugural ball, in her husband's honor, the dance music stopped as a courtesy to her when she entered the room."

"How many terms did he serve?"

"One. It was all he wanted. He accomplished everything he'd set out to achieve in four years. He died less then eight weeks after he left office."

"Good grief. What happened to her?"

"She lived another 42 years. But she remained a significant figure in American society. When the Civil War broke out, her sympathies were with her native South but she also opposed secession. Her home became off limits to all the combatants—high tribute to a First Lady no one remembers today.

"In fact, historical treasures were stored at her house because everyone knew they would be safe there.

"She remained popular until the day she died and her political opinions were sought by many of the men of her time years after the Polk administration ended."

"No kidding."

"By the way, did you know she's related to the artist you have working for the magazine."

"Don? Don Childers?"

"Yeah. The spelling of his name and her maiden name are different, but that's because his branch of the family took a different spelling."

"Does he know this?" I asked.

"Of course he does."

Margaret Smith Taylor

"So, who's next?"

"Next was Zachary Taylor's wife, Margaret. Just before he was elected, the Taylors were ready to retire to a plantation they'd bought in Mississippi. He'd already had a long career in the army and she had followed him from one primitive outpost to another; from the mosquito infested swamps of Florida to the forests of Minnesota—which, incidentally, are filled with snow in the winter and mosquitoes in the summer."

"How many kids did they have?"

"They had five daughters—two of whom died of malaria—and a son. The life of a military officer's wife in primitive America was a tough life. Neither Margaret nor her husband wanted their daughters to marry military men. So, of course, kids being kids, one of them did. She eloped with a West Point graduate who was later to become the President of the Confederacy."

"Jefferson Davis?"

"That's right."

"He was related to a President of the United States by marriage?"

"He was related to two Presidents by marriage."

"Two? Which other one?"

"After his wife died of something called river fever—and they'd only been married three months—he married the aunt of Franklin Pierce's wife."

I made a note of that. "Let's get back to Margaret Taylor. What kind of a First Lady was she?"

"Not much of one—if you were looking for excitement at the White House. She was 61 when her husband became president and she really didn't want to be a society woman. She all but refused to entertain and she more or less confined herself to the family quarters in the White House, just as Letitia Tyler had done. She left all the entertaining to her two surviving daughters.

"And because of this reclusive behavior, she became the subject of much Washington gossip. Rumors had it that she was uncultured and uneducated, when in fact she was one of the first First Ladies to have a decent education. There were even rumors that she wiled away her days sitting in her room smoking a corncob pipe like some sort of bumpkin."

"Did she?"

"Of course not."

"She sounds like she was miserable."

"Her misery didn't last long. Fifteen months after his administration started, Taylor was dead and she died two years later. But from the day her husband died to the day she died, her only memory of her days in the White House was his funeral."

"That's sad."

"As I said, many of the women who became First Ladies didn't want to be."

Abigail Powers Fillmore

"I was thinking of using this talk as the basis for a story in the magazine," I said. "But this is becoming pretty depressing."

"That's too bad because the next First Lady didn't really like the job, either."

"Who was she?"

"Abigail Fillmore, the wife of Millard Fillmore. She was the daughter of a preacher who died when she was an infant. Though he'd left the family in poverty, he also left behind an extensive library, and her mother used it to educate Abigail at home.

It was during Fillmore's administration that piped water was brought into the White House, and Abigail had the first bathtub installed.

"She was a good student. She also taught herself French and how to play the piano. By the time she was 16, she became a school teacher and that's how she met her husband."

"A fellow teacher?"

"He was a student. When she was 20, he walked into her classroom and asked for help. He was just 18. She consented and, while still her student, he began to court her."

"People get fired for that today," I laughed.

Abigail Powers Fillmore

"Their courtship lasted eight years before they married. He became a lawyer and, though a professional man's wife was not expected to work once she married, she continued to teach two more years while he established his law practice in Buffalo.

"Before they went to Washington, their home became a center for the local intellectuals in the Buffalo area, and she was well known for both her learning and her wit."

"What kind of First Lady was she?"

"She delegated the hostess duties to an 18-year-old daughter. But she did institute some changes. It was during Fillmore's administration that piped water was brought to the White House, and Abigail had the first bathtub installed. Also, up until that time, White House cooking was done in an open fireplace in the kitchen and she had the first iron range installed. But what she's remembered for most is establishing the first permanent library in the White House."

"Did she have much influence on her husband's policies?"

"No. But if Millard had listened to just one piece of advice from her, he might have been reelected in 1852."

"What was that?"

"She told him not to sign the Fugitive Slave Act of 1850. The Act made it easy for Southerners to reclaim runaway slaves who fled to the northern states. He thought, by signing it, he would win support in the South that would ensure his reelection. But the Act so infuriated northern abolitionists that many of them left the Whig party, to which he belonged, and joined the new Republican Party. The Whigs, in fact, didn't even renominate him. They chose General Winfield Scott, one of the heroes of the Mexican-American War."

"So, if he'd listened, he might have been reelected," I said.

"Right. But Abigail wasn't sorry to leave the White House. When Franklin Pierce was elected, she and her husband were free to retire. The first thing they did was plan a trip to Europe. They bought maps and books, packed their luggage, and were ready to leave right after they attended Pierce's inauguration. But the weather was cold and drizzly that inauguration day and Abigail got sick. A few weeks later she was dead."

Jane Appleton Pierce

"You keep doing that to me. Tell me Pierce's wife enjoyed her stint in the White House."

"You're out of luck. Jane Pierce was one of the most tragic of First Ladies. She had consumption, her husband was an alcoholic, and just a few months before his administration began, she and her husband were eyewitnesses to the gruesome death of their 11-year-old boy in a train wreck."

I grimaced.

"Two of their other sons were already dead, one as a baby and the other when he was four. With the death of the third one, I think she snapped because she spent most of her time in the upstairs family quarters of the White House composing letters to the dead eleven-year-old."

"Another recluse," I said.

"That's right. She became known to Washingtonians as 'The Shadow in the White House.'"

Harriet Lane

This is getting depressing. Tell me that the next President's wife fared better."

"Can't. The next President was a bachelor."

"That's good news. I mean, that's great news. Who was he?"

"James Buchanan. But, though he never married, he did have a White House hostess. She was his orphaned niece, Harriet Lane. He'd become her legal guardian when she was nine."

"How did Washington society feel about a young niece being the White House hostess?"

"In case you're not catching on, they liked almost all the young hostesses. With the exception of Sarah Polk, Washington had been treated to a string of First Ladies who were withdrawn or sickly. But Harriet was not only bright, she was beautiful and sociable. The song, "Listen to the Mockingbird," was dedicated to her and Washingtonians were glad to have someone who didn't hide upstairs. She became so popular that 'Harriet' became one of the most popular names for baby girls of that time.

"But she was no stranger to the political social scene when her uncle was elected. He'd been appointed minister to London in 1854, two years before he became President, and she went there with him. She was just 24 at the time but she became such a favorite of Queen Victoria that the Queen conferred upon her the rank of Ambassador's wife.

"She toured Europe and met other dignitaries and royalty and was a hit with everyone.

"Her uncle worried about her falling under the spell of all this flattery she received, then returning to the United States with European affectations. Elizabeth Monroe's daughter, Elizabeth Hay, had done that and Washington society resented when she acted as hostess for her mother. But that didn't happen with Harriet. Washington loved her and the White House years were good to her. She enjoyed the experience.

"Buchanan left the White House in 1861 and he and Harriet returned to his estate, called Wheatland, near Lancaster, Pennsylvania. She was then 31 and still unmarried—like her uncle.

"When she turned 36, she married Henry Johnston. They had two sons but, by 1884, her uncle, her two sons, and her husband were all dead."

"You're kidding."

"Nope. The woman who was orphaned at nine was alone again. She had no known living relatives."

"Wow."

"Later in life, she collected art and willed her collection to the Smithsonian. It formed the basis for today's National Collection of Fine Art. Most of the rest of her estate was used to establish the Harriet Lane Outpatient Clinic. It still exists today, as part of John Hopkins Hospital.

Mary Todd Lincoln

I caught a sign out of the corner of my eye. It told me we were going through La Moine.

"Mary Lincoln was probably the most tragic of the First Ladies. Other First Ladies have endured assassinations, scandal, the deaths of children, philandering husbands, but Mary got it all. And to top it all off, she was crazy."

"Crazy? Really?"

"A lot of people thought so including her husband, and if she wasn't she was, at the very least, the most eccentric First Lady we've ever had. Among other things, she claimed she was a psychic and swore she'd fore-seen his election to the presidency. And she was so moody and volatile that Abe often grabbed the kids and got out of the house until her anger passed.

"Often, her rages were fits of jealousy."

"Jealous of what?"

Mary Lincoln was probably the most tragic of the First Ladies. Other First Ladies have endured assassinations, scandal, the deaths of children, philandering husbands, but Mary got it all. To top it all off, she was crazy.

"Any woman who came near him. A lot of historians attribute this to some shrewish part of her nature. But she may have had good reason not to trust Honest Abe. Today, there are medical historians who believe he had contracted syphilis at some point, either before or after he married Mary, and that he transmitted it to her. You may not want to put that in your story because I'm not sure if it's ever been confirmed."

"How far did her jealousy go?"

"Oh, she did some outrageous things."

"Like what?"

"In one famous instance, she arrived late to a ceremony where Lincoln was reviewing troops. When she got there, another woman was riding beside her husband. When the review was over, the woman approached Mary to greet her. Mary let loose with a tirade that included accusations of adultery. By the time she found out the woman was the wife of General Ord, she had already reduced the woman to tears.

"Another woman who witnessed this episode would one day become First Lady herself. She was Julia Dent

Grant, wife of Ulysses S. Grant, and she had seen many of these outbursts. She made it a point to decline invitations to go to the White House or to socialize with the Lincolns because she didn't want to become a target herself. Most people don't know it but the Grants were supposed to be at Ford's theater the night Booth shot Lincoln. Julia had declined the invitation."

"He might have killed them both."

"Might have.

"Her moods and fits of temper became so frequent and public that those around her, including her husband, suspected insanity.

"In spite of this, Lincoln genuinely loved her. The night Booth shot her, he was holding Mary's hand.

...Lincoln became President and achieved greatness in spite of Mary's destructive behavior.

"She was, incidentally, the first First Lady to be widowed by assassination. But she didn't get much sympathy. The public never learned to like her, and newspapermen had a field day with her.

"Even though she came from a slave state—Kentucky—which stayed in the Union during the war, most of her family sided with the South and many of her brothers served the Confederacy. Because of this, she was often accused by Northern critics of being a Southern sympathizer and even a spy. But, if the truth were known, she may have been even more of an Abolitionist than her husband."

"There were others who disliked her because she seemed to give little thought to the war. Remember, Washington, D.C. was never far from the front during the war and there was always the fear of a rebel takeover of the city.

"And still more disliked her because, even though she had pretensions to thriftiness, she was probably the most prodigious spender the White House ever saw."

"Really?"

"Oh, yes. She was unstoppable. Once, when Lincoln saw the bills she'd racked up, he said he couldn't believe she could spend so thoughtlessly when the Union could barely afford blankets for the soldiers. Her debts exceeded his annual income as President.

"By the way, if you're one of those those who thrive on parallels between Lincoln and Kennedy, Kennedy was appalled by the spending sprees of his wife.

"To her dying day, she remained an unpopular figure, hounded by the press and ridiculed even when she was a widow.

"After the death of her third son, she lost it completely. She spoke with imaginary people and continued to pile up debts on her spending sprees, buying things she didn't use and often not even remembering what she bought. She seemed to sink deeper and deeper into psychosis."

"What made her that way?"

"Who knows? It may have been the syphilis some doctors today think she got from Abe.

"She seemed to have had a good childhood. She was one of 15 children but her family wasn't poor. Her father was an influential businessman. People like Henry Clay came to their home on a regular basis and Mary, we know, was well educated for a woman of her time. She often carried on conversations with these guests.

"She was a catch for the bachelors of her time. It's said she was courted by two of the four men who years later contended for the presidency in 1860—Lincoln, the man who was elected, and Stephen Douglas, whose name is forever linked with Lincoln's in history. But I don't know if it's true she was courted by Douglas."

"Her behavior must have been hard on Lincoln."

"Sure. One of the recurring themes in American history is men who succeed because of the women who supported them."

Mary Todd Lincoln

"Like John Adams and James Polk," I said.

"Like Adams and Polk. But Lincoln became President and achieved greatness in spite of Mary's destructive behavior."

I nodded.

"Finally, with her husband and three of her sons dead, and her becoming more and more bizarre, her last surviving son had her committed to an insane asylum."

"Committed?"

"She was only there a few months before one of her sisters and some of her friends got her released. But her bizarre behavior continued. She left the country in 1868—one step ahead of her many creditors—and drifted around Europe for a few years. She didn't come back until 1871 when Congress authorized a pension for her. I should add that the law authorizing a pension would have lost in Congress because some Congressmen refused to vote for the pension unless Sarah Polk was granted one. So you could say Mary Lincoln's pension was granted only because of Sarah's popularity.

Anyway, once she returned, she lived out the rest of her life with the sister who had freed her from the asylum. She died in 1882.

Eliza McCardle Johnson

"Who followed her?"

"Andrew Johnson's wife, Eliza McCardle Johnson."

"Tell me she was happy."

"She was miserable."

"Thanks."

"The Johnsons were one of the few presidential couples both of whom were born into poverty. They married when she was 17 and he was 19. Her father died when she was just a girl, and she herself spent most of her adult life sickly and tubercular. But her mother made sure she acquired an education. Andrew, however, was illiterate when they met and apprenticed to be a tailor. She tutored him, teaching him to read and write, and became the second First Lady to educate her husband.

"What made her miserable?"

"Everything. Her husband wouldn't support the vengeful Reconstruction policies the Republican Congress wanted to impose on the defeated South. So, the Republican majority in the House—his own party, mind you—impeached him and he was tried by the Senate.

"Because of his unpopularity, she lived in constant dread that he would be assassinated, like Lincoln."

"He was cleared by the Senate, wasn't he?"

"By one vote."

"How did Washington society like her?"

"She shunned them and they shunned her. The White House functions she attended could probably be counted on one hand.

"Fortunately, her eldest daughter, Martha, served as hostess, and though Eliza and Andrew were two of the most unpopular people in Washington, their daughter was well liked."

"I'll bet they didn't miss Washington when they left."

"She was relieved when Grant was nominated in 1868 and they could go back to Tennessee.

"Eventually, Andrew was embraced again by his fellow Tennesseans, and he was reelected to the Senate—the body that had tried him—in 1875. But he died that year and she died a year later.

"I'll tell you," I said, "the more you talk, the worse it seems for a woman to be the President's wife."

"Funny you should say that just now because the next First Lady loved the position."

"Well, it's about time."

Julia Dent Grant

"Julia Grant claimed her eight years in the White House were the happiest of her life. Like many First Ladies, she was a woman born into wealth, who ducked below her station to marry a man who later became President of the United States. Also, as with many of those who preceded her, she came from a family of slaveholders. But, because her husband was the only Union general who could stay in the field with Robert E. Lee, he may have been the one man most responsible for the defeat of the South and the fall of slavery."

"Who did her family side with?"

"Like Mary Lincoln's family, most of her family sided with the Confederacy. After the war, both of their fathers moved into the White House to live with them. Need I tell you what happened? Her father still sympathized with the South and his father sided with the Union. The two old men, constantly sniping at each other, became subjects of the national press and amused the whole country."

"You don't hear many good things about Grant," I said.

"Let's face it, he was one of only three great generals that war produced, but he was a failure in almost everything else. He failed at farming, as a clerk in his father's leather goods store, he even failed as a soldier—until the war.

"But, through it all, she stood by him, and loved him.

...She was homely, rather dumpy, and in most photographs we have of her, she's not facing the camera because she was cross-eyed.

"Then the war changed everything. When it started, he volunteered. He had a string of spectacular successes and rose through the ranks until Lincoln chose him to be the man the Union needed to oppose Lee himself."

"Was she a help to him through all this?"

"She was a stabilizing influence on him—one of the few—and she very likely helped keep down his drinking sprees. And he, in turn, was in love with her.

"She was homely, rather dumpy, and in most photographs we have of her, she's not facing the camera because she was cross-eyed. She once told Ulysses she was planning to undergo a surgical procedure that would correct it. He said, 'No.' Her eyes were like that when he fell in love with her and that's how he wanted her to stay. So, she forewent the operation.

"She was a very popular First Lady. The first one since Sarah Polk. One reason was that she befriended so many of the wives of the Congressmen and Cabinet members. These women had lived in Washington for years. They knew the social climate and the ins and outs. Either by design or good fortune she got them on her side and that was more than half the battle to be accepted and respected as the First Lady.

"She created truly democratic White House socials. The women who attended them—by invitation only—came from all walks of life and they dressed according to their means. Julia didn't tolerate snobbery.

"Incidentally, the term 'First Lady' first appeared as a reference to her in a newspaper at this time. But it still didn't see widespread usage until it was used to describe Lucy Hayes several years later."

"It's nice to hear she liked being First Lady."

"She liked it so much that she would like to have seen Grant serve a third term. But, by the end of his second term, his administration was so scandal ridden that, even though he was still one of the most loved men in the country, the Republicans didn't want him in the White House any longer.

"What did he do?"

"It wasn't what he did, and very few people believed him to be at the root of the scandals that plagued his administration. The problem was that he surrounded himself with men who proved to be unscrupulous and, when they were caught, he made the mistake of standing by them."

"I guess his crime was that he was a bad judge of character."

"That and his trusting nature would plague him for the rest of his life."

"Even after he left the White House?"

"Even then. After his presidency was over, he and Julia travelled around the world and they were wined and dined by world leaders from Europe to Japan. But, when they returned to the States, he was once again doomed to failure. There was no job he could hold and, because he was so trusting, he turned his family's fortune over to a shady investment firm and lost everything. His family, so recently secure, was suddenly destitute.

"About this time he was also diagnosed with terminal cancer.

"A publisher, knowing a good thing when he saw it, approached him with a proposal to write his memoirs. Grasping for straws, Grant accepted.

"Mark Twain, the most successful American writer of his time—perhaps of all time—looked at the contract and told Grant he was being taken. He personally offered to underwrite the book and said he'd give Grant an equitable royalty.

"So, Grant wrote the book while he was dying. Much of it on a porch at a resort in the Adirondacks. People came from miles away to stand and

Julia Dent Grant

watch the dying man, the most famous American of his time, sitting there writing his book.

"Have you read it?"

I shook my head.

"It's great. He speaks honestly about himself, how he grew up, and how and why he conducted himself as he did in each of his military campaigns. Someday, teachers in high school and college are going to rediscover it, and they'll assign it as not only a source of U.S. history but as a model of clear and economical writing—or at least they should.

"What he didn't cover in his book was his administration as President. He probably couldn't have even if he had wanted to because he died within days of finishing it.

"It was the only American book to outsell Twain's in the last century.

Suddenly, we were pulling off Interstate 5 and into Ashland.

"There were those who thought Twain had written the memoirs himself. There's no reason to believe so. It's in a simple and elegant style that more writers probably wish they could write in themselves.

"It made a fortune and Ulysses left Julia and the rest of his family financially secure."

"The success of his book inspired her to write her memoirs—she was the first First Lady to do so—but she didn't write like Ulysses did. Her book remained unpublished until 1975, 73 years after she died."

"She must have been the antithesis of Mary Lincoln," I said.

"One of the traits that made Mary infamous made Julia endearing to the public."

"Really? What was that?"

"Both were extravagant spenders. But America was entering the 'Gilded Age' during Grant's administration and people were trying to forget the war. She didn't go through money the way Mary did, but she was a big spender, nonetheless."

"Was she ever accused of influencing her husband's policies?"

"Unlike some other First Ladies, she not only had no influence on her husband's policies, she rarely understood them. On at least one occasion, she placed herself squarely on both sides of an issue."

"Did she leave a mark on the White House itself?"

"Not much I can think of. She had the Grecian columns added. That's about all."

Up ahead I saw Duffy's pickup parked in the parking lot of a restaurant. I had hoped he wouldn't be there yet.

Mac spotted him. "We're at the end of our trip."

The end of the story, I thought.

"Do you think we'll be able to talk about this another time—maybe finish it?" I asked.

"Some time. Do you think your readers would really want to hear more about it?"

I shrugged. "Maybe this is enough." ∆

FARM/GARDEN

Turkeys — fun and profitable and not as dumb as you think

By Dynah Geissal

Turkeys are a lot of fun to raise and can be a good cash crop, too. They're a bit different than other poultry but have unfairly gotten a bad rap. I have raised a lot of turkeys and not one has ever drowned by looking up at the rain. I really have trouble believing that one. They are very friendly (except for an occasional mean old tom) and will follow you around if they are allowed the freedom of the barnyard.

Turkeys can be acquired from a hatchery or from the feed store. The advantages of buying them from the feed store are that they are already started and that you don't have to buy a minimum of 25, as you do from most hatcheries. The advantages of the hatchery are that there is a longer time in which to buy and also a greater variety of breeds to choose from.

I have never had trouble with disease in turkeys, even when I've raised them from chicks. If you have only a few turkeys, it makes some sense to raise them together, if you keep a few things in mind. First of all, turkeys must have feed of at least 21% protein, and 25% is better. Twenty percent is adequate if you also feed milk "free choice." Skim milk is okay.

Turkeys are curious. I once put my 200 chicks and 5 turkeys into their brooder pen, which was enclosed by chicken wire. Two-month-old chickens were outside the chicken wire barrier. The turkey chicks, being shy, ran into the middle of the pen, but the adult turkeys, being curious, stood right at the wire to see what was going on. In a flash, a chicken had one turkey by a toe and was pulling it through the wire. Another chicken had a turkey by its beak. I ran out to get something to cover the bottom part of the pen and, by the time I got back (no more than two minutes), another turkey had been pulled out of the pen. Two of those turkeys died. That sort of thing may be the cause of their reputation for being stupid.

For the rest of this article, we will assume you are raising turkeys in their own brooder. Because of their personalities, turkeys get bored easily, and they'll peck at each other when they're bored. Therefore, give them more space than you would think is necessary. That way, there will be more area for them to explore. Feeding greens from the beginning keeps them busy, too. If they do peck at each other, cover the pecked place with pine tar and correct the situation, so injuries don't recur.

With regard to temperature, you will really have to use judgment here. I'll give you some guidelines, but there is a lot of variation. I like to lower the temperature as soon as possible, so that they feather out early. If they're cold, though, they won't be healthy and nothing is gained.

You can keep the temperature between 95 and 110° F for the first 10 days, or you can begin lowering the temperature immediately if the turkeys seem comfortable with less heat. Either way, when you do lower the temperature, do it gradually. The chart below suggests a schedule for temperature adaptation.

Day 1	95°
Day 3	90°
Week 2	85°
Week 3	80°
Week 4	75°
Week 5	65-75°
Wks. 7-11	Little or no heat

Between the fourth and sixth weeks, turkeys may go outside on a warm sunny day, if there is no wind.

When you initially put the turkeys into their brooder, dip each beak into the water. Later, if one of them does not appear to be eating, dip its beak again. That's usually all it takes.

The waterer should be three inches higher than the floor, so that litter is not scratched into it. Warm water should be given as long as heat is used in the brooder. The waterer should be washed every day in hot soapy water.

Feed turkey starter and fresh tender greens free choice. I try not to give medicated feed to my livestock, but I believe it's a good idea to use it when starting turkeys.

At six weeks, begin offering scratch grains free choice. At this time, 20% protein is adequate. At seven weeks, begin mixing grower into the starter, so that by nine weeks you are feeding all grower. At 11 weeks, mix in one-quarter finisher (70% to 80% corn) or broiler feed with the grower. By 16 to 17 weeks, you will notice that they are cutting back on the milk they consume, if you are feeding that for extra protein. At 19 weeks, feed half grower and half finisher, plus the scratch grain and greens.

Feeders should be washed with hot soapy water every ten days. Stir litter every other day and change it every week.

Butcher at 24 to 28 weeks. Turkeys have been bred to grow faster and bigger. If you think that your turkeys are getting too big, cut down on the grower/finisher and/or milk, but keep feeding scratch grains free choice. Some strains grow faster than others. I changed hatcheries one year and ended up with 42-pound toms. People who had ordered the toms for Thanksgiving were a bit overwhelmed. I have to say that the one I cooked was as tender and juicy as any I've had. But be aware that some birds grow phenomenally.

Try to get your orders early if you plan to sell. People don't want to plan seven or eight months in advance, but if they will, it helps. If you do start to raise turkeys to sell, you will build a following in a couple of years. I sell mine for $1.50 per pound, and people come back year after year.

Turkeys will roost on just about everything, and whatever is beneath a 15 or 20 pound bird will get mighty soiled. I always clip one wing to keep them penned, but it has to be done every time the wing feathers grow back. The birds love to range and can get a lot of their feed that way, so you may want to let them out during the day and pen them up at night. Unlike other birds, turkeys can be led and will respond to calling. They are very difficult to herd, however.

I hope you will enjoy raising turkeys as much as I do. Just try to understand their unique traits, and don't pay too much attention to the stories you may have heard about them. ∆

Visit our web site
http://www.backwoodshome.com

It's an easy way to...

- e-mail staff members
- buy an anthology or book
- re-read articles from back issues
- subscribe or renew your subscription
- link to other self-sufficiency web sites

COUNTRY LIVING

A Backwoods Home Anthology

Learning in the pickle patch

By Jill Fox

What can transform your children into responsible, appreciative, hard working human beings—as they earn money—right on your own homestead? Growing vegetables for the local canning factory, of course. Depending on your location, it could be peppers, tomatoes, or even cucumbers. We grew cucumbers.

For years we had heard about people growing cucumbers for the pickle factory, but I could not get anyone to explain the process. All I ever heard was: "It's hard. Once you do it, you'll never want to do it again."

That didn't discourage my daughter Rachel, then 13, from trying her hand. We (her father, sister Emily, and I) went with her to a meeting for potential growers. My questions were

Emily holds up an example of the ideal pickling cucumber—the kind that brings the highest price.

Rachel displays a five-gallon bucket of the day's harvest.

laughed at by old-time farmers but we were not daunted. We just vowed to avenge ourselves by being a success. So we signed a contract with the pickle plant to grow a quarter acre of "cukes."

We couldn't find anyone willing to plow our plot for us and, lacking a tractor ourselves, we used a couple of garden tillers. My husband and I would pass each other and grin and wave as he tilled up one row and I tilled down another. After several hours of the grueling task, the grinning and waving ceased. But by then we had finished.

Then we planted seeds. While most farmers use an attachment on their tractors to plant, or at least a big-wheeled, push-behind garden seeder, we had neither. This was a job we all did, each using his own technique. Mine was to lay the seeds on the ground at proper spacing and then have Emily, my younger daughter, then 8, push them into the ground with her finger.

Eventually I was left alone to finish planting the last few rows. I took the opportunity to say a little prayer asking God to make our endeavor a success for the children's sake. They were so enthusiastic—I wanted them to learn that hard work does pay off.

Every seed seemed to sprout, but with their emergence came the dreaded cucumber beetle. At present, there is not an effective organic method of controlling these beetles, but I've read about one being developed. The beetles will wipe out a crop if left unchecked. Treating our crop took several hours at a time, using a small home garden sprayer.

The smaller the better

After thinning and side-dressing the cukes with nitrogen, we began the harvest. We were so excited as we picked those tiny little cucumbers. We were

The Fifth Year

Bending over row after row, Rachel picks "pickles" to sell to the local cannery.

told by veteran growers to not let them get any larger than your thumb.

We loaded our maiden harvest into the trunk of our small foreign car (there was no farm truck for us) and headed off to the pickle station. We had never been there, and when I asked where to unload, I again felt like we were the object of snickering.

Then, seeing that we were new, the manager asked us to step closer to see how the pickle sorter works. First the cukes are dumped on a conveyor which shakes them over a series of slots. Each size cuke falls through its respective slot, and they are collected in bins at the bottom. Most of ours were collected in the first bin. That was good: the smallest ones bring the highest price.

They weighed each size separately; the manager did some calculating, made out our check and handed it to us smiling. She said we had the highest check of anyone that day, including growers with larger plots than ours. She went on to say that our "pickles" were unusually pretty and ideally shaped. At that moment I was personally avenged for not being taken seriously by the old-timers at the meeting.

After a couple more days of picking, Rachel and Emily were awakened to what hard work it really is. Emily kept reminding me that it wasn't her idea in the first place so she shouldn't have to pick. Rachel, to my surprise, kept her word and picked her share. I assumed responsibility for picking half, she was responsible for picking the other half, and Emily picked a row or two for us both. This we did without fail three times a week, for about five weeks.

Rachel's countenance began to change from that of an impudent teenager to one of a more appreciative human being. What she said to me that first week was priceless. She admitted it was the hardest thing she'd ever done in her life and that she would never complain about her regular chores again. As she asked me how I could pick for hours and never complain, I sensed that she was developing a greater respect for me and for working people in general.

Picking pickles was the hardest work we'd known, bending over row after row, hour after hour, in the hot sun, with blood rushing to your head. After about 10 rows we would scoot on our behinds or crawl on our elbows—any way we could get them picked.

At first we thought we'd wear skimpy clothing in an attempt to get a suntan, but after being scraped and pricked by the spiny vines which caused unbearable itching, that was out. We had to wear gloves, that's for sure, but they would get heavy and misshapen from dirt and dampness and it became a struggle to keep them on. We also thought flip-flops would be the perfect footwear, especially on rainy days. They only slung the mud up our legs and backs with each step we took until we finally walked right out of them as the suction created by the mud claimed them.

The job had its good side. We developed strength and speed. Each bucketful weighed about 20 pounds, and Rachel and I carried two at a time. We dumped them into feed sacks which weighed anywhere from 60 to 90 pounds when full. Rachel could lift a sackful by herself and toss it into the trunk. One time we had the trunk, back seat, and all the floorboards full—over 600 pounds of cukes.

By speed I mean we could pick the entire patch, load the car, strip our clothes, hose off, throw on some clean clothes and make the 20-mile trip to the station before it closed for the day. I remember us laughing and singing all the way there as we showed the relief of having another day behind us.

Our patch quit bearing about a week early due to the drought. That might not have happened if the ground had been plowed, allowing the roots to go deeper. But even this we considered a blessing. The girls had not become "burnt out" yet, but were ready for the job to be over. We quit with our positive attitudes intact.

God answered my prayer: it had been a rewarding experience for the girls, and yes, for me as well. We'll be reminiscing about those happy pickle pickin' times for years to come. And we can't look at a jar of pickles without wondering, "Did I pick that one?" Δ

Index of articles in previous issues of *Backwoods Home Magazine*

FINDING AN ARTICLE OR A TOPIC

Articles are grouped within categories, such as Animals, Building, Recipes, etc. The complete list of categories is shown on the cover of this Index. Within each category, articles are alphabetized by keywords (shown in **BOLD CAPITAL LETTERS**) that tell you the topic of each article. For example, under the first category (Animals), the first four articles are alphabetized by their topic keywords: Australian Shepherd, birth, calf, and cattle.

There are three ways to obtain the articles you want:

1) Order the back issues that contain them.

2) Order the anthologies that contain them.
   Some back issues are sold out, but their articles can be found in the anthologies.
   (See below for information on our anthologies.)

3) In the case of Issues 41, 42, 43 and 44 only, you can order photocopies of the articles you want. The cost is $2 per article, which includes shipping and handling. We offer this service for those issues because they are sold out, but not yet included in an anthology.

For each article listed, the Index tells you where the article is available.

Here are some examples from the "Animals" category:

"Raising my calf Max" appears in Issue No. 35, which is available for ordering.

"The Australian Shepherd is a good dog choice..." appears in Issue No. 18 and also in the 3-year book anthology, both of which are available for ordering.

"Raising your own feed crops for your livestock" appeared in Issue No. 44, which is sold out, so the listing reminds you that the article is available by ordering a photocopy.

OUR ANTHOLOGIES

Most of the articles (about 90% or 195 articles) from Issues No. 1-12 are available in our 480-page book titled
Backwoods Home Magazine: The Best of the First Two Years, referred to below as the "2-year book."

Most of the articles from Issues No. 13-18 are available in our book titled
Backwoods Home Magazine: The Third Year, referred to below as the "3-year book."

Most of the articles from Issues No. 19-24 are available in our book titled
A *Backwoods Home* Anthology: The Fourth Year, referred to below as the "4-year book."

Most of the articles from Issues No. 25-30 are available in our book titled
A *Backwoods Home* Anthology: The Fifth Year, referred to below as the "5-year book."

BACK ISSUES

Original copies of Issues No. 8, 9, 11, 14, 15, 16, 17, 18, 19, 20, 21, 27, 28, 30, 31, 33, 34, 35, 36, 37, 38, 39, 40, 45, 46, 47, and 48 are available for $5 each. Issues No. 1, 2, 3, 4, 5, 6, 7, 10, 12, 13, 22, 23, 24, 25, 26, 29, 32, 41, 42, 43, and 44 have been sold out, so they are not available.

ORDERING

Send check or money order, your name and address, and the items you wish to order to
Backwoods Home Magazine, P.O. Box 40, Montague, CA 96064. We accept **Visa** and **MasterCard**.
You can place credit card orders by phone at **1-800-835-2418**. (This number is for orders only.)

Article	Located in:

Alternative energy — see Independent energy

Animals

The **AUSTRALIAN SHEPHERD** is a good **DOG** choice for the self sufficient person who values brains and loyalty	Issue No. 18, 3-year book
The miracle of a country **BIRTH** (goat kid)	5-year book
Raising my **CALF** Max	Issue No. 35
Try these smaller breeds of multi-purpose **CATTLE**	Issue No. 37
When Irish eyes are smiling — a love affair with Kerry-Dexters (**CATTLE**)	Issue No. 31
The headless **CHICKEN** and the family picnic — What a sight!	Issue No. 33
Butchering, cleaning, and cooking **CHICKENS**	3-year book
Everything you ever wanted to know about **CHICKENS** Part I	Issue No. 11, 2-year book
Everything you ever wanted to know about **CHICKENS** Part II	Issue No. 12, 2-year book
If you'd like to get started with **CHICKENS** here are the basics	Issue No. 36
Protect your **CHICKENS** from predators by installing this novel electric fence	Issue No. 48
Save time and energy with the fenced **CHICKEN COOP/GARDEN**	Issue 44 (Sold out. Photocopy of article is available.)
You can learn to help **CHICKS** live through "problem hatches"	Issue 44 (Sold out. Photocopy of article is available.)
The great **COW** caper	Issue No. 28, 5-year book
Finding, buying, milking, and living with the family **COW**	Issue No. 36
This St. Bernard backwoods hero saved old Grandma's life (a true **DOG** story)	Issue No. 35
WOLF-DOG HYBRIDS smart, loyal, but they're not for everyone	Issue No. 35
GREAT PYRENEES — a one of a kind guardian of stock (**DOGS**)	Issue No. 11, 2-year book
Lucky **DUCK**	Issue No. 28, 5-year book
The **DUCK** dilemma: they're a lot of fun, and they *do* eat those slugs — *but...*	Issue No. 38
A bit about **DUCKS**	Issue No. 21, 4-year book
The dairy **GOAT** — a gallon of milk a day	Issue No. 21, 4-year book
How to buy your first dairy **GOAT**	Issue No. 21, 4-year book
GOATS are great — I kid you not!	2-year book
Raising **GOATS** as a business is a profitable and fun venture	Issue No. 29, 5-year book
Raising **GOATS** can be profitable	Issue No. 33
GOOD-BYE old friend	Issue No. 27, 5-year book
Father **GOOSE**	4-year book
The **GOSLING** that lived	Issue No. 28, 5-year book
One woman's self-sustaining **GRASSLAND** livestock farm	Issue No. 18, 3-year book
Consider small-scale **HOG** production for delicious food and reliable income	Issue No. 40
Buying the first **HORSE**	Issue No. 21, 4-year book
A first time **HORSE BUYER'S GUIDE**	2-year book
A **HORSE** named Lady	Issue No. 9
Adopting a **WILD HORSE**	Issue No. 31
A **KESTREL** in the coop	Issue No. 11
Animal **LIFESAVERS** — CPR & comfrey	3-year book
Using your "stockman's eye" to **CARE FOR YOUR LIVESTOCK**	Issue No. 15, 3-year book
Raise your own feed crops for your **LIVESTOCK**	Issue No. 44 (Sold out. Photocopy of article is available.)
LLAMAS GUARDING SHEEP? Not such a far-fetched idea	Issue No. 19, 4-year book
It's easy to build your own **MILKING STANCHION**	Issue No. 41 (Sold out. Photocopy of article is available.)
If it's **PERSONALITY** you like, farm animals have a *lot* of it	Issue No. 34
The portable **PIG** machine (movable pen/shelter)	Issue No. 8, 2-year book

How to care for and feed the family **POND**	Issue No. 27, 5-year book
How to raise the best **PORK** you have ever tasted	Issue No. 9
Improve your **POULTRY** with **SELECTIVE BREEDING**	Issue No. 41 (Sold out. Photocopy of article is available.)
RABBIT DISEASES and how to cope with them	Issue No. 17, 3-year book
How to raise **RABBITS** rabbits rabbits rabbits rabbits rabbits rab	Issue No. 12, 2-year book
Raising **RABBITS** — for meat and making money, it's hard to beat this creature on the homestead	Issue No. 40
DAIRYING WITH SHEEP	Issue No. 8
Raising **SHEEP**	5-year book
How to buy your first **SHEEP** (without getting shorn)	Issue No. 32
These are **JACOB'S SHEEP**	Issue No. 37
Trimming feet (**SHEEP**) is important	Issue No. 44 (Sold out. Photocopy of article is available.)
SLAUGHTERING AND BUTCHERING	4-year book
Don't have a cow! (Get a **STEER** instead.)	Issue No. 38
Raising **WATER BUFFALO** — are they better than cattle?	Issue No. 27, 5-year book
INJURED AND SICK WILDLIFE gets a lease on life from this California group	2-year book
WINTERIZE your animals without going broke	Issue No. 48

Building

Building for **INDOOR AIR QUALITY** (IAQ)	2-year book
Design and build a **BARN**	4-year book
Build a **BAT HOUSE** to control insect pests	Issue No. 46
Here's an easier (and cheaper) way to make **WOODEN BEAMS**	Issue No. 43 (Sold out. Photocopy of article is available.)
Make a **SIDEWALK GARDEN BENCH**	Issue No. 47
Don't throw away them **BRICKS**	Issue No. 33
How to build an inexpensive **CELLAR** that works	Issue No. 18, 3-year book
Make your own **LUMBER** with a chainsaw mill	Issue No. 39
Build a fieldstone **CHIMNEY**	Issue No. 27, 5-year book
CHINKING for log homes	4-year book
Solve **CHINKING** woes with a mortar-sawdust mix	Issue No. 41 (Sold out. Photocopy of article is available.)
COB CONSTRUCTION is *literally* dirt cheap	Issue No. 39
Here's a **COLD STORAGE HOUSE** as good as our ancestors built	Issue No. 37
Simplified **CONCRETE AND MASONRY WORK** work	5-year book
CONCRETE DOMES have some impressive advantages	Issue No. 39
COOL your home with this simple device while you also meet your hot water needs	Issue No. 46
How to hang an exterior **DOOR**	Issue No. 8
Here's some sound construction advice for tackling the most important aspect of an **EARTH-SET** dwelling (foundation wall design)	Issue No. 9, 2-year book
Build an **EARTH-SHELTERED LOG CABIN**	Issue No. 27, 5-year book
"What if" planning makes a house **EXPANSION** easier	2-year book
How to build the **FENCE** you need	Issue No. 21, 4-year book
You can cut your costs in half by installing a **CHAIN LINK FENCE** yourself	Issue No. 47
Build an inexpensive but durable **JACKLEG FENCE**	Issue No. 45
Set 100 **STEEL FENCE POSTS** a day with a home-made driver	Issue No. 44 (Sold out. Photocopy of article is available.)
Living with a plywood **FLOOR**	4-year book
Lay **VINYL FLOORING** the foolproof way	Issue No. 45
Build a **HOMESTEAD FORGE** and **FABRICATE YOUR OWN HARDWARE**	Issue No. 36

FOUNDATIONS . . . from pole to slab	Issue No. 15, 3-year book
FRAMING house walls is a cinch	2-year book
Learn the basics of wall **FRAMING**	Issue No. 27, 5-year book
METAL FRAMING — no more mildew, termites, rot, fungus, shrinkage, fire, or knots	Issue No. 33
YESTERDAY'S FURNITURE today — a puncheon bench	Issue No. 46
Build a three-car **GARAGE** for $78	Issue No. 39
How to construct a soundproof **GENERATOR SHED**	Issue No. 8, 2-year book
You can make this effective **GRAY WATER DISPOSAL SYSTEM**	Issue No. 40
Make your own **TOOL HANDLES**	Issue No. 31
HEAT your upstairs by cutting holes in the floor!	Issue No. 14, 3-year book
HEAT your household from the outside	Issue No. 46
Save time and money, and get that custom look, with **HINGES** you make yourself	Issue No. 42 (Sold out. Photocopy of article is available.)
This **HOUSE** was **BLASTED OUT OF SOLID ROCK**	Issue No. 44 (Sold out. Photocopy of article is available.)
A **HOUSE-HEATING SOLAR GREENHOUSE**	Issue No. 12, 2-year book
Building your own **HOME** Part III	Issue No. 27
A little knowledge and sweat can build a **HOME** for under $10,000	2-year book
From domes to yurts, **HOME IDEAS** get their inspiration from the past	2-year book
NEW HOMES FROM OLD HOMES	3-year book
A **HOT TUB** doesn't have to be expensive . . . We made ours for $35	Issue No. 43 (Sold out. Photocopy of article is available.)
From the foundation up, **HOUSE BUILDING IS FORGIVING**	2-year book
INSULATION AND VAPOR BARRIERS	Issue No. 19, 4-year book
LOG BUILDING SCHOOL in woods offers hands-on training	Issue No. 12
What to look for in a **KIT LOG HOME**	4-year book
Build an all-purpose **LADDER**	Issue No. 45
Lessons I learned while building my **LOG HOME**	Issue No. 39
LOG HOMES — fact and fiction	4-year book
Build a **LOG HOUSE** from scratch	Issue No. 9, 2-year book
Building an expensive **LOG HOUSE** — the cheap way, Part I	Issue No. 30, 5-year book
Build an expensive **LOG HOUSE** — the cheap way, Part II	Issue No. 32
How to build a low-cost **LOG LIFTER**	Issue No. 27, 5-year book
Determined woman builds distinctive **VERTICAL LOG STUDIO**	Issue No. 27, 5-year book
Get low-cost, high quality **LUMBER** by investing in an inexpensive planer	Issue No. 45
Roughcut — a cut above? (roughsawn **LUMBER**)	Issue No. 16, 3-year book
The case against **MODULAR HOUSING**	Issue No. 18, 3-year book
MOVING HOUSES — good bargains for backwoods living	Issue No. 18, 3-year book
Understanding **PAINT** and **STAIN**	Issue No. 45
If you build your own (legal) house, you'll have to deal with the **PERMIT PROCESS**	Issue No. 45
Build a cool **POOL** for a refreshing price	Issue No. 34
Steal a **PORCH** from the forest	2-year book
Need a **PRIVY**? Here's the right way to build one	Issue No. 34
PROPANE is a multi-purpose fuel, and it has many key advantages	Issue No. 37
Thermal mass has its place, but **R VALUE** is the more efficient	4-year book
INSTALL RAFTERS ALONE — the easy way	Issue No. 35
RECYCLED MATERIALS add flavor to the Allisons' Oregon home	2-year book
Here's a simple device to **IMPROVE ROUGH ROADS**	Issue No. 31
Building a **ROOF** by yourself can be a big challenge, but a triumph when you are done!	2-year book
Would you believe...a **CANVAS ROOF**? It's simple, quick, durable, and cheap	Issue No. 39
There's nothing like **METAL ROOFING**	3-year book
Wow! — field-fabricated standing-seam **METAL ROOFING**	Issue No. 14, 3-year book

SAVE a bundle of **MONEY BY BUILDING** your home **YOURSELF**	Issue No. 11, 2-year book
Use your own **SAWMILL** to cut lumber prices	Issue No. 29, 5-year book
Here's how I built a 1000-gallon **SEPTIC TANK**	Issue No. 31
Build a **SHAVING HORSE**	Issue No. 15, 3-year book
Riving **SHINGLES** for your roof the old fashioned way	Issue No. 18, 3-year book
She built her own cross-country **SKI LODGE**	2-year book
STACKWALL CONSTRUCTION — it's beautiful, it's affordable, and you can build it yourself	Issue No. 35
...and how about a **STACKWALL CHICKEN COOP**	Issue No. 35
You have to look beyond the building code to create really pleasing **STAIRS**	Issue No. 39
These **DOUBLE-STEEP HALF STAIRS** save space	Issue No. 45
Make a fully functional **COLD STORAGE PIT/MOUND** and enjoy your garden's production all winter	Issue No. 47
STRAW BALE HOUSES — an alternative	Issue No. 14, 3-year book
Women and kids build a **STRAW BALE WALL**	Issue No. 31
Build cheap, **TEMPORARY SHELTERS** for your homestead's temporary needs	Issue No. 33
How to stop an invading army — **TERMITES!**	Issue No. 19, 4-year book
A cautionary tale (**TIRE DUMPING**)	3-year book
A house that a **TORNADO** helped build	Issue No. 16, 3-year book
TRUSSES — low-cost marvels to roof over most large spaces	4-year book
Semi-**UNDERGROUND, SOLAR** house near the Canadian border has some ideas worth crowing about	Issue No. 9, 2-year book
Build your own ferro-cement **WATER STORAGE TANK**	2-year book
A **BRICK WALK** with little work and less money	Issue No. 39
How to design and build a **WATER SYSTEM** for your backwoods home	Issue No. 9, 2-year book
Drive your own **WELL** for next to nothing	Issue No. 21, 4-year book
Protect your small buildings from **WIND DAMAGE**	Issue No. 48
Don't spend a lot of money for your house **WINDOWS**	Issue No. 17, 3-year book
The timberwolf **WOODBOX**	5-year book
Make a colonial **SHOULDER YOKE**	Issue No. 15, 3-year book

Commentary

A history lesson from **AYN RAND**	Issue No. 44 (Sold out. Photocopy of article is available.)
Rewriting the **BILL OF RIGHTS**	Issue No. 18, 3-year book
COUNTRY BUMPKINS	Issue No. 47
FLAG BURNING and **SOBRIETY CHECKS**	2-year book
A **FLAT TAX** makes sense	Issue No. 35
NEWT GINGRICH — man of history	Issue No. 33
The beast is at the door again (Too-**BIG GOVERNMENT**)	Issue No. 28, 5-year book
"Just Once in a Lifetime, **GROUP OF 100**"	Issue No. 12, 2-year book
GUILTY BY DEFAULT? One family's tragedy and a mother's warning	Issue No. 19, 4-year book
Forget the Presidential election: vote for concealed **HANDGUN** permits	Issue No. 42 (Sold out. Photocopy of article is available.)
NATIONAL HEALTH CARE — will it work in the U.S.?	Issue No. 15, 3-year book
Searching for the right American **HEALTH CARE PLAN** — is the **MEDICAL CARE SAVINGS ACCOUNT** the answer?	Issue No. 16, 3-year book
INDEPENDENCE	2-year book
Beyond **IRAQ** — **COPS** too powerful	Issue No. 9, 2-year book
The **FULLY-INFORMED JURY** can restore the "Bill of Rights"	Issue No. 19, 4-year book
Thanks for **NOT KILLING** them	Issue No. 48
Bad **LAWS**, good solutions	Issue No. 29, 5-year book
RUSH LIMBAUGH — champion of "the Right"	Issue No. 11, 2-year book

LUMBER REGS protect big business, not the consumer	Issue No. 21, 4-year book
JAMES MADISON's warning is more important now than ever	Issue No. 31
A **NEWS MAGAZINE** worth reading	Issue No. 45
MEDIA juveniles and Big Government	Issue No. 17, 3-year book
The **MILITIA MOVEMENT**	Issue No. 46
The age of **MISINFORMATON**	Issue No. 39
NEW WORLD ORDER — old world stench!	Issue No. 15, 3-year book
The "Leave Us Alone" coalition and some **ALTERNATIVE NEWS SOURCES**	Issue No. 41 (Sold out. Photocopy of article is available.)
Start your own **NEWSPAPER**	Issue No. 43 (Sold out. Photocopy of article is available.)
NUCLEAR superstition	4-year book
Soviet **NUCLEAR WEAPONS** . . . what effect on our freedoms if terrorists get hold of them?	Issue No. 15, 3-year book
POLITICALLY CORRECT	2-year book
The **POLITICS OF TRAGEDY**	Issue No. 34
The black man's worst enemy is not **RACISM**	Issue No. 16, 3-year book
RECESSION AND AIDS	Issue No. 14, 3-year book
Self reliance means **NO SCAPEGOATS**	Issue No. 36
Politics, **SELF RELIANCE,** and Bill Clinton	Issue No. 30, 5-year book
Born of desperation (benefits of **SELF RELIANCE**)	Issue No. 40
The **TAX PROBLEM**	Issue No. 38
The unfairness of **PROPERTY TAXES**	Issue No. 34
The new frontier (**TECHNOLOGY AND MAKING A LIVING**)	Issue No. 37
There's no stopping **TERM LIMITS**	3-year book
TOLERANCE —both the left and the right lack it	Issue No. 32
The facts of life (some amazing numbers describing the size of the **UNIVERSE**)	2-year book
Don't throw away your **VOTE**	Issue No. 42 (Sold out. Photocopy of article is available.)
A **WAR THAT SHOULDN'T BE**	2-year book

Computer nerd

The saga of the brand name **COMPUTER** and why you should buy a **"CLONE"**	Issue No. 47

Country living

I have a **NEW ADDRESS**…but I didn't move	Issue No. 44 (Sold out. Photocopy of article is available.)
DOROTHY AINSWORTH update: Out of the ashes	Issue No. 38
My Stars and Garters (adventures with homestead **ANIMALS**)	Issue No. 32
Considering life in **RURAL ARKANSAS**	Issue No. 43 (Sold out. Photocopy of article is available.)
BARN CLEANING	Issue No. 20, 4-year book
The saga of **BENJAMIN,** the backwoods, homeschool boy who wanted to get a job	Issue No. 37
Moon over **BOGUS BROOK**	Issue No. 27, 5-year book
CABIN FEVER	4-year book
Give a country **KID** a **CAMERA**	Issue No. 17, 3-year book
Driving and keeping your **CAR** running in winter	Issue No. 31
A few strings attached (to some pesky **CHICKENS**)	Issue No. 41 (Sold out. Photocopy of article is available.)
Winter ch-ch-ch-ch-**CHORES**	5-year book
Pressing **CIDER** and memories	Issue No. 41 (Sold out. Photocopy of article is available.)
CITY BOY, COUNTRY BOY	Issue No. 33
Finding Mr. (or Ms.) Right — when you're in the backwoods (**COMPANIONSHIP**)	Issue No. 11, 2-year book
COOKSTOVE LORE	Issue No. 31

Some thoughts about my **WOOD COOKSTOVE**	Issue No. 30, 5-year book
For a unique taste treat and a lot of fun, grow **NATIVE AMERICAN CORN**	Issue No. 48
Try our **COUNTRY CLICHES QUIZ**	Issue No. 34
The **DANDELION** is a healthful, great-tasting weed you can eat	Issue No. 44 (Sold out. Photocopy of article is available.)
DAVID AND THE D-4...a story about growing up	Issue No. 30, 5-year book
A **DEATH ON THE FARM** farm	Issue No. 33
Close encounters with the **WHITE DEER**	Issue No. 42 (Sold out. Photocopy of article is available.)
Reflections on "**THE DREAM**"	Issue No. 48
DRIVING back country roads	5-year book
DUELING DUCK	5-year book
Farm **ETHICS**	Issue No. 20, 4-year book
FIREPLACE COOKING cures the winter blues	Issue No. 19, 4-year book
Preventing and surviving **STOVE AND CHIMNEY FIRES**	Issue No. 30, 5-year book
GARDENING for blood	Issue No. 32
GOD willing and the creek don't rise	Issue No. 14
GOOD-BYE OLD FRIEND	Issue No. 43 (Sold out. Photocopy of article is available.)
OL' HANK and the John Deere	Issue No. 36
Going **HOME**	Issue No. 27
How we keep humming along on the **HOMESTEAD**	2-year book
Headwaters **HOMESTEAD** backwoods living in the Boston Mountains of Arkansas	Issue No. 17, 3-year book
HOMESTEADING at Hayden Lake	4-year book
Greechie, the **HUMMINGBIRD**	Issue No. 14, 3-year book
Build a bat house to control **INSECT PESTS**	Issue No. 46
Commonsense precautions to help **KEEP KIDS SAFE**	Issue No. 37
Teach your **KIDS** the fun, **SAFE WAY TO SPLIT KINDLING**	Issue No. 14, 3-year book
Orphaned **KITTENS** need special care	Issue No. 41 (Sold out. Photocopy of article is available.)
Having "Escaped from cultivation," **HONEYSUCKLE AND KUDZU** pose a real threat	Issue No. 35
It took a lot of weed-eating fish and work to make our **LAKE** usable	Issue No. 37
Excessive overhang (an amusing encounter with a **LAW ENFORCEMENT OFFICER**)	Issue No. 31
LEARNING in the pickle patch	Issue No. 30, 5-year book
Creating your own **LIFE AT HOME** without special tools	Issue No. 14, 3-year book
Backwoods **LIFESTYLE** misunderstood by people living in the "real world"	4-year book
Everybody *talks* about **LIGHTNING** and yes, there *are* things you can do about it	Issue No. 37
I'm living my **LOG CABIN DREAM**	4-year book
Looking for **LOVE** in rural places	Issue No. 15, 3-year book
Backwoods **LOVE AND DIVORCE** — Don't take the first for granted	Issue No. 35
I remember the day the **LYNX** attacked	Issue No. 44 (Sold out. Photocopy of article is available.)
MARVELS in small packages	Issue No. 14, 3-year book
It's **SPRINGTIME IN MONTANA**	Issue No. 38
MOVING HOUSES — good bargains for backwoods living	Issue No. 18, 3-year book
Fitting in with your **NEW NEIGHBORS**	4-year book
A **NIGHT OUT** at the Lady Griz game	Issue No. 19, 4-year book
Some thoughts on **GROWING OLDER** in the backwoods	Issue No. 16, 3-year book
My backwoods **PHILOSOPHY**	3-year book
PLANNING is an essential key to achieving the country life	5-year book
How to care for and feed the family **POND**	Issue No. 27, 5-year book
In praise of the rural **POST OFFICE**	Issue No. 20, 4-year book
A **POST OFFICE** called Podunk	Issue No. 32
Plant your **IRISH POTATOES** this fall or winter	Issue No. 48
Living with a **FROZEN PRIVY**	Issue No. 19, 4-year book

Open eyes can help you survive your move back to the land
  (**BEING PREPARED FOR PROBLEMS**) ....Issue No. 36
Be a **PURPLE MARTIN** landlord — and find lots of uses for gourds ....Issue No. 38
Some ideas for **REMODELING** and living from Catamount Farm ....3-year book
Inexpensive retired **RUSSIAN MILITARY RIFLES** can be the ideal backwoods meat guns ....Issue No. 47
Explore the world with **SHORTWAVE** ....5-year book
Listening to **SHORTWAVE** broadcasts from
  around the world is informative and fun...............Issue No. 42 (Sold out. Photocopy of article is available.)
SKI FEVER — an alternative to cabin fever! ....2-year book
The first **SLAUGHTER** ....Issue No. 21, 4-year book
I found that **SPECIAL SOMEBODY**, and you can too — with safety ....Issue No. 45
Preparing for **SNOW-INS** ....4-year book
For lots of summer fun, make a **SUPER SQUIRT GUN** ....Issue No. 46
The cholesterol in your **STOVEPIPE** can be fatal ....Issue No. 36
How ya gonna keep 'em down on the farm —
  after they've seen the mall? (**TEENAGERS**) ....Issue No. 28, 5-year book
There's still a lot of life left in **OLD TREES** ....Issue No. 45
Here's how to start your own **SMALL TOWN THEATER COMPANY** ....Issue No. 33
Mom's **WASH** was rainwater clean ....Issue No. 45
The Zen of **WASHDAY** ....Issue No. 36
WINTER in the backwoods is a lot more pleasant if you stay warm and dry ....Issue No. 48
How to cope with **WINTER BLUES** ....Issue No. 31
Outlaw **WISTERIA** ....Issue No. 29
COOKING WITH WOODSTOVES ....Issue No. 14, 3-year book

Crafts

Make a patchwork **BABY BUNTING** from scraps ....5-year book
Make this classic Shaker-style
  BUTCHER BLOCK ....Issue No. 42 (Sold out. Photocopy of article is available.)
Getting more **CASH** from your crafts...Issue No. 14, 3-year book
FELTING is an ancient art that's still useful today..Issue No. 40
FLOWERED CIRCLETS ....Issue No. 19, 4-year book
Make a gold or silver **WIRE CROSS** in 10 easy steps ....Issue No. 48
Make a **DOLL** with real hair.............................Issue No. 42 (Sold out. Photocopy of article is available.)
Make some rustic **BARBIE FURNITURE** ....Issue No. 48
Here's how to make a musical **BAMBOO FLUTE** ..Issue No. 42 (Sold out. Photocopy of article is available.)
Make your own nifty **GIFT BAGS** ....Issue No. 42 (Sold out. Photocopy of article is available.)
KISS CRITTERS — they're cute and they sell ....Issue No. 44 (Sold out. Photocopy of article is available.)
Keep the cooks happy with these
  easy-to-make **KITCHEN HELPERS** ....Issue No. 42 (Sold out. Photocopy of article is available.)
Make a **MATCHBOX CARE ROADWAY** ....Issue No. 35
Making **PAPER** at home is a fascinating process ....Issue No. 47
With **PAPIER MACHE** you can
  make treasures from trash...............................Issue No. 42 (Sold out. Photocopy of article is available.)
Make a beautiful **TIRE PLANTER** ....Issue No. 42 (Sold out. Photocopy of article is available.)
Here are five quick and easy craft **PROJECTS** ......Issue No. 42 (Sold out. Photocopy of article is available.)
Make a **QUILLOW (COMBINATION QUILT AND PILLOW)** ....Issue No. 34
Make a **CRAZY QUILT** ....Issue No. 14, 3-year book
QUILTS — masterpieces of the heart and windows into women's history ....4-year book
This method lets you make **QUILTS**
  that are artistic and very personal ....Issue No. 42 (Sold out. Photocopy of article is available.)

Use this system to make "**QUICKIE QUILTS**" for the whole family ....Issue No. 48
Making a great **RUG** from the rag bag ....Issue No. 18, 3-year book
Creating with **SALTDOUGH** ....3-year book
SEED ART — it's fun to collect the seeds
   and to create these unusual pictures...................Issue No. 42 (Sold out. Photocopy of article is available.)
Instant **SCARFLACE** ....Issue No. 12
Make a "**SLIT SHIRT**" ....Issue No. 30
Want a different look? Try **SPONGE PAINTING** ....Issue No. 33
How to make your own stereo cards (**STEREOPTICON PICTURES**) ....Issue No. 11, 2-year book
Boredom got you tied in knots? Try "**STRING CRAFT**".................................Issue No. 19, 4-year book
Custom crafted **TOILETRIES** make
   very special gifts ....Issue No. 42 (Sold out. Photocopy of article is available.)
Sheetery stitchery — better than paint or wallpaper (decorating **WALLS** with sheets)..................2-year book
Grandma will love this personal "**HELPING HANDS**" **WALL HANGING** ....Issue No. 46
Make quick-as-a-flash "**WINTER WARM WEATHER WEAR**"..Issue No. 31
You can make these beautiful
   pinecone **WREATHS** at home.............................Issue No. 42 (Sold out. Photocopy of article is available.)

Education

Here's 5 reasons adults should **READ KID'S BOOKS** ....Issue No. 46

Farm/garden

Try **ALFALFA** for bigger plants ....Issue No. 45
Combat **APHIDS** by *planting* garlic ....Issue No. 38
Whether they're new or historic varieties, some **APPLES** just belong in a country garden ....Issue No. 31
You definitely want to grow your own **ASPARAGUS** ....Issue No. 38
Grow your own **BAY TREE** ....Issue No. 34
Choosing superior **BEDDING PLANTS** ....Issue No. 21, 4-year book
HIGH BEDS and high production . . . with less work...Issue No. 20, 4-year book
How to build your own **BEEHIVES** ....Issue No. 21, 4-year book
The basics of backyard **BEEKEEPING** ....Issue No. 9, 2-year book
The bonus of **BLACKBERRIES** ....Issue No. 14, 3-year book
BLUEBERRIES are an affordable luxury ....Issue No. 38
Stop **BUGS** nature's way..Issue No. 38
Here's a **CABBAGE** with class —
   Early Jersey Wakefield ....Issue No. 43 (Sold out. Photocopy of article is available.)
Try a **CEMENT BLOCK** garden ....Issue No. 32
Save time and energy with the
   fenced **CHICKEN COOP/GARDEN** ....Issue No. 44 (Sold out. Photocopy of article is available.)
For battling ants or growing earthworms, try **COFFEE GROUNDS** ....Issue No. 12, 2-year book
There are lots of ways to **COMPOST** —
   Find the one that's right for you ....Issue No. 44 (Sold out. Photocopy of article is available.)
Troubleshooting problems with **COMPOST PILES** ....Issue No. 32
SHEET COMPOSTING is a work saver ....Issue No. 41 (Sold out. Photocopy of article is available.)
For a delicious adventure, grow your own **SWEET CORN** ....Issue No. 32
Traditional ways of **KEEPING** your **CORN** crop
   and seed corn are still very effective ....Issue No. 41 (Sold out. Photocopy of article is available.)
Use plastic to get a head start on
   CORN in the fall..Issue No. 41 (Sold out. Photocopy of article is available.)
Enrich your soil with **COVER CROPS** ....Issue No. 41 (Sold out. Photocopy of article is available.)

KRICKET KRAP for your garden	Issue No. 14
Try these fresh ideas in your **HOME DAIRY**	Issue No. 35
DEER discourology	5-year book
Overlooked garden **DELICACIES**	Issue No. 9
The **DUCK** dilemma: they're a lot of fun, and they *do* eat those slugs — *but*...	Issue No. 38
DUCKS contribute to a homestead in many ways	Issue No. 39
Calling **EARTHWORMS**???	Issue No. 19, 4-year book
The **ICHIBAN HYBRID EGGPLANT** is a real producer	Issue No. 38
Follow these eight easy steps to a successful **EGGPLANT** harvest	Issue No. 38
How to keep those **EXCESS EGGS**	Issue No. 30, 5-year book
ELDERBERRIES — the undiscovered fruit	Issue No. 32
Raise your own **FEED CROPS** for your livestock	Issue No. 44 (Sold out. Photocopy of article is available.)
Roll your own bio**FERTILIZER**	Issue No. 20, 4-year book
Raising **FISH** in the **FARM POND**	Issue No. 28, 5-year book
You can make your own **FERTILIZERS**	Issue No. 44 (Sold out. Photocopy of article is available.)
Winter protection and planting of **FRUIT TREES**	4-year book
WILD GARLIC — independent and delicious	Issue No. 46
Native of the forest: a guide to growing **GINSENG**	5-year book
GOATS don't eat zucchini	Issue No. 38
WHIP GRAFTING — the key to producing fruit variety	Issue No. 8, 2-year book
GRAPES — with 3000 varieties, you can grow them almost anywhere	5-year book
A **GREENHOUSE** offers advantages for the organic gardener	2-year book
The instant **GREENHOUSE**	2-year book
How to **CHOOSE A GREENHOUSE**	4-year book
GREENS — delicious, nutritious, and easy to grow	Issue No. 33
Keep fresh **GREENS** in your garden — even in the snow — by using **ROW COVER**	Issue No. 41 (Sold out. Photocopy of article is available.)
Grow winter salad **GREENS** on your windowsill	Issue No. 42 (Sold out. Photocopy of article is available.)
For something different in your garden, try **GROUND CHERRIES**	Issue No. 38
Whose garden is this anyway? (gardener vs. **GROUNDHOG**)	Issue No. 38
Make superior **HAY** the old-fashioned way	Issue No. 44 (Sold out. Photocopy of article is available.)
Fall in the **HERB GARDEN**	Issue No. 11, 2-year book
Tips for cold-climate **HERB** growing	5-year book
How to harvest and dry **HERBS**	Issue No. 9
Self-seeding **HERBS** add random fragrance, beauty, and an "Old World" look to your vegetable garden	Issue No. 12, 2-year book
The 10 most useful **HERBS**	5-year book
Here are a few handy props for **AIR-DRYING YOUR HERBS**	Issue No. 33
HIGH ALTITUDE GARDENING — it's a challenge, but these helpful tips can get you started	Issue No. 38
Your garden has a **HISTORY**	Issue No. 19, 4-year book
Grow **HOREHOUND** for the health of it	Issue No. 38
HOTBEDS — an old but still sound method to get a jump on the growing season	Issue No. 20, 4-year book
Garden **HUCKLEBERRIES** — hardy, easy to grow, and tasty as blueberries	5-year book
Using **HYBRIDS** and creating your own varieties	Issue No. 20, 4-year book
A **HYDROPONIC GREENHOUSE**	3-year book
DRIP IRRIGATION saves a lot of water and weeding	Issue No. 46
A **DRIP IRRIGATION** primer!	Issue No. 16, 3-year book
KIWI fruit — healthy, delicious, low-maintenance	5-year book
LAWN CARE tips	Issue No. 44 (Sold out. Photocopy of article is available.)
LILACS can provide a reliable "thermometer" for planting	Issue No. 38

Make **MANURE TEA** for a more
   bountiful garden ....Issue No. 44 (Sold out. Photocopy of article is available.)
Keep those empty **MILK JUGS** ....Issue No. 21, 4-year book
It's easy to build your own
   MILKING STANCHION ....Issue No. 41 (Sold out. Photocopy of article is available.)
MONEY doesn't grow on trees, but you can grow it in your garden.................................Issue No. 40
For extra production, try **MOUND GARDENING** ....Issue No. 44 (Sold out. Photocopy of article is available.)
Many choices for **MULCH** ....Issue No. 44 (Sold out. Photocopy of article is available.)
The magic of **MULCH** ....Issue No. 9, 2-year book
Build your own backwoods **MULCH MACHINE** .....Issue No. 44 (Sold out. Photocopy of article is available.)
SHIITAKE MUSHROOMS for food and for cash — you "plant" them by inoculating logs ....Issue No. 37
Finding, growing, and eating Asian **MUSTARDS** ....Issue No. 15, 3-year book
As the "green revolution" loses credibility, **ORGANIC GARDENING** makes a comeback!............2-year book
The incredible non-biodegradable food service **PAIL** ....Issue No. 21, 4-year book
PEPPERS for short season growers ....4-year book
Leave space for **PEPPERS**!...Issue No. 33
Grow **WINDOWSILL PEPPERS** the year-round ....Issue No. 48
The **FUYUGAKI PERSIMMON** — it really is "food for the gods" ....Issue No. 37
Friendly alternatives for **INSECT AND PEST CONTROL** ....Issue No. 20, 4-year book
Tips on controlling your garden **PESTS** naturally...2-year book
Try these **ORGANIC CONTROLS** for garden **PESTS** ....Issue No. 38
Repel garden **PESTS** with companion planting ......Issue No. 44 (Sold out. Photocopy of article is available.)
When you're laying out your farm, careful **PLANNING** pays big dividends..................................Issue No. 38
Careful **PLANNING** will make harvesting
   and preserving food a year-long process ....Issue No. 41 (Sold out. Photocopy of article is available.)
Co-**PLANTING** in the vegetable garden..2-year book
Spring **PLANTING** — a lot to do now, plenty of options to consider ....Issue No. 8, 2-year book
How to care for and feed the family **POND** ....Issue No. 27, 5-year book
Home-grown **POPCORN** — the treat you can grow yourself ....Issue No. 32
For some surprises in your garden, grow **POTATOES FROM SEED** ....Issue No. 38
It's cheap and easy to multiply plants by using these **PROPAGATION** techniques ....Issue No. 38
Here's a mighty creative way to **PROTECT YOUR PLANTS FROM ANIMALS** ....Issue No. 39
Try these home remedies for "hare" loss (controlling **RABBITS** in the garden).......................Issue No. 32
Garden for the **RECORD** and ensure a good harvest ....Issue No. 32
ROADSIDE MARKETING: the best of two worlds ....Issue No. 46
Hardy **ROSES** are easy to grow..Issue No. 32
Make a **HEATED SEED GERMINATION FLAT** ....Issue No. 32
SEED STARTING the easy way ....Issue No. 14, 3-year book
SAVING OPEN-POLLINATED SEEDS is one step to self-sufficiency ....Issue No. 35
Build a **SEED STARTER** and make a nice part-time garden income ....Issue No. 46
Self sufficiency and **NON-HYBRID SEEDS** ....Issue No. 18, 3-year book
TRIMMING FEET (SHEEP) is important ....Issue No. 44 (Sold out. Photocopy of article is available.)
SHORT SEASON GARDENING ....5-year book
Rid your garden of
   SNAILS AND SLUGS — organically ....Issue No. 44 (Sold out. Photocopy of article is available.)
Enjoy **SNAP BEANS** — fresh from the garden ......Issue No. 44 (Sold out. Photocopy of article is available.)
Improving poor garden **SOIL** ....5-year book
LEAF MOLD is another way to
   BUILD YOUR SOIL ....Issue No. 41 (Sold out. Photocopy of article is available.)
SOIL AERATION is essential to a
   successful garden ....Issue No. 44 (Sold out. Photocopy of article is available.)
SOIL pH is the secret of a good garden...Issue No. 38

Fall **PUMPKINS AND SQUASH**	4-year book
Grow sweet **TETSUKABUTO SQUASH**	Issue No. 45
It's not too late to **START** your garden	Issue No. 9, 2-year book
You can grow **GOURMET STRAWBERRIES** from seed	Issue No. 43 (Sold out. Photocopy of article is available.)
TOBACCO has some uses that might surprise you	Issue No. 38
There are *lots* of **TOMATO** varieties — choose the ones that suit your garden and your taste	Issue No. 39
Protect your garden with a homemade **TRAP**	Issue No. 21, 4-year book
PROTECT those young **TREES** from frost and vermin	Issue No. 38
TREES enhance any yard, but…if you're planning your garden near trees, remember these tips	Issue No. 44 (Sold out. Photocopy of article is available.)
SCRAP POLY PIPE can be transformed into "training wheels for **TREES**"	Issue No. 38
Next year, grow your own Holiday **TURKEY**	Issue No. 42 (Sold out. Photocopy of article is available.)
TURKEYS — fun and profitable and not as dumb as you think	Issue No. 30, 5-year book
Save your harvest leftovers with a **VEGETABLE STEW MIX**	Issue No. 47
Cracking black **WALNUTS** can be "almost fun"	Issue No. 41 (Sold out. Photocopy of article is available.)

Food preservation

APPLE-DAPPLES — fun to make and even more fun to snack on	Issue No. 41 (Sold out. Photocopy of article is available.)
Here are some simple tips on how to store **APPLES** for a long, long time	Issue No. 41 (Sold out. Photocopy of article is available.)
Canning **BLUEBERRIES**	2-year book
Some healthy advice about canning and **BOTULISM**	2-year book
The magic of home **CANNING** — great food at the best possible price	Issue No. 17, 3-year book
Freeze that **SWEET CORN** and enjoy it all year long	Issue No. 34
They may be old, but they work — a **SOLAR FOOD DRYER**	Issue No. 16, 3-year book
DRYING FOOD — a low cost, easy way to preserve your harvest	4-year book
Some tips on **DRYING FOODS** at home	3-year book
CANNING MEAT	2-year book
DRYING MEAT	2-year book
Keep your **ONIONS** fresh...with panty hose!	Issue No. 41 (Sold out. Photocopy of article is available.)
How to can **PEACHES AND TOMATOES**	2-year book
Here are five ways for gardeners to enjoy summer all year long (**PRESERVING HERBS AND FRUITS**)	Issue No. 35
SALT BLUEBERRIES to preserve them	Issue No. 12, 2-year book
Canning **STEWS AND VEGGIES SOUP**	2-year book
The sensible way to **STORE** and use food	Issue No. 17, 3-year book
Let common sense, your taste buds guide you to **STORING FOOD AT HOME**	Issue No. 12, 2-year book
Those leftover fall **TOMATOES** are a delicious bounty that should be put aside for the future	Issue No. 41 (Sold out. Photocopy of article is available.)
Save your harvest leftovers with a **VEGETABLE STEW MIX**	Issue No. 47
Using and storing **WHEAT** at home	Issue No. 19, 4-year book

Guns and hunting

* NOTE: Articles by **MASSAD AYOOB** are marked with an asterisk [*].

The **.22** — another useful firearm for country living	Issue No. 12, 2-year book
*** ACCESSIBLE TO YOU**, but not the kids	Issue No. 44 (Sold out. Photocopy of article is available.)

ACCESSORIES can make shooting safer, more productive	Issue No. 16, 3-year book
Prepare for hunting season and have some great fun by MAKING YOUR OWN ACCESSORIES	Issue No. 35
Understanding AMMUNITION will make your working guns more useful	Issue No. 15, 3-year book
*Effective rounds for the backwoods (AMMUNITION)	Issue No. 34
*Here are some answers to often asked questions of ANTI-GUNNERS	Issue No. 45
The BOW AND ARROW: low tech tool for food, entertainment	5-year book
The SKS CARBINE — an honest bargain	Issue No. 21, 4-year book
*DEFENSIVE DEADLY FORCE — the ground rules	Issue No. 32
You can make realistic CANVAS DECOYS that work as well as the store-bought kind	Issue No. 35
Harvesting the blacktail DEER	4-year book
They're not just "HIS" firearms (FAMILY firearm safety)	4-year book
*BACKWOODS FIREARMS	Issue No. 31
Using trot lines, set lines, and jug FISHING will increase your fish catch substantially	Issue No. 40
OLD GUNS for the old homestead	Issue No. 48
HANDGUNS are useful tools for the homesteader	Issue No. 27, 5-year book
*The best deals in HOME-DEFENSE guns	Issue No. 42 (Sold out. Photocopy of article is available.)
*The backwoods HUNTER	Issue No. 41 (Sold out. Photocopy of article is available.)
*My choice for the IDEAL BACKWOODS GUN is the four-inch .44 Magnum handgun	Issue No. 37
*Kids, values, and "JUNIOR SHOOTING"	Issue No. 47
Want the KIDS to learn shooting? Try Whittington!	Issue No. 18, 3-year book
*TEACHING YOUR LADY to shoot	Issue No. 43 (Sold out. Photocopy of article is available.)
LEARNING TO SHOOT safely, effectively	3-year book
HAND LOADING YOUR AMMO is far cheaper than buying it	Issue No. 17, 3-year book
*The PRICE OF MACHISMO	Issue No. 40
CLEANING AND MAINTAINING your firearms	Issue No. 20, 4-year book
*The M1A — a rifle that makes a statement	Issue No. 45
*The MARLIN MODEL 60 — It's the classic backwoods home rifle	Issue No. 39
MUZZLELOADERS — art, science, and a piece of history	5-year book
PREPARE YOUR RIFLE before deer season	4-year book
An overview of CENTERFIRE RIFLES	Issue No. 14, 3-year book
Two classic MILITARY RIFLES for the homestead	Issue No. 36
Inexpensive retired RUSSIAN MILITARY RIFLES can be the ideal backwoods meat guns	Issue No. 47
Firearm SAFETY is serious business	3-year book
*SELECTING THE BACKWOODS BATTERY	Issue No. 36
*The price of SELF DEFENSE	Issue No. 33
*Create your own SHOOTING RANGE	Issue No. 35
As a versatile country tool, the SHOTGUN is hard to beat	Issue No. 11, 2-year book
*Mossberg Model 500: the backwoods SHOTGUN	Issue No. 46
TANNING your own hide — a sportsman's guide	Issue No. 36
The right RIFLE for a WOMAN	Issue No. 21, 4-year book
HANDGUN CHOICES FOR WOMEN who want to provide their own defense	Issue No. 19, 4-year book
WOMEN, self defense, and the 20-gauge SHOTGUN	Issue No. 16, 3-year book
SOCIAL CONDITIONING, WOMEN, and self defense	Issue No. 17, 3-year book

Health

NASA says these PLANTS WILL HELP CLEAN THE AIR IN YOUR HOME	Issue No. 37
Use HOUSEPLANTS to improve your INDOOR AIR QUALITY	Issue No. 21, 4-year book
BUILDING FOR INDOOR AIR QUALITY (IAQ)	2-year book
HOLIDAY GOODIES for people with ALLERGIES	Issue No. 12

The amazing **ALOE**	Issue No. 37
ALOE VERA — the magic plant	Issue No. 9
The backwoods **BACK**: the right and wrong ways to do **LIFTING** around the homestead	Issue No. 35
Make your own safe **BAKING POWDER**	Issue No. 11, 2-year book
A **BOTULISM** update for **BABIES**	2-year book
For many people, these natural remedies can **REDUCE HIGH BLOOD PRESSURE**	Issue No. 42 (Sold out. Photocopy of article is available.)
Knowing **CPR** can save a life	Issue No. 42 (Sold out. Photocopy of article is available.)
Country living health hints for **CHILDREN**	Issue No. 11
Remove the toxics from your home — switch to "natural" household **CLEANING AGENTS**	2-year book
Stopping the **DIET**-go-round	Issue No. 12
FIBER — the fact and the fiction	2-year book
Some tips on **FIRST AID READINESS FOR REMOTE AREAS**	2-year book
Praise for a once-perfect food (**FISH**)	2-year book
Here's a new way to remove a **FISH HOOK**	Issue No. 15, 3-year book
NATIONAL HEALTH CARE — will it work in the U.S.?	Issue No. 15, 3-year book
Searching for the right American **HEALTH CARE PLAN** — is the **MEDICAL CARE SAVINGS ACCOUNT** the answer?	Issue No. 16, 3-year book
Surviving a **HEART ATTACK** in the backwoods	Issue No. 41 (Sold out. Photocopy of article is available.)
Ingredients for an **HERBAL FIRST AID KIT** and how you can use them effectively	Issue No. 17, 3-year book
Health care begins at **HOME**	Issue No. 27, 5-year book
HOME REMEDIES	Issue No. 14, 3-year book
How to deal with **HYPOTHERMIA**	2-year book
Teach your **KIDS** the fun, **SAFE** way to **SPLIT KINDLING**	Issue No. 14, 3-year book
What about the **LEAD** in your water supply?	Issue No. 8
Make a **LIFELINE** before you need it	Issue No. 27, 5-year book
Ticks and **LYME DISEASE** — a crippling combination that is difficult to detect!	2-year book
In spite of DEET and Permethrin, the **MOSQUITO** still reigns supreme	Issue No. 8, 2-year book
Tips on dealing with **MOSQUITOES**	2-year book
MUGWORT — From aiding digestion to relieving fatigue, this plant has many good uses	Issue No. 41 (Sold out. Photocopy of article is available.)
Better health from **COMMON PLANTS**	Issue No. 43 (Sold out. Photocopy of article is available.)
POISON HEMLOCK! — Don't get this deadly plant confused with other members of the parsley family	2-year book
Identifying and dealing with **POISON OAK AND POISON IVY**	2-year book
Some **POISONOUS** advice about **SCORPIONS, SNAKES, AND SPIDERS**	2-year book
A **ROAD KILL** could kill you, too!	3-year book
WHITE SAGE — the quintessential chaparral herb	Issue No. 39
Now that a new oat bran study has debunked all the old studies, it's time to study the **STUDIES**	2-year book
The virtues of **VITAMINS** — a megadose of warning!	2-year book
For headache, fever, or even rheumatism, relief is as near as the familiar **WILLOW** plant	Issue No. 40
How to make homemade **YOGURT**	Issue No. 9

History

Bicentennial of the **BILL OF RIGHTS** — would we pay the price again?	Issue No. 12, 2-year book
Feeling nostalgic? Now you'll rave! Here's the story of **BURMA SHAVE**	Issue No. 37
CARVER — he wrote the book on self reliance	Issue No. 31
The genius of John Adams, Thomas Jefferson, and America's **DECLARATION OF INDEPENDENCE**	Issue No. 16, 3-year book
Looking behind the **DECLARATION OF INDEPENDENCE**	Issue No. 28, 5-year book
The **ELECTORAL COLLEGE** — how we elect the President	Issue No. 18, 3-year book

America's earliest **FIRST LADIES** were fascinating (Part I)..Issue No. 29, 5-year book
Former **FIRST LADIES** — beautiful, brilliant, crazy (Part II) ....Issue No. 30, 5-year book
Presidential wives, Part III (**FIRST LADIES**) ....Issue No. 34
Presidents' wives, Part IV — cunning, vindictive, and maybe one murderess (**FIRST LADIES**).Issue No. 35
JOHN FITCH — a forgotten inventor ....Issue No. 31
Your **GARDEN** has a history ....Issue No. 19, 4-year book
GOLD is where you find it — and it's found
 along the Klamath...Issue No. 44 (Sold out. Photocopy of article is available.)
PANNING (GOLD) with nature and history.............Issue No. 44 (Sold out. Photocopy of article is available.)
Solar cell inventor **TONY LAMB** made his breakthrough in 1931 ....2-year book
MEMORIES from the past...Issue No. 8
Remembering the magic of **MOTHER'S KITCHEN** ....Issue No. 18, 3-year book
MUZZLELOADERS — art, science,
 and a piece of history..5-year book
History of the **OREGON TRAIL** ....4-year book
Reliving the **OREGON TRAIL** ....4-year book
Doesn't anyone remember **TOM PAINE**? ....Issue No. 19, 4-year book
Remembering Wisconsin's **PESHTIGO FIRE** — the greatest natural disaster
 in North American history..2-year book
Collecting **OLD PHONOGRAPH RECORDS** is fun and educational.......Issue No. 30, 5-year book
JAMES POLK — a model for modern presidents..Issue No. 32
PROHIBITION: then, now, and always ....Issue No. 45
3 Missouri **QUAKES** of 1811-12 rang church bells in Boston, toppled 150,000 acres of forest.....2-year book
QUILTS — masterpieces of the heart and windows into women's history ....4-year book
LOSING OUR RIGHTS as we watch television .....Issue No. 44 (Sold out. Photocopy of article is available.)
Today it is oil that controls the wealth of nations; yesterday it was **SALT** that made empires ....2-year book
My dad was never home for **SANTA CLAUS** ....2-year book
SCIENCE and **TRUTH** — are they related? ....Issue No. 46
THE SUMMER IT SNOWED ....2-year book
A **TELEPHONE** for Vailsburg ....2-year book
THANKSGIVING — a celebration of freedom and harvest..4-year book
Old **TIN CANS** tell the real story of how pioneers tamed the West........................Issue No. 11, 2-year book
Reliving "The American **WEST**" at the **HART CANYON RENDEZVOUS** ....3-year book
Visiting Laura (Laura Ingalls **WILDER**)...Issue No. 21, 4-year book
Pioneer **WOMEN** on the trail west..2-year book
WORLD SERIES...OF THE PAST ....Issue No. 11, 2-year book
Why does the year begin in **JANUARY**?..3-year book

Homeschooling

ALTERNATIVE EDUCATION — learning in the real world ....Issue No. 20, 4-year book
Homeschool your children using **APPRENTICESHIPS** ....Issue No. 31
A homeschool **ASSIGNMENT** ....Issue No. 20, 4-year book
CHILD-LED LEARNING ....5-year book
How to earn your **COLLEGE DEGREE** outside of the traditional classroom ....Issue No. 31
You can earn a **COLLEGE DEGREE** without ever leaving home, thanks to TVs and computers Issue No. 37
Your family can afford a **COMPUTER**: buy it **USED** ....Issue No. 39
What you do to one side of an **EQUATION** you do to the other to keep it balanced....................Issue No. 38
School at home for **FUN AND PROFIT** ....Issue No. 21, 4-year book
HOMESCHOOLING our teenagers in the backwoods, one of the best decisions we ever made.Issue No. 31
How I've started my child in a program of **HOMESCHOOLING** ....Issue No. 37
Some homeschooling **IDEAS** ....5-year book

Teach your kids **MATH** with the banking game.......Issue No. 41 (Sold out. Photocopy of article is available.)
Help your children to read by teaching them the **PHONIC** basics..........................Issue No. 29, 5-year book
In the classroom and at home, this system will help you grow
   SELF-RELIANT KIDS ....Issue No. 42 (Sold out. Photocopy of article is available.)
Based on years of personal experience, here are **10 GOOD TIPS**
   for homeschooling your kids................................Issue No. 41 (Sold out. Photocopy of article is available.)
Homeschooling children — here is one former teacher's view of how well it **WORKS**
   for his five kids ....Issue No. 9, 2-year book
Home schooling — is it **RIGHT FOR YOUR KIDS?** ....5-year book

Independent energy

Build a **12-VOLT POWER PLANT** from the junkyard ....Issue No. 28, 5-year book
Independent energy runs *BACKWOODS HOME MAGAZINE* ....Issue No. 28, 5-year book
Aluminum-air **BATTERY** gives **ELECTRIC CARS** 750-mile range..........................Issue No. 9, 2-year book
The care of **LEAD ACID BATTERIES** ....Issue No. 28, 5-year book
Charging **RV BATTERIES** with the sun ....Issue No. 14, 3-year book
ELECTRIC CAR RACING — what a gas!...4-year book
ELECTRIC CARS of the 90s — small companies lead the way,
   but the "big three" have entered the race ....Issue No. 11, 2-year book
Converting your gas **CAR** to electric is no shocker ....Issue No. 30, 5-year book
Solar cells, inverters, and your personal **COMPUTER** ....2-year book
CONSERVATION wise choice of appliances key to making PV power work for you Issue No. 8, 2-year book
COOL your home with this simple device while you also meet your hot water needs ....Issue No. 46
MIDWEST RENEWABLE ENERGY FAIR features solar house, electrics, dealers ....Issue No. 15
Sources of **FIREWOOD** ....Issue No. 12, 2-year book
FIREWOOD — how and what to buy ....Issue No. 28, 5-year book
Gathering low cost **FIREWOOD** ....4-year book
Here's the best way to
   SPLIT GNARLY FIREWOOD.............................Issue No. 43 (Sold out. Photocopy of article is available.)
For safety's sake **HOMESTEAD FUEL STORAGE**
   must be handled properly ....Issue No. 43 (Sold out. Photocopy of article is available.)
Don't discount a **GENERATOR**,
   especially a diesel generator, as your primary power source...Issue No. 28
How to keep the **CHINA DIESEL** (**GENERATOR**) purring like a kitten...2-year book
The sunless, windless, waterless alternative energy system
   (**GENERATOR POWER**)...Issue No. 12, 2-year book
How to construct a **SOUNDPROOF GENERATOR SHED** ....Issue No. 8, 2-year book
The case for a **GENERATOR-BASED ELECTRICAL SYSTEM** ....2-year book
DIESEL GENERATOR power is a sensible choice, especially
   when integrated into the total system ....Issue No. 43 (Sold out. Photocopy of article is available.)
Heat and cool inexpensively with a
   GROUND SOURCE HEAT PUMP ....Issue No. 43 (Sold out. Photocopy of article is available.)
GROUNDING AND LIGHTNING PROTECTION for solar-electric power systems .Issue No. 17, 3-year book
Using water hydraulics to help install your house **GROUNDING ROD** ....Issue No. 19, 4-year book
HEAT your upstairs by cutting holes in the floor! ....Issue No. 14, 3-year book
I **HEAT** my house by burning **CORN**......................Issue No. 42 (Sold out. Photocopy of article is available.)
HEAT your household from the outside ....Issue No. 46
Selecting the right **HEATING SYSTEM** ....Issue No. 17, 3-year book
A **HOUSE-HEATING SOLAR GREENHOUSE** ....Issue No. 12, 2-year book
A tour of some alternative energy **HOMES** in the Pacific Northwest ....2-year book

Marrying **SOLAR THERMAL** and **PHOTOVOLTAICS** to create a top notch closed loop solar **HOT WATER** system	Issue No. 15, 3-year book
Using salvaged materials to build a thermosiphon solar **HOT WATER SYSTEM**	2-year book
New **FUEL CELL** may make **HYDROGEN** a practical **FUEL FOR ELECTRIC VEHICLES**	Issue No. 9
Micro-**HYDROPOWER** — a working example	Issue No. 28, 5-year book
For a truly **INDEPENDENT ENERGY SYSTEM**, your choices are solar, wind, and water	Issue No. 28, 5-year book
How an **INVERTER** fits into your solar electric system	3-year book
Solar cell inventor **TONY LAMB** made his breakthrough in 1931	2-year book
Is **METHANE PRODUCTION** on your homestead practical?	2-year book
The sensible, integrated **PHOTOVOLTAIC ENERGY SYSTEM**	Issue No. 20, 4-year book
PHOTOVOLTAICS — Is the big **PRICE** breakthrough just around the corner, or	2-year book
PHOTOVOLTAICS in Arkansas' **MEADOWCREEK** Community help make its self reliant ideas a model for the future	Issue No. 16, 3-year book
PLAN your energy-independent home *before* you begin construction	Issue No. 39
A third world answer to a backwoods power problem — a **POWER CONDITIONING SYSTEM**	2-year book
Using a **PRODUCER GAS GENERATOR** to create electricity	Issue No. 20, 4-year book
Here's a low-cost, low-tech **REFRIGERATOR** that really works	Issue No. 28, 5-year book
A little **PLANNING** makes **LIVING WITH SOLAR** easier than you think	Issue No. 35
Here's one way to build a **SOLAR-HEATED SHOWER**	Issue No. 33
SOLAR CELL improvements make solar desirable as home electricity source	2-year book
SOLAR CELLS power historic ranches off California coast	Issue No. 12
Making and using a **SOLAR COOKER**	Issue No. 30, 5-year book
Getting the most out of a **SOLAR ELECTRIC SYSTEM**	Issue No. 43 (Sold out. Photocopy of article is available.)
Designing for **SOLAR HEATING**	Issue No. 28, 5-year book
PV pioneer describes his successful **SOLAR HOME**	Issue No. 38
Self-reliant couple creates a **SOLAR HOMESTEAD**	Issue No. 35
Try an isolated gain **PASSIVE SOLAR HOUSE**	5-year book
SOLAR PANEL TESTING AND REPAIR	4-year book
SOLAR POWER — is it the answer for your electric needs?	2-year book
Is **STEAM POWER** in your future?	Issue No. 43 (Sold out. Photocopy of article is available.)
Here is a solution to the problem of **TRANSMITTING SOLAR ELECTRICITY** long distance to your home site	Issue No. 11, 2-year book
Semi-**UNDERGROUND, SOLAR** house near the Canadian border	Issue No. 9, 2-year book
Idaho **UTILITY** entry into PV field may be a sign of things to come	Issue No. 21, 4-year book
Selecting the right **VOLTAGE** for your independent home power system	4-year book
Try these simple ways to get started in **SOLAR HOT WATER**	Issue No. 43 (Sold out. Photocopy of article is available.)
How to build a safe, effective wood-fired hot **WATER HEATER**	Issue No. 9, 2-year book
Cool your home with this simple device while you also meet your **HOT WATER** needs	Issue No. 46
TANKLESS WATER HEATERS offer some important advantages, but they have some drawbacks, too	Issue No. 43 (Sold out. Photocopy of article is available.)
The solar-powered silent partner (**SOLAR WATER PUMP**)	5-year book
SOLAR WATER PUMPING — a sensible, reliable alternative	Issue No. 8, 2-year book
WATER SYSTEMS for homesteads with alternative electrical systems	2-year book
WATERPOWER for personal use	Issue No. 16, 3-year book
Design calculations for no-head, low-head **WATERWHEELS**	Issue No. 17, 3-year book
Design calculations for overshot **WATERWHEELS**	Issue No. 18, 3-year book
WIND POWER from the past	4-year book
WIND POWER in the present	4-year book
Small **WIND TURBINES** are a viable alternative	Issue No. 28

Preparing your photovoltaic system for **WINTER** .... Issue No. 19, 4-year book
How to **WIRE** your home **FOR SOLAR ELECTRICITY** .... 2-year book
Hardwoods are the best but pine has its place (**WOOD** as a heating fuel) .... 2-year book
If you are returning to **WOOD HEAT,** here are some **TIPS** that will help .... 2-year book
COOKING WITH WOODSTOVES .... Issue No. 14, 3-year book

Kids

Just for kids — Have a chat with your cat (communicating with **ANIMALS**) .... Issue No. 21, 4-year book
Just for kids — **APPLES,** apples everywhere .... 2-year book
Just for kids — Kids like the **BACKWOODS** too! .... 2-year book
Just for kids — Visit the great prairies (right in your own **BACK YARD**) .... Issue No. 35
Give a country kid a **CAMERA** .... Issue No. 17, 3-year book
Just for kids — **CANDLE MAKING** .... 2-year book
Just for kids — Some good **CLEAN** fun .... 4-year book
Just for kids — A musical houseguest (**CRICKETS**) .... Issue No. 9, 2-year book
Just for kids — Kids' "funny **DRAWING**" contest .... Issue No. 9, Issue No. 11, 2-year book
Just for kids — **FEATHER** your vest .... Issue No. 17, 3-year book
Just for kids — Life in the **FOREST** .... Issue No. 34
Just for kids — A backwoods kitchen **GARDEN** .... 4-year book
Just for kids — Plant a spring **GARDEN** .... 2-year book
Just for kids — **GRANOLA** and the **MOON** .... 2-year book
Just for kids — Fairies in your garden
 (**HUMMINGBIRDS**) .... Issue No. 43 (Sold out. Photocopy of article is available.)
There's a shark in the refrigerator (keeping a child development **JOURNAL**) .... 2-year book
Just for kids — **LADYBUGS AND SPIDERS** .... Issue No. 8, 2-year book
Why I like **LIVING IN THE COUNTRY** .... Issue No. 16, Issue No. 17, 3-year book
Just for kids — Life in a rotten **LOG** .... Issue No. 16, 3-year book
Just for kids — **HELP FOR NATURE'S NURSERY** .... Issue No. 20, 4-year book
Just for kids — You in the big **NIGHT SKY** .... 5-year book
Just for kids — Take a **NITE HIKE** .... 4-year book
Just for kids — Some **PIONEER RECIPES** .... Issue No. 30, 5-year book
Just for kids — Life on the damp side (**POND LIFE**) .... Issue No. 33
Just for kids — A short **POSSUM** tail (tale?) .... Issue No. 18, 3-year book
Just for kids — **LOGIC PUZZLES** .... Issue No. 12, 2-year book
Just for kids — **LOGIC PUZZLES** .... 3-year book
Just for kids — **RAINY DAY MAGIC** .... Issue No. 19, 4-year book
Here's a neat way to expand your child's bedroom and play **SPACE** .... Issue No. 8, 2-year book
Just for kids — **SPROUTS** in a jar .... 2-year book
Just for kids — Some farinaceous folly (**STARCH**) .... Issue No. 36
Just for kids — Some **SUMMERTIME** secrets .... Issue No. 29
Just for kids — **SUN-KABOBS & SOLAR SIZZLE** .... Issue No. 28, 5-year book
Just for parents — Homemade **TEACHING TOYS** .... 2-year book
Just for kids — A can **TELEPHONE** .... 2-year book
Just for kids — Killing some **TIME** .... 5-year book
Just for kids — Knock knock **VINEGAR** .... Issue No. 32
Just for kids — Finger **WEAVING** .... 2-year book
Just for kids — Hard working **WORMS** .... Issue No. 31

Maintenance & repair

Here are 10 ways to beat
    CORROSION in the garage ....Issue No. 42 (Sold out. Photocopy of article is available.)
Ten off-beat **METAL CLEANING** tricks...................Issue No. 41 (Sold out. Photocopy of article is available.)
SMALL ENGINE MAINTENANCE FOR WOMEN ....4-year book
Tips on **MAINTAINING AND DIAGNOSING SMALL ENGINE PROBLEMS**
    around the homestead...Issue No. 33
Seventeen great tips for caring for windows, mirrors,
    and other household **GLASS** ....Issue No. 43 (Sold out. Photocopy of article is available.)
Troubleshoot your own **PC** ....Issue No. 34
Use these tips to avoid problems with your
    SEWING MACHINE ....Issue No. 42 (Sold out. Photocopy of article is available.)
SPRING maintenance hints..Issue No. 8, 2-year book
TRACTOR MAINTENANCE saves you more than money ....Issue No. 32

Making a living

How to get started in **BLACKSMITHING** ....Issue No. 17, 3-year book
This family started a used **BOOKSTORE** for under $2000...Issue No. 40
Low overhead, sense of humor, and personal touch are key ingredients
    to running a **SMALL BUSINESS** ....Issue No. 16, 3-year book
A **CANOE LIVERY** — an honest, clean business ....Issue No. 46
Oklahomans help pave the way for small-scale **CATFISH FARMERS** ....2-year book
SELLING CHICKENS to an ethnic market...Issue No. 18, 3-year book
Making an independent living by **CARING FOR CHILDREN** ....2-year book
Growing **CHRISTMAS TREES** — a year-round part-time business ....Issue No. 14, 3-year book
Clean up with **HOUSE CLEANING** ....3-year book
Be a **CLOWN** — it's fun, and it pays well, too ....Issue No. 35
Getting more cash from your **CRAFTS** ....Issue No. 14, 3-year book
Farming **CRAYFISH** for a living — the demand exceeds the supply ....Issue No. 16, 3-year book
Small-scale **CRAYFISH FARMING** is a profitable business ....2-year book
How to make a living with **WILD CRAYFISH** ....4-year book
Getting into **DESKTOP PUBLISHING** without blowing your budget ....Issue No. 11, 2-year book
Here are two country couples who **DIVERSIFIED** to make a living.......................................Issue No. 40
Good **FARM MANAGEMENT** puts money in your pocket ....Issue No. 14, 3-year book
Getting started in a **FIREWOOD BUSINESS** ....Issue No. 12, 2-year book
Raising **FISHWORMS** as a business ....Issue No. 19, 4-year book
Grow an independent living with a cut **FLOWER** business ....Issue No. 29, 5-year book
Money doesn't grow on trees, but you can grow it in your **GARDEN** ....Issue No. 40
Native of the forest: a guide to growing **GINSENG** ....5-year book
GROWING TREES can pay off, but it takes careful planning, planting, and work ...Issue No. 11, 2-year book
The **GUAYULE** plant — an oil-saving opportunity for an American entrepreneur .....Issue No. 8, 2-year book
Start a home-based **HERB BUSINESS** ....Issue No. 34
Here are some **HOME-BASED BUSINESSES** that are worth trying ....Issue No. 29, 5-year book
Start a **HOME-BASED FOOD BUSINESS** ....Issue No. 27, 5-year book
Consider small-scale **HOG** production for delicious food and reliable income................Issue No. 40
FAMILY works together at successful **HOME-BASED BUSINESS** ....Issue No. 14, 3-year book
Let your **IMAGINATION** guide you to making money in the country ....Issue No. 47
You have to **LEARN** to shovel crap before you learn to be the boss ....Issue No. 29, 5-year book
Here's how to start a part-time, one person **MAIL ORDER** business ....Issue No. 29, 5-year book
MEDICAL TRANSCRIPTION — a recession proof career? ....Issue No. 18, 3-year book

How about them $MUSHROOMS$	Issue No. 46
MULTI-LEVEL MARKETING — is it the road to riches or disaster?	Issue No. 46
Moonlight and **NEWSPAPERS** (delivery)	Issue No. 18, 3-year book
You can have a good career as a **NURSE PRACTITIONER** no matter where you live	Issue No. 40
NURSING — the number 1 country career or business opportunity for both women and men	Issue No. 8, 2-year book
ODD-JOBBIN' can be a country goldmine	Issue No. 29, 5-year book
OSTRICHES AND EMUS — backwoods bonanza or feathered pyramid?	4-year book
PV as a country business? — if you're a jack of all trades	Issue No. 29, 5-year book
PARAKEETS for cash	Issue No. 14, 3-year book
Work at home at your convenience as a **PARAMEDICAL EXAMINER**	Issue No. 15, 3-year book
Opportunity is knocking for the country **PARSON**	3-year book
Now that you have your little slice of heaven, how do you go about **PAYING** for it?	Issue No. 14, 3-year book
PHYSICIAN ASSISTANT — a country career with opportunities galore	Issue No. 12, 2-year book
You don't have to be a historian to make money writing your hometown's **PICTORIAL HISTORY**	Issue No. 48
PLANNING to make a living in the country	4-year book
Boost your income by adding a **PROCESSING STEP** to what you sell	Issue No. 36
Raising **RABBITS** — for meat and making money, it's hard to beat this creature on the homestead	Issue No. 40
A crash course in small business **RECORD KEEPING**	Issue No. 8, 2-year book
ROADSIDE MARKETING: the best of two worlds	Issue No. 46
A **SADDLE SHOP** created self sufficiency for Idaho family	Issue No. 17, 3-year book
SAWMILLS — a firm foundation to homesteading	Issue No. 9, 2-year book
Build a **SEED STARTER** and make a nice part-time garden income	Issue No. 46
Delicious, wholesome, and just enough "crunch," these special **SOYBEANS** sell for $2 a pound	Issue No. 40
Make twenty dollars per hour by baling and selling **STRAW**	2-year book
You can make extra money as a **STRINGER** (writing)	Issue No. 40
TAXES — a good reason for you to start your own **SMALL BUSINESS**	2-year book
Making a living independently by **TEACHING** adults to read	2-year book
Supplement your income by **TEACHING** others your skills	5-year book
SUBSTITUTE TEACHING — the pay is good, but it ain't always easy	Issue No. 46
Making and selling **TIRE GARDENS**	Issue No. 20
A guaranteed-catch, U-catch **TROUT POND** is a fun and profitable business	Issue No. 40
Get paid to take **VACATIONS**	Issue No. 46
Starting a home **VIDEO** business	Issue No. 16, 3-year book
The rise of **GUERRILLA VIDEOS**	Issue No. 16, 3-year book
Got some **WEEKEND RESIDENTS** in your area? Then your home business is waiting to open	Issue No. 40
Collect (almost) free money by gathering readily available **WILD PLANTS AND BOTANICALS**	Issue No. 46
The "**NIGHT CRAWLER** condo" is a great way to make money (**WORMS**)	Issue No. 40
Making a living as a **WRITER**	Issue No. 20, 4-year book
Using **PHOTOS** to sell your **WRITING**	Issue No. 20, 4-year book
If you have some solid how-to knowledge to sell, **WRITING AND PUBLISHING A BOOK** is not that hard	Issue No. 40

Moving to the country

Moving **BACK TO THE LAND** and making it work	Issue No. 15, 3-year book
How we **BOUGHT** our country home	5-year book

How to work with **BROKERS, LAWYERS, TITLE INSURANCE AGENTS**
  when you buy country land..Issue No. 33
The do's and don'ts of **BUYING BACKWOODS PROPERTY** ....2-year book
Making a sunny home in the **CALIFORNIA WILDERNESS** ....2-year book
Living the **COUNTRY LIFE** ....5-year book
Here are some thoughts on finding your **DREAM PLACE** — garden and all....................Issue No. 38
How one man made the American Dream come true (creating a **HOMESTEAD**) ....2-year book
Tepee to cabin to **DREAM HOUSE** ....2-year book
In pursuit of **INDEPENDENCE** ....2-year book
When it comes to **LAND CONTRACTS** — be careful! Here are some critical points to consider.Issue No. 37
LAND REGULATIONS are making it harder to move to the country.....................Issue No. 20, 4-year book
MOVING TO THE WILDERNESS — turning the dream to reality ....Issue No. 36
A tale about tenure in the **NEIGHBORHOOD** ....5-year book
PLANNING a move from the city to the country..5-year book
PLANNING is an essential key to achieving the country life ....5-year book
Trading your city house for a homestead — a **TAXING** move? ....Issue No. 27, 5-year book
Some **TIPS** on moving to your country home ....5-year book
Protect your land **TITLE** before you buy.................Issue No. 42 (Sold out. Photocopy of article is available.)

The natural world

FIRE ANTS on the march in the U.S. ....Issue No. 14, 3-year book
The **BEAVER POND** ....2-year book
The forest king is returning (**CHESTNUT TREES**) ....Issue No. 19, 4-year book
Life of the "prairie tenor" (the **COYOTE**)...Issue No. 18, 3-year book
Understanding the **ENVIRONMENTAL MOVEMENT** ....Issue No. 21, 4-year book
RECYCLING and capitalism shake hands ....2-year book
RODENTS AND RAPTORS — a natural balance ....Issue No. 11, 2-year book
Is it safe to eat the **SHELLFISH** pulled from our coastal waters? ....2-year book
Thoughts on a **SNAKE** ....Issue No. 33
THE SUMMER IT SNOWED ....2-year book
How **CITIES** affect the **WEATHER** ....2-year book
INJURED AND SICK WILDLIFE gets a lease on life from this California group ....2-year book
The **WOLVES** of Mission: Wolf ....Issue No. 15, 3-year book

On-line resources: Homesteading on the electronic frontier

There's plenty of information on the Internet about **BUILDING** and doing **REPAIRS** ....Issue No. 39
CYBRARIAN great Internet job..Issue No. 40
Solar, wind, and other **INDEPENDENT ENERGY**
  information can be found on the Internet.............Issue No. 43 (Sold out. Photocopy of article is available.)
Harvesting the Internet for **GARDENING INFORMATION** ....Issue No. 38
HARVESTING information from the Internet...........Issue No. 41 (Sold out. Photocopy of article is available.)
Don't miss the backwoods on-ramp to the **INFORMATION SUPER HIGHWAY** ....Issue No. 36
Find information fast on the **INTERNET** ....Issue No. 37
Looking for **LOVE** in cyberspace............................Issue No. 42 (Sold out. Photocopy of article is available.)

Profiles

Sweet Alaska gold (**ALASKA HONEY AND POLLEN CO.**) ....Issue No. 21, 4-year book
Most independent woman and man of 1989 (**CECILIA TAYLOR BARRY** and **TONY LAMB**)......2-year book
JERRY BELANGER's network beyond the sidewalk..Issue No. 19

A Backwoods Home Anthology

Dare to dream with **MICHAEL ANDY DARR**	Issue No. 14, 3-year book
Twenty year update: **CARLA EMERY** and her old fashioned recipe book	2-year book
VERNON HOPKINS — wood splitter, trapper, dowser	2-year book
JUNE JAEGER's quilts are works of fine art	Issue No. 37
Solar cell inventor **TONY LAMB** made his breakthrough in 1931	2-year book
The other Texas Frenchman — an interview with **ANDRE MARROU**, Libertarian candidate for President	Issue No. 17, 3-year book
North Dakota self-reliance is **TED NEUMILLER**'s heritage	2-year book
From chimney sweep to stone sculptor to worry wall, **RON PRUITT** has decided his place is in the country	Issue No. 15, 3-year book
MICK SAGRILLO, Wizard of Wind	Issue No. 27, 5-year book
SUNELCO — dealers in the sun	Issue No. 20

Recipes

HOLIDAY GOODIES for people with **ALLERGIES**	Issue No. 12
AMERICAN FOOD — it's as varied as the melting pot	Issue No. 30
From honey apple crisp to French tarts, tasty **APPLE TREATS** are just right for fall	Issue No. 47
APPLES galore	4-year book
This is one way to make **APPLEJACK**	Issue No. 35
...and this is Reverend Dr. Hooker's **APPLEJACK**	Issue No. 35
AUTUMN DELIGHTS: APPLE-STREUSEL COFFEE CAKE, STUFFED WINTER SQUASH, SLICED TOMATOES VINAIGRETTE, PEAR TART	2-year book
Healthy **HOLIDAY BAKING**	Issue No. 18, 3-year book
BARBEQUE — it's America's national cuisine	Issue No. 45
BAR-B-QUE MEATBALLS, HERSHEY BAR SQUARES, DILL PICKLES, FRENCH BREAD	2-year book
BEANS — they may be a poor man's meat, but they are also the gourmet's delight	Issue No. 37
How to homebrew **BEER**	3-year book
Home brew your own **BEER**, Part I	Issue No. 32
Home brew your own **BEER**, Part II	Issue No. 33
BLUEBERRY TOFU FRAPPE, TOFU-CORN CHOWDER, TUNA BURGERS, BROCCOLI CASSEROLE	2-year book
It's good even when it turns out bad! (homemade **BREAD**)	Issue No. 9, 2-year book
WHOLE WHEAT BREAD, SUN TEA, CORN BREAD	2-year book
Three great **BREAD** recipes	Issue No. 27, 5-year book
Quick **BREADS** for summer	Issue No. 16, 3-year book
Try these **BREAD** recipes that are part of our heritage — and still delicious today	Issue No. 37
Making **SOURDOUGH BREAD**	Issue No. 29, 5-year book
Make delicious, eye-catching **HOLIDAY BREADS**	Issue No. 42 (Sold out. Photocopy of article is available.)
Perfect **WHOLE WHEAT BREADS** troubleshooting ideas	Issue No. 40
Country **BREAKFASTS**	Issue No. 9, 2-year book
Make **BUTTER** the easy way	Issue No. 36
Delicious **HOLIDAY CAKES** don't have to be diet-busters	Issue No. 42 (Sold out. Photocopy of article is available.)
CAROB — the chocolate alternative	Issue No. 14, 3-year book
CARROT RECIPE TIPS	2-year book
Emergency **CASSEROLE, TOFU, JAMBALAYA, REBELSAN 100 YEAR SAUCE, DEER JERKY**	2-year book
How to make **CHEESE AND BUTTER**	4-year book
Make your own **STRING CHEESE**	Issue No. 35
CHICKEN with curried rice	Issue No. 19, 4-year book

International ways with **CHICKEN**	Issue No. 15, 3-year book
In search of the perfect bowl of **CHILI**	Issue No. 36
CHILI, DEVILED EGGS, PROVENCAL EGGPLANT, SPAGHETTI,	
BROCCOLI-TOMATO SALAD, CAJUN SHRIMP	2-year book
CHINESE COOKING	Issue No. 28, 5-year book
These **CHOCOLATE** treats make great gifts	
and delicious holiday desserts	Issue No. 42 (Sold out. Photocopy of article is available.)
Lunchbox **COOKIES**	Issue No. 34
You squeezes de tail an' sucks de haid (**CRAWFISH**)	Issue No. 48
Eating **CROW** isn't that bad	Issue No. 38
Old-fashioned **DESSERTS**	Issue No. 29, 5-year book
Elegant **DESSERTS** for entertaining	Issue No. 48
Cooking with **DRIED FRUIT**	5-year book
Make these **HOT DRINKS** for liquid comfort	Issue No. 38
ELISSABURGETTES, HONEY CAKE, TEXAS HASH, NAMELESS SALAD,	
BEAN-BEEF CASSEROLE	Issue No. 9, 2-year book
FISH — this gourmet food is fun to catch, relatively easy to cook, and healthy to eat	Issue No. 47
Your throw-away **FISH** can be keepers if you know how to prepare them right	Issue No. 30, 5-year book
Choosing **FLAVOR ENHANCERS** to make everyday eating an adventure	Issue No. 31
FOUNTAIN TREATS from the fifties	2-year book
GARLIC lovers' delight	Issue No. 35
Try making your own **GRANOLA** dirt cheap	Issue No. 35
Make **GRAPE JUICE** the easy way	Issue No. 41 (Sold out. Photocopy of article is available.)
GREENS and **RHUBARB** are spring tonics	Issue No. 45
Good food for **HARD TIMES** . . . or any time	Issue No. 14, 3-year book
Holiday **HAM** leftovers	Issue No. 48
RED FLANNEL HASH, BACKWOODS CHICKEN, PICKLED BLACK-EYED PEAS, ORANGE HONEY	
PUDDING, SELF-CRUSTING APPLE PIE, CHOCOLATE CHIP CAKE	Issue No. 8, 2-year book
Try **COOKING ON TOP OF YOUR HEATING STOVE**	Issue No. 36
Some **HERB** garden recipes	5-year book
Make **HERBAL WINES** for pleasure and health	Issue No. 34
Wild turkey, goose, and venison for the **HOLIDAYS**	Issue No. 36
Barbecue a whole goat (and more) in an **IMU** (cooking pit)	Issue No. 30, 5-year book
Get the taste of **INDIA** in your kitchen tonight	Issue No. 46
JERUSALEM ARTICHOKE: food for man and beast	Issue No. 46
LASAGNA, TAMALE PIE, PAUL BUNYAN CORNBREAD, BLACK BEANS AND RICE,	
MOONE BISCUITS	2-year book
Spice up your life with **LEMON GRASS**	2-year book
Make **LEMONADE** without lemons	Issue No. 46
LOG HOMES, motorcycles, and good food	4-year book
MANICOTTI, FUDGE MACAROON PIE, CORNMEAL SOUR CREAM BISCUITS,	
CHICKEN CHILI, CHICKEN CACCIATORE, WILD RICE, SALMON LOAF	2-year book
MEDITERRANEAN FOOD — healthful home cooking at its best	Issue No. 34
MUFFIN magic	4-year book
Make your own **OLD WORLD** culinary delights	Issue No. 43 (Sold out. Photocopy of article is available.)
Make quick and easy **PASTA**	Issue No. 39
Try these **PASTA DESSERTS** for unusual holiday fare	Issue No. 48
21 quick, different, and easy **PASTABILITIES**	Issue No. 11, 2-year book
PECTIN — you can rely on the grocer,	
or you can learn to make it yourself	Issue No. 41 (Sold out. Photocopy of article is available.)
PEMMICAN — the all-purpose food	Issue No. 30, 5-year book
It's damn hot, & it's damn good (cooking with **CHILI PEPPERS**)	Issue No. 35

Poor man's shrimp cocktail on **PERCH,** and . . .	Issue No. 30, 5-year book
Enjoy America's sugarplum — the **PERSIMMON**	Issue No. 47
Here are some cucumber **PICKLES** to make at home	Issue No. 41 (Sold out. Photocopy of article is available.)
PIE recipes	Issue No. 15, 3-year book
Make better **PIZZA** at home than you can buy	5-year book
ONE POT MEALS	Issue No. 32
POTATO AND EGG SALAD, BEER BISCUITS, SAUERKRAUT, CHILI, INDIAN PUDDING, ZUCCHINI	2-year book
Safe, delicious, and inexpensive home **PRESERVES**	Issue No. 39
Do you have a good recipe for stir-fried **RATTLESNAKE**?	Issue No. 45
These **ROLLS** will enrich a meal, or even *be* a meal	Issue No. 44 (Sold out. Photocopy of article is available.)
From humble stew to curried root soup, **ROOT VEGETABLES** are an overlooked delight	Issue No. 38
SALADS FOR SUMMER	4-year book
SALADS FOR WINTER	Issue No. 37
These **SALADS** are **HEARTY DISHES**	Issue No. 43 (Sold out. Photocopy of article is available.)
PACKABLE SALADS	Issue No. 17, 3-year book
SANDWICHES for summer	Issue No. 33
SAUERKRAUT the easy way	Issue No. 35
SMOKED TURKEY, SMOKED BRISKET	Issue No. 20, 4-year book
My favorite **SOUP** recipes	5-year book
Homemade **HUNTER'S SOUP**	Issue No. 30
SOUPS for winter	Issue No. 36
SOUPS AND STEWS for late winter	Issue No. 20, 4-year book
Synopsis of **SOURDOUGH**	5-year book
SOURDOUGH with substance	Issue No. 30, 5-year book
Making your own **SOURDOUGH YEAST**	Issue No. 27
SOUTHERN COOKING that doesn't just whistle Dixie	Issue No. 41 (Sold out. Photocopy of article is available.)
The all purpose power food — **SOYBEANS**	Issue No. 14, 3-year book
SQUASH SEEDS are a delicious, nutritious snack	Issue No. 41 (Sold out. Photocopy of article is available.)
Try traditional early American fried **SQUIRREL**	Issue No. 30, 5-year book
If you can boil water, you can make a good **STEW**	Issue No. 44 (Sold out. Photocopy of article is available.)
STOCKS — as important as herbs and spices	Issue No. 21, 4-year book
Make delicious meals all winter with **STORED VEGETABLES AND SPICES**	Issue No. 41 (Sold out. Photocopy of article is available.)
SUN OVER COOKERY	Issue No. 28, 5-year book
Do-it-yourself "**TAKE-OUT**" food	Issue No. 17, 3-year book
How about a delicious **THISTLE SALAD**?	Issue No. 34
TOFU — healthful, delicious, versatile, and you can make it yourself	Issue No. 48
Here are some tasty ways to use those end-of-season **GREEN TOMATOES**	Issue No. 41 (Sold out. Photocopy of article is available.)
The "new" **VEGETARIAN COOKING**	2-year book
Elegant **VEGETARIAN CUISINE**	Issue No. 8, 2-year book
Quick & easy **VEGGIE** food	Issue No. 27, 5-year book
VENISON recipes	4-year book
VENISON recipes	Issue No. 30, 5-year book
VENISON deserves gourmet treatment	Issue No. 41 (Sold out. Photocopy of article is available.)
More **VENISON SAUSAGES**	4-year book

HERBAL VINEGARS — extra zip in your cooking	Issue No. 33
Make delicious **WINE** at home	5-year book
Make "recycled **WINE**" from leftover fruit pulp	Issue No. 41 (Sold out. Photocopy of article is available.)
Rough day? You need to sip some **YELLER WINE**	Issue No. 43 (Sold out. Photocopy of article is available.)
Uncommon **WINES** — another way to save the harvest	Issue No. 16, 3-year book
Hearty **WINTER BREAKFASTS**	Issue No. 19, 4-year book
My best **WINTER MEALS**	Issue No. 18, 3-year book
Enjoy **ZUCCHINI** all year	Issue No. 34
ZUCCHINI MILK	Issue No. 34

Self sufficiency

ACORNS are not just squirrel food	Issue No. 47
Be prepared for "**AFTER THE ACCIDENT HAPPENS**"	Issue No. 47
If you plan to drive the **ALASKA HIGHWAY** for its 50th anniversary in 1992, here are some good travel tips	Issue No. 16, 3-year book
Winterize your **ANIMALS** without going broke	Issue No. 48
Try buying at **AUCTIONS** to save money for just about any item	Issue No. 19, 4-year book
The marvel of **BAKING SODA**	Issue No. 45
How to make your own dressings and **BANDAGES**	Issue No. 34
A local **BARTER** network creates new options	Issue No. 29
How to get started in **BLACKSMITHING**	Issue No. 17, 3-year book
Here's a few old **BOOKS** that are still great books!	Issue No. 16, 3-year book
The **BOW AND ARROW**: low tech tool for food, entertainment	5-year book
Homemade **WAX BULLETS** let you practice shooting on a budget	Issue No. 48
Here's a new idea for a **BURN BARREL**	Issue No. 34
Go **CAMPING** on a low budget or go on no budget at all	Issue No. 45
For float-hunting, you'll want to make a Native American style **CANOE PADDLE**	Issue No. 48
Miles per gallon vs. miles per hour . . . or things to consider when **BUYING A CAR**	Issue No. 15, 3-year book
Tips to make your **CAR** go 150,000 miles!	Issue No. 15, 3-year book
Here are four sure **CATFISH BAITS**	Issue No. 48
The incredible **CATTAIL** — "The super Wal-Mart of the swamp"	Issue No. 43 (Sold out. Photocopy of article is available.)
How to make **CHEESE AND BUTTER**	4-year book
Give the **OLD CHAIR** a lease on life	Issue No. 48
Build a "**SOLAR POWERED**" **CLOCK** — it's fun, educational, and even useful	Issue No. 46
You can earn a **COLLEGE DEGREE** without ever leaving home, thanks to TVs and computers	Issue No. 37
COMFREY is a powerful healing herb	Issue No. 47
How to draw up a **CONTRACT** without having to pay a lawyer	Issue No. 11
Walking that last mile with a loved one . . . a guide to caring for your own **DEAD**	Issue No. 15, 3-year book
Harvesting the blacktail **DEER**	4-year book
Make **DIAPERS** with a flair	Issue No. 48
Seven secrets of **DUTCH OVEN COOKING**	Issue No. 47
Five simple things that make our life **EASIER**	Issue No. 27, 5-year book
SMALL ENGINE MAINTENANCE FOR WOMEN	4-year book
FEED SEVEN on under $300 a month	Issue No. 12, 2-year book
A good plan to help you achieve **FINANCIAL INDEPENDENCE**	Issue No. 12, 2-year book
Protecting your home against the Wild**FIRE** Dragon	Issue No. 9, 2-year book
Protect your home and family from **FIRE**	4-year book
Women play a key role when it comes to making this rural **VOLUNTEER FIRE DEPARTMENT** a success	Issue No. 45

The Fifth Year

Gathering low cost **FIREWOOD**	4-year book
Want to save fuel and money? Try **SQUARE-SPLIT FIREWOOD**	Issue No. 35
We built a **HOMEMADE COMMUNITY FIRE TRUCK**	Issue No. 43 (Sold out. Photocopy of article is available.)
Make your own effective **FISHING TACKLE** while you save money and recycle scrap	Issue No. 44 (Sold out. Photocopy of article is available.)
Want a fun way to cut those food bills? Grab a rod and reel (**FISHING**)	Issue No. 33
Preparing yourself for springtime **FLOODS**	Issue No. 14, 3-year book
Good **FOOD FOR HARD TIMES** . . . or any time	Issue No. 14, 3-year book
The sensible way to **STORE** and use **FOOD**	Issue No. 17, 3-year book
FORAGE for wood lettuce and ground coral and you can spice up your outdoor eating (**EDIBLE FUNGI**)	Issue No. 40
You can become a **HARDCORE FORAGER**	Issue No. 47
Build a **HOMESTEAD FORGE** and **FABRICATE YOUR OWN HARDWARE**	Issue No. 36
FREE SUPPLIES for your homestead	5-year book
What you should know about **GOLD**	Issue No. 20, 4-year book
A chronology of **GOLD** in American history	Issue No. 20, 4-year book
Here's how one couple **BATTLED GOVERNMENT** over an unfair tax assessment — and won	Issue No. 33
A short course in **CUTTING HAIR**	2-year book
HAMFESTS — overlooked goldmines for hobbyists and collectors	Issue No. 20, 4-year book
HARVESTING FROM NATURE	4-year book
Here are seven **HELPFUL HINTS** from Homestead 77	Issue No. 36
HERBS make your canned and frozen foods more appealing	Issue No. 48
HOMEBIRTH — a natural way to come into the world	Issue No. 21, 4-year book
Do **LEATHER REPAIRS** the frugal way, using tools and materials you already have	Issue No. 44 (Sold out. Photocopy of article is available.)
You could furnish an entire homestead at **LEHMAN'S "NON-ELECTRIC" HARDWARE STOVE**	Issue No. 47
Make a **LIFELINE** before you need it	Issue No. 27, 5-year book
Chop 'em, drop 'em, & lop 'em . . . a rank beginner's guide to **LOGGING**	Issue No. 14
"Use it up, wear it out; **MAKE IT DO** or do without!"	Issue No. 16, 3-year book
Our homestead motto: **MAKE-DO**	Issue No. 37
Try these 13 **METAL CLEANING** tips to keep your house shining	Issue No. 44 (Sold out. Photocopy of article is available.)
Here's how to make a really neat and useful non-electric **PASTA MACHINE**	Issue No. 34
10 strong **MILDEW DETERRENTS**	Issue No. 45
PECTIN — you can rely on the grocer, or you can learn to make it yourself	Issue No. 41 (Sold out. Photocopy of article is available.)
Commonsense **PREPAREDNESS** just makes sense	Issue No. 48
Four **PREPAREDNESS EXPOS** scheduled for 1992	Issue No. 15
For this resourceful couple, **PRIMITIVE SURVIVAL SKILLS** are a path to self sufficiency	Issue No. 37
Sometimes a good old bucket of coals is the best solution (**KEEPING YOUR PUMP HOUSE FROM FREEZING**)	Issue No. 43 (Sold out. Photocopy of article is available.)
A **QUAKE PREPARATION** primer!	2-year book
AMATEUR RADIO — a sensible communication alternative for people who are self-reliant	Issue No. 15, 3-year book
New rules for **HAM RADIO** license	Issue No. 15, 3-year book
Improve FM and shortwave reception with a **DO-IT-YOURSELF RADIO ANTENNA**	Issue No. 43 (Sold out. Photocopy of article is available.)
How to maintain a **DIRT ROAD**	Issue No. 48
Recycle those old clothes into a braided **RUG**	Issue No. 20, 4-year book
SAVING is the first step to an independent country life	4-year book

SAWMILLS — a firm foundation to homesteading	Issue No. 9, 2-year book
For safe and effective **SELF-DEFENSE,** try **CAYENNE PEPPER SPRAY**	Issue No. 21
SIMPLIFY, save, grow food, and trade, and you too can afford to work for yourself	Issue No. 40
Make your own Swiss Army style **SNOWSHOES**	Issue No. 36
How to make **SOAP** from fat to finish	2-year book
Homemade **SOAP** — it's easy to make, high in quality, and you can even make a living with it	Issue No. 34
From emergency shower to backpack friend, the **GARDEN SPRAYER** is a real versatile tool	Issue No. 34
STARTING OVER	Issue No. 32
Make a fully functional **COLD STORAGE PIT/MOUND** and enjoy your garden's production all winter	Issue No. 47
Getting **SUGAR** from trees	4-year book
How to make your own "grab and go" **SURVIVAL KITS**	Issue No. 19, 4-year book
A practical **SURVIVAL STRATEGY** in the event of catastrophe	Issue No. 9, 2-year book
Here's how one couple battled government over an **UNFAIR TAX ASSESSMENT** — and won	Issue No. 33
Install a remote **TELEPHONE** line	Issue No. 29, 5-year book
TELLING TIME by the sun and stars is fun, and it's also surprisingly accurate	Issue No. 44 (Sold out. Photocopy of article is available.)
TOBACCO has some uses that might surprise you	Issue No. 38
You can turn **DUMPSTER-DIVING** into an urban treasure hunt (**RECYCLING TRASH**)	Issue No. 34
Try an ex-military **TRUCK** for rugged, reliable service	Issue No. 29, 5-year book
UNCOMMON USES for common substances	Issue No. 11, 2-year book
Create your own **EMERGENCY WATER SUPPLY**	Issue No. 34
Here's a handy chart to help predict your local **WEATHER**	Issue No. 18, 3-year book
Making **TEAS FROM WILD PLANTS AND HERBS**	Issue No. 34
Never underestimate a **WOMAN**	Issue No. 32
WOMEN play a key role when it comes to making this rural volunteer fire department a success	Issue No. 45
Can a **WOMAN ALONE** make a life in the backwoods? Ask Cecilia Taylor Barry!	2-year book
Choosing and using a **WOOD COOKSTOVE**	Issue No. 27, 5-year book

Short stories

The perfect defense	2-year book
Zugswang	2-year book

Think of it this way A column by John Earl Silveira

Just how smart is that **COMPUTER** on your desk?	Issue No. 39
FULLY INFORMED JURIES	Issue No. 33
Just how good of a bet are those **LOTTO** tickets?	Issue No. 37
Want proof of luck, ESP, and **PSYCHIC POWERS**?	Issue No. 40
LOSING OUR RIGHTS as we watch television	Issue No. 44 (Sold out. Photocopy of article is available.)
PROHIBITION: then, now, and always	Issue No. 45
SCIENCE and **TRUTH** — are they related?	Issue No. 46
A little **SKEPTICISM** can be very helpful	Issue No. 34
STEAM-DRIVEN CARS	Issue No. 36
TERM LIMITS — the logic behind it	Issue No. 35

Tools

Long range **ANTENNAS** for the homestead	4-year book
Get a new life for those old dead **BATTERY-POWERED TOOLS** by **CONVERTING THEM TO 12 VOLTS**	Issue No. 35
How to get started in **BLACKSMITHING**	Issue No. 17, 3-year book
Make your own lumber with a **CHAINSAW MILL**	Issue No. 39
Here's a "helping hand" for your **CHAINSAW MILL**	Issue No. 39
Build a homestead **COPY CART**	Issue No. 45
Backwoods **COMPUTERS** — vehicles to independence	2-year book
Set 100 stell fence posts a day with a home-made **DRIVER**	Issue No. 44 (Sold out. Photocopy of article is available.)
Build a **HOMESTEAD FORGE** and **FABRICATE YOUR OWN HARDWARE**	Issue No. 36
The Toolbox — **HAMMERS AND DRILLS**	3-year book
How to make **KNIVES AND SHEATHS**	Issue No. 31
Make your own **ULU** — it's the ultimate backwoods **KNIFE**	Issue No. 45
Build an all-purpose **LADDER**	Issue No. 45
A **DIY LEVEL** that actually works	Issue No. 36
Make **LIFTING** easy with a **ROPE** and the principles of "**MECHANICS**"	2-year book
How to build a low-cost **LOG LIFTER**	Issue No. 27, 5-year book
You can move a piano, even a house by yourself, if you understand the principles of "**MECHANICS**"	Issue No. 8, 2-year book
Get low-cost, high quality lumber by investing in an inexpensive **PLANER**	Issue No. 45
Make your own shopmade **RABBET PLANE**	Issue No. 48
AMATEUR RADIO — a communication alternative for people who are self-reliant	Issue No. 15, 3-year book
New rules for **HAM RADIO** license	Issue No. 15, 3-year book
The James T. Hiteman **OLD TOOL REVITALIZING** process	2-year book
Make your own **ROOTER ROTOR**	Issue No. 12, 2-year book
ROPE as a tool — as versatile as ever	Issue No. 18, 3-year book
Make your own quality **ROPE**	Issue No. 45
Use your own **SAWMILL** to cut lumber prices	Issue No. 29, 5-year book
Build a **SHAVING HORSE**	Issue No. 15, 3-year book
Listening to **SHORTWAVE** broadcasts from around the world is informative and fun	Issue No. 42 (Sold out. Photocopy of article is available.)
Make a colonial **SHOULDER YOKE**	Issue No. 15, 3-year book
Make your own **TOOL HANDLES**	Issue No. 31
Make a colonial **SHOULDER YOKE**	Issue No. 15, 3-year book

Water

The old time **SPRING HOUSE (FOR COOLING FOODS)**	Issue No. 11, 2-year book
Find water, wire, or cable by **DOWSING** with wire coat hangers	2-year book
Water systems for homesteads with **ALTERNATIVE ELECTRICAL SYSTEMS**	2-year book
Create your own **EMERGENCY WATER SUPPLY**	Issue No. 34
Making water **FIT TO DRINK**	2-year book
Try a **GRAVITY FLOW** water system	Issue No. 31
You can make this effective **GRAY WATER DISPOSAL SYSTEM**	Issue No. 40
How to care for and feed the family **POND**	Issue No. 27, 5-year book
Water pump blues? Consider the trusty **RAM PUMP**	2-year book
How to tell if your water supply is **SAFE** to drink	2-year book
Using salvaged materials to build a thermosiphon **SOLAR HOT WATER SYSTEM**	2-year book
The solar-powered silent partner (**SOLAR WATER PUMP**)	5-year book

SOLAR WATER PUMPING — a sensible, reliable alternative	Issue No. 8, 2-year book
Build your own ferro-cement water **STORAGE TANK**	2-year book
How to design and build a **WATER SYSTEM** for your backwoods home	Issue No. 9, 2-year book
WATERPOWER for personal use	Issue No. 16, 3-year book
Design calculations for no-head, low-head **WATERWHEELS**	Issue No. 17, 3-year book
Design calculations for overshot **WATERWHEELS**	Issue No. 18, 3-year book
Drive your own **WELL** for next to nothing	Issue No. 21, 4-year book
Dig a poor man's **WELL** in the country	Issue No. 36
WELL WATER update!	2-year book
How to build a safe, effective **WOOD-FIRED WATER HEATER**	Issue No. 9, 2-year book

Where I live   A column by Annie Duffy

Chasing down **COWS** at Jenny Creek	Issue No. 42 (Sold out. Photocopy of article is available.)
FOUNDER — a hard lesson in horse care	Issue No. 36
Salvaged wood makes a good **GOAT SHED**	Issue No. 37
WORKING for a dad who works at **HOME**	Issue No. 40
Caught in the 'Net (the **INTERNET**)	Issue No. 38
KISS CRITTERS — they're cute and they sell	Issue No. 44 (Sold out. Photocopy of article is available.)
Following in the footsteps of the **MORMON PIONEERS**	Issue No. 47
Nine-patch, baby, and log cabin **QUILTS**	Issue No. 43 (Sold out. Photocopy of article is available.)
GUY SMITH — he fills the dance floor	Issue No. 35
WALKING AND RIDING in the woods	Issue No. 41 (Sold out. Photocopy of article is available.)